When The Town Goes Dry

Articles On Alcohol, Bootlegging, And Prohibition From The Grant County News And The Williamstown Courier

Brandon Simpson

Published by Small Town Press
Dry Ridge, Kentucky
United States of America

www.smalltownpr.net

Editorial Consultant: Paddy McFadden

ISBN-13: 978-0-9816466-8-8

And the LORD God commanded the man, saying, Of every tree of the garden thou mayest freely eat: but of the tree of the knowledge of good and evil, thou shalt not eat of it: for in the day that thou eatest thereof thou shalt surely die.

-Genesis 2:16-17

Contents

Apéritif xvii

1 1890s 1

Suicide And Gambling . . . 1
County Court Orders . . . 1
The Whiskey Habit . . . 2
Burnt Whisky . . . 2
Whiskey Causing Trouble . . . 3
The Whisky Men . . . 3
Whiskey Trust At Work . . . 3
Wells of Wine . . . 4
Very Dry . . . 4
A Dispensary Law . . . 5
Local Option . . . 5
Nine Moonshiners . . . 5
Dispensary Law . . . 6
The Beer Tax . . . 6
W.C.T.U. Notes . . . 6
W.C.T.U. Notes . . . 7
W.C.T.U. Notes . . . 7
Very Dry . . . 8
W.C.T.U. Notes . . . 9
W.C.T.U. Notes . . . 9
W.C.T.U. Notes . . . 9
The Saloon In Chicago . . . 10

2 1900s 11

From 1800 To 1900 . . . 11
Illicit Still . . . 12
The New Woman . . . 12
The Drink Habit Cured . . . 13
Call for Meeting of the Friends of Local Option . . . 13
Local Option Election . . . 13
Resolutions . . . 14
Local Option Outpouring . . . 15

Local Option Election 15
How Local Option Has Killed Franklin 16
Local Option Meetings 16
Local Option Speaking 16
Mason 17
A Splendid Victory 17
Latest Amendment To Local Option Law 18
Enforce the Law 19
Pendleton Goes Dry 19
Dr. Young Lectures 19
Another Victory 20
Wets Win Victory 20
Maysville Not in Dry Belt 20
Cynthiana Voted "Wet" 21
Not Even Free Drinks Allowed in Dry Spots 21
Investigation By Court of Inquiry 21
Taming The "Tiger" 21
The "Tiger" Is Dead 23
For Straight Prohibition 23
Capitol Comment 24
Given Heavy Fine For Selling Booze 24
Madisonville Dry 25
Temperance Rally 25
Well Supplied 25
Went Dry 26
LaRue County Goes Overwhelmingly Dry 26
Liquor Question 26
Chautauqua 26

3 1910s 28

Government Licenses 28
Pendleton and Harrison Counties Vote "Dry" 28
On Charge Of "Bootlegging" 28
Kirtley Barnes Found "Not Guilty" 29
"Blind Tigers" Put To Work 29
Prohibition Repeal Is Carried In Maine 29
Prohibition Candidate 29
Too Much Xmas Booze 30
Drys Will Not Participate 30
The County Unit Law 30
Sunday Drunks Are Fined 31
Bad Whiskey Responsible 31
Are Fined For "Bootlegging" 31
Drunk And Disorderly 32

Costly "Booze" . . . 32
Bootleggers Fined Heavily . . . 32
National Prohibition . . . 32
Wets Are Winners . . . 33
Prohibitionists Won In Nine Counties Monday . . . 33
Prohibition Loses In Ohio . . . 34

4 1920s 35

Moonshine Still Captured In Grant And Owner Arrested . . . 35
Alleged "Moonshiners" On Trial In Covington . . . 35
Law and Order Of State Challenged By Bootlegger And Mountaineer, Says Governor, Urging 120 Officials To Act 36
Carload Of Liquor Seized . . . 37
"Moonshine" Plant Located And Destroyed . . . 37
Alleged Whiskey Bandits Captured In Lexington . . . 37
Three Gallons Of Moonshine Found In Auto . . . 38
Prohibition Enforcement Officers Make Raid And Seize Still. 6 Arrested . . . 38
Prohibition Enforcement Officers Visit Crittenden . . . 39
Doctors Make Defense Liquor Prescriptions . . . 40
Whiskey Stolen After Battle . . . 40
Two Arrested Charged With Liquor Violation . . . 40
Liquor Law Violators Draw Fine . . . 41
To Organize Wets In All The States . . . 41
Liquor Bars Let Down For Fight On Flu . . . 41
Eleven Gallons Of Moonshine "Jugged" Here . . . 42
Heavy Fines Assessed Against Booze Vendors . . . 42
Big Moonshine Still Found In Harrison County . . . 43
Kenton County Sheriff Makes Liquor Arrests . . . 43
6 Sent to Jail on Liquor Charges . . . 43
Heavy Fine For Liquor Law Violators . . . 44
Plans to Stop Liquor Flow At Its Source . . . 44
Dry Raiders Swoop Down On Williamstown . . . 45
Two Arrested Charged With Bootlegging . . . 45
Federal Officers Make Raid At Downingsville . . . 45
Almost In Shadow Of the Court House Booze Is Found . . . 46
Two Places Raided By Co. Sheriff . . . 46
Woman Given Jail Sentence On Liquor Charge . . . 46
Fifteen Gallons Moon Confiscated . . . 46
Many Appeals Are Taken In Liquor Cases . . . 47
Real Beer Is To Be On Sale Soon . . . 47
Two Negroes Escape From County Jail . . . 48
Dry Agents Disguised As Farmers . . . 48
Two Men Break Jail In Owen . . . 48
County Attorney Reports Violations Of Law At Corinth . . . 49
Zion Station Man In Limbo Liquor Charge . . . 49

Drouth Agents Gets Still In Owen County 49
Moonshine Still And 22 Gallons Of Moon Captured 49
Bread And Water For Bootleggers In Nebraska 50
Rich Harvest Off Bootleggers And Plain Drunks 50
Farmer Gets Heavy Penalty For Violation 50
Two Kentucky Distilleries May Resume Runs Soon 51
Federal Officers Find Moon 51
Deserted Car Thought To Be Booze Carrier 51
Boy Says He Bought Booze For Evidence 52
Liquor Law Violator Gets $500 Fine 53
Still Found Near Keefer 53
Anti-Saloon League Speaker To Be Here Next Wednesday Night 53
Bootlegger Captured With The Goods 53
He's Wet! But A Law Enforcer 53
Williamstown Bootleggers Caught In Net 54
Moon Found In Sheriff's Raids 55
Owen County Man Charged With Illegal Possession 55
24 Gallons Rum Seized In Scott 55
Seventy-Three Plead Guilty And Are Fined 56
Streets Of City Flow With Moonshine 56
Large Still Captured In Pendleton Co. 57
Liquor Supply 57
A Temperance Service 57
Moonshine Still Found In Farmer's Home Near Mt. Zion 58
Moonshine Still Found Near Mt. Zion 58
Moon Found In Abandoned Automobile 58
Alleged Moonshiner Arrested 59
Twenty-Eight Gallons Of Moon Destroyed 59

5 1930s 60

Heavy Fine Imposed On Moonshiner 60
Wet Republican Wins In New Jersey Primary 60
Big Year Reported By Raiders 61
Farmer Arrested On Liquor Charge 61
Federal Officers Make Raid, Find Still And Moon 62
Booze Car Goes In Ditch With 25 Gallons Moon 62
Hearst Favors Prohibition Repeal In Address 62
Federal Officers Make Raid On Two Places Tuesday 63
Sherman Man Charged With Possession 63
Modification Of Dry Act Is Urged 63
Alleged Bootlegger Turned Over To Federal Authorities 64
Barrel Of Booze Found In Home 64
Big Still Found On Farm Near Stewartsville 64
Fined $150 And 30 Days In Jail On Liquor Charge 64

Two Held For Having Booze In Possession 65
Possession Of Liquor Gets Man In Trouble 65
Wet Democrat Elected To Congress 65
Seven Officers Of The Law Find Half Pint Moon 65
Four Charged With Illegal Possession 66
Party Can Not "Pussyfoot" In Wet-Dry Fight 66
Beer Tax Bill Is Rejected By House, 228-169 66
Republican Prohibition Plank Fails To Satisfy 67
Church Voices Opposition To Drouth Repeal 68
Federal Officer Makes Raid 68
Held Under $1,000 Bond On Liquor Charge 69
Repeal Is Favored In Kentucky 69
Wets Have Lead In Poll On Congress 69
Repeal Of Eighteenth Amendment Defeated By Narrow Margin 70
Prohibition Repeal Bill Is Passed By House By Good Majority 71
End Of Dry Regime Seen In Passage Of 3.2 Beer Bill 72
Beer Becomes Legal Beverage After 13 Years 73
Beer License Here May Be Fixed At $100 74
License On Beer In Williamstown Fixed At $75.00 74
Beer Flows Freely In Williamstown For First Time In 25 Years 75
Beer Flows In House Restaurant 75
Two More States Fall In Line For Repeal Amendment 75
Old Bay State In Wet Parade. Vote Is 4 To 1. 76
Smashing Victory For Repealists 76
Two More States Fall In Line For Repeal 77
Special Session Of Legislature May Be Called 78
Two Southern States Vote For Repeal 79
Arizona Votes For Repeal Of 18th Amendment 80
Extraordinary Session Of Kentucky Legislature Opened Last Tuesday 81
Missouri In Wet Column By 4-1 Vote 81
Washington in Wet Columns By Three To One 82
Lone Star State Joins Wet Parade By Vote Of 2 To 1 82
Vermont 25th State To Ratify 83
Four More States Vote For Prohibition Repeal Amendment 84
Two More States Vote For Repeal Of Prohibition 85
Virginia Is 32nd State To Ratify 85
Florida Joins Repeal States 86
Four More States Join With 33 Others To Wipe Out Law 86
Constitutional Amendment Is Defeated By Over 2,000 87
Kentucky 33rd State To Ratify Repeal Of Eighteenth Amendment 87
State Wet By Large Majority 87
Liquor Now Flows In Eighteen States Following Repealing 88
Legislature Repeals Rash-Gullion Act 89
Distillery Destroyed By Fire 89

Three Arrested And Held, For Drunkenness 90
Two Arrested For Drunken Driving, Fined 90
Two Arrested Saturday For Intoxication 90
Liquor Dispensaries Must Pay $200 License Fee In Williamstown 91
New Liquor Store Robbed Thursday Night 91
Old Glory Tavern Has New Managers 91
Robbers Are Sentenced To Serve One Year 91
Local Option Election Includes Grant 94
Local Option Elections Ruled Out 94
Vote On Repeal Is Held Valid 95
Four Men Fined On Drunkenness Charge 95
Hijacker Of Beer Truck At Large 95
Several Get Fines For Being Drunk 95
Alcoholic Exhibition Here June 4 96
Booze, Beans And Books In Smash-Up 96
Pulaski County Votes Dry By A Big Majority 96
Adjoining Counties To Hold Local Option Election 97
Four More Counties In State 97
Owen And Pendleton Joins Ranks Of Drys 98
Petition To Close Road House, Filed 98
Road House Closed By Court Order 98
Road House Closing Awaits Court Appeal 99
Crittenden County Votes Dry 2nd Time 99
War Against Drunken Drivers To Be Waged 99
Fined For Drunkenness And Placed on Probation 99
Madison County Goes Dry By A Slim Majority 99
Fifteen In County Jail Monday Night 100
Drys Carry Precinct In Kenton County 100
Local Option Election To Be Held In Sept. 100
2 More Kentucky Counties Voted Wet Last Saturday 105
Local Option Election Set For Sept. 11th 105
Local Option Election For September 11 105
Local Option Election Set For Saturday 105
Wets Win By Majority of 416 Votes 109
Whisky Tax Bill Beaten In House 109
Whiskey To Be Dispensed By Only Four 110
20 Arrested For Drunkenness And Minor Offenses 110
Local Option Election Set For May 14, In Clark Co. 110
Drunken Driver Causes Accident, Two Injured 110
Two Spend Week End In Georgetown Jail 111
Young People To Have Temperance Meeting 111
Few Applications For Beer Licenses Have Been Received 111
Young People Will Have Temperance Meeting, June 12th 111
Liquor Dealers Get Notice That They Can't Get License 111

Retail Liquor Dealers Given 40 Days Grace . . . 112
Beer Dealers Cited In Court, Fines Suspended . . . 112
Wets Win Bath County By 482 Vote Margin . . . 113
Distillery On Kentucky River Declared Bankrupt . . . 113
Arrested For Being Drunk And Driving Car . . . 113

6 1940s 114

Drunken Driving . . . 114
Estill County Local Option Petition Stolen . . . 114
County-Wide Local Option Meeting To Be Held At Dry Ridge . . . 114
Local Option Meeting . . . 115
Another Local Option Mass Meeting . . . 115
Local Option Mass Meeting . . . 116
Eight Grant Countians Are Cited . . . 116
Local Option Campaign . . . 116
Local Option Meeting Friday Night At Williamstown Christian Church . . . 119
Local Option Speaking . . . 119
The Bootleggers And Legalized Liquor . . . 119
Nine Grant County Beer Dealers Have Licenses Suspended . . . 120
Beer Licenses Of Six Suspended . . . 120
Asbury Quartette At Local Option Meet, Sunday Nite . . . 138
Election On Local Option Saturday . . . 138
Drys Carry Grant County By A 212 Majority Vote . . . 138
Boone Countians To Vote on Wet And Dry Issue . . . 139
Boone Goes Wet Nine To Six . . . 139
Pendleton County Voted Dry By 251 . . . 139
Beer-Laden Truck Overturns Near Sherman . . . 140
Pendleton County Local Option Election Contested . . . 140
Wets Win In Gallatin . . . 140
Violator Of Local Option Law Fined . . . 140
Speaking Arranged By Local Option Committee . . . 141
Wets Win In Carroll By Narrow Margin . . . 141
Local Option Election In Grant Called Off . . . 148
Wets Win In Mason . . . 148
Drys Win In Scott By Wide Margin . . . 148
Proprietor Of Rock Garden To Face Liquor Charge . . . 148
Beer Loaded Truck Overturns Near Corinth City Limits . . . 149
Wets Win Election In Bracken County By 108 Majority . . . 149
Beer and Fifth Whiskey Seized By Officers . . . 149
Liquor Tax Raise Of 8 Cents Is Sought . . . 149
Petition Filed For Local Option Election In Grant . . . 150
Attention Citizens . . . 150
Dry Forces To Have Mass Meeting In Dry Ridge . . . 151
Local Option Elections In Grant County . . . 151

Wet Or Dry . . . 151
Federal Judge Says Legalized Liquor Can't Stop Bootleggers . . . 153
Local Option Election To Be Held Tomorrow . . . 154
Murderer Passes Buck . . . 154
Grant County Voted Dry By 591 Votes . . . 165
Drunken Driver Fined $500 And Costs By Pettit . . . 167
Drunken Drivers Occupy Time Of Quarterly Court . . . 167
Prohibitionists To Have Meeting Sunday, Jan. 23rd . . . 167
Dry Forces To Meet Sunday . . . 167
Dry Forces Of Grant County Meet To Elect Committeemen . . . 168
Five Slot Machines Confiscated At Kenton Co. Tavern . . . 168
Local And State Officers Seize Liquor . . . 168
Drys Endorse Sheriff And Judge Candidates . . . 168
Man Charged With Possession Of Spirited Liquors . . . 169
Officers Raid Tavern At Twin Bridges . . . 169
9 Arrested And Fined Over Labor Day Weekend . . . 169
A. A.'s To Have New Year's Party . . . 170
Drunks Land In County Jail Over Holiday Weekend . . . 170

7 1950s . . . 172

Mt. Zion Baptists Protest Liquor Radio Advertising . . . 172
Slot Machine And Alcoholics Destroyed . . . 172
Truck And Drunken Drivers Fined . . . 172
Marvin Mason Says Slot Machine Was Not His Property . . . 172
Officers Stage Raids On Two Road Houses . . . 173
Moonshine And Mash Captured With Still . . . 173
14 Drivers Lose Licenses For Drunken Driving . . . 174
County Board Of Education Rules Against Dancing . . . 174
Woman Fined $100 And Sentenced To 30 Days In Jail . . . 174
Officers Destroy Accumulation Of Beer And Whiskey . . . 174
Motorists Fined In County Court . . . 174
Lewis Henderson Buys Beer Route . . . 175
Rock Garden Raided Twice In Three Days . . . 175
Raid Yields No Booze Or Beer; Slot Holds $5.10 . . . 175
Kentuckians Hit Proposed Whisky Tax Hike . . . 176
Richmond Man Fined Being Drunk On Bus . . . 176
Two Killed In Automobile Crash With Drunken Driver . . . 176
Raid Yields Nine Half Pints Whiskey . . . 177
Man And Woman Fined And Jailed For Drunkenness . . . 177
39 Autos Pile Up Behind Drunken Driver On Dixie . . . 178
Drunken Drivers Have Operator's License Suspended . . . 178
Soldier Shot At Harvie's Tavern . . . 178
44 Half Pints Whiskey Seized In Two Raids . . . 178
Petition Filed For Local Option Election Sept. 6th . . . 179

Mass Rally of Dry Forces Held Last Sunday . . . 179
Four Drunken Drivers Fined $100 And Costs . . . 179
Election Officers Selected To Serve At Local Option . . . 180
Fines Imposed On 8 Persons For Drunkenness . . . 180
Temperance Speaker Scheduled For Talk At Dry Ridge Baptist . . . 180
Drunks Occupy Main Seats In Judge's Court . . . 181
Drys Seek Court Order For Fair Placement Of Election Officers . . . 181
Heavy Vote In Local Option Election Expected . . . 182
Local Option A Very Dry Affair . . . 190
Editor Scorned For Stand On Local Option Election . . . 192
Local Option Election Costs Not Available . . . 193
Raids Result In Arrest Of Two In Grant County . . . 193
Drunks And Hunting Law Violators Draw Fines In Court . . . 193
Four Motorists Fined $100 For Driving Drunk . . . 193
Five Fined For Drunken Driving Over Long Weekend . . . 194
Drunken Drivers Subject To Fines From $100 To $500 . . . 194
Drunken Driver Fined $100 And Loses License . . . 194
Wife's Jaw Broken In Drunken Brawl . . . 194
Fined $100 On Drunken Driving Charge Here . . . 195
Drunken Drivers Get $100 Fines . . . 195
State Whiskey Production Tax Doubled . . . 195
Drunken Drivers Get $100 Fines . . . 195
$100 Fines Meted Drunken Drivers . . . 196
Drunken Youth Goes On Wild Rampage . . . 196
Two Fined $100 On Drunken Driving Charge . . . 196
One Fined For Drunken Driving In Quarterly Court . . . 197
Three Fined For Drunken Driving . . . 197
Six Drunken Drivers Meted $100 Fines . . . 197
Drunk Man Moved To St. Elizabeth . . . 197
Drunk Drivers Fined $100; Lose License . . . 197
Motorist Fined For Driving While Drunk . . . 197
Drunknets Held Illegal . . . 198
Women You Can't Forget . . . 199
Whiskey & Beer Confiscated In Roadhouse Raids . . . 200
Three Motorists Fined $100 For Drunken Driving . . . 200
Two Countians Arrested In Tavern Brawl . . . 200

8 1960s 201

Roadhouse Raided By State Police . . . 201
Early Crouch Fined $200 And Given 60 Days . . . 201
Drunken Driver Chased By Police . . . 201
Three Fined $100 On Drunken Driving Charge . . . 202
Senator Blake Is Fined For Drunken Driving . . . 202
Drunken Driver Wrecks Automobile . . . 202

Two Places Raided Here Wednesday 202
Bootlegger Nabbed In Front Of Court House 203
Bootlegger Fined And Sentenced 203
16-Year-Old Charged With Being Drunk 203
Beer Bottle Thrown Through Auto Window 203
State-Owned Liquor Stores Proposed 203
Webster Votes Against Repeal Of Whiskey Tax 204
Drunk Driving Charge Brings Maximum Mulct 204
Grand Jury To Get "Dry" Case 204

9 1970s 206

Alcohol Abuse Open Forum Scheduled To Be Held Here 206
Whiskey, Beer Confiscated In Raid 206
Grant County Co-Operating In Alcohol Abuse School 206
Drunks May Face Psychiatrist Instead Of Judge Under New Law 207
Grant Countians Invited To Join Alcoholism Study 207
Various Types Attend Alcoholism School 207
Director State Association Alcohol Abuse 208
Train Stopped In Whisky Search 208
Former Resident To Speak On Alcoholism 208
Booze And Drugs Arouse Concern Of Local Schools 208
Drinking And Drug Use Make Bad Memories 210
Students Assess Drug, Alcohol Use 211
Two Arrested With Booze 212

10 1980s 214

Dry Ridge Man Arrested In Liquor Store Hold-Up 214
Gasohol Fuels Farmers' Dreams 215
KSP Cracks Down On Illegal Booze Buys 215
Breathalyzer Updated 216
MADD Program April 28 216
Election Question Brewing 216
Wet/Dry Petitions To Be Filed 217
Petitions Filed 218
Wet-Dry Petitions Probed 218
Two Names Tip Balance On Petition 218
Temperance League Plans Anti-Alcohol Campaign 219
Vote Saturday 219
County Gets 3 To 1 Voter Mandate: Dry 226
Judge Overturns DUI Verdict 227

11 1990s 229

Drunk Drivers Star In Police Video . . . 229
Alcohol Other Drug Council Offers Parent Training . . . 229
AOD Council Promotes Drug Abuse Awareness . . . 230
Alcohol Plays Role In 4 Of 5 Fatalities . . . 231
Alcohol Factor For Most Who Are Jailed . . . 232
Parents' Influence Children To Use Alcohol, Counselor Says . . . 232
Alcohol, Drug Use On Rise Among Teens . . . 233
Alcohol, Drug Abuse Is Problem Of Society, School Officials Say . . . 234
'Dry' County Hosts Happy Hour At GCHS . . . 236
Alcohol, Drug Survey Yields Sobering Results . . . 237
DUI Arrest Refuses To Give Up . . . 238
Student Remains In Critical Condition Following Jeep Wreck . . . 239
State Police Raid American Legion Hall . . . 240
Petition Seeks Special Election On Wet/Dry Issue . . . 240
Lusby Sees No Reason To Roll Out The Beer Barrels . . . 243
Group Of Citizens Does Not Want A Vote On Wet/Dry . . . 243
Wet/Dry Issue Headed To Polls . . . 243
Colson Proud Of Grant County's Past Dry Heritage . . . 244
Personally Speaking . . . 245
County Judge Rejects Wet/Dry Petitions . . . 246
Walters Sees Wet/Dry Debate As A Moral Issue . . . 246
Lyons Gives Her Opinion On Wet Versus Dry Issue . . . 247
Ministers Group, Citizens Form Keep It Dry, Safe Committee . . . 248
Schoenman Says Alcohol Does Not Cause Problems . . . 248
Sipple Offers Reasons To Keep Grant County Dry . . . 249
Sixteen Year Old Fields Weighs In On Wet/Dry Issue . . . 249
Wolfe Gives Reasons To Prove Wet Is Wrong In Grant . . . 251
Lusby Responds To Recent Arguments On Wet/Dry . . . 251
Drinkers Should Move To Wet Area, Suggests Covey . . . 251
Cummins Hopes County Stays Dry . . . 252
County Should Remain Dry . . . 252
Caldwell Against Wet County . . . 253
McMillan Speaks Out On Wet Vote For Community . . . 254
Corinth Man Arrested For Illegal Liquor Sales . . . 254

12 2000s 255

Bingham Against Liquor Sales . . . 255
Williamstown Student Speaks Out On Alcohol . . . 255
Youth Can Live Dreams By Staying Alcohol Free . . . 255
Walters' Class Against Alcohol Sales In County . . . 256
McAdams Upset Over Wallace's Interest In Club . . . 256
Resident Concerned Over Decline In Family Values . . . 257
Wet/Dry Petition Filed With Clerk . . . 257

Court Adopts Entertainment Regulations . . . 258
Wet/Dry Issue Headed To Voters . . . 259
Local Minister Says Wet/Dry Issue Is One Of Safety . . . 262
If Grant County Is Safe, Why Do DUI Cases Clog Courts? . . . 262
Kinmon Encourages Voters To Keep County Dry . . . 263
Personally Speaking . . . 263
Grant County Doesn't Need Saloons . . . 265
Alcohol (Part One) . . . 265
Dry Vote Won't Stop People From Buying Alcohol . . . 265
Business Can Be Successful Without Submitting To Pressure . . . 266
Alcohol (Part Two) . . . 267
Alcohol Contributes To Domestic, Child Abuse Cases . . . 267
For Christians, Voting Is Solemn Obligation . . . 268
Grant County Hasn't Missed Out By Being Dry . . . 268
Wet/Dry Issue Divides County; Voters To Decide July 25 . . . 269
Alcohol (Part Three) . . . 270
An All Purpose Remover . . . 270
Bates Encourages Voters To Keep County Dry . . . 271
County Needs Alcohol Sales Like It Needs Nuclear Explosion . . . 271
Don't Ignore What Is Already Attracting People To Area . . . 272
Instead Of Speaking Out, Make A Real Difference . . . 273
Making People Drive To Get Alcohol Won't Stop Them . . . 273
News Editorial . . . 274
Taylor Encourages Keeping Community Quiet And Small . . . 275
Wet/Dry Issue Sparks Debate . . . 275
Wet Vote Won't Bring Rampant Drunkenness To County . . . 277
Woodyard Says Experience More Truthful Than Figures . . . 277
Voters Decide To Keep County Dry . . . 278
Liquor Store Robbed . . . 279
Children Should Be Taught Alcohol Is Not Essential To Good Time . . . 279
Surprised To Find Beer Cans . . . 280
Corinth To Vote On Alcohol Sales . . . 280
'Moist' Election Set For Jan. 20 . . . 282
Personally Speaking . . . 283
City Residents To Get Say In Jan. 20 Vote . . . 284
Personally Speaking . . . 285
Question Remains Whether Alcohol Sales Will Spur Development . . . 286
In Our Opinion . . . 288
Alcohol Sales Are Not A Solution For Corinth . . . 288
Corinth Goes 'Moist' . . . 289
Corinth's Moist Vote Opens Pandora's Box . . . 290
Reader 'Ashamed' Of Corinth Wet Vote . . . 290
Zero Tolerance For Drinking And Driving . . . 291
Moist Vote On Tap . . . 292

Personally Speaking . . . 293
VisionQuest Gets Praise . . . 294
Voters Get Say On Moist Issue . . . 295
Voters Get Chance To Be Counted Nov. 2 . . . 296
Williamstown Approves Alcohol Sales . . . 297
City Adopts Rules On Alcohol Sales . . . 298
Dry Ridge Voters Tackle Moist Issue . . . 299
Moist Vote Set For Jan. 11 . . . 300
Wet vs. Dry . . . 301
Voters Reject Alcohol Sales . . . 302
What's On Tap? . . . 303
Where Do We Go From Here? . . . 304
Alcohol Sales OK'd But Corinth Still Dry . . . 304
Deputy Jailer Charged With DUI Following Accident In County Vehicle . . . 305
Williamstown Man Seeks Alcohol Answer About Lake . . . 306
DUI, Assault Charges Filed Against Trooper After Wreck . . . 306
Trooper Arrested . . . 307
Ex-Trooper Pleads Guilty In Wreck . . . 307
Alcohol Violation Forces Coach To Step Down . . . 308
Carey Denied Probation . . . 308
Wet Or Dry? . . . 308
Dry Ridge Moist Issue Questioned . . . 310
Citizens Urge Voters To Just Say No . . . 311
Moist Vote Goes To Dry Ridge Voters . . . 311
Alcohol Sales Get Thumbs Up . . . 313
Dry Ridge Adopts Rules Governing Alcohol . . . 314
Dry Ridge Is Moist . . . 315
Country Grill To Reopen, Serve Alcohol . . . 315

13 2010s . . . 317

Alcohol Proponents Start Wet Petition . . . 317
'Wet' Petition Is Now In Clerk's Hands . . . 318
Wet Vote Set For Dec. 22 . . . 318
Wet Proponents Say 'Yes' Vote Will Bring Growth . . . 319
Citizens Organize Against Wet Vote . . . 319
Myths Vs. Realities In The Wet/Dry Debate . . . 321
Wet Or Dry? Vote Is Dec. 22 . . . 322
County Goes 'Wet' . . . 323
Alcohol Voted In Now What? . . . 324
Bottoms Up . . . 326

Digestif . . . 328

Apéritif

This book has been an idea of mine for over ten years. In 2010, I went to France to work as an English-language assistant in a high school in Dijon from October 2010 until April 2011. The school I was assigned to had another English-language assistant from England. In the first few weeks, we went from one class to another to introduce ourselves and talk about our home towns. As my fellow assistant was from England, the description of his home town was not very surprising. When one of the teachers asked me why my hometown was called Dry Ridge, I didn't have an answer for her. I have since learned that Dry Ridge is called Dry Ridge because there were no natural bodies of water at its founding. Since I didn't know that at the time, I told her that I lived in a "dry" county, which means that it's illegal to sell alcohol. Her eyes got really big and she exclaimed, "Really?! I did not know that!" After that, I explained to her and the class the alcohol laws in Grant County.

"There are no bars. No clubs. No liquor stores. No sale of alcohol in stores or in gas stations. The only legal way you can purchase alcohol is to buy it in a restaurant. However, the restaurant must have a 100-seating capacity and 70% of the revenue must come from food receipts."

This subject became an icebreaker for me during my travels in France and surrounding European countries. There were language assistants from various countries around the world and from various states in America, and they all found this topic fascinating. I happened upon a group of Irishmen in Brussels who were having a bachelor party. I had a beer with them and told them about the dry laws in my county. They found it mind-boggling that a country that prides itself on civil liberties and freedom of choice would still have such restrictions.

The primary audiences for this book are those who never knew that prohibition still existed in some capacity in America and those who live or have lived in such areas. As mentioned before, the word "dry" in the context of alcohol means that the sale of alcohol is illegal. The word "wet" in the context of alcohol means that it is legal. These two words have been used in this context in American English for decades. English speakers from other countries such as England and Australia are much less familiar with this application of these two words, and speakers of other languages are even less familiar, if at all.

While the words "dry" and "wet" are often used, in Kentucky we have another word in the context of alcohol laws: "moist." The original definition of a "moist" county was a dry county that had a "wet" city or precinct in it. The modern definition of "moist" is a county, city, or precinct that allows the sale of alcohol in restaurants. Kentucky has some of the strictest and most complicated alcohol laws in the country, if not the world.

After years of having the idea for this book in the back of my mind, I finally decided to put it into action. I figured out that the best way to tell the story of prohibition in Grant County, Kentucky was to research articles in the local newspaper. This book contains every article regarding alcohol, bootlegging, and prohibition from The Grant County News and The Williamstown Courier from the 1890s until 2016. The Williamstown Courier was purchased by The Grant County News in the early 1910s and ceased operations shortly after.

The Digestif section of this book includes sheet music for *Every Day Will Be Sunday When The Town Goes Dry*, a prohibition-era song. It also includes the most current wet/dry map of Kentucky.

Cheers

I want to thank The Grant County News for granting me permission to reprint all their articles into this compilation. I also want to thank the Grant County Public Library for assisting me with the microfilm machine that contained all these articles and the Grant County Historical Society, who recorded all these articles to the microfilm.

Minding Your Ps and Qs

The articles in this book were reprinted exactly as they were originally published. All of the errors, be it spelling, grammar, or punctuation, are intentional. Several of the articles make use of the terms "whisky" and "whiskey." The editorial consultant brought it to my attention that these two words are not interchangeable, as one refers to scotch, and the other refers to Irish whiskey. However, it appears that these two spellings were used interchangeably in the early articles. The articles also contain language of the times, which may include racially and sexually insensitive terms that would be unacceptable in today's world.

1890s

Suicide And Gambling

Two Evils Of Modern Life That Seem To Keep Company

"If we could but obtain accurate statistics, we should find that gambling, was, of all vicious habits, not even excluding hard drinking, the one, which most predisposed it victims to suicide. Yet," continues this writer, one does not quite see at first why gambling should so greatly predispose to suicide. The gambler prima facie ought to be a man trained by his life to bear ill-luck with fortitude." This, of course is true only if there be nothing in the very condition of his life secretly in the very condition of his life secretly disintegrating that fortitude.

Let us see. It is probable that an intelligent jury will always account for the gambler's suicide by supposing that, ere he consummated the deed, he had come under the resistless control of temporary insanity. Hence we must try to discover those facts in the gambler's inward history which lead to this insanity. I believe they are of two classes, according as we study his experience in the light of ethical or of psychological and physiological laws. In the region of moral consciousness, I do not think we need seek far for the cause of insanity. The loss of the man's whole possessions by gambling must work upon a drunken manit awakens him. And now as he looks at the result of his career, at the obligations he has ignored, the relatives he has wronged, even the riches he has lost in pursuit of the gambler's passion, only one word can rise to his mind, and that is, "Fool!" As he glances around, the men with whom he has been gambling look at him in pity and mutter, "Poor fellow!" or "Poor fool!" the very servants who have watched his ruin gaze now at one poorer than they, and call him in their hearts "Poor fool."

I believe that this word of scorn, echoing within and without, filling the atmosphere for that man's ear, accurately describes the shame which he feels. Ashamed, crushed, ruined, despised by the associates who need him no longer, and called to no new and congenial surroundings by any human voice, the wonder is not that so many become insane, but that every ruined gambler is not drawn in the hour of his awakening into the terrible vortex of insanity. The man who loses his all in a legitimate commercial undertaking retains at least his self-respect, and self-respect is the soul of fortitude.Contemporary Review[1]

County Court Orders

Wills Probated And Admininstrators Appointed

License Granted To Sell Liquor At The Elie O'Lee Stand

On motion of E.L. Garvey, D.C. Points was appointed guardian of Bain Frank, and he executed bond, with William Points, Daniel Points and A.W. Spillman as his sureties. Wm. Vallandingham was appointed administrator of B.S. Franks, and executed bond, with B/.F. Menefee as his surety. John T. McClure and D.D. Clements were appointed appraisers. J.I. Harrison was granted license to retail spirituous and vinous liquors at the old Elee O'Lee stand on Fork Lick.[2]

[1] 4 February 1892. *Williamstown Courier.* Author Unknown.

[2] 14 April 1892. *Williamstown Courier.* Author Unknown.

The Whiskey Habit

Permanently And Completely Cured In Twenty-One Days Of Treatment

By Doctor Luther B. Tyson's Vegetable Remedy As Administered By The Williamstown Sanitarium

If You Want Relief From The Worst Of All Habits Apply To This Sanitarium For Treatment

The worst habit to which any man can be a slave in this modern age is without doubt the whiskey habit. Nothing else so completely destroys the usefulness of a citizen to himself and his family and country as to become a slave to strong drink. This fact is agreed to and admitted by all. Doctors have always thought, until very recently, that the whiskey habit was a thing with which medical science had nothing to do and was beyond their skill to treat. That no medicine could control or relieve the appetite of a man who had become a victim to this habit and consequently doctors have done little or nothing in this line until very recently. Doctor Tyson, of Kenton, Ohio, has demonstrated beyond a doubt that the whiskey habit is a disease and can be cured as easily as any other disease to which flesh is heir. The remedy he uses is purely vegetable, it is taken internally, no injections of any kind being used. In a few days treatment the patient looses all desire or appetite for strong drink, his system is built up, the evil effects of long drinking are removed and at the end of a course of three weeks treatment the patient goes forth into the world almost a new man. His desire for whiskey is as completely gone as though he had not tasted a drop of the stuff in his life; the appetite and the taste is completely eradicated. This is not an advertisement in the sense that it is only intended to secure patients for this treatment, but realizing the fact that it is a work of humanitarianism to take a man who is a physical wreck, useless to himself and friends and make him a useful citizen, and give him something for which to live, we desire that this remedy be bought to notice of men who are so unsortunate as to be so afflicted and to all persons who have friends who are useless to themselves and society from the effect of whiskey. One thousand patients have been treated by this remedy and not one has ever returned to drink. If you are a victim of this habit read this and think about it and if you have a friend who is afflicted tell him of this treatment insist on his taking it. Remember in every case a cure is guaranteed or the money is refunded and no charge is made.[3]

Burnt Whisky

Over Eighteen Thousand Barrels of It Destroyed at Owensboro. Ky.

Owensboro, Ky., April 8. The four bonded warehouses of the Glenmore Distilling Co. were burned to the ground Friday afternoon, together with 19,110 barrels of whisky.

The fire caught from sparks from the distillery smoke stack, 200 feet away. A high wind was blowing, and the mammoth frame structures burned like tinder. Nearly a million gallons of burning whisky flowed out on the ground, and was only quenched when it ran off into the Ohio river.

Only the blowing of the wind in a favorable direction prevented the entire destruction of the distillery property, which is one of the largest in this section, together with 500 head of cattle penned up in stalls. The burning whisky ran all over the place, and several times the distillery was in danger. The whiskey was largely two year old, though a large portion was of the crop of 1890. About 3,000 barrels was of the present crop. The total loss is estimated at $335,000 over and above the government tax, which amounts to $765,000. The insurance is $285,000. It is distributed among a large number of companies.[4]

Whiskey Causing Trouble

[3] 5 May 1892. *Williamstown Courier*. Author Unknown.
[4] 13 April 1893. *Williamstown Courier*. Author Unknown.

South Carolinians Will Resist the Dispensary Law With Arms

CHARLESTON, S.C., July 17 The nailed hand of Gov. Tillman made a move Saturday against the blind tigers in Charleston. These have been running now just two weeks, since the dispensary law went into effect. For about ten days the city has been thronged with the governor's spies.

Two days ago the assistant attorney general of the state arrived here, and has been in consultation with the spies and the prosecuting officer of the county. He applied to a magistrate for search warrants, but that official refused to issue them, owing to some legal technicality.

The course of the proceedings, if pursued as now sketched, will, it may be safely said, precipitate a storm very far surpassing any which has yet attended the inauguration of the law.

On the arrest of those accused of violating the dispensary law, and before trial and conviction, the place of business is to be condemned and abated as a nuisance, the premises searched, and the goods and chattels confiscated to the state and carried away.

This is the program mapped out by the dispensary law, and this is the program that Gov. Tillman proposes to enforce. It is no secret that enforcement will be resisted by force if necessary.

In fact, it is no secret that a good many of the inhabitants have armed themselves, and are prepared to defend the sanctity of their premises, and the popular sympathy is entirely on their side.[5]

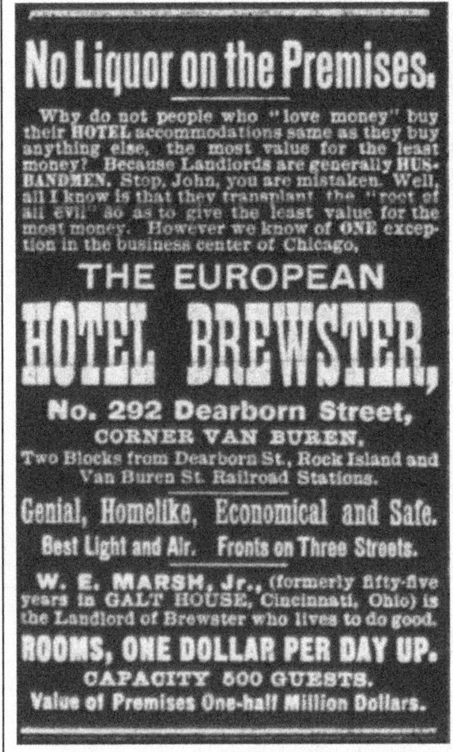

6

The Whisky Men

Fighting for an Extension of the Time for Paying Their Taxes

WASHINGTON, Aug. 18 Senator Frye, of Maine, Thursday introduced in the senate a protest against a bill introduced several days ago by Senator Vorhees, providing for extending six months the bonded period of whisky. Senator Frye stated that his protest had been prepared by the managers of the National Temperance union and gave notice that he proposed to oppose the measure of Senator Vorhees.

Prominent distillers from Pennsylvania, Ohio and Kentucky have been in the city ever since congress convened working up sentiment in favor of extending for a period of six months the bonded period. They finally prevailed on Senator Voorhees, chairman of the senate finance committee, to introduce a bill.

It is probable that his committee will report the measure favorably within a day or two. Senator Fry and several other senators, representing prohibition states, will fight the bill when it comes up in theAuthor Unknown.senate. The whisky men have a big lobby on the ground and it will not permit their bill to be defeated if money can secure adoption.[7]

Whiskey Trust At Work

It Will Endeavor to Have the Senate Increase the Whisky Tax

WASHINGTON, Jan 12. The total amount of spirits now in the entire world is reliably estimated to be 1,356,000,000 gallons. Officially estimated, there are now remaining in bond in the United States 130,561,910 gallons of whisky, of which 4,154,000 gallons are in Illinois and 86,000,000 in Kentucky.

[5]20 July 1893.*Williamstown Courier.* Author Unknown.

[6]Circa July 1893.*Williamstown Courier.*

[7]August 1893.*Williamstown Courier.* Author Unknown.

The trust wants an increase in internal revenue tax, and in justification of its demand the argument is advanced that it would almost immediately give the government an amount more than equal to the entire gold reserve in the subtreasury in New York. The trust has gained one strong point in getting the democratic majority of the ways and means committee to agree to increase the tax from ninety cents to $1 per gallon. If the house committee can be persuaded to accept the increase the scheme is to get the senate to push it up further to $1.25 or perhaps $1.40.[8]

Wells of Wine

The United States Not In It With Italy and Others

WASHINGTON. April 7. Rather discouraging to our own wine growers is the report that comes to the state department from Henry S. Huntington, our consular agent at Castellamare, Italy, as to the enormous wine crop produced in that country during the past two years. He says: "In the last two years here the grape crop has been so abundant that in many districts in southern Italy there were not barrels and demijohns sufficient to hold the pressed juice, and cisterns were emptied of water and filled with wine." Mr. Huntington adds that the great French wine crop by reducing the market in that country for Italian wines will compel large exports to other countries. He shows that Italy is the greatest wine producing country in the world, the crop last year amounting' to $1,200,000,000 in value. The United States stands seventeenth in the list of wine-producing countries with a product last year of but 1,013,729 hecto-litres as against 31,263,877 for Italy, and Mr. Huntington believes that owing to climatic conditions and dear labor we never can compete with Italy in this field.[9]

Very Dry

Saloons in New York Closed Tight on Sunday

Even the Hotels and Cafes Warned by Officers Sent Around for That Purpose Against Selling Liquor on Sunday Great Many Arrests

NEW YORK, Oct. 1. Frightened by the stringent measures of the police, the saloonkeepers Sunday closed their doors tight; not only the front doors and family entrances as well, and even those doors that lead through dark and devious passages from adjacent alleyways to the longed-for goal.

It would not do to state that every saloon in New York was closed, for a good many dealers, after surrounding their places with guards, did a little cautious and tremulous business: but more red tape accompanied the process of getting wet goods in these places than would be necessary to secure an audience with the shah of Persia.

Even the hotels and cafes were warned by officers sent around for that purpose against selling any liquor, except with a regular meal, and if a man wanted to get a drink in an eating house he had to order food and pay for it. The drug stores were also dry.

Down on Park Row there were two saloons which were at great pains to accommodate their patrons. One of them was the place known as the "Beggar's Rest." Standing on an adjacent corner the reporter saw several men walking along by the saloon disappear downward, as if the earth had swallowed them up. Going nearer he found that there was a large trap door in the sidewalk leading into the cellar under the place. Outside a door stood a red-faced man, and a crowd of tough-looking individuals lounged about. At intervals, apparently by signal, two or three of these would disappear down the trap door. But over in Hoboken beer flowed freely, as it always does, and the thirsty went in such crowds to Brooklyn that messengers were sent hurrying from all the big places for extra bartenders.

The Jefferson market police court was crowded with excise cases. Policeman Zimmerman arraigned Charles Bueshong, a bartender.

"Is this man a licensed saloonkeeper?" asked Justice Hogan.

"Yes," replied Zimmerman.

[8] 18 January 1894. *Williamstown Courier.* Author Unknown.
[9] 12 April 1894. *Williamstown Courier.* Author Unknown.

"Did you enter his place?" continued the justice.

"Yes."

"Did you have a warrant or process of law?"

"No," answered Zimmerman.

"I will not entertain this complaint or any other complaint or any other complaints of a similar character. You can take your prisoners when you like. I shall not pass them."

"Are they discharged?" asked the policeman.

"No, sir. I will not pass upon the cases. Take them back. You may do as you please with them," and the officers started back to the station house with fifteen prisoners, who were afterward bailed. There were forty-five prisoners arrested for violating the excise law before other justices, and eight were discharged, the others being held under bond. The police succeeded in making 240 excise arrests during the day. This is the largest number ever made in one day.[10]

A Dispensary Law

Advocated By Georgia Legislators Similar To The Tillman Laws

ATLANTA, Ga., Nov, 17. Upon organization of the present legislature Speaker Flemming appointed on the temperance committee men who are known as determined enemies of the liquor traffic. They have resolved to report for adoption what is known as the Bush bill. This bill provides that it shall be a felony for any citizen of Georgia to engage in the sale of liquor. In place of the present method of selling it is provided that there shall be established in each county a state dispensary, supervised by a discreet man, who shall keep a record of all liquors sold. It is also provided that there shall be a state inspector, who shall test all liquors offered for sale. The officer will also be clothed upon property for purposes of investigation and destroy contraband goods.[11]

Local Option

To Be Discussed By The Georgia Legislature The Temperance Committee Has Agreed Upon A Bill

---

ATLANTA, Ga., Dec. 1. The temperance committee of the legislature has agreed upon a temperance bill, and made their report recommending its passage. The bill provides that in incorporating towns where liquor is now allowed to be sold, venders may sell upon a petition of a majority of the freeholders of the town or city to the mayor and council. He shall then give bond to the ordinary in the sum of $5,000 for faithful observance of the law. He shall pay $100 to the state and all municipal and national tax for one year. He shall only purchase liquor to sell which has been examined by the state chemist as pure and unadulterated, and to retail in quantities not less than one-half pint and shall not sell to minors or habitual drunkards; that no liquor shall be drunk in the premises; that each vender shall only have one place of business, and nothing shall be sold in that place excepting intoxicating liquors, and that it shall be in full view of the street, and there shall be no back doors or back windows or side doors. Each place shall be cleared at 10 p.m. and not opened until 5 a.m. This bill has brought the hottest fight ever made before the Georgia legislature.[12]

Nine Moonshiners

Capture After A Desperate Fight In The Mountains A Thousand Gallons Of Whisky Destroyed

---

MEMPHIS, Tenn., Feb. 5. Deputy Internal Revenue Collector Keller Anderton (of Coal-Creek fame) returned to headquarters Monday, after a raid on Tennessee moonshiners, bringing with him nine prisoners arrested after desperate resistance and hand-to-hand battle in the mountain fastnesses of Hardin county. Gen. Anderton recently received information that an immense wildcat still existed in that county, and with fifteen

[10] 4 October 1894. *Williamstown Courier.* Author Unknown.
[11] 22 November 1894. *Williamstown Courier.* Author Unknown.
[12] 6 December 1894. *Williamstown Courier.* Author Unknown.

deputies, armed with Winchester rifles, the raid was made after a forty-mile ride in the dead of night. The still was located in a dense wood and on approaching the deputies were received with a volley from a cabin near by. The fire was returned and the marshals advanced. After a struggle, in which two deputies were wounded, nine men were captured and 1,000 gallons whisky and the entire plant burned. The prisoners were lodged in jail and Gen. Anderton is the hero of the hour.[13]

Dispensary Law

The Case Goes To The United States Supreme Court On Habeas Corpus Proceedings

---

COLUMBIA, S. C. May 18. – The dispensary law is now on its way to the United States supreme court. A few days ago Constable Beach disobeyed United States Judge Simonton's order of injunction in the case, he having held that no one could interfere with liquor shipped into the state – that the law was unconstitutional in so far as it interfered with interstate commerce. Beach was arrested and put in jail for contempt. Atty. Gen. Barber left here Wednesday for Washington to make application for the United States supreme court for a writ of habeas corpus. The state expects by this method to get the entire case heard by the United States supreme court in the next twenty days.[14]

The Beer Tax

Secretary Carlisle Has About Decided To Raise It To Two Dollars A Barrel

---

WASHINGTON, July 11.It now seems certain that Secretary Carlisle, in his annual message to congress will urge the passage of the bill increasing the tax on beer from $1 to $2 per barrel. The government must have increased revenues, and, in casting about to see how it can best be obtained, it is said that the secretary has practically decided that an additional tax of $1 per barrel on beer would raise the necessary "wind." The eastern brewers will not only not oppose this proposed increase, but are said to look upon it with favor. They believe that such an increase would operate to their advantage, inasmuch as it will enable them to freeze out western competitors, who will be unable to maintain their enormous eastern trade if compelled to pay a $2 tax in addition to paying the long-haul freight charges.[15]

W.C.T.U. Notes

Let local option be the watch word until God gives us victory, for "The battle is the Lord's."

If you are not on the right side, get on the right side and vote for local option, for the protection of home and children, and the banishment of the accursed liquor.

"Woe unto him that giveth his neighbor drink, that puttest thy bottle to him and makest him drunken also." Bible.

You are responsible for yourself alone, for your own influence and your own vote.

Hear the fate of the drunkard in this life, "For the drunkard and the glutton shall come to poverty," and his doom in the life to come, "No drunkard shall inherit the kingdom of God." Shall not we, who are followers of the Lord Jesus Christ, do all in our power to remove the temptation from these slaves to the curse?

If we are true to God and the right "Victory" will soon be our watchword instead of "Work and Pray."

If the nine hundred million of dollars which are yearly expended and wasted in the liquor traffic could be stopped and turned back into the empty pockets of the poor, what poor child would cry for bread, or with aching unclothed feet? R.B. Robinson.

Eight thousand of the twelve thousand saloon-keepers in New York city have served terms in prison. Yet license have been issued to them as men of "good moral character."

[13] 7 February 1895. *Williamstown Courier.* Author Unknown.
[14] 23 May 1895. *Williamstown Courier.* Author Unknown.
[15] 18 July 1895. *Williamstown Courier.* Author Unknown.

Appointments for temperance sermons during District Conference held in Williamstown June 2nd to 5th:

WEDNESDAY, JUNE 3.

Dry Ridge, Rev. J.W. Mitchell.
Salem, Rev. W.A. Cooper.
Grassy Run, Rev. F.T. McIntyre.
Bethel, Rev. L.G. Wallace.
Oak Ridge, J.T. Fiser.
Fairview, Wm. Shoesmith.

THURSDAY, JUNE 4.

Dry Ridge, Rev. G.H. Means.
Salem, Revs. T.F. Taliafero and T.J. Fiser.
Grassy Run, Revs. W.W. Green and W.J. Deran.
Bethel, Revs. J.D. Renaker and P.H. Hoffman.
Oak Ridge, Revs. M.F. Moore and E.K. Kidwell.
Fairview, Revs. J.S. Walker and W.T. Benton.

Services will open at 8 p.m. at the above points. Local talent will please arrange the singing.[16]

W.C.T.U. Notes

Local Option

Temperance is the moderate use of all things helpful, and total abstinence from all things harmful. Union Signal.

We have borne with the evils of intemperance in our midst, even in our town, long enough. It is time for Christian people to rise up in the strength and might of the Lord, and with one blow drive the enemy from the field which he has so long held. God is ready to help. Are you ready to move forward?

The fruits of intemperance are anger, misery, poverty, murder and crimes of all kinds. Have you not seen this verified in your own midst?

Rev. G.W. Young of Richmond, Ky., will speak in Williamstown on next County Court day, June 8. Subject: Local Option. All come and hear him.

From "The Soldier."

The saloon antagonizes the home, the church, the State. On which side are you? That depends entirely upon the way you vote. Not what you say, not how you pray, but what you vote.

We reap as we sow. Sow saloons and reap drunkards. So Prohibition and reap prosperity.

Talk of improving the liquor traffic! You might as well undertake to paint the devil white.[17]

W.C.T.U. Notes

The rain is interfering somewhat with the local option campaign. Never mind it will be "dry" after the election.

Rev. G.W. Young of Richmond, Ky., literally captured the crowd at the court house Monday. It was a large crowd, a grand speech and a great day for local option in Grant.

Let every friend of peace and good order go to the election Monday next and by his vote prefer sobriety to drunkenness, and exalt manhood rather than murder.

The "dry" season will soon set in, in Grant, and the crop of drunk and disorderlies, assaults, fightings, cuttings, and killings, will all be "short" hereafter, in these parts. Selah!

Everything indicates a sweeping victory, for local option, next Monday. The whole county is being aroused this week by public speaking day and night, in every precinct and neighborhood. All the local talent and Rev. W.J. Doran, of Brooksville Ky., a regular temperance Demosthenes, and our own Rev. G.W. Young, of Richmond, Ky., one of the most enthusiastic and effective speakers ever heard in this county, are in the work and are moving steadily forward to assured victory next Monday.

Doran, large-bodied and big-brained, is at the head of one the conquering columns, moving steadily onward like a double header over a smooth track, while Young, thin, [] and sparkling, leads the other. He, himself is so transparent, and his speeches so lucid and clear that no X rays are needed, either to discover his sincerity, or to see the point.

The man who is thinking of excusing himself from going to the polls next Monday to vote for local option on the grounds of being so busy or any other pretext. If he be a pro-

[16] 28 May 1896. *Williamstown Courier.* Author Unknown.

[17] 4 June 1896. *Williamstown Courier.* Author Unknown.

fessed follower of Christ, let him examine Gods word on the subject of strong drink and after he has carefully sudied what it has to say, then if he can conscientiously cast aside all its warnings and admonitions and in the face of them say this is not my fight; I am wholly indifferent to God's word; I am unconcerned about the immortal souls of my friends and neighbor boys. Let him cease praying, quit playing "hide and seek" with the devil; remember his religion and take his stand where he belongs, for it were better for him not to longer continue the part of the hypocrite. Jesus says he that "Gathereth not with me scattereth abroad," and His most scathing denunciations were against the hypocrite. If he be not a christian let him stop and look back down the longline of once noble men and boys whose sorrowful and pitiable wrecks line the history of the liquor traffic. Let him put his ear to the trumpet and hear the wailings of millions of heart broken mothers and fathers, and the distressing cries of innocent and starving children because of this "Demon of Hell," then see if he can deliberately say as an excuse, I am to busy; I have not the time; I care more for a few hours in my crop or business than for all this. Men! if you are men, arouse! wake up! show your true manhood on this the greatest opportunity of your life. Go to the polls early next Monday, work long and hard, say by your actions, this demon shall die, he shall not damn the souls of men in Grant county so long as you can raise your voice and vote in protest against it.

Is there a sensible man in this county who wants his or his neighbors boy to be subjected to the harmful influence of strong drink? Or who wants the quiet, the happiness and the prosperity of his or his neighbors home disturbed, if not destroyed by the awful demon, "whisky?"

Surely, surely, there is not one!

Is there a sensible man in this county who is so careless and indifferent of the future happiness and success of his sons and daughters, and those of his neighbors, as to encourage the traffic of the greatest curse known to the human family, by which men drink even the little shoes from their babies feet and the morsels from their mouth?

If so, may the God of the universe wake that man up to a proper sense of appreciation!

Men of this county, go to the polls next Monday and vote peace, happiness and prosperity to the homes of our county by voting down that awful curse, "whiskey."[18]

Very Dry

Is The Way The Election Went Last Monday

Every Precinct In the County Votes Dry Except Dry Ridge Mt. Zion And Downingsville

The local option on last Monday was a quiet and tame affair. A small vote was polled, but the vote was much larger than either the friends or enemies of the measure anticipated. About 1,900 votes were polled, which is within 1,000 of a full vote. Both the "wets" and the "drys" suffered by the stay-at-home vote, and it is likely that had every vote been out the result would not have been much different, as the stay-at-homes were divided in about the same proportion as the vote that was polled.

The election was extremely quiet and orderly, not a fuss or any of the excitement that usually mars elections took place. In Williamstown the W.C.T.U. (senior organization) took a very active part. They had a free lemonade stand and dispensed non-intoxicating and cooling drinks to all them free of charge. They did much to bring about the result in this place.

The vote at the two Williamstown precincts was exactly two to one in favor of local option, a surprise to even the friends of the law. The opponents of local option did not do much work. They seemed to think the thing was going against them, and put up only a half-hearted fight. Dry Ridge is the only place where a stiff fight was put up and a big vote polled.

From a study of the returns it is apparent that local option could not have been defeated by the most vigorous efforts of the opposition, as the people had their heads that way and were determined to have "no whisky."

Corinth came nearer voting unanimously against whisky that any other precinct in the county, giving 88 votes for local option and 12 votes against it. Cross Roads was a close second,

[18] 11 June 1896. *Williamstown Courier.* Author Unknown.

however, giving 78 for local option to 15 votes against it.

In every place in the county where local option has been the law heretofore the vote was surprisingly large in its favor at this election. The indication is that those places that have tried the measure believe in it and are willing to continue under the law.

It will be nearly twelve months until the last saloon in Grant county is wiped out under the law. Each one will be allowed to run until the license they now hold is out. It will only be a few weeks until some of them will begin to fall by the wayside and others will drop out all during the year until they all quit. Following is the vote:[19]

Precinct	For	Against
E. Williamstown	149	76
W. Williamstown	79	38
Mason	89	21
Corinth	88	12
Dry Ridge	131	200
Stewartsville	62	26
Cross Roads	75	15
Crittenden	108	50
Flat Creek	79	35
Downingsville	51	166
Keefer	35	16
Mt. Zion	55	77
Cordova	95	45
	1096	777
	777	
Maj. for local option	319	
Total vote		1873

W.C.T.U. Notes

The licensed saloon is the open door to perdition.

Alcohol hardens the brain, dulls the nerves and makes the coward more cowardly and the brutal more brutal.

The saloon is where men meet and plan the darkest deeds that ever stain the record of crime.

Whiskey is now being made from old rags. It is time that things have taken a turn, for whiskey has made rags long enough.

The saloon grinds out a grist of paupers, murderers, thieves, and fills our asylums and prisons. Death to this monster; he is now in his death throes, every one strike home to his heart and in God's name we conquer.[20]

W.C.T.U. Notes

The best elements of society, the old residents, the prominent citizens and the farming community are pronouncedly in favor of local option. That class of liquor sellers who defy the law are the same class of men who, under the license system, would sell liquor without a license.

Alcohol produces no desirable effect upon a healthy organism.

Alcohol undergoes no change in the body and cannot be digested and incorporated into any bodily substance, but is a disorganizer of the system, injuring and destroying functions necessary to life.

"I have made a thousand dollars during the last three months," said a saloon keeper boastfully to a crowd of townsmen. "You have made more than that," quietly remarked a listener. "What is that?" "You have made homes wretched, women and children poor and sick and weary of life. You have made my two sons drunkards," continued the speaker, with trembling earnestness. "You have made the younger of the two so drunk that he fell and injured himself for life. You have made their mother a broken-hearted woman. Oh, yes, you have much more than I can reckon up but you'll get your full account some day." – Exchange.

Some one says if we have local option that every day will be like Sunday. Why not? Are we not tired of the staggering, drunken rowdy with his blasphemous oaths and the drunken brawls that occur here every County Court day.[21]

W.C.T.U. Notes

They who sell liquor are poisoners in a general way, and drive men like sheep to hell.

One priest in Ireland secured, in one year, 500,000 signers of the temperance pledge and most of them were kept.

The most advanced medical science is discovering excellent substitute which inspires the hope that even in the treatment of disease that alcohol liquors will yet be wholly superseded.

[19] 18 June 1896. *Williamstown Courier.* Author Unknown.
[20] 16 July 1896. *Williamstown Courier.* Author Unknown.
[21] 30 July 1896. *Williamstown Courier.* Author Unknown.

It is neither right nor politic for the State to afford legal protection and sanction to any traffic or system that tends to increase crime or wasted the national resources to corrupt the social habits, to destroy the lives and health of the people.

There are no considerations of private gain or public revenue can justify the upholding of a system so utterly wrong in principle suicidal in policy and disastrous in results as the traffic in intoxicating liquors.

The encouragement of drunkenness for the sake of profit on the sale of drinks is certainly one of the most criminal methods of assassination for money hitherto adopted by the bravos of any age.[22]

The Saloon In Chicago

There appeared recently in the American Economic Association' an article from the pen of John E. George, of Northwestern University, on "The Saloon Question in Chicago," the purpose of the article being to show that more than 6,500 saloons in Chicago, each having at least three persons the proprietor and two assistants whose interest is to maintain the liquor business, have a large and influential place in the city. In the article referred to it is stated that the annual drink bill of Chicago is estimated at $70,000,000; of this sum $34,000,000 being paid for beer, which at wholesale cost $15,000,000. The city receives from licenses, at $500 each, $3,335,000. Brewing companies are on seventy-five per cent. of the bonds for licenses, and advance one-third of the money. They also own rights and property, and establish agents in cheaply furnished saloons in order to increase the sale. One brewery has 350 saloons that sell beer exclusively. Exchange.[23]

[24]

[22] 1 October. *Williamstown Courier.* Author Unknown.

[23] 28 September 1899. *Williamstown Courier.* Author Unknown.

[24] 26 October 1899. *Williamstown Courier.*

1900s

From 1800 To 1900

Growth Of Religious Bodies In America As Compared With The Growth In Population

The growth in population of the United States from 1800 to 1900 was almost exactly thirteen fold. In 1800 the population was a little more than 5,000,000. It can not be told just what proportion were church members. Statisticians in most religious bodies have made estimates, and if their claims be accepted, it would appear that the proportion of church members to population in 1800 was about 1 in 20. Church membership would seem, therefore, to have beaten the population growth, great as the latter has been, by about four fold. This is conservative figuring. If the rather loose of our day be accepted, the church membership gain over the population gain during the century is about six-fold.

A score or more Methodist Episcopal annual conferences contain more ministers each than there there were in the whole United States in 1900. For example, there were in the opening year of the century 272 Methodist ministers in America. In 1900 there are 37,414. As for Methodist membership, that has grown from 61,351 to 5,200,000 considerably more than eighty-fold. Would Methodist churches of 1800 there were 251 of them average above $500 each in value? Nobody knows. Remember, though, that many of them were log churches and worth far less than that sum. Their value at the rate named would be $125,500. Methodist churches of the United States belonging to the one branch of Methodists North are worth $102,720,000.

Baptists had just one educational institution in 1800 a small affair with an income of less than $8,000 a year. In 1900 the income of the Baptist educational institutions was $3,480,000. Brown University received its name because of a gift of a gift of $5000, one of the largest benevolences known in that day. Baptist educational institutions in 1900 are worth $45,000,000. The income of all Baptist churches in the United States in 1800 was about $200,000. Now their income is $12,500,000 a year. There are 56,682 Baptist churches in all the world.

Presbyterian mission offerings in 1800 were $2,500; now they exceed $2,500,000 by a good many thousands. There were 449 Presbyterian churches in the United States in 1800. Were they worth $500,000? Perhaps. The Presbyterian churches of 1900 are worth $125,000,000. There were practically, perhaps literally, no Presbyterian charities in 1800; in 1900 Presbyterian charities need nine figures to name them. As late as 1829 the income of the Episcopal missionary organization was $10,829. The same organization's appropriations in 1900 were just a little under $600,000. There are thirty-nine Episcopal parishes having incomes in 1900 that are each larger than the incomes of all the Episcopal parishes in American in 1800, and there are fourteen Episcopal dioceses having 1900 more communicant members each than there were members in the whole United States in 1800.

There are eighteen divisions of Lutheran in the United States, besides half a dozen independent synods, and there are eight divisions that have more churches each than there were in America in 1800. The number of Lutheran churches in America in 1800 was 450. Now there are 10,908 or twenty-five-fold, and as for membership, that has increased more than eighty-fold, or more than 6 times as fast as the population. In 1826, when Congregational home mission work started, there were 1200 Congregational churches and a membership of 150,000. During this year the seventy-fifth anniversary of the Congregational home mission work is to be observed, and there are 5,604 churches and 629,874 members to observe it.

In 1800 there were only 100 Roman Catholic churches in the whole United States. Now there are 10,338 and 1723 chapels. In 1826 there was but one priest in all Boston, and none other in all New England. Now there are more priests resident in the city of Boston than there were in all America in 1800. There are five times as many children in Catholic schools to-day as there were members of all Roman Catholic churches one hundred years ago, and the 11,636 Catholic clergy of to-day are five times as many as there were ministers of all religious bodies at the beginning of the century.

Disciples of Christ began as a denomination long after the century did, and their membership long since passed the one million mark. As for property accumulation, that exceeds $16,000,000. Other bodies, rising during the century have made, almost withhut exception, growths exceeding the population ratio. The vast missionary interests which were represented in the Ecumenical Conference on foreign missions last April was wholly the growth of the century just ended. The oldest missionary was organized in 1810. Now the contributions passing through all organized missionary boards is not less than $25,000,000 a year. Ex.[1]

Illicit Still

Moonshine Whiskey Made In Grant Or Owen County

Somewhere about the line between the counties of Grant and Owen on Stevens creek on a clear day a thin blue drifting tongue of smoke creeps out of the hills over the tree tops and floats away into the blue of the sky. Some where beneath that curling smoke safely hidden away among the bluffs and overhanging cliffs of Stevens creek as twists and turns on its way to big Eagle it is said there is an illicit still. That moon shine whiskey is made and sold and that the business has been conducted for a good long time, and it is only recently that the revenue officers have "caught on". We do not know the parties connected with the work or the exact spit at which the still is located. Uncle Sam is likely to learn both the names and the place in a few short weeks unless business is immediately suspended and the parties scatter.[2]

The New Woman

Rev. Thomas B. Gregory, writing in the Chicago American, laments the "passing of woman." He seems greatly worried, and pours forth his regrets as follows:

Mother, as well as the "pies that mother used to make"; wife with the unspeakable charm and beauty that once went hand in hand with her; sister, with the tender endearments that used to be associated with her name and home and its atmosphere of peace and joy, are slipping away from us.

Mr. Gregory thinks that the new woman is "neither wife, mother nor sister," but, "as the Frenchman would put it, simply female." He does not state the case fairly. There has been no change in woman, unless it be for the better. It is true that today more women than formerly are required to toil in order to earn their daily bread. This fact indicates an unsatisfactory condition, but is Mr. Gregory devoting his energies and his talents towards the remedying of this evil?

It is true, also, that women are today taking a more conspicuous part in the formation of public opinion. There are today hundreds of women's clubs and similar societies where none existed a few years ago, but these organizations do injure woman, either individually or in her relation to society. On the contrary, they aid and improve her in both respects.

During our wars, and during every great crisis in the world's history, it has not been thought necessary to keep women in ignorance of the events happening around them. Civilization has nothing to fear from the "new woman" who aspires to an intimate acquaintance with the things which deeply concern society; but it had much to fear from the "old man" who elevates his nose whenever he sees a woman brave enough and energetic enough to earn her own living, when circumstances makes this necessary, or ambitious enough to keep

[1] 24 January 1901. *Williamstown Courier.* Author Unknown.

[2] 7 March 1901. *Williamstown Courier.* Author Unknown.

in touch with the happenings of the world.

The husband, the brother, and the child are better off as well as happier when the wife, the sister, and the mother have, in addition to affection, education and business capacity. The world needs the brain of woman as well as the brain of man, and even more does it need the consciousness of woman.

The Rev. Mr. Gregory will learn, if he will make an impartial investigation, that there has been no such thing as "the passing of woman"; he will learn that our social and political conditions would be more advanced than they are today if the men of America had made the same relative progress during the last fifty years that the women of America have made.

To say that the wife is a helpmeet is better than to say that she had an "unspeakable charm or beauty", to say that a mother instructs, as well as nourishes, her child, is better than to praise the "pies that mother used make." Woman is the complement of man, and neither will suffer if she is his intellectual companion, as well as his wife, his mother, and sister.[3]

The Drink Habit Cured

Home treatment for $15. A cure guaranteed or your money refunded by Dickey's liquor cure, Nerve strengthener, blood purifier, manhood restored, all in one. We make it, we guarantee it to cure any case of the drink habit on earth. We send it to any address in the U.S. upon receipt of $15 and guaranteed a cure or refund the money, Best Bank [] given. Our Business strictly confidential. Address. Dickey Remedy co. or P.O. Box 44, Shelby, Ind.[4]

Call for Meeting of the Friends of Local Option

Preparatory to the Local Option Election the temperance people of the county need a campaign committee, a portion of which should constitute an executive committee. We respectfully request the following persons from the various voting precincts to act on such committee, until permanent committees are named:

Dr. W.H. Daugherty and E.K. Lee, Corinth. Elder E Petty and Henry Ackman, Cordova. Rev. W.G. Baughn and Sam Parker, Keefer. W.H. Beverly and Scott Lam, Downingsville. J.S. Johnson and Nick Searey, Flat Creek. Wm. Calendar and Nelson Kinman, Jonesville. J.W. Crutcher and Joe Violette, Crittenden. Simeon Daugherty and W. Falstich, Sherman. J.B. Sanders and J.F. Vance, West Dry Ridge. Moses McClure and W.F. Bennett, East Dry Ridge. W.H. Davis and Squire Robinson, Mason. J.M. Flege and Dr. Day, Stewartsville. Rev. J.A. Hensley and C. Tomlin, Mt. Zion. Jesse Simpson and Ed Winters, Cross Roads. D.M. Hall, J.H. Webb, Richard Collins, J.D. McMillan, Mrs. Kate Conrad, J.H. Dickey, W.G. Welborn, D.C. Points, Tim Needham, J.D. Cobb and Joe Horner, for the Williamstown precincts.

We desire the above named persons together with all the resident ministers of the county of all denominations, and also preachers who have charge of any congregations in the county, and all residents in the county favorable to meet at the court house in Williamstown on County Court day, Aug. 10, 1903, at two o'clock.[5]

J.A. Davis.
J.D. Redd.

Local Option Election

Town of Williamstown

Grant County Court Held July 13, 1903

Hon. Clay Conrad, Judge, presiding.

H.B. Wigginton and others, petitioners for an election upon the Local Option Question in the Town of Williamstown.

This application is now, on motion of the petitioners, submitted to the Court upon the petition filed herein.

[3]25 April 1901.*Williamstown Courier.* Author Unknown.
[4]6 November 1902.*Williamstown Courier.* Author Unknown.
[5]23 July 1903.*Williamstown Courier.* Author Unknown.

And the Court being sufficiently advised, it is ordered that an election be held in the Town of Williamstown on Wednesday, the 9th day of September, 1903, (at which election all legal voters resident in said town qualified to vote for county officers shall have the right to vote) to take the sense of the legal voters of said town qualified to vote for county officers therein, upon the proposition whether or not spirituous, vinous or malt liquors shall be sold, bartered or loaned therein, it is ordered that the Sheriff of Grant county cause to be opened in said town at the usual voting places therein on the 9th day of September, 1903, a poll for taking of the sense of the legal voters of said town, qualified to vote at elections for county officers, upon the proposition "Whether or not spirituous, vinous or malt liquors shall be sold, bartered or loaned in the Town of Williamstown."

He will cause said polls to be opened at the hour required by law and said election to be conducted according to law, and will cause this order to be published in the Williamstown Courier for two weeks previous to said election, and will further advertise the same by posting up written or printed handbills in at least five conspicuous places in said town for at least two weeks previous to said election.

The Sheriff will duly notify the offices of election required by law to hold the same of the time and places of holding the same. The Clerk of this Court will, within five days after the entry of this order, deliver to the Sheriff a certified copy thereof; and the Sheriff will cause the same to be published in the Williamstown Courier, newspaper, and hand bills aforesaid, within seven days after receiving the same. It is further ordered that the Clerk of this Court cause to be prepared and printed poll books, ballots and other blanks necessary for the proper conduct of said election and deliver same to the Sheriff, to be by him delivered to the officers of election before the opening of said election on the 9th of September, 1903. The Clerk shall have printed on said ballots (in addition to formal parts) proposition "Whether or not spirituous, vinous or malt liquors shall be sold, bartered or loaned in the town of Williamstown," and shall provide the word "Yes" and the "No," with a place at each for the voter to stamp his vote so as to show clearly whether he votes upon said proposition "Yes" or "No." It is ordered that the officers of election now authorized and empowered to hold this election shall hold and conduct same according to the statutes governing elections, and make due returns thereof; and the Clerk of this Court is ordered to supply suitable ballot boxes for said election; and the Sheriff will deliver same to the officers of election; and the Sheriffs of said election will make reports in relation thereto as required by law.

State of Kentucky,

Grant County.

I, R.L. Kinman, Clerk of the County Court for the County and State aforesaid, do hereby certify that the foregoing is a true and correct copy of an order of the Grant County Court on the 13th day of July, 1903, as appears of record in my office. Given under my hand July 10, 1903.[6]

R.L. Kinman,
Clerk.

Resolutions

On Temperance Adopted By The District

Sunday School Conference Recently In Session At Dry Ridge

The Committee on "Temperance" present the following report, which was unanimously adopted by the Conference:

"In asmuch as no more nefarious traffic has insinuated itself into our commercial world and a no more corrupting influence has ever found its way into our political life and nothing can be more blighting, deadening or damning to the church or more detrimental to the family, Sunday School and best government than the present liquor traffic;

"Be it, therefore, resolved by this Sunday School Conference of the Covington district M.E. Church, South, Kentucky Conference, in session assembled in Dry Ridge, Ky.

"That we express our hearty sympathy in the present agitation against the open saloon, the fruitful source of much of the evil prevalent in our State, from which our young life so

[6] 23 July 1903. *Williamstown Courier.* Author Unknown.

greatly suffers and we pledge ourselves to help in every possible way to secure its destruction.

"J.D. Redd,
"L. Robinson,
"T.W. Barker."

Rev. G.W. Young addressed the Conference most forcibly and intelligently on the temperance question.[7]

Local Option Outpouring

A crowd that jammed the court house, filling the aisles and windows and every other available space for sitting, standing or seeing, greeted Drs. G.W. Young, of Georgetown and G.W. Perryman, of Paducah, Monday afternoon. These were the opening guns of the campaign against license in this county, and which will likely grow pretty hot by the second week in September. The speeches of these two able champions of sobriety and good order were both strong and eloquent, and delighted the great throng of friends of local option on the occasion.[8]

Local Option Election

Grant County Court.

J.W. Lancaster and 815 others on petition for vote on Local Option.

Came J.W. Lancaster and 815 others, electors for Grant County and qualified to vote for county officers at an election held for that purpose, and moved the Court for an order directing the Sheriff of Grant county to hold a Special Election in Grant county, Kentucky, on the 12th day of September, 1903, for the purpose of taking the sense of the legal voters of Grant county officers, and of each and all the precincts thereof, as to whether or not spirituous, vinous or malt Liquors shall be sold, bartered or loaned in Grant county and the provisions of this law and prohibition shall apply to druggists.

The said petition having been filed with this Court on the 13th day of July, 1903, at its regular July term, with a sum of money sufficient to pay all the expenses and cost of calling said election. And it appearing to the satisfaction of the Court that the 816 petitioners who have signed said petition is more than twenty-five per cent of the legal votes cast at the November election, 1902, in Grant county, and that the petitioners from each precinct separately are more than twenty-five per cent of the legal votes cast at said election in 1902 in said precincts: It is now ordered by the Court that W.H. Barker, Sheriff for Grant county, shall open a poll and cause an election to be held in Grant county and at each and all the voting precincts thereof on Saturday, the 12th day of September, 1903, at which election all electors of Grant county who are qualified to vote for county officers shall have the right to vote, and submit to the voters of each precinct of said county the proposition as to whether or not Spirituous, Vinous or Malt Liquors shall be sold bartered or loaned in Grant county and the provisions of the local option law and prohibition shall apply to druggist.

The sheriff will within seven days after he has received a certified copy of this order from the Clerk of this Court cause the same to be advertised, giving the time and place and manner of holding said election, by posting written or printed hand-bills in a conspicuous place in each voting precinct of Grant county, and for at least two weeks next before the holding of said election, and he will cause this order to be published in the Williamstown Courier, a weekly newspaper of general circulation in Grant county, for the same length of time, and he will perform all other duties required of him by law in holding said election. He have prepared a ballot for said election one poll book for each voting precinct with the requisite number of ballots in each as required in other elections upon which shall be printed this question: "Are you in favor of the sale of Spirituous, Vinous or Malt Liquors in Grant county, and that the law and prohibition shall apply to druggist?" And opposite this question upon said ballot he shall have printed the word "Yes," and below same the word "No," following each word with a small square

[7] 30 July 1903. *Williamstown Courier.* Author Unknown.

[8] 13 August 1903. *Williamstown Courier.* Author Unknown.

in which the voter shall mark or indicate his vote.

The officers appointed by the Election Commissioners for Grant county shall hold said election and the Sheriff of said county shall notify said officers of the time and place of said election, and he will perform all other duties required of Sheriffs in holding elections.

State of Kentucky,

Grant County Court,

I, R.J. Kinman, Clerk of the County Court for the county and State aforesaid, do hereby certify that the foregoing is a true and correct copy of an order of the Grant County Court made on the 10th day of August, 1903, as shown by the records of my office. Given under my hand August 14, 1903.[9]

R.L. Kinman, Clerk.

How Local Option Has Killed Franklin

Every now and then we hear a fellow exclaim: "If Glasgow only had open saloons it would be the best town in Kentucky, but local option is enough to kill any good town." The Franklin Favorite, edited by Mr. C.C. Pa[]e, whose statement is as good as his oath with all who know him, overcomes this assertion for it can not be dignified by calling it argument like a mountain falling upon it the following:

Sixteen years ago the amount of taxable property in Franklin was $466,159. That was the good year in which saloons were voted out of the town. This year the total amount is $867,574 an increase of $402,215. This fact is certified to by Mr. S.N. Forlin, the present City Clerk and custodian of the records. The corporate limits of the town were exactly the same then as now. This is evidence conclusive that saloons are not essential to the growth and prosperity of a town commercially, to say nothing of moral and spiritual development. Those Tennessee towns now endeavoring to throw off the shackles of the saloon can learn a lesson from this that will serve to refute about the only argument that the friend of the grogshop has to advance. Glasgow Times.[10]

Local Option Meetings

Mrs. Mary E. Balch, of Louisville, very celebrated worker in the temperance movement, will deliver an address Saturday evening at the Baptist church, especially to the ladies, but all are invited. She will also address the public on Sunday morning and evening at the court house. Let everybody hear her.

Wednesday Night.

Rev. Mr. Mitchell, pastor of the First Baptist church at Owenton, will address a mass meeting at the court house on Wenesday evening, Sept. 2, 1903. The public is cordially invited to attend all these meetings.[11]

Local Option Speaking

Thursday night at Mason, J.D. Redd and Brice Goldsboro.

Friday night at Mt. Pleasant, J.D. Redd.

Saturday night at Keefer, J.D. Redd and Brice Goldsboro.

Sunday at Corinth, J.D. Redd and Brice Goldsboro.

Sunday morning and night, mass meetings at the court house in Williamstown, G.W. Young and Brice Goldsboro.

Sunday night at Mt. Zion, Rev. LeBach.

Monday night at Mt. Zion, G.W. Young.

Monday night at the court house in Williamstown, Attorney T.H. Clark, of Columbus, Ohio.

Tuesday night at the court house in Williamstown, Attorney T.H. Clark, of Columbus, Ohio.[12]

[9] 20 August 1903. *Williamstown Courier.* Author Unknown.
[10] 27 August 1903. *Williamstown Courier.* Author Unknown.
[11] 27 August 1903. *Williamstown Courier.* Author Unknown.
[12] 3 September 1903. *Williamstown Courier.* Author Unknown.

Mason

Local Option is the sole topic of conversation in and around Mason at the present time.

Rev. Benton, of the Methodist church closed his services here Sunday night with a rousing temperance lecture, imploping those who believe in sobriety, good government and the welfare of the church to cast their vote for Local Option.

Misses Mary and Fannie Threlkeld, who have been visiting in Cincinnati for several weeks, have returned.

James, the little son of John Fortner, met with a serious misfortune last week by having three fingers of his left hand badly cut and ground into a jelly. The physician who dressed the wound says the fingers, if saved, will be useless to him.

Squire Robinson, who has been on a visit to friends and relatives at Erlanger and Covington, has returned home.

During the thunderstorm last week the lightning struck the residence of Walter Gardner, doing considerable damage, and on Saturday another bolt struck the steeple of our Methodist church almost demolishing it.[13]

A Splendid Victory

The "Drys" Win In Both Town And County

In the Local Option elections held in Williamstown on Wednesday, Sept. 9, 1903, and in the entire county Saturday, Sept. 12, 1903, the "wets" got the worst of it, the town going "dry" by 17 majority and the county by 540. Fourteen of the seventeen precincts in the county went dry by majorities ranging from 5 to 77, and the other three went wet by majorities ranging from 14 to 44. The total vote in the town was 147 65 wet and 82 dry, or a majority of 17 dry. The total vote in the county was 1988 724 wet and 1264 dry, or a majority of 540 dry.

There was a vote taken on Local Option in this county June 15, 1896, when the total vote cast was 1873 777 wet and 1086 dry, or a majority of 319 dry, which shows a gain of 114 in the total vote cast, and 178 for the drys, while the wets show a loss of 54 in the county.

As many precincts went wet in 1896, when we only had thirteen, as went wet Saturday, when we had seventeen. In 1896, Downingsville precinct, which then included Jonesville, gave a wet majority of 115 out of a total vote of 217, while on Saturday the same territory, out of a total vote of 199, gave only 15 majority wet. The other two changes of importance were in Flat Creek and Dry Ridge. Flat Creek changed from a dry majority of 44 in 1896 to a wet majority of 14, Saturday, and Dry Ridge reversed this order by changing from 69 wet in 1896 to 44 dry on Saturday. The other wet precinct is Mt. Zion, which just doubled its wet majority of 22 in 1896, and made it 44 Saturday.

The largest dry majority in any one precinct in 1896 was 76 in Corinth, and Corinth gave the largest again Saturday, 77, with East Williamstown No. 1 a close second in both elections with 73 in 1896 and 74 Saturday, but counting the two East Williamstown precincts as one, as they were in 1896, and the dry majority Saturday would be 118, while in all three of the Williamstown precincts Saturday the majority was 165 dry as against 114 dry in the same territory in 1896.

Now the next thing in order is for the people who have VOTED the town and county DRY to see that the law in impartially and strictly enforced, so as to make and keep them dry according to their expressed will. It is better for both sides that this should be done, so that we may know for a certainty which is better, "wet" or "dry."

Following is the official vote for both elections, as counted and certified by the county election commissioners:

Official Vote

of the Local Option Elections held in the town of Williamstown, Wednesday, Sept. 9, 1903, and in Grant county Saturday, Sept. 12, 1903:

In Williamstown.

Against sale of liquor	82
For sale of liquor	65
Total votes cast	147
Majority against sale	17

In Grant County.

[13] 10 September 1903. *Williamstown Courier.* Author Unknown.

Precinct	For	Against
E. Williamstown No. 1	37	111
E. Williamstown No. 2	24	68
West Williamstown	48	95
Corinth	22	99
Cordova	54	121
Mason	28	78
Keefer	13	33
Cross Roads	10	81
Stewartsville	15	63
Downingsville	65	45
Jonesville	42	47
Flat Creek	75	61
Mt. Zion	94	50
Sherman	35	68
Crittenden	31	69
East Dry Ridge	68	88
West Dry Ridge	63	87
Totals	724	1264

Total votes cast	1988
Majority against sale	540

There are at present eight saloons in the county, four in Williamstown, three in Dry Ridge and one in Downingsville. These will all continue in operation, of course, until the expiration of their State licenses, which were issued to them by the County Clerk, and will close out, of course, on the expiration of these licenses. Under this rule three of them two at Dry Ridge, Mrs. Lafferty's and Fred Hutchinson's, and the one at Downingsville, W.P. Kinman's, will close Nov. 10, 1903; one in Williamstown, Williams Stroud's, Nov. 14, 1903, and W.T. Simmons' in Williamstown, Nov. 16, 1903. This will leave three to run over into the new year, and on Feb. 5, 1904, R.L. Renneckar's license at Dry Ridge will expire, and there will be but two left, both in Williamstown, and of these J.D. Sechrist's will expire April 8, 1904, and the last one, John Perry's, April 11, 1904, at noon, which by the way, will be County Court day. This will give us two more County Courts before the first lot closes, and seven more before the last one reaches a state of innocuous desuetude. This of course, is on the idea that the State license controls, if it does not, and the Town license controls, then William Stroud will run till February 5, 1904, and W.T. Simmons till March 7, 1904, the date at which their Town licenses expire.[14]

[14]17 September 1903. *Williamstown Courier.* Author Unknown.

Latest Amendment To Local Option Law

Published By Request For The Information Of The Public

AN ACT for the better enforcement of an act approved March 10, 1894, entitled "An Act whereby the sense of the people of any county, city, town, district or precinct may be taken as to whether spirituous, vinous or malt liquors shall be sold, bartered or loaned therein," and to amend section 4 of said act.

Be it enacted by the General Assembly of the Commonwealth of Kentucky:

1. In an indictment for a violation of any provision of the act approved March tenth, one thousand eight hundred ninety-four, entitled "An act whereby the sense of the people of any county, city, town, distract or precinct may be taken as to whether spirituous, vinous or malt liquors shall be sold, bartered, or loaned therein," or for a violation of any act amendatory thereof, it shall not be necessary to allege that a vote was taken or an election held, or any other step relative thereto; but it may be simply stated that the act or acts charged were committed in a territory where the said act was in force; and in said indictment it shall be sufficient to designate said act as the local option law.

2. It shall be unlawful for any person to sell, lend, give, procure for, or furnish to another, any spirituous, vinous or malt liquors, or to have in his possession spirituous, vinous or malt liquors, for the purpose of selling them in any territory where said act is in force, and any person so offending shall be fined not less than fifty nor more than one hundred dollars, and imprisoned not less than ten nor more than fifty days.

The possession of United States special tax stamp (commonly called United States license) for carrying on the business of a retail dealer in spirituous, vinous or malt liquors, or the having of such a stamp or license stuck up at the place of business in such territory shall be prima facie evidence of guilt under this section.

3. On the second or any subsequent conviction for a violation of said act, or any of its amendments, the court shall require the defendant to execute bond in the sum of two hundred dollars to be of good behavior for the period of twelve months.

The court may, in its discretion, increase the amount of the bond, and if the bond is not given the defendant shall be committed to the county jail for a period not exceeding ninety days, to be fixed by the court.

4. All the shipments of spirituous, vinous or malt liquors to be paid for on delivery, commonly called "C.O.D. shipments," into any county, city, town, district or precinct where said act is in force shall be unlawful and shall be deemed sales of such liquors at the place where the money is paid or the goods delivered; the carrier and his agents selling or delivering such goods shall be liable jointly with the vendor thereof.

5. Section four of said act is stricken out, and in lieu thereof the following is inserted:

"After the entry of the certificate of the canvassing board as above provided for, in the order-book of the county court, if the vote was given against the sale, barter or loan of spirituous, vinous or malt liquors in the said county, city, town, district or precinct, as the case may be, to any person, except as hereinafter provided; any person who shall sell, barter or loan, directly or indirectly, any such liquors in said county, city, town, district or precinct shall, upon conviction, be fined not less than sixty nor more than one hundred dollars, or be confined in the county jail for not less than ten nor more than forty days, or both so fined and imprisoned, in the discretion of the court or jury, for each offense; and any person who knowingly furnished or rents a house, room, wagon, or any conveyance or thing, in which spirituous, vinous or malt liquors are sold, bartered or loaned, in violation of this act, shall, upon conviction thereof, be fined not less than sixty nor more than one hundred dollars, and the house, wagon, vehicle, land or other thing in which the liquors were sold, bartered or loaned shall be liable for all fines adjudged against the person selling, bartering or loaning the same."[15]

Approved March 11, 1902.

Enforce the Law

There was a large crowd of solid and determined citizens present at the Mass Meeting in the court house, Sunday afternoon, to consider the matter of the better enforcement of the Local Option law. The meeting seemed to be a unit in favor of prompt and energetic measures, and any violators of the law, had better "look a leedle oudt," if they wish to avoid trouble. The law having been adopted, it should be enforced.[16]

Pendleton Goes Dry

Both County And City Vote Against Booze By Substantial Majorities

Falmouth, Ky., Dec. 13. The local option election held in this City today resulted in victory for the drys in all four precincts. The total majority was thirty-six. The result was a surprise to the saloon people, who called the election, fearing that they would be put out of business by the county election to be held next Tuesday, under the unit law.

The fight was waged with vigor and the temperance people are jubilant. Prayer services were held in all the churches, the ladies and children marched through the streets and sandwiches and coffee were served. When the result was learned the church bells rang out the glad tidings and more special services followed.[17]

Dr. Young Lectures

Thinks A Constitutional Amendment

Which Will Prohibit Manufacture Of Whiskey In Kentucky

May Be Sprung By Temperance People At No Distance Date

It is not improbable that within the next few years a constitutional amendment will come before the Legislature of the State of Kentucky, prohibiting both the manufacturing and selling of whiskey in the state. Dr. G.W. Young, Field Secretary for the

[15] 28 January 1904. *Williamstown Courier.* Author Unknown.
[16] 7 July 1904. *Williamstown Courier.* Author Unknown.
[17] 11 December 1906. *Grant County News.* Author Unknown.

Anti Saloon League, made this statement in his address here last Sunday and stated that he believed that such a thing was highly probable.

Dr. Young stated that 96 of the 119 counties in the state are now in the dry belt, 26 of them having voted whisky out within that past five and a half months, and that other elections would shortly be held in Georgetown, Richmond, Cynthiana, Bowling Green and other booze afflicted sections, which would in all probability render them dry. He believes that the state of Kentucky is going to become one of the dryest spots on the map and that the distilleries will have to close down. He does not think, however that this will affect the corn crop, but the people of Kentucky will raise more hogs and less hell.

The doctor delivered a very excellent aadress to a crowded house, which was listened to with marked attention. We have seen pictures on comic valentines that were homlier than is the Doctor, but his good looks do not keep him from getting the attention of a crowd and keeping it, nor from making a subject which is naturally a dry one, rather interesting. He is an enthusiastic worker for the temperance cause, and is very likely doing more to gain converts than any other temperance speaker in the state. He delivered his address in Williamstown Sunday night to a crowded house.[18]

Another Victory

Temperance Win In Richmond By A Substantial Majority

Richmond, Ky., March 14. Tuesday's election to decide whether or not Richmond should remain a "wet" town, or should be "dry" resulted in a victory for the drys, the majority being 148. There are twelve saloons in Richmond, each of which pays into the city treasury $1,000 per annum. The saloons made a hard fight but were defeated. It is estimated that nearly $8,000 was sent into Richmond by outside liquor elements to carry the election for the saloons, and as much as $20 each was paid for votes. The women of Richmond braved the mud and worked hard through the entire day. They established lunch counters at each one of the four precincts from which sandwiches and hot coffee were served. At five o'clock in the morning the church bells began ringing and were kept ringing throughout the entire day. Children of the schools paraded the streets carrying large banners and singing hymns. The licenses of the twelve saloons will expire June 30.[19]

Wets Win Victory

Local Option In Lawrenceburg, Results in a Victory for the Saloons

Lawrenceburg, Ky., Mar. 25 In the local option contest in this city to-day the vote was 231 "wet" and 154 "dry." It was the hottest ever waged in the state under the county unit law.

The tolling of church bells and the blowing of whistles awoke the inhabitants at daylight. Prayer meetings were held in the churches and on the street corners. Two hundred school children, singing religious hymns paraded the streets from early morning, carrying American flags and banners bearing: "Vote to save my boys and girls," and "Vote as you pray and vote for my home."

The whisky interests in this county are very large, there being eight saloons and fifteen distilleries. The most prominent temperance orators in the county delivered address in the campaign. Only one arrest was made to-day. Saloon Keeper Boggs was taken late this afternoon for entering his place of business. His trial is set for to-morrow.[20]

Maysville Not in Dry Belt

Local Option Election Carried By "Wets" By a Substantial Majority Tuesday

Maysville, Ky., May 9. The "wets" won a decisive majority in the local option election here Tuesday, the majority in favor of booze being 348.

[18] 15 February 1907. *Grant County News.* Author Unknown.
[19] 15 March 1907. *Grant County News.* Author Unknown.
[20] 29 March 1907. *Grant County News.* Author Unknown.

The "wets" carried every ward in the city but the Sixth.

Impressive services were held at all the churches by the prohibitionists. In the driving rain women and children paraded behind brass bands, and wemon from various churches were stationed at booths close to the pools serving lunch and hot coffee to the voters.

The "drys" will immediately take steps to hold another election under the Cammack county unit law.[21]

Cynthiana Voted "Wet"

Liquor Element Carries The Bluegrass Town By A Small Majority

Cynthiana, Ky., May 23. By a vote of 492 to 458 Cynthiana voted to keep open saloons Thursday last. The total vote was 950. Another attempt will made to carry the city in July, when the "drys" hope to overcome the small majority registered against them.

There was no disorder and little argument in the booths. Union prayer meetings were held in the Baptist church during the day and the church bells were rung to call the voters to their duty.[22]

Not Even Free Drinks Allowed in Dry Spots

Supreme Court Of Ohio Says One Shall Not Give Away Liquor Where It Cannot Be Legally Sold

By a decision of the Supreme Court of Ohio, rendered Tuesday, it is held that liquor may not be given to a person in a town or village where it may not be legally sold. Heretofore it has been the custom in places where the sale of intoxicants was forbidden to at times evade the law by setting up a free dispensary and giving a drink of liquor or a bottle of beer to callers. The decision is in an Erie county case of Ohio against Linder, but the decision applies all over the State. Linder was prosecuted for selling in a dry township. He set up the defense that the liquor was given without charge. The Court held that liquor could be given away without violation of the law against selling. The prosecutor excepted and went to the Supreme Court and the decision of Tuesday sustains his exceptions and reverses the finding of the Lower Court. Times Star[23]

Investigation By Court of Inquiry

Violations Of Local Option Law Probed By Local Optionists in Williamstown

Williamstown, Ky July 4. The Court of Inquiry suggest by the recent grand jury for the investigation of illegal sale of liquor in Grant county was in session Saturday, and will hold weekly sessions every Saturday from now on as long as they think necessary. The object of the court is to get a line on the blind tigers that are said to exist here and elsewhere in the county and if possible secure sufficient evidence for the conviction of the lawbreakers.

They are making a thorough investigation and probing deeply into the matter, and have already discovered other government licenses than those in existence in Williamstown. It is the purpose of this court to make it extreamely uncomfortable for any who in the future engages in the sale of liquor in Grant county. They invite all good citizens to meet with them every Saturday.[24]

Taming The "Tiger"

Law And Order League At County Seat

Successfully Beard The Great Cat In His Den

[21] 10 May 1907. *Grant County News.* Author Unknown.
[22] 24 May 1907. *Grant County News.* Author Unknown.
[23] 27 June 1907. *Williamstown Courier.* Author Unknown.
[24] 5 July 1907. *Grant County News.* Author Unknown.

And His Prowling Footsteps Will No More Disturb The Midnight Slumberer

WILIAMSTOWN, Ky., July 18. Screwed down and riveted is the way the "lid" has been fastened on in this town during the past week by the city dads with the assistance of the Law and Order League. And if there is a town in the state of like size in which it is harder to buy a drink of the kind that cheers and also inebriates, we would like to have its name. Never before in the history of Williamstown has she been so "dry," and it can also be truly said that never before in her history has there been so little drunkenness.

It has been only a few weeks since the Law and Order League took the matter in hand and determined to stamp out every "blind tiger" that was said to exist here. Today it may be said that their work has been a complete success. It is doubtful if there is now a single drop of intoxicants being sold here. But the Law and Order League is determined that present conditions shall be made permanent, and to accomplish that end they are working night and day to get evidence against parties who are alleged to have been dealing in "fire water." And their work is not in vain. Almost every sitting of the court of inquiry results in some new testimony and new counts against those who are alleged to have violated the law. The court has been sitting every day, and when a county, which amounts to the same thing in this court that an indictment does in the circuit court, is found against any one, no matter what the charge, if the court has jurisdiction, the offender is given immediate trial in the police court before a jury. The result has been heavy fines during the week. In nearly every instance, however, the parties fined have appealed their cases to the circuit court, which will not meet again till October, and have executed bond for their appearance. Witnesses have been summoned before the court of inquiry who have told everything they knew, and their testimony, has resulted in many additional counts being found against alleged violators of the local option law.

A Star Witness

On Friday of last week the court was in session all day. B.F. Lanter was a star witness, and when he left the stand fifty or more additional counts were chalked up against James A. O'Hara. On the same day Louis Myers was tried on a charge of selling whiskey by "bootlegging" methods. He was found guilty and given the limit, $100 and costs. George Pritchard was tried on a similar charge next day and was given a like dose. Pritchard appealed his case to the October term and it is said that Myers will also take an appeal. The trial of C.O. Porter for selling whiskey resulted in a hung jury.

The local option element are are more determined than ever before to stamp whiskey out and to stop the illegal sale of the article. They declare that they will never rest a minute until this has been done. They claim to have no personal feeling against the sellers, but the traffic itself is what they object to, and they will lend those who are now engaged in its illegal sale every assistance in their power if they will but quit and stay quit.

Other "Tigers"

And when they have accomplished this end in Williamstown they propose to turn their attention to other points in the county. They claim that they have the best of evidence that a "blind tiger" exists in Dry Ridge as well as at one or two other points in Grant county, and that they intend to stamp them out just as they have those in Williamstown. They are well supplied with funds which have been freely contributed from every side, tho' they are still soliciting dollar subscriptions from all who feel interested, and promise that such list shall be published in the Grant County News.

A result of the recent crusade is very noticeable. Formerly, and even since the closing of saloons, rarely a day or even an hour has passed without there being more or less signs of drunkenness on the streets, and on some occasions these drunks have been more numerous than in the old days of the wide open saloon. The same old crowd of "booze fighters" as of yore are here yet, but they are just as sober as they ever were in their lives, and a man the least bit under the influence of liquor is the exception rather than the rule. Of course, one can get liquor by having it shipped in, but the class that drink most and are most offensive to the people who care most for the morals of the community are not as a rule a class that has liquor shipped in from other points, but depend largely on "blind tigers" for their supply of thirst quencher.

The police court is presided over by Judge D.S. Clay, who is dishing out justice with quiet, cool dignity, tho' at times the action of the attorneys for the defense in building and ridiculing witnesses and seeking to reflect on the dignity and character of the court, its officers and jurors, has called from his honor an ominous warning note.

The lawyers for the prosecution are Messrs C.H. Beasley and E.K. Wilson, and they are leaving no stone unturned to secure convictions. M.D. Gray and J.J. Blackburn are attorneys for the defense, and they are working hard.[25]

The "Tiger" Is Dead

Peace Declared In The County Seat

Compromise Agreement Reached Between League And "Tiger"

Former Agree To Plead Guilty To All Charges Thus Far Found And Submit To Court's Judgment

---

Williamstown, Ky., July 25. The battle is over, the war is ended, the "tiger" is dead and peace reigns. Where a week ago all was bitterness, recrimination, charges of bribery, subornation of witnesses and bitter feeling generally, today there hovers the white-winged dove of peace, and her love-like cooing, figuratively speaking, is the only sound heard on dusty streets on these hot days in July when the mercury tries to climb out at the top of the bulb.

This result has not been accomplished without a great deal of hard work on the part of those who have been on the trail of the "tiger," but they are satisfied that it has been accomplished at all, and they believe that he is dead beyond the hope of resurrection and that probably never again will one of these animals make his lair among them.

It has been but six weeks since the campaign for the extermination of "blind tigers" in Williamstown was commenced by the organization known as the Law and Order League, and that it has been brought to a successful issue in that length of time seems rather remarkable.

At the meeting of the League Monday night the proposal was made that a committee be appointed to confer with the offenders, those who it was claimed had violated the local option law, and to find out upon what sort of a basis they were willing to settle the matter. The vote on the appointment of the committee developed the fact that there were two factions in the league, the radical and the conservative factions. The radicals were opposed to compromise on any terms, the conservatives favored a compromise. The radicals, headed by the chairman, J.W. Lancaster, withdrew from the league, and the work went on by the remainder.

The committee appointed to confer with the operators of the "tiger" reported and their report was accepted. Under the terms of the agreement it is a compromise and yet not a compromise. Each one of the offenders agrees to plead guilty to each offense already found against him and to pay his fine without further bickering, and to forever stop the illegal sale of liquor, so far as they are concerned in Grant county, while the Law and Order League agrees to pursue their investigations no further. This means that about $5,500 will be paid into the police court of Williamstown, and that after attorney's fees have been paid there will still remain a goodly sum in the treasury of the town.[26]

For Straight Prohibition

H.S. Bonsib, of Indianapolis, a straight out prohibition solicitor, was here from Saturday until Monday and spoke Sunday forenoon at Salem, accompanying Rev. M.S. Clark, the pastor, and at night addressed the congregation of Rev. L.N. Thompson at the Baptist Church.[27]

---

[25] 19 July 1907. *Grant County News.* Author Unknown.
[26] 26 July 1907. *Grant County News.* Author Unknown.
[27] 5 September 1907. *Williamstown Courier.* Author Unknown.

Capitol Comment

Temperance Question Leading Issue

In Coming Election Of State Officers

Lobbyists The Only Danger To Cause Of Prohibition — Frankfort Notes

---

Frankfort, Ky., Sept. 11.

The temperance question is now the leading issue.

Both the leading political parties realize this and are mustering their forces accordingly.

The people at large are the controlling element; the politicians are fully aware that without the assistance of the great common people they are nothing. The people must have what they want. They want prohibition or liquor which?

Ninety counties of the 119 in this Grand Old Commonwealth have voted liquor out. Now the question is shall 29 counties control 90. The people of good old Grant will say no as will the other 89 which are dry.

But there is an element that has not yet been taken into consideration. Dear reader, the first thought that enters your mind is who? The lobbyist is the only man the temperance people have cause to fear.

If he can be kept out of Frankfort during the next session of the Legislature, there is no doubt of the lawmaking body passing a bill whereby the voters of Kentucky may decide as to whether the State shall free herself of the liquor traffic.

Can we keep him out? No, but we must combat him. If every county in the State had a man to represent it who is as true and tried and loyal as the democratic nominee from Grant, there would be no trouble foretelling the result.

Reviewing the past we find that there has always been an element in the General Assembly who failed, at the critical moment, to follow the directions of their constituents.

The whisky lobbyist will be here next January; you may prepare yourself for that.

He will have an unlimited amount of money, and his instructions will be to win regardless of cost.

Frankfort itself is in favor of the traffic, there being no less than forty-seven saloons in north Frankfort. Luckily the residents of the south side at the time they were annexed to the city, had a clause embraced in their charter whereby it would never be possible for the city council or other governing body to issue license for the sale of liquor in their section.

County after county has nominated a candidate for the Legislature, many of them declaring beforehand as to their standing on the question.

The people should make a note of all this and relegate any man to a back seat, who fails to keep his pledge.

This is a question for Democrats and Republicans both to consider. When Grant county went dry, you did not look while in the voting booth for the rooster nor for the log cabin. You voted Yes or No. Now when election day comes will you vote the Democratic ticket because it is Democratic, or the Republican ticket because it is Republican, or will you vote your sentiments? first seeing which party favors your views.

Your Democratic nominee has declared himself on the question. Now watch the Republican and see where he stands.

After the election watch the winner and see how he votes while representing you. If he fails to represent you according to instructions, bury him in political oblivion.[28]

Given Heavy Fine For Selling Booze

Police Judge N.D.C. Mains Is Macadamizing The Pathway Of The Transgressors With Boulders — Making A Rocky Road To Travel

---

Ernest Sharp, son of Gus Sharp, came to town and after loading up on some home made "bug juice" mounted his fine saddle horse and proceeded to give our citizens an exhibition of what his horse could do. He raced up and down Main-cross street pounding his horse in the head with a club and finally landed flat of his back in the mud and a little later Marshal Bishop landed him in jail.

His father came to the rescue and bailed him out. He was arraigned before Judge N.D.C. Mains on a charge

[28] 13 September 1907. *Grant County News.* Author Unknown.

of drunkenness and given a fine of $5 and trimmings.

Sharp confessed that he bought his whiskey from William Crofford, who is a member of the firm Woods & Crofford. They conduct a grocery and restaurant on the corner of Main and Bridge streets in the Randeheimer building.

A warrant was issued for both Arthur Woods and William Crofford. Crofford eluded the officers and went to the country and has not been arrested.

Woods was tried before Judge N.D.C. Mains for furnishing whiskey to be sold on his premises and $100 each in two cases for selling whiskey in local option territory making $320 in all. Woods took an appeal and will carry the case to the Court of Appeals. Woods claims to be a partner with Crofford in the restaurant and grocery, and it also developed that they rent the building in partnership, and pay $30 per month for same.

Crofford holds a government license to retail liquor, but Woods swore he had nothing to do with this.

Ernest Sharp, who testified that he obtained the whiskey from Crofford, is a minor being 20 years of age. - Falmouth Outlook.[29]

Madisonville Dry

Madisonville, Ky., July 8 The local option election held in Madisonville today resulted in a victory for the "drys" by a majority of 37 votes, and since five o'clock this afternoon there has been general rejoicing in the Prohibition ranks all over the city. The campaign has been a warm one for the past three weeks, men, women and children, colored and white, engaging in the fight. There are twelve saloons in Madisonville and each one paid $1,200 annually to the city treasury.[30]

Temperance Rally

The temperance workers of the Second Magisterial District met at Stewartsville Baptist Church Saturday, September 12, and Dr. E. Day was elected chairman, Mace Hampton secretary and J. R. Boles treasurer.

The entire afternoon was spent in arranging plans for the campaign. At 12 o'clock a delightful dinner was served of which all partook heartily.

In the afternoon Revs. J.D. Norris, of Georgia, and J.A. Lee, of Glencoe, delivered addresses, which were greatly enjoyed by everyone present.[31]

Well Supplied

Danville Bootlegger Caught With A Barrel Of Whisky

Chief of Police Logan Wood and Policeman James Dunn arrested Joe Harlan, colored, Saturday afternoon, on the charge of selling liquor in that city, says the Danville Advocate. Harlan had in his possession a barrel of whisky when discovered. He stated that he had brought the liquor from Lexington the night before in a buggy and that he was associated with a Lexington saloon keeper, who had agreed to divide the profits with him. He gave the name of the saloon keeper to the officer, and a warrant was sworn out for him and an officer sent to Lexington to place him under arrest. Harlan pleaded guilty in seven cases, and Judge Puryear handed him a lemon in the shape of total fines aggregating $420 and costs. Harlan left Danville a few months ago under the promise never to return if the fines amounting to more than $400 against him were suspended so long as he remained out of town. Now that he has returned, his total fines and costs aggregate over $1,000; so he is now doomed to serve for about three years in the workhouse. If his behavior is good, he will get out in time to participate in the presidential election four years hence. "The way of the transgressor is hard." The barrel of liquor is in the office of County Attorney W.J. Price.[32]

Is your News subscription paid?

[29] 28 May 1908. *Williamstown Courier.* Author Unknown.
[30] 16 July 1908. *Williamstown Courier.* Author Unknown.
[31] 17 September 1908. *Williamstown Courier.* Author Unknown.
[32] 1 October 1908. *Williamstown Courier.* Author Unknown.

Went Dry

Second Magisterial District Goes For Local Option By Nearly Two To One

Every Precinct Went Dry

The "drys" won a decisive victory in the local option election Saturday in the Second Magisterial District in Grant county and the Jonesville precinct in Owen county. So the last booze dispensary in Grant has gone to join the many that were wiped out some time ago.

The vote by precincts as reported over the phone is as follows:[33]

Precinct	Wet	Dry	Maj.
Mason	16	68	52
Corinth	32	98	66
Keefer	21	42	21
Cross Roads	27	80	53
Stewartsville	40	70	30
Downingsville	65	69	4
Jonesville	66	86	20
	267	513	246
Jonesville in Own			40
Total "dry" majority			286

LaRue County Goes Overwhelmingly Dry

The local option election in LaRue county on Saturday resulted in a sweeping victory for the "drys" by a majority of 1085. There was a light vote polled and the "wets" showed little animation in their flight. The ratio of the vote was about four to one. As it is, LaRue county is totally dry and it was the wets who caused the election in the hope of winning and having an entirely wet county. Several years ago Hodgenville, the only place where whiskey was sold in the county, took a vote and the Prohibitionists won by about 50 majority. This time the majority in the county seat was enormous. - News.[34]

Liquor Question

To be Debated by Editors at Estill Springs

In accordance with a rule laid down for the last midwinter meeting of the Kentucky Press Association, only subjects of immediate interest will be discussed at the regular meeting and outing, which will take place during the latter part of June at Estill Springs.

H.A. Sommers, editor of the Elizabethtown News, is Chairman of the Program Committee, and he has arranged a joint debate between Clarence E. Woods, Mayor of Richmond, and George R. Washburn, editor of the Wine and Spirit Bulletin, as one of the main features of the occasion. The subject of the debate will be:

Resolved, That State-wide prohibition would prove beneficial to Kentucky. The affirmative will be taken by Mayor Woods, who is an ardent Prohibitionist, while the negative will be Mr. Washburn's position.

The Program Committee has many other features of great interest, which will be incorporated in the program for the June meeting, and it is expected that the new system will prove more than successful State Journal.[35]

Chautauqua

Work is Booming

Statewide Prohibition Making Great Headway

The third week of Statewide Prohibition Chautauqua marks a great success. At Vanceburg, Ky., the interest was especially intense, the people at that place soon grasping the significance of this great campaign. At Ashland, although practically no preparation had been made locally, the success was all that could have been hoped for one man was so enthused over the possibilities for Prohibition in Kentucky that he contributed $250 to further the work.

C.J. Hall, of California, Frank S. Regan, the noted tax expert and cartoonist, the Loose family of musicians, L.L. Pickett and J.B. Harris

[33] 1 October 1908. *Williamstown Courier.* Author Unknown.
[34] 28 January 1909. *Williamstown Courier.* Author Unknown.
[35] 22 April 1909. *Williamstown Courier.* Author Unknown.

have been meeting with special enthusiasm. Joe Jameson, the famous humorist and lecturer, declared by Geo. W. Bain and others to be the most eloquent man on the American continent, will be added to the force this week.

People have been enthusiastic in their commendations of this Chautauqua. We give below a few of the kind expressions heard:

A number of fine speakers and excellent music-large crowds have attended each session. - Mt. Sterling Sentinel Democrat.

The music alone is worth the price of admission. - The Oldham Era, La Grange, Ky.

Exhaust your vocabulary and more will be true. - Rev. C.M. Summers, La Grange, Ky.

Every taxpayer should hear Senator Regan he is an eye-opener. - J[]o Frazier, Cashier Bank, Mt. Sterling, Ky.

At first I feared this was a third party movement. I seldom endorse anything but I do endorse this with all my heart. - Dr. Weber. Mt. Sterling, Ky.

Send Regan back and we will have every man in town to hear "The Fool Taxpayer." - B.W. Trimble, Editor Mt. Sterling Advocate.[36]

---

[36] 15 July 1909. *Williamstown Courier.* Author Unknown.

1910s

Government Licenses

By The Wholesale Were Issued To Williamstown's "Bootleggers"

When Internal Revenue Collector, Munson, Caught Them Red Handed

Fourteen Is The Number Alleged To Have Been Issued In One Day

One Of The Gang Said To Tipped The Rest Off To The Revenue Man

Internal Revenue Collector, Munson, swooped down in Williamstown one day last week and compelled fourteen of them to take out a government license, it is reported.

The Collector came to Williamstown some two or three weeks ago and made a quiet investigation. The investigation convinced him that not only was "bootlegging" being indulged in, but that it was being done by the wholesale.

He caught one of the alleged "bootleggers" with the goods on him and informed him that he must take out a government license at once or he would be taken before the Federal Grand Jury to answer the complaint of selling whisky without government license.

This "bootlegger" was a good-natured sort of a fellow and a little tipsy at the time, and thinking he was doing the other boys a favor, he took the internal revenue man around and introduced him to 13 others suspected of "bootlegging." The result was that the whole fourteen agreed to take out government license, and subsequently they did.

Of course, all these sellers of whiskey are now protected from arrest so far as the government is concerned, but the fact that they have a government license will be used against them when the grand jury convenes some three or four weeks hence, and it's not at all improbable that a big batch of indictments will be returned.

Fourteen "bootleggers," each with a government license, ought to be sufficient to keep the average "booze fighter" in Williamstown and the surrounding territory pretty well supplied, and there must be a tremendous profit in the illicit calling of "bootlegging."[1]

Pendleton and Harrison Counties Vote "Dry"

County Seat of Harrison Has Very Small Margin For Temperance

After a hard-fought campaign waged by both sides both Harrison and Pendleton counties voted "dry" Tuesday. The city of Cynthiana voted "dry" by a majority of 35, and the county of Harrison by a majority of 988.

Pendleton county gave the "drys" a majority of 841, and Falmouth a majority of 90. Both counties and the city of Cynthiana were already "dry," and the election was called at the instance of the "wets."[2]

On Charge Of "Bootlegging"

Kirtley Barnes Was Arrested And Tried, But Jury Disagreed

[1] 6 January 1911. *Grant County News.* Author Unknown.
[2] 28 April 1911. *Grant County News.* Author Unknown.

Kirtley Barnes, 21, a son of J.O. Barnes, was arrested on an information from City Attorney J.J. Blackburn, last Monday, and a charge of "bootlegging" preferred. A trial was had of the case Tuesday afternoon, but the jury could not agree and another trial will be had Saturday.

Barnes was accused of having purchased whiskey in Cincinnati for other parties and having made a profit on the whiskey. He testified that he did not make a profit but accepted the money for the whiskey as a matter of accommodation.[3]

Kirtley Barnes Found "Not Guilty"

Trial of Young Farmer Results In His Acquittal

Kirtley Barnes, son of J.O. Barnes, a prominent farmer of near town, who was arraigned the early part of last week on a charge of selling liquor and had a trial Tuesday which resulted in a hung jury, was again tried last Saturday afternoon and the jury found a verdict of acquittal. There was no evidence found that would lead to the conclusion that Barnes had been selling liquor. Another party had given him money to procure a certain quantity of whiskey and Barnes had purchased the goods and turned it over without making a profit. This is not a violation of the liquor laws.[4]

"Blind Tigers" Put To Work

On The Roads And Barrels Of Liquor To Be Emptied Into Gutters

Asheville Enforcing Law

Asheville, N.C., May 22 Four of the "blind tigers" charged with violation of the "search and seize" law were found guilty in the police court this morning and received sentences ranging from eight months to two years on the county roads. In one case prayer for judgment was continued for six months on the defendant's promise that he would never again engage in illegal liquor traffic, and that he would surrender the seized goods, valued at $1,200, to the city authorities.

After papers to this effect had been drawn up the court directed that the contents of the 53 barrels be poured into the city's gutters. It is said that the occasion will be made one of joyous celebration by local prohibitionists.

In the cases where sentence was passed appeals were taken to the superior court. - Atlanta Constitution.[5]

Prohibition Repeal Is Carried In Maine

Augusta, Me., Sept. 18 Complete official returns from the special election of last Monday, when Maine voted on the repeal of the constitutional prohibitory amendment, as canvassed by the governor and council tonight, showed a majority of twenty votes in favor of the repeal.[6]

Prohibition Candidate

For Governor Was Here Last Wednesday

Rev. J.D. Redd, Prohibition candidate for Governor of Kentucky, was here last Tuesday and Wednesday and delivered two brief addresses at the court house. Rev. Redd was formerly pastor of the Williamstown Methodist church and is very well known here, but it does not seem likely that he will cut any very great figure in the Gubernatorial race.[7]

---

[3] 12 May 1911. *Grant County News.* Author Unknown.
[4] 19 May 1911. *Grant County News.* Author Unknown.
[5] 2 June 1911. *Grant County News.* Author Unknown.
[6] 22 September 1911. *Grant County News.* Author Unknown.
[7] 20 October 1911. *Grant County News.* Author Unknown.

Too Much Xmas Booze

And Alvin Hicks Draws A $10.00 Fine For Disorderly Conduct

Alvin Hicks, a former resident of this county, who now lives in Covington, after spending a few days visiting with friends at Mason, spent the day in Williamstown Monday and got too much wildcat whisky. At the depot he got too noisy and after being admonished by Railway Detective F.A. Cunningham to keep quiet, grew opstreperous. Cunningham arrested him and brought him up town, where he was assessed $10.00 for his Christmas frolic.[8]

Drys Will Not Participate

In Local Option Election Called For Georgetown January 25th

At a meeting of the temperance people of Georgetown held at the Baptist church in that city Sunday night, it was unanimously decided that the drys would not participate in the local option election set for January 25th. The conclusion was reached after hearing the report of the executive committee of the law and order league, including a recommendation, based on advice of counsel, that the election be ignored, and after a discussion of the matter by those present.[9]

The County Unit Law

The county unit bill passed by the Senate Thursday provides that at intervals of three years 25 per cent of qualified voters of the unit the countymay petition the County Judge for an election at which the sense of the voters of the unit may be taken as to whether or not there shall be sold in the unit intoxicating liquors. It requires a majority of the legal voters in the county at this election to prohibit the sale of intoxicating liquors or to permit its sale.

Under the provision of this bill, as the Appellate court has constructed Section 61 of the constitution, if the county, the largest unit, votes wet, and the precinct, the smallest unit within the county, dry, there may be sold Intoxicating liquors only in the precincts which vote wet, as the constitution provides for the county, city, township and precinct as a unit. The bill passed is not an original measure. It is an amendment to Section 2560 of the Kentucky Statutes entitled, Liquors Intoxicating."

It provides that the words "cities of the first, second, third, and fourth classes" be stricken from the statute. But for this Amendment the law is the same as the original county unit law; which reads as follows:

"No election in any town, city, district or precinct of a county shall be held, under this article, on the same day on which an election for the entire county is held. (Except that city of the first, second, third and fourth classes may hold an election for the entire county is held.) When an election is held in an entire county and a majority of the legal votes cast at said election are against the sale, barter or loan of spiritous, vinous, malt or other intoxicating liquors, then it shall not be lawful to sell, barter or loan any such liquors in any portion of the county. Is at such an election of the entire county the majority of the legal votes cast are in favor of the sale, barter or loan of such liquors, such election shall not operate to make it legal to grant license to sell, barter or loan such liquors in any territory or division of such county from which the sale, barter or loan has been excluded by an election held under this article, or by special act, but the statues of such territorial division shall remain as if no such election had been held.

"No election shall be held in any election precinct under this act on the same day on which an election is held for the district or city of which the precinct is a part. If an election held for such entire district or city, the majority of the legal votes cast shall be in favor of the sale, barter or loan of spiritous, vinous, malt or other

[8] 22 December 1911. *Grant County News.* Author Unknown.
[9] 12 January 1912. *Grant County News.* Author Unknown.

liquors, then the status in the several precincts thereof shall remain as it was before said election; but if the majority should be against the sale, then the sale, barter or loan of such liquors shall be unlawful in every portion of said district or city."[10]

Sunday Drunks Are Fined

George Chandler Seriously Cut In Sunday Afternoon Affray

George Chandler was seriously cut in the neck by Edgar Whaley Sunday afternoon. Sixteen stitches were taken in the wound, which was inflicted with an ordinary pocket knife. Chandler rallied and was able to appear in court as a witness Monday morning.

Town Marshal Stroud rounded up a bunch of five shortly afterwards and landed them in Ed Landrum's hotel. They were charged with drunk and disorderly conduct. Monday morning Judge Gray tried Bill Hawkins and John Fount Hume, both colored, and Ed. Ransom and Thurston Somers, white, on the charge mentioned, and each of them was given a small fine.

Edgar Whaley was held on a felony charge and had a hearing Thursday morning.

A strenuous effort will be made by the attorney to clean up certain dives that are said to exist and punish the bootleggers.

Elbert Collins refused to tell where he got a pint of whiskey which he secured for Thurston Somers and he was remanded to jail until he sees fit to give the information desired. All that could be got out of him was that he could not remember.[11]

Bad Whiskey Responsible

For Fatal Shooting Affray In Railroad Grading Camp

Woman Struck By Stray Bullet And Instantly Killed

A fatal shooting affray occurred in the railroad grading camp south of Crittenden during the early hours Sunday morning, in which one of the women members of the camp was accidentally killed, and a negro man was shot and seriously wounded.

While the negroes are reticent and not inclined to talk, the following alleged facts were obtained for The News:

Early Saturday night a negro man (not a member of the Crittenden Camp, but of the Dry Ridge camp), went to the Crittenden camp with a large quantity of whiskey which he proceeded to peddle. The negroes all got drunk and late in the night a fight started between the negro bootlegger and Tom Simmons, the camp blacksmith. The bootlegger, it is alleged, opened fire on Simmons with a revolver, and Simmons drew a revolver and fired at the bootlegger.

A shot from Simmon's revolver struck Albert Jenning's wife, and instantly killed here. The same bullet struck the negro bootlegger in the abdomen and inflicted a serious injury. He has been taken to a Cincinnati hospital.

Sheriff Leary went to the scene Sunday, but no arrests were made.

This crew of negroes are all from the South and it is pretty hard to get anything out of them about the shooting.[12]

Are Fined For "Bootlegging"

Two Harrisons Will Board Off The Town For Next 60 Days

Harrison Brown and Harrison Boxley, two colored boys, are in jail as the result of acting as agent for another party in securing whiskey for Thurston Somers, a white man. Somers was arrested last Friday on a charge of drunkenness and told the court he secured his whiskey from the two Harrisons. They were arrested and later fined $60.00 and costs. In lieu of payment of the fines they will

[10] 16 February 1912. *Grant County News.* Author Unknown.
[11] 8 March 1912. *Grant County News.* Author Unknown.
[12] 22 November 1912. *Grant County News.* Author Unknown.

work on the streets for 60 days without pay. They allege that they secured the whiskey from a camp negro. The camp negro was locked up Saturday night when he came out from Cincinnati with a basket of pints and quarts of whiskey and is being held to the grand jury.[13]

Drunk And Disorderly

"Bill" Williams, colored, got drunk Sunday night and as a result was run in by the town marshal. He tried to pull loose from the marshal and was promptly knocked down. Bill is doing penance on the street cleaning department.[14]

Costly "Booze"

Charley Penny Pays Court $65.00 For Selling One Quart

Because he is alleged to have sold one quart of whiskey, Chas. Penny, colored, paid the court $65.00 last Saturday. Penny was accused by the wife of N.G. Roholl, of Mason, who swore to a warrant against him, charging him with accepting money from her husband and delivering him a quart of whisky. Penny made no defense and paid his fine.

Another Stiff Fine

Harrison Brown, also colored, is back in jail to work out a fine of $60.00 and 20 days for the alleged selling of whiskey. This is his third sentence within six months.

Alleged Violator Skips

William Hawkins, colored, has disappeared and his whereabouts are unknown. Hawkins was accused of "bootlegging" whiskey and a warrant was issued for his arrest. When an officer was sent for him he had disappeared and has not been seen since.[15]

Bootleggers Fined Heavily

Well Known Citizen Gets $60 Fine And Ten Days In Jail

Fined For Bootlegging

Martin Stamper, a well known citizen who has been a resident of Williamstown for the past 18 years where he has conducted a restaurant and grocery, and county coroner for eight years preceding the present term, together with Chas. Reed, who was for several months engaged in construction work for the Queen & Crescent Railroad, and later did the excavating for some of the new buildings going up here, were tried on a "bootlegging" charge Wednesday. Stamper was fined $60 and 10 days in jail and Reed was fined $60.00 with no jail sentence. Both were remanded to jail, Stamper to do his 10 days' term and Reed to pay out his fine.

A fine of $50.00 and costs was assessed against Walter Poe for furnishing liquor to a minor, and another fine of a like amount was assessed against Irvin Agee for the same offense.[16]

National Prohibition

Received A Set-Back By War Special Revenue Bill

Washington, September 7. - The war special revenue bill has sounded the death knell of Federal prohibition, for a few years at any rate.

The Government cannot obtain taxes from liquor and prohibit its use at one and the same time. The European war has supplied the liberals with overwhelming argument, and the passage of the additional revenue bill stops for the time being all effective work in behalf of Federal prohibition.

It happens that this situation accords with the views of the Democratic leaders of the House, who have

[13] 30 January 1914. *Grant County News.* Author Unknown.
[14] 1 May 1914. *Grant County News.* Author Unknown.
[15] 22 May 1914. *Grant County News.* Author Unknown.
[16] 5 June 1914. *Grant County News.* Author Unknown.

advocated the submission of the Hobson prohibition amendment to the House on the theory that it would be badly defeated and given a quietus for some time to come. An additional tax will be placed on beer, and possibly on liquors. Brewers and distillers, by paying an additional tax, will have set up a new bulwark against the destruction of their business. This result would have been avoided by a sale of Panama bonds, one of the devices for the raising of additional funds which has been suggested, but that device has had the opposition of both the liberals and the railroads, the latter being influenced to oppose a sale of Panama bonds because of the effect it would have on a money market into which they must soon go for large sum of new capital and the sale of new issues of securities to replace others shortly to fall due.[17]

Wets Are Winners

In Three Kentucky Counties In Local Option Elections

Twelve More Counties Will Vote On Same Question Next Monday

Louisville, Ky., Sept. 21. - In three Kentucky counties Christian, Daviess and McCracken where local option elections were held today the wets scored in every instance over the drys by a majority ranging from 600 to 800 votes.

These were the only counties in which liquor elections were held, 12 others having elected to vote next Monday, September 28. These include:

Fayette, Mason, Carroll, Boone, Henderson, Bourbon, Scott, Montgomery, Clark, Bell, Shelby and Anderson counties.

Davies county, outside the city of Owensboro, went dry by 330 votes, while in the city the wets had a majority of 888.

McCracken county outside the city gave the drys a majority of 564, while the city of Paducah gave the wets a majority of 1382.

In Daviess county where victory had been expected by the wets the advocates of licensed saloons after the vote was known paraded the streets headed by the Third Regiment Band. Cheering crowds greeted the marchers in the business district where the saloons are located but when the paraders traversed the residential thoroughfares they were hissed and jeered.

The drys in McCracken county announced as soon as the result was known that they would be ready three years hence to dispute the right of licensed saloons to do business in the county or the city of Paducah.

Christian county returned a wet majority of 585. The complete unofficial figures are: Wet 4,421 dry 3,836. Hopkinsville returned a wet majority of 630, this, making the county outside of town give a dry majority of 45. This was a big surprise, as the Prohibitionist had been counting on the country precincts to offset the certain wet marity in the town and override it by from 500 to 1,000. The town of the Pembroke, considered dry by a big margin, returned a wet majority of 87, and other precincts were equally as big surprises.

In the local option election held in Daviess county seven years ago, when the city and county voted separately, the county went dry by a majority of 1,500 and the city went wet by 400. Today the election was held under the new county unit law the city and county voting together. The wets had a great dry majority to overcome in the county precincts but for the last month they have been conducting an advertising campaign in the newspapers and sending speaker of national reputation to the rural precincts.[18]

Prohibitionists Won In Nine Counties Monday

Fayette, Henderson And Anderson Remain Wet, While Bell, Bourbon, Boone, Clark, Carroll, Mason, Montgomery, Scott and Shelby Line Up With The Drys

---

Nine more Kentucky counties are in the dry column. In the local option election held last Monday in twelve

[17] 11 September 1914. *Grant County News.* Author Unknown.
[18] 25 September 1914. *Grant County News.* Author Unknown.

counties, 9 cast their votes for prohibition and three against. The counties voting wet are Fayette, Henderson and Anderson.

Those voting dry are Bell, Boone, Bourbon, Clark, Carroll, Mason, Montgomery, Scott and Shelby,

The unofficial majorities in the twelve counties follow:

Anderson, wet, 64; Fayette, wet, 3,264; Henderson, wet 1,053.

Bell, dry, 385; Bourbon, dry, 405; Boone, dry, 530; Clark, dry, 246; Carroll, dry, 517; Mason, dry, 333; Montgomery, dry, 210; Scott, dry, 413; Shelby, dry, 583.

It will be three years before another vote on local option may be taken in any of the counties which voted Monday, and in the meantime they will remain wet or dry as they have voted, unless the Court of Appeals declares unconstitutional the local option law or the provisions of the law.

In all of the counties in which the vote was cast liquor was sold in the county seats, with the exception of Boone, and only two precincts in that county were wet.

While the campaign waged was a redhot one in almost every one of the twelve counties, the election passed of quietly and without any untoward incident to mar it.[19]

Prohibition Loses In Ohio

State wide prohibition lost in Ohio by a tremendous majority, estimated as high as 100,000, and home rule won by a small margin. State wide prohibition was lost in California, is in doubt in Washington, but has apparently won in Arizona, though the returns are meager. Colorado and Oregon have apparently voted dry, though the issue is close.[20]

Is your News subscription paid?

[19] 2 October 1914. *Grant County News.* Author Unknown.
[20] 6 November 1914. *Grant County News.* Author Unknown.

1920s

Moonshine Still Captured In Grant And Owner Arrested

United States Revenue Officer Raids Plant At Stewartsville And Confiscates Two Gallons Of Liquor

Wednesday morning a United States revenue officer accompanied by E. G. Hall, deputy sheriff of Kenton county, came out on train No. 15, drove over to Stewartsville and captured two stills used in the manufacture of whisky. They also arrested S. K. Kroninburg, who it is alleged had charge of the plant and had been engaged in the manufacture of "white mule."

The affair was conducted so quietly that few people knew anything about it in the neighborhood. It is claimed the officers found two gallons of whisky which had been manufactured and took it along as evidence. The officers took the stills and Kroninburg to Covington, passing through Williamstown without making any statement to officials here.

Kroninburg is a brother-in-law of Robert Skoll, who recently conducted a general store at Owenton, and is said, was a partner of Skoll in the general merchandising business.

Skoll and his brother-in-law purchased a small farm at Stewartsville some time ago and have been making preparations for building a store and establishing a business there. Skoll has conducted numerous sales of army goods here and at other points in this and adjoining counties.

It could not be learned here if any charge is to be preferred against Skoll and particulars regarding the raiding of the still and the arrest of Kroninburg are lacking.

Both Kroningburg and Skoll are Jews. They are reputed to be quite well to do, having accumulated their wealth during the past four or five years in the mercantile business.

It is understood that Mr. Hall stated to parties here that information of the "moonshine still" was furnished to revenue officers by a party from the Stewartsville neighborhood who was in the office of revenue department in Covington last Tuesday, and the raid followed this information.

In all the history of the county, in dry times and wet times, this is the first "still" ever confiscated here.

LATER A report current here Thursday morning says that only parts of stills were found by the revenue officer, and that the whisky confiscated was not new whisky, but old, and that part of it was mixed with roots and herbs for medicinal purposes. Nothing further concerning the arrest of Kroninburg had been learned here up to Thursday morning.[1]

Alleged "Moonshiners" On Trial In Covington

S.K. Kroninburg and R. Skoll who were arrested at Stewartsville last week charged with having a still in their possession and with having manufactured whiskey with the same are on trial in Covington Thursday for the offense.

Skoll and Kroninburg are brothers-in-law and claim that they did not manufacture any liquor and that the illicit still does not belong to them, but was left in their hands for safe keeping some time ago. There is a penalty, however, for having a still in one's possession, so it is pretty certain that the men will be let off with a stiff fine.[2]

[1] 21 January 1921. *Grant County News.* Author Unknown.
[2] 28 January 1921. *Grant County News.* Author Unknown.

Law and Order Of State Challenged By Bootlegger And Mountaineer, Says Governor, Urging 120 Officials To Act

Frankfort, Ky., Jan. 23 - "The bootlegger and moonshiner and those allied with them, today challenge the law and order in Kentucky. The impudent, brazen and determined violation of this law is rapidly bringing into contempt all law; is weakening public authority and lessening the confidence of the people of Kentucky in their laws," is the opinion expressed today by Governor Morrow in letters sent to the 120 county attorneys and sheriffs and the chief of police of the cities of the State.

In the letters Governor Morrow said: "As one of the chief law enforcing agents of your county, and as a fellow public servant chargeable also with the enforcement of the laws of the commonwealth, I write you concerning the present shameful violation of the prohibition law in Kentucky.

"I believe in the high integrity; in the capacity and courage of the State's law enforcing agents, and I feel that you will be glad to lend every power of your energy and your office to the suppression of the outbreak of lawlessness.

Says Support Is Assured

"In the enforcement of this law I believe you will have the support of the right thinking men and women of Kentucky. I believe that a quickening and aroused public sentiment will rally to your assistance.

"We can and we must accept the challenge so flauntingly offered, and having accepted it, we must reestablish the supremacy of the law of the land."

In connection with this letter the governor issued a proclamation calling upon the people of the state to cooperate and to throw their irresistible power upon their side of the law, order and decency.

"The will of the people of Kentucky," he said, "must and shall be made superior to the purposes of an outlawed traffic. The power of the bootlegger and the moonshiner must be made to bend before the authority of the sovereign law of the commonwealth."

Impudence Is Charged

The proclamation, preceded by the customary greetings, says:

"The strength of any state is determined by the courage and character of its citizenship. Today the power of the state to enforce law and maintain order is brazenly, notoriously and impudently challenged by the scandalous and open violation of the prohibition law. The moonshiner and bootlegger, and those allied with them are determined to make their will superior to the law of the people of the state.

"The open violation of the prohibition law brings to Kentucky and its people only the known evils of intemperance, but there has come with it, through it, and as a part of it, the intimidation of men and women, threats of violence against all who oppose it, perjury and subordination of perjury, and past experience of the country shows that those engaged in this business do not balk even at debauchery of public officials charged with the enforcement of the law.

"This law-breaking power strikes at the source of all public authority. Confronted with this situation, I call to the conscience of the commonwealth. I appeal to every law-enforcing officer to stand by the law of his state and to exert the utmost energy and determination in its execution and enforcement.

Calls Upon Citizens

"I call upon the people of Kentucky upon its men and women upon the leaders of thought and conduct to unite; to co-operate and to throw their irresistible power upon the side of law, order and decency.

"The will of the people of Kentucky must, and shall, be made superior to the purposes of an outlawed traffic. The power of the bootlegger and the moonshiner must be made to bend before the authority of the sovereign law of the commonwealth."[3]

Carload Of Liquor Seized

[3]28 January 1921. *Grant County News.* Author Unknown.

"Tomato" Label Fails To Disguise $45,000 Whiskey Shipment

Jacksonville, Fla., April 6 With the seizure here of a carload of whiskey valued at more than $45,000 billed as tomatoes, enroute from Herrine, Fla. to Chicago. Federal officials of a nation-wide liquor smuggling syndicate. Announcements of the capture was made today.[4]

"Moonshine" Plant Located And Destroyed

Two Men Working At "Still" Arrested, Brought Here And Released On Bond

A complete "moonshine" still was located and destroyed on the farm of Thos. Clark, of Cherry Grove, by Sheriff L. C. Tanner Friday afternoon. Fifty gallons of mash was being prepared and had reached the fermentation stage. About 20 gallons of the liquor was cooking. No whiskey was found.

Two men, Chas. C. Clark and Grover Jett, who were working at the still, were arrested by the sheriff and brought here to answer to a charge of manufacturing whiskey. They waived examination and gave bond in the sum of $1,000 each for their appearance when the grand jury meets.

Sheriff Tanner states that the men made no effort to escape but that Clark endeavored to make away with the copper pipe used as a "worm." He was unsuccessful and the pipe was brought here as evidence. The worm is about 12 feet long and an inch in diameter.

It has been suspected that "moonshine" was being made near here and quite a bit of it has been finding its way into Williamstown, where it is said it has been disposed of by bootleggers. It was this fact, the sheriff says, that led him to make an investigation. He located the still several days ago but waited until the owners could be caught at their work..

A midnight visit a few days before the arrests were made to a point on the extreme rear end of the Clark farm, disclosed the "still" hidden deep in the underbrush on the banks of a small rivulet that runs into the upper waters of Clarks Creek.

The penalty for manufacturing "moonshine" is not more than a $500 fine and not less than $50, and a jail sentence. For the second offense the penalty is much heavier.[5]

Alleged Whiskey Bandits Captured In Lexington

Following Robbery Of Trucks Laden With Whiskey Near Hinton

Four men, believed to be members of an organized band of 40 desperadoes who have been robbing whisky trucks and banks, were captured in Lexington Tuesday evening. Their arrests were made on John Doe warrants issued by Judge J.R. Lancaster of Georgetown.

The men gave their names as Forrest L. Matthews, 26, F.A. Paulin, 23, [] Grumblin, 21, and Sol Weisman, 30.

The men arrested are alleged to be members of a whisky ring. Two automobiles were seized by the policemen. In the machines were found a 4 cal. Winchester rifle and three revolvers. A bottle of nitroglycerin and a set of surgical instruments were also found.

Raided Trucks Near Hinton

Last Friday two trucks carrying 100 cases of whiskey left Frankfort enroute for New York, traveling under a government permit. About 7 o'clock that night when the trucks were about a mile from Hinton, three machines approached. Five men jumped out of the machines, leveling revolvers and a rifle at the truck driver and commanded them to throw up their hands. The drivers were ordered to get out of the trucks and then were forced into the machines of the thieves. They were carried nearly to Williamstown when they were ordered to get out.

Trucks Abandoned

[4] 8 April 1921. *Grant County News.* Author Unknown.

[5] 20 May 1921. *Grant County News.* Author Unknown.

The trucks driven by the men were found the next day abandoned on the side of the road, and all of the whisky had been [removed]. Sunday morning C.C. Shipley, of Cincinnati, owner of the whisky, drove a high powered car along the Dixie Highway in the hope of meeting the men. Near [] he sighted a Cole 8 automobile which answered the description of one of the machines which the bandits used. Mr. Shipley gave chase and a wild dash across the country followed. Mr. Shipley was overhauling the bandits when they stopped their car, a man got out and throwing a rifle to his shoulder, opened fire. The radiator of Shipley's car was punctured and the chase ended.

The captured men had nearly $1,000 in cash on their persons. They were placed in the county jail at Georgetown and their bail fixed at $1,000 each. They were unable to give bond and are still in jail. It is expected they will have an examining trial this week.[6]

Three Gallons Of Moonshine Found In Auto

Of Pendleton County Man Who Is Charged With Having Whiskey In His Possession In Violation Of State Prohibition Law

---

Saturday night about 11:00 o'clock town Marshal Wm. Stroud arrested James A. McMillan, a Pendleton county man, near the junction of Paris and Main streets, on a charge of having whiskey in his possession in violation of the law. The whiskey was in an automobile which McMillan was driving. A copper coil, supposed to have been part of a moonshine still, was also found in the car.

The whiskey was evidently of home manufacture, or in other words "moonshine," and is said to have been a fairly good grade of article.

McMillan was placed in jail for the remainder of the night and on Sunday morning was released on a bond of $1,000 furnished by Raymond and J.E. Elliott.

McMillan is from near Gardnersville, which is just over the line in Pendleton, east of Crittenden. His arrest followed a telephone message Mr. Stroud received earlier in the night asking him to be on the lookout for a party with a supply of "moonshine." The party using the telephone refused to give his name and his identity is a mystery.[7]

Prohibition Enforcement Officers Make Raid And Seize Still. 6 Arrested

---

About Fifty Gallons Red And White Whisky Confiscated Along With Other Concoctions Containing Unlawful Alcoholic Content. Whisky Poured Out On Street. Accused Men Released On Bond.

Prohibition enforcement officers paid their first visit to Williamstown last Friday and as a result of their work six men were placed under arrest, a large outfit for the manufacture of "moonshine" whisky was seized and a large quantity of illegal beverage was taken and destroyed. Several gallons of red whisky, said to have been manufactured in pre-prohibition days by the Quick distillery near Covington, was confiscated.

The officers were headed by Felix G. Fields, chief agent of the State, and in all eight took part in the raid.

With a display of fire arms such as has seldom been seen here, the officers began their search. The restaurant and grocery of Peter Bolas, was first raided and a quart of moonshine found. Bolas was immediately placed under arrest. The watch fixing place of W.H. McMillin, adjoining Bolas, was next visited. Here it is alleged about two gallons of moonshine in a glass container was found and confiscated. McMillin was also placed under arrest.

The officers then crossed the street to the store of C.W. Barnes, the second floor of which is used as a residence by Kirtley Barnes. A con-

[6] 8 July 1921. *Grant County News.* Author Unknown.
[7] 22 July 1921. *Grant County News.* Author Unknown.

siderable quantity of different kinds of liquors, some of which was real whisky, said too have been made by the Quick distillery and purchased in pre-prohibition days, was found and seized. There were twenty or more containers each holding from a pint to a gallon. There was a wide variety of the liquor found here. Some of it was apparently home brew and had never seen a still. Some was home made wine. All of this was found in Kirtley Barnes' apartments.

In the rear of Barnes' store building, the old Glascock store building, there is a combination garage and stable. The officers searched this place and located a large moonshine still. This still, they said, had not been used recently in manufacturing whisky. There was no copper coil, or worm, which is necessary in making whisky. A large boiler which would hold several hundred gallons, was connected by a steam pipe with the basement of Barnes' store building. The officers destroyed this outfit with the exception of the boiler, which was confiscated and will be sold, they claim,

Both Kirtley and C.W. Barnes were placed under arrest. The officers allege they found enough evidence against the latter to justify the arrest.

The officers then went to the home of Worth Barnes, the old Theobald home, on the Cynthiana pike, about half a mile out. Here they found a wooden keg with a capacity of about 15 gallons and filled with moonshine. They also found a copper coil, or worm at this place. The whisky and worm were both confiscated and Worth Barnes was placed under arrest.

Glenmore Bennett, a nephew of the Barnes Brothers, was caught in the act of destroying a container with about five gallons of moonshine, and he too, was arrested.

A large number of weapons, such as shot guns, automatic rifles, revolvers, etc., were seized in the raid and taen by the officers.

After all of the whisky had been seized that which was rated as moonshine and home-made, was poured out in the street while scores of people watched.

The six men arrested were taken to Covington before Commissioner Roetken for arraignment. They were released on bond, the bond of the Barnes brothers being fixed at $1,000 and the others at $500 each.

They will have a trial on the 19 of July.

In connection with the affair Kirtley Barnes states that the outfit had never been used, that he purchased it shortly before selling out the grocery and butcher business to his brother C.W. Barnes to use in connection with his butcher business and that no whisky had been manufactured on it during the time it has been in his possession. He says he will fight the case.

Attorney John B. O'Neal, of Covington, was employed to represent the defendants.

Commissioner Fields stated to the News that the penalty for operation of a still is a fine of $1,000 and a federal prison sentence of one year, and that the owner is required to pay taxes on all whisky he has manufactured. The penalty for bootlegging is a fine of $500 and six months jail sentence.

The officers state that they have received numerous letters from Williamstown people making complaints of the illegal sale and manufacture of whisky here and this led to the raid. They have evidently received pretty definite information as they went direct to the places raided and seemed to have located them in advance.

Commissioner Fields also stated that the still found had not been in use for some months, in his opinion.[8]

Prohibition Enforcement Officers Visit Crittenden

Five prohibition officers arrived in Crittenden Thursday morning and searched one place. Whether or not they found any illicit booze was not made known by them. They left immediately afterwards for the Flingsville neighborhood where report stated there had been bootlegging.[9]

---

[8] 16 June 1922. *Grant County News.* Author Unknown.

[9] 4 August 1922. *Grant County News.* Author Unknown.

Doctors Make Defense Liquor Prescriptions

Louisville Judge B.J. Bethurum, assistant state prohibition director, heard the testimony in the cases of Dr. George L. Pope, Francis Building, and Dr. J.W. Galvin, Weisinger-Gaulbert Apartments, who were cited to show cause why their permits to prescribe liquor should not be revoked. Dr. Galvin testified that when he prescribed wine in quantities of half a gallon he did not know that an act of Congress had reduced the amount to one quart. Dr. Pope said that he had prescribed whisky to patients he had not seen on information of persons in whom he confided that the person for needed the remedy. Judge Bethurum made no decision in either of the two cases.[10]

Whiskey Stolen After Battle

Covington Men Among Prisoners Who Fall Into Federal Prohibition Agent's Trap

Lexington, Ky., Oct. 18 Eight men with 410 gallons of "red" whisky and 45 gallons of moonshine in four automobiles and a light truck, were captured after a battle this morning by Federal Prohibition agents at the Perryville Bridge in Boyle county, Ky. The men were brought to Lexington and placed in jail. The whisky was removed to a bonded warehouse at Frankfort for storage. The automobiles and truck were placed in a garage here.

The red whisky, which Prohibition Agents believe to be a part of that stolen from the Rugby Distillery at Louisville Monday night, was in possession of three men who say they are Ernest A. Brady, 1701 Holman St., Covington; Lawrence Howard, Covington. The bonds of these three men were fixed by United States Commissioner Charles N. Wiard at $5,000 each, which they failed to provide. They had 220 gallons of the red whisky.

The other five men captured had the moonshine whisky. J.T. Williams, Howard Hayden, Edgar Crawford and Pete Linville, all of Paris, Ky., were in a car with 15 gallons, and Johnny Morys, former jockey, who resides in Lexington, was in a roadster with 30 gallons, officers say. Those five this afternoon were released on bond pending action of the Federal Grand Jury.

Federal prohibition officers in the raiding party were W.H. Kinnard, George Nantz, B.F. Unthank, J.P. Hughe and C.L. Wedding. More than 40 shots were exchanged, but no one was wounded. A riot gun, loaded with buckshot, a rifle and revolvers were found in the various cars, the officers said.

Officers declare the license on a seven-passenger car captured was issued to Brady. The truck, which was new, bore a license issued in Kenton County.[11]

MEDICINAL BEER IS PERMITTED

12

Two Arrested Charged With Liquor Violation

Search Warrant Sworn To By Woman Results In The Capture Of Two Men And 75 Gallons Of Mash

Armed with a search warrant Sheriff's officers went to the farm of T.J. Jump, located about half a mile from Clarks Creek church last Monday night, arrested Newt and Emmett Fornash, father and son, and destroyed about 75 gallons of mash found on the premises. The officers failed to locate a "moonshine still" which it was claimed they were using for the manufacture of the stuff.

The search warrant was issued at the instance of Bertha Lowe, a reputable resident of the neighborhood, who claimed to have direct knowledge of the manufacture of the whiskey. The mash was in process of fermentation.

[10] 20 October 1922. *Grant County News*. Author Unknown.
[11] 20 October 1922. *Grant County News*. Author Unknown.
[12] Circa October 1922. *Grant County News*.

The men were brought here and released on bond and will have a trial later in the week. The mash was found in the residence, which was described in the warrant as being a two story frame. Mrs. Lowe stated that she had seen the still in operation and that it had been moved from place to place.

While the farm is the property of T.J. Jump he has not lived on it for some time, his residence being at Grant, Boone county. The farm was rented by the Fornashes.[13]

Liquor Law Violators Draw Fine

Emmett Fornash Fined $100 And Given Jail Sentence Of 30 Days. Autoists Fail To Give Bond.

In the case of the Commonwealth vs. Emmett Fornash, charged with manufacturing whiskey for the purpose of sale, Fornash was fined $100 and given 30 days in jail by county Judge F.A. Harrison, last Saturday. His father, Newt Fornash, who is said to have been connected with the affair, will have a trial today. Emmett Fornash was placed under bond of $1,000 to prevent his engaging in the same business within one year.[14]

To Organize Wets In All The States

National Body Hopes To Procure Insertion Of Liquor Planks In Platforms Of Both Parties

---

St. Louis, Nov. 20 Steps to organize the wet forces in every state of the country to obtain modification of the Volsted act was discussed at a two-day meeting of the National Association opposed to the Prohibition Amendment which began here today.

Predictions were made by delegates that the liquor question probably would be the principal issue of the 1924 campaign.

Denial that a third major political party favoring amendment of the Volsted law was planned was made by delegates.

George S. Vest, secretary of the Missouri branch of the organization, explained the purpose of the conference was to give the State secretaries a chance to become acquainted. He said the question of what part the organization would play in the next Presidential election would be discussed.

Secretary Vest said the chief aim of the association was to bring about the insertion of "wet" planks in the platform of both Democratic and Republican parties and in this way give the organization the balance of power, which he said has been held by the Anti-Saloon League of America.

William L. Fish, who assisted in the election of Governor Edwards, of New Jersey, to the United States Senate on a light wine and beer platform, emphasized that the prohibition question would be the principal issue in the next general election.[15]

Liquor Bars Let Down For Fight On Flu

Physicians To Be Allowed More Prescription Blanks

Washington, Jan. 23 Orders went out from national prohibition enforcement headquarters to "let down the bars" to physicians whose liquor prescription blank quotas have been exhausted. This action was taken, Acting Prohibition Commissioner J.E. Jones said, to enable doctors to cope with the "flu" epidemic, which has reached serious proportions in some sections of the country.

Under the law physicians are allowed to issue 100 liquor prescriptions every three months. Numerous "flu" cases caused many doctors to use up their quotas of prescription blanks before the expiration of the three months' period.[16]

---

[13] 17 November 1922. *Grant County News.* Author Unknown.
[14] 24 November 1922. *Grant County News.* Author Unknown.
[15] 24 November 1922. *Grant County News.* Author Unknown.
[16] 26 January 1923. *Grant County News.* Author Unknown.

Eleven Gallons Of Moonshine "Jugged" Here

John McNay Held To June Term Of Grand Jury For Possession Of Illicit Booze And Carrying Revolver

John McNay, Newport, Ky., resident, arrested here last Friday after he had failed to heed the warning of town marshal Wm. Stroud to get out of town, was fined $50.00 and costs in Police Court Tuesday morning by Judge Shields for disorderly conduct. He plead guilty to the charge.

McNay was bound over to await the action of the June term of the grand jury on two charges, carrying a revolver and possessing spirituous liquors unlawfully. His bond for revolver toting was fixed at $100 and for possessing liquor $300.

McNay was on streets in an intoxicated condition and was making a nuisance of himself when noticed by the town marshal. Mr. Stroud advised him to get out of town. McNay became abusive. Stroud called deputy sheriff Vallandingham and placed McNay under arrest. It is alleged that he tried to draw a revolver. At any rate a large 45 caliber revolver was found on his person.

McNay's car was then searched. Eleven gallons of white whiskey was taken as evidence and placed in the vault of the Bank of Williamstown for safe-keeping.

McNay is believed to have disposed of several gallons of his booze to a local bootlegger as he had about $90.00 on his person. It is claimed here that the moonshine is of his own manufacture.

Both whiskey, automobile and revolver of McNay's are being held by local officials pending action of the grand jury. Federal officers say that he has been in trouble on the same charge before, having been fined in Newport several months ago on a similar charge.[17]

Heavy Fines Assessed Against Booze Vendors

J. M. Gouge Draws Fines Amounting To $6000 And 90 Days In Jail. Plain Drunks Get $50.00 A Throw

Bootleggers and plain drunks had their inning in Judge Harrison's court last Tuesday. J. M. Gouge was fined $300.00 and 60 days in jail for possessing liquor for purpose of sale in one case, and $300.00 and 30 days in jail for selling liquor in another.

Robert Chance was fined $50.00 and costs for being drunk. A fine of $50.00 and costs was assessed against F. E. Coburn. Chance plead guilty while Colburn plead not guilty. A case against Marion Rankin for drunkenness was continued to the October term of Circuit Court. Rankin implicated Gouge, claiming that he got the liquor from him.

All of the cases were tried before juries. The juries were composed of three men and three women.

The case of Colburn was appealed to the Circuit Court and will be tried at the October term.

Cases tried before the judge for drunkenness without juries will receive fines of $50.00 and costs where the defendant if found guilty. This rule has been established by the court and a precedent made. Offenders are to be given the limit.

Complaints coming from many sources about the state of affairs here have put the officers of the law on their mettle and it isn't going to be safe to get drunk in Williamstown any more.

Allegations have been made that numerous bootleggers are operating in this vicinity and it begins to look like they are going to have to find a more congenial clime in which to work, or else take a chance of paying a heavy fine and going to jail.

In addition to paying a fine any person found guilty of dispensing liquor is put under a peace bond for 12 months, and if he is caught selling booze within that period the bond is forfeited. This makes it extremely hazardous for the bondsmen and renders it rather difficult for a bootlegger found guilty to give bond.

It is a matter of common belief that not only the town, but the county as well, is infested with bootleggers, and they have grown so bold that in many instances they sell almost

[17] 4 May 1923. *Grant County News.* Author Unknown.

openly. It is also common belief that numerous illicit stills exist in the county, and what is true of Grant county is probably true of most all counties in the State.

And while it may not be possible to stop bootlegging entirely, it is pretty certain that it can be curtailed to a large extent and the offenders can be made to be more careful.[18]

Big Moonshine Still Found In Harrison County

Made Of Copper, Coffin Shaped And Had Capacity Of Half A Barrel A Day

Probably the largest moonshine still in captivity in Harrison county was brought into County Judge W.W. VanDeeren's office last Friday by Sheriff John Ingles, Deputy Sheriff Phillip Ammerman and City Policeman George M. Dickey. The officers brought the still into court on information furnished by Robert Beagle, who rents the farm of J.W. Casey who resides in Cincinnati, the farm being located at Casey's Mills, between Renaker and Berry, this county. Mr. Beagle reported to the officials that he and C. Fogle had found the still. It is shaped like a coffin, being eight feet long, fifteen inches wide and eighteen inches deep and probably has a capacity of around 25 or 30 gallons per day.

By following a track which probably was made by dragging the still, a furnace was located nearly half a mile from the point where the still was found. In the bushes were five barrels which had evidently contained mash. The coil was not located. One of the barrels used for mash was a pickle barrel which had been bought of C.W. Kellum, a Falmouth merchant, but Mr. Kellum is unable to recall to whom he sold the barrel.

The officials have a tip that considerable liquor from this still has been sold in Covington.[19]

Kenton County Sheriff Makes Liquor Arrests

Parts of Still Used In Making Moonshine Found By Officer. Men Caught Had Moonshine.

Three white men and three colored youths were arrested near Bracht Station Sunday morning by Deputy Sheriff Armstrong of Kenton county charged with liquor violations.

The men were in an automobile drinking moonshine from a bottle when the officer came up. He placed them under arrest and confiscated their moonshine.

Parts of an illicit still were found in a shock of fodder by the officer. Complaints had been made Saturday night to the officer who came out at midnight and made a search. Failing to located the offenders he returned Sunday morning.

The still it is claimed was being operated on a farm between Bracht Station and Crittenden and had been supplying the thirsty residents of the community for some time.[20]

6 Sent to Jail on Liquor Charges

Heavy Fines And Jail Sentences Imposed And Peace Bonds Required For Good Behavior For One Year

Bootleggers and near bootleggers are being given short shrift in the Circuit Court which began a three-weeks' session Monday. As a result of the court's activities six men are doing penance in the county jail on liquor possession charges and each one was assessed a heavy fine. All of the six were also placed under a peace bond of $1,500 for good behavior for one year.

Russell Crook and Leander Scroggin each drew fines of $100 and 30 days. Porter Holbrook and Ira Webb received the same punishment and Ed Elliott was given $200 and 30 days, there being two cases against Elliott.

John McNay was surrendered by his bondsmen and began serving a

[18] 3 August 1923. *Grant County News.* Author Unknown.
[19] 28 September 1923. *Grant County News.* Author Unknown.
[20] 23 November 1923. *Grant County News.* Author Unknown.

90 day sentence with a $300 fine attached.

The jail's population Monday morning was 15 with a strong probability of this number being augmented before court adjourns.[21]

Heavy Fine For Liquor Law Violators

One Hundred Dollars And Thirty Days In Jail Assessed Against Two Men, And 50 Against Woman

Two men from Newport, Robert Welsh and Harvey Shiels drew fines of $100 and costs each and a jail sentence of 30 days here last Saturday when they were tried for violation of the liquor law.

At the same time, Mrs. May Shiels wife of one of the men, was fined $50 and costs. The men were placed under a peace bond of $1,000 each for one year.

The men and the woman were arrested following a Sunday afternoon carousal in an automobile. At Sherman it is alleged they became abusive and used indecent language in the presence of a mixed crowd which had congregated. They are said to have thrown away a flask containing a small portion of white whiskey which was used as evidence against them.

The party was not arrested until several days following the affair, the Sheriff and deputy Vallandingham failing to overtake them in the county after they had been notified.[22]

Plans To Stop Liquor Flow At Its Source

Chicago, May 4. - Andrew W. Mellon, Secretary of the Treasury, revealed himself today as an optimist regarding the ultimate enforcement of prohibition laws.

"Dry it up at the source," Mr. Mellon said, "and the problem settles itself." Then home brew will be the only hope left for those who can't just worry along without a nip now and then, he declared.

Mr. Mellon is not worrying overmuch, either, he said about the younger generation, sheik and flapper. They are much better than they appear, he remarked.

Stories about hip flask and "mugging" parties do not necessarily indicate a fast slide for perdition, Mr. Mellon said. It is but a surface reflection of a new thrill of economic independence that erupted from the World War, he added.

To the war, and not resentment against the "Volsteadians," Mr. Mellon suggested, can be attributed most of the let down. But it all will come out right in the end, the Secretary predicted.

Mr. Mellon arrived in the private car of C.H. Markham, president of the Illinois Central Railroad. He left later in the day for Jackson, Miss., where he speaks to business men of that section tomorrow. Mr. Markham accompanied him.

Mr. Mellon declined to say anything about the one thing he knows more about, perhaps, than any other American finance. He chatted pleasantly, with every now and then a smile, about many other aspects of the national life.

"I prefer not to discuss the establishment of the gold standard in England," he said pleasantly, "or the Treasury Department. I'm a little afraid of headlines. I would prefer to write it down when I have anything to say."

"The prohibition laws can be enforced," he insisted, "but it will be some time before that is accomplished, partly because so many people do not feel that they are criminals in their drinking. They don't feel the same toward this as they do toward fundamental offenses.

"But my judgment is that if we can dry up the source, if we can stop effectively the smugglers, the question internally will be easy of solution.

"That is a big job. But it can be done, no doubt. And when the smuggling is stopped there will remain the matter of traffic in alcohol. But if we can keep that out, too, we can handle the internal situation.

"We are not employing the navy. That is a mistake. Our efforts to stop smuggling are under the direction of an independent force, and not the navy. Because the Customs and Internal Revenue Departments are under the Treasury, the effort to stop il-

[21] 6 February 1925. *Grant County News.* Author Unknown.
[22] 10 April 1925. *Grant County News.* Author Unknown.

licit importations is under the Treasury direction."

Mr. Mellon thought that perhaps it would be better if the bureau were transferred entirely to the Department of Justice, but since it is not "we are doing the best we can, with indications of ultimate success.

"It's the enormous profit in bootlegging that makes it difficult to suppress," he added.

Mr. Mellon would not agree that the resentment against the prohibition law was at the bottom of what may term a sort of moral letdown on the part of the young folk.

"I attribute it, whatever it may be," he said "to the war. In England I found the same symptoms."[23]

Dry Raiders Swoop Down On Williamstown

Lone Woman Is Taken In Custody Charged With Liquor Law Violations. Several Places Searched.

Wednesday at noon two automobiles loaded with prohibition officers swooped down on Williamstown. There was considerable excitement in the ranks of bootleggers and near bootleggers for a time.

Mrs. Carrie Tate, who resides on the alley running parallel with the Southern railroad, was nabbed by the officers, charged with illegal possession of liquor. While no information was given out by the raiders the report is that a considerable quantity of bootleg whiskey, etc., was found in her possession. The amount alleged to have been found ranges from a quart to six gallons.

Several places suspected were searched, but so far as could be learned no other liquor nor no other incrriminating evidence. The Tate woman was taken away by the officers.[24]

Two Arrested Charged With Bootlegging

Covington Men Captured With Moonshine In Their Possession. Sheriff's Deputy Makes Raid At Crittenden.

Deputy Sheriff, I.O. Vallandingham, went to Crittenden Saturday night and arrested James (Pete) Stephenson and Harry Spencer on a charge of having moonshine in their possession for the purpose of sale. The men were brought here and placed in jail.

Several half pint and pint bottles of moon were seized in the raid.

The two men are residents of Covington. It is claimed they have been peddling moon at Crittenden for some time. The Sheriff's office acted on private information furnished by a citizen of Crittenden. After an investigation Vallandingham came back to Williamstown and swore out a warrant against the men.

The men were found sleeping in a barn at Crittenden, their booze being cached in a hayloft.

Heavy Fine And Jail Sentences

The two men had a trial in the Quarterly Court Wednesday morning when fines of $150.00 and 30 days in jail were assessed against each.[25]

Federal Officers Make Raid At Downingsville

The federal officers who raided Williamstown Wednesday of last week also visited Downingsville. It is claimed a large quantity of moon was found and two citizens of Downingsville were cited to appear for examination at Cynthiana.[26]

Is your News subscription paid?

[23] 8 May 1925. *Grant County News.* Author Unknown.
[24] 21 August 1925. *Grant County News.* Author Unknown.
[25] 28 August 1925. *Grant County News.* Author Unknown.
[26] 28 August 1925. *Grant County News.* Author Unknown.

Almost In Shadow Of the Court House Booze Is Found

Alleged Bootlegger Is Alleged To Have Been Plying Trade With The Grand Jury Sitting A Hundred Feet Away

Following information given the grand jury by Bob Clark, cook for the hotel construction crew here, a search was made of the premises of C.P. Hensley, blacksmith and garage man, at the foot of Paris street, last Thursday.

About a gallon of moonshine whiskey was found by the Sheriff and Hensley was placed under arrest. The grand jury returned a true bill against Hensley and he was later released on bond.

Clark was arrested by the town marshal charged with being drunk. He was fined $57.50 and taken before the grand jury and told that unless he told where he secured his whiskey he would be placed in jail. Clark claimed to have bought the whiskey from Hensley, ensued the search of Hensley's premises and his arrest.

Hensley's place of business is located just across the street from the court house square and the grand jury was in session about a hundred feet away, while Judge Gaines was dealing out law and justice in the court room down stairs.[27]

Two Places Raided By Co. Sheriff

Small Amount of Alleged Liquor Found At One. J.A. Harrison And W.H. McMillan's Places Searched.

Sheriff Chipman and deputies raided two Williamstown business places late Monday in a search for illicit liquor. The places raided were those of J.A. Harrison, local grocer and meat dealer, and W.H. McMillan, jeweler and watchmaker. Both places are in the heart of the business district.

At McMillan's place a small quantity of what is alleged to be moonshine whisky was found and taken as evidence. Nothing in the way of incriminating evidence was found at Harrison's place.

The raid followed an indictment returned by the grand jury earlier in the day, the witness against the two men being John Linn a farmer from the southern part of the county who alleged he had purchased liquor at both places.[28]

Woman Given Jail Sentence On Liquor Charge

Mrs. Carrie Tate, of Williamstown, was found guilty by a jury Saturday of unlawful possession of liquor. She was fined $100 and sentenced to serve 30 days in the county jail. Mrs. Tate is the first woman convicted in Grant County on a liquor charge.[29]

Fifteen Gallons Moon Confiscated

Trio of Colored Men Landed In Jail Charged With Transporting Liquor

The citizens Cynthiana street, in Williamstown, last Saturday afternoon received public demonstration of the fact that the Grant County Sheriff's office is a force to reckoned with by all those who contemplate lawnessness as a mean of livelihood. Deputy Sheriff Ruben Taylor, having received notice that four colored men were acting in a suspicious manner on Cynthiana street, made it a point to be on the job. He found the colored brethren busily engaged in repairing a punctured tire on their Hudson automobile. Investigating, he detected an odor in the vicinity of the machine that certainly did not suggest glue to a natural Kentuckian. Having directed his gaze over the side of the machine he spied three five gallon tin cans and at the same time the repugnant aroma of illicitly distilled corn juice convinced our stalwart deputy that these four darkies had no respect for the prohibition law. Ruben lined the trembling four

[27] 23 October 1925. *Grant County News.* Author Unknown.
[28] 5 February 1926. *Grant County News.* Author Unknown.
[29] 19 February 1926. *Grant County News.* Author Unknown.

up against the shed and confiscated the moonshine whiskey and marched them by columns of twos into the county jail and conveyed the fifteen gallons of mountain dew to the Sheriff's office.[30]

Many Appeals Are Taken In Liquor Cases

The January issue of the Kentucky Law Journal, just out, contains an article entitled, "Comments on Decisions in Criminal Cases in 1924," by Commonwealth's Attorney John J. Howe. The Court of Appeals of Kentucky in 1924 decided 231 criminal cases, only 56 of which were other than homicide or liquor prosecutions. Only 174 criminal cases were decided by the court in 1922.

Errors in the admission of evidence and in instructions to the juries caused most of the 93 reversals of the lower courts.

In the 1924 General Assembly a bill was introduced forbidding jurisdiction to the Court of Appeals in liquor cases. The bill was not passed. Judge Thomas of the Appellate Court recently appeared before a committee of the present legislature urging the passage of a bill limiting appeals in liquor cases to those which by special motion might be granted a hearing. He is quoted as saying that 80 per cent of the appeals in liquor cases were taken for delay. Mr. Howe's article nevertheless states that in 1924 there were 117 appeals in liquor cases and that 47 of them were reversed.[31]

Real Beer Is To Be On Sale Soon

Two Breweries Have Permits To Manufacture Liquor For Sale In Drug Stores Without Prescriptions. "Tonic" to Contain 3.76 Per Cent Alcohol.

Washington, March 29. - People who contend life will be much more endurable for them if they can have beer with a pronounced kick, are to be accommodated by a friendly Government and the Prohibition Department.

Permission has been granted to the Annheuser-Bush Company, of St. Louis, and the Pabst Company, of Milwaukee, to manufacture a malt liquor containing 3.76 per cent malt solids. This beverage will be sold to the public in limited quantities through drugstores without prescriptions or dealer permits.

Both those breweries sought to manufacture such beverages following passage of the Volstead law, but were prevented from so doing.

Now, it is understood the manufacturers have written to wholesalers announcing they soon will have, subject to orders, old "malt extract," containing 3.5 per cent alcohol, and expressing the hope this product "will not find its way into illegitimate channels."

The permits are for a period of six months and contain the proviso that both companies are required to aid the prohibition division in prevention of sale of malt liquor to the public for "beverage purposes."

The malt liquor, it is understood, will correspond to lager beer, as far as the "kick" is concerned, but will carry a much larger proportion of solids. It is described as a "tonic." In a letter to dealers, it is understood that the Pabst Company says the "tonic" is "palatable, but not potable to the extent it can be used as a beverage."

This letter explains that wholesalers will be privileged to sell the product in quantities of five cases weekly to small druggists and 25 cases weekly to large establishments.

The "tonic," it is said is not intoxicating because its solid content is so large that it cannot be consumed in quantities sufficient to produce drunkenness.

No official regulation covering manufacture of the malt liquor, as it is already called, has been issued by the Prohibition Department, and, accordingly, it was said, there are no requirements for dealers permits or bonds to govern its sale.

Details concerning how prohibition officials came to issue the permits could not be learned authoritatively, but is was said they were told

[30] 26 February 1926. *Grant County News.* Author Unknown.
[31] 26 February 1926. *Grant County News.* Author Unknown.
[32] 2 April 1926. *Grant County News.* Author Unknown.

by the brewers that when they were allowed to manufacture and sell this malt extract prior to prohibition that only moderate quantities were sold through drugstores.[32]

Two Negroes Escape From County Jail

Saw Bars And Drop To Liberty. Both Were Awaiting Action Of Grand Jury On Liquor Violation Charges.

Jailer Ed. Arnold lost two of his star boarders some time Tuesday night.

S. Starks and George Crutchfield, negroes, confined in the jail under bond and awaiting grand jury action, sawed the bars in a window and fled.

Jailer Arnold was not aware of the jail break until early Wednesday morning when he went to feed his prisoners. He found the jail bars sawed, the men gone and only one prisoner left. The remaining prisoner is Mrs. Carrie Tate, a resident of Williamstown, who is doing time on a liquor charge. She made no attempt to get out.

Starks figured in a sensational affair at Crittenden March 10th when an automobile which he was driving plunged into another car and overturned. He was captured after a chase of several miles into the country and while being brought back attempted to make his escape from his captors. He was charged with reckless driving, illegal possession of liquor, resisting an officer and driving an automobile while intoxicated. Two other negros were with him at the time, one of whom was placed in jail but was later released.

Crutchfield was captured in Williamstown with several gallons of moonshine last February. Two other negroes with him at the time were released after Crutchfield had assumed the entire responsibility for the liquor.

Sheriff's officers were looking for the escaped jail birds Wednesday but probability of their capture is remote.[33]

Dry Agents Disguised As Farmers

Raid Covington And Newport Places And Make Arrests. One Hundred Search Warrants Issued.

Covington, Ky., May 4 Eleven prohibition agents, disguised as farmers, mechanics, laborers and business men, today invaded Northern Kentucky cities and made many arrests of persons chearged with violating the prohibition law.

The visit of the agents was part of a plan of William O. Mays, prohibition director for Kentucky. Approximately 100 search warrants were issued at Lexington in a program to clean up bootlegging and whisky runners in Kenton and Campbell counties.

The agents were divided into separate parties. One division remained in Covington, another went to Erlanger and the rural districts of Kenton county, a third to Newport and the fourth to Clifton and the rural sections of Campbell.

All of the persons arrested were placed in Covington jail pending their appearance to answer liquor violations before the United States Commissioner at Covington.[34]

Two Men Break Jail In Owen

Owenton, Ky., May 17 Bill Briley and Stallard Anderson, who have been in the Owen county jail since February for violation of the prohibition law, escaped from jail about 2 o'clock this morning. Jailer Joe Kenney says they sawed the door off the hinges and let themselves down by blankets. Two other prisoners, Cleveland Massie and Clarence Wingate, who also might have escaped, preferred not to try it. The prisoners have not been located.[35]

---

[33] 9 April 1926. *Grant County News.* Author Unknown.
[34] 7 May 1926. *Grant County News.* Author Unknown.
[35] 21 May 1926. *Grant County News.* Author Unknown.

County Attorney Reports Violations Of Law At Corinth

County Attorney, L.M. Ackman, was called to Corinth this week to investigate numerous alleged law violations. The violations consist of minor offenses from racing automobiles on the streets to bootlegging and moonshining.

Warrants were issued against more than a dozen alleged violators of the law.[36]

Zion Station Man In Limbo Liquor Charge

Warrant Issued For Desertion Leads To Arrest On More Serious Charge. Fifty Gallons Of Mash Was Fermenting

A warrant issued against Andrew Leach, of Zion Station, for desertion, led to his arrest on a more serious charge last Sunday. Armed by a warrant sworn to by his wife, who lives in Covington, deputy sheriff Ruben Taylor, went to Zion Station to arrest Leach.

Leach surrendered to the officer and went into the house to change his clothes. The officer followed Leach into the house and found fifty gallons of mash in a stage of fermentation in a rain water barrel. The officer poured out the mash, preserving a sample as evidence. No still was found. It is claimed that Leach was suspected of making "moon" prior to his arrest.[37]

Drouth Agents Gets Still In Owen County

Allen Overstreet Arrested And Charged With Selling Moonshine Whisky

Owenton, Ky., June 8. - Prohibition agents made a raid in Owen county last Saturday, arresting Allen Overstreet, accused of selling moonshine whisky, after, according to the officers, they had found two gallons of whisky in his home. They started to the jail at Covington with the prisoner but Overstreet found a man in Grant county to sign his bond and was released till time for the case to be heard.

On the same raid a moonshine still was found in the residence of Oliver Overstreet, a nephew of Allen but Oliver was not found, officers said. Oliver is a tenant on the farm of Ford Costigan in this county.[38]

Moonshine Still And 22 Gallons Of Moon Captured

Jackie Webster Surrenders Himself And Is Fined $300, Thirty days In Jail And Placed Under $1,000 Peace Bond

Sheriff Chipman and his deputies raided the largest moonshine still ever captured in Grant county, Monday. The complete outfit, with 22 gallons of the product of the still and a quantity of mash in process of distillation, was taken in the raid.

The capture was made on the Smoky Row road, near Eagle Creek. The moon was brought to Williamstown as evidence.

Jackie Webster, an aged citizen of the neighborhood, surrendered himself to the authorities Tuesday. He was fined $300.00, 30 days in jail and placed under a peace bond of $1,000 for one year. The illegal booze was poured out.

Webster's home was searched on a search warrant sworn to by Mrs. Russell Fortner, a near neighbor. She claimed that her husband frequently visited the Webster home and became intoxicated while there. The still and accounterments with a very large quantity of mash in process of fermentation, was found in Webster's home.[39]

---

[36] 28 May 1926. *Grant County News.* Author Unknown.
[37] 28 May 1926. *Grant County News.* Author Unknown.
[38] 11 June 1926. *Grant County News.* Author Unknown.
[39] 30 July 1926. *Grant County News.* Author Unknown.

Bread And Water For Bootleggers In Nebraska

Physician Says "It's Murder." Forty Of 60 Days Must Be Served On Slight Nourishment Is Court's Dictum.

Tekamah, Neb., Sept. 7, - Sentenced to serve the first and last 20 days of their 60-day jail sentence on a bread and water diet, because they violated the prohibition laws, Roy Carson, 35 years old, and Thomas Nelson, 50, farmers, arrived at the Burt county jail tonight. Carson weighs 123 pounds and Nelson 150. Each declares he is a heavy eater and can not stand the bread and water sentence, recently affirmed by the State Supreme Court to which they appealed.

A physical examination by Dr. Isaiah Lukens today resulted in a declaration by him that neither man was fit to stand the sentence. "The bread and water diet is not only cruel but murderous, because it damages the vital organs." he asserted.

Sheriff Smith said three previous examinations had been made under the same sentence, but that two men were excused because of physical disabilities. Such sentences, he maintained were necessary to rid the county of liquor law violators.

The case of Carson and Nelson has attracted attention because of their fight in the State Supreme Court.

"No court has the right to injure a man's vital organs because he took a drink of liquor," Dr. Lukens said. "To fully determine if a man could stand such a diet, you would have to place him under examination in a hospital for a week."[40]

Rich Harvest Off Bootleggers And Plain Drunks

Nine Arrested Charged With Various Violations. Fines Assessed Against Several Others In Jail Awaiting Trial.

Violators of the liquor laws came to an unhappy end in Williamstown over the week-end. In all nine arrests of men charged with violations from Bootlegging to plain drunks were made. The offenders were remanded to jail to wait trial. Five of the nine had plead guilty of drunkenness and paid their fines up to Tuesday morning. Fines for drunkenness amounted to $50.00 and costs in each case. It is expected that higher fines will be assessed against bootleggers whose cases will come up the latter part of the week.[41]

Farmer Gets Heavy Penalty For Violation

Of Liquor Law. Jury Finds Jack Webster Guilty Of Possessing Moonshine Still, Manufacturing Liquor, Etc.

In Circuit Court last Friday a jury found Jack Webster, of the Eagle Creek country $425.00, appended a jail sentence of 90 days and the court placed him under a peace bond of $1,000 for one year.

The charge against Webster was possession of a moonshine still, manufacture of liquor for purpose of sale, etc.

Webster was arrested and the plant found at his home several weeks [ago]. He was tried in Quarterly Court and fined $300 and given a jail sentence of 30 days.

Webster employed James Settle, an Owenton attorney, to defend him. He plead not guilty and fought the case through Circuit Court.

He will be required to pay a total fine of $725.00 and costs, and serve the Quarterly Courts sentence of 120 days including the peace bond, and another 90 days inflicted by the jury.

Webster swore before the jury that he did not know anything about the still, that a quantity of mash found at his home was slop for his hogs. It developed, however, that he only had

[40] 10 September 1926. *Grant County News.* Author Unknown.
[41] 17 September 1926. *Grant County News.* Author Unknown.
[42] 22 October 1926. *Grant County News.* Author Unknown.

two hogs and the supply of slop, several barrels, was more than they required.[42]

Two Kentucky Distilleries May Resume Runs Soon

Owensboro, Ky., Nov. 15. - The Glenmore and Davies county distilleries may be again called on to make a run.

No official plans have been received by the local distilleries, but according to an announcement in Washington today, Lincoln C. Andrews, chief of the dry forces, is making plans to permit the manufacture again for medical purposes. The local distilleries are interested in Bourbon liquor only and at the present time the two warehouses in Davies county have about 42,000 barrels of whiskey, which is about equal to 1,260,000 gallons, figuring 30 gallons to the barrel.

According to the announcement made today there is about 15,000,000 gallons in the United States now.

This amount will last about five years, and under the law liquor can not be bottled in bond under four years, and should the manufacturing be allowed the present supply will be about out by the time the new is ready to be bottled.[43]

Federal Officers Find Moon

Large Quantity Said to Have Been Destroyed

Make Raid on Booze Laden Automobile On Baton Rouge Pike. Booze Runners Taken to Covington.

According to a story which reached here Tuesday, federal officers raided an automobile laden with illicit liquor on the Baton Rouge pike, about three miles from Williamstown Tuesday night. It is claimed that they captured a quantity of moon, estimated at 50 gallons. Two men who were in possession of the booze were taken into custody, according to the report.

The booze was poured out by the roadside. The names of the men arrested were not learned here and it is said they were from Newport. The names of the federal officers who made the capture were not made known. For some reason or other the matter has been kept quiet and no information given out. Officers here had no knowledge of the raid, the only information received having come from citizens who live in the neighborhood where the capture was made.[44]

Deserted Car Thought To Be Booze Carrier

What is believed by local officials to be the chief car in a rum-running outfit, is in the muddy field just off the high grade near Joe Ruholl's place, south of Williamstown. The whereabouts of the three men convoying the car is not so well known, though the last seen of them they were sitting in the back end of a truck driving rapidly towards Covington.

The actions of the three men, together with other evidence found at the wrecked car, leads officers to believe the car was loaded with booze which was transferred to the truck. The truck passed through Williamstown about 7:30 Thursday morning, and was noticed by many on account of the speed it was making.

When Deputy Sheriff Ruben Taylor and Captain Strode reached the scene of the wreck, they found a big Studebaker had gone straight down the high embankment and far out into the muddy field. On the car was an Arkansas license, but inside the car, - evidently for emergency use, - were licenses from Kentucky and Ohio. A regular path had been made from the car to where the truck stood, and the officers are certain that the path was made by the men transferring the stuff contained in the car to the truck.

Sheriff Taylor phoned Owenton to find out the owner of the Kentucky license. He was told that the license

[43] 19 November 1926. *Grant County News.* Author Unknown.
[44] 11 February 1927. *Grant County News.* Author Unknown.
[45] 25 March 1927. *Grant County News.* Author Unknown.

belonged to Lewis Robinson, and was for a Ford Car. The local officers notified the officers of Covington to be on the look out for the truck.[45]

Boy Says He Bought Booze For Evidence

Young Man Arrested At Corinth For Purchasing Moonshine Freed at Hearing

---

Grant county in general, and Corinth in particular, is following with closest interest and attention the outcome of the arrest Tuesday of a young fellow in Corinth on charge of buying whisky. From such sources as are available, the boiled down facts seem to these:

On Monday a young man bought a half pint of whisky. On Tuesday a warrant for his arrest on a charge of buying whisky was sworn out in Judge Marshall's court. On Wednesday County Judge R.L. Webb, Commonwealth Attorney Ackman and deputy sheriff Ruben Taylor motored to Corinth to investigate the case. It turned out as many knew that the young fellow was one of the two young men who were brought to Corinth by private citizens to secure evidence against alleged bootleggers. Following a policy that he has stuck to since his election to office, Commonwealth Attorney Ackman did not press the charge against the one who bought the whiskey solely for the purpose of obtaining evidence against the peddler of moonshine.

When Judge Webb, Deputy Taylor, Attorney Ackman and his stenographer reached Junior Hall, where the case was to be heard, they found more than 100 citizens gathered to hear the proceedings. Taking the grounds that the hearing was of the same nature as a grand jury investigation, Attorney Ackman had the roomed cleared of all save those directly interested, and held the hearing behind closed doors.

Back of Wednesday's investigation are whispers of intolerable conditions existing near Corinth, - conditions that the Sheriff's office is powerless to suppress on account of the difficulties encountered in the matter of county lines. With Owen, Scott and Grant converging almost at Corinth's city limits, it is possible for law violators to play hide and seek with officers from the Sheriff's office, escaping from the jurisdiction of one sheriff by hopping into another county.

It is declared that bootlegging flourished to such an extent that citizens of Corinth took it upon themselves to hire a couple of men to "get the goods" on those selling intoxicating drinks. So two young men from the city of Covington were employed for the purpose, and it was one of these who was arrested.

In discussing the affair Wednesday night, Commonwealth Attorney Ackman said that great results could reasonably be expected from the evidence the two men had obtained. He questioned a number of witnesses Wednesday at Corinth, and said he is satisfied that the men are what they represent themselves to be, and that their evidence will be helpful in bringing law violators to justice.

Before the hearing Wednesday, there was much speculation and surmise. It was thought by some that the men were federal agents; by others that they were operators from a private detective agency specializing in nabbing bootleggers; by still other that the men were getting themselves arrested in order to let it be known they were "spotters," so that they could "shake-down" those from whom they had bought whisky.

It is learned that the men are neither federal officers, detectives, or "shakers"; but men highly recommended to the citizens of Corinth by a minister of Covington.

A humorous angle is presented by a rumor that the ones who had sold the fellow moonshine were the ones who swore out the warrant for his arrest. The rumor has it that, after selling the half pint of booze, the man selling it heard the fellow was a federal agent, and, as it has been repeatedly ruled that federal agent has no legal right to buy whiskey, thought to beat the fellow to the "immunity bath" by turning state's evidence.

Some are wondering if these fellows' activities will result in as much benefit as the Sheriff's haul of some six months or more ago, when more than $1,300 in fines was taken in, in one day's court held at Corinth.[46]

Liquor Law Violator Gets $500 Fine

[46]8 April 1927. *Grant County News.* Author Unknown.

A fine of $500 and a ninety day jail sentence, besides being assessed the costs, was given John L. Anderson, of Corinth, Thursday morning by County Judge Webb after Anderson had plead guilty to five separate charges of liquor law violations. Anderson is the first of six men of the Corinth section for whom warrants have been issued to appear before Judge Webb for a hearing.

County officials are profuse in their praise of Corinth citizens for the splendid co-operation given in the city-wide effort to rid Corinth of bootleggers. County Attorney Ackman stated that the people of Corinth were almost solidly behind city Marshal New, and the county officials, in waging a war on prohibition violators.

Judge Walter Marshall resigned more than a week ago, but no successor has been named.[47]

Still Found Near Keefer

A 50 gallon still was captured on the farm of T. M. Cook, near Keefer, last Saturday. Deputy Sheriff Ruben Taylor was in the neighborhood armed with a warrant for Buford Cook, who was charged with being drunk and accidentally ran across the still which was concealed in a dug-out in a clump of undergrowth. The still was of 50 gallon capacity. About 120 gallons of mash in process of fermentation was found at the still. T. M. Cook, owner of the farm, denies any knowledge of the still and its ownership is in doubt.[48]

Anti-Saloon League Speaker To Be Here Next Wednesday Night

Dr. R. H. Bennett will address a mass meeting at the Baptist church Wednesday night, May 11, at 7:30. He is an Anti-Saloon League speaker and is rated as one of the leading orators of the South.[49]

Bootlegger Captured With The Goods

Drunken Brawl Among Show People Lead To Arrest of Dry Ridge Man. "Moon" Home Brew and Apricot Extract Found.

Blaine Dawalt, young Dry Ridge farmer, is in jail doing penance of 30 days, with a $300 fine and $1,000 peace bond attached for bootlegging.

Dawalt was captured Saturday by deputy sheriffs Ruben Taylor and Walter Conrad. He had in his possession 41 bottles of home brew, about two gallons of "moon," and a quantity of apricot extract with which he colored the "moon." The liquor was brought here as evidence and was later poured out.

Dawalt was operating in the extreme northern section of Dry Ridge, out side the corporate limits. It is claimed that he had been engaged in dispensing hard drinks to the thirsty for several months.

His arrest followed a drunken brawl on Friday night which resulted in the arrest of several members of an itinerant show company. Members of the company were given a clean bill of health and ordered to leave town after they had turned state's evidence.[50]

He's Wet! But A Law Enforcer

Kenton Democrats Are Told At Smith Meeting. "Up From Rank of Poor, He Is Now Outstanding Candidate For White House."

Covington, Ky., May 14. - Attorney Shelly D. Rouse, of Covington, former Chairman of the Kenton County Democratic Executive Committee, was the principal speaker last

[47] 22 April 1927. *Grant County News.* Author Unknown.
[48] 6 May 1927. *Grant County News.* Author Unknown.
[49] 6 May 1927. *Grant County News.* Author Unknown.
[50] 17 June 1927. *Grant County News.* Author Unknown.

night at a meeting of the Covington Al Smith Club in Good Will Hall, Fifth Street and Madison avenue, Covington.

Mr. Rouse paid tribute to Al Smith as one of the outstanding Democrats who proved his worth by having been elected Governor of New York four times.

"A man who time after time has received the support and confidence of the people of his state," Mr. Rouse declared, "is entitled to represent the people of the nation in the White House.

"He has come up through the ranks of the poor. He has known personal suffering and want. He has been in touch with every condition in his home state, politically, socially and otherwise. He is a man that has the courage of his convictions and it will be recalled that in his message to the New York Legislature that stood solidly for law enforcement.

"Although he does not believe the Volstead law to be effective, he recognized that it is a law and stands for enforcement. He is called wet.' Don't you believe it would better to have a wet' President who will enforce the law than a dry' candidate who will not?

"Al Smith is a man who has stood the test. Next November I shall be proud to vote for him."

The meeting was attended by a large group of Democrats from Kenton and nearby counties.

There was a delegation from Grant county, headed by R. L. Westover, of Williamstown, editor of the Grant County News, who stated that the Democrats of his county would line up solidly for Al Smith and that an instructed delegation would be sent to the district and state convention at Lexington, June 14.

Uulie J. Howard, Commonwealth Attorney of Kenton County presided; John W. Mittendorf, Clerk of the Kenton County Court, was secretary. In the audience were a number of women members of the Kenton County Democratic Women's Club, which is assisting in the Al Smith movement in Kenton county.[51]

Williamstown Bootleggers Caught In Net

"Snooper's" Visit Results In Saturday Raid. Four Cited To Appear In Federal Court. All Released On Bond.

As a result of a raid made by federal agents, W. C. Thompson, E. B. Henson and Mat Wilson, four Williamstown men were cited to appear in federal court in Covington Monday on liquor violation charges.

The defendants are Dr. A. L. Abbott, alleged to have been selling whiskey, hearing set for July 7 and bond fixed at $1,000. Jim Purnell, possessing and selling whiskey, hearing set for July 5, bond fixed at $500. J. W. Barlow possessing and selling home brew, waived examination and held to grand jury.

The federal agents visited Williamstown shortly after noon Saturday and armed with search warrants proceeded to search the places of those mentioned. Several half pints of "moon" were found in Dr. Abbott's place. Dr. Abbott was absent when the raid was made and the officers broke through the door.

A small amount of home brew was found in Barlow's place and a considerable quantity at the home of Jim Purnell. It is claimed that nothing was found at Hensley's but he was cited to appear on evidence of a "spotter" who spent last County Court day in Williamstown.

This "spotter" it is alleged claimed that he purchased near beer and whiskey from the parties mentioned and it was he who swore to a search warrant.

A small flask of "moon" was found on the person of a farmer who was in "Red" Mitchell's place, but was released after being taken to Covington, presumably on the ground that the agents had no authority to search him.

Nothing was found in the way of intoxicants at "Red" Mitchell's nor at other places searched.

On Wednesday of last week Dr. Abbott's place was searched by Sheriff Chipman, following evidence given by a man named Buchanan, who was arrested on a charge of drunkenness and disturbing religious worship at the Baptist church. Several bottles of homebrew were found by the Sheriff and Abbott was placed under bond to await action of the grand jury which meets in June.

[51] 18 May 1928. *Grant County News.* Author Unknown.

The "spotter" is alleged to have visited Jim Purnell's home some time ago where he asked for near beer. He was furnished with a bottle and told that there was no more to be had. He then requested Purnell to make up a batch of the stuff, and Jim, being of an accommodating nature, proceeded to do so. It was this beer that was found at Purnell's.[52]

Moon Found In Sheriff's Raids

Williamstown Citizens Are Cited For Illegal Possession Of Whiskey And Home Brew

Sheriff Chipman and his deputies raided four places last Saturday afternoon but had only small success. M. H. Hensley was charged with having in his possession of a small amount of moon. Wm. Barlow was cited for having a small amount of home brew and less than a half pint of moon.

Two other places were raided without disclosing anything in the nature of alcoholic stimulants. "Red" Mitchell's restaurant and soft drink place, was thoroughly searched after complaint had been made by a party who claimed he had bought the goods that made him drunk there. Nothing was found, despite the fact that the officers went back the second time. This was the second time "Red's" Place had been searched recently without results.

Clarence Hensley's garage at the foot of Paris street, was also searched. Nothing was found. The officers were armed with search warrants.

John C. Ackman took to the bushes when he was chased by the sheriff. He broke up a container alleged to have contained two or three gallons of moon on the concrete pavement south of Williamstown, thereby destroying the evidence. Ackman was not captured.

The Sheriff is not authorized by law to search any place unless he is armed with a search warrant, sworn to by some reliable party.[53]

Owen County Man Charged With Illegal Possession

Of Liquor Is Held Under Bond Pending Trial. Quantity Of Booze Found In Automobile.

Chas. M. Dent, of Owen county, arrested at Keefer last Friday, charged with illegal possession of liquor, was arraigned before Judge Webb. He was held under bond for appearance Friday of this week.

Dent is alleged to have had quite a quantity of "moon" in his car when he was arrested. He had been indulging too freely in his goods which led to his arrest.[54]

24 Gallons Rum Seized In Scott

93 Empty Containers, Coloring Material Also Confiscated.

Georgetown, Ky., Jan. 1 Twenty-four gallons of moonshine whisky, ninety-three empty five gallon moonshine containers, and a quantity of material used in coloring the liquor to give the moonshine a red liquor tint, was confiscated today by Lexington Federal prohibition agents in a raid on the dairy farm operated by Otis Ashurst on the Dixie Highway, two miles from here.

Ashurst was arrested following the raid and was taken to Lexington. He later gave $1,000 bond and was released for appearance next week before United States Commissioner Charles N. Waird for examining trial at Lexington.

According to the agents, Ashurst had liquor hidden so securely that they were forced to tear practically the entire floor of a living room of his home. The liquor, empty cans and the coloring matter were taken from a trap under the floor, the agents said.

The agents say they believe Ashurst has been selling colored moonshine for red liquor for the last year.

[52] 25 May 1928. *Grant County News.* Author Unknown.

[53] 28 July 1928. *Grant County News.* Author Unknown.

[54] 31 August 1928. *Grant County News.* Author Unknown.

[55] 4 January 1929. *Grant County News.* Author Unknown.

Ashurst's trial probably will come up at the February term of Federal Court at Lexington.[55]

Seventy-Three Plead Guilty And Are Fined

In Federal Court At Lexington for Selling Malt Sirup. Fines of $25 Each Assessed.

Lexington, Ky., Jan. 15 Seventy-two defendants charged with having sold malt sirup pleaded guilty of violation of the prohibition law in Federal Court here today and paid fines of $25 each.

After the fines had been paid, managers of three chain store systems, employers of the defendants, promised that no more alleged "home-brew" materials would be sold in their stores. Sawyer A. Smith, District Attorney, then announced that he intended to stop the sale of the materials throughout the eastern part of Kentucky.

The companies paid fines of $500 each. They are the Kroger Grocery Company, with its subsidiary, the Piggly Wiggly Company; the Great Atlantic & Pacific Co. with its subsidiary, the Quaker Maid, and the Glass Chain Store Company, a Lexington concern.

"Now we are going after the higher-ups, the manufacturers and the agents for the malt," said Mr. Smith.

The malt, he said, makes beer of 4 1-2 per cent. alcohol content, which is in violation of the United States code making it unlawful to advertise, manufacture, sell or possess any preparation, compound or substance intended for use in the illegal manufacture of intoxicating liquor.

Fines and costs in the cases totaled $3,565.

After District Attorney Smith had made his statement, attorneys for the stores declared that their clients hadn't intended to violate the law, but realized they were guilty techncally and were willing to pay fines and agree to take the malt stocks out of their stores.

Judge A. M. J. Cochran said he appreciated the position of the defendants, whom he described as "respectable men engaged in a respectable business," but he said the only way to define the law clearly, was to impose fines on those who had laid themselves liable, however unwittingly.

Besides the chain store companies and their employees the following independent dealers paid fines of $50 and costs of $20 each: Aurice M. Willis, William E. Barret, J. L. Bales, George Faig, Alex Hughes, Ray Hensley, Ben Hambrick, Fred S. Johns, William Montague, J. B. Wallace, Fletcher P. Vick, and Ellis M. Overstreet.

Henry M. Petrie, employed by Mr. Faig, and Weldon Adams, employed by Mr. Bales, received suspended fines of $25 each. The only defendant who declined to enter a plea of guilty was A. Michael, proprietor of a general store, who declared: "I am not guilty and I am not going to plead guilty."[56]

Streets Of City Flow With Moonshine

When Federal Agents Apprehend Two Automobiles Loaded With The Liquor Here Last Week

---

The streets of Williamstown ran with alleged moonshine whiskey last Friday evening. Federal agents from Covington captured two automobile parties who were conveying the illicit goods and who stopped here to get a meal. The names of the federal officers could not be learned as they hurried away with their captives.

In one car, containing a party of white people, 15 gallon cans filled with moon were found. In another carrying colored people a smaller quantity was found.

The federal officers placed both parties under arrest and took them to Lexington. The moon is said to have been secured in a Northern Kentucky city. With the exception of a small quantity from each car which was kept for evidence, all of the moon was poured to the gutter.[57]

---

[56] 18 January 1929. *Grant County News.* Author Unknown.

[57] 1 February 1929. *Grant County News.* Author Unknown.

Large Still Captured In Pendleton Co.

Nine Barrels Of Mash And Equipment Captured In Raid Of Falmouth Officials

Falmouth, Ky., Feb. 18 Operating under a search warrant issued by County Judge Early Cummins, Sheriff J. L. Bradford and Deputy J. W. Wright, found a 100-gallon copper still at the home of Arlie Slater on Hog Ridge, about 15 miles west of Falmouth last Friday afternoon.

Sheriff R. S. Kitchen and Deputies Florence and Kitchen of Harrison county came to Falmouth that day with warrants for the arrest of three men who were supposed to be at the home of Slater. When the officers reached the Slater home they found no one on the premises except three girls about 10, 11 and 12 years of age. The girls said their father was in the hospital and that their mother had gone to the hospital to see him. A complete distilling outfit was found which occupied the entire floor space of one room. Nine barrels of mash were also in the room ready to "run." The outfit was equiped with gasoline burners and was one of the most valuable that has ever been captured in this county. The mash was poured out and the distilling outfit was too large to bring to Falmouth in the automobile and parts of it were destroyed. The still had been operated for some time and much whisky has been made in it.

Arlie Slater owns the farm of 67 acres on which the still was found. One of the girls found at the home is a daughter by a former marriage. The other two girls are Mrs. Slater's by a former marriage. She was the divorced wife of Kirtley Wright, and she was married to Slater several months ago.

Slater met with an automobile accident about six weeks ago when his machine struck a telephone pole on Hog Ridge. He received injuries to his hand and was taken to the St. Elizabeth Hospital, Covington, where he has reported that Slaters' hand was amputated last week. Mrs. Slater was at the hospital with her husband at the time the raid was made on her home. A warrant has been issued for Slater charged with operating a still.[58]

Liquor Supply

In Kentucky Drying Up, Even In Mountains State Prohibition Administrator Declares

Louisville, Ky., Sept. 11 Kentucky's liquor supply, W. O. Mays, Federal prohibition administrator for Kentucky and Tennessee, said today, is fast drying up and even in the mountains the manufacture and sale of liquor is noticeably on the wane.

Praise of Dr. James H. Doran, Federal Prohibition Comimssioner, has been given to the dry agents in the two states for their work in the four months period ended Aug. 31, Mays said.

In the four months, 2,939 persons were arrested, 775 stills were destroyed and 720,803 gallons of liquor poured out by the agents, Mays reported. Automobiles to the number of 178 were seized.[59]

A Temperance Service

There will be a Temperance service at the Baptist church Sunday, evening, Sept. 22 at 7:30 o'clock. All the churches of the town are cooperating. All the choirs and singers of the town are invited to assist in the singing.

Dr. A. C. Graham, of Louisville, Sept. of the Anti-Saloon league, of Kentucky, will bring the message. The subject will be, "The Greatest Nation in The World." He is a great speaker, and a large crowd is expected. Everybody is cordially invited to attend.[60]

Moonshine Still Found In Farmer's Home Near Mt. Zion

[58] 22 February 1929. *Grant County News.* Author Unknown.
[59] 13 September 1929. *Grant County News.* Author Unknown.
[60] 20 September 1929. *Grant County News.* Author Unknown.

Largest And Best Equipped Plant For Manufacture Of Liquor Ever Found In County. Men In Charge Of Plant Make Escape.

Sheriff Chipman and his deputies acting in conjunction with Boone county officers, captured a large moonshine still on the Mt. Zion-Verona pike, near the Boone county line in Grant county, early Thursday morning.

In connection with the still between five hundred and six hundred gallons of mash was also found. Only a small amount of whiskey was secured, which was taken for evidence. A wooden keg with a capacity of two or three gallons, was among the loot. From this it was evident that it was the intention to age the booze in wood, or at least a small part of it.

The still was found at the home of Frank Chandler, a tenant on the farm. There was no one at the house when the raid was made, the owners of the still having evidently got wise to the fact that the officers were after them.

Grant and Boone county officers were searching for a convict from Iowa, for whom there is a reward. It is claimed that this convict is chearged with murder of a woman in Iowa.

The man really wanted is not Chandler, though he seems to have been in the game, but the escaped convict who is alleged to have been engaged in teh illicit liquor trade in Grant county for several months past. The man is a familiar figure in the northern part of the county and is said to have been the source of supply for the bootleggers in that part of the county. He has frequently been seen in Crittenden in company with a young woman, who is said to be another man's wife.

Sheriff Chipman stated that he believed that the escaped convict and Chandler made their escape not more than five minutes before the raid was made. An automobile passing the raiding party on the road is believed to have carried them away.

Reports have been current for some time past that the escaped convict was operating a still and delivering its output to numerous bootleggers in Grant and adjoining counties. His identity was not secured, however, until Mr. Chipman received a post card carrying his picture, and offering a reward for his arrest.

Officers were hopeful Thursday morning that a capture of all those concerned would be effected before night. However, as he had a good start on the officials he may be two or three hundred miles away by this time.[61]

Moonshine Still Found Near Mt. Zion

Second Large Plant Found Near Mt. Zion During Past Week. Operators Make Escape.

Armed with a search warrant Sheriff Chipman and his deputies, went to the farm of Mrs. Voyle Franks, near Mt. Zion, last Saturday, and located a large moonshine still.

The still was at the home of Wm. Cummins, who lived on the farm, as a tenant. No one was at home and no arrests were made. Sheriff Chipman reports that he found the still, a quantity of mash, some home brew and a small amount of moon.

This was the second still to be located by Sheriff Chipman in the same neighborhood within a week. The other still was captured Thursday morning of last week. The operator of the first still, believed to have been "Pedro" Jones, wanted in Iowa on a charge of wife murder, is still at large. A man named Chandler, said to have been connected with "Pedro" in the manufacture of moon, was a tenant on the farm, and it was at his home the still was found.

Both stills are in possession of the Sheriff, but the culprits have so far eluded arrest. "Pedro" Jones is said to have operated on a large scale in northern part of the county.[62]

Moon Found In Abandoned Automobile

Twenty-Six Gallons Of Liquid Refreshments Brought To Williamstown By County Patrolman

[61] 27 September 1929. *Grant County News.* Author Unknown.

[62] 4 October 1929. *Grant County News.* Author Unknown.

George Lanter brought to Williamstown Thursday morning twenty-six gallons of moon found in an abandoned automobile at the grade crossing south of Dry Ridge.

Lanter, who was patrolling the highway, noticed the car which had a broken steering wheel. An examination of the car revealed the moon. The consignment was turned over to Judge Webb as evidence.

The car carried an Ohio license tag and according to Fred Conrad, who lives near the crossing, was left there about four o'clock Thursday morning. Lanter found the booze about 8:00 o'clock.

The driver of the car had missed the grade crossing and ran into a ditch, breaking the steering wheel. As a change had been made in the crossing the driver probably attempted to cross at the old crossing and met with bad luck. There is no clew as to the identity of the car.[63]

ALLEGED MOONSHINER ARRESTED

BEN CHANDLER PICKED UP HERE BY SHERIFF. CLAIMED THAT HE OPERATED STILL NEAR MT. ZION.

Ben Chandler, alleged moonshiner and bootlegger, was arrested here by local officials Monday. Chandler was driving through in a big automobile when he was picked up by the minions of the law.

Chandler is charged with having operated a moonshine still at his home near Mt. Zion. The still was found in his home when the Sheriff and his deputies were looking for an alleged wife murdered of Iowa going under the alias of "Pedro," several weeks ago. Chandler and Pedro are claimed to have been operating the still and dispensing the output to thirsty people in the Northern part of the county.

Both Chandler and Pedro made their get-away. Pedro evidently left this part of the country as no trace of him has been found. Chandler was recognized as he passed through Dry Ridge and Sheriff Chipman was notified and lay in wait for him here.

Chandler was released on bond and the date of his trial has not been fixed.[64]

TWENTY-EIGHT GALLONS OF MOON DESTROYED

There was plenty of moon in Williamstown last Thursday. Twenty-eight gallons which was confiscated by patrolman, Geo. Lanter when he found it in an abandoned car near Dry Ridge Thursday morning, was taken to the office of Judge Webb. After taking a small sample as evidence Judge Webb ordered the liquor poured in the gutter. There were four five gallons cans and eight one gallon cans of the liquid which smelled a good deal like wood alcohol. The owner of the abandoned car has not been located.[65]

Is your News subscription paid?

[63] 13 December 1929. *Grant County News.* Author Unknown.
[64] 20 December 1929. *Grant County News.* Author Unknown.
[65] 20 December 1929. *Grant County News.* Author Unknown.

1930s

Heavy Fine Imposed On Moonshiner

Large Still Located At Dry Ridge Together With 15 Gallons Of Raw Whiskey And 12 Barrels Of Mash

Wm. Martin, Dry Ridge farmer, was fined $250.00, given a jail sentence of 30 days and placed under a peace bond of $1,000 Tuesday when he plead guilty to a charge of manufacture and sale of moonshine whiskey. He was tried before Judge Mullins of the County Court.

The Sheriff's office was notified of the location of the still after two young men of the neighborhood had got into a fight with Martin. Monday night they went to Dry Ridge and had no trouble in locating the still which was not in operation but was still hot, having been closed down for the night.

Martin was arrested and brought here for trial. He decided not to fight the case as he was caught with the goods. He reprieved his fine but will have to serve a month in jail.

This was the first still captured by local officials in several months. Judge Mullins has the outfit at his office but destroyed the moon. Martin claimed that he had been operating the still about two weeks and that it had a capacity of 5 gallons an hour.[1]

Wet Republican Wins In New Jersey Primary

Will Oppose Wet Democrat In November Election. Victory Is Overwhelming.

Dwight Morrow, White Hope of the Republican party, for president two years' hence, and advocate of the repeal of the 18th Amendment, was the overwhelming choice of New Jersey Republicans for United States Senator last Tuesday. There is not much doubt that he will win in November.

Newark, N. J., June 18 The plurality of Dwight W. Morrow, landslide victor in the contest for the Republican senatorial nomination in yesterday's primary, advanced to more than 267,000 today as late returns were reported.

With 223 of the State's 3,304 districts missing, the vote was: Morrow, 374,267; Franklin W. Fort, 107,174; Joseph H. Frelinghuysen, 43,093.

Morrow will be opposed for election next fall by Alexander Simpson, wet Democrat, who was nominated for the six-year term without opposition, and for the unexpired term of former Senator Walter E. Edge by Miss Thelma Parkinson, the only Democratic candidate for that term.

Fort and Frelinghuysen conceded Morrow's nomination a few hours after the polls closed, and early returns indicated an emphatic victory for the ambassador. Both sent telegrams congratulating him on his victory and pledging their support in the fall election.

Late Voting Heavy

The returns indicated that Morrow had carried many of the dry rural districts, from which Fort was expecting his chief strength.

Balloting was light in the fore part of the day, but there was a rush to the polling places before they closed at 8 p. m., as commuters thronged home from New York and Philadelphia.

Ambassador Morrow sat quietly in his Englewood home reading Herodotus, while the votes indicating his victory were being counted. He refused to comment, saying he would wait until the complete vote was tabulated.

[1] 30 May 1930. *Grant County News.* Author Unknown.

"However," he said smilingly, "I seem to have carried my own ward."

He expressed great pride in the vote given him by his neighbors in Englewood.

Despite the overwhelming defeat of Fort, Dr. James K. Shields, superintendent of the Anti-Saloon League is still in the fight and we are here to stay. We thought he would make a better showing than that."

Urges Repeal

Morrow opened his campaign May 15 with an address in which he declared that if elected he would be prepared to vote for a resolution submitting to the States a constitutional amendment which would restore to the States the power to determine their policy toward the liquor traffic. He said:

"I look forward to the time when the old leaders in the temperance movement will appreciate that they have not reached a final solution of a world old problem by the present Eighteenth Amendment.

"I look to the time when the moral teachers of the country will realize that in the battle for a great social reform there was wisdom in the old system of experimenting in 48 laboratories rather than in one."[2]

Big Year Reported By Raiders

Of Kentucky And Tennessee Stills Property Worth $749,991 Destroyed, Official Reveals.

Louisville, Ky., July 1 Activity of Federal prohibition agents, as outlined in a report made by Joseph Phillips, acting Deputy Administrator of Western District of Kentucky and former Assistant Prohibition Administrator for Kentucky-Tennessee District, showed a substantial increase over the fiscal year of 1928-29.

Phillips said that the department's activities for the month of June, 1930, were the longest of any single month in the history of the department.

The figures for June were approximated by Phillips and the report sent to Washington, where it will be filed. Phillips was in charge of the department for the last fiscal year.

The 1929-1930 fiscal year, ending June 30, 1930, showed 6,634 persons arrested by Federal agents for violation of liquor law. Persons arrested by state and city officers assisted by Federal agents 1,383; prosecutions in Federal Courts for liquor violations 8,377; number of stills seized and destroyed, 2,960; gallons of spirits (whisky, beer, wine, alcohol, etc.) seized and destroyed, 59,439; gallons of mash seized and destroyed 2,473,709.

Approximately 607 automobiles were seized during the year. The value of the property seized and destroyed amounted to $747,991, and the amount of property seized and not destroyed amounted to $205,596.

The reports of the year 1928-29 showed number of persons arrested by Federal officers, 6,496; arrests by state officers, assisted by Federal officers, 1,343; prosecutions, 7,502; stills, 2,604; gallons of spirits, 41,530; gallons of mash, 2,590,545; automobiles seized, 462; property seized and destroyed, $541,246, and property seized, $167,270.[3]

Farmer Arrested On Liquor Charge

Quantity Of Mash And Moon Found At Home. Abandoned Still Found Near Crittenden.

Thursday of last week the Sheriff and his officers arrested Alfred Rice, farmer, of near Crittenden, on a charge of possessing and manufacturing liquor. A small quantity of home made liquor and two barrels of mash was found at Rice's home. He was brought to Williamstown and later placed under a $1,000 appearance bond.

Abandoned Still Found

On a farm about two miles west of Crittenden, where the Crittenden and Verona pike crosses Bullock Pen creek, an abandoned moonshine still was located last Saturday. The still was a completed whiskey making outfit, with a copper boiler and burner.

[2] 20 June 1930. *Grant County News.* Author Unknown.

[3] 4 July 1930. *Grant County News.* Author Unknown.

Information reached the sheriff's office that the still was lying on the bank of the creek.

There was no one near the still when sheriff's officers reached the place and it was brought in. It is believed that the owners of the still were transporting it to some other locality when they became frightened and abandoned it.[4]

Federal Officers Make Raid, Find Still And Moon

Federal officers from Covington located a still on the farm of Raymond Jones, 6 miles east of Williamstown, in Pendleton county, last Friday, and a small quantity of moon and mash was found. The still was destroyed.

Jones was taken to Covington where he was released on $1,000 bond for his appearance. He does not live on the farm and claims that he had no knowledge of the still. A search was also made of Jones' garage on Paris street, here, by officers, but nothing of an incriminating nature was found. The officers came back Saturday and made a further search but found nothing.[5]

Booze Car Goes In Ditch With 25 Gallons Moon

Driver Arrested, Fined And Placed Under Peace Bond. Liquor Poured In Gutter.

The driver of an automobile travelling south, was hit by another car, travelling north, on the Dixie Highway, two miles north of Dry Ridge, Wednesday morning shortly after 8 o'clock, and forced over an embankment and wrecked.

County patrolman, Geo. Lanter, happened along about that time and stopped to see if he could render assistance. He found the wrecked car contained 25 gallons of white mule, mostly in 1 gallon cans and placed the driver under arrest.

The man who gave his name as Wm. Frost was brought here along with the booze, plead guilty before county judge G. C. Mullins, and was fined $150.00, given a 30 day jail sentence and placed under $1,000 peace bond. The booze was poured in the gutter.

The driver of the other car, H. L. Miller, is said to have caused the wreck. His car was not damaged and he proceeded on his way. Both cars bore Ohio license tags.[6]

Hearst Favors Prohibition Repeal In Address

Urges Government To Borrow $5,000,000,000 To Restore Prosperity. Could Pay Off Debt In Five Years.

New York, June 2 William Randolph Hearst, head of the Hearst newspapers, tonight in a radio address urged the Government to borrow $5,000,000,000 to restore prosperity, and suggested that it could pay off the debt in five years by abolishing prohibition.

"This is not a time for reducing the national debt through burdensome taxation and thereby reduce prosperity," he said.

"It is time to increase the national debt and increase the expenditure of the Government in public works in the employment of labor, and thereby increase prosperity.

"Then out of prosperity pay off the debt."

Prosperity, he continued means increased incomes and values out of which the government would "eventually get, even with moderate taxation, an increased income to pay off the loan."

"And," he added, "if the Government desires further to increase its income let it end this folly of prohibition, which does not prohibit and substitute government control of the man-

[4] 21 November 1930. *Grant County News.* Author Unknown.
[5] 12 December 1930. *Grant County News.* Author Unknown.
[6] 16 January 1931. *Grant County News.* Author Unknown.

ufacture and distribution of alcoholic beverages and secure for itself, on the basis of the figures of Canada's excise income, an additional income of $1,000,000,000 a year.

"That excise income to the United States Government of $1,000,000,000 would in itself pay off in five years $5,000,000,000 borrowed and spent to restore prosperity."

Mr. Hearst gave "overcapitalization" as the cause of the depression. He criticized income it received during the period of prosperity for "higher wages and shorter working hours" for its employees.

"It this had been done," he said, "the shorter working hours would obviously have prevented any lack of employment.

"And if wages had been increased in proportion to the productivity of modern machinery and the consequent increase in the profits of industry, the purchasing power of the public would have been increased and the consumption of all kinds of goods and products would have been maintained at a high level or raised to a still higher level."

Instead, he said, industry so increased its capitalization that there was no money left to build up the purchasing power of the masses and maintain the conditions which made for prosperity.[7]

Federal Officers Make Raid On Two Places Tuesday

Federal officers raided two places here Monday. A small amount of liquor is said to have been found in both. Warren Renaker was arrested on a charge of violating the liquor law. C. P. Hensley was also arrested on the charge and both were taken to Lexington. Their bond had not been fixed.

The federal officers came armed with search warrants sworn to by an undercover man named Thomason who is said to have spent several days in Williamstown recently digging up evidence.[8]

Sherman Man Charged With Possession

Of Home Brew And Moonshine, Arrested Tuesday By County Officials. Bond Fixed At $300.

Ben Hunter, of Sherman, was arrested by Sheriff Conrad Tuesday afternoon, charged with illegal possession of home brew and moonshine whiskey.

A search of Hunter's home revealed about a half gallon of moon, several quarts of home brew, etc. Judge Mullins held him under $300 bond for his appearance at the October term of court. He gave the bond.[9]

Modification Of Dry Act Is Urged

As Best Way Of Ending Intolerable Conditions. Congressional Move Is Aim Of Committees.

Washington, September 7 Modification of the Volstead Act is certain to be a major issue in every presidential campaign, and in every congressional election, until the law is changed and changed it will be!

Henry Clay Hansbrough, for 18 years a member of the United States Senate from North Dakota, so declared today in accepting the National Chairmanship of the League for the Modification of the Volstead Act, with headquarters here.

Senator Hansborough will serve also as Chairman of the league's Committee on Senate Legislation.

Directs House Activities

Rowland B. Mahany, Washington attorney, formerly a member of the House from Buffalo, and American Minister to Escuador, is Chairman of the Committee on House Legislation.

Hollins N. Randolph, of Atlanta, is Chairman of the league's Advisory

[7] 5 June 1931. *Grant County News.* Author Unknown.
[8] 3 July 1931. *Grant County News.* Author Unknown.
[9] 10 July 1931. *Grant County News.* Author Unknown.

Committee. Chesley W. Jurney, long identified with legislation activities at the Capitol, is the league's President.

Senator Hansbrough said:

"We have no quarrel with those urging the seemingly impossible task of having the Congress, as well as the 48 states, take the Eighteenth Amendment out of our Constitution, but we do believe that modification of the Volstead act, so as to permit beer and wine without bricks is the shortest, surest and most practicable road toward ending the intolerable conditions imposed upon us by so-called prohibition.

Cause Of Depression

"It has added immensely to the expense of Government, and, at the same time, is demoralizing the youth of the nation.

"In a large measure it is accountable for the increase in crime. And, by just so much as it has reduced the farmer's output of barley and hops, of his orchards and vineyards, it has added automatically to his production of wheat and cotton, and is, therefore, largely responsible for the prevailing depression."[10]

Alleged Bootlegger Turned Over To Federal Authorities

Howard Greenwell, Crittenden garage owner, was turned over to federal authorities last Friday when his case came up for trial. He was charged with having, possessed liquor for purpose of sale. Monday he had a hearing and was held under $1,000 bond.

Glenn McGill, colored, who was arrested at the same time, was tried and given a fine of $100 and 40 days in jail and placed under a peace bond of $1,000. He will have to serve 90 days in jail to pay the fine.[11]

Barrel Of Booze Found In Home

Mrs. Maggie Webster Is Held Under $1,500 Appearance Bond, Pending Hearing

---

A fifteen gallon barrel containing about 10 gallons of alleged whiskey was found at the home of Mrs. Maggie Webster, about 7 miles west of Williamstown, on Chipman Ridge, by deputy sheriffs Tuesday.

The deputies, Ira Caldwell and William Taylor, armed with a search warrant, went to the Webster home. The barrel of booze was in plain view and easy of access to those who cared to imbibe.

Pending a hearing Mrs. Webster was placed under a $1,500 bond for her appearance at a later date.[12]

Big Still Found On Farm Near Stewartsville

R. E. Goaley, of near Stewartsville, reported to the Sheriff's office Tuesday that he had found a large moonshine still on his farm and asked the officers to come out and get it.

The officers brought the still in late in the afternoon and it is now on exhibition at the Sheriff's office. The still is one of the largest liquor making outfits ever found in the county.

Evidence that whiskey had been made from the still for some time was apparent when 7 barrels which had contained mash, were located nearby. The barrels were empty, the mash having been emptied.[13]

Fined $150 And 30 Days In Jail On Liquor Charge

Mrs. Maggie Webster, at whose home a barrel of booze was found last week, plead guilty to a charge of possession and selling in Judge Mullins' Court last Saturday and was assessed a fine of $150 and 30 days in jail. She was placed under a peace bond of $1,000. She will be required to serve 90 days in jail unless she pays the fine. Mrs. Webster was allowed

---

[10] 11 September 1931. *Grant County News.* Author Unknown.
[11] 2 October 1931. *Grant County News.* Author Unknown.
[12] 2 October 1931. *Grant County News.* Author Unknown.
[13] 9 October 1931. *Grant County News.* Author Unknown.
[14] 9 October 1931. *Grant County News.* Author Unknown.

to go home and straighten up matters before beginning her sentence.[14]

Two Held For Having Booze In Possession

Tom Jump, Jr., and Francis Jump, were arrested Tuesday night in an alley in the rear of the court house charged with illegal possession of booze. The men are said to have had a gallon of the happy water in their possession. They had not given bond Wednesday afternoon and are being held in the county jail.[15]

Possession Of Liquor Gets Man In Trouble

Erlanger Man Is Fined $100.00 and 30 Days in Jail. Had Eight Gallons of Whiskey In Automobile.

R. C. Wagner, of Erlanger, was fined $100.00 and given a jail sentence of 30 days when he plead guilty to possession of liquor Thursday of last week.

Unfortunately for Wagner he had a flat tire when he reached a point on the Dixie Highway, near Dry Ridge. He stopped to charge tires, parking his car on the pavement. Again, unfortunately for him, the county patrolman arrived on the scene while he was changing the tire.

A search of the car revealed the liquor and Wagner was brought here where he plead guilty before Judge Mullins, who fined him the amount stated.

The liquor was of red variety and was poured into the gutter. Many longing eyes watched the proceeding as the contraband was poured out.[16]

Wet Democrat Elected To Congress

In Normally Republican District In New Hampshire Democratic Membership Now 200 Compared to 214 Republicans

---

Manchester, N. H., January 5 Former Congressman William N. Rogers, Democrat, advocate of prohibition repeal, was elected today to represent the First New Hampshire Congressional District, complete returned showed tonight.

Rogers defeated Former Governor John H. Barlett, Republican by 2,048 votes in an ordinarily Republican district, and will succeed the late Representative Fletcher Hale, Republican.

The Final Vote Rogers, 27,453; Barlett, 24,505.

Rogers' election to the seat once held by Daniel Webster swelled Democratic membership in the House to 220, compared to 214 Republicans, and cut into what normally is Republican territory. The outcome was forecast by recent Democratic gains in the municipal elections. Manchester, largest city in the district, inaugurated a Democratic administration for the first time in 10 years.

Rogers had served to a term in the house previously and retired in 1924 to practice law. His opponent was a member of the International Boundary Commission, former First Assistant Postmaster General and had been backed by Senator George H. Moses.

Both candidates stressed unemployment relief in pre-election speeches, Barlett pledged himself to support a $3,000,000,000 bond issued. Rogers, ridiculing the Hoover administration, said Barlett's proposed bond issue was not in keeping with the Hoover policy and had no chance.[17]

Seven Officers Of The Law Find Half Pint Moon

It took seven officers of the law to find a half pint of moonshine whiskey in Williamstown last Saturday afternoon.

A search warrant was issued against Joe Harrison's place, armed

---

[15] 20 November 1931. *Grant County News.* Author Unknown.

[16] 18 December 1931. *Grant County News.* Author Unknown.

[17] 8 January 1932. *Grant County News.* Author Unknown.

with which the Sheriff, two deputies, the town marshals of Crittenden, Dry Ridge, Corinth, and the county patrolman, went in quest of the forbidden liquor.

After a search of half an hour a half pint of moonshine whiskey was found in the bathroom. Harrison denied either ownership or knowledge of the liquor.

Harrison and R. B. Caldwell were taken before Judge Mullins and immediately released on their own regconnaisance without bond.[18]

Four Charged With Illegal Possession

Of Whiskey Making Outfit. Sheriff's Officers Ferret Out Still By Sense Of Smell.

An acute sense of smell enabled sheriff's officers to locate a whiskey making outfit Monday. The officers went to the home of James F. Jacobs, five miles southeast of Williamstown, to serve a summons on one of the men.

They smelled booze and investigated. A complete whiskey making outfit was found in the house together with a large quantity of mash, some barrels and others paraphernalia.

The two Jacobs', Tom Seeler and Harry Casey were arrested. All except Casey were charged with possession of apparatus used for the purpose of manufacturing. Casey was arrested on a charge of aiding and abetting. He plead guilty and submitted to a fine. The others will have a trial this week.[19]

Party Can Not "Pussyfoot" In Wet-Dry Fight

Plea That Democrats Make Fearless Stand On Prohibition Is Voiced At Connecticut Convention. Roosevelt Wins In Kansas; Garner Launches Another Attack On Hoover.

Hartford, Conn., May 16 A plea that Democrats unite in a fearless stand on the prohibition question was voiced tonight by Jouett Shouse, chairman of the Democratic national executive committe, in opening the part's state convention.

The convention Tuesday will elect 16 delegates to the national convention, with every indication they will be instructed to support Alfred E. Smith for the presidential nomination. A minority of the group, favoring Gov. Franklin D. Roosevelt, will be allowed to vote as it chooses on other convention questions.

"This is no time for straddling or pussyfooting," Mr. Shouse said in his keynote address. "In other words nobody can misconstrue, misunderstand or misinterpret, we must pledge ourselves on prohibition, regardless of the circumstance that all our party is not in accord."

Shouse also urged the party to be explicit in its attitude on the tariff and unemployment relief measures and to avoid the "weaselworded and double-meaning sentences," of the 1928 Republican platform. He assailed President Hoover's administration for he continuance of strained business conditions.

"The Republicans are pinning their last hope for November," he said, "on a bitter struggle in the Democratic convention. That hope will fail.

"There will be lively rivalry undoubtedly for the presidential nomination, but when the Chicago convention has completed its work it will find all factions lined up solidly behind the nominee, whoever he may be."[20]

Beer Tax Bill Is Rejected By House, 228-169

May And Spence Are Only Kentucky Congressmen Voting To Raise Federal Funds By Levy On Brew

Washington, May 23 The house rejected beer-for-revenue today, but in so doing rounded out for the 1932 campaign the most complete prohibition record of any congress since the Volstead act became law.

[18] 18 March 1932. *Grant County News.* Author Unknown.
[19] 25 March 1932. *Grant County News.* Author Unknown.
[20] 20 May 1932. *Grant County News.* Author Unknown.

The vote was 228 to 168 against a motion to bring up the O'Connor-Hull bill to tax 2.75 per cent beer at three cents a pint. May and Spence, Kentucky Democrats voted for it. All the other Kentucky congressmen present voted against it, Chapman, who was absent, was paired against it.

Party lines were obliterated, just as when submission of the prohibition issue in a proposed new amendment to the Constitution was defeated last March, 227 to 187.

Joining with 85 Democrats for the bill were 83 Republicans and one Farmer-Laborite. The March vote on submission brought together 90 Democrats and 97 Republicans.

Floor and galleries were crowded, during the balloting, but there was a noticeable lack of the tension that marked the submission rollcall. Today, as then, the vote was forced through with a discharge petition signed by 145 members.

Debate was limited to 30 minutes, but even before discussion began Representative Blanton (D. Tex.), a prohibitionist, sought to block the vote with a parliamentary objection. He contended a second vote relating to the Eighteenth amendment was not in order.

O'Connor (D., N. Y.,), coauthor of the beer bill, and La Guardia (R., N. Y.) contested this interpretation, and Speaker Garner overruled Blanton's objection.

Following the custom that speakers vote only in case of a tie, Gardner was not recorded on the beer ballot.

The only Kentuckians voting for the bill were Spence, of the Sixth District, and May of the Tenth District.[21]

Republican Prohibition Plank Fails To Satisfy

The prohibition plank adopted by the national Republican convention early Thursday morning fails to satisfy either the wets or drys. It is characterized in the Cincinnati Enquirer as "Weasel Word" plank.

Text Of Prohibition Plank

Chicago, June 15 The text of the administration prohibition plank adopted by the Republican Resolution's Committee tonight follows:

The Republican party has always stood and stands today for obedience to and enforcement of the law as the very foundation of orderly government and civilization. There can be no national security otherwise.

The duty of the President of the United States and of the officers of the law is clear. The law must be enforced as they find it enacted by the people. To these courses of action we pledge our nominees.

The Republican party is and always has been the party of the Constitution. Nullification by nonobservance by individuals or state action threatens the stability of government.

While the Constitution makers sought a high degree of permanence, they foresaw the need of changes and provided them. Article V. limits the proposals of amendment to two methods: (1) Two thirds of both houses of Congress may proposed amendments, or (2) on application of the Legislatures of two-thirds of the states a national convention shall be by Congress to propose amendments. There after ratification must be had in one or two ways: (1) By the Legislatures of three-fourths of the several states or (2) by conventions held in three-fourths of the several states. Congress is given power to determine the mode of ratification.

Referendums without constitutional sanction cannot furnish a decisive answer. Those who propose them innocently are deluded by false hopes; those who propose them knowingly are deceiving the people.

A nation-wide controversy over the Eighteenth Amendment now directs attention from the constructive solution of many pressing national problems. The principle of national prohibition as embodied in the amendment was supported and opposed by members of both great political parties. It was submitted and ratified by State Legislatures of different majorities. It was not then and is not now a partisan political question.

Members of the Republican party hold different opinions with respect to it and no public official or member of the party should be pledged or forced to choose between his party affiliations and his honest convictions upon this question.

We do not favor a submission limited to the issue of retention or re-

[21] 27 May 1932. *Grant County News.* Author Unknown.

peal. For the American Nation never in its history has gone backward, and in this case the progress which has been thus far made must be preserved, while the evils must be eliminated.

We, therefore, believe that the people should have an opportunity to pass upon a proposed amendment the provision of which, while retaining in the Federal Government power to preserve the gains already made in dealing with the evils inherent in the liquor traffic, shall allow states to deal with the problem as their citizens may determine, but subject always to the power of the Federal Government to protect those states where prohibition may exist and safeguard our citizens everywhere from the return of the saloon and attendant abuses.

Such an amendment should be promptly submitted to the states by Congress, to be acted upon by state conventions called for that sole purpose in accordance with the provisions of Article V. of the Constitution, and adequately safeguarded so as to be truly representative.[22]

Church Voices Opposition To Drouth Repeal

Methodists Take Uncompromising Stand Against Any Change in Eighteenth Amendment

---

Lexington, Ky., September 4 In adopting the report of its committee on temperance and social service, the 112th session of the Kentucky Conference of the Methodist Episcopal church, South yesterday afternoon condemned both the Democratic and Republican party planks on prohibition, and took an uncompromising stand against repeal or modification in any form whatsoever of the Eighteenth amendment.

The report further calls on "our people to meet unwaveringly the serious obligation which has been thrust upon them in the coming election, by voting for those candidates only who believe that prohibition ought to be the law. It further urges that each candidate be required to state his position in relation to repeal or modification of the Eighteenth amendment, and recommends "that a citizens" movement for prohibition, law observance and law enforcement be organized and maintained in each county throughout the state."

The report follows substantially the attitude toward the prohibition question and the forthcoming national elections expressed by Bishop James Cannon, Jr., chairman of the General Board of Temperance and Social Service, who addressed the Kentucky Conference Thursday afternoon. It was signed by the Rev. M. S. Clark, of Irvine, chairman, and read to the conference by Mrs. Ludie Day Pickett, of Wilmore, president of the Kentucky W.C.T.U., and secretary of the conference committee.

The only other matter dealt with in the report was the question of world disarmament, which was urged in approval of the calling by President Hoover of the Geneva World Disarmament Conference for June 22 of this year.

Other members of the conference committee on Temperance and Social Service are: Rev. Paul C. Gillespie, Williamstown; Rev. O. B. Crochett, Danville; Rev. W. H. Cardwell, Mt. Olivet; Rev. W. B. Garriott, presiding elder of the Danville district; Mrs. Elizabeth Pigg, Berry; T. F. Brooks, Apox; C.E. Rankin, Flemingburg, and R. H. Morris, Crestwood.[23]

Federal Officer Makes Raid

Large Quantity Of Homebrew And Gallon And Half Of Moon Found In Wigginton Flats

---

A federal officer from Lexington made a raid on the rooms of George Kennedy, located in the Wigginton building last Monday afternoon. One hundred and twenty-one quart bottles of homebrew, 250 empty bottles and one and one-half gallon of moonshine whiskey was found. Most of the stuff was dumped into the ditch but a part was kept for evidence.

It is claimed that Kennedy had been operating a homebrew joint for the past several months and was doing

[22] 17 June 1932. *Grant County News.* Author Unknown.

[23] 9 September 1932. *Grant County News.* Author Unknown.

a large business.. He was held under bond for action of the United States Court grand jury.

Farmer Found With Mash

The same federal officer searched the home of Wm. Souder, near Stewartsville, Saturday and found several barrels of mash used in making moon. Souder was released on bond for his appearance before the federal grand jury.[24]

Held Under $1,000 Bond On Liquor Charge

E. C. Gardner was placed under $1,000 bond on a liquor charge last week. If he is proven guilty and convicted it will be his second offense for which the law provides imprisonment in the reformatory. He will have a trial at the coming term of Circuit Court.[25]

Repeal Is Favored In Kentucky

By All Democratic Nominees For Congress, While At Least Three Republicans Oppose It.

Louisville, Ky., September 27 Announcement that Democratic nominees for Congress in Kentucky favored early repeal of the Eighteenth Amendment and that the three Republican nominees so far replying were against it was made here today by the Kentucky branch of the Women's Organization for National Prohibition Reform.

No answers have been received from Maurice H. Thatcher, Republican, and Alben W. Barkley, Democratic candidates for the senate.

The questions, submitted by registered mail September 1, were as follows:

Question 1 If elected, will you support a resolution for the straight repeal of the Eighteenth Amendment and the restoration to each state of its power to regulate the manufacture, sale and transportation of intoxicating beverages within its own limits? Such resolution to be submitted to conventions in the several states for ratification or rejection.

Question 2 If elected, do you further pledge yourself to exert power and influence to have the above-mentioned resolution presented before the Seventy-third Congress at the earliest possible date after it convenes?

The organization announced all Democratic Congressional candidates replied "yes" to both questions except C. R. Carden, who said he was a Democrat and would stand and vote for the entire party platform.

On the Republican side, Robert Blackburn checked his answers "no;" William Lewis wrote "I will not," and Hugh H. Asher telegraphed, "I am personally a dry and do not favor repeal of the Eighteenth Amendment." The other six Republican candidates have not replied.[26]

Wets Have Lead In Poll On Congress

Anti-Prohibition Candidates Exceed Dry 11 to 1, Group Reports

---

Washington, Oct. 23 The Women's Organization for National Prohibition Reform reported today that, in a poll it is conducting, "wet candidates for the Seventy-third Congress exceed drys eleven to one."

An announcement issued by Mrs. William B. Mason, chairman of the District of Columbia division, which is the national legislative department of the organization tabulated replies of 607 candidates from forty-five states.

The organization classified 553 fo those replying as "wet" and 54 "dry." The "wet" classification included 474 candidates who were listed as supporting a resolution for those replying as "wet" and 54 either repeal or submission with qualifications."

Democrats Wetter

[24] 16 September 1932. *Grant County News.* Author Unknown.
[25] 23 September 1932. *Grant County News.* Author Unknown.
[26] 30 September 1932. *Grant County News.* Author Unknown.

"Democratic candidates are still leading Republicans more than two to one for straight repeal in the poll which already covers over 50 percent of the candidates and which will be continued right up to election day," Mrs. Mason said.

"The arrival of a militant wet group in the new Congress after March 4 is definitely forecast. Wets have real cause to be jubilant. These latest returns of the Congressional poll spell defeat for the drys, and a new deal for the drys, and a new deal for prohibition reform advocates is on the horizon."

"I think it is particularly interesting that 322 Democrats are standing on their national plank, with 135 Republicans, avowed repealists, have parted company with the Republican restrictive plank."

The organization asked the candidates:

"If elected will you support a resolution for straight repeal of the Eighteenth Amendment and the restoration to each State of its power to regulate the manufacture, sale and transportation of intoxicating beverages within its own limits? Such resolution to be submitted to conventions in the several States for ratification or rejection."

Mrs. Mason reported that ten Kentucky Democratic Congressional nominees answered "yes," and four Republicans answered "no." In Indiana, four Republicans and nine Democrats replied "yes"; one Republican and one Democrat were listed "wet with reservations," and three Republicans answered "no."[27]

[27]28 October 1932. *Grant County News.* Author Unknown.

Is your News subscription paid?

Repeal Of Eighteenth Amendment Defeated By Narrow Margin

Repealists Fail To Secure Necessary Two-Thirds Majority By Six Votes. "Lame Duck" Congressmen Responsible For Defeat.

Washington, Dec. 5 A bold and unprecedented attempt by the Democratic leadership to force its party's outright prohibition repeal proposal through the House failed today and dimmed prospects of further action on the issue of further action in that branch during the remainder of the short session.

The action was interpreted on Capitol Hill as foreshadowing a special session of the new Congress next spring after President-elect Roosevelt is inaugurated, so the Democrats can carry out their pledge for flat repeal.

Despite defeat of the resolution by the narrow margin of 272 to 144 two-thirds majority being required for adoption the Democrats planned immediate attack on the problem of modifying the Volstead law. Speaker John N. Garner hopes a beer bill will be ready for action before Christmas holidays.

Eighty-one "lame duck" members not returned to the next Congress, and 33 Democrats reelected in November, voted against the measure. Sixty-nine defeated incumbents voted for it. A shift of six votes from the negative to the affirmative would have sent the resolution to the Senate.

Altogether 168 Democrats, 103 Republicans and 1 Farmer-Labor, voted for the measure; 44 Democrats and 100 Republicans voted against it. Eleven of the Democrats opposing are "lame ducks," while 70 are Republicans.

Spectacular in its inception, swiftness of action and failure, the Democratic effort will go down in history as the first to bring a constitutional amendment before legislative branch of the Government under procedure preventing any amendments and curtailing debate to 40 minutes.

It was the first test in Congress on flat repeal of the Eighteenth Amendment since it was voted into the Constitution in 1917, although the Beck-Lintchicum submission proposal was defeated last spring by 227 to 187.

Speaker Garner was greeted warmly as he vigorously walked into the chamber promptly at 12 o'clock to open the House. The galleries were packed with leading persons, even the seldom-used executive and diplomatic sections. Senators and members of the Cabinet were on the floor to watch.

Dispensing with the opening formalities as quickly as possible, the Vice President elect then discarded all custom by recognizing Representative Henry T. Rainey, of Illinois, party floor leader, to offer the resolution.

Several attempts were made to extend debate time, but the Wets apparently were so confident of victory they prevented it.

Coming down into the historic well of the House to open the brief debate, Rainey read the Democratic and Republican wet planks. He called upon his forces to support the measure, declaring it conformed "with the wording of both platforms."

Procedure Is Rapped

Attacking the procedure invoked by Speaker Garner, Representative Bertrand H. Snell, of New York, Republican leader said: "You are not only breaking the precedents of 150 years, but you are not showing proper respect to the office of President by passing important legislation before the usual notification of meeting and receiving any message the President desires to send us."

With the conclusion of the debate the roll was called amid unusual silence. Every member and the 700 spectators crowded into the galleries listened to check the vote of each member.

"Two-thirds not having voted, the resolution is lost," Speaker Garner said in announcing the vote.

Questioned by Representative Earl C. Michener, Republican, Michigan, if he would "consider a similar resolution brought up in the regular manner," the Speaker said: "The Chair will decide that when it's brought up."

Immediately after the House adjourned, however, Garner told newspapermen:

"I shall not give a vote on any other resolution except the Democratic resolution. Either you are going to pass Democratic repeal or nothing.

"I would oppose anything except the Democratic resolution."

Garner said he would be "willing" to bring up the Democratic proposition if it were passed by the Senate.

Meanwhile, he added, the plan to pass a beer bill by Christmas would be carried out. Hearings are to be begun Wednesday before the House Ways and Means Committee on a beer bill introduced by Representative John J. O'Connor, Democrat, New York, and a measure to legalize light wines proposed by Representative Clarence F. Lea, Democrat, California.[28]

Prohibition Repeal Bill Is Passed By House By Good Majority

Vote Is 289 to 121, 15 More Than Necessary. States To Ratify Amendment. Given Seven Years.

Washington, Feb. 20 Congress today proposed to the states that national prohibition, after its 13 years of turbulent trial, be done away with by repeal of the Eighteenth Amendment.

The house by a vote of 289 to 121, 15 more than necessary, approved the repeal resolution passed last week by the senate. Under it, for the first time in American history, conventions of the people are to decide whether the states shall ratify or reject a change in the Constitution.

Thirty-six of the 48 states must ratify the resolution in order to carve the Eighteenth amendment out of the national charter and substitute for it a Twenty-first. By its terms, also the ratifications must all occur within seven years from today. With repeal, the amendment carries a specific prohibition of intoxicating liquors into any states remaining dry.

With enough legislatures now in session to dispose of the amendment this year if they take action, leaders in many sections of the country lost no time in getting things started.

As the first of the states were acting, President-Elect Roosevelt in New York expressed gratification at th decision of congress. He coupled it with hopes that this short session of congress would carry out one more proposal of the Democratic platform of last year by passing beer legislation.

In Boston, by prior arrangement, Governor Ely had the legislature ready for a joint session to which, immediately upon the vote in Washington, he delivered a message asking for early legislation to call a convention. He specified that the delegates

[28] 9 December 1932. *Grant County News.* Author Unknown.

[29] 24 February 1933. *Grant County News.* Author Unknown.

standing for election to the convention should list themselves definitely for or against ratification.[29]

End Of Dry Regime Seen In Passage Of 3.2 Beer Bill

Local Attorneys Are Of Opinion That Legal Beer May Be Sold In Kentucky Without Modification Of State-Wide Prohibition Law

---

According to the opinion of local attorneys beer may be sold in Kentucky under the present state-wide prohibition law, if the bill before Congress and which is sure to be enacted, becomes the law of the land. Whether this will be permitted in small towns and communities under the county unit law, is a matter to be determined. However, if the United States Government, through its law-making bodies, decides that beer is not an intoxicating liquor it is hard to see how it can be banned. Towns and counties, however, may collect local tax the same as on cigarettes.

Covington, Ky., March 15 Samuel W. Adams, Covington City Solicitor, yesterday was studying various city ordinances as well as the state prohibition law preparatory to drafting an ordinance licensing and regulating sale of beer. City Manager H. D. Palmore said the city would take immediate action in passing the necessary ordinances.

It was the opinion of City Solicitor Adams yesterday that immediately after passage of Legislation by Congress, permitting beer of certain alcoholic content, and the signing of the bill by the President, beer could be sold in Kentucky. This opinion also was given by other attorneys.

The Kentucky dry law makes no reference to the alcoholic content of any beverage and attorneys say that it has been left to juries to determine the amount of alcoholic content that has been illegal.

What amount of license will be imposed upon those handling beer is problematical. Cafe licenses were fixed at $300 in an ordinance passed in 1914, this being payable semi-annually.

It was recalled yesterday that an ordinance providing for licensing and regulation of malt beverages was passed by Commissioners more than 10 years ago in which a license of $120 was fixed. This ordinance was not enforced, however, as the city was enjoined from its enforcement by an order of Kenton Circuit Court.

Washington, March 14 By the overwhelming vote of 316 to 97, more than three to one, the House of Representatives today passed the Cullen bill modifying the Volstead Act by legalizing the manufacture and sale of 3.2 per cent beer and taxing it $5 a barrel.

Members of the House jumped to their feet and cheered lustily when Speaker Henry T. Rainey announced the vote, and the turmoil lasted several minutes.

The bill, when passed by the Senate and signed by President Roosevelt, will legalize the manufacture and sale of beer in all parts of the United States where it is not prohibited by local or state law. Predictions were made freely that beer will be on sale shortly after April 1.

Before Senators Today

Immediately after being advised that the House had passed the bill, Senator Pat Harrison, Mississippi, Chairman of the Senate Finance Committee, called a meeting of the committee for 10 o'clock tomorrow morning to consider the House bill.

It is to be taken up in the Senate just as soon as the Senate committee can report it favorably, provided the President's economy bill has been disposed of. Prompt action in the Senate is anticipated, although the debate is expected to last longer than it did in the House because of the rule of unlimited debate in the upper branch.

Both the Senate Finance and Judiciary Committees reported favorably on a beer bill in the last session of Congress, and sentiment for legalizing beer is much stronger in this Senate than in the preceding body.

Margin Is Surprise

Senator Joseph T. Robinson, of Arkansas, Senate majority leader, gave assurance at the White House yesterday that the beer bill would be passed promptly in the Senate, and similar assurance came today from Senator Henry F. Ashurst, of Arizona,

Chairman of the Judiciary Committee, which will pass on the taxing provisions of the bill.

Sentiment among Senators tonight was preponderantly in favor of passing the bill as it came from the House and this likely will be done as quickly as a vote can be taken.

The result in the House today was no surprise save in the size of the majority for beer. Democrats and Republicans joined in the final rout of the dry forces, who were making their last desperate but futile stand in the body they had controlled for more than a decade.

End Of Dry Regime

Although prohibition repeal has been submitted to the states, the vote today is the one that actually marks the end of bone dry prohibition in the United States.

Voting for the bill were 238 Democrats, 73 Republicans, and the five Farmer-Labor members from Minnesota. The 97 negative votes were split among 58 Democrats, chiefly from Southern states, and 39 Republicans, the majority of whom represented rural districts.

The 316 affirmative votes was the highest wet vote that ever has been cast in the House since national prohibition was adopted, and for several years before. It exceeded appreciably the vote by which the repeal of the Eighteenth Amendment was submitted to the states.

Announcement was made on the floor during the debate that large breweries in St. Louis already have considerable quantities of 3.2 per cent beer made and aging under Government supervision and that this beer will be ready for bottling and prompt distribution as soon as the bill goes into effect, which will be 15 days after President Roosevelt signs it. In the event the beer bill failed of passage, these breweries intended to dealcoholize the product and sell it as near beer.

Certain Of Approval

Passage of the beer bill in response to President Roosevelt's 72-word special message yesterday cleans the slate for the House and puts it in a position, according to Speaker Rainey, to take a three-weeks' recess whenever the Senate passes the economy and beer measures.

Speaker Rainey announced further that the House bill in the form it passed today is acceptable to the White House and that there will be no delay in obtaining the President's signature to it if the Senate passes it without material changes.

Debate on the bill was limited to three hours, the roll call starting shortly before 4 o'clock. The debate was turbulent, but the outcome never was in doubt from the beginning.

Unanimous consent to take up the bill today was obtained on the proposal of Representative Joseph W. Byrns, of Tennessee, Democratic floor leader. Dry leaders realized that the only effect of objection would be the adoption of a drastic rule that would limit the time for debate to a much shorter period that the three hours provided in the Byrns proposal. [30]

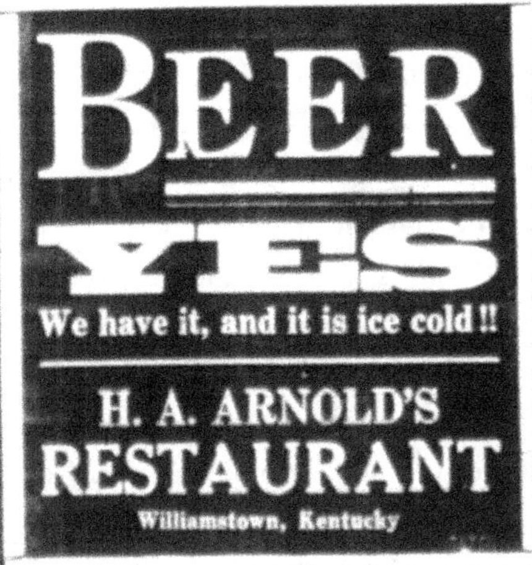

[31]

Beer Becomes Legal Beverage After 13 Years

Kentucky One Of Fourteen States Which May Handle Same Without Change In Present Law

---

With the passage of the bill legalizing beer in both houses of Congress, Tuesday, beer of 3.2 per cent. in volume will become legal beverage for the first time in 13 years. The bill was sent to President Roosevelt, who affixed his signature Wednesday.

Only fourteen states in the union will be permitted to handle beer as a beverage until existing laws are changed. Among the fourteen are Kentucky.

Beer Law In Brief

---

[30] 17 March 1933. *Grant County News.* Author Unknown.

[31] 21 April 1933. *Grant County News.*

Washington, March 22 The principal provisions of the beer bill:

Legalizes wine and beer of 3.2 per cent alcohol by weight, or 4 per cent by volume.

Levies a Federal tax of $5 a barrel of thirty-one gallons.

Becomes effective fifteen days after enactment.

Leaves all regulation as to distribution to States.

Protects dry States by reaffirming Webb-Kenyon act preventing interstate shipment into those having laws prohibiting sale of beverages of more than 1-2 of 1 per cent alcoholic content.

Provides that brewers must pay annual Federal license fee of $1,000 for each brewery.

Continues existing law calling for $50 annual fees for wholesalers and $20 for retailers.

Amends dry laws affecting Hawaii, Alaska and Porto Rico to permit sale of 3.2 per cent beer and wine.

Makes manufacturers bear burden of proof that products do not contain more than 3.2 per cent alcohol.

Reaffirms Volstead act penalties on violators of provisions, including forfeiture of license.

Permits advertising by newspapers and other publications.

Beer and wine may be sold in fourteen States as soon as legalized: Kentucky, Indiana, California, Illinois, Missouri, Montana, Nevada, New Jersey, New York, Oregon, Pennsylvania, Washington and Wisconsin.

Three other States permit beer to be sold after specified times : North Dakota, July 1; West Virginia, May 9; Wyoming, May 18. [32]

Beer License Here May Be Fixed At $100

While beer may be sold legally in Williamstown after the 7th day of April, the town board of trustees may fix the license so high that it will be prohibitive to many of the smaller places.

No definite agreement had been reached by the town board of trustees up to Wednesday, but some members, and probably a majority favor fixing the license at $100.

If this is done it is not likely that many will be able to pay the license. On the other hand there are a number of road houses in the county outside of the corporate limits of the town which will not be required to pay a license fee.

The board of trustees were expecting to call an extra session before they meet in regular session next Monday night to work out the matter which will not be passed until the regular session. [33]

License On Beer In Williamstown Fixed At $75.00

Several Places In Williamstown Expected To Take Out Licenses To Sell "Suds." Will Be Available Today.

Beer will again be available in Williamstown today, or at least as soon as those who desire to pay licenses and handle it can get a supply.

The Town Board of Trustees in monthly meeting passed an ordinance fixing the license fee at $75.00 per annum. Those who take out the license may sell beer at 3.2 per cent alcoholic content immediately if they can secure a supply. The entire ordinance is published in this issue of The News.

Some were in favor of fixing the license at $150.00, and some at $100.00. An agreement was reached presumably satisfactory to both the members of the board and those who propose to handle the "suds."

It is understood that several will take out licenses in Williamstown. Some will sell only in bottles while others will have draft beer. Three or four applications have already been made.

So beer has come back after 13 years, and will be sold legally in Williamstown. [34]

---

[32] 31 March 1933. *Grant County News.* Author Unknown.

[33] 31 March 1933. *Grant County News.* Author Unknown.

[34] 7 April 1933. *Grant County News.* Author Unknown.

Beer Flows Freely In Williamstown For First Time In 25 Years

Two Places Open For Sale Of Bottled Goods Last Friday. Heavy Sales Reported By Both.

For the first time in more than 25 years beer is flowing freely in Williamstown.

It is good oldtime stuff too. Only bottled goods are being sold and this in only two places. So far only two places of business have taken out licenses. These are the D. H. Restaurant and the half-way house.

The local license is $75.00, the state license $75.00 and the federal license $20.00.

Judging by the way the old and new timers went after the amber fluid it is going to be very popular. One place reported sales of more than 100 cases in two days. The other probably did equally well.

At this rate it will not take long for the profits from sales to equal the tax. The beer is retailing at 15 cents per bottle.

Equally strong demand was in evidence in the big towns. A leading hotel in Cincinnati telephoned one place here Sunday offering $1.00 on each case on hand. The offer was rejected. Newport and Covington reported shortages.

Local places were well supplied and were able to fill the needs of all customers. There was no drunkenness reported. The few mildly intoxicated persons were apparently drinking the old homemade moonshine, which is still plentiful.

Twenty states are open for the sale of beer and many more will be open in a short time. Those who have drunk the beer assert that it is as good as the old time brew. [35]

Beer Flows In House Restaurant

For First Time In 30 Years, Congressmen and Their Guests Enjoy the 3.2 Beverage

Washington, April 17 In the same House restaurant where real beer last was sold 30 years ago, thirsty Congressmen, their guests and secretaries today downed 720 bottles of the new 3.2 beverage.

But unlike the scene of 30 years ago the new beer was sold only at tables.

Promptly at 12 noon it went on sale. The first to be on hand were Representatives Delaney and Boylan of New York, Berlin, of Pennsylvania and Fernandez, of Louisiana. And from the time they clinked glasses and cried "Prosit!" "Skal" and "Here's How!" until the stock of 30 cases finally gave out there was a stream of searchers for the foamy brew.

Many of the buyers were not Congressmen, for the beer was served, as well, in the section of the restaurant that is open to the public. But whoever drank it, the beer was gone in about four hours.

Thirty cases more were ordered for tomorrow, with the real boss of the restaurant Chairman Lindsay C. Warren, Democrat, North Carolina, of the Accounts Committee promising:

"It will be handled in orderly fashion, and sold only to people who come in, sit down and drink."

Warren expects the beer sales to decrease the House restaurant's $10,000-plus annual deficit. But it will not be sold in the cloakrooms adjoining the House floor, one story above, nor have arrangements been made for its sale in the Senate restaurant at the other end of the Capitol. [36]

Two More States Fall In Line For Repeal Amendment

Illinois and Indiana Are Latest To Join Wet Procession, Six More States To Vote This Month

For repeal of the Eighteenth Amendment, 12.

Against repeal, 0.

[35] 14 April 1933. *Grant County News.* Author Unknown.
[36] 21 April 1933. *Grant County News.* Author Unknown.

That is the score at the present time for the repeal of the Eighteenth amendment.

Monday, Illinois voted for repeal by a majority of more than 10 to 1. Tuesday Indiana followed suit by a majority of more than 2 to 1.

Indiana had long been considered a stronghold of the drys. Tuesday's victory for the wets was a knock out blow.

Up to the present time 10 states have voted and all have voted wet by overwhelming majorities.

During the month of June, 6 more states vote on the amendment. These states are, Massachusetts, June 16; Connecticut, June 20th; Iowa, June 20th; New Hampshire, June 20th; California, June 27th; West Virginia, June 27th.

With the exception of Iowa and West Virginia all of these states are certain to vote for repeal and both Iowa and West Virginia are expected to do so.

If all six vote for repeal, 16 states in all will have voted for repeal.

Tuesday, Delaware voted wet on local option by a majority of 3 to 1.

Kentucky cannot vote this year unless a special session of the legislature is called, which is not probable. By the time Kentucky votes it is probable all will be over but the shouting.[37]

Old Bay State In Wet Parade. Vote Is 4 To 1.

Massachusetts Is Eleventh State To Vote Approval Of Repeal Amendment. Score Now Is 11 To 0.

Boston, June 13 Massachusetts Wets swept Dry resistance aside today and elected every one of 45 delegates to a constitutional convention which will act on repeal of prohibition.

The Wet victory made Massachusetts the eleventh state to register approval of the repeal amendment and placed her in company with Wyoming, Illinois, Indiana, New York, New Jersey, Michigan, Rhode Island, Delaware, Wisconsin and Nevada.

The margin of success for the Wets ran more than 4 to 1 throughout the state, but in Boston it was near 10 to 1. The 15 congressional districts gave a high combined district total for the Wets of 441,195, as compared to 98,884 for the Drys.

James Roosevelt Wins

Riding high on the wave of Wet success was James Roosevelt, son of President Roosevelt, who was chosen from the Ninth District, which included parts of Cambridge, and Boston.

Besides voting on repeal ratification delegates, most all of the communities passed on the question of local license. The results showed a big overturn for the Wets with only a few scattered towns standing firm against license as most of the communities had in 1924 when the last vote was taken.

Among the prominent Drys who went down to defeat were Mary E. Woolley, President of Mount Holyoke College, and Professor S. Ralph Harlow, Smith College.

As the repeal-pledged delegates rolled up large majorities, David F. Sibley, Secretary of the Allied Repeal Forces telegraphed President Roosevelt.

"We are proud to deliver Massachusetts to you as the eleventh state in the union to join the parade of the state in the repeal of the Eighteenth Amendment." [38]

Smashing Victory For Repealists

In Connecticut, New Hampshire And Iowa. Score Is Now 14 To 0 For Striking Out Eighteenth Amendment.

Three more states were added to the repeal column Tuesday as the result of elections to select delegates to conventions to pass on the Eighteenth Amendment.

---

[37] 9 June 1933. *Grant County News.* Author Unknown.
[38] 16 June 1933. *Grant County News.*

That makes a total of 14 states to vote for repeal, a clean sweep in elections held to date.

Connecticut voted eight to one for repeal. New Hampshire gave good majorities and Iowa, which had been claimed as strongly dry, was piling up a surprisingly large anti-prohibition vote.

States to vote previously were Michigan, Wisconsin, Illinois, Indiana, New York, Massachusetts, Wyoming, Rhode Island and Delaware, all of which gave sizable majorities to repeal delegates.

New Haven, Conn., June 20 Connecticut reemphasized her opposition to prohibition today by voting 6 to 1 for repeal of the Eighteenth Amendment, which it never ratified.

Fifty delegates pledged to vote at the state convention for ratification of the Twenty-first Amendment which would strike prohibition out of the Federal Constitution, were elected.

Unofficial returns from the state's 169 towns showed:

For repeal, 236,942. Against repeal, 35,349.

Even before compilation of the vote was completed, Governor Wilbur L. Cross set July 11 as the date for the convention. The 50 delegates, 15 at-large and the others representing the 35 senatorial districts, will gather in Hartford to record Connecticut formally for repeal.

Victory Is Assured

Manchester, N. H., June 20 With a vote of more than two to one, repealists were certain of victory in New Hampshire tonight as the wet vote continued to pile up with more than half the state, including most of the largest cities already reported.

Only a dozen of the smaller communities cast a majority vote in favor of retention of the Eighteenth Amendment as the 10 delegates-at-large, favoring repeal, received large majorities over their dry opponents.

With 260 towns and city wards reported the vote was:

For repeal, 75,337. Against repeal, 30,337.

The town of Deering, home of Daniel A. Poling, national dry leader voted 46 to 35 in favor of repeal, while the town of Haverhill, home town of Senator Henry W. Keyes, a dry, voted 508 to 290 for repeal.

Iowa Going Along

Des Moines, Iowa, June 20 Prohibition was taking a drubbing in this one-time stamping ground of the Drys tonight as returns from today's special election gave an ever-increasing majority to advocates of repeal of the Eighteenth Amendment.

Returns from 2,272 of the 2,435 precincts in the state were:

For repeal, 364,473. Against, 239,858.

The vote was light, which had been taken as an encouraging sign by the Drys.

Although Iowa recently voted to permit sale of 3.2 per cent beer the state rallied its dry forces and presented an organized fight against the proposal to repeal the Eighteenth Amendment.

Feeling ran high and billboards carrying advertisements for the repealist cause were burned in Washington county. [39]

Two More States Fall In Line For Repeal

Wet Victory Estimated At More Than Two To One In East And West. California And West Virginia Join Wet Parade. Score Is Now 16 To 0 For Prohibition Repeal.

Advocates of repeal on opposite sides of the continent took commanding leads Tuesday in California and West Virginia.

As early returns trickled in from the Golden Bear state, giving anti-prohibitionists a more than two-to-one advantage, tellers in West Virginia had counted up a vote of 123,098 for repeal and 70,130 against, with about half the state reported.

In West Virginia, listed as dry for two decades, those favoring ratification of the Twenty-First amendment at first enjoyed a better than two to one lead, but later returns from the rural districts cut down this percentage.

The first returns from California came principally from the Los Angeles district, and when totaled with scattered ballots from other sections gave 122,464 for repeal and

[39] 23 June 1933. *Grant County News.* Author Unknown.

43,731 for retention of the prohibition amendment.

The Pacific coast state's referendum gave opportunity not only for a popular mandate on repeal but also on whether pari-mutual betting on horse races should be permitted.

Meanwhile, 150 repeal delegates eleceted by an overwhelming majority in New York state in May gathered in Albany for formal ratification of the amendment repealing the prohibition amendment. Former Gov. Alfred E. Smith, long a repealist, was unanimously chosen president of the convention.

In Texas both advocates and opponents of the dry law gathered at Austin to choose the candidates that will stand for their sides at the state election on August 26th.

By an almost two to one vote the Oklahoma house of representatives during Tuesday voted to Gov. W. H. Murray to permit the special session of the legislature to permit the people of the state to vote on the repeal question. The senate has yet to vote.

The 14 states that have gone on record previously in favor of repeal are Michigan, Wisconsin, Rhode Island, Wyoming, New Jersey, New York, Delaware, Nevada, Illinois, Indiana, Massachusetts, New Hampshire, Connecticut and Iowa.

Charleston, W. Va., June 27 West Virginia, regarded as one of the dryest of the dry states for 20 years, tonight became the fifteenth consecutive state to ratify repeal of the Eighteenth Amendment.

A wave of ballots that rolled in from the populous centers which cradle the state's great industries towered far above the comparatively meager majorities from 19 dry rural counties to give repeal a lead of 73,810 with two-thirds of the precincts reported.

West Virginia had been dry seven years longer than the nation. It was the first state with strong Southern traditions to vote on repeal.

Therefore both wets and drys regarded the vote as a "pivotal one;" prohibition's foes labored to the last minute to get out a strong vote; its friends conducted many prayer meetings.

F. Scott McBride, superintendent of the Anti-Saloon League, said that if West Virginia voted nay, repeal would be blocked; leaders of the United Repeal Council predicted victory by 50,000 to 100,000; drys also predicted triumph.[40]

Special Session Of Legislature May Be Called

To Enact Legislation To Tax Beer And Set Up Machinery For Repeal Of The Eighteenth Amendment. Ten-Day Session Proposed.

Frankfort, Ky., July 3 Executing a sharp about-face in policy, Governor Ruby Laffoon in letters sent to members of the 1932 session of the General Assembly today indicated he was not averse to calling a special session of the Legislature.

The Governor in his letter to the legislators expressed the opinion that a special session to enact legislation to tax beer, would not be unwise, though he held the view that the session should not be continued more than 10 days. He also asked the members if they would agree to limit themselves to actual traveling expenses so the cost of the seession would be reduced to a minimum. Their daily pay of $10 would be paid.

The Governor's action came as a surprise to wet and dry forces alike. He previously had stated he would not call a special session under any circumstances, saying the "the time was too short" before the regular session is convened in 1934.

August Date Looms

The statement that he would not call a special session was made after the Court of Appeals had held the state tax being collected on beer illegal.

Should replies from the Legislature be favorable, the Governor is expected to call a special session to convene in August, 10 days or two weeks after the primary elections.

Prohibition in all of its phases is possible for consideration at the special session, if it is held.

Immediately after the Governor's letter was made public many persons began advocating plans to persuade Governor Laffoon to include the re-

[40] 30 June 1933. *Grant County News.* Author Unknown.

peal of the Rash-Gullion Act and provide for an election to enable voters of the state to express themselves on repeal of the Eighteenth Amendment to the Federal Constitution.

Without a special session, Kentucky voters will be unable to ballot on national repeal until the summer of 1934. If arrangements were made at a special session the question could be submitted for decision at the polls at the regular election this fall.[41]

Two Southern States Vote For Repeal

Alabama And Arkansas Join Wet Parade. Dry Hopes Dashed In Dixie. Prohibition To Be Off Books by First Of Next Year.

An Associated Press Dispatch says:

Two traditional strongholds of prohibition, Arkansas and Alabama, apparently capitulated to the rising tide of repeal sentiment yesterday and piled on what political leaders throughout the country deem the last straw on the dry camel's back.

As the count of returns from yesterday's special elections on repeal progressed this morning the Wets of both states maintained comfortable margins.

Latest returns from Arkansas, from 962 of the state's 2,103 precincts, including the most populous centers were: For repeal 51,880; against 32,676.

The vote in 1,084 of Alabama's 2,137 precincts: For Repeal 63,958; against, 41534.

Hopes Based Upon South

Dry leaders all along have staked their hopes of stopping repeal upon holding fast for prohibition the long-dry bloc of Southern states and have conceded little chance for retaining the Eighteenth Amendment for even another year if they lost more than one Dixie state.

Anti-prohibition forces were jubilant over the apparent defeat of the Drys in Arkansas and Alabama and predicted confidently that prohibition would be off the books by the end of this year.

Alabama and Arkansas bring to 18 the number of states that have voted for repeal. This is exactly half the 36 required for ratification of the repeal amendment.

No state has voted for retention of prohibition.

Tennesee Is Next

Repealists expect another victory in Tennessee, which votes Thursday, the third Southern state to do so this week.

Sixteen other states have set dates for repeal elections this year, and Postmaster General James A. Farley has predicted that all will vote wet. If they do so, and the repeal majorities are maintained in Alabama and Arkansas the number of states favoring repeal will be brought to 35 by November 8.

Governor O. K. Allen, of Louisiana, has said that his state will be called to act as soon as it would "do any good toward accomplishing repeal." Virginia and Utah also may decide to vote this year. Thus, it is possible that repeal may be approved by the required 36 states before the new year.

Other Dates Set

Other states, besides Tennessee which have set voting dates are: Oregon, July 21; Missouri, August 17; Texas, August 26; Washington, August 29; Vermont, September 5; Maine, September 11; Maryland and Minnesota, October 10; North Carolina, South Carolina, Ohio and Pennsylvania, November 7.

Repeal has been approved by New York, New Jersey, Rhode Island, Illinois, Michigan, Nevada, Delaware, Wyoming, Indiana, Wisconsin, Massachusetts, Connecticut, New Hampshire, Iowa, West Virginia and California.

The balloting was light in Arkansas and Alabama but the count was slow. The first Arkansas precinct to report gave an overwhelming vote for repeal, 44 to 1. This was in Upperhill Township. The lone vote was cast by Mrs. B. C. Purvis, wife of an election official. Purvis voted wet.

The appeal of President Roosevelt, calling for Democratic voters in the South to support the party declaration made in Chicago, was believed to have swung many normally dry voters. The recent speaking tour made through the South by Postmaster General Farley, was accepted as a contributing factor.

H. K. Toney, Speaker of the Arkansas House of Representatives,

[41] 7 July 1933. *Grant County News.* Author Unknown.

said he had been called into conference in Little Rock today with Governor J. M. Futrell and others and that if Arkansas stayed in the repeal column he would urge an immediate session to legalize beer.

Toney said he would propose that a beer tax be levied for the benefit of the state's common schools.

An unusual situation existed in at least two Arkansas Counties where Dry candidates for delegates to the state repeal convention next month were shown in early returns to be leading but the county vote on the direct question of repeal gave Wet majorities. This was in Lonoke and Saline Counties.

Under the law setting up machinery for the repeal referendum however, the convention is bound as a unit to cast the state's vote for or against repeal in accordance with the statewide result of the voting.

Should a majority of the convention delegates elected be dry and the referendum result show a majority for repeal, Dry leaders intimated they would contest this provision of the referendum act.

Oklahoma City, Okla., July 18 Governor William H. Murray today signed the legislative resolution setting up machinery for a state-wide vote on repeal of the Eighteenth Amendment, thus assuring a vote after December 5. Unless a special election is called, the vote would be at the state primary next July.[42]

Arizona Votes For Repeal Of 18th Amendment

States Favoring Repeal Now Number 21 With None Against. Votes Is 3 To 1 Against Prohibition.

Phoenix, Ariz., August 8 A steady tide of wet votes swept Arizona today toward the list of 20 other states advocating repeal of the Eighteenth Amendment.

When returns from more than two-thirds of the state's 444 precincts had been tabulated dry voters were inundated more than three to one.

The Drys conceded defeat following the recent overwhelming repeal of the state prohibition law. They failed to place any names of delegates on the ticket elected to cast Arizona's official vote and make this the twenty-first state in the repeal column.

The vote in 302 precincts was: For repeal, 28,211; against repeal, 8,752.

Mrs. Isabella Greenway, Democratic Committeewoman for Arizona and friend of the family of President Roosevelt, had a long lead in the primary race for the congressional seat vacated by Lewis W. Douglas now Federal Director of the Budget. She was leading her nearest opponent in the Democratic primary, Harlow Akers, young Phoenix attorney, who was an unsuccessful candidate last year for the United States Senate, 15,830 to 7,764 in the incomplete count. William Coxton, former Secretary of the Arizona Corporation Commission, the only other aspirant, had polled 3,022.

In her campaign, Mrs. Greenway had stressed her acquaintance with personages at the national capital, acquired during her incumbency as National Committeewoman, but had sought to discourage voters in believing her acquaintance with the family of the President would redound to the benefit of Arizona should she win the post.

The Democratic nomination is tantamount to election unless the Republican State Central Committee puts a candidate in the field before election day. The only other party aspirant in the primary, Dillworth E. Sumpter, Socialist, was nominated without contest, but had no hope of election next October 3.

The Republicans have indicated no desire to brave the state's Democratic strength this year.

Denver, August 8 Colorado was assured a place among the states to vote on prohibition repeal this year when the House late today adopted a measure to submit the 21st amendment to popular vote September 12. The measure had passed the Senate and Governor Johnson has indicated he will approve it.[43]

---

[42] 21 July 1933. *Grant County News.* Author Unknown.

[43] 10 August 1933. *Grant County News.* Author Unknown.

Extraordinary Session Of Kentucky Legislature Opened Last Tuesday

Session Called By Governor To Pass Legislation And Set Up Machinery And To Submit Ratification Of Prohibition Repeal

Frankfort, Ky., Aug 14 Members of the Kentucky General Assembly gathered here today in preparation for an extraordinary session convoked by Governor Laffoon to meet tomorrow to pass relief legislation, obtain necessary revenues to finance relief work and to submit ratification of prohibition repeal to the voters of the state.

The Democratic caucus met tonight and selected Representative Frank Lebus, Harrison County, as its speaker, taking the place held in the regular session by Representative John Brown, Lexington, who resigned his Legislative position when elected to Congress.

Representative Clarence Evans, Simpson County, was elected caucus Chairman and Democratic floor leader.

Lebus was Governor Laffoon's choice for the Speakership.

To Give Free Hand

Anti-administration forces in both branches said they would give to Governor Laffoon a free hand in organization of the Assembly. They took the position the Chief Executive had called the session and had the responsibility for it. They wished to give him control with a view to maintaining his responsibility for the session and for its actions.

There were indications from all quarters that harmony would be restored in Democratic ranks and that Governor Laffoon would have full opportunity to obtain action on the program he will present to the Assembly tomorrow.

Senator Allie W. Young, Senate Democratic leader, has been in conference frequently with the Governor. Although it was understood he was not fully in agreement with the Governor on certain views, leaders close to him said there would not be any effort to perpetuate the anti-administration bloc that existed in the last (regular) session of the Assembly.

This, also, is planned with a view to making the responsibility Governor Laffoon's throughout.

Republicans will line up wholeheartedly in the enactment of necessary relief legislation, Senator Ray B. Moss and Representative Joseph Bosworth, minority leaders in the two branches said.

Revise Present Law

"The situation of our people is too serious for anybody to play partisan politics in such a time," Senator Moss said.

Bills have been prepared covering all phases of Governor Laffoon's proposals to the Assembly, and will be ready for presentation by Administration spokesmen immediately after the Governor delivers his message at noon tomorrow.

The major question before the Assembly is the producing of new revenues. Increased taxes will be the Assembly's principal task. Governor Laffoon had prepared specific recommendations concerning sources from which additional revenues should be derived and the manner of raising them.

A principal feature of this program, it is understood, will be revision of the present graduated sales tax law. This law was passed at the 1930 session and was aimed principally at store chains and at the larger merchants. It imposes a graduated scale of taxes according to the volume of business done by the merchant. The tax is nominal on small stores and increases progressively with sales until the rate is 1 per cent on all sales of more than $1,000,000.

Governor Laffoon will recommend, it is understood, that the rates in the lower brackets themselves be cut down so that the higher rates would apply at lower sales levels. Exemptions allowed in the present law would be stricken.[44]

Missouri In Wet Column By 4-1 Vote

St Louis votes 20 To 1 For Repeal; Kansas City By 10 to 1

[44] 17 August 1933. *Grant County News.* Author Unknown.

St. Louis, Aug. 19 A mounting wave of wet votes from rural sections and cities tonight made Missouri the twenty-second State under the banner of prohibition repeal.

As unofficial and incomplete returns flowed in from three quarters of the precincts in the State, the preponderance of wet votes indicated the "show-me" State had cast a vote of more than four to one for repeal of the Eighteenth Amendment.

Returns from 3,053 of the 4,126 precincts showed: For repeal 459,381; against repeal, 110,995.

The sweeping strength of the repeal vote was evident when incomplete returns indicated only twenty-one of the 115 counties in the State had given dry majorities. These were rural counties, always considered extremely arid in any test of wet and dry strength. Many other counties hitherto classed as rigidly dry, swung into the wet column.

Returns indicated almost a negligible dry vote in St. Louis and Kansas City. In St. Louis, center of anti-prohibition sentiment when the dry movement was at its crest incomplete returns from more than half of the precincts showed a twenty to one ration for repeal. Nearly complete tabulation of the Kansas City and Jackson county votes showed a ten to one ratio.

Complete returns from St. Louis showed: For repeal, 172,565; against repeal, 8,201. In Jackson county, which includes Kansas City, the vote in 494 out of 544 precincts was: For repeal, 123,418; against 13,185.

The lightness of the vote, attributed to lack of interest and absence of many drys from the polls after urging by their leaders, was shadowed in nearly every return from both city and rural sections.[45]

Washington in Wet Columns By Three To One

Incomplete Returns Indicate Sweeping Victory For Repeal of Prohibition Amendment

Seattle, Wash., Aug 29 Washington's voters showed a strong trend toward repeal of prohibition tonight as early returns from today's special election were tabulated.

Reports from 469 of the State's 2,682 precincts gave wet delegates to the repeal convention October 3 a total of 78,485 votes to 28,556 for dry delegates.

Although the state-wide total will have no bearing on determining whether Washington will become the 24th state to vote for repeal, or the first to reject it, since delegates are chosen by legislative districts, the district votes follow generally the total vote.

Elwha precinct, in the Olympic mountain section of the 24th legislative district, was the first voting unit to report 100 per cent for repeal. The precinct cast its 93 votes solid for repeal.[46]

Lone Star State Joins Wet Parade By Vote Of 2 To 1

In Twenty-Third State To Ratify Amendment To Repeal Prohibition With None Against. Washington Follows Suit.

Dallas, Texas, August 27 The dream of Senator Morris Shepard to make this the first of 13 states to block repeal of the Eighteenth Amendment was left behind tonight in a storm of wet votes.

Returns today from 239 of the state's 254 counties, including 40 complete, as compiled by the Texas Election Bureau, showed 279,567 votes for repeal and 165,082 against.

Texas also voted 283,725 to 155,419 to amend its state constitution to legalize 3.2 per cent beer.

Sheppard, fifty-eight-year-old Democratic Senator, frequently called the "father of the Eighteenth Amendment," because of his efforts in writing prohibition into the National Constitution, stumped the state's 31 senatorial districts preceding Saturday's referendum.

Under a blazing August sun, the Texas-born Senator carried his plea

[45] 24 August 1933. *Grant County News.* Author Unknown.
[46] 31 August 1933. *Grant County News.* Author Unknown.

that the Lone Star State eschew beer and halt the anti-prohibition drive.

"Keep the lid on John Barleycorn's coffin," he urged, but it was a losing fight.

Against him was arrayed the full force of the National Administration of his own party. Another native son, Vice President John Nance Garner, exhorted this wide-spread area of the "Solid South" to support the measure advocated by President Roosevelt and supported in daily expressions of confidence by James A. Farley, the National Democratic Chairman and Postmaster-General.

Even Sheppard's home city of Texarkana voted for repeal, showing a margin of 335 votes against the Eighteenth Amendment to boost a statewide majority of more than 100,000.

Senator Sheppard tonight said prohibitionists should receive "fresh hope" from the referendum despite the majority of more than 110,000 by which the state went wet.

"The militant and aggressive fight by the Drys in Texas and the relatively large vote they polled in the face of such tremendous odds ought to give fresh hope and enthusiasm to prohibitionists everywhere," Sheppard said.

Governor Miriam A. Ferguson, whose husband, James E. Ferguson, opposed Sheppard in a speaking campaign, hailed the referendum's result as a "return to sanity." She expressed hope "we will be rid of political hypocrisy that has been a painful incident to prohibition."

Farley, in New York, said he was "not surprised at the result because I have been confident from the outset that every state in the Union would vote in favor of repeal when given the opportunity to do so.

"The vote in Texas," the Democratic chieftain continued, "justifies the prediction I have made repeatedly that the Eighteenth Amendment will be repeal by November 7."

Texas yesterday also approved a $20,000,000 bond issue for relief purposes to meet a warning by the Federal Relief Administration that it must provide additional state aid before it could hope to obtain Federal assistance.

The larger cities of the state supplied the biggest margins for repeal, with San Antonio and Galveston recording majorities of more than 7 to 1. Prohibitionists received their greatest strength in rural districts.

Numerous elections were conducted in precincts and counties to decide upon local option, with most of them showing a trend against prohibition.

Texas was the twenty-third state to ratify the twenty-first, or Repealing Amendment.

Washington, voting tomorrow will be the twenty-fourth to signify its sentiment, and at least 13 other states are scheduled to conduct referenda this year. The approval of 36 is required to void the Eighteenth Amendment.[47]

Vermont 25th State To Ratify

Amendment To Repeal Prohibition Has Long Been A Rockbound Prohibition Stronghold. No State Has Voted For Amendment.

Montpelier, Vt., September 5 Vermont, long a rockbound prohibition stronghold, today joined the parade of states favoring repeal of the Eighteenth Amendment.

It was the twenty-fifth consecutive state to record itself in opposition to retention of prohibition in the Constitution. No state has voted for the amendment.

Complete returns from the 248 towns and cities in Vermont gave: for repeal, 41,279, against 20,572.

The vote in St. Albans, near the Canadian border, the first city to report a complete vote, was 1,812 for repeal and 295 against.

Rutland City went 3,532 to 681 for repeal.

The vote in other communities was: Bennington, for repeal 1,884, against 332; Brattleboro, for 1,358, against 535; Burlington for 3866, against 1,099; Plymouth birthplace of President Coolidge, for 28, against 10; Rupert against 94, for 35.

Only two counties were recorded in the dry column Lamoille, one of the smaller, located in the north central part of the state and with few large communities within its borders, and Orleans, adjoining it on the northeast and of similar rural character.

The turnout of voters generally was light, there being no other statewide question on the ballot.

[47] 31 August 1933. *Grant County News.* Author Unknown.

On the opposing tickets of candidates for places in the ratification convention which will be held September 26, were two former Governors. John E. Weeks opposed repeal and Franklin S. Billings favored it. There were 14 candidates on each ticket, one from each county.[48]

Four More States Vote For Prohibition Repeal Amendment

Maine, Maryland, Minnesota and Colorado Join in Wet Parade by Heavy Majorities. Kentucky Selects Delegates.

Maryland rushed quickly into the mounting repeal column yesterday as majorities in Minnesota and Colorado lifted the anti-prohibition lineup to 29 states.

The vote in Maryland with 1,256 of the state's 1,397 precincts reported gave the repeal forces a majority of about five to one. Minnesota recorded a vote of 268,478 for repeal and 124,229 against in 1,675 of the 3,693 precincts in that state. Colorado in 1,061 out of 1,547 precincts counted 112,528 for and 49,595 against repeal.

Maryland's vote for repeal was 191,991; against, 37,051 and 3,452 votes for an uninstructed repeal convention.

While Maryland, Colorado, and Minnesota were voting today, Maine was completing the count of ballots that yesterday placed that original dry state in the wet column. With 42 precincts missing, the Maine vote was 112,626 for repeal and 51,817 against.

The vote from Baltimore alone, where the total was 119,019 for repeal and 11,295 against, was sufficient to insure a majority for the repealists.

The other sections of Maryland however, followed suit. Apparently but one county had gone dry. Dorchester county on the eastern shore with 20 to 29 precincts reported, showed 1,207 against repeal to 915 for.

Other former dry strongholds on the eastern Maryland shore swung over to the repeal side.

The Maryland vote was cast for six delegates-at-large and for three delegates from each of the six congressional districts. The lead of the wets in the First and Sixth districts, both of which are outside of the city of Baltimore, appeared to be commanding.

Gov. Albert C. Ritchie, a repeal pioneer, in a statement last night said the result "is a splendid justification for the stand against the Eighteenth amendment which the Maryland people have consistently taken."

George W. Crabbee, superintendent of the Maryland Anti-Saloon League, in conceding victory for repealists, said "from reports in known bootlegging sections it is plain that bootleggers voted wet as all sensible persons knew they would. From other sections it looks like many good people were mixed up in bad company."

Minnesota Goes Wet

Minnesota, the home state of Andrew Volstead, "father" of the prohibition enforcement law, had voted repudiation of the Eighteenth amendment on the basis of incomplete returns.

Representative reports, in some cases meager, but in others, fairly complete continued to show a majority for repeal of slightly more than two to one in Minnesota.

The drys displayed surprising strength in scattered areas in Minnesota. They drew their chief support in the strictly rural sections and in some instances, either carried small cities and villages or were forced to concede narrow margins to repealists.

Hennepin county, in which is located the state's largest city, Minneapolis recorded 13,106 votes for repeal to 3,246 against on the basis of returns from 50 out of 405 precincts.

Following Maryland and Minnesota into the wet column, Colorado became the 29th state to vote for expulsion of prohibition.

Fifteen delegates will attend a constitutional convention September 26th at Denver to formally ratify the 21st (repeal) amendment.

Only eight of the 63 Colorado counties had reported dry majorities in the early returns.

The vote in all 314 Denver precincts was not tabulated but 250 precincts in the city reported 48,885 for repeal and 9,756 against.

Outside of Denver in 693 precincts the vote was 55,676 for repeal and 34,064 against.

Seven counties outside of Denver, with all precincts reported, returned

48 7 September 1933. *Grant County News.* Author Unknown.

overwhelming majorities for repeal. All seven counties are in the metal mining country.

Repeal Slate Named

Louisville, Ky., Sept. 12 A list of 19 candidates for the state repeal convention at Frankfort, November 27, who will be balloted on in the November election was announced today by Mrs. James Ross Todd, chairman of the United Repeal Council of Kentucky as bearing the endorsement of the repeal group.

The repeal council, recently organized to conduct the campaign for repeal in Kentucky, is made up of groups interested in repeal of the Eighteenth amendment, Mrs. Todd said. The aim of the council is to elect 19 delegates in the state-at-large election who will put Kentucky in the repeal column.

The candidates endorsed by the wet organizations are:

First district Mrs. J. G. Gaither, Hopkinsville; Roy M. Shelbourne, Paducah.

Second district Mrs. James Ross Todd, Louisville; Brue Haldeman, Louisville.

Third district G. Lee McClain, Bardstown; C. C. Boldrick, Lebanon.

Fifth district R. C. Simmons, Covington; Harry J. Allington, Newport.

Sixth district Miss Laura Clay, Lexington; Russell des Cognets, Lexington.

Seventh district Henry D. Fitzpatrick, Prestonsburg; Dr. W. J. Smith, Belfry.

Eighth district Dan S. Keenan, Ashland; D. E. See, Maysville.

Ninth district Mrs. William M. Martin, Harlan; Beecher Smith, Somerset.

State-at-large Charles P. Farnsley, Louisville.[49]

Two More States Vote For Repeal Of Prohibition

The Score Is Now 31 For And 0 Against Repeal Of Eighteenth Amendment New Mexico and Idaho Join Wet Parade.

Repealists are counting Idaho and New Mexico as states No. 30 and 31 in the mounting anti-prohibition column on the basis of early but substantial leads in Tuesday's balloting.

New Mexico's vote to abolish the Eighteenth amendment was running nearly three to one. Idaho's polling was much closer, but a member of the state council of the Idaho allied drys conceded the state for repeal with approximately one-fourth of the precincts reported.

In unbroken succession, 29 states have voted to ratify the repeal amendment. Thirty-six are needed.

In Arizona, one of those which has ratified, the state supreme court Tuesday dismissed an appeal from a lower court's refusal to issue an injunction to stay the repeal election held August 8.

Votes from 416 of Idaho's 819 precincts gave 44,183 for repeal to 31,943 against repeal. Thirty-nine counties of the 44 in the state had reported by 9:30 p. m. and of those 29 gave majorities for repeal, compared with 10 against.

Returns compiled from 45 of 785 New Mexico precincts showed a vote of 5,638 for repeal and 1,801 against.

The vote on the New Mexico state constitutional dry law from 43 precincts was 5,860 for repeal and 1,722 against.[50]

Virginia Is 32nd State To Ratify

Twenty-First Amendment. Score Is Now 3 to 0. Four More States Needed.

Richmond, Va., Oct. 3 Virginia, the second state to ratify the Eighteenth amendment, today became the thirty-second to vote its repeal.

Both urban and rural Virginia contributed to the slightly less than two to one margin held by repeal with approximately three-fourths of the precincts reported. It was from the large centers of population, however, that the wet tide set in strongest.

Repeal, in the van with the first scattering returns, gathered momentum as Richmond, Norfolk, Lynchburg, Newport News, and Roanoke counted out majorities that ranged from slightly less than two to one to almost five to one.

---

[49] 14 September 1933. *Grant County News*. Author Unknown.
[50] 21 September 1933. *Grant County News*. Author Unknown.

Many of the counties, especially those adjacent to the cities, swelled the anti-prohibition margin with the western counties apparently the chief dry stronghold.

With 1,246 of the state's 1,690 precincts reported, the repealists lead 90,742 to 50,886. Advocates of repeal of the state prohibition law and the substitution of a liquor control plan were in the van 83,301 to 45,403. Slightly fewer precincts had reported in the referendum on state prohibition.[51]

Florida Joins Repeal States

Wets Are Ahead by More Than Four to One, Tabulation In About Half of Precincts Reveals.

Jacksonville, Fla., Oct. 10 Florida today became the thirty-third state to vote for repeal of the Eighteenth amendment, the wets leading by approximately four and a half to one with more than half of the state's precincts counted.

With the vote tabulated from 749 of the 1,273 voting places in the state the count stood: For repeal 75,523; against, 17,542. Incomplete returns had been received from 52 of the state's 67 counties.

The repealists started off early with a landslide, first showing a lead of 8 to 1 that steadily dwindled but the drys never came close enough to leave any doubt as to the outcome.

The cities piled up huge majorities for the Twenty-first amendment and for the most part the rural sections were not far behind. The drys were not leading in any county from which returns had been received.

Duval (Jacksonville) county, was showing a margin of 10 to 1 for repeal and Hillsborough (Tampa), where Postmaster General Farley spoke last night in the interest of the repeal cause, showed 12 to 1 against retention of prohibition.

Fashionable Palm Beach county, winter playground of the wealthy, balloted 9 to 1 against the Eighteenth amendment.

In Dade (Miami) county the vote was about 5 to 1 for repeal.

In Orange (Orlando) county the wets held a comparatively small lead of 2 to 1.

The balloting was to select 67 delegates to the state convention in November.[52]

Four More States Join With 33 Others To Wipe Out Law

First Returns From Kentucky Indicate Repeal Measure Has Carried By An Overwhelming Majority

The Eighteenth Amendment is dead.

Thirty six states, the necessary number, voted for repeal Tuesday, and Kentucky on first returns shows a decided trend toward repeal. The matter is only a question of majority. Louisville, was voting 10 to 1 for repeal and Kenton and Campbell counties in about the same ratio. Country counties, believed to be dry are joining the procession on first returns. The state has probably voted as much as 150,000 for repeal.

Grant county, with only three precincts out of 19 reporting Thursday morning, showed a slight margin for repeal. The vote in the county will probably be close. The three precincts reporting are the two east side precincts and Zion Station, representing less than one-third of the vote cast.

The constitutional amendment to take the tax off real estate, is probably beaten, although first returns from over the state show a slight lead for the amendment.[53]

Constitutional Amendment Is Defeated By Over 2,000

[51] 5 October 1933. *Grant County News.* Author Unknown.

[52] 12 October 1933. *Grant County News.* Author Unknown.

[53] 10 November 1933. *Grant County News.* Author Unknown.

Final Count In Kentucky Election Shows Repeal Amendment Carried By Nearly 150,000

Louisville, Ky Nov. 21 Ten days after the ballots were cast in the November 7 election, the Kentucky vote count was completed today and unofficial returns bore out the trends established in the tabulation.

Final returns gave repeal of the Eighteenth Amendment to the Federal Constitution a majority of 144,482 votes. The count from the states, 4,204 precincts was: For repeal, 384,081; against 239,599.

On the repeal issue the 120 counties were evenly divided, 60 favoring repeal and 60 opposing it. Of the nine congressional districts five favored repeal and four opposed it.

Sixty-six counties favored the state tax amendment and 54 opposed it. By congressional districts the count was 6 to 3 for the amendment.[54]

Repeal

District	For Repeal	Against Repeal
First	24,914	25,445
Second	37,757	39,098
Third	102,960	20,899
Fourth	26,909	30,396
Fifth	47,194	13,858
Sixth	43,165	36,506
Seventh	35,186	8,930
Eighth	36,110	27,214
Ninth	28,896	37,253
	—	—
Totals	384,081	239,599

Kentucky 33rd State To Ratify Repeal Of Eighteenth Amendment

Momentous Occasion In Kentucky A History Making Day', Governor Laffoon Declares In Calling The Convention To Order.

Frankfort, Ky., Nov. 27 Kentucky today became the thirty-third state to ratify repeal of the Eighteenth amendment to the federal Constitution.

Nineteen delegates, elected at the regular November election, met in convention here today and at 11:47 o'clock this morning voted to repeal national prohibition.

The convention was called to order by Gov. Ruby Laffoon and the oath of office was administered to the delegates by Chief Justice W. H. Rees, of the court of appeals.

Bruce Maldeman, of Louisville, was made permanent chairman and Miss Laura Clay, of Lexington, temporary chairman of the convention. C. C. Boldrick, of Lebanon, was elected secretary.

The resolution calling for Kentucky's ratification of the proposed twenty-first amendment repealing the Eighteenth amendment was presented to the convention by Mrs. James Ross Todd, of Louisville, one of the leaders for national prohibition reform.

"Momentous Occasion," - Laffoon.

In calling the convention to order Governor Laffoon declared "this is a momentous occasion in Kentucky a history-making day in the old commonwealth."

"For the first time in history of the state, duly elected delegates have assembled for the purpose of ratifying an amendment to the Constitution of the United States."

After the repeal of the Eighteenth amendment, the governor said, the mode of handling liquor industry of the country would be materially changed and expressed the hope that it would not mean the return of the "open saloons."[55]

State Wet By Large Majority

As Official Returns Are Certified To State Board. Constitutional Amendment Rejected By Majority of 3,250.

Frankfort, Ky., Nov. 27 Complete official returns certified to the State Board of Election Commissioners today by Secretary of State Sara W. Mahan showed Kentucky ratified repeal of the Eighteenth Amendment by a majority of 152,236 and repected the proposed amendment to authorize the Legislature to remove the state tax on

[54]24 November 1933. *Grant County News.* Author Unknown.

[55]1 December 1933. *Grant County News.* Author Unknown.

real estate by a majority of 3,250. The final figures were:

For repeal, 386,653; against repeal, 234,417.

For the tax amendment, 132,780; against amendment 136,030.

Sixty counties voted for repeal and sixty against. Sixty-six counties voted in favor of the tax amendment and fifty-four counties against.

The State Election Board accepted returns from all 120 counties as regular. Certificates of election were issued to 143 candidates who were successful in the November 7 election. Certificates in districts composed of one county or less are issued by the County Clerks.[56]

Liquor Now Flows In Eighteen States Following Repealing

Repeal Of Eighteenth Amendment Becomes Effective When Utah Becomes Thirty-Sixth State To Ratify Twenty-First Amendment

---

Washington, Dec. 5 Utah late today wrote finis to national prohibition liquor flowed freely immediately in 18 states, and almost at once President Roosevelt proclaimed the fact at the same time calling upon Americans to help restore respect for law and order.

President Roosevelt's proclamation, an unusual one, followed one by William Phillips, Acting Secretary of State, certifying that the necessary 36 states had approved the Twenty-First, or Repeal Amendment to the Constitution.

Liquor shops in 18 states virtually were opened by Utah's action. Half a dozen other states were completing plans for legalized sale under their own laws. Rest of the nation remained dry.

Special Taxes Die

The National Recovery Act made it mandatory that the Chief Executive proclaim the end of prohibition in order to abolish a series of special taxes.

The President made a special plea that no state authorize return to the saloon, either in its old form or in a new guise, and said the objective being sought through a national policy was education of every citizen toward greater temperance.

In asking for cooperation with the Government in an effort to restore respect for law and order, the President enjoined all citizens and others in the United States to confine their purchases of alcoholic beverages solely to licensed dealers.

Old Evils Banned

"The policy of the Government will be to see to it that the social and political evils that have existed in the pre-prohibition area shall not be revived nor permitted again to exist," he said.

"We must remove forever from our midst the menace of the bootlegger and such others as would profit at the expense of good government and law and order."

Mr. Roosevelt said the observance of his request for purchases solely from licensed dealers or agencies was made "personally to every individual and every family" in the nation and would result in consumption of beverages which had passed Federal inspection, in the break-up and eventual destruction of the "notoriously evil, illicit liquor traffic," and payment of reasonable taxes for support of the Government.

The proclamation directed special attention' to authority given the Government by the repeal amendment to prohibit transportation or importation of intoxicating liquors into dry states.

In concluding, the President said:

"I trust in the good sense of the American people that they will not bring upon themselves the curse of excessive use of intoxicating liquors to the detriment of health, morals and social integrity."

Word that Utah the thirty-sixth state had ratified repeal was flashed to the Capital a few hours after Pennsylvania and Ohio. But a little later, the final formalities were completed with the issuance of proclamations by the State Department and President Roosevelt declaring prohibition at an end.

There was little ceremony at the signing of the presidential or the State Department proclamations, but in wet states and certain dry ones there were celebrations.

Uncle Sam Ready

[56] 1 December 1933. *Grant County News*. Author Unknown.

Nearly 14 years of alcoholic draught enforced by the Eighteenth Amendment of World War day inception, was ended by the Utah vote.

It found the Federal Government prepared to control the flow of liquor in wet states, through a virtual dictatorship over the industry, and to protect the arid ones. Several of the 18 states where liquor could be sold immediately, however, were without regulations.

Repeal celebrations, however, found liquor supplies for immediate consumption restricted in certain sections.[57]

Legislature Repeals Rash-Gullion Act

Proposal Repeals State Prohibition Enforcement Act And Provides For Restricted Sale Of Spirits

Frankfort, Ky., Mar. 13 Legislative action on liquor control and liquor taxation bills was completed today as the senate approved, without amendment, house measures on those subjects and made them ready for Gov. Ruby Laffoon.

In addition, the senate passed, with an amendment, the house bill to appropriate approximately $700,000 to the school teachers in 43 counties and sent it back to the house, thereby clearing from its slate all of the so-called major bills except that calling for consolidation of the offices of jailer and sheriff. Action on the jailer-sheriff merger is slated for Wednesday.

With only comparatively minor house bills still to be acted on in the remaining two days of the session, the senate decided to forego a night session and adjourned until Wednesday morning.

Repealing the Rash-Gullion act by which the state prohibition amendment was enforced, the liquor control bill sets up a new system for handling distilled spirits in Kentucky and provides for their sale with certain restrictions, by the drink and in unbroken packages. Yesterday the senate approved the house bill to submit to the voters at the November, 1935, election the question of repealing the state prohibition amendment.

Senator Hiram Brock (R), of Harlan, championing the liquor control bill, termed it an embodiment of recommendations made in both the majority and minority reports of the governor's liquor control commission, but "largely following" the minority "or dry" report.

Senator W. C. Farmer (R), of Albany, opposed the bill on the ground "it provides for the doing of things prohibited by the constitution."

After debate on the bill itself had subsided, several amendments were offered and all were voted down at the request of Senator James H. Thompson, of Paris, administration floor leader, who insisted that the bill be passed in its present form to avoid the necessity of sending it back to the house.[58]

Distillery Destroyed By Fire

In Lexington One of Most Historic In America, Established in 1870, Loss Estimated At $5,000,000. Reconstruction Arrangements Under Way.

Lexington, Ky., April 30th Smouldering ruins mark the site of a major portion of one of the most historic distilleries in America the James E. Pepper plant near Lexington, established in 1870.

Fire that started about 1:00 a. m., Saturday when a watchman threw gasoline into a heating stove, quickly swept four warehouses, the gauging room and bottling plant, destroying 20,000 barrels of whisky, some of it twenty-one years old. Loss was estimated at $5,000,000.

The night watchman, Stanley Travis, 24, died early this morning in a Lexington hospital.

Lexington firemen battled the flames for three hours, bringing them under control in time to save a new $400,000 building nearing completion.

The property is owned by the Schenley Products company of New York, Fred Pauley, manager, said all the company's insurance was handled in New York and the he felt certain most of the loss was covered.

[57] 8 December 1933. *Grant County News.* Author Unknown.
[58] 16 March 1934. *Grant County News.* Author Unknown.

The Schenley Products company owners of the James E. Pepper plant at Lexington, has its Cincinnati offices in the Carew tower. It operates a distillery at Lawrenceburg, Ind., and Lester Jacobi, vice president of the company, who is a Cincinnati man, is in charge of the local operations, Lew Rosenstiel, another Cincinnatian, is president of the company; Grover A. Whalen, former police commissioner of New York city, is chairman of the board. Only recently the officers and salesmen of the company came west on a private train and inspected the various distilleries of the concern, including the James E. Pepper plant at Lexington.

Henry Pogue, Covington, Ky., in charge of plants, left immediately for Lexington.

Jacobi said that it was too early to make an estimate of the loss. It was fully covered by insurance but the whisky consumed by the flames is irreplaceable, he added.[59]

Three Arrested And Held, For Drunkenness

Holbrook's Garage, At Dry Ridge, Scene Of Disturbance; Men Unable To Pay Fines.

Three men were arrested last Saturday noon by county authorities at Holbrook's Garage, Dry Ridge. They were charged with drunkenness in a public place. They gave their names as: Warren Hall, Logan Hall and Fred Hale, all of Detroit, Michigan.

Monday morning, the case was heard and the men were fined $10.00 and costs each. Being unable to pay their fines they were returned to the county jail.

Another man, and a woman, who were accompanying the three, were not arrested.[60]

Two Arrested For Drunken Driving, Fined

Covington Men Arrested Last Saturday On Affidavits Of Bus Driver And Deputy Sheriff

---

J. H. Cress and Russell Mitchell, both of Covington, were arrested last Saturday afternoon at 4 o'clock for drunken driving and intoxication in a public place, with Mitchell also charged with resisting an officer, on affidavits of Julian Clay, bus driver, and Deputy Sheriff Frank Vance. The two men were accompanied by two women who were released.

Clay, formerl a resident of Williamstown, first noticed the actions of the car which was driven by Cress, as the bus being driven by Clay reached a point just south of Erlanger. Following the car to Williamstown, Clay notified authorities here and the arrest was made by Vance.

Appearing before Judge Pettit Monday morning, Cress was fined $100.00 and costs when he plead guilty of the charge of being drunk on a public highway, a second charge of drunken driving against him being filed. He paid his fine and was released. Mitchell pleading guilty to charges of drunkenness and resisting an officer, was fined $25.00 and costs. Unable to pay his fine, he was returned to the jail to serve out his sentence.[61]

Two Arrested Saturday For Intoxication

Bob Lawrence Breaks Window Out Of Corinth Jail, Is Held On Three Counts; Ben Cummins, Jailed.

Robert Lawrence, of Corinth, who was arrested some weeks ago, fined $50.00 and costs and sentenced to 30 days in jail, but who was released on $100.00 bond two weeks ago in order to receive treatment at a hospital in Cincinnati, was arrested last Saturday afternoon in Corinth on three warrants, namely, breach of peace, drunkenness in a public place and driving an automobile while intoxicated.

[59] 4 May 1934. *Grant County News.* Author Unknown.
[60] 10 August 1934. *Grant County News.* Author Unknown.
[61] 14 September 1934. *Grant County News.* Author Unknown.

Lawrence, following his release from jail two weeks ago, went to the hospital, where he underwent an operation. Returning from the hospital last week, he was arrested by Marshall Wainscott, Corinth. After being placed in the Corinth Jail, Lawrence caused quite a disturbance, in the course of which he broke out some of the windows of the jail, he then was removed to Williamstown for safe keeping.

Monday, Lawrence appeared before Judge Pettit and was fined $10.00 and costs on the charge of being drunk in a public place. The remaining charges against him were not tried Monday. Being unable to pay his fine, he returned to jail.

Ben Cummins, of near Williamstown, was arrested Saturday for being drunk in a public place. He was tried Monday and fined $10 and costs. Cummins also returned to lay out the fine.[62]

Liquor Dispensaries Must Pay $200 License Fee In Williamstown

---

At a meeting of the town board Monday night the question of a liquor dispensary license was discussed and voted upon.

There had been some discussion as to whether or not the town would grant a person the right to operate a liquor store. The board consulted an attorney and was advised that they could not refuse to grant such a license.

A skeleton ordinance was drawn and will be published in The News. A fee of $200 was fixed by the board as license for a liquor dispensary.[63]

New Liquor Store Robbed Thursday Night

One Hundred Thirty-Eight Pints of Whiskey Stolen. Five Williamstown Men Held Under $3000 Bond.

Five Williamstown men were being held Friday in Williamstown jail charged with house breaking. The five were Ikey Stewart, Edward Hensley, Garrett Ryans, Florian Jacobs and Jim Jacobs.

These men are charged with breaking into the back window of the liquor store operated by Russell Collins Thursday night and removing 138 pints of government liquor. Stewart and Ryans confessed entering the store and removing the whiskey.

According to County Attorney, R. L. Vincent, the liquor was removed to Edward Hensley's where it was divided. Ryans hid his share at home of his uncle, where he later led officers to its hiding place. Hensley and Stewart poured their share into unlabeled bottles. This part of the loot was caught in the possession of Jim and Florian Jacobs by deputy sheriffs.

The men waived examining trial and are being held for action of the grand jury which will convene next June. Their bond was set at $3000 each.

The penalty for this offense is from one to five years in the state penitentiary.[64]

Old Glory Tavern Has New Managers

Mrs. Floyd Caldwell and Francis West have rented Ole Glory Tavern and assumed management of the filling station and restaurant last Monday morning. William Williams has operated this place of business for the past two and a half years.[65]

Robbers Are Sentenced To Serve One Year

Three Sent To Penitentiary For Store Breaking. Hensley Indicated On Same Charge Will Be Tried At October Term.

---

[62] 21 September 1934. *Grant County News.* Author Unknown.

[63] 8 March 1935. *Grant County News.* Author Unknown.

[64] 15 March 1935. *Grant County News.* Author Unknown.

[65] 10 May 1935. *Grant County News.* Author Unknown.

Ikey Stewart, James and Florian Jacobs, charged with robbing a liquor store here several weeks ago, were tried in Grant Circuit Court Thursday and sentenced to serve one year each in the penitentiary.

Edward Hensley, indicted on the same charge is out on bond and will be tried in October. Garrett Ryan, who also was indicted escaped jail a few weeks ago and has not been apprehended.

The court suspended the sentence of Floyd Wilson, who was given two and one-half years. He is on probation and unless he fails to provide $8.00 per month toward the support of his child, his sentence will not be imposed.

No other criminal cases were tried at this term of court.[66]

---

[66] 21 June 1935. *Grant County News.* Author Unknown.

THE SECRET IS OUT! JIM SPREAD THE NEWS

"Charlie, I shouldn't tell you this yet, but HEIDELBERG is coming out with a new WINTER BEER. It packs a big wallop for winter drinking. Warms you up. Look at me! I just had a sample and I'm almost sweating . . . and you, you look frozen stiff."

. . . And Charlie tried WINTER BEER, the new *strong* member to the famous Student Prince hearty family. Now he's passing the news along.

. . . And Saturday, and all winter long, you, too, can enjoy this NEW, HEAVY BODY WINTER BEER *brewed with a real kick for zero drinking.* It has all the goodness and outstanding qualities of regular BLACK LABEL *plus.* This new beer brings back all the pleasures of summer drinking.

ON SALE BY ALL PROGRESSIVE DEALERS

The Heidelberg Brewing Company[67]

[67] 22 January 1937. *Grant County News.*

Local Option Election Includes Grant

Forty-Nine Counties To Hold Local Option Election In Three-Fold Dry Campaign Throughout State. Aim Is The Defeat Of Repeal Amendment.

Louisville, Ky., Sept 25 Forty-nine counties of Kentucky will hold local option elections this year, it was announced here by Dr. Henry W. Bromley, general chairman of the Kentucky State Citizens' Committee, which is conducting a three-fold dry campaign throughout the State this fall. The Citizens' Committee has as its aims the defeat of the repeal amendment at the November election, the promotion of local option elections, and an educational campaign against the use of liquor as a beverage.

Elections have been called by County Judges in the following counties, it was announced: Allen, Adair, Bath, Bell, Bourbon, Boyd, Calloway, Carlisle, Carter, Casey, Clay, Crittenden, Edmonson, Fleming, Fulton, Gallatin, Garrard, Grant, Graves, Greenup, Harlan, Harrison, Henry, Hickman, Jackson, Jessamine, Johnson, Knox, Laurel, Lawrence, Letcher, Lincoln, Magoffin, Mason, McLean, Mercer, Montgomery, Morgan, Nicholas, Ohio, Owen, Pendleton, Powell, Pulaski, Robertson, Trimble, Wayne and Whitley.

Dr. Bromley announced that the dry committee was perfecting precinct organizations in practically every county in the State and that speakers planned to conduct meetings in every community schoolhouse, country church and court house.

Last year about a dozen counties held local option elections and went dry, but these elections were invalidated by the Court of Appeals, which held that elections could only be held on regular election days. More than 100 of the 120 counties in Kentucky were dry before prohibition, Dr. Bromley explained, and he said that he expected the drys to carry the State overwhelmingly in November.[68]

Local Option Elections Ruled Out

Kentucky Court of Appeals Upsets Plans Of More Than A Score of Counties To Conduct Local Option Elections

Frankfort, Ky., October 9 Knocking out the local option section of the 1934 alcoholic control act, the Kentucky Court of Appeals Tuesday upset plans of more than a score of counties to conduct local option election November 5 to determine whether or not trafficking in liquor should be permitted under the 1934 act.

Supplementing a previous opinion that held local option elections could not be conducted on any other day than a regular election day, today's opinion, written by Judge James W. Stotes of Louisville and concurred in by the whole court, barred the holding of local option elections on any day so long as the seventh amendment is in the constitution. The question of repealing the seventh amendment, prohibiting the manufacture, sale or transportation of intoxicating liquor except for medical, sacramental or scientific purposes, will be voted on at the general November 5 election.

Judge Stotes's opinion was given on the petition of Charles D. Ball, suing as a citizen and taxpayer of Bell county, for a temporary injunction to prevent the holding of a local option election in Bell county on November 5. Bell Circuit Court refused the injunction of Bell county and other officials. The election was called under provisions of the alcohol control act.

The opion referred to another Appellate Court decision given last November and forbidding the holding of any election on "a day other than the regular election day in each year, except where the constitution specifically so authorizes." In the decision, Appellate Court did not determine whether a local option election could be held on regular election day, but held that the prohibition amendment repealed Section 61 of the State Constitution which directed the Legislation to provide for the holding of local option elections.

Judge Stotes pointed out that the alcohol control act itself expressly for-

[68] 27 September 1935. *Grant County News.* Author Unknown.

[69] 11 October 1935. *Grant County News.* Author Unknown.

bids the holding of local option elections on a regular election day.[69]

Vote On Repeal Is Held Valid

Mandate Is Issued At Once So Governor Can Make Usual Proclamation. Decision Approves Method of Submitting Pension Law In Effect.

Frankfort, Ky., Dec. 3 Kentucky's 16-year-old prohibition amendment was repealed validly in the November 5 election, Kentucky Court of Appeals held today, and Governor Laffoon may proclaim the official result as soon as the necessary arrangements can be made.

The Governor's official proclamation required by the Constitution, will be forthcoming probably this week, the Governor said, at which time the state's seventh amendment, repeal, automatically will be taken off the books.

Because of the importance of the case, the Appellate Court ordered its mandate of final judgment issuel immediately, without prejudice to the right of the losing party to file a petition for a rehearing within 30 days. Ordinarily mandates are not issued until after the time for filing rehearing petitions expires.[70]

Four Men Fined On Drunkenness Charge

Four men, Rynie King, Stafford Crosthwaite, Jess Coleman and Alvin Kidwell were arrested at the Two-Way House, charged with drunkenness and disorderly conduct. The men were fined $35.00 and costs each and they paid. Crostwaite was armed with a revolver and claimed to be a deputy sheriff.

Bill Teagarden was arrested at Eibeck's place south of Williamstown on a charge of drunkenness and disorderly conduct. He resisted arrest and had to be subdued. He is now languishing in jail, paying off a $35.00 cost and fine.[71]

Hijacker Of Beer Truck At Large

Driver Knocked Senseless And Badly Beaten By One Whom He Had Befriended. Steals Truck And Makes Get-Away.

Ed Joy, 45, driver of a beer truck was knocked senseless and severely beaten by a hitch-hiker whom he had befriended last Thursday night.

Mr. Joy reported to officers that he was returning from Cincinnati to Knoxville, Tenn., last Thursday when he picked up a hitch-hiker. He said they were in the north end of Scott County when he stopped his truck to make a minor repair and the man aprached him from the other side of the truck and hit him over the head with a piece of iron, beat him unmercifully and threw him over an embankment believing him to be dead. Mr. Joy said he was in no condition to defend himself and pretended to be dead because he believed his attacker would otherwise have killed him. The man robbed him and started back north with the truck load of beer.

Mrs. Grace Dunn, proprietor of Wapella Inn, told officers that "Buck" Dickerson, a local man, came to her roadhouse Thursday night and tried to sell her some beer. She said she did not believe him to be a representative of any beer dispensary and refused to buy.

The truck was found on the Barnes road Friday morning, it was loaded with 150 cases and 30 half barrels of beer.[72]

Several Get Fines For Being Drunk

Drunkenness And Breach Of The Peace Land Several In Jail. Some Pay Fines And Some "Sit It Out." Monday Busy day In Judge's Court.

---

[70] 6 December 1935. *Grant County News.* Author Unknown.
[71] 17 January 1936. *Grant County News.* Author Unknown.
[72] 14 February 1936. *Grant County News.* Author Unknown.

Monday was a busy day in Judge Pettit's court. Several arrests were made over the weekend and prisoners were tried before the judge Monday morning. Companions are still in jail.

Clem Richards, G. C. Giss, Jim Allen, of Fayette and Jessamine counties were charged with being intoxicated on the public highways. Each was fined $15 and cost. Giss was released after his father came to Williamstown and paid the fine. His two companions are still in jail.

E. Cooke, of Covington, and Harry Lonkard were arrested for being drunk in front of the residence of Joe Cook who was said to have been on his death bed. They were fined $40 and costs.

Oval Webster, Chester Boling and Jeff Updike were arrested and placed in jail for being drunk at a dance hall in the Stewartsville community Saturday night. They also were fined $10 and costs, one man paid the fine and was released.

Harold Workman was given a fine of $10 and costs for breach of the peace.

Anie Lakes was brought in by county patrolman, charged with speeding on the public highway. His case was continued.[73]

Alcoholic Exhibition Here June 4

Educational Exhibit Explains Actions Of Alcohol On Inanimate Substances And Value of Same Outside The Human Body

---

The Williamstown W. C. T. U. organization is sponsoring an alcoholic educational exhibition Thursday night, June 4th at 7:30 o'clock at the Baptist church.

It is a rare privilege for the people of Grant and surrounding counties to hear these speakers of national reputation. Pastors of all the churches and all who might be concerned are asked to announce to their congregations and friends the coming of the "Crusade Caravan" and its speakers, Miss May B. Macken, National Field worker and Mr. and Mrs. A. W. Killip, owners of the Crusader.

Only a free-will offering to help pay traveling expenses will be made.

The Crusader is a sixteen foot auto trailer, painted silver, and contains the Alcohol Exhibit. It may be parked on the streets of any town or city and opened to the public.

Some of the things explained are the characteristic actions of alcohol on inanimate substances, the value of alcohol outside the body, the harmful effects upon the body, the narcotic effect, the destroying of the cell protoplasm. The effects of alcohol in the blood, and the slowing of the reaction time, bringing in the drinking drive and the part he plays in accidents.[74]

Booze, Beans And Books In Smash-Up

Traffic Was Halted When Three Transfer Trucks Figured In A Wreck Which Spilled Booze, Beans And Books On Highway.

Three transfer trucks, loaded with booze, beans, and books, figured in an early morning accident at the end of the Piner road on the Dixie Highway, near Huff's roadhouse, Wednesday morning.

Two of the trucks collided and one of them ran into an approaching one. One truck was completely burned, the second had one side burned off and the third was badly wrecked.

As a result, booze, beans and books were scattered all over the road and traffic was halted. It is reported that a bus stopped and passengers got aboard laden with whiskey.[75]

Pulaski County Votes Dry By A Big Majority

Of Seven Counties Which Have Held Local Option Elections, Only One Has Voted Wet.

---

[73] 22 May 1936. *Grant County News.* Author Unknown.
[74] 29 May 1936. *Grant County News.* Author Unknown.
[75] 14 August 1936. *Grant County News.* Author Unknown.

Pulaski and Martin counties voted dry Tuesday in local option elections.

Pulaski county cast an overwhelming dry vote but drys carried Martin county by only 23 votes.

The Pulaski vote was 5,913 for local option to 1,164 against with 62 out of 66 precincts reporting. The four missing precincts will not report until Wednesday. Somerset, county seat, voted 998 to 444. Only one precinct in the county voted wet.

Martin county voters cast 724 ballots for local option to 701 against.

Pulaski, the largest county in Kentucky to invoke the new local option law in a wet and dry referendum, voted 7,049 to 2,177 last year against repeal of the state prohibition amendment. The vote today was on whether or not to prohibit the sale of liquor within its own borders.

Of the seven counties that have held local option elections only Lee county voted wet. Lee joined the wet column the first time in its history after drys carried it in the statewide referendum last November. The only other reversal of form occurred in Magoffin county which converted a 1,291 wet majority last fall into a 5,035 dry majority at the local option election. Other counties that voted dry both on the repeal amendment and at the local option elections were Taylor, Edmonson, Bracken, Clinton and Clay.

Other counties that hold local option elections this month are, Owen, Thursday; Allen, Saturday; Whitley, Thursday; Barren, September 26; Rowan, September 29, and Warren, September 30.

In a county which votes dry under the local option law possession of liquor is regarded as primar facie evidence of guilt.[76]

Adjoining Counties To Hold Local Option Election

Owen and Pendleton counties are scheduled to hold local option elections December 12th. Nearly a score of local option elections have been held in the State this year and nearly all of them voted "dry" by large majorities. What Owen and Pendleton will do is not very much in doubt.[77]

Four More Counties In State

Join in Ranks Of The Drys. Three Vote Wet. Nineteen Counties Have Outlawed The Sale of Intoxicants.

Alcoholic beverages were outlawed Saturday in four Kentucky counties, but three voted wet, returns from local liquor option elections disclosed.

While Lawrence, Marshall, Metcalfe and Barren returned dry majorities, Henry, Trimble, and Rowan counties voted to continue of liquor.

Dry forces were leading in Knox county's election, but the county was incomplete. Returns from 10 of the 56 precincts gave: dry 634, wet, 380.

Saturday's elections boosted the total of dry counties to 19 of the 120. In addition to the three counties voting wet, Carroll county joined the wet column Friday, which also includes Lee and Johnson counties. They voted earlier this year.

Dry majorities Saturday were: Lawrence 186; Marshall 789; Barren 611 and Metcalfe 750. The wet margins were Trimble 112, Henry 422 and Rowan 404.

Court injunctions prevented elections in Wolfe and Kenton counties. An election scheduled at Burkesville was postponed because the court ruled the petition seeking an election was invalid. Dry forces are preparing a new petition.

Three city precincts voted overwhelmingly wet at Bowling Green, Friday, but dry forces believe the result will be nullified when a countywide election is held in Warren county early next year.

Fifteen other counties previously have voted dry. They are Crittenden, Whitley, Breckinridge, Pulaski, Martin, Magoffin, Taylor, Bracken, Edmonson, Russell, Clinton, Clay, Menifee, Leslie and Morgan.

The state court of appeals, however, recently held the Crittenden county election invalid.[78]

---

[76] 18 September 1936. *Grant County News.* Author Unknown.

[77] 20 November 1936. *Grant County News.* Author Unknown.

[78] 11 December 1936. *Grant County News.* Author Unknown.

Owen And Pendleton Joins Ranks Of Drys

Owen and Pendleton counties held local option elections last Saturday, and both joined the ranks of the drys.

Owen's vote was 1,639 dry, against 1,407 wet, majority, 232. Pendleton's vot was 1,650 wet, against 1,575 dry, a majority of 35. The vote in Pendleton was closer than had been expected.

About three-fourths as many votes were cast in Saturday's election as in the November election in both counties.[79]

Petition To Close Road House, Filed

County Attorney, R. L. Vincent, filed a petition in the County Court a few days ago to close the Eibeck road house.

It is alleged in the petition that the Eibeck road house has violated the license issued to it by the County Judge in that:

1. They permitted drunken and boisterous persons to congregate in and near the premises.

2. That they permitted people to congregate at the road house for immoral and unlawful purposes.

3. That they had operated the road house later than mid-night the hours stated on the license.

The road houses out side of incorporated towns, which are located in the County, must obtain a license to operate from the County Judge, and that license must be approved by the County Attorney. The law provides that if any road house proprietor violates the law its license may be revoked on proper hearing before the County Judge.

The County Attorney states that many complaints had been received against the Eibeck road house, and that every effort will made to close the place.[80]

Road House Closed By Court Order

The Commonwealth Introduces Witnesses To Prove That Road House Was Being Operated In Disorderly Manner

Eibeck's road house, two miles south of Williamstown, was closed by order of court, Monday. Witnesses were introduced to prove that the house was operated in a disorderly manner, that gambling was permitted on the premises along with other allegations. The order of the court reads as follows:

Special Term of the Grant County Court held at Williamstown, Kentucky on January 4th, 1937. Hon. Chas. A. Pettit, County Judge, present and presiding.

Commonwealth of Kentucky,
Plaintiff.

Vs.

Judgment and Order Revoking License to Operate a Road House.
Sadie Eibeck and William Eibeck,
Defendants.

This cause coming on to be heard and the defendants, Sadie Eibeck and Wiliam Eibeck, having due notice of this proceeding, and being represented by attorney, G. L. Tucker, each side announced ready for trial. The Commonwealth introduced numerous witnesses in support of its charges and allegations that the defendants had violated the rules set out in granting them a license to operate a road house in Grant County, Kentucky, in that: they had kept the place open later than twelve o'clock at night; that they had permitted drunken and disorderly persons to congregate in and near the place; that they had permitted persons to gather at said place for unlawful purposes.

After the Commonwealth had presented its evidence the defendant presented a number of witnesses denying such charges and allegations. After all the evidence was introduced the defendant's attorney, G. L. Tucker, presented his argument to the court, followed by the argument of R. L. Vincent, County Attorney, in behalf

[79] 18 December 1936. *Grant County News.* Author Unknown.
[80] 1 January 1937. *Grant County News.* Author Unknown.

of the plaintiff. Whereupon the court being sufficiently advised the orders and adjudges that the defendants are guilty as charged in plaintiff's petition, and it is further ordered and adjudged by the court that the license issued to William Eibeck on the 29th day of June, 1936, by the County Court of Grant County, Kentucky be and is hereby revoked and held for naught.

There being no further business it is ordered that court adjourn.

CHAS. A . PETTIT

Judge, Grant County Court.

It is reported that an appeal will be taken.[81]

ROAD HOUSE CLOSING AWAITS COURT APPEAL

It was stated in last week's News that the Sadie Eibeck road house, on the Dixie Highway, two miles south of Williamstown had been closed by order of court.

The place is still in operation and awaiting an appeal taken by her attorney, G. L. Tucker, Mr. Tucker stated. It may take several weeks to decide the matter. In the meantime the road house is still in operation.[82]

CRITTENDEN COUNTY VOTES DRY 2ND TIME

Marion, Ky., Feb. 21 Crittenden County voted dry at a local liquor option election yesterday. The vote was 1,295 dry, 297 wet. The liquor ban will become effective sixty days from March 8.

This was the second liquor election in the county. Last September the county voted dry, but the vote was declared void on the grounds that the election had not been advertised properly.[83]

WAR AGAINST DRUNKEN DRIVERS TO BE WAGED

When district headquarters for the State Patrol have been established in Williamstown, it is a sure thing that war will be waged against drunken drivers. Some ten members of the patrol will be permanently located here with offices in the Wigginton building. Drunken drivers have long been a menace to the public and it has become necessary to do something about it.

There are many road hogs on the highways who are not drunk and who constantly endanger the lives of those who travel in automobiles. There are also those who refuse to give their dimmers at night, this is nothing short of being courteous and it only takes a second to turn your dim lights on.[84]

FINED FOR DRUNKENNESS AND PLACED ON PROBATION

Harold Workman was given a suspended fine of $10.00 and costs on a drunkenness charge in Police Court, Monday.[85]

MADISON COUNTY GOES DRY BY A SLIM MAJORITY

BUT CITY OF RICHMOND GIVES TWO TO ONE IN FAVOR OF WETS. BELL COUNTY ELECTION SET FOR JUNE 12TH.

Madison County voted dry by the narrow majority of 199 Tuesday as Richmond voted wet by a 2-to-1 majority in a county-wide local option election.

The vote was: For local option, 3,942; against, 3,743.

Five precincts in and near Berea gave the drys a vote of 1,401 to the

[81] 8 January 1937. *Grant County News.* Author Unknown.
[82] 15 January 1937. *Grant County News.* Author Unknown.
[83] 26 February 1937. *Grant County News.* Author Unknown.
[84] 26 March 1937. *Grant County News.* Author Unknown.
[85] 7 May 1937. *Grant County News.* Author Unknown.

wets' 193. Richmond's wet plurality was 1,034 votes. The wets carried twenty-six of the county's forty-three precincts, and the drys carried seventeen.

The poll was the first under the 1936 Local Option Election Law to be held in a city of Richmond's size.

The Court of Appeals, Tuesday upheld the validity of the Laurel County vote by which that county voted dry. The suit attacking the election was filed by Richard Campbell.

In another opinion, the court invalidated the local option election held in Martin County on the grounds that it had been irregularly advertised and called. The ruling reversed the judgment of the Martin Circuit Court which sustained special and general demurrers to the petition attacking the election.

At Pineville, Circuit Judge J. M. Gilbert granted a mandatory injunction ordering Bell County election commissioners to name officers for a local option election set for June 12. The commissioners had refused to name the officers, claiming that since wet-and-dry elections already had been held in two Bell County precincts, no election can be held for three years. The case will be taken immediately to the Court of Appeals.

Meanwhile, wets and dry looked forward with interest to fourteen county liquor elections scheduled before July 7, the deadline until next fall under the law forbidding a vote less than thirty days before or after an election. The primary election date is August 7th.

According to the Associated Press, the standing is thirty-eight to eight in favor of the drys, in forty-five local option elections already held in Kentucky.[86]

Fifteen In County Jail Monday Night

Whiskey And Gasoline Does Not Mix. Fifteen Jailed As Result Of Drunken Driving, Disorderly Conduct, Etc.

Fifteen men were spending their holiday-night in jail here, Monday. Most of them were arrested because of drunken driving. Some paid fines and some preferred to "lay it out" behind the bars.

Two men from Georgetown, B. Parsons and George Davis were arrested by Grant County officials Monday night and lodged in jail awaiting the arrival of the Scott County Sheriff. They were said to have caused a wreck south of Corinth in Scott County and left the scene.

Deputy Sheriff C. B. Martin arrested three men at the Half-Way House, Monday morning. Daniel Williams, Bruce Lyken and Earl Bruce of Morgan County were charged with disorderly conduct. They entered the Half-Way House from a bus, ordered beer and refused to pay for it. They were fined $10 and costs.

Frank Johnson, Charlie Hart and Roy Gibbons were arrested for being drunk and disorderly. Hart and Gibbons were fined $13.85 each and released, Johnson is still in jail.[87]

Drys Carry Precinct In Kenton County

A local option election held in the Stephenson precinct in Kenton county, which borders on the Grant county line, held last Friday, resulted in a victory for the drys by a majority of approximately five to one.[88]

Local Option Election To Be Held In Sept.

If Plans Of Drys Go Through. Petitions Now Being Circulated. Approximately 1,000 Voters Must Sign.

If present plans of the drys go through, an election will be held some time in September for the purpose of prohibiting the sale of alcoholic liquors in Grant county.

Ministers of various churches in the county attended a meeting held at the Baptist Church, Monday night and it was unanimously agreed that the sale of all kinds of intoxicating liquors, including whiskey, wine, gin,

[86] 21 May 1937. *Grant County News.* Author Unknown.
[87] 4 June 1937. *Grant County News.* Author Unknown.
[88] 11 June 1937. *Grant County News.* Author Unknown.

beer, etc., should be banned from the county under the local option law.

Petitions are now in circulation and approximately 1,000 voters must sign them in order to call the election which will be set for some date in September.

Nearly on-half the counties have voted on the question, and approximately three-fourths of them have voted dry.

The petitions will have to be filed by the necessary number of voters in order to call the election next month, and the election will have to be advertised in a newspaper in the county at least two weeks before the election.

Pendleton county voted dry some months ago but the election was declared illegal because it had not been properly advertised. The drys carried the county by a small majority.

What Grant county will do is a moot question, but is assured that a hard fight will be made by both the wets and drys.[89]

---

[89] 11 June 1937. *Grant County News.* Author Unknown.

An Appeal To Reason

As long as men are not born free and equal; as long as privation, sickness, old age, and death is our heritage, just that long will people drink.

You who would give water to the guests at the wedding feast, must remember that though the bride and groom need no wine, the guests may need a little something to make them remember that they, too, once were young. As long as men drink, there will be those who make it and sell it, and no laws that you can make or no penalties that you may invoke will keep them from doing it. Men get drunk to escape from a world that they are either unwilling or unable to cope with. It is to this type of person that "Lazy stream of dreams where vain desires forget themselves."Or, they drink because they have lost or never have had full physical vigor. Drink restores them temporarily to full mental and physical capacity, at least in their own mind.

Young folks are full of energy and need no stimulants.—They are not acquainted enough with reality to want to get away from it, so alcohol means nothing to them. But, young folks are adventurous, and they quickly change from Treasure Island, Robinson Crusoe and Swiss Family Robinson to the whiskey bottle if you forbid it, and make it an adventure. Don't misunderstand me, I believe if all whiskey could be banished from the earth, the world would be a better place to live, but you cannot rid yourselves of it. It is a heritage of civilization. The ostrich sticks his head in the sand and fools himself into thinking his whole body is hidden.—We cannot vote it out, and say that, now it is gone; for we know it is not gone and never will be. It has just become illegal, and when it becomes illegal, you give the bootleggers standing in our community, and give thieves and robbers an easy means of livelihood by manufacturing it.

Whiskey is not a pauper. It pays more than half the taxes in this State and affords gainful employment to many a good citizen who would otherwise be on the relief rolls. It has a definite place in medicine and when properly used, has a definite place as a beverage. The Frenchman would no more do without his wine, the German without his beer, and the Englishman his Scotch and Soda, because someone made a fool of himself, than we would do without food because some of us had dispepsia.—You must not judge whiskey by the drunk on the corner any more than you must judge the community by the people who are in it's jail. He is just a weak sister, that can't take it; and like some of us know no moderation in eating, drinking, or any of the other functions of life, and he pays for his weakness.

When you can assume the burden of taxation that whiskey carries, and give means of livelihood to those engaged in making and selling it legally, when you can make this world such a pleasant place to live that none wants to drink—then, I say, vote Dry, but until then, vote for Liquor Control and Law Enforcement.

- - - TAXPAYERS LEAGUE

[90]

[90]Circa June 1937. *Grant County News.*

To the Thinking Man and Woman of Grant County:

DO YOU WANT--

The depression to return?

A half dozen bootleggers in each block and all up and down the country roads?

Do you want Jamaica Ginger and Wood Alcohol and Poison Liquors, and Blindness and Paralysis and Jake Leg and Death?

Do you want to lose the thousands of dollars revenue paid to the towns, to Grant County and the State by bonded dealers?

Do you want the greatly increased jail costs and court costs that a dry county begets?

Do you want to make our towns dead and drive business into neighboring counties of Scott, Kenton and Pendleton?

In short, do you want Prohibition, which causes all of these things, again?

Does anyone remember what was called the depression?

The depression started during prohibition times and DID NOT END until prohibition was over. JUST AS SOON AS PROHIBITION WAS OVER things began to improve and in the space of a little over a year, business was good, there were jobs for all who wished to work, and things were back to normal.

Many persons have the mistaken impression that there has been more lawlessness in Grant County since Prohibition than during it. That such is not the case, is shown by a comparison of the following figures taken from the Jail Register of Grant County Jail, as follows:

During the years 1930, 1931, 1932, and 1933, all of which were Prohibition years, Charles Race, Jailer, was paid for keeping county prisoners and attending court alone, the sum of $10,918.26.

During the years 1934, 1935, 1936 and through May of 1937 (as far as the records are complete), during all of which time the county has been Wet, John Davis, Jailer, has received for county prisoners and attending court, the sum of $3,615.52.

Mr. Race received an average of $228.09 per month, and Mr. Davis, an average of $88.18 per month for county prisoners and attending court. If Mr. Davis' average continues during the rest of 1937, as in the first part, he will receive for his four years the sum of $4,232.78.

It will thus be seen that Grant County was compelled to pay its Jailer for keeping county prisoners and attending court $6,715.48 MORE during the last four years of Prohibition than it has had to pay him for the same services for the four years following Prohibition during which time the County has been wet.

We could give many other startling facts and figures if we had space. Please just remember

PROHIBITION IS THE WORST BREEDER OF CRIME THAT HAS EVER BEEN INVENTED.

THINK THE QUESTION OVER VERY CAREFULLY BEFORE YOU VOTE.

—Beer Dealers Association of Grant County. [91]

[91] Circa June 1937. *Grant County News.*

LEST WE FORGET

The Eeighteenth Amendment became an effective part of the Federal Constitution in 1919, and remained effective for 14 years. During that time we had a worst physical drouth in history, and yet, taking these 14 years and comparing them with any 14 years in history of the United States, we had:

Greater Prosperity and Less Drinking.

Less Automobile Fatalities in Proportion to the number of cars.

Less Cost of Enforcement of Liquor Laws, and Better Enforcement Than Now.

Payment of Federal Debts; and Now, an Increase yearly of Debts.

VOTE "YES" FOR LOCAL OPTION AND ON SEPTEMBER 11 PUT GRANT COUNTY "DRY."

—Grant County Dry Citizens Committee

92

[92]Circa June 1937. *Grant County News.*

2 More Kentucky Counties Voted Wet Last Saturday

Two more Kentucky counties are wet and the rainfall had absolutely nothing to do with it.

Bell and Grayson counties voted down prohibition in local option elections held last Saturday.

Bell county went wet by almost 200 votes in 7000 cast. Grayson slipped on the damp side by 200 votes.[93]

Local Option Election Set For Sept. 11th

Petition Filed With County Clerk. Signed by 1,451 Voters: More Than The Required Two-Thirds Necessary.

A petition was filed with County Clerk, R. F. Lanter, Monday, asking for an election to be held on the 11th day of September to determine whether the county of Grant shall remain wet or shall join the ever-increasing number of dry counties in Kentucky.

The petition carries the signatures of 1,451 registered voters of the county, about 200 more than the number required.

After the petition is recorded by the County Clerk, he will present to the Sheriff, who will see that it is properly advertised after a court order has been made by the County Judge.

It is estimated that there are around fifty beer saloons in the county and about one-third as many places where hard drinks are dispensed, most of them by package. No one has a license to sell whiskey by the drink in Williamstown or its environs.

The tax on products of this kind is considerable in this county and brings in quite a bit of revenue both to the State and county, especially in Williamstown.

Approximately 50 counties in the State have voted on the question and at least three out of every four have voted dry. There is no knowing what Grant county will do, but the general opinion is that she will be voted dry, especially if all those signing the petition cast their vote that way, as there will probably not be more than 3,500 votes cast in the election.[94]

Local Option Election For September 11

Voters of Grant County Will Vote on Whether Or Not Intoxicating Liquors Shall Be Sold

This week's News carries an advertisement for a local option election to be held September 11. It will be decided at this election whether spirituous, vinous or malt liquors may be legally sold within the boundaries of Grant county.

Spirituous liquors are whiskies, brandies, gins, or other concoctions containing a certain prescribed per cent. of alcohol. Vinous liquors pertain to wines and malt liquor to beer, containing more than a certain per cent. of alcohol.

It is expected that a hard fight will be made both by the local option forces and those who are opposed to a return to prohibition, as it existed during the prohibition era, ending a few years ago.

The News will publish paid advertising for either side, but will not handle free propaganda for either, and will be absolutely neutral.

If the drys win, the sale of beers, wine and whiskey, as well as other intoxicating liquors, will be forbidden by law 60 days after the election.[95]

Local Option Election Set For Saturday

Voters of The County Will Determine Whether Or Not The County Shall Remain In The Wet Column

[93] 18 June 1937. *Grant County News.* Author Unknown.
[94] 16 July 1937. *Grant County News.* Author Unknown.
[95] 20 August 1937. *Grant County News.* Author Unknown.

Wets and drys will fight it out in an election to be held in the various precincts of Grant county, Saturday. While both sides are advertising heavily and the drys are holding nightly meetings, there does not seem to be a great deal of enthusiasm manifested by the voters.

While there are approximately 5,000 registered voters in the county, it is not expected that nearly all will be cast, but no one can tell until Saturday night, nor can they tell what the outcome will be.

The ballots have been furnished the County Clerk by The News office, and they will be in hands of the precinct officers so that voting may start by six o'clock. The polls will be open from six until four o'clock.

The simple question to be voted on is "yes or no." A vote of "yes" is for local option and a vote of "no" is opposed to it.[96]

---

[96] 10 September 1937. *Grant County News.* Author Unknown.

To The Children Of Grant County:

You are very dear to us because you are helpless and must look to us for protection. When infantile paralysis or scarlet fever threatens you, we invoke the law to protect you and by its aid, we throw around you the safeguard of a quarantine.

We also seek to improve your minds, and with our taxes, pay for your education; and we build the churches in which to teach you the moral truth.

We realize that a great licensed industry also has its eyes on you, because it must make you it's customer for tomorrow. The men who drink liquor today furnish the money that makes the industry profitable, and as they die off, you will have to step into the ranks or the profits will disappear.

We know that no quarantine is perfect, and that no school can benefit every child, and that no church can save every soul, but we believe in these institutions.

On Saturday, September 11th, at the polls in Grant County, we shall endeavor to build a quarantine about you, and though we realize that some men will violate the law and will attempt to make money by selling illegal liquor, still we know that the quarantine will help, and our conscience will know that if you, our children, become drunkards of tomorrow, you will not be drinking poison that our vote made it legal to advertise and sell to you in supposedly decent places of business.

Because of this we shall

Vote "*YES*"

FOR LOCAL OPTION

- - - Fathers and Mothers of Grant County

97

[97]Circa September 1937. *Grant County News.*

VOTE 'NO'

Saturday, Sept. 11th

Here's What Doctors Say ABOUT Beer:

WHAT DO THE DOCTORS SAY ABOUT BEER?

[illegible]

TONIC FOR APPETITE

[illegible]

... **I have never seen a beer alcoholic.**"

[illegible]

"I regard beer as a food and a good beverage and not intoxicating in the amounts that one could consume it."

THE ECONOMIC, SOCIAL, MORAL, HEALTH AND FOOD VALUE OF BEER

[illegible]

FARM MATERIALS USED

[illegible]

FOOD VALUE OF BEER AS COMPARED WITH MILK

[illegible]

Vote "No" . . . [X] On Local Option

- - - Grant County Beer Dealers Association

98

[98]Circa September 1937. *Grant County News.*

Wets Win By Majority of 416 Votes

Local Option Election Held In Three Counties In State, Saturday. Drys Win Two While Grant Votes Wet.

The wets carried Grant County in her first local option election last Saturday by a majority of 416 votes. A larger vote was cast than had been anticipated by either the drys or the wets. Thirty-six hundred and fifty-four votes were counted, 1619 voted "Yes" and 2035 voted "No", giving those against local option a majority of 416. The counting was over by 8:30 Saturday night.

Drys won in Mercer county by a vote of approximately 4 to 1. Caldwell county drys won by 2,067 to 1,544 over the wets. The registered majority of the county is 6,500.[99]

Whisky Tax Bill Beaten In House

Extra Tax On Whisky Would Have Increased Old Age Pension. Governor Says He Asked Bill To Be Killed And Is Delighted.

Frankfort, Ky., Jan. 25 Within little more than an hour, the House of Representatives today approved and then killed a bill to double the whisky production tax and use the extra revenue to increase old age pensions.

The final action, climaxing a disorderly session featured by a sharp exchange of words between Gov. A. B. Chandler and several members of the House, left the bill virtually dead tabled to be brought back to life.

The reverse play followed one of the quickest and most unusual parliamentary maneuvers in the House in years and found many members switching their votes. Gov. A. B. Chandler informed the House, after the final roll call, that the reversal was effected and the bill killed at his request.

Waterfield Starts Fight

Representative H. L. Waterfield, Clinton, started the fireworks when he moved that the House take from the Kentucky Statutes Committee No. 1 his bill doubling the whisky production tax and earmarking the extra revenue for old-age pensions.

Representative Frank Daugherty, Bardstown, moved to table Waterfield's motion, which would have killed the bill then and there. His motion lost by a vote of 58 to 27, and opponents of the bill then sought unsuccessfully to adjourn to block first reading of the bill. They lost and the House gave the bill first reading by a vote of 52 to 35 after taking it from the committee.

Leading the fight against consideration of the measure were Daugherty, Joe Robinson, Lancaster; Tyler Munford, Morganfield, and Ferd Gnau, Louisville. Their efforts included an attempt to forestall action today by automatic adjournment, but the bill's sponsors blocked that move by having the session extended indefinitely.

Arguments On Bill

Principal arguments against the bill were that the whisky industries could not stand additional taxes. Proponents of the measures contended the industry could afford an additional 5 cents a gallon tax "to help the infirm an aged of this State."

Governor Chandler was advised immediately by his House leaders of the action and came to the House himself. While his leaders rallied votes to reconsider the bill and kill it, a group of Administration Representatives engaged in a filibuster on two minor judicial bills which finally were passed.

Proponents of the whisky bill, sensing what was in the making, sought to effect adjournment before reconsideration could be had but were blocked when Speaker John Kirtley refused to recognize Representative Sam Milam, Russellville, to make the adjournment motion. Milam had been recognized and put his motion when the enrolling committee reported, halting all other action. He could not regain recognition thereafter and Representative Rodes Myers, Bowling Green, was recognized to make a motion to recommit the whisky tax bill.[100]

[99] 17 September 1937. *Grant County News.* Author Unknown.
[100] 28 January 1938. *Grant County News.* Author Unknown.

Whiskey To Be Dispensed By Only Four

Four Merchants Now Selling Liquor, Law Will Not Allow Operation Of More Dispensaries, Should Anyone Desire Such Occupation.

The City Council of Williamstown has recently passed an ordinance whereby the number of whiskey dispensaries in the City of Williamstown is limited to four. Hertofore, any man who paid the licenses as required by law, had the right to sell whiskey.

In as much as liquor is legal in Kentucky and Grant County has voted wet, it would seem logical that the number of dispensaries should not be limited. The city would enjoy revenue from the sale of licenses should anyone desire to go into the liquor business and incidentally, taxes might be lowered as a result of such sales.[101]

20 Arrested For Drunkenness And Minor Offenses

Over Week End. Several Sent to Georgetown Jail And Had Trials Monday. Fines Assessed In Some Cases. Others Let Go On Probation.

The State patrol and county peace officers arrested 20 men over the week end for minor law violations in Grant county.

Starting at the north boundary line of the county the State patrol found 20 men Saturday afternoon and night who were more or less intoxicated, or were disorderly at various road houses, on the Dixie Highway and in Williamstown.

Some of the men were taken to Georgetown jail and kept over until Monday. Others had immediate trials. Fines were assessed against several of the men. Most of those fined paid up, but some were unable to pay and were let out on probation with the caution to go home and stay home.

They were also warned that any future violations would meet with heavier punishments. The trials were held before his honor, Judge Ernest Chipman.

Judge Chipman declined to reveal the names of the law violators to a News reporter, but we had no intention of publishing them anyway.[102]

Local Option Election Set For May 14, In Clark Co.

Winchester, Ky., Feb. 14th County Judge Joe S. Lindsay, acting on a petition presented today by the Clark County Dry Committee, set Saturday, May 14, as the date for a local option election.

The petition, filed with County Clerk Linville Jackson and then presented to the County Judge, carried the names of 1,939 Winchester and Clark County voters, representing more than 25 per cent of the total votes cast in the last general election.

The petition was presented by the Rev. Charles M. Neal, pastor of the Main Street Church of Christ, who acted as chairman of the Petition Committee of the Dry Committee, which was organized several weeks ago.[103]

Drunken Driver Causes Accident, Two Injured

Fine of $103.50 imposed And Driver's License Suspended For Six Months

Charged with driving a truck while intoxicated, Archie Morton, 150 No. Eastern Ave., Cincinnati, was fined $103.50, and given a suspended driver's license for six months. His sister, Sarah Earler, 512 W. 4th street, Cincinnati, who was riding with Morton, was fined $14.50 on a charge of drunkenness.

[101] 11 February 1938. *Grant County News.* Author Unknown.
[102] 11 February 1938. *Grant County News.* Author Unknown.
[103] 18 February 1938. *Grant County News.* Author Unknown.

It was claimed that Morton caused an accident which occurred on a sharp curve, two miles north of Williamstown, on Dixie Highway, which resulted in an injury to C. Cook, his left hip being broken, his left eye cut and other multiple bruises.

Cook was taken to St. Elizabeth's Hospital, first aid being rendered by Dr. Harper, Dry Ridge physician.

Arresting officers were McMillan, Osborne and Wyrick. The accident occurred at 1:00 o'clock Tuesday morning. Harry Poe, who was following Cook, who was driving a motorcycle, in an automobile, was a witness to the accident. The trial was held before Judge Ernest Chipman.[104]

Two Spend Week End In Georgetown Jail

Luther Scroggin, local truckman, was arrested Sunday night, charged with operating his truck while intoxicated. Denver McComas, who is said to have been drunk, tried to intervene and was also taken into custody. Both were taken to Georgetown jail and locked up pending trial here, Monday.[105]

Is your News subscription paid?

Young People To Have Temperance Meeting

A young people's temperance meeting will be held at the Christian Church in Williamstown, Saturday afternoon, 2:30. All young people of the county are urged to attend. A troupe of young people from Lexington will be here to conduct the meeting.[106]

Few Applications For Beer Licenses Have Been Received

Frankfort, Ky., June 7 C. M. C. Porter, Malt Beverage Administrator of the Department of Revenue, reported today that only a few hundred applications for beer licenses have been received.

Porter said there were nearly 7,000 beer retailers in the State. Each of these is required to secure a new license from the Department of Revenue to do business July 1st. No applicant for beer license is entitled to credit for any fee which he may have paid to the county to sell beer at retail. Applications for licenses must be received by June 15, Porter said, if licenses are to be issued by the date required. The County court clerks cannot issue beer licenses as heretofore.

Porter said that it would be illegal for any retailer to buy, sell, or possess beer without a license after July 1, and that the license of any distributor might be revoked for selling to a retailer who was not properly licensed.[107]

Young People Will Have Temperance Meeting, June 12th

A young people's temperance meeting will be held at the school auditorium Sunday evening, June 12th at 6:30 o'clock. All young people in Williamstown and throughout the community are invited and urged to be present.

A band of young temperance workers from Lexington will have charge of the program.[108]

Liquor Dealers Get Notice That They Can't Get License

Notices have been received by retail liquor dealers in Grant county, whether they sell by the package or by the drink, that unless their place of business is in incorporated towns, they will not be granted a license to continue. Incorporated town liquor dealers have not received any notice

[104] 22 April 1938. *Grant County News.* Author Unknown.
[105] 22 April 1938. *Grant County News.* Author Unknown.
[106] 13 May 1938. *Grant County News.* Author Unknown.
[107] 10 June 1938. *Grant County News.* Author Unknown.
[108] 10 June 1938. *Grant County News.* Author Unknown.

and it is presumed that they will secure licenses.

There are five applicants for licenses in Williamstown and one in Dry Ridge, for package sales. There are 12 in the county outside of incorporated towns, only one of whom sells by drink. Their licenses expired yesterday, June 30th and all of them are closing out the stock on hand at reduced prices.[109]

Retail Liquor Dealers Given 40 Days Grace

Political Move Seen In Edict Of Gov. Chandler. Sales Continue In Incorporated Towns.

Governor Chandler issued an edict last week giving retail licenses, a 40 day of grace, on the plea of depression.

In view of the fact that practically all dealers had made applications for license and their certified checks are on file at Frankfort, and that the extension of time carries the matter over until one day after the primary election, the attitude of the Governor is ridiculous, and is regarded as a move to hold a club over the dealers until after the election.

While package dealers in Williamstown and other incorporated towns in Grant and other counties, have not yet obtained their license, they have not been notified to the effect that license will not be granted them and they are proceeding to sell just as they have in the past.[110]

Beer Dealers Cited In Court, Fines Suspended

Forty Days Of Grace Given Hard Liquor Dealers Believed No To Apply In Unincorporated Towns

Sheriff Ben Kinman cited three men last Sunday on a charge of selling beer on Sunday.

When the men appeared before County Judge, Ernest Chipman, they stated that they had been informed by "outside" parties that they could sell on Sunday and would not be bothered. After hearing the statements of the men Judge Chipman gave each of them a suspended sentence with a warning that they must observe the law in the future else he would be forced to fine them and revoke their license.

The penalty for a violation of the law which prohibits the sale of beer on Sundays is a fine from $50.00 to $500.00 and revocation of the license.

Sheriff Kinman stated to The News that he had been ordered by the County Judge to cite any one guilty of a violation of the Sunday liquor law. He also stated that he expected to do his duty as a peace officer and that any one found guilty of violating the law would be arrested.

In the county there are about a dozen places outside of incorporated towns that sold hard liquor prior to June 20th, when their license expired. All of these places with one exception, are still selling hard liquor by the package.

Governor Chandler declared a moratorium until after the August primary on liquor dealers on the plea of a "depression." However, this edict does not apply to those outside of incorporated towns.

Those who applied for license, sent their certified checks to Frankfort for $100.00 each. The checks have been cashed but the fee has not been refunded. The dealers seem to think that they have a right to continue to sell until they have received their money back and are continuing on that assumption. There is no doubt that the 40 days of grace was granted to the liquor dealers by Chandler to hold as a club over the heads of the liquor dealers, but he fails to realize that the liquor dealers are not easily fooled.[111]

Wets Win Bath County By 482 Vote Margin

[109] 1 July 1938. *Grant County News.* Author Unknown.
[110] 8 July 1938. *Grant County News.* Author Unknown.
[111] 22 July 1938. *Grant County News.* Author Unknown.

Owingsville, Ky., Sept. 11th Official tabulation today of votes in the Bath County local option election yesterday showed a majority of 482 for the Wets. The vote was: Wets, 1,708; Drys, 1,226.

Hopkins County voted wet yesterday by a majority of 544.[112]

Distillery On Kentucky River Declared Bankrupt

The Belle of Anderson County Distilling Co., located at Camp Nelson, Jessamine County, on the Kentucky River, is bankrupt, Federal Judge H. Church Ford ruled Monday.

Officials of the firm who had fought the bankruptcy proceeding argued the distillery was solvent. The principal point of issue was the value of the Camp Nelson property.[113]

Arrested For Being Drunk And Driving Car

Clay Renaker was arrested by policeman Russell McMillan, Friday for operating a motor vehicle while being intoxicated. He gave bond and will be tried next Tuesday morning.[114]

---

[112] 16 September 1938. *Grant County News.* Author Unknown.

[113] 31 March 1939. *Grant County News.* Author Unknown.

[114] 8 December 1939. *Grant County News.* Author Unknown.

1940s

Drunken Driving

Do the people of this county feel that drunken driving should be controlled?

The law in this county reports that juries turn loose people that should be convicted of drunken driving.

How would you feel if a drunken driver ran over your child, and killed it, especially after the same man had been turned loose by a jury in a previous case?[1]

Estill County Local Option Petition Stolen

Petition Bearing 1,766 Names, Was Taken From County Judge's Office. Man Held For Questioning.

Irvine, Ky., Aug. 10 On the day County Judge W. M. Noland was to have ruled on a petition requesting that he call a local option election to decide whether liquor may be sold in Estill County, County Clerk Maggie Wolfinbarger reported this morning the petition had been taken from her office.

Although urged by C. A. Ellis, Paris, representing the Citizens Temperance League, to order the election, Judge Noland declined to do so in absence of the petition, and continued the case until September 14th.

Petition Filed August 3

Several hours after the County Clerk reported the petition was missing, Sheriff Ancil Powell, Jr. announced he had picked up for questioning a man whose name was written on a paper found on the floor of the clerk's office.

The petition, bearing 1,766 signatures, was filed with the County Judge August 3 and given to the County Clerk for safekeeping.[2]

County-Wide Local Option Meeting To Be Held At Dry Ridge

The County-wide meeting in interest of Local Option, will be held in the Dry Ridge Baptist Church Sunday afternoon at 2 o'clock. Dr. O. W. Robinson, Pastor of the Williamstown Methodist Church will preside.

We are reaping the results of a liberal administration in Grant County. It is up to the good citizens of the County to "put a stop" to this crime wave. During the past few weeks, a place has been entered and the slot machine robbed. Last Sunday evening there was a shooting scrape at one of the notorious dives of the county. There is no use dodging the issue, these places are dives that are not only engendering the lives of our folk, but they are succeeding in making drunkards and worse of our young people. We do call upon the good citizens of Grant County to arise in indignation. We should demand of our law enforcement officials, enforcement of the laws.

Petitions will be circulated immediately for the purpose of calling the Local Option election. We plead with all good citizens to sign these petitions. Can you afford to play up to the lawless group by not doing so?

O. W. Robinson, Chairman
A. Threlkeld, Vice-Chairman

[1] 31 May 1940. *Grant County News.* Author Unknown.
[2] 14 August 1942. *Grant County News.* Author Unknown.
[3] 4 September 1942. *Grant County News.* Author Unknown.

J. O. Carter, Sec'y.-Treas.[3]

Local Option

Mass Meeting

2:00 O'CLOCK P. M.

Sunday, September 6

DRY RIDGE BAPTIST CHURCH

The meeting will be addressed by

Former Governor

Flem D. Sampson

COME AND BRING YOUR NEIGHBOR

4

LOCAL OPTION MEETING

The first Mass Meeting on the interest of the Local Option campaign was held last Sunday afternoon in the First Baptist Church, Dry Ridge. A large and enthusiastic audience, estimated between 500 and 600 was assembled to hear former Governor Flem D. Sampson deliver the keynote address. Dr. O. W. Robinson, County Chairman, presided. Every member of the Executive Committee with one exception was present. Every precinct of the County was represented. Rev. J. O. Carter, Secretary-Treasure of the organization, read the minutes of the first meeting held some two weeks ago in the Williamstown Baptist Church. Hon. L. M. Ackman, of Williamstown in a very splendid manner, presented Gov. Sampson. The Governor was in fine form, and did not hesitate to pay his respects to all classes of law violators. One point he stressed was that in his Courts he found that the great majority of crimes could be traced to the use of intoxicants. Judge Sampson is Circuit Judge in three Counties in Southern Kentucky, all of which are dry, and he pointed to the fact that there is less law violations, and that bootlegging is at a very low ebb. Petitions are being circulated throughout the County. These petitions will be presented to County Judge C. A. Pettit in the near future, requesting the Court to call an election. The response to these petitions is highly satisfactory.

Another County Mass Meeting will be held Sunday afternoon, Sept. 20th at 2:30 o'clock at the Williamstown Court House, with a well known speaker bringing the address. One of the encouraging features of the campaign is the fine manner in which the Woman's Committee is taking hold of the work. Mrs. Anna Clinkscales and Mrs. E. C. Vice, of Williamstown and Mrs. T. F. Simon of Corinth are heading up the Women's work. The women of every part of the County are being urged to form groups and have speakers to come in and address their group. All petitions should be ready to turn over to the Executive Committee on Sunday afternoon, Sept. 20th.[5]

ANOTHER LOCAL OPTION MASS MEETING

SUNDAY AFTERNOON AT 2:30 AT THE COURT HOUSE. DR. W. W. STOUT TO SPEAK.

The Local Option movement in Grant County is gaining in momentum. Much enthusiasm is being shown in all sections of the county. The petitions are being circulated and signed enthusiastically. Our citizens are a determined group and will see to it that Mr. John Barley corn makes his exit!

Again, all the God-fearing, righteous-loving and sober-minded people of Grant County will meet in a great County-Wide Mass Meeting. This meeting will be at the Court House at 2:30 p. m., Sunday, Sept. 20th. Dr. W. W. Stout, an outstanding citizen of our State, an ardent dry, an orator of renown, will be the main speaker. Dr. Stout will say many things that we all need to hear. There were over 500 present for the first Mass Meeting and the drys expect many more for this one. Join this crusade for righteousness, sobriety and purity and march with the majority to a great victory!

All those with petitions are urged to come and bring them for a brief meeting at 2 o'clock. This is urgent and very necessary. The petitions must be checked before the Mass Meeting.[6]

---

[4]Circa September 1942. *Grant County News.*

[5]11 September 1942. *Grant County News.* Author Unknown.

[6]18 September 1942. *Grant County News.* Author Unknown.

ANOTHER

Local Option Mass Meeting

2:30 P. M.

Sun., Sept. 20

AT COURT HOUSE

Speaker: DR. W. W. STOUT, Georgetown.
Special Music: Olivet Quintette, Olivet, Ill.

600 WANTED! 600 WANTED!
(Those with petitions are asked to bring them in at 2:00 p. m.)

[7]

Local Option Mass Meeting

The mass meeting in the interest of the coming Local Option campaign held last Sunday afternoon in the Williamstown Court House, was a very enthusiastic affair, the court house being filled with delegations from all sections of the County. Dr. W. W. Stout, pastor of the First Baptist Church of Georgetown was the speaker. Dr. Stout is a very forcible, and at the same time, entertaining speaker. He held his audience in an address of almost an hour's length. He stressed the fact that the liquor and slot machine groups are wholly responsible for the present campaign, pointing out the fact the they have never kept within the limits of the law. He also stated that many were claiming that when Local Option becomes the law, men with money invested in the liquor business lose their investment, and livelihood. He granted their plea, but pointed to the fact that addicts to the liquor habit and those who did not have the strength to pass up the slot machine, became good and productive citizens.

Dr. Stout also stated that there is not one good thing that can be said about the two businesses liquor and slot machines. The leaders of the movement in Grant County were greatly pleased with the response in the signing of the petitions. Many times the required number have already signed, and daily calls are coming from different sections of the County, asking for additional petitions. Dr. Stout also paid high tribute to the Editor of The News in his fair and impartial manner of treating the news of this campaign. The audience on Sunday afternoon was heartened by the good news that three additional counties of the State had voted dry on last Saturday. This makes a total of 63 dry counties in Kentucky.[8]

Eight Grant Countians Are Cited

To Appear Before The Alcoholic Beverage Control Board At Frankfort This Week For Liquor Violations

The following news dispatch from Frankfort appeared in last Friday's Kentucky Post:

Frankfort, Ky., Sept 25th Eight Grant County beer and liquor dealer must appear before the Alcoholic Beverage Control Board next week in response to citations for violations of the state beverage laws.

Two of the dealers, N. Dunn, Dry Ridge, and J. L. Mitts, Williamstown, are accused of violations of both liquor and beer regulations, while the others must answer charges of violation of their beer license only.

Others named are:

Chester Campbell, Mason; Otis Dunn, Williamstown; Mrs. Sara Beckman, Williamstown; Mrs. Yuelita McAtee, Williamstown, and Clarence Lawrence, operating as Fisher's Camp, Corinth.

Accusations include violation of the law against Sunday sales; selling liquor on premises where only beer may be sold; sales to minors and conducting the premises in a disorderly manner.

Hearings in the Grant County cases will be held Thursday and Friday.[9]

Local Option Campaign

The petitions requesting the County Judge, Hon. Charles A. Pettit, to call an election for the purpose of taking a vote on Local Option for Grant County, was presented to the Judge yesterday. He will pass on it at the October term of the County Court, and the date of the election will be set. A very fine response greeted the

[7] Circa September 1942. *Grant County News.*
[8] 25 September 1942. *Grant County News.* Author Unknown.
[9] 2 October 1942. *Grant County News.* Author Unknown.

men and women who had these petitions. Very few people throughout the County refused to sign. Several times the required number of names are on the petitions.

Law abiding men and women of the County feel that the hour has come to put a stop to the continued violations of the laws by roadhouses and the saloons that have so openly defied every known decency. Many men who have been classed as liberals are coming to those who have charge of the present campaign and saying we intend to vote dry, and then we intend to see that the dry laws are observed.[10]

- Committeemen.

---

[10] 2 October 1942. *Grant County News.* Author Unknown.

[11]

[11] Circa October 1942. *Grant County News.*

Local Option Meeting Friday Night At Williamstown Christian Church

The local option committee will meet Friday night at 7:30 at the Williamstown Christian Church. Supper will be served at that time, every precinct in the County is planning to send a representative to this meeting.

The leaders of the movement are planning a complete organization of the County, they are confident that the sentiment is overwhelming in ridding the County of the liquor interests and the destructive influences that surround same, but realize the need of a strong organization to fully arouse the people and get the voters to speak with their votes on the day of election.

A large portion of the County has been covered with petitions asking for an election. The reaction from these petitions has been more than the committee had expected and they're strongly impressed with the sentiment of the people in Grant County for law and order. They realize that respect for law and order, and good citizenship in the County greatly attacked by a vicious element that has no regard for the laws of the land, they see in the aim of the destructive interests to disregard morals, law and decency.

Last Saturday saw four more Counties of the State vote dry, making 67 Counties in the State in the dry column. The better element of the people is saying by their vote that the only way to deal with this evil is to get rid of it. They believe the freedom of our County cannot be maintained unless the value of life is sustained.[12]

- A Committeeman.

Local Option Speaking

Tuesday evening at the Methodist Church, Hon. Fred A. Harrison and Dr. O. W. Robinson will deliver addresses in the interest of the coming Local Option election that is soon to be held in the County. All are cordially invited to hear these addresses.[13]

The Bootleggers And Legalized Liquor

In a short time the voters of Grant County are going to be called upon to vote on the WET and DRY issue. There are many questions arising in the mind of the average voter when a proposition of this kind is placed before him. We find one of the first questions to be that concerning the bootlegger. We would be led to believe by the liquor interests that the bootlegger was a creature of Prohibition, that prohibition produced him and is responsible for him, and that he has disappeared under the licensed system. When we vote, let us do it intelligently. Has the bootlegger disappeared since the return of the saloon?

Let The Following Facts Speak For Themselves

Thirty-one persons, including several millionaires, held before the U. S. District Court for smuggling 1,000,00 gallons of liquor into the U. S. by land and sea under legal liquor. This report is from U. S. District Records.

"U. S. Government estimates 50,000 gallons of bootleg liquor manufactured in New York City monthly."

Two thousand (2,000) bootleg plants with an average of over 300 gallons per day each, confiscated in Illinois, Wisconsin, and Indiana under Repeal. (Alcohol Tax Admr.)

In Ohio, 183 bootlegging joints raided, 21 stills, 20 transporters, and $12,510 in fines, for one week's work under legal liquor. Enforcement Chief Humphrey gave this statement.

Here is the report of the Kentucky Alcohol Tax Unit: 588 stills were seized, 1,321 persons arrested and 234,414 gallons of whiskey and mash confiscated in the fiscal year ending last June 30th. "In one single day in the U. S. court at Paducah, 48 bootleggers were sentenced to Federal prisons. In wet Princeton (1937) out of 60 arrests for drunkenness, 58 were drunk on bootleg liquor according to the evidence given in court. Rowan county voted wet; a short time later

[12] 2 October 1942. *Grant County News.* Author Unknown.
[13] 9 October 1942. *Grant County News.* Author Unknown.

two men were killed on poison liquor and later nine illicit distillers were arrested.

This is a statement made by Jos. H. Choate, former Chief of the Federal Alcoholic Administration. "One half of all liquor now sold in the U. S. two years ago was illicit liquor."

George T. Stewart of the Kentucky Alcoholic Beverage Control Board in a survey made in one of our Counties, stated that 65 percent of all liquor sold in that county was moonshine liquor. And why not? The legal liquor and whiskey joint have become the outlet for this illicit liquor.

Has the bootlegger and moonshiner disappeared under Repeal? THEY HAVE NOT. They have but multiplied. We must also remember that the liquor question is one of right and wrong. We cannot let the scare of the bootlegger keep up from voting against a traffic wrong in itself and which cannot and does not produce good.[14]

- O. W. Robinson, Chairman of Local Option Committee.

Nine Grant County Beer Dealers Have Licenses Suspended

Louisville, Oct. 21 (Special) Suspensions, ranging from 5 to 45 days, were given sixteen Kentucky retail beer licenses by the State Alcoholic Beverage Control Board, Harry D. France, State Director of Brewing Industry Foundation. Kentucky Committee, was notified today Nine of the outlets are in Grant County; four in Scott County and three in Hopkins County. All suspensions were ordered after Committee field representatives appeared before the State Board in September and October and testified to law violations. The charges included: sales on Sunday, sales to minors, sales after hours and operating a disorderly place.

Suspensions included: Grant County: Mose Teagarden, Town Tavern, Corinth, and Chester Campbell, Rock Garden. Mason, 45-days; Kirtley Bennett, Wayside Inn, U. S. 25; Mrs. Emma Younger, Hilltop Tavern, Williamstown J. L. Mitts, Mitts Restaurant, Williamstown; N. Dunn, Dry Ridge and Otis Dunn, Kentucky Colonel, Williamstown, 30 days; James E. Falls, Mayflower Skating Rink, Williamstown, 20 days; and Mrs. Sara Beckman, Jake's Place, Williamstown, 15 days.

Scott County, Clarence Lawrence, Fisher's Camp, U. S. 25, and Ezra Sellers, Dixiana Service Station, Sadieville, 45 days; Lewis Mulberry Service Station, Sadieville, and A. Weisenberger. Dover House, Georgetown, 30 days.

Hopkins County: Mrs. Ada Troop, Dreamlite Club, 5 days; H. C. Wadlington, Wadlington's Tourist Camp, 8 days and Mrs. Bonnie Day Carter, Lattle Club, 45 days. All the Hopkinsville County outlets are near Madisonville.

The suspensions became effective at midnight October 21st.

"Such disciplinary action clearly demonstrates to citizens of those counties where local option elections are being sought that strict control is the solution for anti-social practices, wherever found, in licensed malt beverage outlets. Such places are visited, and can be at all times, by law enforcement officers without the benefit of a search warrant. This is not true of the bootleg places. In order to catch the bootlegger, enforcement officers must first obtain evidence upon which the warrant is based. It is the policy of the Committee to cooperate with law enforcement and licensing agencies in regulation retail beer outlets. By improving conditions in outlets the Committee hopes to help preserve the vast revenues our Federal, State and local governments derive from the legal manufacture and sale of malt beverages," Director France said in announcing the suspensions.[15]

Beer Licenses Of Six Suspended

Six Grant County retail beer licenses and one in Scott County are under suspension on order of the State Alcoholic Beverage Control Board. The rulings followed inspections of the outlets by the Kentucky Committee of Brewing Industry Foundation.

Charged with selling beer on Sunday and their licenses under suspension for 15 days are: Fred Price,

[14] 16 October 1942. *Grant County News.* Author Unknown.

[15] 23 October 1942. *Grant County News.* Author Unknown.

Wilbert Brown and John Goodpaster, all of Williamstown; Daisy May Angle, RFD 3, Corinth and George M. Jeurgens, RFD 1, Mason.

Licenses held by Wm. Schulte, Crittenden, and James Foster Smith, RFD 3, Corinth (Scott County) are under suspension for 30 days. They are charged with Sunday sales of beer and employing a female as barmaid.[16]

---

[16] 20 November 1942. *Grant County News.* Author Unknown.

Why Should You Vote Wet?

VOTE WET IN ORDER THAT YOUR **BOYS** AND **GIRLS** MAY CULTIVATE A TASTE FOR BEER AND LIQUORS AND THUS FURNISH THE **NEW CUSTOMERS**, WITHOUT WHICH THE **LIQUOR BUSINESS** COULD NOT **SUCCEED.**

VOTE WET TO FURNISH A **SAFE** AND SECURE PLACE WHERE **SLOT MACHINES** AND **GAMBLING** DEVISES MAY **OPERATE** FOR THEY WILL NOT BE TOLERATED IN RESTAURANTS, GROCERY STORES AND OTHER PLACES OF BUSINESS WHERE **LIQUOR** and **BEER** ARE NOT SOLD.

VOTE WET TO ENABLE THE BEER AND WHISKEY DISPENSARIES, DELIVERY TRUCKS, AND PRODUCERS TO FURNISH EMPLOYMENT TO THOUSANDS OF **HUSKY** MEN AND WOMEN WHO OTHERWISE WOULD BE **FORCED** TO FIND A JOB IN **WAR INDUSTRIES** OR ON THE **FARM,** WHERE ALL THEY COULD DO WOULD BE WORK, FIGHT AND GIVE TO MAKE OUR **DEMOCRACY** LIVE.

VOTE WET SO THE **KEELY CURE** SANATORIUMS MAY CONTINUE TO MULTIPLY AND FURNISH PROFIT AND EMPLOYMENT TO THE STRONG and SKILLED **DOCTORS** AND **NURSES** WHO OTHERWISE WOULD BE **SERVING** YOUR **BOYS** AS THEY **FIGHT** AND **DIE** TO PROTECT YOU. (IN 1930 THERE WAS ONLY ONE KEELY CURE SANATORIUM IN THE UNITED STATES.)

VOTE WET SO THAT THOSE WHO ARE **AFRAID** TO FACE **LIFE** MAY FIND AN ESCAPEMENT IN INTOXICATION AND THUS **WEAKEN** THEMSELVES AND **BREED** MORE FLAKS THAT WILL DEMAND A HEAVIER DOSE OF THIS SAME **POISON** TO OVERCOME.

VOTE WET SO THAT THE **CORN** AND **GRAIN** THAT IS SO DESPERATELY **NEEDED** BY THE **ARMIES** OF FREEDOM MAY BE CONVERTED INTO **BOOZE** THAT WILL ENSLAVE THE INDIVIDUAL.

> EVERY NATION IN THE PAST THAT HAS SUCCESSFULLY FOUGHT FOR ITS LIFE HAS BEEN FORCED TO BECOME A SOBER NATION. YOU CANNOT TRAIN A WINNING FOOTBALL OR BASKETBALL TEAM ON BEER AND WISKEY, AND YOU CERTAINLY CANNOT **TRAIN** A WINNING **ARMY** OR **NAVY** ON THIS DIET.

VOTE WET SO THAT WE MAY RECEIVE THE **TAXATION** FROM BEER AND WHISKEY THAT WILL ENABLE US TO PAY A **SMALL** PORTION OF THE **COSTS** TO THE TAXPAYERS INCIDENT TO THE **IMPRISONMENT** OF MEN WHO BECOME **CRIMINALS** WHEN THEY ARE TOO DRUNK TO EXERCISE THEIR JUDGMENT.

> THE BUREAU OF CRIMINAL INVESTIGATION COMPOSED OF SCIENTISTS, WHO ARE WITHOUT BIAS, HAS REPORTED THAT 85 PER CENT OF THE MEN NOW SERVING IN OUR PENAL INSTITUTIONS ARE THERE BY REASON OF CRIMES COMMITTED WHILE UNDER THE INFLUENCE OF ALCOHOL.

NO, **NONE** OF THIS SUITS YOU, BUT IT'S **PLAIN** SIMPLE **TRUTH.**

ALCOHOL IS A **NARCOTIC** AS DEADLY AS **MORPHINE,** OR **COCAINE,** AND JUST AS HABIT FORMING. IF YOU PERMIT MEN AND WOMEN TO DO BUSINESS IN GRANT COUNTY WITH THIS DEADLY STUFF WHERE YOUR **BOYS** AND **GIRLS** SEE IT, SMELL IT, AND WATCH OTHERS **DRINK** IT, THEN BE PREPARED TO HAVE THE YOUNGER GENERATION GROW UP AND BECOME THE **CUSTOMERS,** WHOSE MONEY CONTRIBUTES TO THE **WEALTH** OF THE **BREWER,** THE **DISTILLER,** AND THE MEN WHO CLAIM THEY CAN **BOSS** GRANT COUNTY.

Vote "*Yes*" for Law Enforcement

Grant County Committee For Local Option

17

[17] Circa November 1942. *Grant County News.*

TO ALL PERSONS INTERESTED IN THE LOCAL OPTION ELECTION

The News will not publish arguments for or against local option unless they are paid for at the regular advertising rate and run as advertising.

The News has many subscribers who are dry and many who are wet. To publish matter for the local option group free, and not for the other group would be manifestly unfair.

So, if you wish to argue the question through this newspaper, be prepared to pay space rates.

We will publish without cost, notices of speakings and other matter that we consider news, free of charge.

18

[18]Circa November 1942. *Grant County News.*

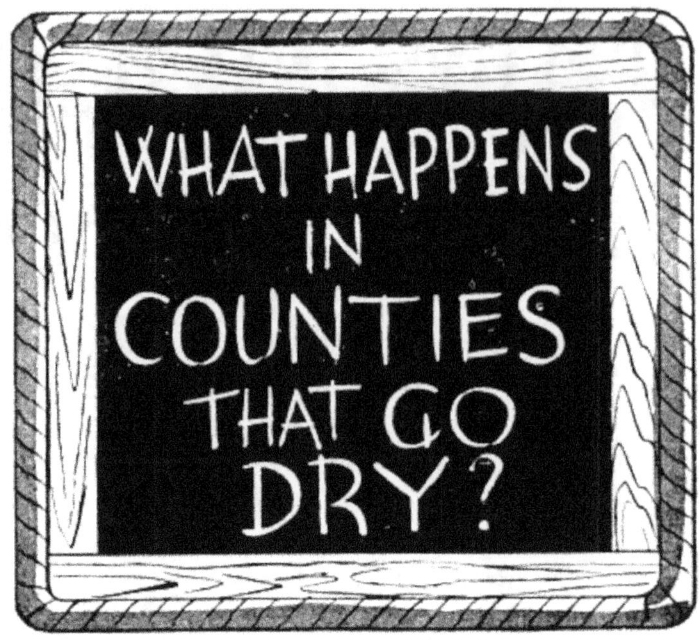

PROHIBITION laws are designed to prevent the sale of alcoholic beverages. Such laws do prohibit *legal* sales in *licensed* places—but they do NOT and never have prevented *illegal* sales by bootleggers. The history of Prohibition—federal, state and local—is one of complete failure.

Here is a concrete example: consider the experience of Clark County, right here in Kentucky. In 1938, Clark County voted dry. In June, 1941, it held another election, and this time voted for legal control.

According to records of the Clark County Court and the Winchester Police Court, during the last 11 months that Clark County was "dry", 28 persons were convicted of drunken driving and 11 were convicted of bootlegging. During the first 11 months since Clark County has restored legal control, drunken driving convictions were cut 60%, and only one was convicted of bootlegging.

This is the record where prohibition has been tried and rejected. Doesn't that record speak for itself?

HARRY D. FRANCE, State Director 1182 STARKS BLDG., LOUISVILLE, KY.[19]

[19] Circa November 1942. *Grant County News.*

What Shall It Profit A Man?

From 1935 to 1941, the Federal Government and the State Government of Kentucky sought to collect all posible taxes through unrestricted sale, under loose license system, of whiskey and beer. During this same period, the policy of "eat, drink and be merry" failed to make adequate provisions for the safeguarding of moral values beyond price, and for this failure we began to pay at Pearl Harbor.

During the last twelve months, in the desperate agony of mortal peril, we the people, have spent and committed ourselves to spend more money than the whiskey and beer business can ever pay in taxes in the next two hundred years. However, our wealth,our factories, our taxes and the whiskey industry cannot save us and our institutions, but we must turn for protection to boys 18, 19 and 20 years old, not yet old enough to vote but old and brave enough to die in order to save our wealth, our liberty and our way of life.

The total taxes from the whiskey industry amounted to about One Billion Dollars a year (Grant County's share is some $500.00), and yet, the Federal Government reports that the total cost of crime in the United States is Nineteen Billion Dollars annually. And the Bureau of Criminal Investigation has reported that 85 percent. of the crimes stem from intoxication and debauchery.

This year the National Brewers Organization, through its Digest, advised the world that with the unrestricted sale of beer, the brewery business had the greatest opportunity every known to teach the young soldiers to like their product and recruit the greatest body of customers that any business ever enjoyed.

If the people of Grant County and of this country have the courage to whip Hitler, Mussolini, and Hirohito, then certainly they ought to have the courage to whip a business whose profit depends upon making drinkers out of our boys and girls.

In 1917 and 1918, the United States of America had a dry navy and a dry army, due to the stern insistent demand of General John J. Pershing, Josephus Daniels, and Newton D. Baker. That army and navy never suffered a major reverse, and within twelve months from the time it contacted the enemy, sober soldiers and sailors under the stars and stripes, had won victory and peace for our country.

Our national policy will be determined by what the Counties do, for in a democracy the power moves from the bottom up. If you want your boys to return home strong, healthy, sober and self-respecting, help make the policy of temperance a military law by voting Grant County Dry.

Vote "YES" To Protect Your Boys And Girls Not Yet Old Enough To Vote.

Be sure and register at the County Clerk's office so you can vote.

TO VOTE "DRY" VOTE "YES", On December 12th

Grant County Committee For Local Option

[20]

[20]Circa November 1942. *Grant County News.*

Are you against the bootlegger?

You know the BOOTLEGGER.

He is the one who sells liquor and beer in violation of the law.

The dealer who SELLS on SUNDAY is a BOOTLEGGER.

The dealer who SELLS to YOUTH under eighteen is a BOOTLEGGER.

The dealer who SELLS after closing hours is a BOOTLEGGER.

The dealer who SELLS to an intoxicated man is a BOOTLEGGER.

The dealer who maintains a slot machine on his premises is a BOOTLEGGER.

Recently thirthy-one indictments were returned in this County charging this same violation of the law over a period of about thirty days.

Out of the THIRTY-SIX who hold license to sell beer or liquor or both in Grant County EIGHTEEN of them were FOUND, by the very liberal State Alcoholic Control board, to be BOOTLEGGERS.

Here is the reason. Since it became known that a Local Option election was to be held in Grant County the State Board of Alcoholic Control has TRIED and found EIGHTEEN of the license holders in this County to be GUILTY of violating the laws of the State and has revoked their license for a certain period of time, BUT THEY HAVE NOT BEEN FINED ONE CENT.

You have heard of the TRADITIONAL BOOTLEGGER, the old LOOSE OVERCOAT or the baggy shirt that would hold a half dozen pints. He went to jail for THIRTY DAYS and paid A HUNDRED DOLLAR FINE and everybody condemned him.

The next time one of these shiny five ton trucks, filled eight feet high with beer cases, crowds you off the highway or blocks Main Street, take a pencil and paper and figure how many overcoats or hickory shirts it would take to lug that five tons of booze around.

Liquor is now traveling on air, in high society, made lawful by the laws of your State and County, BUT IT STILL BRINGS PROFIT TO A FEW AND DISGRACE AND DEATH TO MANY.

If you want to find out whether slot machines are back in Grant county, ask the school boys, they can tell you?

TO GET RID OF THESE BOOTLEGGERS, VOTE DRY ON DECEMBER the 12th

[21]

[21] Circa November 1942. *Grant County News.*

Would You Sell Our Boys and Girls

FOR LESS THAN TWO PENNIES?

WOULD YOU VOTE TO MAKE DRUNKARDS OF THE BOYS AND GIRLS OF GRANT COUNTY BY KEEPING LIQUOR UNDER THEIR NOSE EVERYWHERE THEY GO?

WHEN GRANT COUNTY VOTES DRY, IT MEANS A LOSS OF LESS THAN TWO PENNIES

FOR EVERY MAN, WOMAN AND CHILD IN THE COUNTY IN REVENUE FROM THE STATE'S LIQUOR CONSUMPTION AND LICENSE TAXES

HERE'S THE PROOF -:- READ FOR YOURSELF

Proof taken from actual figures in the report of Kentucky's Dept. of Revenue, Year closing June 30, 1942

THE TOTAL WHISKEY CONSUMPTION TAX RECEIVED BY THE STATE FROM ALL sources, fiscal year ending June 30, 1942 was	$2,906,746.05
Total state beer consumption tax, same period was	1,234,273.28
Total state wine consumption tax, same period was — — — — — — — —	182,022.35
Grand total consumption tax for this period was — — — — — — — —	**$4,323,041.68**

THIS TOTAL CONSUMPTION TAX OF $4,323,041.68 RECEIVED BY THE STATE, if divided by the 2,839,927 people in Kentucky, would amount to $1.48 for every man, woman and child in the state.

AT $1.48 PER CAPITA, GRANT COUNTY'S 9910 POPULATION PAID into the state's general fund for the year ending June 30, 1942:

A total liquor consumption tax of — — — — —	$14,666.80
She sent the state for whiskey license fees — — —	800.00
Her state beer license fees at $25.00 per store were — — —	725.00
Her grand total sent the state for liquor revenue was — — — — — — — — —	**$16,191.80**

THIS $16,191.80 IS THE SUM THE STATE WILL LOSE AND NOT GRANT COUNTY when this county votes dry December 12. This county is only one o fthe 120 counties of the state sharing in the general fund. So this county will lose ONLY her 120th part of this $16,191.80, which totals ONLY $134.93.

This $134.93 is this county's only loss in state revenue, less than 2c a peron.

THE ONLY OTHER LIQUOR REVENUE GRANT COUNTY WILL LOSE BY VOTING DRY is the small amount received by the county from local license fees charged liquor and beer stores. This small amount does not begin to pay for caring for the drunks.

WHEN GRANT COUNTY VOTES DRY SHE WILL CONTIUE TO RECEIVE HER SHARE OF the $9 157,255.20 total liquor revenue pouring into the state's general fund from 64 distilleries, 7 breweries, 100 wholesale distributors and 5,000 beer and whiskey saloons.

GRANT COUNTY PEOPLE PAID OUT FOR BEER AND WHISKEY LAST YEAR APPROXIMATELY $146,370.70. This equals $14.77 for every man, woman and child. Figure for yourself how much this staggering sum would have contributed to the peace and prosperity of the county had this amount been spent for useful things!

LET'S VOTE THE LIQUOR JOINTS OUT OF GRANT COUNTY DECEMBER 12

TO VOTE DRY, VOTE "YES" **GIVE OUR BOYS AND GIRLS A BREAK!** 22

---

22 Circa November 1942. *Grant County News*.

NOTICE OF LOCAL OPTION ELECTION

TO THE VOTERS OF GRANT COUNTY, KENTUCKY:

There will be an election at the various places of [illegible] in Grant County, Kentucky, on the 12th day of December, 1942, same being Saturday, the polls opening at 6 o'clock A. M. and closing at 4 o'clock P. M.

Upon the question as to whether or not spirituous, vinous and malt liquors shall be sold, bartered or loaned therein.

Given under my hand as Sheriff of Grant County, Kentucky, this [illegible] day of November, 1942.

(Signed) LEWIS HENDERSON, [illegible]
Grant County, Kentucky.

ORDER
GRANT COUNTY COURT

Regular term held October 12, 1942
Hon. Chas. A. Pettit, Judge, present and presiding.

In the matter of L. M. Ackman, and others, on petition.

WHEREAS, there has been filed with the County Court Clerk of Grant County, Kentucky a petition signed by L. M. Ackman, and others, requesting this Court to enter an order directing an election be held not sooner than sixty days nor later than ninety days after October 1, 1942 in Grant County, Kentucky, for the purpose of taking the sense of the legal voters of said County upon the proposition as to whether or not spirituous, vinous or malt liquors shall be sold, bartered or loaned therein, and

WHEREAS, it further appears to the Court that the number of signers to said petition, totaling 1417 legally qualified voters of Grant County, is equal to twenty-five per cent, or more, of the votes cast in said County at the last preceding general election, and that said signatures bear the date of the signing and the post office addresses of said petitioners.

IT IS THEREFORE ORDERED that an election be held in Grant County, Kentucky for the purpose of taking the sense of the legal voters of said County upon the proposition of whether or not spirituous, vinous or malt liquors shall be sold, bartered, or loaned therein, and said election shall be held on SATURDAY, THE 12TH DAY OF DECEMBER, 1942, A. D.

The proposition to be voted upon shall be stated on the voting ballot without emblems and two spaces left upon the right side of same, one for votes favoring the proposition to be designated by the word "YES" and one for votes opposing it designated by the word "NO". The voter shall designate his vote by a cross mark placed opposite the word "YES" or the word "NO".

The question to be submitted shall be in words and figures as follows, to-wit:

ARE YOU IN FAVOR   YES ......
OF ADOPTING PROHIBITION
IN GRANT COUNTY, KENTUCKY   NO

The county court clerk of Grant County shall within five days from the entering of this order give to the Sheriff of Grant County, Kentucky, a certified copy of this order, and it shall be the duty of the said Sheriff to have same published in The Grant County News, a newspaper of general circulation in Grant County, Kentucky, for at least two weeks (14 days) before the election and in all issues of said paper during said period up until the election, and in at least two issues thereof, and also to advertise same by written or printed hand bills posted at not less than five (5) conspicuous places in each of the voting precincts of said County for at least two weeks (14 days) before said election; and it shall be the further duty of the Sheriff to report in writing to the County Court that said notices have been duly published and posted.

The said election, including the canvass and counting of the ballots, shall be held in accordance with the provisions of the general election laws of the State of Kentucky and the said laws, including penalties for violations, shall apply to the said election excepting where the said laws are inconsistent with Chapter 242 of House Bill No. 271 of the Acts of 1942 of the General Assembly of Kentucky, regular session, and approved March 5, 1942, and effective as of October 1, 1942.

The costs of the election shall be borne by Grant County. The County Court Clerk of Grant County will also send a certified copy of this order to each of the Election Commissioners of Grant County, Kentucky.

(Signed) CHAS. A. PETTIT,
Judge Grant County Court, Kentucky.

STATE OF KENTUCKY }
GRANT COUNTY } SCT.

I, Lawson Taylor, Clerk of the County Court for the County and State aforesaid, do certify that the foregoing is a true, correct and complete copy of the aforesaid petition as recorded in Grant County Court Order Book X, pages 72 and 73 of the Grant County Court records, Williamstown, Kentucky.

Witness my hand this the 15th day of October, 1942.

LAWSON TAYLOR, CLERK.
BY JUNE W. TAYLOR, D. C.

(Signed) LEWIS HENDERSON,
Sheriff Grant County, Ky.

[23]

[23]Circa November 1942. *Grant County News.*

500 DIE IN COCOANUT GROVE NIGHT CLUB AT BOSTON.

Scene Of Wholesale Death

Operators of the Boston Cocoanut Grove Night Club violated the law forbidding the hiring of youths under eighteen years of age; also the law providing for a lock that would permit pressure from the inside to open a safety door, also the law forbidding the use of inflammable decorations, and forbidding intoxication. As a consequence, more than 500 persons are dead today and hundreds more are fighting for their lives in the hospitals of Boston.

The crowd that had met to celebrate a football game with DRINK and song, many of whom were soldiers in uniform, or college boys and girls, died like sheep in the slaughter pen, because—

THE WHISKEY BUSINESS IS ALWAYS AN OUTLAW.

These DIVES don't care for the boys and girls, their SAFETY, or their CHARACTER—all they want is MONEY.

This fire was started by a boy employee, 16 years of age, who under the law, could not have been employed or present.

The safety door was out of order and LOCKED so that it would not swing out.

The decorations were so inflammable that the flames RACED entirely around the hall in just an instant.

The patrons were so BEFUDDLED that they forgot their manhood and became screaming, clawing beasts.

How much TAXES will it take to PAY for these LIVES

IF YOUR BOY OR GIRL HAD BEEN IN THIS NIGHT CLUB, HOW WOULD YOU VOTE ON DECEMBER 12?

VOTE "YES" AND SAVE PROPERTY, LIVES AND SOULS.

Money or Morals, Which Will You Choose?

What Shall it Profit a County to Have all its Taxes Paid and Lose the Souls of its People?

Christ said: "Man does not live by bread alone." Counties cannot live on money alone.

An Old Testament prophet warns: "Woe to him that buildeth a town with blood and a city with iniquity." (Habakkuk 2:12). Liquor money is BLOOD money and the price of human SOULS.

Solomon, the wisest man who ever lived, said: "He that loveth silver shall not be satisfied with silver—but those riches shall perish by evil travail." (Ecclesiastes 5:10, 14).

Liquor interests have staked their all on their right to bribe civilization with a little tax money for the privilege of exploiting the souls of men, women and youth. They claim that civilization and prosperity was born with their aid and will die without them.

Who gets the REAL BENEFIT, THE TAXPAYER OR THE LIQUOR DEALER? They took over $146,000.00 out of this county last year. They got $14.77 for every man, woman and child in the county. THEY ARE INTERESTED IN THIS PROFIT ALONE.

Who pays the insurance losses in accidents? Who pays the hospital bills? Who pays for the jails and penitentiary? Who pays for the keeping of mentally deranged and insane inebriates? Who takes care of the beggars reduced to poverty by liquor? Or the families of drunken paupers? Who pays for the divorces and broken homes, for the lost souls and ruined lives?

WHICH DO YOU THINK CONTRIBUTES MORE TO YOUR COUNTY AND ITS GROWTH . . . . YOUR CHURCHES AND THEIR LEADERS, OR THE SALOONS AND THEIR CRIMES?

Will you SELL SOULS and the GOOD NAME of your Community for a LITTLE FILTHY LUCRE which will NOT keep the prisoners in JAIL? You must choose—MONEY or MORALS?

24

---

[24]Circa November 1942. *Grant County News.*

Grant County Deserves The Best
. . . And Is Getting It!

Local Option Mass ∵ Meetings ∵

DECEMBER 6-11, 1942

SPEAKERS OF NATIONAL REPUTATION

EACH NIGHT AT 7:30

DECEMBER 6TH— (Sunday)	WILLIAMSTOWN CHRISTIAN CHURCH Speaker—Dr. Ira M. Hargett
	JONESVILLE BAPTIST CHURCH Speaker—Hon. Walter J. Hoshall
DECEMBER 7TH— (Monday)	DRY RIDGE BAPTIST CHURCH Speaker—Dr. Ira M. Hargett
	MASON BAPTIST CHURCH Speaker—Hon. Walter J. Hoshall
DECEMBER 8TH— (Tuesday)	CRITTENDEN HIGH SCHOOL Speaker—Dr. Ira M. Hargett
	STEWARTSVILLE BAPTIST CHURCH Speaker—Hon. Walter J. Hoshall
DECEMBER 9TH— (Wednesday)	CORINTH HIGH SCHOOL Speaker—Dr. Ira M. Hargett
	VINE RUN BAPTIST CHURCH Speaker—Hon. Walter J. Hoshall
DECEMBER 10TH— (Thursday)	LAWRENCEVILLE BAPTIST CHURCH Speaker—Dr. L. C. Ray
	MT. PLEASANT CHRISTIAN CHURCH Speaker—Hon. Walter J. Hoshall
DECEMBER 11TH— (Friday)	**Prayer Meetings in All Churches in County**
	Combined Prayer Service WILLIAMSTOWN BAPTIST CHURCH Leader—Dr. L. C. Ray
	Combined Prayer Service DRY RIDGE CHRISTIAN CHURCH Leader—Hon. Walter L. Hoshall

Attend The Mass Meeting Closest To You.

Grant County Local Option Committee

25

[25] Circa November 1942. *Grant County News.*

NOTICE!

TOBACCO GROWERS

You May Be Next!

YOUR BIGGEST SOURCE OF INCOME

MAY BE TAKEN AWAY FROM YOU.

The Drys and Professional Prohibitionists who are Conducting the local option election in Grant County to prohibit the sale of Alcoholic Beverages are also trying to take Bread and Butter from You and Your Family by prohibiting the sale of tobacco . . . . .

Read what the Women's Christian Temperance Union and organizations representing the Anti-Saloon League Say in their Booklet which they are circulating throughout the country in their crusade TO STOP THE SALE OF TOBACCO.

The following excerpts are from "Tobacco, Can It Be Defended?" - - - circulated by the Women's Christian Temperance Union, Evanston, Ill.

Page 7: "From a physical, moral and spiritual standpoint, tobacco is the worst enemy of humanity, I make no exception to that. Alcohol is a terrible curse to humanity, but tobacco is more subtle in its influence upon the body."

Page 23: "In no instance is the sin of the father more strikingly visited upon his children than the sin of tobacco smoking."

Page 18: "A baby born of a cigarette smoking mother is sick. It is poisoned and may die within two weeks of birth . . . Sixty per cent of all babies born of mothers who are habitual cigarette smokers die before they are two years old."

Page 25: "Few more revolting crimes can be charged to a parent than the murder of his child. As a result of indulgence in tobacco by parents, thousands of children die prematurely because their progenitors have been conscious sinners or unconscious, and thousands more are compelled to drag out puny existence for the same reason."

Important Notice

These statements Are TRUE— Let the poor misguided Drys DENY them!

These are the Dry's own Statements

FROM "TOBACCO, TOMBSTONES AND PROFITS": "I believe tobacco shortens more lives and kills more people than alcohol ever did, not because tobacco is more deadly, but because it is more widely used than whiskey.

HERE ARE THE FACTS:

The Statiscal Abstract of the United States for 1941 shows that the increase in Tobacco consumption was 6.05 pounds per capita in 1934 to 6.50 pounds per capita in 1939. The Statiscal Abstract of the United States for 1941 shows that the death rates per 1,000 births for infants under one year of age were:

1920—85.8	1930—64.6	1938—51.0
1925—71.7	1935—55.7	1939—48.0

Death rate on infant mortality decreased from 85.8 per 1,000 births in 1920 to 48.0 per 1,000 in 1939. This represents a decrease of over fifty per cent in the death rate on infant mortality.

Important Notice

The Drys would stop the SALE of all cigarettes, cigars, and tobaccos!

What would this do to tobacco growers?

Go to the Polls, Saturday, Dec. 12

and VOTE NO

Register NOW - - - VOTE NO

SIGNED BY,

HAROLD BREWER, Dry Ridge
W. M. OSBORNE, Dry Ridge, R1
W. A. SIMPSON, Crittenden
S. L. McCOY, Dry Ridge
J. A. REDNOWER, Corinth
D. W. ROBINSON, Corinth
HOWARD BREWER, Dry Ridge
O. O'BANION, Mason

The Largest Tobacco Growers & Land Owners in Grant County

Remember Prohibition - - - Don't Let It Happen Again!

26

[26]Circa November 1942. *Grant County News.*

Answer these questions, Yes or No . .
Then Make Up Your Own Mind

1: Do people stop using alcoholic beverages if their county votes dry? ☐ Yes. ☐ No.

2: Would liquor be illegally sold by bootleggers and consumed in these counties? ☐ Yes. ☐ No.

3: Is illegal sale of beer or liquor, by bootleggers, better than legal sale by decent, regulated dealers? ☐ Yes. ☐ No.

4: Has Prohibition ever been a success, either locally or nationally? ☐ Yes. ☐ No.

5: Since national Prohibition failed dismally—with the federal government behind it—is it possible to *enforce* local prohibition today when alcoholic beverages are so easily transported? ☐ Yes. ☐ No.

6: Bootleggers pay no taxes; futile enforcement costs money. Can we afford to substitute this loss for legal beer that pays its way in taxes? ☐ Yes. ☐ No.

7: Isn't it better to control the sale of alcoholic beverages in legally operated places which can be inspected at any time, as against bootleg places which cannot be inspected legally without a search warrant based on sworn evidence of law violations? ☐ Yes. ☐ No.

KENTUCKY  **COMMITTEE**

BREWING INDUSTRY FOUNDATION

HARRY D. FRANCE, State Director **1182 STARKS BLDG., LOUISVILLE, KY.**

[27]

[27] Circa November 1942. *Grant County News.*

Let's Vote Liquor Out

Vote Dry Of Grant County, Saturday December 12 **Vote "Yes"**

Liquor Revenue and Old Age Pensions

Again the wets have sought to scare the old-age recipients into voting wet by saying that they may lose their old-age assistance if the revenue from liquor is cut off. Read what Dr. W. A. Frost, Dept. of Welfare, Frankfort, says in a letter dated Dec. 2, 1942. (He is a member of the Board of Controls of the Anti Saloon League.)

"For anyone to state that revenue from liquor is used specifically for old-age assistance is a misrepresentation of the facts, either from a lack of information or wilfully.

"It is little less than criminal for anyone to disturb these aged and dependent people by threatening their mere existence if they do not vote the way they are told to vote, and for this reason I have determined if at all possible that they shall not be [illegible] and harassed by mercenary people.

"Sincerely yours,
"Signed: W. A. FROST, Commissioner
"Department of Welfare."

[illegible]

The Tobacco Issue
TWO FACED AND SLY

The liquor people try to borrow respectability from the tobacco growers of Grant County.

Because tobacco DOES NOT enslave and make beasts of men VOTE AGAINST WHISKEY.

Because tobacco DOES NOT break up homes and debauch our children VOTE AGAINST WHISKEY.

Because tobacco DOES NOT corrupt our politics and defeat the processes of justice VOTE AGAINST WHISKEY.

Grant County voters are too shrewd to be deceived by a smoke screen. There is no defense for whiskey. THE LIQUOR CROWD HAS TO RAISE A FALSE FACE TO COVER THE SKULL AND CROSS BONES.

TO VOTE DRY—VOTE "YES"
AT LOCAL OPTION ELECTION DEC. 12TH

[illegible] GRANT COUNTY IS CALLED [illegible] VOTE "YES" DECEMBER 12TH.

THE SALOON BUNCH
HIDING THEIR SLIMY BUSINESS BEHIND THE FOLDS OF THE FLAG

How the liquor crowd shout their so-called patriotism and love for our boys in service! THEY SAY that an unfair and sinister advantage is being taken of the boys in service by holding a Local Option Election while they are absent. We believe this is an UNFAIR and UNWARRANTED REFLECTION upon the youth of Grant County. Acting upon this belief, we interviewed the following parents and we give herewith their signed statement. READ IT:

We, the following Grant County parents, resent the insinuation in the statements of the booze crowd that our sons, who have gone out to serve under the flag of their country are in favor of the sale and use of intoxicating liquors and would so vote in the coming election. We hereby state that such a statement is unfair and untrue. We feel that we know our sons better than anyone else and that if they were at home they would vote dry, as we [illegible].

Mr. and Mrs. A. N. Skinner	Mr. and Mrs. A. W. Glasgow
Mr. and Mrs. Roscoe Jump	Rev. and Mrs. J. W. Gilbert
Mr. and Mrs. J. M. Ackman	Mr. and Mrs. E. M. Lawrence
Mr. and Mrs. Gus Delaney	Mr. and Mrs. H. V. Price
Mr. and Mrs. H. B. Caldwell	Mr. and Mrs. Howard Colvin

Mr. and Mrs. Ruben Taylor

Only these couples were interviewed. They signed [illegible] many other signatures [illegible] REMEMBER 60 COUNTIES IN KENTUCKY VOTED [illegible]

CITIZENS OF GRANT COUNTY ARE NOT FOOLED
THE LIQUOR BUSINESS DOES NOT PAY ITS OWN DAMAGE

THE BOOTLEGGER

DURING PROHIBITION 2500 FEDERAL AGENTS were the greatest number employed to enforce the law against bootlegging.

NOW, with legalized booze the Federal Government has MORE THAN 4500 AGENTS to raid moonshine stills and run down bootleggers and [illegible] as [illegible].

The Federal Alcohol Tax Unit Reports for the fiscal year ending June 30, 1942, 11,569 moonshine stills captured, 185,747 gallons of spirits, 5,451,993 gallons of mash, and 20,174 bootleggers and moonshiners arrested. BOOTLEGGERS ARE EVERYWHERE—the smoke screen of legal liquor hides them. The Liberty Magazine stated recently: "We have the worst system of bootlegging ever known." LET'S GET RID OF THEM.

ANOTHER PLEA FOR OUR BOYS

Hear the words of a personal letter from an Adjutant of the Army Air Corps:

"Of all the boys that have been in trouble, not one has been sober. Surely people will see the light soon and get rid of such an evil influence. Incidentally, there is a nice term awaiting anyone who brings liquor on the Post. A man can't be depended on who drinks. THE FELLOWS REALLY ADMIT THAT THEY WOULD BE BETTER OFF WITHOUT IT. I wish I could be in Grant County the 12th to tell all the MOTHERS, DADS and EVERYONE else TO HELP OUR BOYS BY DRIVING IT AWAY FROM ONE SMALL AREA—the best one I know.

"As Ever,
"Signed: A. B. COLVIN."

The Revenue Question

Grant County has to waste $146,370.79 in debauchery each year in order to procure a total tax of $16,191.80 which goes to Frankfort to be divided between 120 counties, of which amount Grant County gets ONLY one one-hundred-twentieth [illegible] or $134.93.

REVENUE IN WILLIAMSTOWN

Williamstown, in order to collect some $1,200 in license taxes has to EXPOSE ITS CHILDREN to more than half of the licensed saloons in the county and BRAND ITSELF as the center of DRUNKS, SLOT MACHINES, GAMBLERS and the attendant vices that are not mention in polite society.

The city of Williamstown collects the saloon taxes for ITSELF, and when the "good" customers are arrested for being drunk and disorderly, they lay their fines out in jail AT THE EXPENSE OF THE TAXPAYERS OF GRANT COUNTY.

TO THE PEOPLE OF GRANT COUNTY:

I have never before seen in any form such a cheap method of advertising as has been used by a group of citizens of our county.

I refer you to a statement of Secretary of State [illegible] [illegible] upon receipt of a note handed him by Japan's [illegible] [illegible] I have never seen a document that was more [illegible] with [illegible] falsehoods and distortions. It would not have surprised me to see such an advertisement signed by the overseers of the liquor interests [illegible] of the names which were signed to the article referred to above I can see no incentive for that particular group of citizens to try to [illegible] the people of our county [illegible] propaganda.

"In a second issue of the News, one of our citizens made a statement to this effect: 'It is funny that we have to let our boys of the Armed Forces [illegible] that we cannot trust them to stop drinking at [illegible].' THIS MATTER IS NOT FUNNY at all, but it is PATHETIC and AN APPALLING FACT that a large number of our boys [illegible] their [illegible] a soldier's over-indulgence is in many cases, the Guard House, and in some occasions, death. We now have a full account of our [illegible] at Pearl Harbor. If this is not a [illegible] I shudder to think WHAT WOULD HAVE TO HAPPEN TO WAKE US UP?

"A few weeks ago it was necessary for me to cause an individual to be [illegible] highly intoxicated, and had no control of his emotions. I understand that he was given a large fine and paid it by BOARDING IT OUT AT OUR EXPENSE. I wonder if the tax receipts from the liquor he bought and consumed was sufficient to pay his board and room rent. This does not mention the damage he caused prior to his arrest.

"I am one of the 'poor misguided drys' and I am doubting the 'true statements' of the 'wets.' The drys of Grant County have in mind THE BEST INTERESTS of our people and certainly have no intention of taking bread and butter away from our children. I say again that the notice to tobacco growers, along with its threats, will have no effect on the Local Option Election to be held Dec. 12, 1942. (These statements should be erased from our minds as highly irrelevant.)

"Yours for some careful and deliberate thinking.
"FRANK W. COLLINS."

IF YOU VOTE FOR LIQUOR— WHO IS GOING TO DRINK IT?

The liquor traffic MUST have ONE OUT OF EVERY THREE BOYS AND GIRLS as NEW drinkers EVERY year to take the place of those dying from alcoholism. Some men claim they do not drink but will vote for liquor "so the other fellow can have it." WHO IS THIS OTHER FELLOW, is it their son—their daughter—the man who marries their daughter—the hired help— their bus drivers— the friend who is driving the car in which they were riding? Remember friends, if you vote to keep liquor in Grant county SOMEBODY MUST DRINK IT if the liquor dealers and brewers continue to make money. If you MUST vote for liquor WHY NOT BE FAIR AND DRINK IT YOURSELF?

Give Our Boys and Girls A Chance - - - Vote Liquor Out!

Commissioner of Revenue, Ward J. Oates, stated at Frankfort on Friday, Dec. 4th, that the sale of whiskey and beer to minors in Kentucky has reached serious proportions as a study of 380 charges preferred against whiskey and beer licenses showed the sale to minors leading all other offenses. But what does the liquor crowd care so long as they get their blood money! Let's vote them Out! . . . . . If you love Grant County and are proud of her independent freedom, VOTE OUT THE BUSINESS that is trying to be the political boss of your native county so that it can DEBAUCH, ROB and STEAL without fear.

The WHISKEY BUSINESS is the only business in Grant County that can afford to SPEND MONEY to corrupt a county election in order t oget an underhold. THE WHISKEY BUSINESS IS ALWAYS AN OUTLAW.—

NOW IS YOUR CHANCE TO BANISH LIQUOR FROM GRANT COUNTY, GO TO THE POLLS DEC. 12 AND VOTE "YES".

28

[28]Circa November 1942. *Grant County News.*

Remember Prohibition - - Don't Let It Happen Again!

Nailing The Dry Lies to The Cross of Truth

The Drys, in their ad in The Grant County News, Friday, November 27th, said: GRANT COUNTY ONLY RECEIVES TWO PENNIES FOR EACH MAN, WOMAN AND CHILD FROM THE ALCOHOLIC BEVERAGE INDUSTRY . . . . These weeping and wailing brothers, who devote their time to promoting Local Option Elections, prevert the truth to suit their own ends. These poor misguided Drys, who weep tears over the boys and girls and women who are drinking themselves to ruin . . . . they promise that their Local Option and Prohibition schemes will stop drinking, compel temperance, and eradicate crime? Are they philanthropists, actuated by a love of humanity, giving their time freely to the reformation of the human race? The weeping and wailing Drys and their brothers and sisters of the Anti-Saloon League and the W.C.T.U. are **INTERESTED IN CASH AND POWER ONLY.** Take that away from them and see how quickly they lose interest in Local Option and Prohibition.

Let's Look At The Record And See What The Real Truths And The Actual Facts Really Are!

THESE FIGURES ARE FROM THE UNITED STATES COLLECTOR OF INTERNAL REVENUE, WASHINGTON, D.C. WHY DON'T THE DRYS QUOTE THESE FIGURES? . . THEY DON'T WANT THE TRUTH! — HERE ARE THE COLD FIGURES, AND THEY CANNOT BE DISPUTED.

The Records of The United States Collector of Internal Revenue Show That: SINCE THE RETURN OF REPEAL, GRANT COUNTY HAS PAID TO THE STATE AND FEDERAL GOVERNMENT THE AMAZING SUM OF $3,912,928.12. YES, LET'S REPEAT THIS AMOUNT, $3,912,928.12. DOES THIS ANSWER THE DRYS' SICKLY WAIL? WOULD BOOTLEGGERS, GANGSTERS, CRIMINALS, RACKETEERS AND PROHIBITIONISTS PAY THIS?

Figure out how many Fighting Planes, Machine Guns, Tanks and other War Equipment this has bought to help defeat the Axis! This amounts to $21.46 every month for EVERY MAN, WOMAN AND CHILD IN GRANT COUNTY WOULD HAVE TO PAY IN TAXES TO THE FEDERAL AND STATE GOVERNMENT IF PROHIBITION WAS IN EFFECT.—HOW WOULD THE PROHIBITIONISTS TAKE CARE OF THIS REVENUE?—During the year of 1941-42 Grant County RECEIVED from the GENERAL FUND of The State of Kentucky $9,735.09 TOWARD THE SCHOOL FUND. Will the DRYS pay this amount if Grant County votes in favor of local option? Will THESE weeping and wailing brothers and sisters PAY THIS INCREASE IN TAXES FOR YOU TAXPAYERS? ASK YOUR DRY LEADERS TO ANSWER THIS.

Here Is Grant County's Record During Prohibition, Taken From The Judgment Book in the County Judge's Office:

There were 549 convicitions in Grant County DURING PROHIBITION for drunken driving, drunks, possession of moonshine liquor, transportation of intoxicating liquor and possession of moonshine stills. Approximately 85 percent of these were committed to the county jail and served time at the EXPENSE of the TAXPAYERS OF GRANT COUNTY.— DO YOU WANT HISTORY TO REPEAT ITSELF?

GO TO THE POLLS SATURDAY AND VOTE 'NO'

A Vote "No" means a vote for Legal Control, and Against Control by Bootleggers, Criminals, Gangsters and Hoodlums.

Remember Prohibition - - Don't Let It Happen Again!

[29]

[29] Circa November 1942. *Grant County News.*

SOLDIERS, SAILORS, MARINES OF BOTH WORLD WARS

In the dark days of World War No. 1 when you brave defenders of America were fighting your hearts out in France to preserve democracy, free speech, freedom of religion and unrestricted voting the prohibition forces at home took advantage of your absence, disfranchised you and voted national prohibition.

National prohibition, installed behind your backs, by the stay-at-homers, proved a failure and a national blunder and one of the first steps to end the depression was to enact repeal and restore control, and undo the wrong that had been done you.

A local option election was held in Grant county in 1937 when all of you soldiers, sailors and marines of both wars were here at home with us. At that time Grant county rejected prohibition and local option.

Now, on December 12th, 1942, while you brave defenders of America are again on the foreign battlefields and in the distant army camps, the prohibition forces of Grant county are again taking advantage of your absence, and disfranchising you by holding a local option election in your home county at a time when you cannot vote.

It is the duty of the Grant county heroes of World War No. 1 to see that the prohibition forces of this county are not successful in taking advantage of the Grant county heroes of World War No. 2. LEAVE GRANT COUNTY LIKE IT IS UNTIL THE BOYS RETURN. It's not fair to change it while they are AWAY. BE A 100 PERCENT AMERICAN!

VOTE NO DEC. 12

Register Properly Before December 12th

QUOTING—

WALTER WINCHELL [illegible]

[illegible]

. . . . .

FREDERICK [illegible] COLLINS [illegible] LIBERTY MAGAZINE of June 27, 1942:

"After several months of [illegible] surrounding military camps, in state capitals, and especially in Washington where the [illegible] lobby flourishes as never before—I am convinced that Prohibition is already with us, and presently, if we don't watch out, it will be on us. At a time when we are [illegible] all to a war for the four freedoms—freedom from fear, freedom from want, freedom of speech, and freedom of worship—a small but alert and [illegible] well heeled minority is again planning to rob us of the greatest freedom of all, the freedom of choice."

VOTE "NO" For Yourself and for the Boys in the Service

AND THE DRYS WOULD REPEAT

[illegible] Raymond Clapper [illegible] the African desert. "The canteen serves cold American beer and hot American hamburgers and hot dogs with catchup and raw onion. The men gang around, and that one hour brings [illegible] These are the things that [illegible] of the men." The whole matter is summed up in a [illegible] Secretary of War Stimson: "This policy has caused a degree of temperance among Army personnel which is not [illegible] communities now, nor was as high a degree of temperance attained either in or out of the Army during the days of national Prohibition. Under this policy, military personnel are encouraged to remain on the reservation and enjoy refreshments under conditions conducive of temperance."

The statements are put on record because the prohibitionists are again urging laws which will deny to soldiers the privileges of ordinary civilians. [illegible] How the scheme worked the country over, when tried before, need not be recalled. How it worked in the Army appears in the report of Surgeon General Magee in 1941. "An Army graph for the period 1919-1940 shows that the last upsurge of alcoholism in the Army was exactly coincidental with the prohibition period between 1920 and 1932, and that there has been a constant and gratifying decline in alcoholism and a corresponding increase in moderation since beer was legalized in 1933. From a low of 2.5 per 1,000 men in 1919, the hospitalization rate jumped to 11.5 in 1922 and was over 6 per 1,000 in every year of the dry era. It was 2.7 in 1940."

VOTE "NO"

WAR BONDS

Mr. and Mrs. Taxpayer, these are FACTS:

The banner month for Grant County in War Bond sales was September. Did you KNOW that sixty percent of THESE BONDS were BOUGHT by MEMBERS OF THE GRANT COUNTY BEER DEALERS AND THEIR FAMILIES.

If you vote "YES" Dec. 12th you will help the Japs.

If you vote "NO" Dec. 12th you will HELP OUR BOYS, WHEREVER THEY MAY BE.

VOTE "NO"

[illegible] IS POPULAR AMONG OUR FIGHTING MEN ABROAD

[illegible]

. . . . .

RAYMOND CLAPPER [illegible]

. . . . .

[illegible]

PATRIOTISM

[illegible] liberty and freedom. The drys are at their old trick again. We do not want these boys to find that THESE RIGHTS have been taken away from them at home while they are FIGHTING for you and us abroad. [illegible]

MR. and MRS. TAXPAYER [illegible] WHO WILL PROFIT MORE, THE LAWYERS OR YOU? STOP AND THINK.

VOTE "NO"

REMEMBER DECEMBER 7TH, 1941

THE JAPS STABBED OUR BOYS IN THE BACK AT PEARL HARBOR. LET'S NOT STAB THEM THE SECOND TIME. GO TO THE POLLS DEC. 12TH AND VOTE "NO."

VOTE "NO"

VOTE FOR THE RIGHTS OF THE BOYS—VOTE NO

[illegible] THE RIGHTS OF THE BOYS away who are FIGHTING FOR FREEDOM and LIBERTY and their rights to their own opinion on reform matters, would you. Let us be 100 PERCENT AMERICANS WHILE THEY ARE FIGHTING OUR BATTLES FOR US.

VOTE "NO"

MR. AND MRS. TAXPAYER

Do you know why Lawyers are always interested in Local Option Elections [illegible] to bring back Racketeers, Bootleggers, Moonshiners and Hoodlums.

That should be easy, they get enormous fees to defend them in all their rackets. While YOUR BOY may drink cold water that the Axis have fixed for him in a scorching desert in Africa. Your Government is shipping to your boy, Beer in cans today, insuring him of something pure to drink.

Mr. and Mrs. Taxpayer, you NOT ONLY help YOURSELF when you VOTE NO December 12th, you HELP THE BOY AND GIRL, who may give his or her life for YOU today.

VOTE "NO"

War Mothers and Fathers

Will you stand for a sneak attack by the professional dry forces, Saturday Dec. 12--that is equal in principals, to the sneak attack by the Japs on Pearl Harbor, Dec. 7, 1941? Go to the polls and vote-"NO" Dec. 12th to offset this sneak attact. Your boy would be proud to know that you were taking his part while he gives all for all of us on the battle field of honor.

VOTE NO

30

[30] Circa November 1942. *Grant County News.*

NOTICE

TO VOTERS

We, the undersigned, in SERVICE FOR OUR COUNTRY respectfully ask you to vote "NO" on December 12, 1942 and let US have a VOICE in our HOME COUNTY as well as abroad WHEN WE RETURN, IF EVER.

Signed,

Wilbur Clark Doane
Logan J. Mullikin
Harry Dunaway
Porter Kinman
Marvin Harrison
Arnold Brewer
Albert Clemons
Herbert R. Beach
Pvt. John R. Evans
Cpl. Henry C. Crowe
Ralph Cummins
George Fortner
Hubert Breeden
Hobart Dailey
Jesse R. Richerson
Charles R. A. McGee,
M O M M I C Co. 20
Barracks 13-W
New Orleans, Louisiana.
Pfc. Alford C. Stamper,
Co. E. 40th A. R.
N. Camp Polk, Louisiana.

[31]

[31] Circa November 1942. *Grant County News.*

LIQUOR IS A CURSE!

To The Citizens and Boys and Girls of Grant County

LET'S VOTE IT OUT!

VOTE DRY

VOTE DRY

SAMPLE BALLOT

For Local Option Election, Dec. 12, 1942

Are you in favor of adopting Prohibition in Grant County, Kentucky?

YES ☒

NO ☐

The Liquor Dealers Say:

That we lose state and county revenue when Grant County votes dry December 12th.

The Facts Are:

To Vote Dry--Vote Yes

AT LOCAL OPTION ELECTION DEC. 12TH

GRANT COUNTY IS CALLING A HALT

VOTE YES DEC. 12

Let's Have The Whole Truth About Liquor!

68 Counties Dry!

And Every County Satisfied

Let's Vote Grant Dry

The Liquor Dealers Say:

Local Option Does Not Work

THE FACTS ARE - -

THE LIQUOR DEALERS SAY - - -

It's not a question of "Wet or Dry" - It's Legal or Illegal Liquor.

WHAT ARE THEY CRYING ABOUT?

THE LIQUOR DEALERS SAY:

LET THE DEALERS READ THE FOLLOWING AND WEEP

Prohibition Stopped Liquor Advertising

LEGAL LIQUOR IS NOW ADVERTISED AND UNDER OUR NOSE EVERYWHERE

Did you have all this during Prohibition? DID YOU?

Prohibition Decreased Drunkeness 70 Pct.

SINCE REPEAL GENERAL DRUNKENNESS HAS INCREASED 300 PERCENT according to the Federal Bureau of Investigation. WERE CHILDREN AND YOUNG PEOPLE UNDER AGE. MOST PEOPLE DRINK BECAUSE IT IS HANDY. GIVE THE UNFORTUNATES IN THIS COUNTY A CHANCE TO CLEAN-UP. DON'T KEEP LIQUOR UNDER THEIR NOSE EVERYWHERE THEY GO.

Prohibition Decreased Crime 54 Pct.

SINCE LEGAL LIQUOR RETURNED UNDER REPEAL general crime has increased, according to "G-man" J. Edgar Hoover. He further stated in 1937 that the past three years have been the most terrible in the criminal history of America. J. M. Walter, director of the division of correction of the State Welfare Department at Frankfort, declared recently that "Unless something is done, crime is going to bankrupt the State." In wet Floyd County the grand jury declared that murder was on the increase in that county due to the increased sale of liquor at roadhouses. We have 1,000 more men in Kentucky prisons than we had in 1935.

Not By My Vote!

NOT BY MY VOTE

NOT BY MY VOTE

NOT BY MY VOTE

NOT BY MY VOTE

NOT BY MY VOTE

NOT BY MY VOTE

NOT BY MY VOTE

NOT BY MY VOTE

Let's Make Grant County A Clean Place to Live In!

THE LIQUOR DEALERS SAY:

THE ONLY LIQUOR MONEY THAT REMAINS IN this county NOW is what goes in the pockets of the dealers.

TO VOTE DRY - - VOTE YES

THE LIQUOR DEALERS SAY:

THAT WHEN GRANT COUNTY VOTES DRY, OLD AGE PENSIONS AND OUR SCHOOLS WILL SUFFER.

THIS IS WRONG. Hon. A. Y. Lloyd, State Director of Public Assistance, declares that "such a statement is false." And he ought to know. Old age pensions and our schools receive support from the state's general fund. Liquor revenue is NOT earmarked for these agencies. BOTH WILL CONTINUE TO RECEIVE THEIR USUAL SUPPORT. As a matter of fact Grant County, WET OR DRY, will continue to receive her share of the over nine million dollars in liquor revenue coming from the distilleries, breweries, wholesalers and 5,000 beer and liquor saloons over the state. THIS COUNTY'S ONLY LOSS in state revenue amounts to LESS THAN TWO CENTS PER PERSON.

TO VOTE DRY -- VOTE YES

GRANT COUNTY LOCAL OPTION COMMITTEE

THE LIQUOR DEALERS SAY:

VOTE YES DEC. 12 AND REMOVE THIS SMOKE SCREEN.

CLEAN UP THESE DEPLORABLE CONDITIONS! DRIVE THESE UNDESIRABLE AND DANGEROUS CRIMINALS OUT IN THE OPEN WHERE THEY MAY BE DETECTED AND CAPTURED.

TO VOTE DRY - - VOTE YES

The Voters Have Had All They Wanted of So-Called "Regulated Liquor." They Are Going To The Polls Saturday, Dec. 12th, and Outlaw All Liquor!

32

[32]Circa November 1942. *Grant County News.*

VOTE DRY! VOTE YES!

SAMPLE BALLOT
For Local Option Election, Dec. 12, 1942
Are you in favor of adopting Prohibition in Grant County, Kentucky? YES ☒ NO ☐

Be sure to register at the County Clerk's office.

TO VOTE DRY VOTE "YES" DEC. 12TH
Liquor stores, beer joints and road houses are far worse than the old saloon. The people grew sick and tired of the old saloon—they are sick of the present set-up. GRANT COUNTY IS CALLING A HALT! ...... VOTE "YES".

Grant County Local Option Committee

33

Asbury Quartette At Local Option Meet, Sunday Nite

The Asbury College Quartette, famed in America and popular in foreign lands, will render several selections at the Local Option Mass Meeting at the Christian Church, Sunday evening, December 6th at 7:30 o'clock. The public is invited to be present.[34]

Election On Local Option Saturday

Wets And Drys To Fight It Out At The Polls Saturday, Dec. 12. Both Sides Optimistic.

Whether or not whiskey and beer will continue to be sold in Grant County will be decided at the polls Saturday, Dec. 12th. Both sides, the wets and the drys, are optimistic over the outcome. Advertising for and against local option appears in this issue of The Grant County News. The pages of advertising are informative, read them and decide which way you intend to vote Saturday. It is the right and the duty of every citizen of voting age to cast his vote in all elections.

There has apparently been little discussion in regard to the issue, that is, in so far as News representatives have learned. However, a surprising number of voters may go to the polls.[35]

Drys Carry Grant County By A 212 Majority Vote

Grant County went dry last Saturday by a majority of 212. The total vote cast was 1,516 dry to 1,304 wet, a total of 2,820. There were very few spoiled ballots. The votes cast represents approximately 50 per cent. of the total vote of the county, and was fairly heavy considering the fact that the weather was very disagreeable. A light snow fell throughout the day and the roads became slick and dangerous for traffic toward evening.

No doubt the vote would have been much heavier had the weather been better. Also it must be taken into consideration that more than 400 Grant County voters are serving their country in the armed service; also that many tobacco farmers were busy stripping their tobacco and did not take time off to go to the polls. The drys are highly pleased, the wets are thoroughly disgusted with the result.

Leading workers for the wet movement have stated to The News that they would file an injunction aiming to set aside the election. On just

[33] Circa November 1942. *Grant County News.*
[34] 4 December 1942. *Grant County News.* Author Unknown.
[35] 11 December 1942. *Grant County News.* Author Unknown.

what grounds, The News is not informed. Such an injunction might postpone matters for a while, even if it does nothing else. If there is no postponement the county will be dry within 60 days from date of the election.[36]

Official Vote Of Local Option, Held Dec. 12th

Precinct	Yes	No
West Williamstown	155	164
E. Williamstown No. 1	100	100
E. Williamstown No. 2	121	118
East Dry Ridge	113	77
West Dry Ridge	136	174
Sherman	46	56
Crittenden	130	116
Mt. Zion	79	30
Flat Creek	64	46
Zion Station	13	20
Jonesville	94	50
Downingsville	22	38
Holbrook	31	32
Stewartsville	50	37
Cross Roads	55	25
Keefer	35	43
Mason	92	39
Corinth	121	96
Cordova	59	43
Total Vote	1516	1304
"Yes" Majority	212	

WIEDEMANN'S
Draft Beer
The Only Draft Beer In Williamstown

DENT'S
POOL ROOM
1 DOOR SOUTH OF THE NEWS OFFICE

37

Boone Countians To Vote on Wet And Dry Issue

The voters of Boone County will vote on local option Saturday, March 13th. Both Boone County papers, The Walton Advertiser and The Boone County Recorder are carrying full page advertisements for both wets and the drys this week.[38]

Boone Goes Wet Nine To Six

Boone County went wet in last Saturday's local option election, by 9 to 6. Sixteen hundred sixteen voted wet, while 987 voted dry.

The drys carried only four of the 17 precincts in the county, Walton, Belleview, Bullitsville and Burlington No. 1.[39]

Pendleton County Voted Dry By 251

Pendleton County was voted dry Monday in a local option election in which the dry forces were led by Rev. R. S. Moore, pastor of two Pendleton County churches and principal of Simon Kenton High School, Independence.

The vote in the county's 23 precincts was 1,772 dry against 1,521 wet. The county will go dry sixty days from the first day of May, providing certification of the result is not held up thru court action by the wets.

Pendleton is the 79th of Kentucky's 120 counties to be voted dry. A local option was held in 1937 at which time the drys were defeated by a vote of 2,066 to 1,693.[40]

---

[36] 18 December 1942. *Grant County News.* Author Unknown.
[37] 1 January 1943. *Grant County News.*
[38] 5 March 1943. *Grant County News.* Author Unknown.
[39] 12 March 1943. *Grant County News.* Author Unknown.
[40] 14 April 1944. *Grant County News.* Author Unknown.

Beer-Laden Truck Overturns Near Sherman

A truck driven by Donald Nunley, 18, Sadieville, traveling south laden with 250 cases of beer overturned one mile south of Sherman, Saturday afternoon, causing damage estimated at $700 and delaying traffic for several hours. The driver was not injured.

According to Sgt. Buford Wainscott and Patrolman Lawrence Rankin of the State Highway Patrol, the truck was owned by George Hayden, of Corinth. The driver attempted to pass an auto on a curve and caught the front part of the truck on the rear fender of the auto when it was necessary to get back to avoid hitting an on-coming car head-on.

Damage to the truck was placed at $400 and the entire shipment of beer valued at $300 was lost. Glass was strewn over the highway for hundreds of feet. It took four hours to completely clear the roadway Sgt. Wainscott said.[41]

Pendleton County Local Option Election Contested

The local option election held in Pendleton County, April 10th at which time the drys emerged victorious, has been contested according to a petition filed at the Falmouth court house. The contest is based on the date of selecting officers.[42]

Wets Win In Gallatin

Louisville, Ky., Sept. 26 Victory of "wet" forces in the Gallatin county local option election yesterday marked an interruption to the "dry" trend in Kentucky, and was the first local option election to be won by Kentucky wets' in seven contests held so far this year.

Official returns in the Gallatin county election gave the "drys" 615 votes and the "wets" 996.

Kentucky now has 84 counties in which the sale of alcoholic beverages is prohibited by law, the state Anti-Saloon League said.

Ninety-five "dry" precincts are scattered through the 36 remaining counties which have voted to stay "wet" or which have not voted on the question, the league added.

Kentucky's wet-dry map shows that non-prohibition areas are around the metropolitan centers and in the Blue Grass region. Two precincts in Jefferson county are "dry" as are 21 precincts in McCracken county, around Paducah.[43]

Violator Of Local Option Law Fined

J. L. Mitts Fined $800.00 On Charges Of Violating Local Option Law And The Suffering Of Slot Machines

J. L. Mitts was fined $100 each on three indictments for violation of the local option law and sentenced to serve thirty days in jail. He was also fined $500 for suffering five slot machines. Four other indictments against him for violation of the dry law were dismissed, following the fine and sentence on the other charges. He paid the fine and is serving the term, in jail, to which he was sentenced.

Slots Ordered Destroyed

By order of the court, the jailer, Perry Scroggin and the sheriff, Lewis Henderson, are to take the money from the five slot machines which the sheriff confiscated from Mitts and pay it over to the circuit clerk of the court for the use of the state, and they are further ordered to burn or destroy the slot machines and report their action to the court in due time.[44]

[41] 19 May 1944. *Grant County News.* Author Unknown.
[42] 19 May 1944. *Grant County News.* Author Unknown.
[43] 29 September 1944. *Grant County News.* Author Unknown.
[44] 12 October 1945 *Grant County News.* Author Unknown.

Speaking Arranged By Local Option Committee

Walter J. Hoshal, prominent Dry Leader of Kentucky, will speak in the interest of the coming local option election Sunday afternoon at 3:00 o'clock at the Dry Ridge Baptist Church.

An ad announcing the speaking appears on page six of this issue.[45]

Wets Win In Carroll By Narrow Margin

By the small margin of 74 votes, the wet forces of Carroll County won a local option election in the county's fifteen precincts April 8th.

This leaves the number of Kentucky's dry counties at 87, almost three-fourths of her 120.[46]

[45] 12 April 1946. *Grant County News.* Author Unknown.
[46] 12 April 1946. *Grant County News.* Author Unknown.

Who Pays The Liquor Revenue?

The Drinkers and Home Pay The Revenue

It's an old and truthful saying that "the consumer always pays the freight." The liquor outfit love to boast of the revenue they pay. As as matter of fact, liquor revenue is 99 percent based on consumption. Whiskey is made for 50 cents per gallon. Where then does the fabulous price of from $15 to $25 per gallon to the drinker come in? Very easy. Uncle Sam grabs $9.00 per gallon of his share of the boodle, Kentucky gets $1.20 per gallon, the wholesaler gets his take and the retailer is happy because the higher the tax, the more profit he gets. And the retailer is right. The Kentucky Fair Trades Act gives the dealer the right to base his profit on a percent of the cost and the tax. The higher the tax, the more PROFIT. That is why the industry never squawks when the tax is raised on liquor. WHY SHOULD THEY when the CONSUMER PAYS THE TAX? Judge Wm. B. Ardery in passing on this fair trade act at Frankfort, said it meant millions more in profit to the dealers and that liquor had a knife at the public's throat. The DRINKERS PAY THE REVENUE and NOT the liquor industry. YES! Saloons get the money—the drinker contributes the profit and settles for the revenue—the public gets the headache and the TAXPAYERS PAY THE BILL for damages in crime, drunkenness, misery, broken homes and pauperism. ARE WE FOOLISH OR JUST PLAIN CRAZY?

To pay the liquor revenue, drinkers consumed nearly 8 billion dollars worth of liquor for the year ending June 30, 1945, according to the U. S. Department of Commerce. This amounted to $58.00 for every man, woman and child in the nation.

Louisville Loses Money On Liquor Revenue Declared Former Mayor Scholtz

Former Maylor Scholtz in an address before the Legislative Council at Frankfort, December 14, 1937, asked for more revenue from liquor. "Louisville's cost for liquor law enforcement has increased steadily and we are now losing money," the Mayor stated. He added that "Outlays are greater from year to year for the keep of prisoners, the medical treatment and care of dependents of liquor addicts."

THE MAYOR WAS RIGHT. ALL the revenue from liquor did not pay for taking care of the drunks or families put on relief by liquor. So the taxpayers paid the bill. SMART FIGURING, ISN'T IT?

YES! Saloons Get The Money-- The Public The Headache-- And Sucker Taxpayers Settle For The Damage.

THE CONSUMER "PAYS THE FREIGHT"

One fact should be made clear. While the industry is proud of its role as tax collector, it recognizes that it does not pay excise taxes. It merely collects them. The consumer pays them. —The Distilled Spirits Industry

THE LIQUOR OUTFIT CAN'T MAKE SUCKERS OUT OF GRANT COUNTY TAXPAYERS BY TRYING TO GET THEIR OPEN SALOONS AND ROADHOUSES BACK.

LET'S KEEP 'EM OUT

Vote "YES" -- To Vote Dry

Wednesday, May 15, 1946

—GRANT COUNTY LOCAL OPTION COMMITTEE.
Rev. G. R. Henson, Chairman; Rev. C. N. OGG, A. Threlkeld, L. M. Ackman, J. W. Bennett.

THE OLD LIQUOR GANG IS TRYING TO GET BACK IN GRANT COUNTY

THIS IS THE GANG WHO SHOUTED LONG AND LOUD THREE YEARS AGO . . . "DON'T VOTE GRANT COUNTY DRY—YOU CAN'T ENFORCE THE LAW."

NOW!—THIS SAME GANG—WHO HAVE BEEN DELIBERATELY BREAKING OUR LOCAL OPTION LAW AT EVERY OPPORTUNITY—ARE SHEDDING PIOUS TEARS AND YELLING FOR SO-CALLED "REGULATED" BOOZE, WHICH MEANS THE RETURN OF OPEN SALOONS AND ROADHOUSES. WORKING WITH THEM, ARE THEIR "BUDDIES"—THE CRIMINAL ELEMENT—GANGSTERS, RACKETEERS, BOOTLEGGERS, THE BREWERS, DISTILLERS AND VARIOUS TYPES OF LAW BREAKERS—ALL LOOKING FOR EASY MONEY MADE FROM GAMBLING, VICE, AND EVERYTHING THAT GOES WITH SO-CALLED "REGULATED" LIQUOR.

"IT'S HARD TO BELIEVE"

– THE MODERN OLIVER TWIST CAN BE SO FAT AND ASK FOR MORE

THE YOUTH OF AMERICA
MORE! MORE! MORE!
ALCOHOLISM
PROFIT MAD LIQUOR TRAFFIC
DRUNKARDS
CRIMINALS
HARLOTS
WASTRELS
SLACKERS
AMERICAN BUSINESS MENS RESEARCH FOUNDATION CHICAGO No 1025

THE LIQUOR BOYS ARE BLUBBERING BUCKETS OF TEARS over the high school students and the little ones tottering into "Blind Tigers." To cure the bootleg evil they would **legalize** it, **protect** it, and **increase** it. To cure the imaginary youthful tendency to drink, they would make liquor easy to get and legal. They would put booze back in every drug store, restaurant, hot-dog stand, grocery store . . . . EVERYWHERE under the nose with enticing window displays, dancing, juke boxes blaring and neon signs flashing a welcome. To cure criminals and give the law enforcement officials a new birth of honesty, they propose the simple expedient of bringing back legalized liquor, which has been the faithful ally of every vicious element in American life. It protects criminals, fosters social evil and bribes politicians, juries and legislatures.

THE GOOD PEOPLE OF GRANT COUNTY ARE NOT FOOLED BY THEIR FALSE PROPAGANDA. If we MUST have booze around, then give us the "BLIND" Tiger instead of OPEN SALOONS with wide open eyes to deceive and snare the innocent.

We must remember that the law cannot give a man a **license to sell liquor** and by so doing make a **law abiding citizen out of him.** It only tends to make EVERY man who goes in the business honest or otherwise . . . . a law breaker and a CRIMINAL. 47

47 Circa April 1946. *Grant County News.*

IT'S THE LAW!

The retailing of beer in Kentucky is subject to strict legal regulations. For six years the Kentucky Committee of the United States Brewers Foundation has been actively cooperating with law-enforcement agencies in seeing to it that these regulations are observed.

The program is one of education, vigilance and Self-Regulation. Its sole aim is to maintain wholesome conditions wherever beer is legally sold.

Licensed retailers are fully informed of their social responsibilities and refuse to deviate from the standards which they have pledged to uphold. Failure to co-operate is not tolerated.

Self-Regulation works!

KENTUCKY COMMITTEE
UNITED STATES BREWERS FOUNDATION
HARRY D. FRANCE, State Director
1523 HEYBURN BUILDING
LOUISVILLE

Sample of the Local Option Election Ballot to be Voted Wednesday, May 15, 1946

(Consecutive No.)

Name of Voter ....

Residence .... Reg. No. ....

— — — — Perforated Rule — — — —

Are you in favor of continuing Prohibition in effect in Grant County, Kentucky?

YES .... ☐

NO .... ☐

— — — — Perforated Rule — — — —

(Consecutive No.)

Name of Voter ....

Residence .... Reg. No. ....

I, Emerson Lowe, Clerk of the county court, in and for the State of Kentucky, County of Grant, do hereby certify that the sample Local Option Election Ballot printed above is a facsimile of said ballot which is to be submitted to the qualified voters of Grant County, Ky. at the Local Opton Election to be held Wednesday, May 15, 1946.

In witness whereof I have set my hand and seal of the office of ounty Court Clerk at the court house in the city of Williamstown, y., on this 1st day of May, 1946.

Emerson Lowe

(Seal) County Court Clerk of Grant County, Ky.

Prepared, posted and published in compliance with section 1550-15 Carroll's Kentucky Statutes. [48]

[48] Circa April 1946. *Grant County News.*

Saloons -- Booze -- Drunks

All Over The Place In Wet Counties

All This Tragic Mess Will Come Back To Grant If Saloons Return

READ THESE PARAGRAPHS

If We Don't Want This In Grant We Can Keep The Saloons Out

IF PROHIBITION WAS SO TERRIBLE, then what is wrong with these figures? In 1929 Louisville arrested 2,155 for drunkenness. In 1933, the first year of repeal, over 6,000 were arrested, of which 400 were boys and girls under age. In 1934, 10,600 were arrested including 1,400 boys and girls. In 1937, 12,200 were arrested, of which nearly 4,000 were boys and girls under age!

WARD J. OATES, ACTING COMMISSIONER OF REVENUE OF KENTUCKY, claimed in an interview that some of the records of the wholesale liquor outfit are "so rotten they stink." Allan Trout, special writer on the Courier-Journal staff, figures that a county is going dry in Kentucky on an average of one every six weeks.

ONE OF THE HIGHEST POLICE OFFICIALS OF LOUISVILLE, as quoted in a Courier-Journal editorial, claims that 50 per cent of the persons operating saloons in Louisville have criminal records. Recently, every saloon-keeper in the city was fingerprinted. Where else would you look for this law defying crowd. There are 1,200 SALOONS IN THE CITY.

FIFTEEN SOLDIERS TOLD A POLICE OFFICIAL that in a certain saloon in Louisville they had caught a venereal disease from girls hanging around the place. THERE ARE 1200 SALOONS IN THE CITY.

THE COURIER-JOURNAL STATED editorially about a year ago, commenting on an article by Michael Griffen, that "vice control in the city has virtually disappeared. Any citizen can find evidence for himself. He can walk along most any downtown street at night and see and hear the sordid manifestations." Nothing strange about this. Liquor, prostitution and gambling go hand in hand. Liquor is the greatest cause of vice. THERE ARE 1200 BREEDERS OF THIS SORT OF THING IN THE CITY. Why not attack this whole mess AT ITS SOURCE?

MAJOR KIMBERLING OF THE LOUISVILLE POLICE FORCE is reported in the Courier-Journal as testifying that the usual night crowd in a certain saloon in the city was "composed of drunks, prostitutes, known criminals, thieves and soldiers." THERE ARE 1200 SALOONS IN THE CITY.

IN A CERTAIN SALOON IN LOUISVILLE, the polices found that girls between the ages of 14 and 17 years were hired to entice soldiers to drink. Their pay was a nickel for each 20c drink they sold. The girls were served water "just capped" with whiskey. One girl testified she drank thirty-one such "capped" drinks in one night. THERE ARE 1200 SALOONS IN THE CITY.

LOUISVILLE LEADS ALL OTHER CITIES in its population class in crime, according to the FBI. Saloons do breed crime. THERE ARE 1200 OF THESE CRIME BREEDING CESSPOOLS IN THE CITY.

BY CAREFUL SURVEY, HON. W. A. FROST OF THE KENTUCKY PAROLE BOARD found that 85 per cent of all in Eddyville Prison were there because of drink. The population of Kentucky prisons has increased by over 1,000 in four years.

DR. ISHAM KIMBELL, SUPERINTENDENT OF CENTRAL STATE HOSPITAL at Lakeland, stated recently that "Alcoholics who must be treated in mental institutions are on the increase in Jefferson County." "In the opinion of many people," Dr. Kimbell said, "Alcohol is the greatest public health problem at the present time which is not being systematically handled." THERE ARE 1200 DISEASE BREEDING SALOONS IN LOUISVILLE creating these "Alcoholics" for the taxpayers to care for.

LOUISVILLE ARRESTED 900 DRUNKEN DRIVERS LAST YEAR. Probably a small number compared to those not caught. Several hundred people were killed or injured. OVER 1200 SALOONS IN THE CITY are turning these potential murderers loose on our streets. What are we doing about it?

FIFTY-EIGHT DRUNK ON MOONSHINE LIQUOR and only two on legal liquor, was the evidence brought out when 60 drunks were convicted in wet Princeton, Caldwell County, Kentucky, during July and August, 1937—four months before that county voted dry.

"SIXTY-FIVE PER CENT OF ALL LIQUOR SOLD IN HARLAN COUNTY IS ILLICIT LIQUOR" stated George Stewart, Spirits Administrator of the State Alcohol Control Board in 1940—two years before that county voted dry.

DON'T LET SALOONS RETURN

VOTE DRY -- VOTE YES -- KEEP THEM OUT

Grant County Local Option Committee—G. R. Henson, Chairman. [49]

[49] Circa April 1946. *Grant County News.*

Booze - Drunks - Lawlessness

Under The Guise Of "Regulated" Saloons Are Trying To Get Back In Grant

BREWERS AND DISTILLERS OF LOUISVILLE, CINCINNATI, ST. LOUIS AND MILWAUKEE ARE BACK OF A VICIOUS MOVEMENT TO OPEN SALOONS AND ROADHOUSES ALL OVER THE COUNTY.

From The Temperance Advocate Courtesy of The National Voice Los Angeles 13, Calif.

This Brood Is Responsible For:

50 PER CENT OF ALL CRIME— 60 PER CENT OF JUVENILE DELINQUENCY— 78 PER CENT OF UNWED MOTHERS— 90 PER CENT OF VENERAL DISEASES —40 PER CENT OF AUTOMOBILE ACCIDENTS— 90 PERCENT OF DIVORCES— 49 PER CENT OF ALL DESTITUTE CHILDREN— 60 PER CENT OF PAUPERS.

THE UNITED STATES SUPREME COURT HAS SUMMED IT ALL UP IN THESE WORDS: "THE STATISTICS OF EVERY STATE SHOW A GREATER AMOUNT OF CRIME AND MISERY CAUSED BY LIQUOR THAN ANY OTHER SOURCE."

Saloons And Roadhouses Will Not Get Back In Grant County By My Vote Because:

THE POLICE SAY: Liquor and gasoline cause accidents.
THE MURDERER SAYS: Liquor caused me to kill..
THE JUDGE SAYS: Liquor causes most of the crime before me.
THE DOCTOR SAYS: Liquor weakens resistance and shortens life.
THE LADY SAYS: A liquor breath is very repulsive.
THE LAWYER SAYS: Liquor causes most of the divorce cases.
THE UNDERTAKER SAYS: Liquor speeds up my business.
THE MOTHER SAYS: Liquor robs my home of peace and happiness.
THE CHILDREN SAY: Liquor makes our daddy drunk and dangerous.
THE PASTORS SAY: Liquor robs souls of eternal life.
THE BIBLE SAYS: A drunkard shall not inherit the kingdom of God.
THE LIQUOR CROWD SAYS: I am voting for all this.

WHAT DO YOU SAY?

YOU CANNOT STAND WITH THE CHRISTIAN FORCES OF GRANT COUNTY— THE HOME AND OUR CHILDREN—IF YOU VOTE TO BRING SALOONS BACK TO GRANT COUNTY.

TO VOTE DRY . . VOTE YES

Wednesday, May 15, 1946

LET'S KEEP GRANT COUNTY DRY

Grant County Local Option Committee—
Rev. G. R. Henson, Chairman; Rev. C. N. Ogg, A. Threlkeld, L. M. Ackman, J. W. Bennett. [50]

[50] Circa April 1946. *Grant County News.*

Why You Should Vote Wet

VOTE WET in order that your BOYS and GIRLS may cultivate a taste for beer and liquors and thus furnish the NEW CUSTOMERS without which the LIQUOR BUSINESS could not SUCCEED.

VOTE WET to furnish a safe and secure place where slot machines and gambling devices may operate, for they will not be tolerated in restaurants, grocery stores and other places of business where LIQUOR and BEER are not sold.

VOTE WET to enable the beer and whiskey dispensaries, delivery trucks, and producers to furnish employment to thousands of HUSKY men and women who otherwise would be forced to find a job in industries or on the farm where all they could do would be work, fight and give to make democracy live.

VOTE WET so that the KEELY CURE sanatoriums may continue to multiply and furnish profit and employment to strong and skilled DOCTORS and NURSES who otherwise would be SERVING your community and trying to protect you. (In 1930 there was only one Keely Cure Sanatorium in the United States).

VOTE WET so that those who are AFRAID to face LIFE may find an escapement in intoxication and thus WEAKEN themselves and BREED more fears that will demand a heavier dose of this same POISON to overcome.

VOTE WET so that the CORN and GRAIN that is so desperately NEEDED to save the starving children of Europe may be converted into booze that will destroy the youth of our nation.

> You cannot train a winning football or basketball team on beer and whiskey, and you certainly can not TRAIN a winning life on this diet.

VOTE WET so that we may receive the TAXATION from beer and whiskey that will enable us to pay a SMALL portion of the COSTS to the taxpayers incident to the IMPRISONMENT of men who became CRIMINALS when they were TOO DRUNK to exercise their judgment.

> The Bureau of Criminal Investigation composed of scientists, who are without bias, has reported that 85 percent of the men now serving in our penal institutions are there by reason of crimes committed while under the influence of alcohol and law enforcement last year cost the taxpayers TWENTY-ONE BILLION DOLLARS.

VOTE WET so that the places that bootleg a LITTLE liquor now, but have to keep their customers FAIRLY SOBER for appearances sake, can sell all they'll hold, until they drink themselves into a DRUNKEN STUPOR across the tables and on the floor, and YOUR BOYS help to LOAD them into a conveyance, homeward bound.

No, NONE of this suits you, but it's PLAIN, simple TRUTH.

ALCOHOL is a NARCOTIC as deadly as MORPHINE, or COCAINE, and just as habit-forming. If you permit men and women to do business in Grant County with this deadly stuff where your BOYS and GIRLS see it, smell it, and watch others DRINK it, then be prepared to have this younger generation grow up and become the CUSTOMERS whose money contributes to the WEALTH of the BREWER, the DISTILLER, and the men who claim they can BOSS Grant County.

VOTE "YES" FOR LAW ENFORCEMENT

Wednesday, May 15th, 1946

—Grant County Committee For Local Option. [51]

[51] Circa April 1946. *Grant County News.*

LET'S KEEP OPEN SALOONS AND ROADHOUSES OUT OF GRANT COUNTY

NOTE—If there is more liquor sold NOW ..... what are the liquor boys yelling about? Why do they want the saloons and roadhouses back? You can bet your old sock that all that old baloney about MORE liquor sold in dry counties is pure bunk. Sure some is sold. When we find a law that will stop all that, the same law could stop all stealing and lawlessness. Some people are bound to break the law for easy money. But that doesn't mean we have to make it handy for them to drink.

LET'S KEEP GRANT COUNTY DRY!

TO VOTE DRY -- VOTE YES

Wednesday, May 15, 1946

GRANT COUNTY LOCAL OPTION COMMITTEE, Rev. G. R. Henson, Chairman; Rev. C. N. Ogg, A. Threlkeld, L. M. Ackman, J. W. Bennett.

52

[52]Circa April 1946. *Grant County News.*

Local Option Election In Grant Called Off

At a special term of the Grant County Court held May 4, 1946, Judge Charles A. Pettit presiding, the court allowed the motion filed by C. McGee, et al, to withdraw their petition calling for a local option election, which the court had already allowed, and had called an election for May 15, 1946.

The expense attendant on printing ballots and other court costs is ordered charged to the petitioners.

A copy of the petition and order is given in the following paragraphs.

Petition

"Special Term of Grant County Court held at Williamstown, Ky., this, the 4th day of May, 1946, Hon Charles A. Pettit present and presiding.

"Comes C. McGee, et al, petitioners herein and moves the court permit them to withdraw the petition heretofore filed on March 11, 1946 calling for a local option election to be held in Grant County, Ky. on May 15, 1946 and to enter an order cancelling and calling off the local option election for May 15, 1946 for Grant County, Ky.

"Wherefore, they pray the ruling of the court on this motion.

"(Signed) C. McGee.

"Filed May 4, 1946

"Charles A. Pettit, Judge."

Order

"It appearing to the court that C. McGee, et al, filed a petition on March 11, 1946, with the required number of petitioners, calling for a local option election for Grant County, Ky. to be held on May 15, 1946.

"It further appearing to the court that an order was entered calling for the election to be held on said date.

"It further appearing to the court that C. McGee, et al, have this day filed a motion requesting the court to enter an order permitting them to withdraw said petition, and to enter an order to cancel the order calling for said election. It is therefore considered and adjudged by the court that the motion be, and the same is hereby sustained.

"C. McGee, et al, are, hereby permitted to and they do hereby withdraw the petition heretofore filed on March 11, 1946 calling for a local option election and said order heretofore entered calling said election is hereby cancelled, set aside and held for naught.

"The sheriff is hereby directed to publish a notice of the cancellation of the order calling said election.

"The petitioner is hereby ordered and directed to reimburse the county for all its cost herein expended.

"(Signed) Charles A. Pettit, County Judge."[53]

Wets Win In Mason

By a majority of 1,379 votes the county of Mason favored continuation of the sale of beer and liquor in a local option election held May 15th. The vote was: wet 4,360, dry 2,981. This was the first local option election since 1915, and brought a near record vote.[54]

Drys Win In Scott By Wide Margin

By a margin of 1,050 votes, the dry forces of Scott County won a local option election June 22nd. 2,775 persons voting "yes" in favor of continuing prohibition in the county, and 1,705 voting "no."

Only three precincts gave the wets a majority and two of them are in Georgetown. The other precinct voting wet was Stonewall.[55]

Proprietor Of Rock Garden To Face Liquor Charge

William Updike, proprietor of Rock Garden, was arrested last Friday by Sheriff Lawrence Caldwell and deputy sheriff Elmer Ballard after a

[53] 10 May 1946. *Grant County News.* Author Unknown.
[54] 24 May 1946. *Grant County News.* Author Unknown.
[55] 28 June 1946. *Grant County News.* Author Unknown.
[56] 2 May 1947. *Grant County News.* Author Unknown.

warrant had been issued. Updike's place of business was searched and officers found beer and whiskey.

On motion of the defendant's attorney, E. H. Walton, Judge C. A. Pettit continued the cast until May 9th when Updike will face trial.[56]

Beer Loaded Truck Overturns Near Corinth City Limits

A tractor-trailer left the road near the city limits of Corinth Tuesday night, went over a 40-foot embankment and overturned. The driver, Harold Porter Brown, was not injured.

The vehicle, owned by E. F. Pritchard, Lexington, was loaded with 450 cases of beer. Estimated damage was $1,500 to the truck and $300 worth of beer.[57]

Wets Win Election In Bracken County By 108 Majority

A local option election in Bracken county last Saturday was won by the wets with a majority of 108. It was the first held in the county in the past five years, on a petition of the drys. In a previous election the wets carried the county by a 250 majority.[58]

Beer and Fifth Whiskey Seized By Officers

Officers Raid Three Road Houses. Operators Released Under $500 Bond. Slot Machine Found At Rock Garden.

Sheriff Lawrence Caldwell, Deputy Sheriff Elmer Ballard, Patrolman Paul Dunn, and City Policeman Russell McMillan raided three Grant county road houses Tuesday on affidavits signed by Harry and Cecil Scroggin.

At Rock Garden, near Mason, the officers found four cases of beer, a fifth of whiskey, a half pint of gin, and a twenty-five cent slot machine. Rock Garden is owned and operated by Chester Campbell.

Mac's Castle, at four corners on the Taft Highway, operated by Ervie Starns, was raided and nine cases of beer was seized.

The Dog House, U. S. 25, a mile north of Williamstown, was the third place the officers visited, the find there was 19 bottles of beer. Dewey Sebastian, operator of the establishment, had been arrested shortly before Christmas when The Dog House was raided and whiskey and beer was found. His trial for that offense was set for Saturday, Jan. 10th, he will be tried on both charges. Sebastian and Starns were released under $500 bond each. B. F. Kinman, judge pro-tem, said Chester Campbell had not been brought before the court Wednesday morning.

Harry and Cecil Scroggin, who signed the affidavits, were taken into custody Tuesday by county officers in connection with thefts in Boone, Kenton and Grant Counties.[59]

Liquor Tax Raise Of 8 Cents Is Sought

Clements' Bill Expected To Bring State $220,000 In New Revenue

Frankfort, Ky., Feb. 24th An 8-cent-a-gallon increase on the State's present $1.20 distilled-spirits consumption tax was proposed in a bill introduced today in the Legislature.

The bill was one of several measures offered by leaders of Governor Earle Clements' Administration. Representative John C. Watts, Nicholasville, majority floor leader, told reporters the bills would gather up loose ends of the Governor's legislative program.

The tax, paid eventually by the public, would increase the levy on a pint from 15 cents to 16 cents. The raise is expected to yield $220,000 a year in new revenue. It was offered by Representative Edward F. Prichard, Paris.[60]

[57] 23 May 1947. *Grant County News.* Author Unknown.
[58] 23 May 1947. *Grant County News.* Author Unknown.
[59] 9 January 1948. *Grant County News.* Author Unknown.
[60] 27 February 1948. *Grant County News.* Author Unknown.

Petition Filed For Local Option Election In Grant

1,029 Voters Sign Petition Calling For Local Option Election. Date Set For July 3rd

A petition signed by 1,029 voters has been presented in open court requesting that same be filed and requested the presiding Judge, Hon. Chas. A. Pettit, to enter an order calling for a local option election in Grant County.

Being sufficiently advised, the court permitted said petition to be filed. The election is to be held the first Saturday in July, the 3rd.

The required number of persons signing such a petition is 25 percent. of the votes cast at the last general election. The number signing the local option petition is equal in number to almost 75 percent of votes cast at the election last November.

The last local option election was to have been held in the county May 15, 1946 but at a special term of county court, the court allowed a motion to withdraw the petition calling for the election. At that time the drys had formed an organization opposing the sale of spirituous beverages and conducted an extensive campaign to defeat the return of legal sales in the county.

A local option election was held here Sept. 11, 1932 at which time the wets won by a majority of 523 votes.[61]

Attention Citizens

It is indeed very much regretted that the wet forces of Grant County are attempting to vote liquor back into the County, especially when the majority of the voters have expressed their desire for it to remain dry. The great Apostle Paul said, "Hold fast to that which is good." We, the dry forces of Grant County, believe that prohibition has done us more good than having a wet county.

If it did not mean money in the pockets of the profiteers of the liquor industry to make a county wet, there would be no point in calling an election. Filthy lucre is sought at the expense of damning the souls and lives of our youth. No regard is given to their success in life as long as it means blood money in the pockets of a few selfish, greedy, grasping people.

If you have the smallpox, the government may take you out of your own home and put you in a pest house. It may quarantine your property and prevent people from coming to see you and also prevent your family from leaving home. It may burn your goods without compensation, lest they spread the disease, but if you want to go into the business of spreading alcoholism, "The fourth health problem," the government licenses you and takes a part of the profits.

The American housewife is saying, "My children need milk and meat." The liquor industry is saying, "No, there is not enough profit in it." The starving children of Europe are saying, "Please, please send us food or we perish." The liquor industry is saying, "No, no, my coffers must be filled. I must grab all I can while the time is ripe. Let other peoples of the world starve and perish, but I must have mine at any price."

Did you know that they are trying to include in the Marshall Plan 142,000,000 of American wine to go to Europe, while they are so desperately in need of food and clothing? - Protestant Voice. "Did you know that after eleven years of legalized drunkenness we now have: (1) The highest rate of juvenile delinquency in our history; (2) The greatest period of crime in the history of the Nation; (3) Venereal diseases so frightful in their prevalence that health and medical authorities refer to one of them, syphilis, as Public Health Menace No. 1; (4) Jails, penitentiaries and asylums are more crowded than ever before; (5) Traffic fatalities are more terrible than the statistics of American deaths in battles of this last war; (6) The highest tax rate on record; (7) The largest public debt in the Nation's history; (8) Sickening spectacles of corruption in government; (9) The gloomiest post-war prospect of public morality that ever confronted our people; (10) We have 437,000 liquor outlets and 40,000,000 drinkers?

-Signs of The Times.

[61] 14 May 1948. *Grant County News.* Author Unknown.

Do you think it will pay to have a wet county when our coming generation of boys and girls grow up to be drunkards? The chances are too many against them for that; they will become addicts to drink if the county goes wet.

We plead with you fathers and mother . think of your children and grandchildren; think of your neighbor's children; think of the happiness of your home; think of your respectability as a citizen who can be counted on to do that which is right in the sight of God and man. Remember, we will all have to stand in the presence of God some day and give account of the deeds done in the body. Yes, even how we voted on election day when our God-given conscience told us which was right and wrong. Choose the right and you will not regret it. Choose the wrong and everyone will regret it.

There will be a MASS MEETING of the DRY FORCES of Grant County at the DRY RIDGE BAPTIST CHURCH SUNDAY AFTERNOON, MAY 23 AT 2:30 P. M. (E.S.T.) ALL URGED TO ATTEND! Walter J. Hoshal, State Superintendent Anti-Saloon League, Louisville, will be the speaker.

- Better Government League of Grant County.[62]

Dry Forces To Have Mass Meeting In Dry Ridge

The dry forces of Grant County, known as the Better Government League, will have a mass meeting at the Dry Ridge Baptist Church Sunday afternoon, May 23rd at 2:30 o'clock. The State Superintendent of the Anti-Saloon League, Walter J. Hoshal, of Louisville, will be the speaker.

All persons interested in retaining prohibition in the county are invited to attend the meeting.[63]

Local Option Elections In Grant County

In the May 4th issue of The News in the story captioned, "Petition Filed For Local Option Election in Grant," it was stated, in the last paragraph that a local option election was held here Sept. 11, 1932. This was an error, whether typographical or we got our dates mixed, we do not know. At any rate, the year was 1937. All persons reading the article were no doubt aware that it was a mistake as there was no local option law in 1932.

It was also stated in the same article that the number of persons signing the petition was equal in number to almost 75 percent of the votes cast at the last general election. Again we erred, the percentage was some 40.3 percent.

Reports of two local option elections held in Grant County as taken from the files of The Grant County News are:

Issue of Sept. 16, 1937, election held Saturday, Sept. 11, 1937; Wets 2,035, Drys 1619. Wet's majority 416.

Issue of Dec. 18, 1942, election held Saturday, Dec. 12, 1942; Drys 1516, Wets 1304. Dry's majority 212.[64]

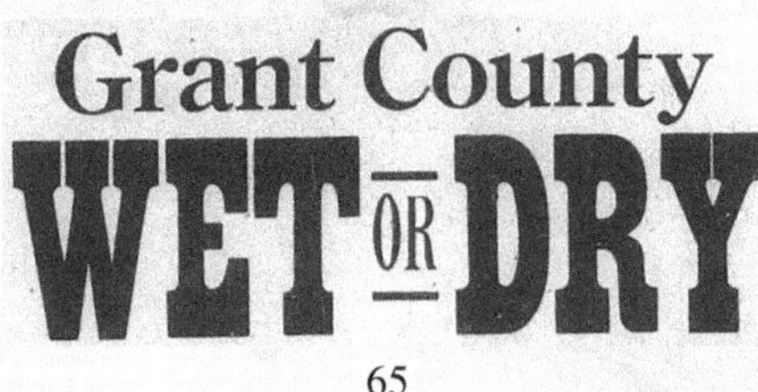

65

Wet Or Dry

Read What Editor Roscoe I. Downs Of "The Hancock Clarion" Has To Say On That Stale Chestnut About Bootleggers Voting Dry — Moonshine In Dry Counties And Liquor Revenue

---

Answering Commissioner Clyde Reeves And The Local Option Question

---

[62] 21 May 1948. *Grant County News.* Author Unknown.
[63] 21 May 1948. *Grant County News.* Author Unknown.
[64] 21 May 1948. *Grant County News.* Author Unknown.
[65] 21 May 1948. *Grant County News.*

State Revenue Commissioner Clyde Reeves speaking before a training school for agents of the Alcoholic Beverage Control Department at Frankfort last week, made some very remarkable statements in relation of question of liquor sale and the spreading local option regulation. Some of these statements reveal the real sentiment of the Commissioner in relation to the sale of liquor and that sentiment is very much in opposition to the spread of the dry movement that has voted ninety-three out of the 120 counties of the state dry, and some of the statements made by him are very candid and state the truth even stronger than do the drys.

Commissioners Reeves starts out by stating, as reported by the Associated Press, "that church forces unwittingly find themselves allied with bootleggers in campaigns to adopt prohibition at local option elections."

This statement of the Commissioner is not true as he very well knows, if one shall take the true meaning of the word, "allied." Standard Dictionary defines "allied bound by or as by an alliance; united, confederated or leagued."

If Mr. Reeves in his unholy alliance with the so-called legal liquor sale for the purpose of bringing more revenue into the state treasury used the word "allied" inadvertently, then he should so state, but if he used the word knowing full well the meaning as well as the application made, then he should apologize to the great majority of Kentuckians who are known as drys, for surely they are in the majority or they would not be able to vote ninety-three of the counties dry.

To state that the church forces of Kentucky are allied with bootleggers, as the meaning of "allied" is defined, is as untrue and basely false as is the whole liquor industry. To say that the church forces of Kentucky are "united, confederated or leagued" with bootlegging and bootleggers is not true and Commissioner Reeves knows it is not true. The dry force of Kentucky, and the church people, if you please, are not allied with the bootleggers and never have been, even "unwittingly" as the Commissioner states. If local option breeds bootleggers it is not the fault of the law but the failure of those who are charged with the enforcement of the law.

And it was to the very ones whose duty it is to enforce the liquor laws of the state to whom Mr. Reeves was speaking. If there is an alliance it must be between the bootlegger and the moonshiner and those who are sworn to enforce the laws, for there is where the breakdown is. Mr. Reeves should endeavor to break up such an alliance if there is such.

The Revenue Commissioner goes still further in his censure of church people when he states: "When clergymen take part in pushing prohibition movements, they inadvertently find themselves in cahoots with bootleggers." Again Mr. Reeves uses a word "cahoots" that is unfortunate if used unthinkingly and another base untruth if spoken knowingly. Again we use the Standard Dictionary to define the word "cahoot" and it says: "cahoot to be partners; partnership." Again we say, to state that our clergymen "who push prohibition movements" are partners with bootleggers and have formed partnership with bootleggers is false and the Commissioner knows it is false.

It is just the sort of statements that the Commissioner of Revenue made whether inadvertently or deliberately, that is doing more to make Kentucky counties dry than any other one thing, because they attempt to bring ridicule and contempt upon those who sincerely and wisely endeavor to bring better moral and spiritual conditions in our state. And we are sure that Mr. Reeves is aware of the fact that it is not only the "clergymen and church people" who are active in bringing prohibition in Kentucky: there is a great host of people in our state who are very much against the sale of liquor, both legal and illegal, and it is this great movement by the people that is bringing about the result of which he speaks. To say they are in league with bootleggers is just as false as when he states that the clergymen and church people are in league with them.

As we stated in paragraph above that the blame for bootlegging rests on the law enforcement agencies, is verified by the Commissioner when he is represented as saying:

"Kentucky has tried to stop the spread of prohibition with everything but strict enforcement of the laws. He recommended that the agents be fair but tough' in policing the retail dealers who violate laws."

And in a following paragraph Mr. Reeves states a truth that we all know, and in that statement says the very thing that we "church people" and the "clergymen" stand for and have voted ninety-three counties dry. We quote:

"One bad license can sour the sentiment in a wide area. I'D VOTE DRY, TOO, IF I LIVED IN SOME COUNTIES I KNOW."

What he says about "some counties he knows" is true about all counties where the sale of liquor is had, either legal or illegal. They just will not obey the law when it comes to the sale of liquor. It is doubtful if there ever was a seller of liquor who at all times strictly obeyed the laws governing that sale. If the legal seller breaks the law in his trade then he becomes a bootlegger in just the same manner as does the illegal seller.

The Commissioner states much more in this report of his address to the agents of the Alcoholic Beverage Control Department, and through it all runs the threadbare tale of "what would we do without the revenue that liquor produces." Nothing is ever said about the added cost of enforcing or attempting to enforce the liquor laws. It is evident that the cost of policing and courts having to do primarily with liquor violations and the resultant causes mount much higher than do the revenue produced.

Only a few days ago it was reported that the illegal manufacture of liquor at Owensboro and Daviess county was more than that produced legally in the great distilleries there. No one seemed to know about this and it was smoothed over very quickly and quietly. Owensboro and Daviess county have the legal sale of liquor and therefore, according to those who condemn the drys and say that moonshining and bootlegging are in the dry counties, the question is: how does it happen that so much moonshining is done in that great wet county? Are the clergymen and church people responsible for the condition, and are they in league with those moonshiners as so reported?

At the same meeting Julian Elliott, state beer administrator, urged the agents to make a special effort to report licensees who cater to minors. This is just another example of the nefarious trade that will not be legal even if so declared. It is one instance where it is verified that the seller of liquor never obeys the law.

It would seem by the address of the State Revenue Commissioner that we are committed to the condition that the liquor interests in Kentucky have long wanted: Sympathy for their trade among those who are in authority. There is but one remedy for the eradication of such condition, and the drys know what that is and how to do it.

LET'S KEEP SALOONS OUT OF GRANT COUNTY

- Better Government League of Grant County[66]

FEDERAL JUDGE SAYS LEGALIZED LIQUOR CAN'T STOP BOOTLEGGERS

Charlotte, N. C. - Federal Judge E. Yates Webb, of Shelby, holding court here, commented from the bench that "You can't stop bootlegging by having legalized liquor stores."

It was during trial of a defendant who said he was from South Carolina.

"It just goes to show," the Judge commented, "that you can't stop bootlegging by having legalized liquor stores. There are more blockade stills in South Carolina today than there were during prohibition. Liquor stores breed bootlegging. They embolden bootleggers.

"Some people say that they advocate legalized stores because they will reduce taxes. They don't reduce taxes; they never have done it. I suppose if one of these people were to see a friend lying in a drunken stupor in a gutter, he would urge him to get up so he could buy more liquor and thereby further reduce taxes.

"Alcoholism is killing more people in the United States than cancer. It killed 135,000 persons in this country last year. Liquor is the scourge of mankind. It is responsible for murder, suicide, patricide and every other horrible crime. People often ask me why I am so opposed to liquor.

"I am opposed to liquor," Judge Webb concluded, "because I love my fellowman."

- Better Government League of Grant County[67]

---

[66] 11 June 1948. *Grant County News.* Author Unknown.

[67] 2 July 1948. *Grant County News.* Author Unknown.

Local Option Election To Be Held Tomorrow

A local option election will take place in Grant County tomorrow, Saturday, July 3rd. The polls will be open from 6 a. m. to 4 p. m.

It is the privilege of every citizen of the county 21 years of age or older who is properly registered, to vote. The question to be voted is, "Are you in favor of the sale of alcoholic beverages in Grant County, Kentucky?" If you are "dry," vote "NO"; if you are "wet" vote "YES." Whatever your conviction, vote. Your vote determines the outcome of the election.[68]

Murderer Passes Buck

California Man Sentenced To Death Tries To Avoid Consequence

Sacramento, Calif., May 27thFrank Arktru when called by the Superior Court of California to be sentenced to death, said in response to the Judge's questionIf he had anything to say why judgment should not be passed upon him.

"I have! Your honor, you have asked me a question, and now I ask, as the last favor on earth, that you will not interrupt my answer until I am through."

"I stand here before this bar, convicted of the wilful murder of my wife. Truthful witnesses have testified to the fact that I was a loafer, a drunkard, a wretch, that I returned from one of my prolonged debauches and fired the fatal shot that killed the wife that I had sworn to love, cherish and protect."

"While I have no remembrance of committing the fatal deed, I have no right to condemn the verdict of the twelve good men who have acted as jury in this case, for the verdict is in accordance with the evidence."

"But may it please the court, I wish to show that I am not alone responsible for the murder of my wife."

The startling statement created a tremendous sensation. The judge leaned over the desk, the lawyers wheeled around and faced the prisoner, while the spectators could hardly suppress their intense excitement.

The prisoner paused a few seconds and then continued in the same firm distinct voice:

"The judge on this bench, the jury in the box the lawyers within the bar, and most of the witnesses, including the pastor of the old church, are also guilty before Almighty God, and will have to stand with me before His Judgment Throne, where we shall be righteously judged."

"If it had not been for the saloons of my town, I never would have become a drunkard, I would not be here now, ready to be hurled into eternity! Had it not been for the inhuman traps, I would have been a sober man and an industrious workman, a tender father and a loving husband. But today my home is destroyed, my wife murdered, my little childrenGod bless and care for them!cast out upon the mercy of the world!whilst I am to be hung by the strong arm of the State¡'

"God knows I tried to reform, but as long as the open saloon was in my pathway, my weak, diseased, will-power was not matched against the fearful, consuming, agonizing appetite for liquor. For one year our town was without a saloon. For one year my wife and children were happy and our little home was a paradise."

"I was one of those who signed remonstrances against the re-opening of the saloons of our town. One-half of this jury, the prosecuting attorney on this case, and the judge who sits on this bench, all voted for the saloons! By their votes and influence the saloons were re-opened, and they made me what I am!"

The impassioned words of the prisoner fell like coals of fire upon the hearts of those present, and many of the spectators and some of the lawyers were moved to tears.

The Judge made a motion as if to stop further speech, when the prisoner hastily said:

"No! No! your honor, do not close my lips. I am nearly through."

"I began my downward career at a saloon barlegalized and protected by the voters of this town. After the saloons you allowed have made me a drunkard and a murderer, I am taken before another Barthe Bar of Justice, and now the Law Power will conduct

[68] 2 July 1948. *Grant County News.* Author Unknown.

me to the place of execution, and hasten my soul to Eternity. I shall appear before another Barthe Judgment Bar of Godand there you, who have legalized the traffic will have to appear with me! Think you that the Great Judge will hold me, the poor, weak, helpless victim of your traffic alone responsible for the murder of my wife?"

"Nay!"

"In my drunken, frenzied, irresponsible condition I have murdered one, but you have deliberately voted for the saloons which have murdered thousands, and they are in full operation today with your consent."

"All of you know in your hearts that these words of mine are not the ravings of an unsound mind, but God Almighty's truth."

"You legalized the saloons and made me a drunkard and a murderer and you are guilty with me before God for the murder of my wife."

"Your honor, I am done. I am now ready to receive my sentence and be led forth to the place of execution. You will close by asking the Lord to have mercy on my soul. I will close by solemnly asking God to open your blind eyes to your own individual responsibility, so that you will cease to give your support to this dreadful traffic."[69]

---

[69] 2 July 1948. *Grant County News.* Author Unknown.

Booze-- Drunks-- Lawlessness

Caused by so-called "Regulated" Saloons Are Trying To Get Back With Us.

BREWERS AND DISTILLERS OF LOUISVILLE, CINCINNATI, ST. LOUIS AND MILWAUKEE ARE BACK OF A VICIOUS MOVEMENT TO RETURN OPEN SALOONS AND ROADHOUSES ALL OVER THE COMMUNITY.

THIS BROOD IS RESPONSIBLE FOR:

50 PER CENT OF ALL CRIME—60 PER CENT OF JUVENILE DELINQUENCY.
78 PER CENT OF UNWED MOTHERS—90 PERCENT OF VENEREAL DISEASES.
40 PER CENT OF AUTOMOBILE ACCIDENTS—90 PER CENT OF DIVORCES.
49 PER CENT OF ALL DESTITUTE CHILDREN—60 PER CENT OF PAUPERS.

THE UNITED STATES SUPREME COURT HAS SUMMED IT ALL UP IN THESE WORDS: "THE STATISTICS OF EVERY STATE SHOW A GREATER AMOUNT OF CRIME AND MISERY CAUSED BY LIQUOR THAN ANY OTHER SOURCE."

SALOONS AND ROADHOUSES WILL NOT RETURN TO GRANT COUNTY BY MY VOTE – BECAUSE:

THE POLICE SAY: Liquor and gasoline cause accidents.
THE MURDERER SAYS: Liquor caused me to kill.
THE JUDGE SAYS: Liquor causes most of the crime before me.
THE DOCTOR SAYS: Liquor weakens resistence and shortens life.
THE LADY SAYS: A liquor breath is very repulsive.
THE LAWYER SAYS: Liquor causes most of the divorce cases.
THE UNDERTAKER SAYS: Liquor speeds up my business.
THE MOTHER SAYS: Liquor robs my home of peace and happiness.
THE CHILDREN SAY: Liquor makes our daddy drunk and dangerous.
THE PASTOR SAYS: Liquor robs souls of eternal life.
THE BIBLE SAYS: A drunkard shall not inherit the Kingdom of God.
THE LIQUOR CROWD SAYS: I am voting for all this.

WHAT DO YOU SAY?

YOU CANNOT STAND WITH THE CHRISTIAN FORCES OF GRANT COUNTY AND THE BEST INTEREST OF YOUR HOME AND COMMUNITY IF YOU VOTE WITH THE LIQUOR CROWD.

You Make Your Choice Saturday, July 3

LET'S KEEP GRANT COUNTY DRY

REV. SAM MORRIS

Will Speak at The

Baptist Church, Williamstown

Friday Evening, July 2nd at 8:00

—Better Government League of Grant County. [70]

[70] 2 July 1948. *Grant County News.*

We Don't Want to Argue --- Nor to Sling Any Mud

But We DO Want to State a Few

FACTS AND PRINCIPLES

1

Local Option in Grant County is a farce. With wet counties both north and south of us, and with several bootleg places right here in our county, it is absurd to say that our citizens do not drink, or that Grant County is dry.

2

Local Option is causing an enormous loss of business to Grant County business men. When people drive to a wet county to purchase alcoholic beverages, they frequently buy their groceries, clothing, etc., there. It is estimated that this is costing Grant County between $50,000.00 and $100,000.00 per year.

3

Local Option is costing us several hundreds of dollars in license taxes every year. Since we have liquor anyway, it seems foolish not to have it sold locally and legally, and thus make it bear its share of the cost of our county government.

4

We admit that a liquor store, if not drastically regulated, frequently becomes a public nuisance. We understand that the new Alcoholic Beverage Control Board at Frankfort plans to improve conditions in the liquor business in Kentucky, and that retailers who violate the law are going to have a very rough time. We heartily endorse this program of law enforcement.

5

Last week the Drys published in this newspaper their favorite piece of advertising tripe—the old Hen and her chickens— to show some evils that result from the liquor trade. A pretty good temperance lesson, but a mighty poor argument for Local Option. Because it fails to point out that liquor bought in another county or from a local bootlegger will produce the same evil results.

6

Prohibition is the rankest kind of foolishness. The moderate use of an alcoholic beverage for personal or social enjoyment is neither a sin nor a crime. 70 percent of the grown-up people of the United States use beverage alcohol; but only about THREE percent. use it to excess. How silly it is to meddle with the personal habits and tastes of 70 people, merely because THREE of them go too far. Let's try to find a way to help the three "problems," but leave the 67 normal people alone!

7

Many of our county's best citizens are Wets. The Drys try to make it appear that all Wets are rifraff, trash, scum of the earth. But we know a lot of Wets who are among our most substantial and most respected citizens. Many of them do not drink at all. Many are devout church members. In short, they are fine people, who do their own thinking, and are too intelligent to be fooled by the worthless arguments and empty promises of the Prohibitionists!

8

Surveys made in Grant County show that the sentiment here is more than 60 percent. wet. This means that if ALL voters go to the polls and vote, the Wets will win every time. If the Wets lose this election, it will be their own fault— it will be BECAUSE THEY DID NOT GO AND VOTE. Let's not make that mistake. Let's all go to that election, and—

Vote Yes- Saturday July 3

Grant County Citizens Committee

For Legal Sale Of Alcoholic Beverages

"DOC" GILLILAND	ONIE BATES
G. C. ELLIOTT	MRS. OLA WILSON
M. A. SOWARDS	PETE MANCHIKES
J. B. MILLER	GORDON TRUE
DOUGLAS WOOD	GEORGE HAYDEN
JEFF WEBB	CLARENCE LAWRENCE
FRANK MARKSBURY	CUTHBERT McCOMAS
LINZIE O'BANION	DEWEY PETTIT
ALVA ENGLE	HAROLD BREWER
J. A. READNOWER	JOHN FARRELL
BOB ECKLER	W. J. MULLIKIN
HOMER McMILLAN	AUSTIN VEST
DALTON LOWE	JOHN DAVIS
H. G. BATES	BILL HOWE

AND MANY OTHERS

[71]

[71] 2 July 1948. *Grant County News.*

SAMPLE BALLOT

A SAMPLE OF THE PROPOSED LOCAL OPTION BALLOT.
Election to be held Saturday, July 3rd, 1948.

Are you in favor of the Sale of Alcoholic Beverages in Grant County, Kentucky?

YES .... ☐

NO ...... ☐

_ _ _ _ _ _ _ Perforated Rule _ _ _ _ _ _ _ _

(Consecutive Number)

Name of Voter____________________

Residence ________________ Reg. No.________

Commonwealth of Kentucky,
Grant County—Sct.

I, Emerson Lowe, Clerk of the County Court in and for the State and County aforesaid, do hereby certify that the Sample Local Option Ballot printed above is an exact facsimile of said ballot to be submitted to the qualified voters of Grant County, Ky., at the Election to be held Saturday, July 3rd, 1948.

In witness whereof, I have hereby unto set my hand and the seal of office of County Court Clerk, at the Courthouse in the City of Williamstown, Ky., this 22nd day of June, 1948.

EMERSON LOWE,
County Court Clerk of Grant County, Ky.

(Seal)

Prepared, posted and published in compliance with Section 119.190 Kentucky Revised Statutes 1946.

72

[72] 2 July 1948. *Grant County News.*

Speaking Schedule

FOR LOCAL OPTION

All To Begin At 8:30 P. M., Fast Time

Williamstown—Saturday, June 26th at Courthouse
Rev. Stephen H. Zukor

Mt. Zion—Saturday, June 26th at Clyde Franks' Store
Rev. G. R. Henson

Zion Station—Tuesday, June 29th at Pleasant View Church—Rev. W. M. Wilson

Cross Roads— Wednesday, June 30 at Lawrenceville Baptist Church—Rev. C. N. Ogg

Corinth—Wednesday, June 30th at Corinth Church of Christ—Mr. Franklin Webster

Jonesville—Thursday, July 1st at Baptist Church
Rev. Willie Davis

Holbrook—Thursday, July 1st at Betha[illegible] Church
Rev. L. N. Stamper

Folsom—Thursday, July 1st at Folsom Lodge Hall
Rev. Gerald Knopt

[73]

[73]2 July 1948. *Grant County News.*

TO VOTE DRY VOTE "NO"

For God, Country and Home

Don't Vote For Revenue And Not Get It!

For Less Than Two Cents Would You Vote Saloons Back in Grant County?

FOR LESS THAN TWO PENNIES WOULD YOU VOTE TO PUT LIQUOR BACK UNDER THE NOSES OF OUR BOYS AND GIRLS EVEYWHERE THEY GO IN THE COUNTY?

SINCE GRANT COUNTY VOTED DRY, IT HAS MEANT THE LOSS OF LESS THAN TWO PENNIES PER PERSON IN REVENUE FROM THE STATE'S LIQUOR CONSUMPTION AND LICENSE TAXES.——THE ONLY OTHER REVENUE GRANT COUNTY HAS LOST SINCE VOTING DRY IS THE LOCAL LICENSE FEES CHARGED SALOONS. THESE LOCAL FEES NEVER DID NOR NEVER WILL EVEN PAY FOR THE CARE OF THE DRUNKS THE SALOONS CREATE.

IF YOU WANT THE PROOF

READ THE REPORT OF KENTUCKY'S DEPARTMENT OF REVENUE, YEAR CLOSING JUNE 30TH, 1947.

SINCE GRANT VOTED DRY

SHE HAS CONTINUED TO RECEIVE HER FULL SHARE OF THE REVENUE POURING INTO THE STATE'S GENERAL FUND FROM 73 DISTILLERIES, 6 BREWERIES, 150 WHOLESALE DISTRIBUTORS AND OVER 4,000 BEER AND WHISKEY SALOONS OVER THE STATE. And WET or DRY she will CONTINUE to receive HER SHARE of this revenue.

SINCE GOING DRY, GRANT COUNTY HAS SAVED HUNDREDS OF THOUSANDS OF DOLLARS FOR THE NECESSITIES OF LIFE AND EVEN MANY LUXURIES. THIS SUM IS NOW CONTRIBUTING TO THE CONTINUED PEACE AND PROSPERITY OF THE COUNTY.

WHY?

DID SEVEN COUNTIES VOTE TO REMAIN DRY?

Trimble, Scott, Letcher, Madison, Knott, Lewis and Boyd Counties voted saloons out by a combined dry majority of 3,313. TWO YEARS AGO these same Counties voted to keep saloons and roadhouses from coming back by a combined majority of 7,729. And the soldier boys were all back home. ——LET THE LIQUOR BOYS ANSWER THAT ONE.

PROHIBITION IS A SUCCESS——
NO BETTER PROOF THAN THIS!
LET'S JOIN THOSE SEVEN COUNTIES
SATURDAY, JULY 3, 1948.

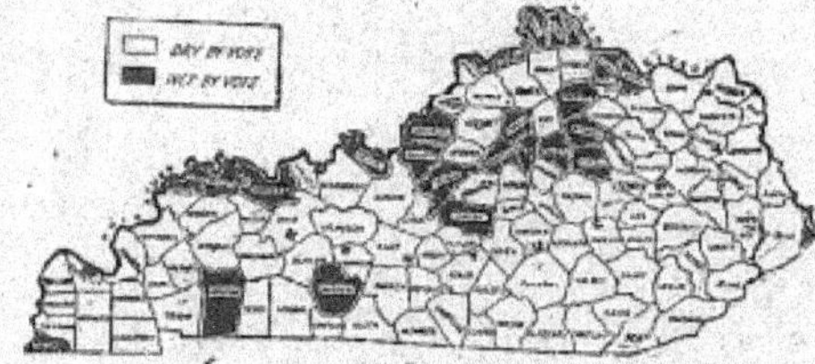

WET AND DRY MAP OF KENTUCKY, JULY 1, 1946
The ninety-three dry counties appear white. One hundred and five dry precincts, scattered in fifteen wet counties, do not sho wexcept McCracken County, which is all dry except Paducah and two precincts in the county. Ten precincts are dry in the southern half of Union County.

WHO?

PAYS THE LIQUOR REVENUE?

The LIQUOR INDUSTRY ADMITS the DRINKERS PAY it. Read what they say—THE CONSUMER "PAYS THE FREIGHT."

"One fact should be made clear. While the industry is proud of its role as tax collector, it recognizes that it does not pay excise taxes. It merely collects them. The consumer pays them."—The Distilled Spirits Industry.

MOTHERS—CHILDREN—AND THE HOME PAY LIQUOR'S REVENUE IN TEARS, MISERY AND SUFFERING.

DON'T LET SALOONS BACK IN GRANT COUNTY.
VOTE NO TO KEEP THEM OUT
SATURDAY, JULY 3, 1948.

VOTE NO AND KEEP GRANT COUNTY DRY

Don't Let the Liquor and Beer Joints Back in Grant County —— Keep Them Out!

SAMPLE BALLOT
For Local Option Election July 3rd
Are you in favor of the Sale of Alcoholic Beverages in Grant County, Kentucky? YES ... ☐ NO .... ☒

BETTER GOVERNMENT LEAGUE
FOR GRANT COUNTY

THE SALOONS AND DIVES ARE KNOCKING AT THE DOOR OF YOUR HOME, ASKING YOUR PERMISSION TO COME IN. TELL THEM

[74]

[74] 2 July 1948. *Grant County News.*

A Little Chat With

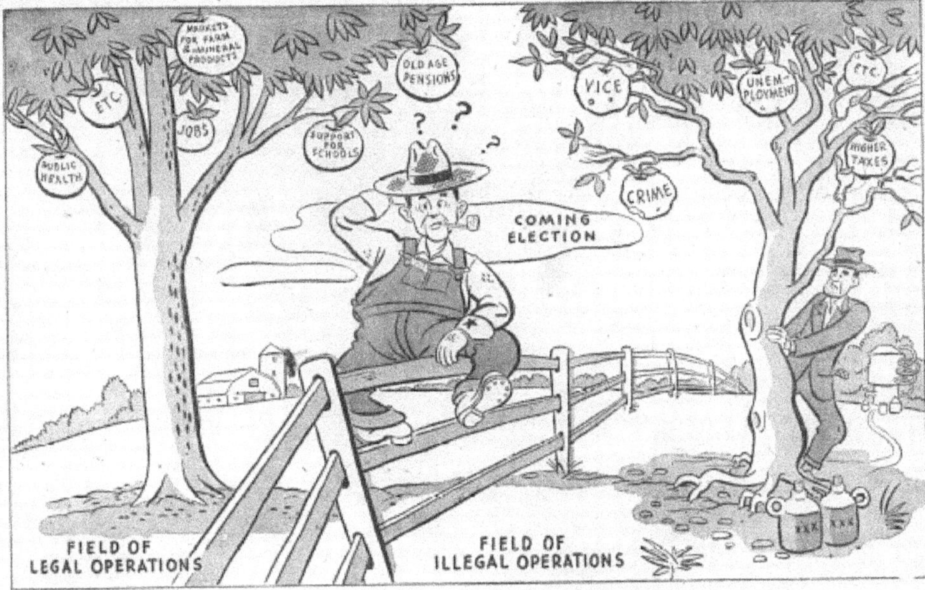

A Man On The Fence

Hello there, Neighbor!

We want to offer you our deepest sympathy.

We can see how uncomfortable you are — sitting astride that fence with a foot dangling on either side.

We can see, too, that a lot of your discomfort is because you are terribly confused. You're trying to figure out something.

Ah, we get it! You want to get off that fence, but can't make up your mind which side to get down on. Suppose we tell you a few things that may help you decide—O. K.?

Look, now! On your right side (and we do mean THE RIGHT side) is the FIELD OF LEGAL OPERATIONS. The soil there is WET and very productive. The chief plant thriving there is the REVENUE tree, which bears some very fine fruit—such as Support for Schools, Public Health, Old Folks Pensions, Employment for Labor, Markets for Farm and Mine Products, etc.

And the amazing thing is that this tree requires so little attention. Just prune it now and then with the Shears of LEGAL CONTROL, and it will cause practically no trouble.

Now glance at the field on your left side (rather we should say the WRONG side). That field is called the FIELD OF PROHIBTION or ILLEGAL OPERATIONS. See how DRY the soil is? Trees that bear GOOD fruit will not grow on that side. Instead, you have trees that produce such unpalatable fruits as Higher Taxes, Unemployment, Vice, Crime, etc.

And wait! There's something else you ought to know! That DRY field produces some wild underground crops, known as Moonshining, Bootlegging, Rum-running, Gangsterism, etc. Sometimes the people try to destroy these crops with an "exterminator" called Law Enforcement; but it just seems impossible to get rid of them.

We're quite suspicious that, 'way down deep, that "dry" soil is actually much wetter than the WET field on your right. But its wetness benefits nobody but a few dozen racketeers who don't mind working underground.

Well, we've told you how things are on each side of the fence. But THE DECISION IS UP TO YOU.

Oh! You've decided already! You're going to get down on the RIGHT SIDE, the WET side.

That's fine, neighbor! Proves what a sensible fellow you are.

So long now! We'll be seeing you—at the polls on SATURDAY, JULY 3D.

We'll All

VOTE "YES"

Grant County Citizens Committee For Legal Sales Of Alcoholic Beverages

75

[75] 2 July 1948. *Grant County News.*

A Famous Editorial Speaks For Grant County

Henry Grady Still Lives In The Hearts Of The People!

THE ELOQUENT DEFENSE OF WOMANHOOD, childhood and the home against the liquor traffic made by Henry Grady, famed journalist of the past generation, is still remembered. Mr. Grady was opposing the return of saloons to his home city, Atlanta, Georgia:

"MY FRIENDS, HESITATE BEFORE you vote liquor back . . . now that it is shut out. DON'T TRUST IT. It is powerful, aggressive, and universal in its attacks. Tonight it enters an humble home to strike the roses from a woman's cheeks, and tomorrow it challenges this republic in the halls of Congress.

"TODAY IT STRIKES THE CRUST from the lips of starving children, and tomorrow levies tribute from the government itself. There is not cottage humble enough to escape it . . . no palace strong enough to shut it out.

" . . . IT IS THE MORTAL ENEMY of peace and order. The despoiler of men, the terror of women, the cloud that shadows the face of children, the demon that has dug more graves and sent more souls unshriven to judgment than all the pestilences that have wasted life since God sent the plagues of Egypt, and all the wars since Joshua stood before Jericho . . .

"IT CAN PROFIT NO MAN by its return. It can uplift no industry, revive no interest, remedy no wrong . . . It comes to destroy, and it shall profit mainly by the ruin of your sons and mine. It comes to mislead human souls and crush human hearts under its rumbling wheels.

"IT COMES TO BRING gray-haired mothers down in sorrow to their graves. It comes to turn the wife's love into despair, and her pride into shame. It comes to still the laughter on the lips of little children, and to stifle all the music of the home and fill it with silence and desolation. It comes to ruin your body and mind, to wreck your home . . ." Don't let the saloon back."

NO! MR. GRADY . . LIQUOR'S NOT GOING TO COME BACK IN OUR COUNTY BY MY VOTE

WHAT DO YOU SAY?

SIGNED, Committee of Veterans of World War II

Donald Bingham
John Lawrence
Orville Cook
John Ackman
Hugh Bingham
Paul Lawrence
Wilbur Bingham
Raymond Lawrence
Melvin Hutton
Allen Caldwell
Douglas Ackman
Kenneth Kenner
Willie Cook
R. N. Barnes
Russell Brown
Wes Havicus
Omer Brown
Ray Bates
Otis Brown
J. W. Howard
Rual Brown
Earl Jones
Robert Hisel
John Sullivan
Kenneth Holbrook
Keith Kinner
Harold True
Glinden Beach
Alvin Sipple
Irvin Jump
Kirt Hutton
Victor Steger
William Lillard
Earl Jones
Robert Hisel
Denver Wynn
Hubert Lusby
Richard Baston
Donovan Hedger
Charles F. Colcord
Holton Carnes
Norris Delph
Alvin Barnes

SIGNED, Committee for Dry Forces of Grant County

Bertie Richardson
W. G. Atha
Elzie Webster
Everett Webster
Harold K. Connely
L. N. Stamper
Mrs. Harold Connely
William Blaine
O. G. Ramsey
J. B. Landrum
Louis Smith
Bernard Pelfrey
Clay Bennett
Mrs. J. B. Landrum
G. R. Henson
F. M. Scroggin
Fred Vice
Cecil Ballard
Howard McKinsey
Ed Alexander
Mrs. Jennie Renaker
Finley Hubbard
W. W. Hon
C. H. Ferrell
Earl Stone
Roscoe Jump
K. R. Connely
Mrs. Roscoe Jump
Mrs. Earl Stone
Mrs. Floyd Martin
Mrs. W. W. Hon
W. C. Franks
Hobart Varner
A. C. Gross
Herman Carnes
Robert Blackburn
Mrs. Calvin Points
Mrs. Ray Lawrence
Fred Turpin
L. M. Menefee
Marion Belew
A. L. May
Ira T. Caldwell
J. R. Stephens
Mrs. Marion Belew
Everett Latimer
Mrs. Franklin Webster
June Lusby
Mrs. L. M. Ackman
Mrs. Calvert Hulett
Russell Lawrence
Mrs. Ruben Taylor
O. O. Frakes
C. B. Acree
Cauley Davis
Mrs. William Howell
John Henry
Wilbur Odor
Mrs. Loyal Epperson
C. C. Ackman
Estell Hopper
Nancy Mortis Ackman
L. A. Ackman
Elmer Brooks
Floyd Dunn
Mrs. Ernest Ackman
Willie Hook
W. F. Dunn
Lescal Taylor
A. Threlkeld
Mrs. Lescal Taylor
Mrs. Walter Epperson
John Mitts
Ethel Fortner
Ernest Ackman
Mrs. L. B. Simpson
Ernest Gray
John Brown
Sol Brown
Julian Caldwell
Mrs. Edith Chipman
R. C. Stewart
Forest Taylor
A. W. Collins
J. H. Colcord
Floyd Osborne
Jake Berkley
Kirtley Caldwell
Mrs. Kirtley Caldwell
Everett White
L. A. Rogers
Raymond True
Herman Jones
Charlie Shannon
Beuford Wainscott
Mrs. W. K. Childers
Mrs. Violet Harrison
John Poe
John A. Chapman
Thurman Poe
Perry McComas
Ola Taylor
W. M. Wilson
Mrs. Thurman Poe
Kelley Kennedy
Harold Hedger
Gilbert Longbons
Joe Points
Elbert Points
Mrs. Mary Beach
J. T. Stephenson
Russell Osborn
R. H. Morris
John Sullivan
Robert Hedges
Steve Zukor
Denver Dunn
Mrs. Denver Dunn
Thomas D. Webb
Mrs. Raymond Stewart
Mrs. Floyd Osborne
Ernest Chipman
Perry Scroggin
A. N. Skinner
Everett West
Herbert Caldwell
Clyde V. Caldwell
Wilbur Woodyard
Mrs. F. M. Clinkscales
Mrs. Perry Scroggins
Mrs. Herbert Caldwell
Mrs. Everett West
Otis Kells
Mrs. Otis Kells
J. W. Bennett
L. M. Ackman
Chester Caldwell
George Ammerman
Franklin Webster
Florian Link
James Epperson
W. P. Colson
Jesse Colson
John McClain
Mrs. Walter Epperson
Garvey Fortner
Mrs. Garvey Fortner
Harold Snell
Mrs. Harold Snell
Mrs. Ethel Fortner
Lutie Cook
Mrs. Lutie Cook

SATURDAY, July 3rd, 1948, between 6 A. M. and 4 P. M. is Grant County's time of testing. ---If you don't vote, you vote "Wet".

TO VOTE "DRY", VOTE "NO"

76

[76] 2 July 1948. *Grant County News.*

GRANT COUNTY CITIZENS HAVE

THE VOTERS' CHOICE!

If you vote "DRY" you get . . .

1. BOOTLEGGING!
2. POOR QUALITY OF ALCOHOLIC BEVERAGES, AT HIGHER PRICES!
3. LOSS OF REVENUE!
4. LOSS OF MONEY AND BUSINESS TO WET COUNTIES!
5. CONDITIONS ALMOST IMPOSSIBLE TO CONTROL!

If you vote "WET' you get . . .

1. LEGAL SALE OF LIQUORS!
2. GOOD QUALITY OF ALCOHOLIC BEVERAGES, AT RIGHT PRICES!
3. GAIN IN REVENUE!
4. MONEY AND BUSINESS KEPT IN GRANT COUNTY!
5. CONDITIONS EASY TO CONTROL!

YOU CAN'T STOP THE SALE OF LIQUOR - - - BUT YOU CAN CONTROL IT AND MAKE IT PAY TAXES TO THE COUNTY!

VOTE "YES"

SATURDAY, JULY 3rd

—Grant County Citizens Committee for Legal Sale of Alcoholic Beverages.

[77]

[77] 2 July 1948. *Grant County News.*

The Old Saloon Keepers Are Getting The Jitters

In their Feverish Scramble to get back in GRANT County they are blaming everything on

PROHIBITION

"IT'S HARD TO BELIEVE"

THAT ANYBODY CAN BE SO BLIND-

They Don't Like Prohibition . . . It Puts Them Out Of Business.

[78]

[78] 2 July 1948. *Grant County News.*

Grant County Voted Dry By 591 Votes

Drys Carry All Precincts In The County Except Four. Vote At Holbrook Tied 40-40.

Grant County was voted dry last Saturday by a majority of 591. The total vote cast was 3,297, exclusive of 94 spoiled ballots, 1,944 dry and 1,353 wet. The vote cast represents approximately 42 ¡ percent. of the total vote of the county and was considered fairly heavy. According to the registration there are 7,763 voters in Grant County. The voting list has not been purged in at least three years, The News was informed by the county clerk's office.

The dry forces had a strong organization. They started out to win the election. Open meetings were held in all parts of the county from the time those interested in retaining prohibition in Grant County formed their organization. Speakings were held in all sections of the county and are reported to have been well attended. The drys are highly pleased with the outcome of the election while the wets express themselves as being thoroughly disgusted.

An unexpected even took place Saturday which has caused considerable comment. Those opposed to the sale of alcoholic beverages in Grant County had challengers at the polls. It is the law that a person who is a registered voter, must, if he removes from one precinct to the other or if he is a new resident in the county, go to the office of the county clerk and register. Otherwise, he shall be denied the right to vote. Every voter in Grant County who is a subscriber to The Grant County News should be aware of the law as this newspaper has never failed to publish in due time, the deadline for registering and inform the public that is absolutely necessary for persons under the category just named, to go to the clerk's office and register properly. In the issue of June 4th, 1948 The Grant County News at the top of column three, page 1, the following news appeared:

June 9 Last Day To Register

"Wednesday, June 9th is the last day to register for the August primary or the local option election, July 3rd.

To be eligible to vote, it is necessary that new residents of Grant County or persons removing to different precincts since the last election, go to the office of the county court clerk and register or be present and have someone register for you."

Some voters are reported to have been challenged who have voted in the same precinct for as long as thirty years even though they did live in a different precinct on July 3rd.

The wets were virtually unorganized or, if they were their organization did not take advantage of the right to challenge. Leading workers for the wets have stated to The News that they will possibly file an injunction to have the election set aside.

However, it is not believed a sufficient number of votes were challenged to swing the election for either the wets or the drys. The large majority proves overwhelmingly that Grant Countians are definitely opposed to the sale of alcoholic beverages.

Every precinct in the county's 19 voted dry except 4, West Williamstown, West Dry Ridge, and Downingsville voted wet, and a tie vote was registered at Holbrook.

Perry county voted wet Saturday by a margin of 2,419 in a turnout of more than 6,900 voters. Of Kentucky's 120 counties, 92 are dry.[79]

Official Count In Local Option Election, July 3rd

Precinct	Yes	No
West Williamstown	148	139
East Wmstown No. 2	142	178
East Wmstown No. 1	111	129
West Dry Ridge	200	189
East Dry Ridge	79	142
Cordova	64	86
Corinth	99	144
Keefer	26	47
Mason	35	118
Cross Roads	17	72
Holbrook	40	40
Downingsville	61	24
Jonesville	24	104
Stewartsville	45	62
Flat Creek	49	65
Zion Station	22	29
Mt. Zion	58	98
Sherman	42	96
Crittenden	91	186
Total "No" Votes		1944
Total "Yes" Votes	1353	
Plurality of "No" Votes		591

[79] 9 July 1948. *Grant County News.* Author Unknown.

WE THANK YOU

We thank everyone who helped to vote our county "dry" July 3

1. We are thankful to God first.
2. We thank everyone on the precinct committee.
3. We thank all churches and pastors in the county.
4. We thank every voter who came to the polls and voted "dry".

CENTRAL COMMITTEE FOR LOCAL OPTION

G. R. Henson	Herbert Caldwell	C. N. Ogg
Forest Taylor	L. M. Ackman	J. W. Bennett
Roscoe Jump	Augustus Threlkeld	

[80]

[80] 9 July 1948. *Grant County News.*

Drunken Driver Fined $500 And Costs By Pettit

Driver's License Also Suspended For One Year. Other Fines Meted Out In Quarterly Court.

Joseph Hannah, of Orlando, Florida, was fined $500 and costs last week in Judge C. A. Pettit's Quarterly Court when he plead guilty to a charge of operating a motor vehicle while under the influence of intoxicating liquor. His driver's license was also suspended for one year.

The Floridian's auto figured in a wreck on the Dixie Highway near Dry Ridge several days ago in which an Ohio honeymooning couple were seriously injured. Hannah was released from a Covington hospital last week and returned here for trial.

In other cases before the Quarterly Court last week, Gerald Montgomery, of West Chester, Ohio was fined $10 and costs on a charge of being drunk in a public place; William Daugherty Jones, Corinth, breach of peace, $25 and costs; William Owen Cook, Corinth, operating a motor vehicle under the influence of intoxicating liquor, $100 and costs.

Thomas Barber, Danville, Ill., and Carl O'Hara, Mason, charged with being drunk in a public place, were each fined $25 and costs.[81]

Drunken Drivers Occupy Time Of Quarterly Court

Drunken drivers continue to occupy a great part of the time of Judge Chas. A. Pettit in Grant Quarterly Court. It is noted that a majority of arrests are of persons out-of-the county and often out-of-the state.

Cases heard last week and the past Monday are: Arson C. Warner, Columbus, Ohio, charged with reckless driving, fined $10 and costs. Charles Webster, Jr., Rising Sun, Ind., $100 and costs on a charge of issuing a cold check. Clay Kells, Falmouth, was fined $1.00 and costs on a like charge. Charles F. Johnson, Georgetown, was arrested on a charge of drunken driving and was fined $150 and costs. A fine of $150 and costs was imposed on Marion Sloan, Dayton, Oh., for driving a motor vehicle while under the influence of liquor. Cisrow Turner, Georgetown, William H. Hill, Cincinnati, and Walter Feltner, Cincinnati, were each fined $25 and costs for being drunk on a public highway.

Fred George Lazaris and Jack Brown, 15 and 17 years of age respectively, were fined $50 and costs each on charges of reckless driving and $50 and costs each on breach of peace charges.

Preliminary hearing for Noel E. Lawson, Lexington minister, was scheduled for today.[82]

Prohibitionists To Have Meeting Sunday, Jan. 23rd

The prohibitionists of the county have called a meeting for Sunday afternoon, Jan. 23rd at 3:00 o'clock at the Dry Ridge Baptist Church. All voters of the county who are interested in electing county officials who will carry out law enforcement are invited to attending a meeting according to their advertisement on another page of this issue of The News.

The "drys" fought a vigorous battle to keep the county free of the sale of alcoholic beverages when a local option election was held last summer and won.[83]

Dry Forces To Meet Sunday

The advertisement appearing in last week's News announcing a meeting of the Dry Forces of Grant County carried last Sunday as the date for the meeting. The advertising copy furnished The News carried the wrong date, it should have been January 30th.

[81] 15 October 1948. *Grant County News.* Author Unknown.
[82] 5 November 1948. *Grant County News.* Author Unknown.
[83] 21 January 1949. *Grant County News.* Author Unknown.
[84] 28 January 1949. *Grant County News.* Author Unknown.

A meeting is called for Sunday afternoon, January 30th at the courthouse in Williamstown.[84]

Dry Forces Of Grant County Meet To Elect Committeemen

The Dry Forces of Grant County in a meeting at the courthouse last Sunday afternoon, elected a steering committee of five men to select a chairman from each of the County's 19 precincts to complete to act in selecting a candidate for the office of Sheriff of Grant County and Judge of the County at the coming primary election in August. The five men comprising the steering committee are: Fred Turpin, chairman; Mike Satterwhite, G. R. Henson, Thomas D. Webb and A. Threlkeld.

The steering committee has selected the chairmen from the various precincts who have been notified to meet at the courthouse tonight (Friday) at 7:30 to decide upon the candidates for the offices of Sheriff and Judge.

Herbert Caldwell was re-elected chairman of the Dry Forces of Grant County at the meeting Sunday afternoon.[85]

Is your News subscription paid?

Five Slot Machines Confiscated At Kenton Co. Tavern

State Troopers who entered Huff's Place, a roadside tavern north of Crittenden, with a warrant for the arrest of a person by the name of Smith last Saturday night, confiscated five slot machines.

Sgt. R. E. Osborne stated that it was the sworn duty of State Troopers to do their duty when they observe the law being broken whether or not they possess a warrant.

Joe Kennedy, operator of the tavern, was fined $750 and costs by Judge William E. Wehrman in Kenton County Court on a charge of possessing the five slot machines.[86]

Local And State Officers Seize Liquor

Quantity Of Illegal Liquor And Beer Confiscated In Raid On Rock Garden. Proprietor Released Under $500 Bond.

Eleven half pints of whiskey, six fifths, three pints and five half pints of gin and three cases of beer were [seized] by state and county officers who raided Rock Garden, south of Williamstown, Monday night. The confiscated illegal liquor and beer is held as evidence by Sheriff Lawrence Caldwell.

The proprietor of Rock Garden, Chester Campbell, was charged with selling intoxicating beverages in a dry county. He was released on $500 bond and ordered to appear today before Judge C. A. Pettit.[87]

Drys Endorse Sheriff And Judge Candidates

John S. Mitts And F. B. Taylor To Run For Offices On Dry Ticket

---

John S. Mitts, Lawrenceville precinct, has filed for office of Sheriff of Grant County, thus becoming the second candidate to make official announcement for the office. Otto Johnson, Elliston, made his formal announcement last week. Elmer Ballard, deputy sheriff, is to be a candidate for the office but has not made formal announcement to date.

F. B. Taylor, Baptist minister at Jonesville, will be a candidate for the office of County Judge. Both, Mr. Mitts and Mr. Taylor have been endorsed by the Citizens League for Better Government, whose members are among the dry forces in the county. These two candidates will have the support and backing of the

---

[85] 4 February 1949. *Grant County News.* Author Unknown.
[86] 25 February 1949. *Grant County News.* Author Unknown.
[87] 4 March 1949. *Grant County News.* Author Unknown.

league. Mr. Taylor is pastor of Macedonia Baptist Church, Jonesville. Former pastorates are Mason, Oak Ridge, Lawrenceville, Bethany and Crittenden.

Buford Wainscott, former highway patrolman, will be Mr. Mitts running mate for deputy sheriff.

Otto Johnson stated that he was running on "his own" and was not being backed by any group, wet or dry. Mr. Johnson maintains his home on the Mt. Zion and Eliston road.

Rumor still has it that Rasho Marksberry and R. Lester Mullins will be candidates for judge. If they enter the race it will be farmer, preacher and school teacher.[88]

Man Charged With Possession Of Spirited Liquors

State police last week arrested Orville Sydnor in Harrison county for being drunk in a public place. He was also charged with illegally possessing and transporting two cases of whiskey and two cases of beer which officers found in his truck.[89]

Officers Raid Tavern At Twin Bridges

Two Men Arrested And Held To Grand Jury Under $500.00 Bonds. Beer, Whiskey, And Slot Machines Confiscated.

State police, the sheriff's office and W. O. Mitchell, of the State Alcoholic Control Board, Frankfort, raided Early Crouch's tavern at Twin Bridges last Sunday. Arrested in the raid were Crouch and Wallace Barnes, of Newport. The latter was reportedly operating a five cents slot machine.

Twenty-four cases of beer, a fifth of whiskey and a five cents slot machine were confiscated by the officers.

Placed under arrest, Crouch was charged with possession of alcoholic beverages in dry territory. Barnes was charged with operating a game of chance. The men were given a hearing before Judge Chas. A. Pettit Monday morning and released under $500.00 bonds each for action of the grand jury.[90]

9 Arrested And Fined Over Labor Day Weekend

Weekend Fines Total $335. One Placed Under $250 Appearance Bond For September 12th.

Nine persons were arrested and given fines in County Court for offenses during the Labor Day weekend.

Estelle Wilson, 2339 Harper Ave., Norwood, charged with drunken driving, was fined $100 and costs.

A fine of $100 and costs on a charge of drunken driving was imposed upon James B. Comer, of 1618 Main St., Cincinnati.

Will Daugherty Jones, Corinth, charged with operating a motor vehicle without an operator's license, to which he plead guilty, was fined $10 and costs. Jones was also charged with driving while under the influence of intoxicating liquor and was held under $250 bond for appearance September 12th.

Audrey Ballou, Lafollette, Tennessee, and Clarence Amburgey, Williamstown, were fined $10 and costs each for being drunk in a public place.

George W. Shearer, 412 Wyoming Ave,., Wyoming, Ohio was charged with reckless driving and fined $15 and costs.

Walter Kaminski, 8070 Badger Ave., Detroit, Mich., charged with reckless driving as a result of a collision between the automobile he was driving and one operated by Rassie Cook, Grant County, made satisfactory settlement for repairs to Cook's car and was released.

Lonnie Jones, 21 Back St., Cincinnati was fined $100 and costs on a charge of being drunk in a public place.[91]

---

[88] 11 March 1949. *Grant County News.* Author Unknown.
[89] 18 March 1949. *Grant County News.* Author Unknown.
[90] 1 July 1949. *Grant County News.* Author Unknown.
[91] 9 September 1949. *Grant County News.* Author Unknown.

A. A.'s To Have New Year's Party

A. A.'s of Northern Kentucky will have their second annual New Year's party at 4 p. m. on New Year's Day. A buffet lunch consisting of old Kentucky ham, turkey, etc. will be served in the evening. Games will be played and refreshments will be served during the party, an A. A. member announced. Music furnished by out of town talent will be an added feature.

A. A.'s families and anyone interested in the organization are cordially invited to attend.[92]

Drunks Land In County Jail Over Holiday Weekend

New Year's Drinkers Are Warned To Keep Off The Roads. Heavy Fine Imposed For Driving Auto While Drunk.

Officers were busy during the Christmas holiday weekend bringing in drunks who learned before it was all over that liquor and gasoline does not mix.

Fourteen were arrested and fined for drunken driving or being drunk in a public place, others for driving without an operator's license or for breach of the peace. They were all given hearings before Judge Chas. A. Pettit and fined.

Those arrested were as follows: Ben Temple (colored) Cincinnati, was fined $10 and costs for driving without an operator's license.

Ervin J. Privitt, Cincinnati, fined $10 and costs for being drunk in a public place.

Robert McLin, Dayton, fined $1 and costs for breach of the peace, and $25 and costs for being drunk in a public place.

Lewis T. Sheldon, Lexington, $10 and costs for being drunk in a public place.

Lum Lore, fined $1 and costs for breach of the peace, and $25 and costs for being drunk in a public place.

Lowell Leming, Williamstown, fined $10 and costs for being drunk in a public place.

Charles Eagleton, Cincinnati, fined $100 and costs for drunken driving, and $2 and costs for driving without an operator's license.

Tom Holder, Williamstown, $100 and costs for drunken driving, and $2 and costs for operating an automobile without a license.

Paul Cole, Lexington, $100 and costs for drunken driving.

Delbert Capps, Dayton, $10 and costs for reckless driving.

George W. Crockett, Cincinnati, $10 and costs for reckless driving.

William Langford, Detroit, and Curtis Weimeyer, Orlando, Fla., each fined $10 and costs for reckless driving.

Sam Jones, Cincinnati, $25 and costs for being drunk in a public place.

Russell (Buck) Sweitzer, Corinth, $10 and costs for being drunk in a public place.

Boyd Flynn, Cincinnati, $100 and costs for drunken driving.

George F. Greenwell, Demossville, $100 and costs for drunken driving.

Leland McElvoy, Cincinnati, and Leonard Withrow, Dayton, Oh., were fined $100 and costs each for drunken driving.

A Warning

Those who intend to celebrate the New Year holiday by drinking, are warned to stay off the road, Anyone arrested for operating a motor vehicle while drunk is sure to be jailed and fined.[93]

[92] 30 December 1949. *Grant County News.* Author Unknown.

[93] 30 December 1949. *Grant County News.* Author Unknown.

Medicine Looks At Alcoholics Anonymous

DR. W. W. BAUER, broadcasting under the auspices of THE AMERICAN MEDICAL ASS'N.,— Bureau of Health Education, has given us permission to reprint his remarks on the radio program, DOCTORS AT HOME, given February 9, 1946, over the NBC network:

"Why do men and women drink to excess? Is it because of an appetite for the taste of alcohol? Probably not, because most people have to learn to like alcoholic liquor. Is it because they crave the effect? Many of them dislike the effects. Is it because of a drug addict, like morophine? No. It is now generally recognized that the chronic alcoholic becomes so by reason of difficulty with his personality. It is true that he deteriorates from abuse of alcohol, but he would not abuse it if he were not already lacking. His apparent addictions to alcohol are an effort to escape from reality. The normal man who uses alcohol can take or leave his drink. The person who becomes a chronic alcoholic never knows to what his first drink will lead. There are, in short, persons who ought never to drink.

A solution to the alcoholic problem which works in more than 60 percent of instances has been found by a group of men and women who call themselves ALCOHOLICS ANONYMOUS. The title describes them exactly. They have been alcoholic, and they remain without name."

HARRY M: TIEBOUT, M. D., Greenwich, Conn., made the following remarks on THERAPEUTIC MECHANISM OF ALCOHOLICS ANONYMOUS in the American Journal of PSYCHIATRY, January 1944: "The work of Alcoholics Anonymous has a three-fold aspect. First, the group has weekly gatherings where experiences are related and problems discussed. Second, all are urged to read their book, 'ALCOHOLICS ANONYMOUS,' which contains their tenets and must be read if one is to arrive at any understanding of their program. Third, the members work with prospects who are making their initial contact with the group. Helping others is a two1way situation since it not only assists the beginner in his first efforts but it also aids the helper who derives from his efforts something which is essential for his continued sobriety. Statistics at the New York office of the organization reads as follows.

5 recovered at the end of the first year.
15 recovered at the end of the second year.
40 recovered at the end of the third year.
100 recovered at the end of the fourth year.
400 recovered at the end of the fifth year.
2,000 recovered at the end of the sixth year.
8,000 recovered at the end of the seventh year.
75,000 recovered at the end of the fourteenth year.

A Special Meeting Will Be Held On Tuesday, November 29th

AT THE ST. WILLIAM HALL, WILLIAMSTOWN, KY., AT 8:00 p.m., E.S.T. THE GENERAL PUBLIC IS INVITED. A PROMINENT BUSINESS MAN, FORMERLY OF AKRON, OHIO, WHERE A.A. WAS ORGANIZED IN 1935, WILL BE THE SPEAKER OF THE EVENING.

On November 1st, a prominent insurance executive from Cincinnati (graduate of the University of Cincinnati and Harvard Law School) was our guest speaker. Other good speakers, such as Lawyers, Doctors, Dentists, Salesmen, Radio Announcers, Bankers, Business Men of all kinds, Farmers Truck Drivers, Bartenders, Members of the Clergy, Etc., will speak at later dates.

A. A.'S OF GRANT COUNTY

P. O. BOX 55, WILLIAMSTOWN, KY.

94

[94]Circa December 1949. *Grant County News.*

1950s

Mt. Zion Baptists Protest Liquor Radio Advertising

The Mt. Zion Baptist Church, composed of 363 members, voted unanimously in a business meeting to write Columbia Broadcasting System, Inc., protesting the advertising of liquor on the radio.

The following excerpt from Columbia Broadcasting Company's letter to the church follows:

"Your letter gives us an opportunity to advise you that we have never accepted the advertising of spirituous liquors on the Columbia network and that we have no intention of changing this policy.

"As you know, discussion and comment on such a subject can give rise to incorrect reports, and we are glad to be able to clarify our position to you."[1]

Slot Machine And Alcoholics Destroyed

Sheriff Elmer Ballard destroyed a case of beer and several full pints and broken pints of whiskey in front of the courthouse Wednesday afternoon. A slot machine containing $1.75 was also mutilated.

The whiskey, beer and slot machine had been confiscated some time ago. Officers got the 25 cents slot machine from Marvin Mason, and the beer and whiskey from Edward Helton, Raymond Grubbs and Elmer Mersch.[2]

Truck And Drunken Drivers Fined

Ten truck drivers were fined by Judge R. L. Mullins $15 and $10 costs each, for driving trucks loaded above the weight limit. They were Jack Burnette, Miami, Fla.; Emory Clark, Orlando, Fla.; Ed Harrison, Valdosta, Ga.; Edward S. Carson, Akron, Oh.; William B. Jackson, Atlanta, Ga.; George A. Smith, Thomasville; William B. Vickers, Newport; Robert Nichols, Hartford, Mich.; Fred Hall, Greenville, Tenn., and Robert Farmer, Cincinnati.

Robert McQueen, Harrison, Oh., was fined $15 and $10 costs. Jesse J. Cox, Cincinnati, and Leonard Wright, Owenton, were fined $100 and $5 costs each for drunken driving. Marvin Hughes, Owenton, was fined $25 and $10 costs for being drunk in a public place. A fine of $2 and $10 costs was imposed upon Rosella Chipman, Williamstown, for driving without an operator's license. Ronald Weatherbee, New York, was fined $15 and $10 costs for reckless driving.[3]

Marvin Mason Says Slot Machine Was Not His Property

The News published an item of news in the issue of Jan. 20 captioned, "Slot Machine And Alcoholics Destroyed," which information was obtained from Sheriff Elmer Ballard. In the second paragraph the item read, "Officers got the 25 cents slot machine from Marvin Mason."

Mr. Mason stated to The News that the slot machine was left in his place of business, during his absence, by someone unknown to him and that he notified county officials to call for it.

[1] 20 January 1950. *Grant County News.* Author Unknown.
[2] 20 January 1950. *Grant County News.* Author Unknown.
[3] 20 January 1950. *Grant County News.* Author Unknown.

Following is the court order relative to the above mentioned news story:

"GRANT QUARTERLY COURT

"To The Sheriff of Grant County.

"You are hereby directed to destroy a 25c slot machine, that is lodged in the Grant County Jail, having been taken from the property of Marvin Mason, Mason, on or about the [...] day of June, 1949, and the same being unclaimed, and the owner unknown, you shall destroy said slot machine in front of the Courthouse in Williamstown, Ky., and make due return thereon, and any money found in same shall be turned over to this court.

"Witness my hand this 18th day of January, 1950

"R. Lester Mullins,

"Judge Grant Quarterly Court."[4]

Officers Stage Raids On Two Road Houses

Fines And Jail Sentence Follow Seizure Of Slot Machines And Alcoholic Beverages In Saturday Night And Early Sunday Morning Raids

---

Action took place in Grant County Saturday night and early Sunday morning when two road houses were raided and a quantity of gin, whiskey, beer and three slot machines were brought in as evidence.

The raids were made by Sheriff Elmer Ballard, Deputy Sheriff Julian Foree, Sgt. Roy E. Osborne of the State Police, and State Troopers Chester Harp, Harold Kinman and Paul Dunn. They had a warrant signed by County Judge R. Lester Mullins.

Two slot machines and alcoholic beverages were seized by the officers at Ethel's Place (Sunny Hill) on the Dixie Highway, south of Williamstown. Cited to court Monday morning, Mrs. Ethel McAtee, proprietor of Ethel's Place, was relieved of prosecution when her son, Stanley Luttrell, who said he was associated in business with his mother, claimed the slot machines and liquor were his. He was given 30 days in jail and fined $100 and costs on the liquor charge and fined $250 each on the two slot machine charges.

Found at Ethel's Place was a fifth of gin, a part of a fifth of whiskey, nine cases of beer and 11 cases of empty beer bottles.

Officers confiscated a slot machine at Clarence's Truck Stop, at the intersection of the Dixie Highway, and the Keefer Road. Clarence Purcell, proprietor, was cited into court and fined $250 and costs for suffering a slot machine in his place of business.

Sheriff Ballard destroyed the whiskey and the slot machines in front of the courthouse, Monday. $72.50 taken from the slot machine goes to the state.

The beer and all other beer now lodged for safe keeping in a padded cell in the Grant County jail, will be turned over to the Alcoholic Control Board.[5]

Moonshine And Mash Captured With Still

Sheriff And Federal Officer Find Moonshine Still. Accused To Be Tried In Federal Court Next Month.

Sheriff Elmer Ballard and Robert Perkins, federal officer, captured a 15-gallon moonshine still, 7 gallons of "moon" and 60 gallons of mash on the farm of Ralph Cummins, west of Elliston, last week. Sheriff Ballard said Robert Cummins, brother of Ralph Cummins, was in a smoke house operating the still when he and Mr. Perkins walked upon the scene. Cummins saw the officers and fled down a hill but was captured when he was found lying in some bushes. Claiming ownership of the still, Ralph Cummins was arrested and is now free under $300 bond. He will be tried in federal court in Convington.

This is the first time a moonshine still has been captured in Grant County for many years. Sheriff Ballard said he had been on the alert for the still for the past two months.[6]

---

[4] 27 January 1950. *Grant County News.* Author Unknown.

[5] 27 January 1950. *Grant County News.* Author Unknown.

[6] 10 February 1950. *Grant County News.* Author Unknown.

14 Drivers Lose Licenses For Drunken Driving

Through Wednesday morning, March 22nd, fourteen automobile drivers this month had been convicted for drunken driving and had their licenses revoked for six months.[7]

County Board Of Education Rules Against Dancing

The County Board of Education, in session March 6th, ruled against dancing in any of the schools in the county system, it was learned this week.

Action of the Board took place when a ruling was asked by citizens of Corinth where a controversy had arisen over whether square dancing should take place in the school in that city.[8]

Woman Fined $100 And Sentenced To 30 Days In Jail

Pleading guilty to a charge of selling beer in dry territory, Helen Fredericks was fined $100 and sentenced to 30 days in jail before County Judge R. Lester Mullins, Monday.

Miss Fredericks was cited by agents of the State Alcoholics Beverage Control after she is alleged to have served them beer at Rock Garden, Saturday.

The men from the State Board, Russell Fryman and Joe Fredericks , bought the beer and returned to Williamstown where they obtained a warrant. Upon returning to Rock Garden to search the place, they were unable to find any beer.[9]

Officers Destroy Accumulation Of Beer And Whiskey

County Judge R. Lester Mullins and Deputy Sheriff Julian Foree destroyed approximately 80 bottles of beer and a quantity of whiskey by opening the bottles and pouring the contents in front of the courthouse last Saturday morning.

Alcoholic beverages confiscated when arrests are made is kept for a period of time and then destroyed.[10]

Motorists Fined In County Court

Since June 18th, the following cases have been disposed of in Grant County court:

June 22, Abram E. Hurst, Florence, S. C., was fined $500 and $5 costs for operating an overweight truck on a public highway.

June 24, Walter Phillips, Covington, was fined $100 and $5 costs for driving a motor vehicle while under the influence of alcohol.

June 24, Wilbur E. Lawrence, Cincinnati, Oh., was fined $100 and $5 costs for operating a motor vehicle while under the influence of alcohol. Lovelace was fined $2 and $10 costs on the same day for driving without an operator's license.

June 24, Norman F. Taylor, Cincinnati, was fined $10 and $10 costs for improper passing.

June 23, Robert Daugherty, Dayton, Oh., was fined $5 and $10 costs for driving without an operator's license.

June 24, William A. Williams, Jr., Ludlow, was fined $100 and $5 costs for driving while under the influence of alcohol.

June 18, Clifford Gregory, Cincinnati, was fined $10 and $10 costs for improper passing.

June 24, Robert A. Hartman, Covington, was fined $100 and $5 costs for driving while under the influence of alcohol.

June 25, Clarence Wiles, Lockland, Oh., was fined $100 and $5

[7] 24 March 1950. *Grant County News.* Author Unknown.
[8] 24 March 1950. *Grant County News.* Author Unknown.
[9] 24 March 1950. *Grant County News.* Author Unknown.
[10] 28 April 1950. *Grant County News.* Author Unknown.
[11] 30 June 1950. *Grant County News.* Author Unknown.

costs for driving while under the influence of alcohol.

June 25, Clarence Jump, Williamstown, was fined $100 and $5 costs for driving while under the influence of alcohol.[11]

Lewis Henderson Buys Beer Route

Lewis Henderson has bought from Moody Crouch his beer distributor's route.

Mr. Henderson will distribute four brands of beer in the counties of Kenton, Boone, Gallatin, Carroll and Harrison and will operate two trucks.[12]

Rock Garden Raided Twice In Three Days

Woman Arrested In Both Raids Released Wednesday Under $1500 Bond. Place On Taft Highway Raided.

Alcoholic Control Board agents, Sheriff Elmer Ballard and his deputies and State Police raided Rock Garden, six miles South of Williamstown Sunday morning. Local officers made the second raid on the tavern Tuesday morning at 11 o'clock.

Helen Fredericks, waitress, who served a 30-day jail term early this year for serving alcoholic beverages in dry territory, was arrested in the Sunday raid. She was given a hearing Monday morning before Judge R. Lester Mullins and bound over to the October grand jury. She was released under $500 bond. Helen Baughn, waitress, was arrested by officers when the raid was made. She also was released under $500 bond and bound over to the October grand jury.

Local officers made a second raid on Tuesday morning at Rock Garden and arrested Helen Fredericks again for serving alcoholic beverages. She remained in jail in default of bond until Tuesday afternoon when she was released under $1500 bond.

Chester Campbell, ordered by officers to remain at the place during the raid, fled. A warrant was sworn out for his arrest, but he had not been apprehended Wednesday.

In the raids, officers confiscated quantities of beer and whisky. A slot machine, which Sheriff Ballard said was old and apparently not in operation, was also confiscated.

Sunday, the officers made a raid at a roadside place of business on the Taft Highway near Twin Bridges and arrested Arthur Edwards and confiscated three cases of beer. He was charged with possessing and selling alcoholic beverages in dry territory and suffering gambling on the premises. He was given a hearing before Judge Mullins Monday morning and pleaded guilty to the charge of possessing and selling alcoholic beverages and was fined $100 and given 30 days in jail on each charge. He was bound over to the grand jury on the gambling charge.[13]

Raid Yields No Booze Or Beer; Slot Holds $5.10

March Of Dimes Gains $5.10 From Slot Machine Taken Following Raid On Road House On U. S. 25

Sheriff Elmer Ballard raided the Southern Queen, a roadhouse south of Mason on the Dixie Highway, Tuesday, but found no whiskey or beer. According to Sheriff Ballard, W. D. Roberts, owner and operator of the establishment was arrested on an affidavit bearing the statement that Roberts had sold whiskey. He is charged with selling alcoholic beverages in dry territory.

Officers found a slot machine in a dwelling adjacent to the roadhouse containing $5.10 which was turned over to the March of Dimes. William Hunter claimed ownership of the slot machine, saying he had brought it here to try to sell for another party.[14]

---

[12] 18 August 1950. *Grant County News.* Author Unknown.
[13] 25 August 1950. *Grant County News.* Author Unknown.
[14] 19 January 1951. *Grant County News.* Author Unknown.

Kentuckians Hit Proposed Whisky Tax Hike

Revenue Commissioner H. Clyde Reeves and Guy C. Shearer, chairman of the State Alcoholic Beverage Control Board, have filed protests in Washington against a proposed $3 per gallon increase in the federal whisky tax. The protests were requested by Governor Lawrence Wetherby.

Shearer recommended that the tax be reduced to $6 per gallon. He said Congress had agreed to a reduction upon the end of World War II emergency.

Arguing that as long as whisky may be legally sold, it should be kept within the price range of the average consumer. He said, "If the $12 per gallon excise tax legislation passed, it will not only bring out the hillside moonshiner, but moonshining will again move into the big-time business classification."[15]

Richmond Man Fined Being Drunk On Bus

Owen Young, Richmond, Ky., was fined $10 and $12 costs after he plead guilty to being drunk in a public place Tuesday. Young was arrested on complaint of a bus driver.[16]

Two Killed In Automobile Crash With Drunken Driver

Mrs. Russell Lawrence And C. Liston Hempfling Meet Instant Death. Drunken Soldier Causing Collision Expires.

Mrs. Russell Lawrence, 42, met instant death in an automobile accident on U. S. 60 near Beaver Dam early last Saturday night. C. Liston Hempfling, passenger in the car driven by Mr. Lawrence was also killed and a third passenger, C. C. Weisman, of Elizabethtown, suffered a broken arm and leg. Mr. Lawrence suffered a compound fracture of the right leg. Both are in St, Joseph Hospital, Louisville. I. B. Pyson, 30-year-old soldier and driver of the car which collided with the one driven by Mr. Lawrence, died at 10:30 Saturday night in an Owensboro hospital.

The accident occurred when the automobile driven at high speed by Pyson, rounded a curve on the wrong side of the highway. Mr. Lawrence swerved his car to the left in an attempt to avoid a head-on crash. The two cars crash-sidewise. Mrs. Lawrence was seated on the right side in the front seat and Mr. Hempfling on the right side in the rear. The car was completely demolished. Pyson was later cited for drunken driving.

Mr. and Mrs. Lawrence and Mr. Hempfling had been to Paducah where they attended a State Conference of Production Credit Association Directors and Secretaries. They were taking Mr. Weisman to his home in Elizabethtown; he is Secretary of the Nolin Production Credit Association in Elizabethtown, and Mr. Lawrence holds the office of Secretary of Northern Kentucky Production Credit Association.

Mrs. Lawrence was the daughter of James H. and Jessie Northcutt Colcord and was born in Grant County. She and Mr. Lawrence were married November 1, 1930, they had no children. Besides her husband and father, she is survived by two brothers, Harold Colcord, Lexington, and Chas. Colcord, Verona, and two sisters, Mrs. Anabel Reis, Cleves, Oh., and Mrs. Ethel Mattingly, Louisville. She was an active member of the Dry Ridge Christian Church and Williamstown Woman's Club.

Funeral services were conducted from Dry Ridge Christian Church Wednesday afternoon by Rev. Jack Candy and Rev. J. L. Roberson. Burial was in the Williamstown cemetary with Elliston and Stanley in charge.

Mr. Hempfling was vice president of the Northern Kentucky Production Credit Association and a member of the board and executive committee. He was also Chairman of the Board of Supervisors of Soil Conservation Service in Boone County, a director of the Hebron De-

[15] 16 March 1951. *Grant County News.* Author Unknown.

[16] 31 August 1951. *Grant County News.* Author Unknown.

posit Bank, a member of Hebron Lodge No. 757 F. & A. M., member of the governing body of the Hebron Lutheran Church and a prominent Boone County farmer and orchardist. He is survived by his wife, Mrs. Lizzie Mae Hempfling; a son, Vaughn Hempfling, and a brother, Charles L. Hempfling, both of Taylorspuort; a sister, Mrs. Nita Betham, Baltimore, Md.; his mother, Mrs. E. O. Hempfling, Taylorsport, and three grandchildren. He was 55.

Services for Mr. Hempfling were conducted Tuesday afternoon at 2 o'clock at the Hebron Lutheran Church, burial was in the Hebron cemetary. Services by the Masonic Order were held Tuesday evening.[17]

Raid Yields Nine Half Pints Whiskey

Nora Hunter's Place Raided Wednesday Afternoon, Nine Half Pints Booze Confiscated.

Sheriff Elmer Ballard seized nine half pints of whiskey in a raid on Nora Hunter's place in Dry Ridge late Wednesday.

Assisted by State Police, Sheriff Ballard found the whiskey in a trailer at the rear of the small concrete block building where Mrs. Hunter operates a restaurant and filling station. It is understood she occupies the trailer as living quarters.

The warrant bore the names of Nora Hunter and Lee Landrum. Landrum operates a garage next door to Mrs. Hunter's restaurant. Both were brought to Williamstown and place under bond in the amount of $300 each. They will be given a hearing Tuesday morning, October 16th in quarterly court.[18]

Man And Woman Fined And Jailed For Drunkenness

Sheriff Chases Man As He Flees When Being Placed Under Arrest, Found In Wooded Area.

Sheriff Elmer Ballard "ran a race" with an offender of the law Tuesday when the latter attempted to make his getaway after he had been stopped by the sheriff on the Dixie Highway near Sherman. He is Jasper Russell, arrested for driving while under suspension and without an operator's license.

Sheriff Ballard and Deputy Julian Force were driving north when they met Russell. With him was Elizabeth Bamforth, who was taken into custody and charged with being drunk on a public highway. Arraigned before Judge R. Lester Mullins Wednesday morning they plead guilty to the charges and were committed to jail until they pay their fines. Mrs, Bamforth was fined $15 and $12 costs; Russell was fined $5 and $12 costs for operating a car without a license and $150 and $7 costs for driving while under the influence of liquor.

The arresting officers said Russell ran when he was accosted. He fled across the railroad tracks into a wooded area but was caught after Sheriff Ballard shot twice into the air as a warning for him to stop.

Others fined in quarterly court since October 18th were:

Herschel G. Rutherford, Cincinnati, fined $45 and $10 costs for being drunk on a public highway.

Thomas N. Stewart, Jr., Danville, $5 and $10 costs for driving without an operator's license.

Thomas N. Stewart, Jr., for improper registration on car, $10 and $10 costs.

Arvil J. Mills, Artemus, Ky., for improper registration, $10 and $10 costs.

Hubert C. Riggs, Toledo, Ohio, weaving on the highway, $15 and $15 costs.

Thomas N. Epperson, Flat Lick, Ky., improper registration, $10 and $10 costs.

Thomas E. Farris, Dayton, Oh., speeding at 80 miles an hour at night and improper passing, $25 and $10 costs.

Hugh Rolls, Cincinnati, for being drunk on a public highway, $10 and $14.50 costs.

Alex Newby, Corinth, for being drunk in a public place, $10 and $10 costs.

Clarence Fox, Owen County, for driving while under the influence of

[17] 5 October 1951. *Grant County News.* Author Unknown.

[18] 12 October 1951. *Grant County News.* Author Unknown.

liquor, $100 and costs and a year's suspension of driver's right as he was driving without an operator's license. This was his second offense.

Lee Wells, Hamilton, Oh., no operator's license, $2 and $10 costs. He was also fined $10 for improper parking.

Henry Long, Cincinnati, for being drunk on a public highway, $10 and $15.50 costs.

Everett Roland, Cincinnati, was charged with issuing cold checks. He was fined $1 and $10 costs on one charge and $1 and court costs suspended on the second charge with the provision that he pay the checks which were for $2 and $3 each.[19]

---

39 Autos Pile Up Behind Drunken Driver On Dixie

Thirty-nine automobiles, trucks and police cruisers were piled up Sunday afternoon on the Dixie Highway between Crittenden and Dry Ridge because of a car operated by a drunken driver. He is Oram Gillespie, Sadieville, who was fined $200 and costs of $5 and had his operator's license suspended in quarterly court.

The long line of traffic was relieved of congestion after Gillespie was stopped by State Troopers at Sixth District Headquarters.[20]

Drunken Drivers Have Operator's License Suspended

$100 Fines And Court Costs Meted Drunks. Truckers Fined For Exceeding Maximum Gross Weight.

Upon conviction of operating a motor vehicle while under the influence of liquor, six persons were fined and had their licenses suspended for six months in quarterly court.

A $100 fine and $5 costs was imposed on Arnold Maddox, of Cleveland, Tenn. Receiving the same fine and court costs were James R. Reed, Cincinnati; Horace Kearney, Richmond, Ky.; Russell Barrett, Beattyville; Eugene Wolfe, Cincinnati, and Fred A. Connelly, Dearborn, Michigan.[21]

Soldier Shot At Harvie's Tavern

Cpl. Elton G. Robinson, 38, veteran of the Korean conflict, was shot through both legs by a bartender, Arthur Havicus, 44, of Walton. The shooting reportedly took place at Harvie's Tavern, operated by Alex Harvie, former Williamstown resident, last Saturday when the soldier is said to have forced his way into the tavern after throwing an 8-pound stone through a window. He is also reported to have destroyed a number of glasses and dishes after entering the establishment.

Removed to St. Elizabeth Hospital, where his wounds were treated, Robinson is said to be in satisfactory condition. He gave his home address as Cynthiana.[22]

---

44 Half Pints Whiskey Seized In Two Raids

Arrested Men Held To Grand Jury Under $1,000 Bonds. State Agents Secure Warrants For The Raids.

Agents of the state alcoholic beverage control board, assisted by Sheriff Elmer Ballard, his deputies and state police, conducted raids on two places of business in the county Saturday morning. Two men arrested were charged with selling intoxicating beverages in dry territory. They are George Curry, who operates a place of business known as Kanary Korner in the southern corporate limits of Williamstown, and Orville Sydnor of Corinth, operator of Dixie Sandwich Shop.

---

[19] 26 October 1951. *Grant County News.* Author Unknown.
[20] 30 November 1951. *Grant County News.* Author Unknown.
[21] 30 November 1951. *Grant County News.* Author Unknown.
[22] 14 December 1951. *Grant County News.* Author Unknown.

W. C. Isaacs, ABC agent from Frankfort, Deputy Sheriffs Julian Foree and Porter Martin seized 11 half pints of whiskey, one half pint of whiskey with a broken seal and 63 bottles of beer when they raided Curry's place. State police and Sheriff Ballard raided Sydnor's establishment where they found 33 half pints of whiskey and some partly filled bottles of whiskey with broken seals.

Warrants were obtained by Isaacs and J. P. Hoard, another state agent, from the county court.

Arraigned before Judge R. Lester Mullins Monday morning, Curry and Sydnor waived examining trial and were held to the grand jury under $1000 bonds which they provided.[23]

Petition Filed For Local Option Election Sept. 6th

A petition bearing a sufficient number of signatures was presented in the clerk's office Wednesday afternoon requesting that it be filed and that the presiding judge, Hon. R. Lester Mullins of Grant County Court, enter an order calling for a local option election in this county September 6th.

Twenty-five percent of the number of votes cast at the last general election is the required number of persons signing such a petition.

The last local option election held in the county was in 1948 when the county voted dry by 591 votes.[24]

Mass Rally of Dry Forces Held Last Sunday

All Sections Of County Represented At First Meeting To Fight Return Of Whiskey To Grant County

A mass rally of the dry forces of the county was held Sunday afternoon, July 20th at the Dry Ridge Baptist Church.

A large number of laymen and laywomen and ministers came together in an enthusiastic meeting in which an organization of the county was begun to carry the fight to every precinct to keep the county dry. Citizens from most of the county's 19 precincts attended. There were nineteen ministers of the gospel present from over the county.

The organization is to be headed by Augustus Threlkeld and he is to be assisted by a number of very able assistants. Plans are being perfected and will soon be in operation.

A petition has been filed in the office of the county clerk for a local option election September 6th.[25]

Four Drunken Drivers Fined $100 And Costs

Drivers Rights Suspended For Six Months. Others Are Fined In Quarterly Court.

Three Ohio residents and two Kentuckians were given the maximum fine of $100 and court costs for operating motor vehicles while under the influence of intoxicating liquor. Pleading guilty before Judge R. Lester Mullins in quarterly court were James Cornelius and Frank DeRose, Cincinnati; Walter Teaters, Fayettsville, Oh.,; Leroy Rucker, Covington and Luther Baker, Barbourville, Ky.

Raymond Purnell, Grant County, Edith Cornelius, Cincinnati, Darwin Skirvin, Dry Ridge, and James Boyle, Cincinnati, were each fined $10 and costs for being drunk in a public place.

John H. Bledshaw of Lexington, was fined $10 and costs for weaving on the highway. Harold E. Barnes of Columbus, Ohio was fined $10 and costs for the same offense.[26]

[23] 11 January 1952. *Grant County News.* Author Unknown.
[24] 4 July 1952. *Grant County News.* Author Unknown.
[25] 25 July 1952. *Grant County News.* Author Unknown.
[26] 22 August 1952. *Grant County News.* Author Unknown.

Election Officers Selected To Serve At Local Option

Sheriff Elmer Ballard, chairman of the Board of Election Commissioners, and Commissioners Jean H. Blain of Dry Ridge, and R. H. Barnth of Corinth, announce the names of the election officers to serve at the local option Saturday, September 6th. The officers were selected at a meeting of the board held last Friday night.[27]

Fines Imposed On 8 Persons For Drunkenness

Four Pay $100 And Costs And Have Driver's Rights Revoked. All Enter Guilty Pleas

Entering pleas of guilty, eight persons were fined in quarterly court for operating cars while under the influence of intoxicating liquor or being drunk on the highway.

James Roland Rowles, colored, Cincinnati, entered a plea of not guilty when he was brought into court on a charge of driving while drunk. He and a companion, James Franklin Willis, also of Cincinnati, were arrested by Trooper Jesse Hamilton Sunday night as they were returning to their home from Paris, Ky. Willis, charged with being drunk on a public highway, also plead not guilty. Rowles was fined $100 and $5 costs and had his driving rights suspended for six months, and Willis was fined $10 and $10 costs. Trooper Hamilton produced a half pint of whiskey found in the glove compartment of their car evidence.

Others entering pleas of guilty when arraigned before Judge R. Lester Mullins on charges of drunken driving were Clyde LaFevers, Broadhead, Ky.; Cecil T. Baker, Dayton, Ohio and William O. Hamilton, Williamstown. They were each fined $100 and $5 costs.

Those paying fines of $10 and $10 costs for being drunk on a public highway were Raymond S. Steinke, Betkins, Oh.; Ernest C. Brown, Coxton, Ky.; Leslie Burgan, Dayton, Ohio, and Robert L. Ballard, Tipp City, Ohio.

Robert L. Clase of Gasstown, Oh., and L. B. Rains of Williamsburg, Ky., were each fined $10 and $10 costs for improper driving.[28]

Temperance Speaker Scheduled For Talk At Dry Ridge Baptist

Rev. Walter C. House, Executive Superintendent of the Temperance League of Kentucky, with headquarters at 21 McDowell building, Louisville, will speak at the Dry Ridge Baptist Church Tuesday night, September 2nd, at 8 o'clock.

He has spoken on the alcohol problem in over 300 churches, clubs and civic meetings since 1951.

Mr. House is a Baptist minister and has held pastorates in Kentucky and Indiana. He is a member of the Executive Committee of the National Temperance League with headquarters in Washington, D. C., a member of the American Business Men's Research Foundation of Chicago, a member of the Kentucky P.T.A., a member of the Rotary Club, a member of the Gideons International, a member of the Kentucky Peace Officers Association and is listed in Who's Who of the Midwest, and more recently has been listed in Who's Who of the South and Southwest.

The subject as announced by Mr. House will be "What Time is it."

The Temperance League of Kentucky led in organizing the successful Local Option Campaigns last year in Roberson County, Falmouth, Sturgis and other places in Kentucky. Mr. House was elected by the participating church groups of the State to act as the Lobbyist for the dry forces at Frankfort during the Legislature this year.[29]

Drunks Occupy Main Seats In Judge's Court

[27] 29 August 1952. *Grant County News.* Author Unknown.
[28] 29 August 1952. *Grant County News.* Author Unknown.
[29] 29 August 1952. *Grant County News.* Author Unknown.

The front seat in quarterly court continues to be occupied by drunks with nine sitting on the reserved side during the holiday weekend.

Jake McBee of Cleveland, Oh., was brought in by Trooper Jesse Hamilton and fined $100 and costs and had his driver's license revoked in the state of Kentucky for six months. He was charged with drunken driving.

Sheriff Elmer Ballard arrested Darwin Skirvin for breach of peace August 28th. He is serving his time, six days, at "Hensley's Hotel."

Everett Colston, Corinth, was fined $10 and costs for being drunk August 28. He was escorted to the local jail by Sheriff Ballard.

Edward M. Whitlock, Lexington, was arrested by Trooper Hamilton for improper driving and was fined $10 and costs. The trooper also brought in five others for being drunk on a public highway. They were Jerry F. Hetch, Chicago, $10 and costs; Alonzo C. Stafford, Gainesboro, Tenn., $10 plus costs; Milton E. Cox, Dayton, Oh., $10 and costs; Ross R. Murray, Chicago, $10 and costs; Norman Honea, Detroit, $10 and costs. All entered pleas of guilty.

Herbert Dishman of Anderson, Ind., was taken into custody by Trooper Hamilton for driving while drunk. He was given the maximum fine of $100 and costs and lost his driving rights in the state for six months.

Zemer Sydnor, Grant County, was fined $10 and costs for being drunk in a public place. Sheriff Ballard was the arresting officer.

Deputy Sheriff Julian Foree arrested Everett Colston for being drunk in a public place. His fine was fixed at $10 and costs. This was Colston's second offense in less than one week.[30]

Drys Seek Court Order For Fair Placement Of Election Officers

---

Committee Charges Discrimination By Election Commission

The dry forces are seeking a court order to compel the election commissioners to give a fair placement of election officers in the local option election to be held tomorrow.

The election officers in each precinct consist of two judges, one sheriff and one clerk. To be fair to both sides, the drys and the wets are entitled to one judge and equal lists of sheriffs so far as is possible.

Augustus Threlkeld, Chairman of the Committee for the Drys, stated that the drys, upon receiving the August 28th issue of The Grant County News in which appeared a list of election commissioners, were confronted with the idea that the dry forces had been discriminated against for a fair deal in the local option election in selection of the election officers. Mr. Threlkeld said they have asked the election commission to make corrections and give them the change to which they were entitled. Two of the commissioners assured them, Mr. Threlkeld said, that this would be done and they held a meeting at 1 p. m. Tuesday, Sept. 2nd, to make this adjustment. They failed to do so, and the only resort the drys had to get this done was to ask for an injunction from Judge Ward Yager's court to compel the commissioners to give this relief.

The dry forces presented a list of four names from each precinct from which the election commission would select two of the officers from their list. Out of 19 precincts in Grant County, the dry forces have the break in three precincts with a judge and sheriff, and the wets have a break in 16 precincts, Mr. Threlkeld said. In three precincts both judges were selected from the wet forces.

The dry forces executive committee consists of Augustus Threlkeld, G. R. Henson, Franklin Webster, O. W. Robinson, Herbert Jones, M. J. Belew, L. M. Hamilton and Don Smith. A. Threlkeld is chairman and Don Smith is secretary. The sheriff of Grant County, by virtue of his office, is chairman of the election commission. Mr. Threlkeld said, "The sheriff has consistently refused to recognize this committee with the power to act for the dry forces. We feel that we have not been dealt with fairly in this way and only seek that which, accord-

[30] 5 September 1952. *Grant County News.* Author Unknown.

[31] 5 September 1952. *Grant County News.* Author Unknown.

ing to the statute of law of the state, we are given this right." The hearing on the petition before Judge Yager was at 8 o'clock last night, September 4th.[31]

Heavy Vote In Local Option Election Expected

Predictions vary as to the possible total vote to be cast here in the local option election Saturday. Some have placed the figure as high as 4,000 while others predict not more than 2500 will vote. In 1948 there were 3297 votes cast in the local option election exclusive of 94 spoiled ballots.

There are 7,545 registered voters in Grant County. The county clerk's office has been busy the past few weeks registering new voters and transferring registrations from one precinct to another. When the registration books closed August 27th, 249 had registered as new voters and there were 269 transfers.

The polls will be open Saturday from 6 a. m. to 5 p. m.[32]

[32]5 September 1952. *Grant County News.* Author Unknown.

NEVER FORGET

1. **NEVER FORGET** that by countless decisions of state and United States Supreme Courts the sale of alcoholic liquor (and that includes beer and wine) is declared to be in **a different class from every other business** and can only be carried on by the express permission of the people.

2. **NEVER FORGET that despit claims** of brewers, distillers and wine makers, the consensus of scientific findings proves beverage alcohol in any form to be a narcotic poison, dangerous alike to the drinker and to those with whom he associates.

3. **NEVER FORGET** that the experience of social workers proves that wherever liquor is sold there is social deterioration and lowered standards of living, both normally and economically.

4. **NEVER FORGET** that liquor is no longer a social necessity. Today there are so many wholesome ways of refreshment, relaxation and inspiration, that resorting to the use of alcoholic bevarages is scarcely a sane way of escape from the commonplace grind of life.

5. **NEVER FORGET** that liquor today is a tragic menace on the highways of community, state and nation, and even the liquor makers urged their patrons not to drink before driving. Nevertheless the National Safety Council states that one in every five fatal traffic accidents involves liquor, involving millions of dollars in accident costs.

6. **NEVER FORGET THAT ALCOHOL IS NOT WANTED IN BUSINESS.** It never has been, but with all the constantly growing competition and multiplying care and responsibility required for skill, judgment and salesmanship, liquor is "out" and the business man does not wish to hire or keep a drinking employee in his organization.

7. **NEVER FORGET THAT LIQUOR FOR 51 YEARS HAS BEEN BANNED ON THE RAILROADS OF THE UNITED STATES,** and a survey of the 70 leading lines recently made, shows that the attitude of railway officials is more emphatically against its use by employees, and **"that"** they say repeatedly, **"includes beer."**

8. **NEVER FORGET THAT LIQUOR DEBAUCHES AND DEGRADES YOUTH.** Judge Braude, Chicago, finds that at least 33 per cent of all child delinquency is due to drink. J. Edgar Hoover, Director of the Federal Bureau of Investigation, declares that youthful crime has grown so rapidly that it now challenges the American people.

9. **NEVER FORGET** that, most tragic of all, liquor, wherever legalized, always exploits childhood, the innocent but helpless victim of its blight. The opening of a saloon means that **some** boys and girls in its vicinity will be deprived of the love and care of a father or mother, their family safeguards broken down and shattered, and their whole future jeopardized.

10. **NEVER FORGET THAT LIQUOR IS ALWAYS A COSTLY AND UNFAIR COMPETITOR OF ALL LEGITIMATE RETAIL BUSINESS IN ANY COMMUNITY.** It must be, for in millions of cases, it takes from the family pocketbook hard earned dollars that all too often are needed for food, clothing, shelter, home comforts, and education.

11. **NEVER FORGET** that liquor multiplies crime, causing accidents, spreads destitution and always and forever increases unemployment and social disorder.

12. **NEVER FORGET** that every liquor trade magazine today betrays increasing fear of rising public sentiment of the traffic's law-defying record. The trade leaders sense danger ahead.

13. **NEVER FORGET** that while in the nation at large, the liquor men boast of paying back to local, state and federal governments, taxes equalling an average of $18.38 per capita— they soft pedal the fact that they take out of the people's pockets **—and largely divert from the local merchants**—grocery, dry goods, meat market, hardware, clothing, boot and shoe shops— no less than $55.93 per capita.

14. **NEVER FORGET** that besides all this, the cost of liquor-bred crime, disease inefficiency, etc., in the country at large, conservatively estimated, now averages at least $37.00 per capita, additional, **a total gross loss to the public** due to liquor of over $90.00 per capita.

15. **NEVER FORGET,** every town where liquor is permitted to be sold contributes to this loss.

16. **But, also, NEVER FORGET** any town that says so and means it, can steadily reduce liquor sales and liquor loss to the vanishing point if they wish to, and stand upon their rights as American citizens.

TO VOTE DRY . . . VOTE "NO"

- - - - Grant County Committee For The Drys

33

[33]Circa September 1952. *Grant County News.*

Charged With Murder

"Prisoner at the bar, have you anything to say why sentence of death should not be passed upon you?"

A solemn hush fell over the crowded court room, and every person waited in almost breathless expectation for the answer to the judge's question.

The judge waited with a dignified silence.

Not a whisper was heard anywhere, and the situation had become painfully oppressive, when the prisoner was seen to move, his head raised, his hand clinched, and the blood rushed into his dull, careworn face.

Suddenly he arose to his feet, and in a low, but distinct voice, said:

"I have! Your honor, you have asked me a question, and now I ask, as the last favor on earth, that you will not interrupt my answer until I am through.

"I stand here, before this bar, convicted of the wilful murder of my wife. Truthful witnesses have testified to the fact that I was a loafer, a drunkard, a wretch, that I returned from one of my prolonged debauches and fired the fatal shot that killed the wife that I had sworn to love, cherish and protect.

While I have no remembrance of committing the fatal deed, I have no right to condemn the verdict of the twelve good men who have acted as jury in this case, for the verdict is in accordance with the evidence.

But may it please the court, I wish to show that I am not alone responsible for the murder of my wife."

The startling statement created a tremendous sensation. The judge leaned over the desk, the lawyers wheeled around and faced the prisoner, while the spectators could hardly suppress their intense excitment.

The prisoner paused a few seconds and then continued in the same firm distinct voice:

"I repeat, your honor, that I am not the only one guilty of the murder of my wife.

"The judge on this bench, the jury in the box, the lawyers within the bar, and most of the witnesses, including the pastor of the old church, are also guilty before Almighty God, and will have to stand with me before His Judgment Throne where we shall be righteously judged.

"If it had not been for the saloons of my town, I never would have become a drunkard, my wife would not have been murdered, I would not be here now, ready to be hurled into eternity! Had it not been for the inhuman traps, I would have been a sober man and an industrious workman, a tender father and a loving husband. But today my home is destroyed, my wife murdered, my little children—God bless and care for them! —cast out upon the mercy of the world!—whilst I am to be hung by the strong arm of the State!

"God knows I tried to reform, but as long as the open saloon was in my pathway, my weak, diseased, will-power, was no match against the fearful consuming, agonizing appetite for liquor. For one year our town was without a saloon. For one year my wife and children were happy and our little home was a paradise.

"I was one of those who signed remonstrances against the re-opening of the saloons of our town. One-half of this jury, the prosecuting attorney on this case, and the judge who sits on this bench, all voted for the saloons! by their votes and influence the saloons were re-opened, and they made me what I am!"

The impassioned words of the prisoner fell like coals of fire upon the hearts of those present, and many of the spectators and some of the lawyers were moved to tears.

The judge made a motion as if to stop further speech, when the prisoner hastily said:

"No! No! your honor, do not close my lips. I am nearly through.

"I began my downward career at a saloon bar—legalized and protected by the voters of this town. After the saloons you allowed have made me a drunkard and a murderer, I am taken before another Bar— the Bar of Justice, and now the Law Power will conduct me to the place of execution, and hasten my soul to Eternity. I shall appear before another Bar— the Judgment Bar of God—and there you, who have legalized the traffic will have to appear with me! Think you that the Great Judge will hold me, the poor, weak helpless victim of your traffic, alone responsible for the murder of my wife?

Nay!

In my drunken, frenzied, irresponsible condition I have murdered one, but you have deliberately voted for the saloons which have murdered thousands, and they are in full operation today with your consent.

"All of you know in your hearts that these words of mine are not the ravings of unsound mind, but God Almighty's truth.

"You legalized the saloons and made me a drunkard and a murderer, and you are guilty with me before God for the murder of my wife.

"Your honor, I am done. I am now ready to receive my sentence and be led forth to the place of execution. You will close by asking the Lord to have mercy on my soul. I will close by solemnly asking God to open your blind eyes to your own individual responsibility, so that you will cease to give support to this dreadful traffic."

TO VOTE DRY . . . VOTE "NO"

- - - - Grant County Committee For The Drys

34

[34] Circa September 1952. *Grant County News.*

HEAR

Rev. Walter C. House

of the

Temperance League Of Ky.

Tuesday, September 2

8:00 P. M.

Dry Ridge Baptist Church

"WHAT TIME IS IT"?

IS THE SUBJECT OF HIS TALK ON THE ALCOHOL PROBLEM

MR. HOUSE HAS SPOKEN ON THIS PROBLEM IN OVER 300 CHURCHES, CLUBS AND CIVIC MEETINGS SINCE 1951.

ATTEND THIS MEETING AND LEND YOUR SUPPORT TO HELP KEEP GRANT COUNTY DRY.

—Grant County Committee for the Drys.

[35]

[35]Circa September 1952. *Grant County News.*

STAND UP AND BE COUNTED

The liquor business lives by the death of its customers. The aim and goal of its advertising is to lead every citizen to be a regular and steady drinker. Every steady drinker is dying a slow death.

No man who has any regard for human welfare is in the liquor business. When a man becomes decent he gets out of the liquor business. The liquor dealer knows that his product causes want, misery, murder, adultery, divorce, crime, and death but the love of easy money has blinded his eyes and deadened his conscience.

When a man takes the side of liquor he becomes the enemy of Christ and his church. He becomes the enemy of little children. He becomes the enemy of all that is decent. He becomes the friends of crime, murder, adultery, lawlessness, and despair. Let's make up our mind which side we are on. No man can be on both sides.

A man that would vote liquor back to save himself a few dollars in taxes is both stupid and criminal. He is stupid because the cost of liquor to the taxpayer is far greater than the revenue. He is criminal because he would sell his neighbor into slavery for a few dollars.

The liquor business would destroy the church if it could. We must either destroy the liquor business or be destroyed by it. No Christian that prays will vote wet. No Christian will vote wet who will picture himself before Almighty God on the last day.

STAND UP AND BE COUNTED. WHICH SIDE ARE YOU ON?

—DRY RIDGE BAPTIST CHURCH.

[36]

[36] Circa September 1952. *Grant County News.*

WEIGHED IN THE BALANCES
AND FOUND WANTING

YOUR HOME
SCHOOL AND
CHURCH.....

HOME
SCHOOL
CHURCH

WHISKEY
BEER

OR

BEER JOINTS
DISPENSARIES
AND DRUNKS
?

On Which Side Will You Vote?

"NOW THEREFORE BEWARE, I PRAY THEE,
AND DRINK NOT WINE NOR STRONG DRINK,
AND EAT NOT ANY UNCLEAN THING."
—Judges 13:4.

To Vote, Dry In The Local Option Saturbay, Sept., 6,

VOTE NO . . . 

—Grant County Committee For The Drys.

[37]

[37]Circa September 1952. *Grant County News.*

*From Report of Legislative Commission to investigate Problem of Drunkenness in Massachusetts ---- House document No. 2000.

---

1. "50% OF THE FELONIES COMMITTED IN MASSACHUSETTS ARE RELATED TO ALCOHOLISM"—PAGE 21*

2. "85% OF THE COMMITMENTS FOR MISDEMEANORS ARE DUE TO ALCOHOLISM OR CRIMES RELATED THERETO"—PAGE 21*

3. "25% OF THE POPULATION AT THE REFORMATORY FOR WOMEN ARE ALCOHOLICS"—PAGE 31*

4. "IN ONE BOSTON COURT ONE OUT OF EVERY EIGHT CHILDREN WAS UNDER THE INFLUENCE OF LIQUOR WHEN HE GOT IN TROUBLE"—PAGE 32*

5. "25% OF THE POPULATION IN MENTAL HOSPITALS IS DUE OR STRONGLY RELATED TO CAUSES GROWING OUT OF THE INTEMPERATE USE OF ALCOHOLIC BEVERAGES"—PAGE 33*

6. "61 MILLION DOLLARS A YEAR IS TANGIBLE COST OF DRUNKENNESS IN MASSACHUSETTES—REVENUE FROM LIQUOR ONLY SLIGHTLY OVER 13 MILLION"—PAGE 36*

7. "20 THOUSAND ALCOHOLICS IN MASSACHUSETTS NOW"—PAGE 36*

---Grant County Committee For The Drys

[38]

[38]Circa September 1952. *Grant County News.*

SUBMARINE ATTACK ON BOOZE

THE BEN FRANKLIN MUTUAL CASUALTY INSURANCE COMPANY IN SENDING OUT ADVERTISING MATTER FROM ITS OFFICES IN CHICAGO, INCLUDES COPY OF SAFETY BULLETIN NO. 5, OF THE ILLINOIS STEEL CO., WHICH, UNDER THE ABOVE CAPTION, READS AS FOLLOWS:

"FOR THE MARRIED MAN WHO CANNOT GET ALONG WITHOUT DRINKS, THE FOLLOWING IS SUGGESTED AS A MEANS OF FREEDOM FROM BONDAGE TO SALOONS:

"START A SALOON IN YOUR OWN HOME. BE THE ONLY CUSTOMER (YOU'LL HAVE NO LICENSE TO PAY). GO TO YOUR WIFE AND GIVE HER TWENTY DOLLARS TO BUY A GALLON OF WHISKEY, AND REMEMBER THERE ARE SIXTY-NINE DRINKS IN A GALLON. BUY YOUR DRINKS FROM NO ONE BUT YOUR WIFE, AND BY THE TIME THAT THE FIRST GALLON IS GONE SHE WILL HAVE EIGHTY DOLLARS TO PUT IN THE BANK AND TWENTY DOLLARS TO START BUSINESS AGAIN.

"SHOULD YOU LIVE TEN YEARS AND CONTINUE TO BUY BOOZE FROM HER, AND THEN DIE WITH SNAKES IN YOUR BOOTS, SHE WILL HAVE MONEY ENOUGH TO BURY YOU DECENTLY, EDUCATE YOUR CHILDREN, BUY A HOUSE AND LOT, AND MARRY A DECENT MAN, AND QUIT THINKING ABOUT YOU ENTIRELY."

---GRANT COUNTY COMMITTEE FOR THE DRYS

[39]

[39]Circa September 1952. *Grant County News.*

TOMMY BROWN

"What is your name?" asked the teacher.

"Tommy Brown, ma'am," answered the boy.

He was a pathetic little fellow, with a thin face, hollow eyes and pale cheeks, that plainly told of insufficient food. He wore a suit of clothes evidently made for somone else. They were patched in places with cloth of different colors. His shoes were old, his hair cut square in the neck in an unpracticed manner in which women sometimes cut boy's hair. It was a bitter day, yet he wore no overcoat, and his bare hands were red with cold.

"How old are you, Tommy?"

"Nine years old come next April. I've learned to read at home and I can cypher a little."

"Well, it is time for you to begin school. Why have you never come before?"

The boy fumbled with a cap in his hands, and did not reply at once. It was a ragged cap with frayed edges, and the original color of the fabric no man could tell.

Presently he said, "I never went to school 'cause—well, mother takes in washin' an' she couldn't spare me. But Sissy is big enough now to help, an' she minds the baby besides."

It was not quite time for school to begin. All around the teacher and the new scholar stood boys that belonged to the room.

While he was making his confused explanation some of the boys laughed, and one of them called out, "Say, Tommy, where are your cuffs and collar?" And another sang out, "You must sleep in the rag-bag at night by the looks of your clothes!" Before the teacher could quiet them, another boy had volunteered the information that the father of the boy was "old Si Brown, who is always drunk as a fiddler."

The poor child looked around on his tormentors like a hunted thing. Then, before the teacher could detain him, with a suppressed cry of misery he ran out of the room, out of the building, down the street, and was seen no more.

The teacher went to her duties with a troubled heart. All day long the child's pitiful face haunted her. She could not rid herself of the memory of it. After a little trouble she found the place where he lived, and then two kind ladies went to visit him.

It was a dilapidated house. When they first entered they could scarcely discern objects, the room was so filled with steam of the soap-suds. There were two windows, but a tall brick building adjacent shut out the light. It was a gloomy day, too, with gray, lowering clouds that forbade even the memory of sunshine.

A woman stood before a wash tub. When they entered, she wiped her hands on her apron and came forward to meet them.

Once she had been pretty, but the color had gone out of her face, leaving only sharpened outlines and haggardness of expression.

She asked them to sit down; then taking a chair herself, she said, "Sissy, give me the baby."

A little girl came forward from a dark corner of the room carrying a baby that she laid in its mother's lap, a lean, sickly looking baby with the same hollow eyes Tommy had.

"Your baby doesn't look strong," said one of the ladies.

"No, ma'am. I ain't very well, and I expect it affects her."

"Where is your little Tommy?" asked one of the visitors.

"He is in there in the trundle-bed," replied the mother. "Is he sick?"

"Yes'm, and the doctor thinks he isn't going to get well." At this the tears ran down her thin and faded cheeks.

"What is the matter with him?"

"He was never very strong, and he's had to work too hard, carrying water and helping me lift the wash-tubs, and things like that. Of late he has been crazy to go to school. I never could spare him till this winter. He thought if he could get a little education he'd be able to take care of Sissy and baby and me. So I fixed up his clothes as well as I could, and last week he started. I was afraid the boys would laugh at him, but he thought he could stand it if they did. I stood at the door and watched him going.

"I can never forget how the little fellow looked," she continued, the tears streaming down her face. "His patched-up clothes, his poor little anxious look. He turned around to me as he left the yard and said, 'Don't worry, mother, I won't mind what the boys say.' But he did mind. It wasn't an hour before he was back again. I believe the child's heart was just broken. I thought mine was broken years ago. If it was, it was broken over again that day. I can stand most anything myself, but oh! I can't bear to see my children suffer." Here she broke down in a fit of convulsive weeping. The little girl came up to her quietly and stole a thin little arm around her mother's neck. "Don't cry, mother," she whispered; "don't cry."

The woman made an effort to dry her tears, and she wiped her eyes. As soon as she could speak with any degree of calmness, she continued:

"Poor little Tommy cried all day; I couldn't comfort him. He said it was no use to do anything. Folks would only laugh at him being a drunkard's boy. I tried to comfort him before my husband came home. I told him his father would be mad if he saw him crying. But it wasn't any use. Seemed like he could not stop. His father came and saw him. He wouldn't have done it if he hadn't been drinking. He ain't a bad man when he is sober. I hate to tell it, but he whipped Tommy and the child fell and struck his head. I suppose he'd been sick anyway. But oh! my poor boy. My sick suffering child!" she cried. "How can they let man sell a thing that makes the innocent suffer so?"

One of the ladies went to the bed. There he lay, poor little defenseless victim. He lived in a Christian land, in a country that takes great care to pass laws to protect sheep, and diligently legislate over its game. Would that the law was more jealous of little waifs' rights!

His face was flushed and the hollow eyes were bright. There was a long purple mark on his temple. He put up one little wasted hand to cover it, while he said, "Father wouldn't have done it if he hadn't been drinking." Then, in his queer, piping voice, weak with sickness, he half whispered, "I'm glad I'm going to die. I'm too weak ever to help mother anyhow. Up in heaven the angels ain't going to call me the drunkard's child, and make fun of my clothes. And maybe, if I'm right up there where God is, I can keep reminding him of mother; and he will make it easier for her."

He turned his head feebly on his pillow, and then said in a lower tone, "Some day—they ain't goin'—to let—saloonkeepers open. But I'm afraid—poor father— will be dead —before then." Then he shut his eyes from weariness.

"For the wages of sin is death; but the gift of God is eternal life through Jesus Christ our Lord." —Rom. 6:23.

Vote No To Keep This Out of Grant County

- - - - Grant County Committee For The Drys

[40]

Local Option A Very Dry Affair

The Majority In Favor Of Keeping County Dry Is 1331. Election Commission Ordered By Court To Revise List Of Officers.

The people of Grant County on last Saturday, Sep 6th, turned out in large numbers, 2911 of them, to vote upon the question submitted to them by reason of a petition for a local option election filed by the "wets" of Grant County.

After all the machinery of the election had been set up, the officers appointed, ballot boxes delivered and the lists of persons registered in the county made out by the County Court Clerk, the election proceeded on Saturday in a very orderly and decorous manner.

The results surprised nobody. The number of persons voting to repeal the local option law in Grant County was 790, and 2121 persons voted to retain this law. The results prove that practically three persons out of every four in Grant County are in favor of local option. The majority on last Saturday in favor of the "drys" was 1331.

An interesting sidelight is in the vote in the three precincts in Williamstown. At the 1948 local option election, West Williamstown went "wet" by 10 votes; East Williamstown No. 1 went "dry" by 18 votes, and East Williamstown No. 2 went "dry" by 36 votes. This gave the three precincts in Williamstown in 1948 a "dry" majority of 44 votes.

On last Saturday, West Williamstown went "dry" by a majority of 43 votes; East Williamstown No. 1 went "dry" by a majority of 89 votes, and East Williamstown No. 2 went "dry" by a majority of 117 votes. The three Williamstown precincts on

[40] Circa September 1952. *Grant County News.*

September 6, 1952, gave a "dry" majority of 249 votes.

Even more interesting is the result of Saturday's election in the two precincts at Dry Ridge. In 1948 West Dry Ridge went "wet" by 11 votes and East Dry Ridge went "dry" by 63 votes. On last Saturday, West Dry Ridge went "dry" by a majority of 145 votes and East Dry Ridge went "dry" by a majority of 121 votes; giving a total "dry" majority in the two Dry Ridge precincts of 266 votes.

These totals are significant in the light of the fact that in 1948 there was a "dry" majority of only 591 votes in all of Grant County.

Downingsville was the only precinct in the county favoring the repeal of the local option law; the majority was in favor of the "wets."

It is also worth noting that in 1948 with a total vote of 3297 cast in the local option election, there were only 1944 "dry" votes, while on last Saturday, with a total vote of 2911 cast, there were 2121 "dry" votes.

This should indicate that Grant County is overwhelmingly in favor of denying to the brewers and distillers the right to vend their wares in Grant County.

Many thoughtful citizens of Grant County are chagrined to think that this unnecessary election, with its costs borne by the taxpayers, was forced upon them at a time when the county's money is so urgently needed for road machinery and road improvement.

Augustus Threlkeld, a nationally known farm leader, was chairman of the "dry" organization, and Herbert Caldwell of Williamstown was secretary-treasurer.

A few days preceding the local option election, the dry forces sought a court order to compel the election commission to revise their list of selected election officers to serve at the election Saturday. They charged in their petition that the commissioners had failed to give the dry forces an equal distribution of officers. The "drys" and the "wets" are each entitled to one judge and an equal number of clerks and sheriffs. They further charged in their petition that the dry forces had been given but one judge in three precincts.

The hearing in Judge Ward Yager's court in Warsaw, lasted approximately three hours and resulted in a decision by Judge Yager that the election commission meet on Friday, September 5th and revise the list of election officers. The judgment of the court follows in part:

"It is ordered by agreement of the parties, that the election commissioners of Grant County, Kentucky shall meet in the courthouse in Williamstown, Grant County, Ky. at 9 o'clock a. m. on Friday, September 5, 1952, and from a supplemental list to be filed at that time by the plaintiffs herein by and through their accredited chairman, Augustus Threlkeld, and select for each precinct in Grant County, Kentucky, one judge and either a sheriff or clerk for the said special election to be held on Saturday, Sept. 6, 1952, who possess the qualifications as such officers as set out by the law of the State of Kentucky and that the persons so selected by the Grant County Election Commissioners shall be notified, as by law required, and shall be election officers at the said special election, subject to emergencies as provided for by Kentucky election laws."

In pursuance of the above order and agreement, the Grant County Election Commission met on Friday, September 5, 1952, and from the original list submitted by Augustus Threlkeld, Chairman of the Committee for those opposing the repeal of the local option law in Grant County, Ky., and from the supplemental list submitted by said chairman, Augustus Threlkeld, corrected any ommissions and submitted said corrected list to the plaintiffs and by agreement of the parties said list is hereby made a part of hereof and attached hereto and is hereby ordered and direct-to be the list of election officers, provided however, in the event any fail to serve, his successor shall be named in the manner provided by the general election laws of Kentucky."

Defendants in the case were the election commissioners, Elmer Ballard, Robert Barnes and Jean Hart Blain. They were represented by R. L. Vincent and R. R. Vincent, attorneys.

L. M. Ackman and William Threlkeld, attorneys, represented the plaintiffs who were Augustus Threlkeld, G. R. Henson, Franklin Webster, O. W. Robinson, Herbet Jones, M. J. Belew, L. M. Hamilton and Don Smith.[41]

Is your News subscription paid?

[41] 12 September 1952. *Grant County News.* Author Unknown.

To The Citizens Of Grant County

Last Saturday, the citizens of Grant County were asked again as to where they stood on the Liquor question. They answered in no uncertain way by their vote as to where they stood. The question has been thrust at the people at different times for the past several years. The answer in last Saturday's election should suffice to last many years.

All praise to the voter who took time to discharge this privilege in casting the vote. Many churches and church people stood up against this evil and said, "NO, THIS SHALL NOT COME TO PASS IN GRANT COUNTY." To them and to all who helped to win this great victory, your Committee for the Drys want to thank you and to say, "WELL DONE."

—Committe for the Drys

42

Editor Scorned For Stand On Local Option Election

Editor, Grant County News,
Williamstown, Kentucky.

Dear Editor:

You being editor of the Grant County News, or as some call it the Grant County bible, could be way behind in old and late news items that maybe you never heard about.

On the front page of the Grant County News of September 12th, I noticed in one paragraph about many thoughtful Citizens of Grant County being chagrined to think that this was an unnecessary election, with its cost borne by the taxpayers, and was forced upon them at a time when the County's money is so urgently needed for road machinery and road improvement.

Do you know that I, C. McGee of Dry Ridge Kentucky pay enough taxes myself to hold a wet and dry election every three years, thereby it really cost the rest of you taxpayers nothing.

Here is more news that you don't know that every three years as long as I live, and enough of the so called criminals as referenced to by the Drys of Grant County will sign a petition for a local option you will have one.

Do you know that Grant County is democratic by a large majority and if they are dry that they have for the past 16 years supported a wet bunch in Washington by their vote, why do they vote this way and drink and vote dry in a county election.

Don't you know that some of the leading Drys live to-day on land that was payed for by their (pappas) by money derived from the Likker Business.

Don't you know that if I was that dry that I would sell that land which was purchased with Likker money and give the money derive from it to some institute or preacher who would lick their chops like a Hound Dog in thin gravy and enjoy it as much.

Do you know that who ever represents the wets or drys that they got on the side if possible that will pay the most money.

Do you know that the advertising of all the lousy bunk run in your paper in regard to the Local Option Election was paid by the drys and that the leading wets bought no votes, hauled no voters and took no interest whatever in the election.

Do you know that the Likker places that surround Grant County really love the dys for the saveing the day for them, I suppose the dry voters all ready know this for you can see quite a few of their cars parked at the joints in Kenton County, it looks like a Grant County Parade for sure on weekends.

Do you relize that there is more money spent for tobacco which is the largest money crop in our county. All this money could be spent for food instead of cigarettes, chewing tobacco, etc, which is the argument of the Drys in favor of local option.

Do you know that tobacco will be raised for years to come and used by wets and drys even if it injures their health or kills them, all for the love of money.

Don't you know that God put all these things here for you to use, Tobacco, whiskey, beer, fast horses, and a thousand other things that may not be good for you if you over do it.

Maybe I should say, Lord forgive them they know not what they do, Instead I will say, Lord forgive them for they no what they do.

In closing Dear Editor, This is old and late news items which I believe you all ready know, you may use them as news items, if you do not care to give space to this, send me the bill and I will be glad to pay you with

42 Circa September 1952. *Grant County News.*

money which I made from the beer business as Distributor for the George Wiedemann Brewing Company, Newport, Kentucky.

Signed, C. McGEE,

PS: More late news. I have been approached by some of the leading business men in Dry Ridge to promote a News Paper to be published at Dry Ridge.

— The above letter was published as submitted and has not been edited for spelling or punctuation. - Editor.[43]

Local Option Election Costs Not Available

Astor B. Kinman, county court clerk, stated Wednesday that the total cost of the local option election could not be determined until it is decided who will pay the expense of the court costs in the case before Judge Ward Yager in Warsaw the week of the election.[44]

Raids Result In Arrest Of Two In Grant County

Ervie Starns And Nim Dunn Arrested For Selling Intoxicants In Dry Territory

Investigation of two places of business by Osmyn Botts, of the State Alcoholic Beverage Control Board, resulted in the arrest of two men in Grant County last Sunday. Charged with selling intoxicating beverages in dry territory the two men, Nim Dunn of Dry Ridge, and Ervie Starns, proprietor of Four Corners on the Taft Highway, were released under $500 bond. Judge R. Lester Mullins said their examining trials were set for September 30. Assisting in the raids were Sheriff Elmer Ballard and Deputy Sheriff Julian Foree.

Botts reported he bought a bottle of beer at Four Corners Saturday night and that when he returned Sunday with a search warrant, six bottles of beer and 32 empty beer cases were found. He said he purchased a half pint of whiskey from Dunn Sunday but when he returned with a warrant to search his store he found no intoxicants.[45]

Drunks And Hunting Law Violators Draw Fines In Court

Samuel E. Harding, Cincinnati, plead guilty to a charge of driving while intoxicated and was fined $100 and costs in quarterly court. Suspension of operator's license in the state of Kentucky for six months is automatic when one is convicted on such a charge.

Joseph C. Vaskuhl, Covington, was fined $10 for improper driving.

A Cincinnati resident, Robert Fitterer, was fined $15 and $10 costs for hunting with a resident license. He was also fined $15 and $10 costs for hunting with an unplugged gun.

Charles Fitterer drew a $15 fine and court costs of $10 for hunting with an unplugged gun.

William Burg, Cincinnati, was arrested for hunting without a license and was fined $15 and $10 costs.

For being drunk in a public place, Ray Goodpaster, Williamstown, was fined $10 and costs. Sammy Harper, colored, of Middlesboro, was also fined $10 and $10 costs for drunkenness.[46]

Four Motorists Fined $100 For Driving Drunk

Others Fined In Quarterly Court. Drunken Drivers' Permits Suspended On Conviction.

Four motorists were fined $100 each and court costs for driving drunk and had their permits to drive in Kentucky suspended for six months. Those receiving fines were Charles Henson, Owenton, fined $100 and $23.25 costs. He plead not guilty and was tried before a jury of six men

[43] 19 September 1952. *Grant County News.* Author Unknown.
[44] 19 September 1952. *Grant County News.* Author Unknown.
[45] 19 September 1952. *Grant County News.* Author Unknown.
[46] 19 December 1952. *Grant County News.* Author Unknown.

and found guilty. He paid the fine and was released. Others fined for drunken driving and losing their right to drive for six months in Kentucky were Wayne E. Walters, $100 and $5 costs, William Fryman, $100 and $5 costs, and Harry T. Barber, $100 and $5 court costs suspended.[47]

Five Fined For Drunken Driving Over Long Weekend

Among those fined in quarterly court of the 4th of July holiday weekend were three women on charges of drunkenness. All arrests were for traffic violations or having to do with intoxicating beverages. Those fined were:

Drunken driving: Frank D. Dugger, Stockbridge, Mich., Virgil Wolfinbarger, Independence, Robert Helton, Miamisburg, Oh., Ernest Creek, Cincinnati, and Dock Ison, Georgetown, each fined $100 and $5.00 costs.

Drunk in public place: Charles Huskins, Danville, Guy Stanley, Dry Ridge, Gene Stewart, Cincinnati, Ky Huffman, Miamisburg, Ohio, each fined $10 and $16 costs. Earl Leon Peterson, Detroit, $10 and $16 costs.

No registration plate on motor vehicle: Eugene Marksberry, Dry Ridge, $10, costs suspended.

Improper registration in motor vehicle: Foster W Haley, Burlington, $10, costs suspended.

No operator's license: Bobby G. Hampton, Lexington, $5 and $10 costs; Opal Stewart, $2.00, costs suspended.

Improper driving: Ray Penick, Dayton, Ky., Donald L. Shultz, Clement, Indiana, Charles Feiger, Covington, Carlos Dusmore, of Science Hill, and Merle Mullins, Covington, each fined $10 and $10 costs. Clifton Chreet, Pineknot, $10 fine, costs suspended. Walter G. Arvin, Irvine, $15 fine, $10 costs.

Drinking beer on public highway, Frances Penick, $10 and $10 costs.

Drunk on public highway: Helen Creech, Cincinnati, $10 and $10 costs.[48]

Drunken Drivers Subject To Fines From $100 To $500

Persons convicted of driving while drunk are subject to a fine of not less than $100 and not more than $500 plus court costs. In addition, a driver's permit is automatically suspended for six months in Kentucky when convicted on such a charge.

In the July 23rd issue of The News, it was stated through error that the maximum fine for driving drunk was $100; this should have been $500.[49]

Drunken Driver Fined $100 And Loses License

Richard Israel, Cincinnati, was fined $100 and $5 costs when arraigned before Judge Pro Tem H. S. Needham, Wednesday. Israel was convicted of drunken driving and was remanded to jail upon failure to pay his fine. He automatically loses his right to drive in the state of Kentucky for a period of six months.[50]

Wife's Jaw Broken In Drunken Brawl

Clyde Collier, arrested Nov. 21 on a charge of breach of peace, is being held in the Grant County jail for examining trial Nov. 30.

Collier is alleged to have broken his wife's lower and upper jaw on the right side of her face when he was under the influence of liquor, Judge R. Lester Mullins reported. Mrs. Collier was removed to St. Elizabeth Hospital.[51]

[47] 22 January 1954. *Grant County News.* Author Unknown.
[48] 9 July 1954. *Grant County News.* Author Unknown.
[49] 30 July 1954. *Grant County News.* Author Unknown.
[50] 29 October 1954. *Grant County News.* Author Unknown.
[51] 26 November 1954. *Grant County News.* Author Unknown.

Fined $100 On Drunken Driving Charge Here

Charged with operating an automobile while under the influence of liquor, J. D. Duncan was fined $100 and costs when tried before a jury in circuit court last Friday. He entered a plea of not guilty. Duncan had been tried on the charge in city court, was fined $200 and appealed to circuit court.

Last Friday was the final day of the October term of Grant Circuit Court. Many cases were settled out of court and there were a number of equity suits.[52]

Drunken Drivers Get $100 Fines

Fifteen law violators were fined in quarterly court the past ten days. Two drew $100 fines and $5 costs each and had their drivers license suspended; they were William T. White of Dunville, Ky. and Bradley Jones of Williamstown.

Others fined were: Jack D. Shirley, weaving on highway, $10 fine and $10 costs; Leroy Henry, Williamstown, improper passing, $10 fine and $10 costs; Herman Kurt Willer, Milwaukee, Wis., improper passing, $10 fine and $10 costs; Wm. Bill Simpson, Williamstown, drunk in public place, $10 fine and $16 costs; Jimmy D. Doolin, Williamstown, speeding, $10 fine and $10 costs; John Fount Hume, Williamstown, drunk in public place, $10 fine and $16 costs; Betty McIntosh of Raven, Va., drunk on public highway, $10 fine, costs suspended; Perry Hawkins, Owenton, improper driving, $10 fine and $10 costs; Marvin Hughes, Cincinnati, drunk in public place, $10 fine and $10 costs; Bobby L. Bowen, Williamstown, speeding, $10 fine, costs suspended; Lawrence Cooper, Revelo, Ky., improper passing, $10 fine and $10 costs.[53]

State Whiskey Production Tax Doubled

Repeated efforts to kill the controversial whiskey tax bill before the General Assembly failed and on the last day of the regular session of the legislature the tax was raised from 5 to 10 cents a gallon.

The Senate first voted to cut a proposed boost in the tax from five to 20 cents a gallon to a total of 10 cents, and the House after five roll calls and parliamentary hassling finally concurred. The Senate vote was 25 to 9. The final House vote on the amended bill was 60 to 14.

The governor's executive secretary sat in the House gallery during the roll calls and took a tally of the vote.

Administration leaders said that Governor Chandler would not veto the whiskey tax boost, which was fought to the bitter end by opponents. Both the Senate and House galleries were full most of the day with employees from distillers in Frankfort, Lexington, Owensboro and Bardstown.

Under the present 5 cents tax a gallon, the whiskey tax brought $4,067,593 in the last fiscal year. The tax boost would double the revenue.[54]

Drunken Drivers Get $100 Fines

The maximum fine for drunken drivers was imposed on two Michigan motorists in quarterly court. Lyle Churchill and Arnold W. Rowlett, both of Monroe, Mich., were fined $100 and $14.75 costs each and had their drivers licenses suspended for six months in Kentucky.

Others fined $10 and $10 costs for traffic violations were Clarence O. Patrick, Walton; William McFarland, Detroit; Earl Thomas, Hamilton, Ohio; Leonard Spencer, Pontiac, Mich.; Orville Crumbie, Dry Ridge. Albert Dansion, Junction City, Oh., Linzie Brown, Union, Ky.; Russell Switzer, Corinth; Jeff Baker, Scalf, Ky., and John Kindle, Cincinnati.

Frank Lynn, Williamstown, was given 10 days in jail for being drunk in a public place.

[52] 21 October 1955. *Grant County News.* Author Unknown.

[53] 3 February 1956. *Grant County News.* Author Unknown.

[54] 24 February 1956. *Grant County News.* Author Unknown.

James Thurman of Frankfort, fined $10 and $10 costs for being drunk on a public highway; Virgil Brown, Corinth, $10 and $10 costs for being drunk in a public place; and Leonard Mills, Scalf, Ky., $10 fine and $10 costs for public highway drunkenness.[55]

$100 Fines Meted Drunken Drivers

Twenty-one defendants were fined on charges to which they plead guilty in quarterly court. Two were fined $100 and costs and had their driver's licenses suspended for six months for driving while under the influence of liquor.[56]

Drunken Youth Goes On Wild Rampage

Escapade Leads Officers To Make Raid On Early Crouch's Tavern

---

A drunken-crazed youth went on a rampage Sunday afternoon and destroyed property at a farm home that could not be replaced for $1,000, the farm owner said.

The 16-year-old boy, who is the son of a tenant on the Omer Chipman farm on Chipman ridge, told officials that the last thing he remembered Sunday afternoon after drinking a number of bottles of beer at Early Crouch's tavern, was sitting in a rocking chair and watching the television.

Mr. and Mrs. Chipman and their daughters went to Louisville Sunday to visit their daughter and son-in-law, the Rev. and Mrs. Hansel Eason. They returned home about 8 o'clock and found the interior of their home "turned up-side-down," Mrs. Chipman said. She related that the youth had broken twelve window sashes and five storm windows, had turned over the television, broken a record player, thrown the contents of the refrigerator out of the window and two pitchers of milk on the walls and floor, had cut all the clothing belonging to Mrs. Chipman and her daughters into shreds, (only a vest of Mr. Chipman's had been cut) one of the dresses was the graduation formal of their daughter, Betty. The Venetian blinds were torn from the windows, eggs had been thrown against the walls and spattered over the floor. Mrs. Chipman said the boy was lying on the floor asleep where he had vomited.

Mr. and Mrs. Chipman said the boy was a good worker and had not ever been in any kind of trouble to their knowledge. He was paroled to the custody of Mr. Chipman and agreed to work to try to pay for the damage.

The escapade led Sheriff Julian Foree and his deputy, Porter Martin, Sgt. Harold L. Kinman and Trooper Lawrence Gay of the state police on a raid of Crouch's tavern Monday morning at 10:30. The warrant was signed by Joseph Crammer.

Sheriff Foree said Crouch was not at home but the officers were admitted by his wife. He said they found six half pints of whiskey, a quantity of empty half pint whiskey bottles, 12 empty beer bottle caps and a bucket full of beer bottle caps. Crouch was arrested in Dry Ridge for possession of intoxicating beverages in a dry county and for sales of the beverage. He waived examining trial and was bound over to the grand jury. He was released under $1,000 bond, $500 on each count.[57]

Two Fined $100 On Drunken Driving Charge

Fourteen persons were fined in quarterly court for: issuing cold check, drunk and abusive, drunk in public place, drunken driving and other traffic violations. Two of the offenders were fined $100, $2 tax and court costs and had their drivers licenses suspended for six months in Kentucky.

All were brought before Judge R. Lester Mullins and plead guilty as charged.[58]

---

[55] 9 March 1956. *Grant County News.* Author Unknown.
[56] 27 April 1956. *Grant County News.* Author Unknown.
[57] 1 June 1956. *Grant County News.* Author Unknown.
[58] 24 August 1956. *Grant County News.* Author Unknown.

One Fined For Drunken Driving In Quarterly Court

James Botkin, Berea, pleaded guilty of the charge of drunken driving before Judge pro tem Ben F. Kinman in Grant Quarterly Court and was fined $100, $2 tax and $5 costs. His driver's license was suspended for six months in the state of Kentucky.[59]

Three Fined For Drunken Driving

Three persons were found guilty in Grant quarterly court before County Judge R. Lester Mullins last week on the charge of drunken driving. Each was fined $100, state tax $2, costs $5, and six months' suspension of driving rights in the State of Kentucky. There are: Earl Osborne, Jr., Cincinnati, Arthur F. Kinman, Cincinnati, and Porter Hammond, Dry Ridge.[60]

Six Drunken Drivers Meted $100 Fines

Thirty-one persons were arraigned before Judge R. Lester Mullins in quarterly court during the past two weeks on charges of drunkenness and traffic violations.

Six were given the maximum fine of $100 for operating motor vehicles while under the influence of intoxicating liquor. Each fine carried a court cost of $5 and $2 State tax and offenders had their driver's license suspended for six months, in the State of Kentucky. They were George A. Deitsch, Cold Springs, Ky., Claude B. Burrell, Ferndale, Mich., John W. Baer, Dayton, Ohio, Otha Head, Cincinnati, Eddie Cummins, Dry Ridge.[61]

Drunk Man Moved To St. Elizabeth

Emerson Carter, 65, a resident of Indiana, was arrested by Sheriff Julian Foree at the farm of B. Rose, Holbrook, Sunday night.

Sheriff Foree said he had been called to the Rose home the day before because Carter was reported to be drunk and disorderly. He said he was unable to find him when he went to the Rose farm at Holbrook. Receiving another call, he found Carter and took him into custody. He became very ill after being placed in jail and on advice of a physician, Carter was removed to St. Elizabeth Hospital. The sheriff said he had a bottle of rubbing alcohol in his pocket, half full.[62]

Drunk Drivers Fined $100; Lose License

Four men were fined $100 each by Judge R. Lester Mullins on charges of drunken driving and had their drivers license suspended for six months.[63]

Motorist Fined For Driving While Drunk

Eugene J. Collins, Cincinnati, charged with drunken driving was fined $100.00 and six months suspension of his driving rights in Kentucky, by Police Judge John J. Blackburn Tuesday morning.

Collins was arrested and placed in jail Monday night as he and his wife were driving through town enroute to Berea. Police officer Charlie Hudson said the motorist was very drunk and became extremely abusive. No charges were placed against Mrs. Collins but she remained at the jail with her husband, the officer said.[64]

[59] 26 October 1956. *Grant County News.* Author Unknown.
[60] 29 March 1957. *Grant County News.* Author Unknown.
[61] 6 September 1957. *Grant County News.* Author Unknown.
[62] 18 October 1957. *Grant County News.* Author Unknown.
[63] 6 December 1957. *Grant County News.* Author Unknown.
[64] 17 January 1958. *Grant County News.* Author Unknown.

Drunknets Held Illegal

Drunknets, roadblocks used by state police to catch drinking drivers, are illegal according to an opinion offered by the Attorney General's office.

Asst. Attorney Gen. David B. Sebree wrote that roadblocks used to check licenses are legal. They become illegal, he said, when the primary motive of checking the license is to see whether the driver is intoxicated. Such arrests he said have the effect of requiring the motorist to give evidence against himself.

Sebree suggested that evidence can be used against a driver on a drunk driving charge if he has been stopped in good faith for the sole purpose of checking his license.

This amounts to the observance by the arresting officer of a misdemeanor being committed in his presence, Sebree said.

The opinion was written for Safety Commissioner Don Sturgill after the legality of drunknets was questioned in a Jefferson County case.

Sebree acknowledged there was a difficult line of reasoning in the case of drunknets as opposed to ordinary roadblocks and suggested the matter be presented to the Court of Appeals as soon as possible.[65]

---

[65] 24 January 1958. *Grant County News.* Author Unknown.

WOMEN YOU CAN'T FORGET

CARRY NATION'S BATTLE OF THE BOTTLE

(By Herb Michelson)

"The Hatchet Lady was always ready for action 'to do good for humanity.'"

JOHN L. SULLIVAN . . . The Great John L., the hard-knuckled ringmaster who would yield to no man but Gentleman Jim Corbett . . . was now a bit worried, and all because of a little old lady.

The little old lady was waiting downstairs, outside John's saloon. She wanted to see John. Wanted to tell him she didn't like the "mean things" he was saying about her.

John didn't want to see her. Didn't want to get any closer to her than he was. John L. was scared. He told the lady's messenger, "Tell her I'm sick . . . Not on my life will I see her."

Thus was averted a meeting between Sullivan and Carry Nation, "The Lady with a Hatchet," "The Smasher," "The Loving Home Defender."

MOST REPORTS call her Carrie, but upon her birth in Kentucky in 1846 her unlettered father inscribed her name in the family Bible as Carry.

She changed the spelling as an adult . . . and tried to change other things. Only at the first revision was she entirely unsuccessful.

* * * *

MODERN historians will long ponder why this Kentuckian, this particular woman fought so long, so hard, so bitterly against man's alcoholic adventures. It may have been her times, it may have been her background, it may have been none of these.

There was bound to be one crusader, though, who would make himself or herself a name. In this case, it just happened to be Carry Nation.

If one individual is due credit for Carry's crusading, it would have to be her first husband, a doctor named Gloyd.

This tireless country doctor was also a tireless country drinker. Matter of fact, it was drink that killed him— 18 months after his marriage and one year after becoming a father. He died in agony of delirium tremens.

This was what moved Carry close to her mission.

* * * *

A WIDOW at 25, Carry soon married Missouri newspaper editor David Nation, but at the turn of the century the marriage collapsed— Nation wasn't in sympathy with Carry's crusades.

During divorce proceedings, she told Nation, "God has given me a mission. I dare not turn back. Shall I hearken unto God or man? Judge ye."

Now free from the objections of any spouse, Carry began her historic campaign— The 12 Year War, a fight that took her from Kansas to New York, from Canada to Scotland, from Mexico to England . . . a battle that found her behind bars on 33 occasions.

THE CAMPAIGN was launched in Kiowa, Kans., in '99. She organized a county temperance union, bought several dozen bright and shiny hatchets, armed her followers with them and moved on the bigger dens of iniquity.

In December of 1900, the Nation people marched on Wichita, entered one of the more plush nighteries, where hung an oil painting of Cleopatra at the Roman bath.

Carry, clad in cape and beaded poke bonnet, flung a rock at the hapless Cleo then hurled a second stone through a $1,500 mirror adorning the bar, shouting, "I came to the governor's town to destroy the finest saloon in it."

This was "Hatchetation."

TWO YEARS later, her crusade making headline after headline, Carry came to New York City, ready for her biggest battle on the bottle.

Unfettered by razzing, she strode into the headquarters of Colonel Murphy, Gotham's No. 1 cop, and asked him, "Don't you think New York is an awful bad place . . . Don't you think it's full of hell holes and murder factories?

"I only came to do New York good. I want to do good for humanity. I want to do something for you."

Murphy wanted nothing done for himself. He called Carry "crazy" and asked her to leave quietly.

But Carry did nothing quietly. She stormed New York, from Carnegie Hall to the Bowery, crying, "Take me to some hellholes . . . down with 'Hellbroth' (beer)."

* * * *

WHEN SALOON keepers heard she was on the prowl, they'd close down rather than do battle with colorful Carry. Although men were her chief adversaries, she often lashed out at her own sex. Carry was as anti-corset as she was anti-alky, warning women not to make their "hearts and livers into one solid lump."

New York rocked with laughter at her escapades. She lectured in Carnegie Hall, tried to teach a Sunday School class in a tough, all-male Democratic drinking club. Her finest hour came, though, in the ornate Victoria Hotel.

In the Victoria's lobby stood a figure of Diana, clad only in bow and arrow. Whipping out her hatchet, Carry told all who would listen, "She ain't got a thing on . . . it ain't respectable . . . Would you like your wife to see that?"

* * * *

SHE DIDN'T LIVE to see prohibition effected. She doubtless would have prepared a great speech for the occasion had she been there. But at 65, Carry passed on in 1911, after an unsuccessful attempt to found a school for young prohibitionists in Eureka Springs, Arkansas.

Hatchet Hall, the school was to be called. But the first class never met. In 1936, prohibitionists tried to gather funds to make Hatchet Hall a national shrine, but again no success.

* * * *

CARRY was laughed at, she was harassed, she was denounced. Her enemies were legion, her supporters faithful to the end. She felt she had a mission on earth and gave her all in its support.

This above all, is the greatest truth in the legend of Carry Nation.

66

[66] 9 May 1958. *Grant County News.* Herb Michelson.

Whiskey & Beer Confiscated In Roadhouse Raids

Thirty-nine full half pints of whiskey, eight 6-can cartons of beer, ten cans of beer and 29 bottles of beer were seized in raids of two roadhouses south of Williamstown late Wednesday afternoon, May 14.

Judge R. Lester Mullins reported that three ABC officials made purchases of beer and whiskey at Ervie Starns' place of business and Grant Taylor's restaurant the day of the raid and obtained warrants for their arrest. The whiskey and beer was seized when the Alcoholic Board of Control representatives, Sheriff Porter Martin and Alva Ransdell, deputy sheriff, went to the roadhouses that night.

Starns and Taylor waived examining trial before Judge Mullins and were held to the grand jury under $500 bond each. The Starns warrant bore the signature of Carl Harmon and Taylor's that of Charles R. Reed.[67]

Three Motorists Fined $100 For Drunken Driving

The maximum fine of $100 and cost was imposed on three motorists arranged in quarterly court during the past week on charges of operating a motor vehicle while drunk. In addition to the fine, they were required to pay $5 court cost and $2 state tax.

Nineteen cases were tried between Sept. 24 and Sept. 30 but three of the defendants were charged with two offenses.[68]

Two Countians Arrested In Tavern Brawl

John H. Cheeseman, 38-year-old Walton man, thought to have been the victim of a road house brawl Saturday night, died of natural causes, Dr. E. L. Smith, Kenton county coroner, ruled Monday. Dr. Smith said Cheeseman died of a hemorrhage not caused "by any blows."

Cheeseman's body was found near the entrance to Johnny and Fay's Tavern, about 1 1/2 mile south of Walton.

Arrested in connection with his death and held for investigation were two Grant county people, Lawrence J. Stewart, 27, Crittenden, and Lula Mae Sturgeon, 33, Elliston.

Officers reported the three had been together in the tavern and apparently the men got in a fight over the woman after they left the building and entered the victim's car.

The report said Stewart contended that he knocked Cheeseman down and the Sturgeon woman "stomped him." She said she was merely "suffing" with the two men.

Stewart was arrested at a nearby tavern and Lula Mae Sturgeon, who was said to have left the scene in a car was taken into custody at a Grant County farmhouse Sunday morning.

Officers reported the pair apparently were unaware the victim was dead but thought he was unconscious. They indicated that Cheeseman must have lain on the lot more than an hour before State Troopers were called to the scene.

Mr. Cheeseman leaves his mother, Mrs. Emma McClure Cheeseman, Walton, three brothers, Robert and Raymond, Walton, and Morris Cheeseman, Morning View; four sisters, Mrs. Nellie Collins, Mrs. Helen Rich and Mrs. Tillie Smith, all of Walton, and Mrs. Emma Anderson, Petersburg.

Services were held at 2:00 p. m.. Tuesday at Chambers & Grubbs Funeral Home, Walton. Burial was in the Independence cemetary.[69]

Is your News subscription paid?

[67] 23 May 1958. *Grant County News.* Author Unknown.
[68] 3 October 1958. *Grant County News.* Author Unknown.
[69] 5 May 1959. *Grant County News.* Author Unknown.

1960s

Roadhouse Raided By State Police

A roadhouse on Taft Highway was the scene of a raid by Kentucky State police last Sunday afternoon at 3 o'clock. Police reported the establishment of Early Crouch was raided and 28 cases of beer and 15 half-pints of whiskey were confiscated.

Arrested were Neal Elliott, 75, Route 1, Dry Ridge, a 15-year-old boy, Harold McClure, 33, Route 1, Glencoe, and Early Crouch, 62. Crouch and the boy were charged with selling alcoholic beverages in local option territory. Neal and McClure were charged with public drunkenness.

Crouch is out on bond and is scheduled to be given a hearing before Judge R. Lester Mullins, Friday. Judge Mullins could not be contacted to make a statement regarding the juvenile. McClure and Elliot were placed in jail on drunkenness charges. Elliot was released to his son Sunday night, and McClure was released Monday morning.[1]

Early Crouch Fined $200 And Given 60 Days

Charged with selling alcoholic beverages in local option territory, Early Crouch, 62, plead guilty when arraigned before Judge R. Lester Mullins. He was fined $200 and given 60 days in jail.

Crouch, operator of a road house on Taft Highway west of Dry Ridge, was arrested February 7 when his establishment was raided by State police. Judge Mullins said 28 cases of beer and 15 half-pints of whiskey confiscated in the raid, will be turned over to the Alcoholic Control Board for disposition.

A 15-year-old boy, arrested in the raid and charged with selling alcoholic beverages in dry territory, was placed on probation.

Harold McClure, Jr., 33, Glencoe and Neal Elliot, 75, of Dry Ridge, also arrested at the time of the raid and charged with public drunkenness were fined $22 each.[2]

Drunken Driver Chased By Police

A 1954 automobile, being driven at a high rate of speed, was wrecked as it was being pursued by Harold Elliston. Dry Ridge police officer, on the Taft Highway Monday morning. Although the automobile was completely demolished, the driver, registered as Garland Perkins of Owenton, was uninjured. He was arrested and charged with driving an automobile while under the influence of alcoholic beverages. He was fined $100 and costs. Charged also for driving on a revoked license, he was fined $50.

Officers said Perkins' automobile ran into a fence on the farm of Jas. Gordon, tearing down some 40 feet of the fence and went over a steep embankment.

A passing motorist saw the car as it went over the bank and got out to investigate. He parked his car, officers said, and was walking back to the wreck when he fell over a fence and suffered a dislocated shoulder. He was unidentified.[3]

[1] 12 February 1960. *Grant County News.* Author Unknown.
[2] 19 February 1960. *Grant County News.* Author Unknown.
[3] 20 May 1960. *Grant County News.* Author Unknown.

Three Fined $100 On Drunken Driving Charge

Three motorists were fined $100 in quarterly court on charges of driving while under the influence of alcohol. In addition to the fines, court cost and state tax of $7 was assessed and driver's licenses revoked for six months in Kentucky. Fined were Louis Hiter, Dunnville, Ky.; Wilburn L. Barnes. Mt. Vernon, Ky., and Homer V. Thornton, Bromley, Ky. Mr. Barnes was also fined $14 for driving without an operator's license.[4]

Senator Blake Is Fined For Drunken Driving

Paris, Ky., Nov. 21 H. Stanley Blake, 65, of Carlisle, member of the Kentucky Senate from the 30th District since 1937, was fined $200 and $3 costs and given a retroactive one-day jail sentence in Paris Police Court tonight on a charge of driving while drunk.

Police Judge Thomas Johnston said that Senator Blake, long known as the dean of the Kentucky Senate because of his length of service, was credited with serving the one-day jail sentence for the time spent in the lockup after his arrest here early on the morning of November 8th, election day.

Senator Blake appeared in court tonight for his trial and entered a plea of not guilty through his attorney, William Blanton of Paris.

Paris Police Officers Melvin Howard and Clarence Heflin, the arresting officers, said they followed Senator Blake's car from near the court house out East Main Street about three-fourths of a mile then stopped him and arrested him. He was fined $100 and costs on a similar charge in Fayette County Quarterly Court on August 30, 1956.

Grant County is in the 30th Senatorial District which is represented by Mr. Blake.[5]

Drunken Driver Wrecks Automobile

Elmer Rogers, from the southern part of the state, was arrested Monday afternoon after he ran into and wrecked the automobile of Mrs. R. A. Greene, parked in front of her home on North Main St. Damage to the car was $300 or $400 Mr. Greene said.

Rogers was charged with driving while under the influence of intoxicating liquor and having no driver's license. He was fined $100 and $7.50 costs on the first charge and $2 fine, $10 costs and $2 tax on the second charge. On failure to pay his fine, he was placed in jail.[6]

Two Places Raided Here Wednesday

A quantity of whiskey, beer and wine was seized by officers here Wednesday when two business establishments in the city limits of Williamstown were raided.

Conducting the raids were Sheriff Alva Ransdell, Deputy Byron D. Martin and state police. The officers raided the Dog House, owned and operated by Goldie Taylor and located on the west side of U. S. 25 north of Williamstown. Seized were 94 bottles of beer, four half pints of whiskey six years old and three pints of wine.

The Kanary Corner, operated by Erva Starnes and located on the east side of U. S. 25 south of Williamstown, was also raided and taken from this place of business were 219 bottles of beer, two four-fifths of whiskey and eleven half pints of whiskey.

Taylor and Starnes were arrested and charged with illegal possession of alcoholic beverages. They were released under $500 bond and ordered to appear for examining trial before Judge R. Lester Mullins Monday morning.[7]

[4] 3 June 1960. *Grant County News.* Author Unknown.
[5] 25 November 1960. *Grant County News.* Author Unknown.
[6] 9 February 1962. *Grant County News.* Author Unknown.
[7] 8 June 1962. *Grant County News.* Author Unknown.

Bootlegger Nabbed In Front Of Court House

Observing suspicious activities taking place in front of the court house Saturday, around an automobile, Sheriff Alva Ransdell and Deputy Byron Martin, investigated and took one man into custody for bootlegging whiskey. He is Frank Hutcherson of Pendleton County.

Sheriff Ransdell said they saw Hutcherson give a man something out of his automobile and asked if he was selling whiskey and he replied that he was not. They found the man, Ransdell said, behind the court house and asked him how much he paid for his whiskey and he told them $2.

They questioned Hutcherson further, the officer said, and he admitted that he did sell the man whiskey. They searched his car and found 12 bottles of whiskey and 72 bottles of beer.

Hutcherson was placed under arrest and upon making bond of $500 was released.[8]

Bootlegger Fined And Sentenced

Frank Hutcherson plead guilty to a charge of bootlegging whiskey, in Judge Lester Mullins court, Monday, and was fined $100 and sentenced to thirty days in jail. He is now serving the sentence in the county jail.

Hutcherson was arrested September 14 by Sheriff Alva Ransdell and Deputy Byron Martin after they investigated suspicious activities taking place between Hutcherson and a man in front of the court house. After questioning both parties Hutcherson admitted that he had sold a bottle of whiskey for $2.

Twelve bottles of whiskey and 72 bottles of beer were uncovered when the officers searched his car.[9]

16-Year-Old Charged With Being Drunk

A 16-year-old Pendleton County youth was removed to a Lexington hospital early Sunday morning, December 27 following an accident on Ky. 22 in which he was injured.

State police said Gary D. Hutchinson, Route 1, Falmouth, was traveling east on Ky. 22 two miles east of Williamstown when he ran off the left side of the road and was thrown out of the truck he was driving, into a field. He was taken to Grant County Hospital and transferred to Central Baptist Hospital, Lexington. He suffered a broken shoulder, severe cut of the left ear and cut over the right eye.

Police said he was charged with being a public drunk.[10]

Beer Bottle Thrown Through Auto Window

Deputy Sheriff Byron Martin said the rear window of the late model automobile belonging to Elmer Cruey was broken last Saturday night when someone threw a beer bottle through it. The car was parked in front of Mr. Cruey's home on Broadway in Dry Ridge.

The officer said the previous week, the windshield of Mr. Cruey's car was broken when someone hit it with a rock. Deputy Martin said he did not report the first incident to the sheriff's office.

Finger prints were taken from pieces of the broken beer bottle, Mr. Martin said.[11]

State-Owned Liquor Stores Proposed

Reports from Frankfort are that the state administration is considering asking the General Assembly to switch Kentucky to a system of state-owned liquor stores as a means of meeting school financial needs.

The governor's special education commission suggested that state-owned package liquor stores might held solve the teacher salary crisis.

---

[8] 20 September 1963. *Grant County News.* Author Unknown.

[9] 4 October 1963. *Grant County News.* Author Unknown.

[10] 1 January 1965. *Grant County News.* Author Unknown.

[11] 30 April 1965. *Grant County News.* Author Unknown.

No official estimates are available on how much money state-owned stores would realize. Unofficial estimates are that the yield might be somewhere between $8 and $15 million a year of gross profit on sales. From this would be deducted the cost to the state for administration, acquisition or rental of stores, salaries and other cost items.

Governor Breathitt said he was neutral about the question. He named the commission a few weeks ago to look into ways to boost teachers' salaries.

The liquor store proposal came as a surprise. Bills have been offered in the legislature many times but have never won approval.

If the General Assembly puts the proposal into law Kentucky would become the 18th liquor-monopoly state. Much opposition is expected from both the wets and drys, according to press reports.

Henry M. Schulman, executive secretary of both the Kentucky Retail Liquor Association and the Louisville Retail Package Liquor Dealers Association, said his group would offer "determined opposition" to state-owned liquor stores.

The Rev. Walter C. House, consultant to the Temperance League of Kentucky, said the league was also opposed because state ownership "puts the individual directly in the liquor business."

The Rev. Mr. House questioned the wisdom of a bond between schools and liquor.[12]

Webster Votes Against Repeal Of Whiskey Tax

Franklin Webster, State Representative from Grant County and Owen County voted against repeal of the tax on whiskey production. The bill passed and reduces the tax two cents a year starting July 1, 1967. Each cent of the tax brings in approximately a million dollars a year to Kentucky.

Upon learning of the passage of H. B. 140, the bill repealing the tax, Grant McDonald, President of the Kentucky Chamber of Commerce, the organization sponsoring the bill said, "This is indeed a wonderful day for Kentucky which reflects the maturity of our legislative and executive branches of government in dealing with the problem of the production tax which, for some thirty years, has been a punitive and vindictive tax against this important industry. Kentucky's economic future is greatly enhanced by the removal of the tax which now permits this industry to compete fairly in the market place."[13]

Is your News subscription paid?

Drunk Driving Charge Brings Maximum Mulct

Lexingtonian Pays $100 Fine and Costs. Loses Permit.

Fifteen defendants of various infractions of the law faced R. Lester Mullins, Grant county judge, during the past week in quarterly court. A Lexington autoist received the maximum penalty for operating his car while under the influence of intoxicating liquor - $100 fine, court costs and automatic suspension of his drivers permit for six months.[14]

Grand Jury To Get "Dry" Case

Trio Gives Bond For Appearance

The case of three men charged with illegal transportation of alcoholic beverages in local option (or dry) territory was removed from Dry Ridge city police court Wednesday on agreement of City Attorney John Lane Ackman and Rudy Yessin, Frankfort, attorney for the defendants.

Police Judge Eric McBee said the charges were not within his court's jurisdiction and the matter was referred to the Grant county grand jury session in July. The defendants, Louis R. Richerson and William Allen Stewart of Dry Ridge and Charles M. McComas of Williamstown, gave bond for their July 1 appearance before the grand jury.

[12] 11 February 1966. *Grant County News.* Author Unknown.
[13] 18 March 1966. *Grant County News.* Author Unknown.
[14] 17 June 1966. *Grant County News.* Author Unknown.

Richerson and McComas are the present commander and commander-elect, respectively, of the American Legion Post 137 at Williamstown.

The charges were brought by State Police Sgt. W. O. Bradley and State Police Detective Ben Harney.[15]

---

[15] 30 May 1968. *Grant County News.* Author Unknown.

1970s

Alcohol Abuse Open Forum Scheduled To Be Held Here

Many people are talking about it, a few people who want to do something about it are seeking your help. These are inviting you to participate in an Open Forum on Alcohol Abuse one of the frustrating and neglected problems of this community.

The Northern Kentucky Mental Health Mental Retardation Regional Board has appointed a joint Ad Hoc Committee on Alcohol Abuse to coordinate planning for treatment and education programs in this eight county region. The Committee is made up of board members and at-large citizens from the area who are dealing actively with or are knowledgeable about this major problem.

Citizens of Grant County are invited and urged to attend this meeting at the court house in Williamstown, Tuesday, July 11.

The purpose of the forum is to hear your statement of the problem as you see it, to explore with you resources that currently exist to manage the problem, and to consider with you additional resources we should plan together to provide necessary treatment and to promote prevention.[1]

Whiskey, Beer Confiscated In Raid

State police raided Charlie Starns Grocery on U.S. 25 in the south city limits of Williamstown at 4 p.m. December 16. Found were 40 half pints of whisky and 108 bottles of beer.

Starns was charged with sale of illegal alcoholic beverages in local option territory, also possession of illegal alcoholic beverages in local option territory.

Starns plead guilty as charged and was fined $100 on each count and sentenced to 30 days in jail by Judge Byron D. Martin. The jail sentence was probated.[2]

Grant County Co-Operating In Alcohol Abuse School

Nineteen Northern Kentucky county or city police courts are co-operating in the Northern Kentucky Comprehensive Care School of Alcohol Abuse.

Dr. Clarence Lassetter of the CCC staff and director of the school released the list.

The school holds "classes" in two locations, at the City-County Building, Covington, and the City Building in Carrollton. The school is open, he said, for all those who wish to learn more about the problem of alcoholism.

At the same time he reported that 57 took part in the sessions during the first period of 1973 from mid-January to mid-February. Eight faculty members aided in the discussions, the showing of films and the dialogues.

Present at several sessions to help in their work were student nurses from the Northern Kentucky Vocational School.

Courts who have notified Dr. Lassetter of their agreement to participate include:

Bellevue police court, Boone county court, Bromley police court, Campbell County Court, Carroll County Court, Carrollton city court, Covington police court, Crescent Springs police court, Dayton Po-

[1] 7 July 1972. *Grant County News.* Author Unknown.

[2] 22 December 1972. *Grant County News.* Author Unknown.

lice court, Erlanger police court, Florence police court, Ft. Mitchell police court, Ft. Wright police court, Gallatin county court, Grant County court, Kenton county court, Ludlow police court, Newport police court, and Silver Grover police court.

However, Dr. Lassetter also emphasized that the school is open to those who termed "self-referrals."[3]

Drunks May Face Psychiatrist Instead Of Judge Under New Law

Within a few days drunks who face Kentucky judges might find themselves talking to a psychiatrist rather than a jailer.

A new law goes into effect in Kentucky on July 1. It will be administered by the Kentucky Department of Mental Health which has been given powers to set up rules and regulations to carry out the mandate of the General Assembly.

Workings of the new law were explained by John Richardson, alcohol program abuse program developer from Northern Kentucky Comprehensive Care Center at an eight-county meeting in Ft. Mitchell. Grant county is included.

The department, he said, will take over co-ordination of alcoholism programs throughout the state. Judges will have an alternative to a jail sentence.

It is hoped, Richardson said, that detoxification centers can be set up on a 24 hour basis in population centers and that treatment programs can be established in existing general hospitals.

In one area, those whose condition merit it, may get inpatient care, whenever a diagnosis reflects serious alcohol-related mental disturbances. Treatment and prevention is also a part of the program with emphasis on helping teen-agers and young adults.[4]

Grant Countians Invited To Join Alcoholism Study

A six-day school on alcoholism featuring U.S. Senator Harold Hughes of Iowa will open at Covington's Quality Inn-Riverview at 4 p.m. Sunday, July 8.

Sponsored by the Kentucky Department of Mental Health, the School for Alcoholic Studies will bring to Northern Kentucky authorities from Florida, Alabama, Canada, Louisiana, the University of Kentucky and authorities from the department at Frankfort.

John Richardson, alcohol program developer for the Northern Kentucky Comprehensive Care Centers, is coordinating local efforts. Further information may be obtained from him at XXX-XXXX.

Following the Sunday session and banquet at which Senator Hughes will speak, the school moves to the campus of Thomas More College for the remainder of the five days.

Richardson reported the gathering is open especially to those working on alcoholism problems in Comprehensive Care's Region. Seven which includes Kenton, Campbell, Boone, Pendleton, Grant, Owen, Gallatin and Carroll counties.

Senator Hughes, three times governor of his state, is a World War Two veteran. A recovered alcoholic, he is spear hearing efforts to find solutions at the national level.[5]

Various Types Attend Alcoholism School

Officials of the Northern Kentucky Comprehensive Care Centers are evaluating the recent six-day school on alcoholism conducted at Thomas More College, Ft. Mitchell.

The institute attracted social workers and even former alcoholics from the eight counties of Region Seven, Kenton, Campbell, Boone, Pendleton, Grant, Owen, Gallatin and Carroll.

One expert, James Whitt, director of the office of alcoholism for the sponsoring Kentucky Department of Mental Health, pointed out that Americans "often reach for a pill to al-

[3] 30 March 1973. *Grant County News.* Author Unknown.

[4] 29 June 1973. *Grant County News.* Author Unknown.

[5] 6 July 1973. *Grant County News.* Author Unknown.

leviate the slightest distress and often turn to alcohol to blot out an unpleasant experience to enhance a situation."

A University of Alabama sociologist, Dr. Gerald Giobetti, explained that alcoholics may come from any background, from homes where alcohol is taboo or from other homes where it is used to an excess.

The six-day study was coordinated in Region Seven by John Richardson, director of comprehensive care is program on alcohol abuse.[6]

Director State Association Alcohol Abuse

Raymond P. Daugherty of Lexington has been named Executive Director of the Kentucky Association on Alcohol Abuse and Alcoholism, Inc.

As head of the year-old organization, Daugherty will direct its statewide efforts in promoting education about alcohol abuse and alcoholism and encouraging development of services for persons with alcohol problems. One of the first projects will be the KAAAA annual meeting, which will take place November 1, 2, and 3, at the Galt House in Louisville. This event will offer educational workshops, entertainment and the featured banquet speaker, Vernon Johnson.

Daugherty, a graduate of Georgetown College, was previously manager of the Department for Human Resources' SID Services in Lexington, which provides care, counseling, and referral for intoxicated persons. While serving in the U.S. Army, he helped establish the army's first Alcohol and Drug Rehabilitation and Education Team in Japan.

In carrying out its program, the Association hopes to bring about greater communication among all those concerned about alcohol problems. KAAAA membership, which is presently 300, is open to anyone interested. The offices are at 212 Washington Street in Frankfort, Kentucky.

Daugherty is the son of the Rev. and Mrs. R. T. Daugherty of Williamstown.[7]

Train Stopped In Whisky Search

Police stopped a train on the L & N track in Gallatin County Tuesday to search the cars after they had received reports that someone was throwing bottles of whisky from the train along the tracks.

The trainload of whisky originated the Decoursey yards, Covington.

A state policeman at LaGrange said someone began throwing objects from the train in Grant County and continued for some 20 miles. He said he "wasn't sure what was being thrown from the train but they think it was whisky."[8]

Former Resident To Speak On Alcoholism

Ray Daugherty, well known in Grant County, will be the speaker tonight (Thursday, Dec. 11) at 7:30 p.m. at the Comprehensive Care Center, Second and Greenup Streets, Covington.

Daugherty, now of Lexington, chairman of the Kentucky Association on Alcohol Abuse and Alcoholism, will meet with the Regional Council on Substance Abuse headed by Richard Murray, Covington pharmacist.

The council includes representatives from eight Northern Kentucky counties including Grant, Pendleton and Owen.[9]

Booze And Drugs Arouse Concern Of Local Schools

Parents Need To Help, Educators Say

First In A Series

---

[6] 3 August 1973. *Grant County News.* Author Unknown.

[7] November 1974. *Grant County News.* Author Unknown.

[8] 4 June 1975. *Grant County News.* Author Unknown.

[9] 11 December 1975. *Grant County News.* Author Unknown.

The letter was impassioned. The writer was upset no, furious. A young girl in the county apparently drank alcohol after taking medication while riding on a school bus. She passed out at school.

"She could have been seriously hurt or killed," wrote C. Switzer of Corinth.

"We can't blame the bus driver, Who do we blame? I cannot honestly answer that question but I do know we must work together in some way to change this system. Maybe next tine instead of a 14-year-old it could be a five-year-old or six-year-old. Maybe next time it will be too late for stomach pumps," wrote Switzer.

Concerned about the situation, THE GRANT COUNTY NEWS began investigating the incidents of drugs and alcohol in local schools.

Was the use here widespread? How did it compare to other school systems? And what are the schools doing to cope with it?

The following story by staff writer Joyce Daugherty is the first in a series about the problem.

Grant County High School Principal Carl Webster said he had come to expect about three incidents of alcohol abuse at the school during a year. But in November he dealt with that many incidents during a two-week period.

He said that bus drivers have found empty fifth and pint sized bottles on their buses, as well as empty medicine bottles in which students apparently sneak liquor to school. But he said he believes most of the drinking, when it does occur, happens before the kids get on the bus.

And he indicated it is alcohol, not drugs, that is the biggest problem in schools.

"More of them (students) have access to alcohol than to any other drug. They can get it just over the (county) line in any direction. I think many of them have access to it at home," he said.

In Williamstown, Principal Sonny Fentress, in his first year at the school, said he hasn't detected such problems there but acknowledged "we do have people here who have had problems but as far as for using it in school, we don't have that problem."

The city and county high schools do employ school psychologists and both schools have embarked on drug education programs.

But Dr. Thomas Hagler, superintendent of Grant County Schools, said, "I'm very much puzzled by this feeling that we (the schools) are going to deal with all the family's problems. Parents don't want to discipline their kids. It's not the responsibility of the teachers or a school bus driver. People in this county have to start exercising parental authority over their kids."

Webster said that, of those students who appear to have drinking problems, "most of them are drinking in the morning.

"The problem is now that the parents have settled for kids drinking. They say I would rather that my kids drink than smoke marijuana.' It's a lot more approved.

"We have some that we are going to recommend to Compcare," relayed Webster, "but I don't think they'll go."

He said the parents are aware of the problems of these children but very few of them or their kids will admit that the problem exists.

"They are not likely to admit it unless they (the kids) are pretty far gone."

"I'm terribly afraid that the kids don't know what they are doing to themselves," said Fentress.

Apparently there is an interest in drug education at the Williamstown school. Fentress reports that the school is having to order additional books on the subject as those that had been in the library were for the most part, stolen.

"Well, maybe someone is using them," sighed Fentress.

The Williamstown principal said drug education in class is handled mainly through the school's health and physical education programs and that the school sponsors assembly programs on the subject for the upper grade levels.

Teachers at both schools have been trained to recognize various drugs by sight, odor and symptoms.

Officials in the Grant County school system are preparing to upgrade their drug education program for the 79-'80 school year and plan to put a new emphasis on it.

"We don't want to glamorize drug use," said Hagler who offered the opinion that most of the films made to warn students of the dangers of drugs inadvertently glamorize them.

"They instill in their minds that there's something there that they (the students) don't even know about."

In the new approach, physical and legal ramifications will bear the main emphasis.

He hopes to have some sort of program in operation for the fifth through twelfth grades by next year.

"They are going to get a dose of what's bad about drugs...cold hard facts," said Hagler. "We hope to deal with the problems of peer group pressures, it's the biggest problem as to whether or not a kid uses drugs...but the deterioration of the family is number one in the long run."

"We're going to try to involve as many people in the community as possible," Hagler said of the new program.

The Kentucky State Police, Comp Care and clergymen throughout Grant County should be involved Hagler said.

Webster heartily approves of the new program and says that it is an aftershot to try to educate students about drugs when they have reached the high school level.

"It doesn't do any good to preach at them," said Webster. "It won't change their ideas at all."

In-school drinking does exist at Grant County. Though it's been just about impossible to catch anyone in the act of sneaking a drink, empty and half-full bottles have been found on the premises.

"They don't disguise it too well," said Webster, "but they don't carry it. They leave it somewhere."

Webster feels that the lack of parental guidance and the amount of teenage drinking is well evidenced by "cases of beer and empty bottles on parking lots on Monday mornings. Generally adults don't do that."

"I know a lot of people make a big distinction between drugs and alcohol but what difference would it make when a kid kills himself?"[10]

Drinking And Drug Use Make Bad Memories

Second In A Series

Last week THE GRANT COUNTY NEWS interviewed Grant County and Williamstown school administrators about the drug/alcohol problems of the students in their schools.

This week the NEWS talked to two young men who went through personal drug and alcohol abuse problems during their teen-age years.

Proms, football games, first loves and learning how to drive are all part of most folks memories of their teenage years.

Those who have undergone the agony of overdosing on drugs, spending hours throwing up and having their stomachs pumped don't recall those memories of their high school and early post-high school years fondly.

Art Guyton of Xenia, Ohio, and Revel Dawson, of Louisville, shared similar experiences through their teen-age years.

Both began drinking long before they were old enough to legally by liquor. Smoking marijuana and being sick from ingesting various other drugs illegally are all part of their teen-age memories.

Guyton and Dawson are now in their early 20's and students at Cumberland College in Williamsburg, Ky. Through their religious faith they say they have overcome the desire for alcohol and other drugs and are spending time in an effort to deter others, especially youngsters, from the path they followed early in life.

At a drug education assembly program for Williamstown High School students Friday, Guyton, now the preacher at Clark's Creek Baptist Church, and Dawson talked about their experiences..

The 21-year-old Dawson related that he began drinking at the age of 12.

Many of his friends were older and peer pressure played an important role in his initiation to drink.

"I had to be accepted by them because I didn't have a car," he said.

Dawson thought that knowledge of his father's experiences would keep him away from alcohol.

"Because he was an alcoholic I though I wouldn't get (in drinking) but I needed a release."

At the age of 14 Dawson was smoking marijuana.

[10]7 December 1978. *Grant County News.* Joyce Daugherty,Staff Writer.

"It was either sniff pain or smoke a joint. I always said I'd never smoke a joint but I did."

A strongly-built man, Dawson said he was a good athlete in high school. He felt that because of this other students looked up to him and he felt additional pressure to be "cool".

"Basically it was just social acceptance," he said, adding that he began using cocaine and mescaline during his sophomore year.

Dawson said that he "overdosed" twice on mescaline and cocaine to the point where he passed out for "a couple of hours."

"The last thing I remember saying was, I'm dying.'"

Dawson indicated that those who were with him were afraid to call for emergency help and were busy getting high themselves.

Dawson also said that he would take amphetamines "speed" regularly and blames the rotting of some his molars on that drug.

"It was at the point to where I had to have speed."

"Drugs would wind me up so tight I'd come down and need it again."

"It wasn't an escape from reality," said Dawson.

"All the things I was doing to myself was that I was just afraid to face responsibility."

"Jesus delivered me from it."

Art Guyton was raised in a country area similar to Grant County.

He considers his life up until he was 15 as average.

At the time he decided to take a class in drafting at the high school.

Fifteen of the boys in the class began to socialize together on a regular basis.

"All of us would go drinking and to dances."

Guyton said his parents were aware of his problems as they progressed. "My folks weren't out of the ordinary in what they were doing (to help him)."

"I put my folks through a lot of hell and I'm sorry for that."

Being accepted by those he considered his friends also played a role in Guyton's drinking and using drugs.

"I had to find something to impress people."

He also said he hadn't intended to smoke marijuana or take drugs.

"I really wasn't sure I wanted to do that but everyone else was doing it so I did it."

"It was totally peer pressure all the way for me."

Guyton remembered the tables turning as he grew older and the pressure he later exerted on friends and cousins to use drugs.

Guyton does offer some simple advice for students, "strive while in high school, especially junior high to find out who you are, be an individual and don't do something for somebody else."[11]

Students Assess Drug, Alcohol Use

Third And Final Part Of A Series

This week, in the third and final part, of a series in which THE GRANT COUNTY NEWS investigated incidents of drinking and drug use in local schools, the students speak up.

Twenty-four Williamstown students in grades 9-12, as well as 15 from Grant County High School, were interviewed for this story. Because students were reluctant to respond openly to questions to be used for publication, we agreed to use no names.

Their responses, however, add an interesting insight to the problems addressed by school administrators and person who experienced problems with alcohol and drug use.

Booze and drugs come into Grant County schools from "outside." Most students will tell little more than that. They say only "friends" or "older kids" travel over the county line to buy it for them.

Nearly half of the Grant County High School students interviewed said that their homes and families supplied the alcohol, although none from Williamstown did. A number of the Grant County students singled out Kenton County as a likely place to go to find drugs and alcohol.

And although most students acknowledge drinking is a much more widespread problem than drugs they say their parents' warning against its use are not as firm.

[11] 14 December 1978. *Grant County News.* Joyce Daugherty,Staff Writer.

"They know I drink on occasion," said one Williamstown senior, "but I'm not supposed to drive. They are against any kind of drugs."

One Grant County High School student said of his parents' warnings against drug use, "we should be telling them since we're more experienced."

Another whose parents learned of his drug use lamented the adults' attitude. "They told (warned) me over and over again and said they didn't want me because I did it. They would rather send me away than help me," the student said.

A little less than half of the students questioned said they really didn't consider ever being arrested for drug use. Those who did said they know they would "get in big trouble" but that the "trouble" would only come from their parents. One students felt if he were caught with alcohol by the police "not much" would happen but if caught with drugs felt he would probably "get killed." Only one student at Williamstown had considered the possibility of going to jail. Another feared he would be grounded. A number at Grant County High School students had considered being sent to jail, others believed they would be fined or put on probation.

Three of 20 Williamstown students interviewed said they had seen students using drugs or alcohol in school. Each of the 15 questioned at Grant County said they had.

Most students agreed that as many as 80 to 95 percent of the students at both high schools had "gone out drinking," and from 40 to 70 percent were smoking marijuana.

And what about drug education in school? One student believed a drug education class should be mandatory. Another said, "it should be available to more people." But most felt it did little good.

One Williamstown student described the drug education program there as a "useless Sonny Bono film."

Finally, we asked them how they felt about the public exposure THE GRANT COUNTY NEWS was giving the problem.

One Grant County High School student retorted, "they put us down and Williamstown up."

In the original story school administrators in the county district admitted that the school had problems with drug and alcohol abuse. Williamstown administrators believed abuse there was not widespread.

Eight of the Williamstown students interviewed said they believed drinking did occur in the school.

All but four of the Grant County High School students agreed with Superintendent Dr. Tom Hagler's view that responsibility for the problem rests at home. And one said he felt THE GRANT COUNTY NEWS stories should have been written "long before now."[12]

This story concludes THE NEWS' formal series on alcohol and drug problems in the schools. We will, however, report periodically on the problems as we learn more about them.

THE EDITOR

Two Arrested With Booze

Two Williamstown residents in their mid-20s were arrested Monday afternoon and charged with seven misdemeanor counts of illegal possession and sale of drugs and alcohol.

Ronald Lee McClure, of 511 Helton Heights, has been charged with sale of an alcoholic beverage in a dry territory, illegal sale of alcoholic beverage, illegal possession of an alcoholic beverage for the purpose of sale, possession of marijuana, trafficking in marijuana and possession of prescription drugs not in their original container.

McClure arrested by the Kentucky State Police with the assistance of the Grant County Sheriff at the apartment of Rosalie Simpson Jackson at 154 N. Main Street, Williamstown.

Twenty-three half-pints of T.W. Samuels whiskey were confiscated as evidence at the apartment.

Jackson was also arrested and charged with the misdemeanor offense of trafficking in marijuana.

In the line of duty, KSP Sgt. Les Simpson arranged to make an illegal buy of alcohol from McClure which transpired on Sunday.

[12] 21 December 1978. *Grant County News.* Joyce Daugherty,Staff Writer.

McClure and Jackson were arraigned on January 22 and pleaded not guilty to all of the charges.

They were released from custody on an unsecured bail bond and are scheduled to appear in court on February 19.[13]

---

[13]25 January 1979. *Grant County News.* Author Unknown.

1980s

Dry Ridge Man Arrested In Liquor Store Hold-Up

A Dry Ridge man has been arrested and warrants issued for the arrest of his brother in connection with the armed robbery of Collett's Carry Out, U.S. 42 and Tanners Lane, Florence last week, according to Florence police.

Earl Grant Hibbard, Jr., 33, Rt. 1, Dry Ridge, has been arrested and charged with criminal intent to commit murder, robbery in the first degree, and wanton endangerment, according to Florence Sgt. William Minnick. Warrants have been issued for the arrest of his brother, Rick Hibbard, in connection with the same incident, Sgt. Minnick stated.

The criminal intent to commit murder and wanton endangerment charges resulted from a high speed pursuit by police after the armed robbery about 8:45 p.m. last Thursday. One of the suspects allegedly fired shots at Florence Sgt. Jack Sturgeon during that pursuit.

According to Detective Jesse Baker, of the Boone-Florence Felony Squad, an armed man in his late teens entered Collett's Carry Out last Thursday night. The man was described as a 5'8" to 5'9", 140 pounds, slender build, with short dark brown hair and clean shaven. He was described as wearing a tan coat, length just below the waist and wearing a knit cap.

Det. Baker stated that the clerks at the store reported that the young suspect came in and picked up some liquor. He instructed the clerk he was holding up the store, but she apparently misunderstood according to Det. Baker as she asked him to show his driver's license. As he revealed his revolver a customer entered the liquor store, according to Baker. The robber then allegedly left the store.

As the clerk called to her husband in the rear of the store, he went outside to check the area, according to Det. Baker. The husband allegedly returned into the store at gunpoint in front of the robber. The armed man then ordered the male clerk and the customer to the rear of the store, according to Det. Baker. He then ordered the woman to empty the cash register and took the money from her, police reported.

After the suspect fled the store, the clerks then reportedly called Florence police. With a description of the car used in the getaway a yellow Chevy Nova Florence police were joined by Boone County and Kentucky State Police in pursuit of the car west on U.S. 42 and south on I-75.

The chase reached high speeds at times, according to Det. Baker. One of the suspects allegedly leaned out his window and fired shots at Sgt. Sturgeon as he followed behind in his cruiser on I-75.

The suspects pulled off the interstate near Crittenden and fled on foot, according to police. Police from all three departments, as well as officers from the Boone County Sheriff's department, Walton police and Kenton County police reportedly covered the area in search of the suspects.

Earl Hibbard, Jr. was allegedly arrested by Kenton County police as he was coming on foot out of the woods in Kenton County between Walton and Crittenden.

The robbery at Collett's Carry Out last week was not the first at the store in its 20 years of business in Florence. Last November, Bob Collett noted that he's always aware of the possibility of another robbery.

"I think no matter what kind of business you have, you always worry. You can't help it," Collet said last November during a rash of armed robberies in the county.

"More people are wanting extra money and they figure it's the easiest way to get it."[1]

[1] 28 February 1980. *Grant County News.* Author Unknown.

GASOHOL FUELS FARMERS' DREAMS

The Department of Agriculture has vowed to make farmers instrumental in the search for energy alternatives.

Agriculturists seem determined to glean fuel for the next generation from this generation's corn crop.

The stills of Kentucky, they say, may once more be activated. This time with the approval of the notorious "Revenooers."

What they are talking about is not Kentucky moonshine. It is the Blue Grass answer to the gas crisis. It is called gasohol.

An abandoned distillery in Cynthiana, once operated by Seagrams. will begin production of ethanol this summer. Willitt Distributing Company in Bardstown will add gasohol to its products list if federal, local and private funding is obtained.

Farmers and bankers have joined hands with distillers and fuel barons to promote the production of gasohol, a blend of 10% ethanol and 90% unleaded gasoline.

Supporters of gasohol production see it as a double blessing, an alternative to foreign energy dependence and a boom to the American farmers suffering from the low value placed on bountiful crops of golden corn.

The United States Department of Energy has recently established a new department to serve prospective gasohol producers in the midwest. The department which is known as the Office of Alcohol Fuels will handle millions of federal loan guarantee dollars available to gasohol producers.

In an attempt to develop fuel alternatives, President Carter has pledged government money to subsidize gasohol operations. In order to get in on the ground floor, Kentucky legislators have pledged state subsidies to match those federal funds.

According to the Kentucky Department of Energy, priority for financing will be given to smaller communities with populations under 25,000.

The enthusiasm for small scale distilleries operated by farmers is mellowed with skepticism.

"Making gasohol is much more difficult than making alcohol to drink," warns Wayne Sininger. Grant County Conservation Agent.

"Alcohol to be mixed with unleaded gasoline must be 200 proof: on a regular farm still the alcohol is usually 150 to 160 proof. And, often there is water in it."

According to Sininger, if water seeps into the alcohol and gasoline mixture, it will become an inefficient and ineffective fuel.

"It takes more complex equipment to produce alcohol to be used as a source of fuel," Sininger continues. "In order to distill it properly, it might take more energy than could be produced."

In addition, certain procedures must be followed before alcohol can be produced on a farm legally. "You have to have a federal permit from the United States Treasury Department." says Sininger.

The Bureau of Alcohol, Tobacco and Firearms has already approved approximately 60 permits for experimental stills in the State of Kentucky, and expects to approve many more before year-end.

Still, experts say that big businessmen with the financial capacity to build or improve upon already existing distilleries hold the key to the success or failure of gasohol production.

It is currently estimated to cost about $1.50 per gallon in its first year of production.

Current estimates are that gasohol could cost as much as $1.75 per gallon to produce during the first year.

But, if gasoline prices continue to rise at the unbelievable rates of the past several years, gasohol could be the domestic answer to OPEC blackmail.

That is, if the "Revenooers" continue to believe that the moonshine made in the hills of Kentucky will be used to fuel automobiles and not their drivers.[2]

KSP CRACKS DOWN ON ILLEGAL BOOZE BUYS

The Kentucky State Police cited several businesses with unlawful transaction with a minor and permitting the sale of alcoholic beverages to a minor recently, according to Kentucky State Police Post 6 Public Affairs Officer Jim Dolwick.

[2] 17 April 1980. *Grant County News.* Author Unknown.

The charges were levied following three, allegedly illegal "buys" in December, 1981 and January, 1982. According to Sergeant Phil Harney, three Kentucky State Police Troopers, Tom Lanter, Rob Elliott and Jim Daley, and two 18-year-old males visited each business which was cited. While the two 18-year-old minors purchased the alcoholic beverages, the troopers would observe the transaction, he stated. Kentucky laws stipulates a person must be 21 years of age, or older, to purchase alcoholic beverages.

"The buys were made on three different dates: December 19 and 20, 1981. and January 9. 1982," Sergeant Harney said.

Among the businesses cited for transactions made on December 19 and 20, 1981 were Shamrock Inn. Bracht Station Road, Dixie Highway, Crittenden and Breeze Inn, Box 271, Route 1, Crittenden, according to Kentucky State Police reports.

Bartenders who served the alcoholic beverages were cited for unlawful transaction with a minor. Criminal complaints for permitting the sale of alcoholic beverages to a minor were also served on the person in charge of each business.

Additional businesses cited on December 19 and 20, 1981 were Spanish Villa, Florence; Round up, Erlanger; Comi Si Chiama, Newport; The Cottage, Southgate; Camp Springs Tavern, Melbourne; and Swanee Villa, Melbourne.

Criminal complaints were signed against the Kwik Shoppe, Melbourne; King Kwik, Newport; Palmers Transfer Liquor, Newport; and Poppy's Carry-out, Newport on January 22. Each business was cited for permitting the sale of alcoholic beverages to a minor, according to police reports.

"These types of investigations will continue." Sergeant Harney emphasized.[3]

Breathalyzer Updated

Law enforcement officials throughout Grant County are undergoing a recertification process that will enable them to better use breathalyzer equipment. The equipment, used to determine a level of intoxication for drunken subjects, will be kept at the Grant County Jail.

The recertification was necessitated when 129 breathalyzers were purchased with federal monies by the Commonwealth of Kentucky. The breathalyzers are a modernized version of the breathalyzer previously used by police.[4]

MADD Program April 28

The Grant County Jr. Woman's Club will present a program on April 28, at 7:30 p.m. at the Williamstown High School Cafeteria on Mothers Against Drunk Driving:

MADD is an organization of victims, survivors and concerned citizens determined to reduce deaths and injuries resulting from driving under the influence. Mothers Against Drunk Drivers encompasses all types of people: young, old, male, female, mothers, fathers, sisters, brothers, any citizen concerned with the problems of driving under the influence.

Mr. and Mrs. Edward Kentrup with the Northern Kentucky Chapter of MADD will present the program.[5]

Election Question Brewing

As many registered voters in the county are aware, there is a movement afoot that may result in a local option election on June 29. Should that election occur, the question on the ballot would ask voters if they are in favor of allowing the sale of alcoholic beverages in the county.

Some voters have been approached personally with requests to sign a petition, but the most visible activity thus far has been a mail campaign asking registered voters to sign up. The return address is to J.K. West at a post office box in Williamstown. "J.K. West" is Judy West, a county resident who is the only person publicly associated with the effort thus far.

[3] 28 January 1982. *Grant County News.* Author Unknown.
[4] 3 March 1983. *Grant County News.* Author Unknown.
[5] 14 April 1983. *Grant County News.* Author Unknown.

West had little comment on the petition drive as of Tuesday. She did note that she has had some negative feedback in the return mail. West also said that she has been working on the petition since November.

According to Kentucky law, any petition drive for a local option election must garner signatures from registered voters equal to 25 per cent of the votes cast in the affected territory during the previous general election. In November's election, which should be applicable in this case, 4,711 votes were cast, according to county clerk John S. "Corn" McCoy. That means that West needs 1,178 signatures in order to mandate a local option election, a number that would comprise 17.4 per cent of the county's 6,783 registered voters.

The election date can either be set by the county judge/executive, or the petitioner can request a specific date. The petition form included with West's letter requests a local option election on of June 29, a Saturday. That date was presumably chosen since it falls a month after the primary election on May 28. According to McCoy, voting machines must remain sealed for 15 days after a primary election. That would leave approximately two weeks to reset the machines for a local option election, which is feasible, according to McCoy. Kentucky law stipulates that the cost of local option elections is to be borne by the county.

According to figures supplied by the judge/executive's office, last November's election cost the county in excess of $8,500. That figure includes fees for election officers, the board of elections, poll rental, advertising and the printing of ballots. Although the cost of advertising and the printing of ballots should be considerably less for a one-issue, election, the cost could still be substantial.

When asked if a local option election could cost the county somewhere in the vicinity of $3,000, Grant County Judge/ Executive B. D. Martin replied: "I'd say you're probably right."

However, Judge Martin noted that Kentucky law leaves him no choice in the matter. "If they get enough legitimate names, I'll have to issue the orders for a special election." Martin and McCoy will work together to determine which signatures are valid.

West is asking that signatures be returned to her by February 15. The law stipulates that the signatures must be filed with the county clerk more than 60 days. and less than 90 days, before the date of the election, which means that the names will most likely be submitted sometime between the latter part of March and the end of April.

Such an election cannot be held on the same day as a general or primary election, nor may it be repeated any oftener than once in every three years. Should there be a special election in June and the issue is defeated, the question cannot be put up for election again until 1988.[6]

Wet/Dry Petitions To Be Filed

Not much is brewing right now in Judy West's campaign to get a wet/dry issue in front of the voters this summer, even though she had asked for signatures to be returned by February 15.

"I'm getting everything together now," said West, who anticipates filing the petition for a local option election by April 1. West needs the signatures of 1.178 registered voters in the county to force a special election asking voters if they favor the sale of alcoholic beverages in the county. That number is equal to 25 per cent of the votes cast in last November's election, the number of signatures required by Kentucky law.

"I'm confident I'll have the names," said West. "I don't really know what the final total is." Several other people are helping her collect names and not all of them have returned their petitions, according to West.

West's next stop is to file the signatures with the county clerk, who will work with the county judge/executive to authenticate the signatures. West said the petition and signatures would be filed by her lawyers, whom she did not identify.

If a sufficient number of signatures are determined to be valid, the county is required by law to hold a local option election at its expense. West has requested June 29, a Sat-

[6]24 January 1985. *Grant County News.* Author Unknown.

[7]21 February 1985. *Grant County News.* Author Unknown.

urday, for the election, a day off for many people.

"It will give everybody, even if they want to vote 'no', a chance to vote," said West.[7]

Petitions Filed

The machinery has now officially been set in motion that may result in a local option election in Grant County on June 29. On that date countians will be asked to decide whether or not they are in favor of the sale of alcoholic beverages locally.

Holbrook resident Judy West, who has worked since November collecting signatures on a petition requesting the special election, turned in 318 pages of signatures at 11:03 a.m. on Monday. The signatures were turned over to County Clerk John S. McCoy, who is required by law to join forces with county judge/executive B.D. Martin in validating the signatures. If a sufficient number of the signatures are found to be authentic, the county is required to hold the special election.

In order to force a special election on the question, 1,178 valid signatures are needed. That number is equal to 25 per cent of the votes cast in last November's general election, the percentage mandated by statute. Although the signatures on West's petition have not yet been tabulated, it would appear that there are a sufficient number to mandate the special election, assuming that the signatures are validated.

McCoy and Martin will probably get started on validating and tabulating the signatures next week, according to McCoy.[8]

Wet-Dry Petitions Probed

As of Monday afternoon, Grant County Judge/Executive B.D. Martin and county clerk John S. McCoy had worked their way through signatures from nine precincts, determining which were valid and which were not. The signatures are affixed to petitions requesting that the county hold a local option election in June which concerns only one issue, the sale of alcoholic beverages within the county. There are 13 precincts in the county.

Martin and McCoy estimated that they would be comparing signatures on the petitions with voter registration cards until some time yesterday. McCoy said that 1,376 signatures had been submitted. Based on the turnout in last November's election, 1,178 valid signatures are needed to force the special election.

McCoy said it took three days of preparation before he and Martin could even begin comparing signatures. They started examining the signatures on April 9, according to McCoy, after he had eliminated duplicate signatures and arranged the remainder by precinct. He said that a number of signatures had been eliminated, but said he didn't know how many.

"What we've pulled we haven't counted," said McCoy. "And we're not gonna count 'em till we're done."

McCoy estimated that 500 new voters had been registered since Holbrook resident Judy West began the petition drive in November.[9]

Two Names Tip Balance On Petition

It wasn't a resounding victory, but those local residents who petitioned the county to hold a wet/dry election in June will have their way. Petitioners submitted 1,376 signatures. Of those. 1,180 were deemed valid by the county clerk and judge/executive, exceeding the required number by a mere two signatures. The petition drive was started last November by Judy West, of Holbrook.

In an order dated April 17, Grant County Judge/Executive B.D. Martin ordered county clerk John S. "Corn" McCoy to start preparing to hold the special election on June 29, Saturday. McCoy will be operating on a tight schedule, since the special election follows hard on the heels of the May 28 primary. McCoy will not be able to reset the voting machines for 15 days after the primary in case a recanvass is required. That waiting period is specified by statute. The wet/dry issue must be a special election since not all voters in all precincts are qualified to vote in the primary, due to party affiliations.

[8] 4 April 1985. *Grant County News.* Author Unknown.
[9] 18 April 1985. *Grant County News.* Author Unknown.

The wet/dry issue will affect the county as a whole, according to Catherine Staib, general counsel for the Department of Alcoholic Beverage Control (ABC) in Frankfort. If a majority of the voters in the county vote in favor of the sale of alcoholic beverages, the entire county will be wet.

"However, after the whole county has gone wet, precincts that are really upset about it can go dry," said Staib.

At present, according to Staib, individual precincts cannot choose to opt for the sale of alcohol. Neither can cities of the fifth class or smaller. However, a decision is pending in the Kentucky Supreme Court that could allow precincts to vote themselves wet, which would make the size of the city irrelevant as it relates to that issue. At present, however, all cities in Grant County are either fifth class or smaller.

Should the issue pass, the first licenses would be issued a minimum of 60 days after the election, according to Staib.

"No license can be issued until 60 days after the results of the election are certified," she said, adding that the first licenses would probably be for beer, since they are the easiest ones to obtain. They allow package sales as well as consumption on the premises.

The other type of license, the quota license, is more difficult to obtain. It allows package sale of wine and distilled spirits. The number of those licenses issued is based on population; one license can be issued per 2,300 residents, which would mean a half-dozen licenses would be available in Grant County.

The number of beer licenses is not set by statute, but, said Staib: "The marketplace generally takes care of that without too much trouble."[10]

Temperance League Plans Anti-Alcohol Campaign

A large-scale battle of the ballot is shaping up as the recently activated Grant County Temperance League gears up in an attempt to defeat the wet-dry issue being presented to the voters on June 29. That election came about as the result of a petition drive spearheaded by Judy West, a Holbrook resident.

The league hopes to ensure the defeat of the issue with a publicity campaign which will probably begin in the next two to three weeks. The publicity committee of the league was slated to meet Tuesday night after press time to discuss strategy.

The overall campaign is under the guidance of a 17-member steering committee, composed of local residents. Reverend Murrell Crockett, of the Sherman Baptist Church, is the chairman. The treasurer is Bill Cull, of Dry Ridge. Although Cull was not contacted before press time, a reliable source indicated that the league already has approximately $2,000 in its war chest as the result of a May 5 mass meeting at the Williamstown Baptist Church, and donations sent in from local churches.

Also assisting in the effort will be Dr. Delbert L Butts, the executive director of the Temperance League of Kentucky, as well as another man who led a successful wet-dry fight in Murray, Kentucky. Both men will be depended upon for advice as to what means will be effective in persuading voters to vote against the issue.

In addition to advertising, the steering committee will be using word-of-mouth to present their case. A captain will be appointed to head the effort in each of the county's 13 precincts. Each captain will, in turn, enlist the aid of several volunteers to help cover the precincts, which should lead to a sizable volunteer force.[11]

Vote Saturday

It's probably safe to assume that you know there is an election this Saturday. The special election will be history early on Saturday evening, and after that Grant County will either remain dry, or a new era will begin with the sale of alcoholic beverages here for the first time in several decades.

We might mention in passing that, if you are a registered voter, you should rake a few minutes on Saturday to voice your opinion. Complaints after the fact are just so much hot air. However, we don't think there will be too much problem enticing the

[10] 25 April 1985. *Grant County News.* Art Ranney,Staff Writer.

[11] 16 May 1985. *Grant County News.* Art Ranney,Staff Writer.

voters of the county to turn out this weekend, if street corner discussions are any indication of the interest people have in this issue. It might not be too far-fetched to suppose that coffee sales have increased in local restaurants as folks linger over a second or third cup to talk about the upcoming vote and assess the prospects.

Also, as regular readers of THE NEWS know, there have been numerous articles on the subject, as well as extensive advertising. Both serve to keep the issue in front of the public, stimulate interest, and more than likely help to generate a large voter turnout.

We would like to voice one concern, however. It's possible that the issue and all the rhetoric it has sparked will cause ill will that lasts long beyond the June 29 election. This should not be allowed to happen.

Yes, there are fundamental philosophical differences between the two camps. The political issue is alcohol, but the "yea" and "nay" people are divided at a more basic level than politics. Up to this point, though, the diverse elements in our community have managed to exist peaceably enough, and it would be a shame to let a single issue polarize us to the point that people quit speaking to each other, or stop doing business together. We don't know that it will happen, but anything is possible.

What we're trying to do is to keep the peace before the conflict. We would like you to think about the issue, and make up your mind. Next, go to the polls and vote on Saturday. Finally, no matter which way it goes, continue to be kind to each other. Life is too short...[12]

---

[12] 27 June 1985. *Grant County News.* Author Unknown.

Look At What Happened In The Following Counties After Going Wet!

1982 and 1983 Uniform Crime Reports for Kentucky,
published by the Kentucky State Police

	Rowan Co.		Floyd Co		Pike Co		Logan Co.		(For Comparison:) Grant Co.	
	82	83	82	83	82	83	82	83	82	83
	Dry	Wet	Dry	Wet	Dry	Wet	Dry	Wet	Dry	Dry
DUI Arrests	251	420	287	619	146	485	113	357	279	263
Drunkenness Arrests	381	464	744	962	274	542	104	490	165	165
Legal Sales Began	Dec. 82		Fall 82		July 83		July 83		....	

VOTE DRY — VOTE NO JUNE 29

Pd. for by Grant County Temperance League. Bill Cull Treasurer. Rt. 1 Dry Ridge, Ky. 41035

N6271p

13

[13]Circa June 1985. *Grant County News.*

14

[14] Circa June 1985. *Grant County News.*

Local Option Issues And Answers

If Grant County were to vote in favor of the sale of Alcoholic Beverages on June 29, 1985, there are some important facts that we will have to face. We need to know before we vote how things would be if the sale of alcoholic beverages is legalized.

QUESTION: Would we have state-owned liquor stores?

ANSWER: No. There is no such thing as state-owned liquor stores in Kentucky. All are individually or privately owned.

QUESTION: How many package liquor stores could Grant County have?

ANSWER: The law permits one for every 2,300 people. Grant County could have 7.

QUESTION: How many beer outlets would Grant County have?

ANSWER: There is no limit on the quota of the number of beer licenses that can be issued. The number, according to KRS 242.060, would be at the discretion of the state A.B.C. board.

QUESTION: Does the county fiscal court have the authority to forbid beer joints.

ANSWER: The opinion of the Attorney General (OAG 64-905) says no. The state A.B.C. board has that authority and not the fiscal court.

QUESTION: Who would be the county A.B.C. administrator?

ANSWER: KRS 241.110 says that our County Judge/Executive would be the county administrator. Or he may appoint someone to that position to serve "at the pleasure" of the county judge.

QUESTION: How much will the county have to pay the A.B.C. administrator?

ANSWER: No one will do this job for free. Estimated $8,000 per year for someone part-time. With all the headaches involved it could require a full time employee.

QUESTION: Could we vote dry in a few months if we didn't want to stay wet?

ANSWER: No. The law forbids another such vote for a minimum of at least three years. (KRS 242.030).

QUESTION: What is the maxiumum amount that the county could collect for liquor and beer licenses?

ANSWER: A license to sell liquor has a maximum of $400 annual fee for license. The annual maximum fee that can be charged for each beer license is only $200 per year.

QUESTION: Can beer be consumed on the premises?

ANSWER: Yes, all that is necessary is for the proprietor to have a beer license.

A Quick Look At The First Year's Revenue (Gains or Losses) Using MAXIMUM FIGURES.
Note: No County Charges Maximum Fees.

POPULATION OF GRANT COUNTY 14,381

	MAXIMUM FEE	NUMBER ALLOWED	TOTAL
Retail Package Distilled Spirits and Wine License	$400. each	7	$2,800.
Malt Beverage (Beer) License (No Limit)	$200. each	40 est.	$8,000.
Special Restaurant (Wine License (No Limit) 50 or more seats	$300. each	10 est.	$3,000.
			TOTAL $13,800.

COST FOR ALCOHOL BEVERAGE CONTROL	
One Administrator Part Time	Approximately $8,000. per year
Just One Additional Law Enforcement Officer	Approximately $12,000 per year
Just One Additional Cruiser for that Officer	Approximately $10,000. per year
	TOTAL $30,000. per year

This does not include court costs, clean up costs, incarceration costs for those arrested or any cost except for the main items listed.

TAX DOLLARS ARE SENT TO STATE AND FEDERAL LEVELS. NO TAX DOLLARS WILL BE REALIZED IN THE COUNTY EXCEPT AS THEY ARE REDISTRIBUTED BACK TO YOUR COUNTY. BEING A WET OR DRY COUNTY MAKES NO DIFFERENCE, WE WILL GET OUR FAIR SHARE EITHER WAY.

TOTAL TAKEN IN BY LICENSE FEES ESTIMATED	+13,800.
TOTAL COST FOR CONTROL ESTIMATED	-30,000.
	TOTAL DEFICIT $ -16,200.

GUESS WHERE THE DEFICIT MONEY WILL COME FROM? FROM YOU (THE TAXPAYER) OF COURSE!!!

Paid for by Grant County Temperance League, Bill Cull, Treasurer, Rt. 1, Dry Ridge, Ky. 41035

N627lp [15]

[15]Circa June 1985. *Grant County News.*

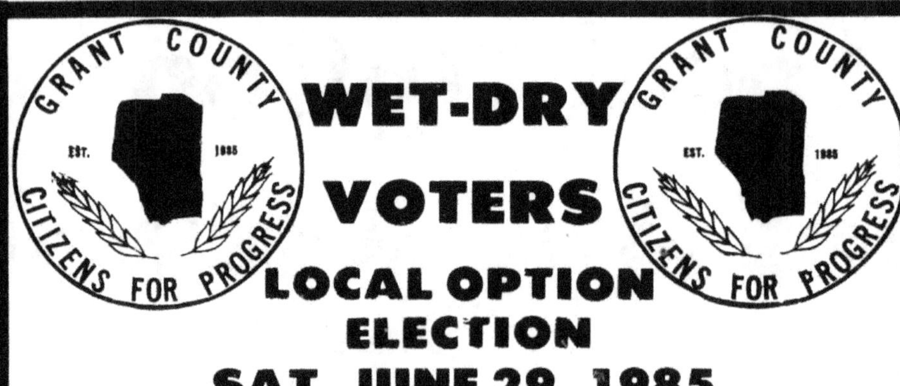

ELECTION

SAT. JUNE 29, 1985

We have all heard, read & seen the fear tactics of the dry people. Now let's calmly and realistically examine the facts. Grant Co. has been dry since 1944. Meanwhile most of the adjoining counties were wet. Records indicate that Grant Co. has a higher ratio of alcohol related accidents, felonies and misdemeanors than our neighbor counties.

Although Grant Co. is dry, people in the most remote areas have access to alcoholic beverages within 10 minutes.

Just what have we accomplished with our dry legislation?

1. We have forced Grant County people to spend thousands of dollars every year in other counties and cities. Food, beverages and other related items are purchased at a one stop shopping center and brought back to their homes and recreational facilities in our county.
2. We have denied local restaurant and motel owners the chance to compete with other eating places in neighboring counties.

The dry people have used the attitudes and platitudes comedy with pictorial references as follows:

"Fill it up" referring to filling a glass with whiskey.

"Fill it up" referring to a gas tank being filled with gas for a Drunk Driver.

"Fill it up" referring to a grave being filled with dirt.

Let's add one more line **"fill it up"** referring to the pockets of our business competitors in other counties.

No matter how complicated or complex the dry people try to make it, it should be obvious to any mature adult that this election is not to determine if drinking alcoholic beverages is morally right or wrong. If moral standards could be set by an election then all problems world wide could be solved.

The real question that this election will answer is **"DO WE WANT THE MONEY SPENT HERE TO HELP INCREASE OUR ECONOMY AND TAX DOLLARS OR DO WE WANT TO CONTINUE TO GIVE IT TO OTHER COUNTIES?**

The campaign to petition for a local option election was started early in 1985. It attracted tremendous pressure from local political powers. Whatever the final results show we have once again proved that a few people cannot dictate our freedom of choice at the election polls. This also assures us that Grant Co. is still part of the United States of America.

VOTE "YES" SATURDAY JUNE 29

[16]

[16] Circa June 1985. *Grant County News.*

WET VS. DRY ISSUE

FACTS:

1. No bars will be allowed.
   Because of the classification of Grant County (based on population), state law prohibits selling liquor by the drink. Only 6 package stores will be licensed.
2. More jobs and more money for Grant County. Motels and restaurants will locate here.
3. Residents choosing to drink will buy locally.
4. We are against driving and drinking.

We feel Grant Countians can decide this important issue for themselves without influence from outsiders with fancy ads and bumper stickers.

Let Your Voice Be Heard On Saturday, June 29

Please Vote (Wet or Dry) But Vote

YOUR Opinion Not Someone Else's.

We would like to thank the people that signed the petition and supported this issue thereby giving Grant Countians an opportunity to vote on this important issue.

Paid for by Grant County Citizens for Progress. Judy West, Treasurer, Rt. 1 Williamstown, Ky. 41097

17

[17]Circa June 1985. *Grant County News.*

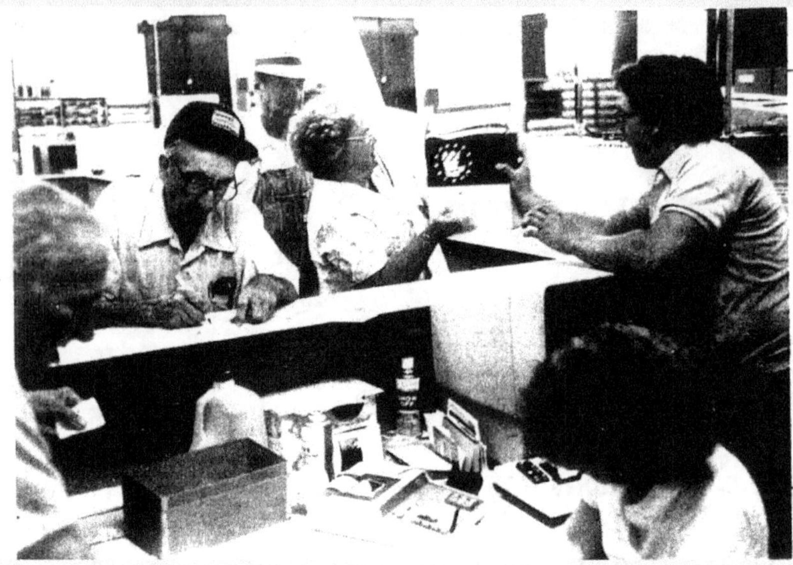

The electoral process at work: Election official Mary Ellen Baker signs in during a lull in the action at Precinct II [Mt. Zion] so she can take her turn at voting. Joe Rose, the precinct's sheriff, is in the background. At left, Ralph Nicholson and Mary Johnson turn in their materials from Precincts 4 and 10, respectively. At right, wet advocate Judy West holds the return sheets behind her as she sees the handwriting on the wall. [Staff photo by Ranney]

18

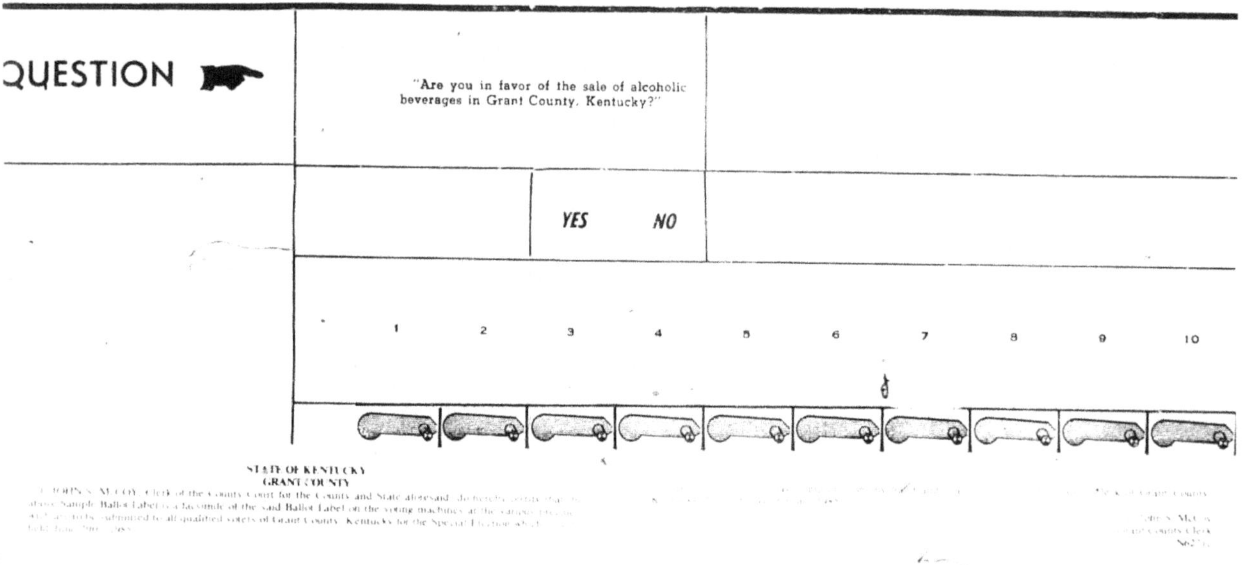

7410 U.S. 42 - Florence, Ky.

Special Election, June 29, 1985, Grant Co., Ky.

QUESTION

"Are you in favor of the sale of alcoholic beverages in Grant County, Kentucky?"

YES NO

1 2 3 4 5 6 7 8 9 10

STATE OF KENTUCKY
GRANT COUNTY

19

County Gets 3 To 1 Voter Mandate: Dry

It was a relatively quiet campaign, and the results of last Saturday's local option election proved that the wet, dry issue here was no more than a rumble in rumps. Anti-alcohol forces brought out the sate to defeat the issue by a margin of nearly three to one.

Out of an official total of 4,944 votes cast. 72 percent, or 3,559 were negative At the time of the election, there were 7,750 registered voters in the county. The official tally of total votes cast represents 63.8 percent

[18]Circa June 1985. *Grant County News.*
[19]Circa June 1985. *Grant County News.*

of those voters. a respectable turnout comparable to May's primary election. In that election, 59.2 percent of the registered voters went to the polls.

The strongest turnout of the individual precincts was registered in Precinct 6, Jonesville. Out of 195 registered voters there, 73.8 percent went to the polls, defeating the issue by a greater than 3-1 margin, 110 votes to 33. The lightest turnout. percentage-wise, was recorded in Precinct 10, in Crittenden, the area of the county with the easiest access to alcohol. Only 53.9 percent of the precinct's 1,109 voters went to the polls, but those who did vote were emphatically in favor of keeping the county dry. 383-165, a better than two-to-one ratio.

The outcome of the election was apparently a foregone conclusion to most people. The basement of the courthouse wasn't even crowded, a contrast to the May primary when the area was jammed. Judy West, the Holbrook resident who headed up the petition drive to get the issue on the ballot, was the only obvious supporter of the issue in the crowd of 20 or 30 who staved to hear the total read. West was wearing a black and white jersey emblazoned with "end the drought" on the front and "vote wet" on the back.

The jersey was obviously not going to be enough as the precinct reports started arriving, but West was hoping to carry at least one precinct. Even that was not going to happen, however, and the dry forces dutifully applauded the final totals for the television crew, even though the ending was anticlimactic.

According to state law, the issue cannot appear on a ballot again for three years. A possible exception to that may occur in the near future, depending on the outcome of a case currently under submission to the state Supreme Court. The case which was instigated by Magoffin County and joined later by others, asks the court to give individual precincts the right to permit alcohol sales.

According to Catherine Stalls. general counsel for the cabinet of Alcoholic Beverage Control, oral arguments in the case were presented on March 14. She said it was not uncommon to wait this long for a decision, adding that she had waited as long as a year for a decision to be handed down.

Recapitulation sheets for Saturday's election are located on page 4 of this issue of THE NEWS.[20]

Judge Overturns DUI Verdict

A guilty verdict against a Paris man who was charged with driving under the influence after a car accident in Grant County last year, has been overturned by District Court Judge Stan Billingsley.

The case received wide spread publicity in August because officials at University Hospital in Cincinnati refused to release the blood alcohol records of John Wood, who was apparently driving under the influence at the time of the accident in the county. The records were needed to convict Wood of DUI and Billingsley wrote to the hospital administrator and said he would cite the hospital for contempt of court if the records were not sent.

The hospital finally complied with the request and Wood was recently found guilty of DUI by a Grant County jury and sentenced to 180 days in the Grant County Jail. Last week, however, Billingsley directed a verdict of acquittal in favor of Wood and dismissed the case.

According to the order written by Billingsley, "The court finds that viewing all the evidence presented, that reasonable minds could not find guilt beyond a reasonable doubt. The evidence presented by the Commonwealth is as consistent with innocence as with guilt."

Confusion over the case stemmed from the testimony of Henry Stanfield. At the scene of the accident, Stanfield told the arresting officer that Wood was driving the vehicle, but in court, Stanfield changed his testimony and said he was driving the car.

Jim Purcell, county attorney, said he planned to appeal the ruling, but even if the appeal is won, Wood can not be punished. "We are not willing to concede that Wood was not the driver," Purcell said. "But the appeal is for certificate of law to determine whether the ruling was correct. It can have no effect on the defendant."

[20] 4 July 1985. *Grant County News.* Art Ranney,Staff Writer.

[21] 5 November 1987. *Grant County News.* Author Unknown.

Purcell said a decision on whether to try Stanfield had not been made.[21]

Is your News subscription paid?

1990s

Drunk Drivers Star In Police Video

Beware drunk drivers, speeders and other law breakers. You could find yourself in the starring role of a Kentucky State Police video.

KSP Post 6 in Dry Ridge, as well as the other state police posts in Kentucky, now have two video cameras on patrol as part of a criminal patrol unit.

The cameras have been installed for about three months and according to Trooper Coy Cox, he has made at least 15 driving under the influence arrests during that time.

The video camera automatically comes on when a trooper's blue lights are activated. It can also be activated manually and it records images and audio.

"When you have a camera with film it's not just your testimony against theirs because you have the audio," Cox said.

The video recording can be used in court and by law police officers are not required to tell the person they stopped that they are being taped.

"I feel like this is the most valuable piece of equipment given to a law enforcement officer," said Cox, a four-year veteran of the KSP.

Cox and his partner, Hobert Strange are the only officers at post 6 who have the cameras. Both have been given special training in how to use the equipment and they have been trained as criminal patrol officers to go beyond a citation. A special police dog is being trained to assist Cox and Strange.

On routine patrol once the blue lights in the cruiser are activated the video camera begins rolling. The date and time flashes in the corner which is also helpful if an arrest is made.

The recorder which is on the officer is also activated and will remain on until the blue lights are turned out or the machine is shut off. Each tape holds six hours of taping.

According to Cox, so far the video camera has been the most helpful in DUI cases.

"The person you stop may say that they have only had a few drinks and then not be able to pass any of the sobriety tests given by the officer and then in court they will be neatly dressed and present a different side to the judge, so to back you up you have the tape," he said.

Florida was the first state to begin using video cameras for police.

According to Cox, a Florida Mother's Against Drunk Driving (MADD) group raised funds and purchased cameras for all officers.

"We would love to see cameras in every vehicle and we are hoping to get a federal grant over the next few years to make it possible," Cox said.

The only negative side, to the cameras, according to Cox, would be if the camera malfunctioned and didn't run a tape.

"I feel the positives far and above outweigh any negatives because these machines could also save police officer's lives in the instance where an officer pulls a car over and gets shot," Cox said.

"A picture and license plate of the car and possibly the suspects will be on tape," he added.

According to Cox, Florida and Kentucky's use of the video tape is causing other states to take notice. A police department from Washington is scheduled to come look at Kentucky's system.[1]

Alcohol Other Drug Council Offers Parent Training

A major training program aimed at parents of teenagers has been intro-

[1] 2 August 1990. *Grant County News.* Jamie Baker-Nantz.Editor.

duced to the Northern Kentucky area and will be taught in Grant County.

"Parent to Parent" will be taught for four consecutive weeks at the Williamstown United Methodist Church.

The program combines video presentations, student workbooks, audio tapes and class exercises with a workshop facilitator to help teach parents how to help their teenagers deal with facing drug and alcohol problems.

"Parent to Parent" is a cooperative venture among the Grant County Alcohol and Other Drugs (AOD) Council, Grant County Schools, the Pendleton County AOD Council, Pendleton County Schools and the AOD Council of Northern Kentucky.

The program was developed by PRIDE (Parents' Resource Institute for Drug Education Inc.) in Atlanta and is targeted specifically to help parents see that their children avoid drug and alcohol problems. "Parent to Parent is a very positive program that helps parents to get in touch with the feelings of their children," said Rev. Frank Spillman, minister at the Williamstown United Methodist Church.

"Parents bring their resources together to work through any problems," he added.

The program will begin at 7 p.m. on Feb. 28. Each session will last from 7 p.m. to 10 p.m.

Refreshments and a nursery will be provided.

Parent to Parent can be presented in businesses, schools, churches or even at home.

For additional information contact Sherry Mason at XXX-XXXX or Gail Wilson at XXX-XXXX.[2]

AOD Council Promotes Drug Abuse Awareness

Editor's Note: This is the first of a month-long series during April on alcohol awareness. April is Alcohol Awareness Month.

Although Grant County's Alcohol and Other Drugs (AOD) Council is fairly new to the area, the members have high hopes of educating the community about drug and alcohol abuse.

"Our purpose is to make people more aware of alcohol and other drugs and the effect it has on their lives," said Dorothy Powers, chairman of the local AOD.

Even though Grant County's AOD is only a year old, the group has been active in promoting drug abuse awareness.

Grant County's AOD Council is composed of Powers, Terry Evans of the Kentucky State Police, District Judge Stephen Bates, Jim Brown, Gene Wynn, Sharon Faulkner, Lynn Faulkner, Lanette Whalen, Frank Spillman, Carol Woodyard, Jill Collins and John Eckler.

The AOD sponsored a Red Ribbon campaign last fall.

The council also sponsored a "Parent to Parent", training program that combines video and audio tapes and class exercises with a workshop facilitator.

This program helps to teach parents how to help their teenagers deal with facing drug and alcohol problems in February at the Williamstown United Methodist Church.

According to Rev. Frank Spillman, council member, another "Parent to Parent" group began Tuesday evening at Crittenden-Mt. Zion Elementary.

"This program basically helps parents come together to learn to raise their kids drug free," Spillman said.

According to Powers, 12 to 15 parents attended the first session at the Williamstown Methodist Church.

"A lot of people think they have to have a drug problem in their family before they can participate but they don't because the tapes teach how to be a better parent," she said.

"Parent to Parent" consists of four consecutive sessions on Tuesdays. The program lasts from 7 p.m. to 9:30 p.m.

"I think it is a very good program," Spillman said. "It is positive parenting that uses common sense parenting skills."

"Parent to Parent" was developed by PRIDE (Parents' Resource Institute for Drug Education Inc.) in Atlanta and is targeted specifically to help parents see that their children avoid drug and alcohol problems.

"Parent to Parent" can be presented in businesses, schools, churches or even in homes. Spillman and Powers hope that others will be-

[2] 7 February 1991. *Grant County News.* Jamie Baker-Nantz,Editor.

come interested and request a "Parent to Parent" class.

For more information on "Parent to Parent" contact Spillman at XXX-XXXX; Sherry Mason at XXX-XXXX or Gail Wilson at XXX-XXXX.

Throughout April, Grant County's AOD Council has planned several community activities.

On April 25, Doug Flynn, a former member of the Cincinnati Reds, will be traveling to all the schools in the county and discussing drug abuse with students.[3]

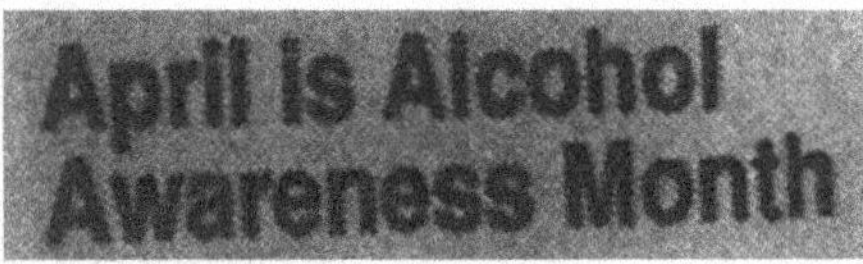

4

Alcohol Plays Role In 4 Of 5 Fatalities

Editor's Note: This is tile second of a month-long series during April oft-alcohol awareness. April is Alcohol Awareness Month.

Four of five deaths that occurred in Grant County during 1989 were alcohol related.

Figures for 1990 are not yet available.

Also in 1989, Grant County had 829 accidents that were investigated by state and local police agencies. Of those 829, 42 had alcohol as a contributing factor.

During 1989, teenage drivers in Kentucky were involved in 37,526 accidents. One hundred and forty eight of those accidents were fatalities and 1,199 were alcohol related.

Of those 42 accidents in 1989 that occurred in Grant County, 22 people were injured and four were killed.

By examining Grant County's accident figures some may assume that the county is "wet."

However, Grant County has been "dry" (a place that prohibits the sale of alcohol) for many years.

According, to John "Corn" McCoy, county clerk, the last time the wet/dry issue was on the ballot before Grant County voters was June 29, 1985.

The measure was defeated by a margin of three to one. There were 1,362 votes in favor of Grant County being a "wet" county and 3,559 votes against.

"As far as the number of DUI (driving under the influence) and alcohol intoxication arrests go, you would think the county was wet," said Lt. Terry Evans of the Kentucky State Police Post 6 in Dry Ridge.

"Everything around the county is wet and the county is close to a metropolitan area and a lot of people work there which leads to people drinking elsewhere and traveling back to Grant County," Evans said.

Evans said that the number of DUI and AI (alcohol intoxication) arrests in Grant County could be attributed to 1-75 but in order to determine how the location of an interstate affects alcohol related arrests the would require further study.

According to John Lile, commander of Post 6, the number of drunk driving fatal accidents is declining, but the percentage remains too high.

According to Lile, in an effort to combat the number of drunk drivers, the KSP will be using the BAT Mobile (a mobile breathalyzer van) more frequently.

The Dry Ridge Police Department and the Crittenden Police Department also have portable video cameras that they use to tape suspected drink drivers.

Penalties for first-time driving under the influence charges and repeated offenses have continued to stiffen during the years.

For driving under the influence penalties, please see the accompanying chart.[5]

DRIVING UNDER THE INFLUENCE PENALTIES

1st Offense: \$200 to \$500 fine or 48 hrs. to 30 days jail

2nd Offense: \$350 to \$500 fine and 7 days to 180 days jail and 10 days to 180 days community labor

3rd Offense: \$500 to \$1,000 fine and 30 days to 365 days jail and 10 days to 365 days community labor

Loss of Driving Privileges as follows: **Minimums**
1st Offense - one month
2nd Offense - 12 months
3rd Offense - 24 months

Any offense if driver is under 18 - suspended until age 18. and Mandatory Substance Abuse Treatment or Education
1st Offense - 90 days
2nd Offense - 12 months
3rd Offense - 12 months

and All Cases: Service Fee is \$150 plus court costs of \$67.50 and Insurance Premiums will double in amount until five years from date of conviction

As of 7-1-91 many of these penalties will increase, none will decrease.

6

[3]4 April 1991. *Grant County News.* Jamie Baker-Nantz,Editor.

[4]Circa April 1991. *Grant County News.*

[5]11 April 1991. *Grant County News.* Jamie Baker-Nantz, Editor.

[6]Circa April 1991. *Grant County News.*

Is your News subscription paid?

Alcohol Factor For Most Who Are Jailed

Editor's Note: This is the third of a month-long series during April on alcohol awareness. April is Alcohol Awareness Month.

Ninety percent of the prisoners who are housed in the Grant County Jail are there on alcohol related offenses, says Jailer Gary "Louie" Jump.

"Most everyone that comes in is alcohol or drug related somehow," said Jump.

"They might have been brought in for other charges but in many cases they commit a crime such as burglary or theft to get money to help buy drugs or alcohol," he added.

Jim Purcell, county attorney, agrees with Jump that many of the cases that he prosecutes are alcohol related.

"I don't see a lot of cases where the offender is under 18 and you don't really see many where the person is under 21," Purcell said.

"The majority of cases involve people between their mid '20s and mid '40s," he added.

Purcell said that he believed that Interstate-75 was a definite factor in the number of cases of alcohol-related offenses.

"There is no question that I-75 is a factor," he said.

Both Purcell and Jump say that whenever possible local judges sentence many who are unable to pay fines for alcohol-related offenses to do public service work in the community.

"I try to use these people whenever we can," Jump said. "I have used them to mow yards and to paint."

According to statistics released by the National Council on Alcoholism, 55 percent of all arrests are alcohol related.

Statistics also show that 80 percent of fire deaths, 65 percent of drownings, 22 percent of home accidents, 77 percent of all falls, 36 percent of pedestrian accidents and 25 to 33 percent of all suicides and homicides are committed by alcoholics.

In addition, statistics by the AOC also indicate that 30 percent of divorce and juvenile delinquency cases are associated with alcohol in a family member and as many as 90 percent of reported child abuse cases implicate alcohol.[7]

Parents' Influence Children To Use Alcohol, Counselor Says

Editor's Note: This is the last of a series during April on alcohol awareness. April is Alcohol Awareness Month.

The drug of choice for many area youth is alcohol and according to Bill Bettner, coordinator for Comprehensive Care Centers' Rural Services for Mental Health and Substance Abuse, parents' attitude is the single most important factor influencing teenagers to use drugs and alcohol.

"How parents view drugs and alcohol has a lot to do with how they use it. Until parents teach them, by example, the value of living clean and sober, then we are just blowing in the wind," he said.

Bettner doesn't rule out biological, psychological and social factors as also having a part in alcohol and drug use.

Comprehensive Care Center provides treatment for Grant, Owen, Carroll and Gallatin counties for teenagers with chemical dependencies.

Jennifer Skirvin of Williamstown, also works with Bettner as a chemical dependency counselor.

She does intervention work that focuses on "at-risk" youth.

Williamstown High School has started a program focusing on early intervention and Grant County High School is expected to begin one in the fall.

Student representatives and guidance counselors from Grant County and Williamstown attended a team leadership conference in Boone County last weekend that taught how to implement programs in their individual schools.

[7] 18 April 1991. *Grant County News.* Jamie Baker-Nantz,Editor.

According to Bettner, the conference focused on self esteem, peer pressure and communication.

"Almost any kid could be at risk," Bettner said.

"People may say its not happening in their county, but it is," he added.

According to Bettner, intervention programs are usually geared to the middle school level because that is where experimentation with alcohol and drugs begins for most kids.

According to Joyce Doyle, principal at Grant County Middle School, there isn't a serious problem with alcohol.

"I'm sure it exists to some extent, but I haven't noticed a serious problem that drink while at school," she said.

The National Institute on Drug Abuse reported the following:

10 percent of sixth graders report drinking

33 percent of eighth graders report drinking

56 percent of ninth graders report drinking

92 percent of twelfth graders report drinking

"I find that in county's where the people, the schools and the judges recognize that there is a problem, then that admission goes a long way towards helping the problem," Bettner said.

Bettner suggests that parents need to talk to their children about alcohol and drugs before it is too late.[8]

Observable Behaviors Which *May* Indicate Drug Abuse

1. Withdrawing from extra-curricular activities, including sports.
2. Grades dropping or consistent under-achievement.
3. Transferring/dropping classes.
4. Lack of or a decline of interest or motivation.
5. Frequent or patterned absences (Mondays, Fridays, afternoons).
6. Class-cutting.
7. Open defiance of school or parental authority.
8. Verbal abuse of peers, instructors, friends or siblings.
9. Disorientation or confusion.
10. Depression.
11. Crying with no apparent reason.
12. Nervousness or paranoia (suspiciousness).
13. Sleeping in class.
14. Changes in appearance or hygiene.
15. Unusual weight changes.
16. Peer group changes.
17. Personality changes (not mood swings but changes in basic attitudes, outlook, belief systems and relationship values).
18. An odor of alcohol or marijuana.
19. Bloodshot or glassy eyes.
20. Not "tracking" - an inability to follow a train of thought in a conversation.
21. In possession of drug paraphernalia (rolling papers, pipes, bottles, marijuana seeds in pockets or drawers.
22. An unexplained increase or disappearance of material possessions.
23. Running away.
24. Withdrawing from family activities.
25. An increase in dishonesty - lying or stealing.

9

Alcohol, Drug Use On Rise Among Teens

SADD Releases Survey Results

The Grant County High School Chapter of Students Against Drunk Driving has released the results of a survey the chapter conducted in April 1992.

The subject of the survey was students at Grant County Middle School and the object was to see how prevalent alcohol and drug use was among the students.

This survey was used in comparison to the same survey given two years ago.

The students were asked if they drink or have drunk alcoholic beverages. The reply was 53 percent yes, compared to 47 percent two years ago.

Of the students who replied yes to drinking, 10 percent said that they drink weekly, compared to 3 percent two years ago. Those students were also asked why they drink. Thirty-five percent replied "because tt's fun," compared to 28 percent two years ago.

When asked how many of their friends drink, the reply of "most" went up eight percent.

Eighty-one percent of the students said that they had at one time been with someone who was drinking or had been drinking. this percentage is up 5 percent.

Thirty-seven percent of the students that said they drink, said that their parents know that they drink. This is up by seven percent.

The students were also asked if their parents drink. Forty-six percent said yes (a two percent increase). Fourteen percent of those students said that their parents drink most of the time. This is a five percent decrease.

The students replied to what their parents drink this way: beer - 83 percent (13 percent decrease), wine - 30 percent (eight percent increase), hard liquor - 10 percent (four percent increase), all of the above - 21 percent (six percent increase).

However, the students replied to what they drink this way: beer - 47 percent (three percent increase), wine - 17 percent (two percent increase), hard liquor - 15 percent (six percent

[8] 25 April 1991. *Grant County News.* Jamie Baker-Nantz, Editor.

[9] Circa April 1991. *Grant County News.*

increase), and all of the above - 27 percent (12 percent increase).

The students were questioned on whether or not they use or have used drugs. Forty-one percent of the students said yes. This percentage increased over two years by 16 percent.

The students replied they have experimented with the following drugs: prescription drugs - 47 percent (same percentage), over the counter - 35 percent (four percent increase), marijuana - 27 percent (five percent increase), other - 19 percent (same percentage), all of the above - 10 percent (five percent increase).

Maria Osbourne, president of Grant County's SADD chapter, said the most surprising aspect of the survey was the increases over the previous survey.

"The fact that everything increased since the last survey was the most surprising," she said.

She said the same survey is given every two years because there is a new group of students at the school every two years.

"We have taken into consideration that there is some margin of error to the survey," she said.

She said the point of releasing the results of the survey is to let the community and students know the extent of substance abuse.

"It seems like it is a problem more for the middle school," she said. "They understand what these things can do to your body, but they have never experienced it themselves."

The fact that some of these students may be bragging was taken into consideration.

"But, then again, they could be bragging about the extent of their substance use," she said.

Roger Humphrey, Dry Ridge police chief, said he has seen a trend in alcohol-related offenses, such as possession. However, there has not been an increase in driving under the influence among teens.

He pointed out that finding teens with alcohol is not an everyday occurrence, but it is something that is happening in the community.

"I have been told that sometimes these kids bring alcohol from home, or they have somebody older buy it for them," he said.

He added that, fortunately, the trend of using inhalants to achieve a high has not surfaced in Grant County.

"Let's hope it doesn't because that is dangerous," he said. "That stuff can be fatal on the first time."[10]

Alcohol, Drug Abuse Is Problem Of Society, School Officials Say

---

Officials at Grant County Middle School said they feel the problems of drug and alcohol use among teens is a problem of society and their school isn't isolated from it.

Ron Livingood, principal at Grant County Middle School, questioned the validity of a survey conducted by the Grant County High School chapter of Students Against Drunk Driving. The results of that survey were printed in last week's Grant County News.

"I questioned the validity of the survey because of it's casualness," he said. "I don't know the actual number of students that participated in the survey. I can only look at the pragmatic evidence."

According to Livingood, of the 556 students at the middle school, there have been three specific cases involving three students related to drug and alcohol abuse.

"Drug and alcohol abuse is definitely a problem of society and the schools aren't isolated from society," he said. "We try to deal with the individual student's needs.

If see an individual that is exhibiting behavior that is a problem and other than the normal adolescent behavior, we try to get that student into counseling."

He said the students with drug and alcohol problems are referred to treatment facilities, such as St. Elizabeth's chemical dependency unit.

Larry Davis, Grant County high school principal, said although locking some of the bathroom doors at the high school is one way to avoid drug sales and use in the school, it is not the only reason.

Davis said the doors to some bathrooms are locked to also reduce vandalism and eliminate smoking in the bathroom.

At the middle school, Livingood said that the bathrooms at the upper end of the middle/elementary school complex are kept unlocked because they cannot be supervised.

---

[10] 18 March 1993. *Grant County News.* Jon Paul McKinney,Staff Writer.

However, the one at the lower end of the hallway, nearer to the elementary school, is locked because it is used for both middle school and elementary students.

To combat the problems of drug and alcohol abuse, Livingood said the schools have been trying a preventative maintenance plan.

"There is a need to be more proactive against these issues and not deal with them as they arise," he said.

Although there is no on-going anti-drug program, there are programs at the middle school to promote positive attitudes and strong self-esteem.

"We also try to instill in the students strong decision-making skills," he said. "We want the students to have a good self-concept."

He said what turns some students on to substances is the same as it was 15 years ago - peer pressure.

However, Livingood attributes substance abuse nowadays to two new factors - the breakdown of the family and the proliferation of the media.

He pointed out that teenagers are exposed to more drug and alcohol glorified subjects on stations such as MTV.

"For instance, characters on television programs are now allowed to say things that if a student repeats at school, he or she will get in trouble for," he said.

As far as the breakdown of the family, he said no one is to blame.

"Probably both parents are working or the student is from a single parent family," he said. "Mom or Dad has custody and has to work two jobs just to get by."

According to a teacher at the middle school, there may be some experimentation by some students at the school.

Patti Hund, an art teacher at the school for six years said that she feels there may be some students that have experimented with drugs or alcohol at the middle school.

"There has been no research done on this - I base it strictly on language, an interest in cigarettes and alcohol," she said. "You also have to decide how much is talk and how much is real. But, I believe if you cut everything a student said in half, there may be an element of truth there."

Another teacher at the high school, who did not wish to be identified, said that the self-esteem programs at the school may work, but believes the reason some teenagers experiment is out of boredom.

"The problem hasn't been addressed because some do not believe the problem exists," the teacher said. "Some people don't believe there is such a thing as drinking in moderation."

The teacher also said they have heard of drug deals happening in the school.

"Some kids have told me they have seen it, but I never have," the teacher said. "In my class, I have never had a student under the influence of drugs. I do believe there is a group of students in the school that have access to drugs. It could be all hearsay."

For two middle school students, the decision to be drug and alcohol free is a subject that has already been decided.

"I have never tried it and I won't," said Danny Mann, 14, an eighth grader at the school.

For another student, the decision to stay clean and sober is one made from experience.

Krissy Ford, 14, also an eighth grader at the school said she has chosen to be alcohol and drug free because of alcohol abuse in her family.

"I also went through D.A.R.E. (Drug Abuse Resistance Education program taught in the schools by the Grant County Sheriff's Department and Deputy Cynthia Covington) and thought that helped," she said.

She added she has received guidance from her mother and contacts at church.

Mann said he also went through the D.A.R.E. program, but he had decided long before that through talks with his parents.

"They have always talked to us and told us about drinking," he said. "I know what I can and cannot do."

Both students don't idolize any sports figures or teachers. Mann credited his parents and Ford singled out her mother as their main role models.[11]

'Dry' County Hosts Happy Hour At GCHS

---

[11] 25 March 1993. *Grant County News.* Jon Paul McKinney,Staff Writer.

As it was poured into the glass, the golden-brown liquid grew a white foamy head that led the way to the top of the glass.

The can of beer would be one of many that would be consumed throughout the course of the afternoon.

But the circumstances for the partaking wasn't a party or a fishing trip.

The beer and liquor were being downed for a class sponsored by the Department of Criminal Justice Training and hosted by the Crittenden and Dry Ridge Police Departments at Grant County High School.

The alcohol was being drunk by volunteers who allowed themselves to be used as guinea pigs for the 19 police officers, three of whom were from the Grant County area, to test the officer's abilities in determining the levels of intoxication in people.

Taking classes were Chief Gary Humphrey of the Crittenden Police Department, Deputy Troy Hagedorn of the Grant County Sheriff's office, and Officer Chris Hankins of the Williamstown Police Department.

According to Humphrey, the classes were part of a certification process an officer must complete each year. A police department must have one officer trained in this field in order to receive grants from the state.

The DUI Standardized Field Sobriety Test is aimed to train officers in how to determine if a person is legally drunk.

"It gives us some idea about how alcohol affects the body," Humphrey said. "We (the officers) had no idea which ones would have been arrested."

The hosting police agencies solicit volunteers who are willing to drink during the course of the afternoon.

Those volunteering are each given different amounts during a two-hour time span.

One of those who volunteered, Jenna Pelfrey, said she learned as much as the officers did that afternoon.

"It was very interesting to learn how your coordination works after you have been drinking," Pelfrey said. "There is a world of people who go fishing and sit around and drink then get in the car and drive and everybody thinks they are o.k."

She said she also realized a few points about alcohol when it came time to go home.

"They don't let you leave the building until you have blown .00 on the breathalizer," she said. "And, when I felt perfectly fine, I was still blowing .06."

The law classifies being legally drunk as having a blood/alcohol level at .10.

Officials from the Department of Criminal Justice Training do not let the subjects leave until all the alcohol has left their system. For Pelfrey, she was free to leave at 7:30 p.m. The volunteers began drinking at noon.

To illustrate how alcohol affects people individually, the officers were divided into groups and they each took turns testing the subjects.

"Only the first group would have arrested me," she said.

However, another subject, Kay Covey, would have been arrested by all five groups of officers despite only registering .09 during a breathalizer test.

The experience was eye-opening for Covey.

"I learned I can't drink," she said. "I'm really glad I took part in this - I learned a whole lot."

She said she also didn't realize that it would take nearly five hours for the alcohol to work it's way out of her system.

"Some people would say 'yeah, I'm ok to drive,' and they will still be legally impaired," Humphrey said.

Another subject said the experience made her aware of how much training officers must take.

"That's their job and they are trained to know what to look for," said Angela Ghent, who drank six ounces of vodka and grapefruit juice.

She said, although she only registered .06 on the breathalizer test, four of the five groups would have arrested her.

"But they gave me that test when I was sober and I still couldn't do it," she said.

The tests involved a "walk and turn," a "one-leg stand" and a horizontal gaze test, in which the subject is to focus on an object held by the police officer as they move it side to side.

The test is to detect involuntary jerking by the eye, which is heightened by alcohol.

Humphrey said the involvement of the volunteers is imperative for the success of a course like this.[12]

[12] 16 June 1994. *Grant County News.* Jon Paul McKinney,Staff Writer.

ALCOHOL, DRUG SURVEY YIELDS SOBERING RESULTS

"It's 10 o'clock, do you know where your kids are?" This public service ad from the 1970's might still apply today. Or better yet, do you know what your kids are doing?

The results of a survey of Grant County and Williamstown students by the Alcohol and Other Drugs Council and the University of Cincinnati Department of Sociology might surprise some parents.

The good news is that 61 percent of the students in grades 9-12 responded that they had not used alcohol during the 30 days prior to the survey. The bad news is that 39 percent, or 245 children in this community, had used alcohol within 30 days and 456 students indicated it was easy to get alcohol.

And that's not all, 271 students said it was "ok" to get drunk as long as they were not driving.

One and one-half years ago. Lanette Whalen, rural coordinator for the AOD of Northern Kentucky, Inc. asked for support of the survey from Jerry Reid, Lynn Ritchey and P. Neal Ritchey, professors in the Department of Sociology at the University of Cincinnati.

A total of 630 students were surveyed during the spring of 1993 536 were from Grant County High School and 94 students were from Williamstown Independent High School. They were 15 to 18 years old; 50 percent were female; 50 percent male; 75 percent had a B or C grade average; 73 percent lived with two parents (biological or step-parent); and 75 percent listed their religious preference as Protestant.

The results of the survey, which included questions about alcohol, tobacco and other drug use, were discussed at a meeting hosted by the local AOD Council on June 13.

Committee member Clay Parks said that the council sent a notice of the meeting to school counselors. principals, mayors and law enforcement people. There were 11 people in attendance.

In Kentucky it is illegal for anyone under the age of 21 to drink. purchase alcohol, or be in possession of alcohol. And no one under the age of 16 may purchase cigarettes or any other form of tobacco. So where are these young people getting these illegal substances? Many at the meeting felt they were either getting it from their parents' home or they had older friends buy it for them.

"Some parents think it's okay to offer it (alcohol) to their children, but the parents are disobeying the law the same as the bar that sells it to underage boys and girls. Parents are violating this law," said District Judge Stephen Bates.

Some other statistics from the survey were:

over one-third, or 232 students, reported riding in a car in the past year with someone who had been drinking

11 percent reported driving after three or more drinks at least one time during the past year

292 students indicated that it is easy to get marijuana

39 percent reported that it was their perception that most adults get drunk two or more times per month (according to national figures, this is not actually the case)

85 percent believe it is easy to develop a serious alcohol problem

Males are at higher risk to use alcohol and other drugs (44 percent) than females (34 percent).

The survey also indicated a strong relationship between the use of tobacco and the use of alcohol and other drugs. Of those students (89 percent) who reported using some form of tobacco, 94 percent of them had also used alcohol or marijuana in the past 30 days. Over one-half (69 percent) of those with D or F grades reported using tobacco in the past 30 days.

There was a lively discussion at the meeting about the causes of children using alcohol and other drugs as well as ways for adults to get involved.

"We can certainly look at the tremendous impact that the peer group does have that's a big one and it's hard for adults to intervene and have a counter impact," Reid said.

"There is tremendous evidence that they are angry and I'm not sure of the reasons.... Some of it may come from a sense that there is no place for them in today's society, that they are not going to be successful, that society is too confusing and overwhelming. In some cases, they are simply not getting enough attention; not respected as a group."

"Parents don't often communicate with their kids as adults there is this big gulf between us and them;

we don't talk about things. And, of course, we don't model very well; we drink an awful lot, express attitudes that we want them to have, but they are going to do what we do," he said.

Joyce Doyle, Director of Pupil Personnel for Grant County Schools, brought up the fact that there were very few childen who were not involved in the church. Many of those present agreed.

"I wish we had a survey of the parents' perception of their own youngsters. Children are going to church on Sunday morning after drinking on Saturday night aren't the parents naive' about what is going on?" questioned Parks.

"We need to tell our children to think about 'Who are you influencing? You are very important as a human being what is your life doing for other people'" Doyle said. "It is evident our young people need us and, Lord knows, we need them and we need in the right frame of mind."

Doyle said their school is starting a program next year, after a training this summer, that will include 10 juniors and seniors who are going out to the 8th grade and doing a program called "Say 'Wait' to Sex."

"They will tell these 8th graders, 'I do not have sex,' and it's going to take 10 children who are willing to stand up and say that. At the same time, I think we can work it into the program, '...nor do I do drugs or alcohol,'" Doyle said.

Doyle said their yearly October revival of "Just Say 'No' to Drugs and Alcohol" has been very successful, with over 3,000 people attending. After the revival, many say they will never drink or use drugs, but she said that it's not enough to do something once a year. She suggested having monthly events, like holding anti-drug and alcohol dances or carnivals.

Doug Markesbery, Pastor of United Methodist Church, questioned if the students involved in the survey were questioned about having nothing to do in this community. Reid said that 16 percent of the students felt there was almost nothing to do on weekends except to get drunk or high.

Within the 259 square miles of the county, with a population of approximately 18,000, there is not much for teens, or adults, to do at night or on weekends in Grant County no movie theatre, no bowling lane, no skating rink. Many young people cruise the fast-food restaurants in Dry Ridge or head north to find entertainment.[13]

DUI Arrest Refuses To Give Up

Crashes Deputy's Cruiser

An initial traffic stop in Crittenden led to a chase involving various county police agencies that ended with a wrecked Grant County Sheriffss cruiser and a slightly wounded officer on the afternoon of Feb. 16.

Crittenden Police Chief Gary Humphrey stopped Flem Patterson Jr. of Williamstown driving a 1986 Plymouth north on U.S. 25 near Case Lane in Crittenden around 2:45 p.m.

Humphrey said he was going to originally cite Patterson for speeding and having a loud exhaust. He then found out Patterson's license was suspended because of an earlier driving under the influence charge.

Patterson, 34, was also allegedly intoxicated and Humphrey charged him with DUI.

While Humphrey told Patterson he was going to be placed under arrest. Patterson fled to his car and took off south on U.S. 25.

Before the chase ended, Patterson was charged additionally with wanton endangerment, a felony charge; attempting to elude; no registration or insurance in his possession and resisting arrest.

Grant County Sheriff's Deputy Troy Hagedorn and Kentucky State Police troopers came to the aid of Humphrey, who was in pursuit of Patterson.

Troopers cleared U.S. 25 of traffic near Post 6 and Hagedorn did the same by Sherman Estates.

Hagedorn then set up a moving road block with his cruiser in an attempt pull Patterson over.

Patterson paid no heed to Hagedorn and attempted to pass him by crossing over the lane divider into oncoming traffic, running a car off the road, Humphrey said.

Hagedorn said he pulled over some to give Patterson room if he tried to pass again against oncoming traffic.

[13] 23 June 1994. *Grant County News.* Linda Morris,News Correspondent.

"I'd rather him get past me than him hit someone head on," Hagedorn said.

Patterson again attempted to pull past the cruiser, but by this time traffic coming north on U.S. 25 had been stopped.

Hagedorn said traffic was clear ahead so he attempted to force Patterson off the road when he pulled along side him.

Patterson rammed in the side of the deputy's car as the two vehicles cruised down U.S. 25 at around 40 mph, according to Hagedorn.

Hagedorn returned the hit with his cruiser and forced Patterson to stay behind him. Hagedorn then turned his car and blocked both lanes.

"I had to do something," Hagedorn said. "I couldn't afford to let him get past me."

Police said Patterson leaped from the car and began to scuffle with Hagedorn and Humphrey.

Hagedorn grabbed him from behind while Humphrey was able to handcuff him.

"He was wanting to fight again," Humphrey said.

In the scuffle, Humphrey bashed his knees on the ground and had to go to the hospital for X-rays.

Humphrey requests the individual driving a dark blue or black General Motors vehicle that was allegedly almost hit and forced off the road by Patterson south of Sherman to call the Crittenden Police Department at XXX-XXXX.[14]

Student Remains In Critical Condition Following Jeep Wreck

Alcohol, Speed Contribute To Crash

A Grant County High School junior is in critical condition after an alcohol related accident in Dry Ridge left her pinned under a Jeep.

On a night when visibility at times was measured in feet, 17-year-old Christina Bowen and two friends were tossed about the 1979 Jeep 4x4 when it lost control. The Jeep spun out into an embankment and crashed on its side. The cause, according to the Grant County Sheriff's Office was alcohol.

The driver, Billy Leiner, 21, of Covington was charged with driving under the influence, and unlawful transaction with a minor in the third degree because he knowingly gave alcohol to Bowen. He was also charged with three counts of not wearing a seatbelt, one count for each unbelted person in the Jeep.

Emergency medical technicians performed CPR on Bowen after she was drug from the overturned red Jeep on rain soaked Dry Ridge-Mt. Zion Road late May 24.

Fellow passenger Danny Marksbury, 20, of Dry Ridge suffered cuts and bruises and complained of head and back injuries said Deputy Chuck Dills.

Deputies said rain, a curve and excessive speed contributed to the accident.

"(Letner) had a little bit of everything going against him." said Dills.

Bowen was taken to St. Elizabeth/Grant County Hospital and later transferred to University of Cincinnati Hospital, while deputies booked Leiner into the Grant County Jail.

She suffered head injuries, according to police, but Diana Cline, assistant public information officer at U.C. Hospital. listed them as only "general trauma at this point."

Marksbury, who was also transferred to U.C. Hospital was released on May 25.

Deputy Randy Middleton said Bowen was sitting on the center console of the jeep between Loner and Marksbury. He said the trio was heading to take Bowen to her Crittenden home at 11:24 p.m. after hanging out in Dry Ridge.

The Jeep spun 130 feet before flipping on its side and sliding another 25 feet, police said.

"She was trapped underneath," said Middleton of Bowen.

Letner had a .111 blood alcohol content making him legally drunk. said Dills, though pointing out that the test wasn't given until more than an hour after the accident.

"At the time of the accident he would have been at a higher limit." he said. Letner admitted to police that all three had been drinking and that he had drunk a 12 pack of beer one and a half hours before the accident, according to police.

[14] 23 February 1995. *Grant County News.* Eric Wessel,Staff Writer.

[15] 1 June 1995. *Grant County News.* Eric Wessel,Staff Writer.

Dills pulled out three full Bud Light beers from the Jeep.

"He was going too fast and drinking," said Middleton.[15]

State Police Raid American Legion Hall

---

141 Cases Of Beer Confiscated

Charges Pending, Police Say

Members Decline To Comment

American Legion Hall members faced the sobering reality of possible criminal charges after a June 30 raid in which police confiscated 141 cases of beer.

The Kentucky State Police continues its investigation into the Williamstown American Legion Hall for allegedly selling beer in a dry county and expects charges to be filed in the next few weeks.

"Some form of charges will be filed," said Trooper Russell Harney.

Harney said the charge would probably be distributing alcoholic beverages in a dry territory which is a misdemeangor charge. Harney would not comment on the number of individuals that could face charges.

Grant County was voted to be a dry county by residents years ago using the state's local option rule, which means no alcoholic beverages may be bought or sold in the county.

Legion members are keeping quiet over the incident.

"Right now we're not making any comments because we don't know what's going on," said legion member James Adkins.

County Attorney Jim Purcell said the investigation is also looking at reports of beer being sold inside to members.

Purcell said before the raid, his office had never officially had a complaint about alcohol at the legion hall.

"Have I heard rumors? Yes," he said.

Purcell said the laws interpretation of prohibition is stringent. He said that it is not only illegal to buy and sell beer in a dry county, but to also buy beer outside the county and bring it in to distribute without a charge.

"You may possess alcohol for personal consumption, but the moment you transfer it in any way that's illegal," he said.

Sgt. Robert Huepel said the post had received numerous complaints about the legion's alleged practice of selling alcohol in the hall and also in bulk to drink elsewhere.

"Complaints have been coming in that beer has been going out the door," said Trooper Jan Wuchner, spokesman for Post 6.

Huepel said it was a coincidence that the raid took place days before the Independence Day holiday.

"Its just the way it all came together," Huepel said. "It was just by sheer coincidence. Nothing was planned."

Harney said that the investigation should be completed in the next few weeks.

The raid consisted of members of the KSP, Williamstown Police Department and the Grant County Sheriffs Office.[16]

Petition Seeks Special Election On Wet/Dry Issue

Should Grant County be wet or dry?

That is the question Boyd Kiser is hoping registered voters in Grant County will get the opportunity to decide in a special election on Dec. 7.

Kiser, a retired Kentucky State Police officer, sent out a survey to all registered voters in the county on Sept. 11. The survey asked registered voters who favored Grant County to be wet, or for liquor to be sold here, to sign a petition and return it to him.

The survey contained a cover letter, return envelope and petition.

The letter said, "A group of open minded citizens is surveying the opinions of the people of Grant County concerning whether or not alcohol should be available for sale in the county."

The petition orders the county judge-executive to schedule a special election on the wet/dry issue. Wet/dry issues, by law, cannot be held during a regular election.

[16] 13 July 1995. *Grant County News.* Eric Wessel,Staff Writer.

Kiser said he decided it was time for citizens to decide if they wished to be able to purchase alcohol in the county and he came to that conclusion after having discussions with various groups in the county.

Giving individuals the right to chose, is why he said he picked the name "American Way" for his effort.

The last time the wet/dry vote was held was in 1985. The vote was 3-1 in favor of the county remaining dry.

"I think it's a good idea for the county," he said. "We've got an influx of new people in the county now."

Kiser believes if liquor sales are permitted, it would help to attract "nice motels and restaurants" to the area.

"Just think of the tax revenue this would generate" he said.

To get a special election, Kiser must obtain signatures from at least 25 percent of those who voted in the last general election.

According to County Clerk Judy Fortner, there were 3,623 votes cast last November. That means 906 signatures must he obtained on the petitions.

Fortner said once her office receives the petitions, they will turn them over to the judge-executive and his office has the responsibility to check the validity of the signatures.

Kiser said the response he had been receiving to the survey was in favor of alcohol sales.

John DiGirolamo, owner of The Country Grill Restaurant in Dry Ridge, said if alcohol sales are approved he sees it as an added service for customers, but doesn't foresee a big increase in his receipts.

"It might help in my case the out of town customers who sometimes ask for beer or wine with their meal, but I know this community and I know it will be a controversial issue," DiGirolamo said.

Law enforcement officials, however, weren't exactly keen on liquor sales.

Willimastown Police Chief Ronnie West said if approved he expects more problems.

"Since the DUI (driving under the influence) laws have gotten tougher, those offenses have decreased, but I would expect you'll see more fights and domestic calls that would arise from alcohol sales." West said.[17]

---

[17]26 September 1996. *Grant County News.* Jamie Baker-Nantz,Editor.

Alcohol and Other Drugs Council

The AOD Council at Grant County High School consists of back row, Will Allstock, Candy Doyle, Patrick Flerlage, Hannah Haynes, Kristi Howe, Matt Howe, GenaKay Livingood, Wade Napier, JoAnn Sterneberg and Sasha Sterneberg, along with JoAnn Brill, guidance counselor. Not pictured are Wade Napier and Anitra Fields.

"Without the direction of Lanette Whalen of the Northern Kentucky AOD office and the Grant County Adult Council, the success of this program could not be a reality. I am proud to be the chairperson for the Grant County AOD Council.."

-Joyce Doyle, AOD chairman

The AOD Council at Williamstown High School consists of back row, Jim Brown, guidance counselor; Shawn Hurston, Carol Ann Dennison, Adria Combs, Lori Beth Brown, Hollie Hammons and front, Heather Dixon, Nicole Fortner, Daniel Beighle, Michael Hagedorn and Elizabeth Rich.

Local youth take pledge against drugs, alcohol

The Grant County AOD (Alcohol and Other Drugs) Youth Council is a very active and dedicated group of teenagers. The youth council is made up of 10 Grant County High School students and 10 Williamstown High School students.

These young people are very much aware of what drugs can do to the human body and are dedicated to the idea that they would like to see a drug free school.

Each year the youth council goes to the elementary schools presenting plays for the younger students and providing a time for questions and answers.

Also at Halloween, the students dress in costume and go to the St. Elizabeth Hospital's pediatric ward and give out treats to patients. They also explain how important it is to remain drug free.

These teenagers are to be commended. They believe and try to pass on to others the benefits of remaining drug free.

The Adult Council consists of Doyle, Lisa Wiggins, Angie Jent, Jim Brown, Gay Napier, JoAnn Brill, Judy Martin, Ros Reade, Dr. Clay Parks, Al Rich, Sharon Faulkner, Deborah Reed and Lanette Whalen.

This anti-drug message is brought to you by The Grant County News. The content of this special section was produced by the Grant County Alcohol and Other Drugs Council. Questions or comments on the content should be directed to Lanette Whalen, rural coordinator for the Northern Kentucky AOD at 282-7880.

Please take time and assist your child in reading the section. You should talk to your children about drugs before someone else has a chance to.

Alcohol related?

Accidents(?) Involving Alcohol

In 1993 alcohol was a major contributing factor in 6,679 automobile accidents(?). In 1994 there were 5,995 accidents(?) involving alcohol. In Grant County alone there were 25 accidents(?) involving drinking drivers. In those 25 accidents(?), 15 were injury accidents(?) with 23 people injured and 10 property damage accidents(?). The severity of these injuries ranged from minor to disabling. The property damage was in the thousands of dollars.

As you can see there is was a 11 percent decrease in alcohol related accidents(?) in 1994 compared to 1993. I commend all those involved in this reduction of alcohol related accidents(?). This 11 percent reduction is great but it's only the start. With more patrols, tougher laws along with stricter penalties, and education we can take the **QUESTION MARK OUT OF ACCIDENTS** Remember it's not an **ACCIDENT** that a person decided to drink and drive.

OTHER FACTS INVOLVING ALCOHOL AND ACCIDENTS IN KENTUCKY

In 1993 Kentucky ranked 15th out of 50 states in teenage motor vehicle deaths There were a total of 142 teenage deaths (source NAIL).

In Grant County as of October 7, 1995 there have been a total of 38 fatal accidents compared to 25 last year at this time.

In the Kentucky State Police Post 6 area Troopers have arrested 456 DUI'S as of October 7, 1995 compared to 369 in 1994.

Between 1990 and 1994 there has been a total of 1,332 arrests for DUI in Grant County. 1,018 of those arrested were convicted of DUI for a percentage rate of 76.4 (source KTC-95-19)

Alcohol related fatalities have averaged 319 per year for the past five years. If the cost of an average motor vehicle accident is used, the estimated annual cost of alcohol related accidents in Kentucky is about $105 million. (source KTC-95-19)

Information gathered by Lt. Al Rich, Kentucky State Police

18

[18]Circa September 1996. *Grant County News.*

Lusby Sees No Reason To Roll Out The Beer Barrels

Dear Editor,

Better stop and think if asked to sign a petition for a "wet/dry" election.

Consider: "In the end [alcohol] bites like a snake and poisons like a viper. Your eyes will see strange sights and your mind imagine confusing things... 'They hit me,' you will say, 'but I'm not hurt! They beat me, but I don't feel it! When will I wake up so I can find another drink?' " (Proverbs 23:32-35 NIV).

Isn't it interesting that a very large crowd could have such a good time at the Marigold Festival gift in Williamstown without the "benefits" of barrels of beer and kegs (or whatever) of wine?[19]

Sadie Evelyn Lusby
Mason

Group Of Citizens Does Not Want A Vote On Wet/Dry

Dear Editor,

We, the people, listed below of Grant County, would like to state that we do not want alcohol in our county.

Also, we do not want to see it on the ballot to vote for or against.[20]

Thank you,
Concerned citizens,
Charles Nicholson
Myra Nicholson
Peggy L. Lewis
Mr. and Mrs. Allen Vance
Dr. and Mrs. Paul Bodenhamer
Sue Hillman
Patty Nicholson
Marie Bishop
Logan and Bonnie Murphy
Laverne Spegal
Joe White
Jewel Bruce
Benny Bivins
Shirley Masters
Edward Souder
Jenifer Bivins
Arlie and Edith Frasure
Joe and Jo Ann Martin
Steve Nicholson
Les and Betty Taylor
Pat and Darrell Caldwell

Wet/Dry Issue Headed To Polls

Question Arises Over Whether Dec. 7 Can Be Date For Election

It looks like the voters in Grant County will have an opportunity to decide whether they want liquor to be sold here or not.

Boyd Kiser, a retired state police officer, was expected to file his petition requesting a special election early this week in the county clerk's office.

Kiser, said in a phone interview on Monday, he had more than enough signatures and expected to turn in about 1,200.

According to County Clerk Judy Fortner, Kiser needed 906 signatures (or 25 percent of the votes cast in the last general election) before the issue could be decided upon in a special election.

Once the wet/dry petition has been filed with the clerk's office, she will then turn it over to Shirley Howard, county judge-executive, and the fiscal court for the signatures to be verified.

The petition requests that the special election be held on Dec. 7.

Kiser said he chose that particular day because it is the anniversary of Pearl Harbor and a reminder that Americans have choices.

"We should have the right to chose whether we would like a drink with our meal," he said.

Dec. 7 is on a Saturday and according to state law, elections, including special ones that are not in conjunction with a general election, must be held on Tuesday.

State law prohibits a wet/dry election from being held at the same time of a general election.

The law also allows for a date of a special election to be specified and if it is not it is up to the judge executive to set the date.

Because Dec. 7 falls on Saturday, Howard is researching as to the legality of the petitions and the date.

[19] 26 September 1996. *Grant County News.*
[20] 3 October 1996. *Grant County News.*

"I don't know at this point if that date being a Saturday or not has any bearing on the validity of the petitions." Howard said. "We are looking into that question at this time."

Kiser said he was pleased with the response and had heard very few negative comments about the county being "wet." He said he had also received phone calls from people who did not receive petitions.

Kiser used the voter registrations rolls as a guide for mailing out petitions. After he received the list of registered voters, he then randomly chose those who would receive a petition.

"I guess maybe I should have done it according to precincts, but really it was just a random choice," Kiser said.

A lack of funds prevented him from mailing them to everyone on the registered voter's list, he said.

Local church leaders and some citizens, however, have quite a bit to say about the wet/dry issue.

A meeting was held last week at the Williamstown Christian Church for anyone interested in airing a concern over the issue.

"This is not a personal issue, but what is the best possible environment for our community," said James Craigmyle, pastor of Williamstown Baptist Church.

Craigmyle said last week's meeting was held to let local ministers and other concerned citizens have a chance to let their feelings be heard.

"We're not going after any particular person," Craigmyle said. "This is about what is best for all of Grant County."

The wet/dry debate is already causing accusations and heated words in the community.

John DiGirolamo, owner of The Country Grill Restaurant in Dry Ridge, said he felt like he had been attacked because of his recent zone change along Wilorn Drive.

"There's absolutely no connection between the zone change and the wet/dry issue," he said. "I'm not behind this."

DiGirolamo had requested a zone change on the property he owns behind the restaurant so he can build more parking spaces if the state's widening of KY 22 takes away his front lot parking area.

When he previously asked for a zone change on the property two years ago, he wanted to use the house as a meeting/party room.

"It upsets me for people to accuse me of this," he said. "I've worked in businesses where I've had to baby-sit drunks all night long and I don't want to do that again."

DiGirolamo said he didn't, however, see any problem with people wanting to have a drink with a meal.

Under rules from the state's Alcohol Beverage Control, because Grant County doesn't have any cities with a population of 3,000 or more, bars won't be permitted and beer or wine will be permitted only in businesses who derive 50 percent of their profits from food sales.

Based on the county's population, the state would only grant licenses for seven or eight package liquor stores.

Editor's Note: This is the second of several articles concerning the wet/dry issue.[21]

Now's your chance Grant County!
Should liquor sales be allowed by law in Grant County?
If you have an opinion on the wet/dry issue, The Grant County News wants to hear from you.
Letters to the editor must be signed and include the writer's phone number. Phone numbers are for verification only and will not be published in the paper.
Letters should be limited to 250 to 300 words. They will be edited for clarity, libel and grammar.
Send letters to: Letters to the Editor, The Grant County News, P.O. Box 247, Williamstown, Ky 41097 or Fax them to 606-824-5888.

22

Colson Proud Of Grant County's Past Dry Heritage

Dear Editor,

I am writing due to the article where Mr. Kiser, a former state policeman wrote. He said many new people coming into our county want liquor sales.

If they want liquor so badly - let them move to a wet county.

[21] 3 October 1996. *Grant County News.* Jamie Baker-Nantz,Editor.

[22] Circa October 1996. *Grant County News.*

Having come to Grant County 50 years ago in 1946 - and having five sons who do not drink - I am proud to be from Grant County.

As a former state trooper, does he not remember terrible accidents that happened?

If he needs a liquid with a meal there are plenty available - Coke, fruit juice, milk and all types of soft drinks - which are much healthier than liquor.

Young people are tempted to drink, if it is easily available.

When I was a teenager in Illinois in 1941, we couldn't walk on one side of the street - business side -because of the drunks and spit on the walk.

Believe me - when I say as a mother of six children raised in Grant County - I am proud they are good citizens.

Former U.S. Senator George McGovern writes that in 1995, 125,000 people, many of them young people, died due to alcoholism. That is more than were killed in the Vietnam War.[23]

Sincerely,
Eleanor M. Colson

Personally Speaking

Common Sense Needed When Voting Wet Or Dry

Last night, after a long, back-breaking day at the word processor, I had a beer.

I drank it from a mug glazed in frost, chilled to perfection in my freezer. As I poured it from the bottle, it gushed over the side and onto my jeans before settling into foamy, golden stasis.

When it was gone, I heated left-over chicken and made some of those fake mashed potatoes that come in a box. I washed the meal down my throat with a second beer, and after that, I turned in for the evening.

Two beers in one evening. Maybe tonight, I'll have two more. Or maybe even three.

And what happened to me after those two beers entered my bloodstream?

Absolutely nothing.

I did not get behind the wheel and smash into a bus load of nuns. I did not stumble to the nearest tavern and start a rumble. I did not beat up my girlfriend or my mother. I did not pass out in the gutter face down in my own vomit. I did not cause the degradation of society, whatever that means.

And though every church leader in the community will throw Bibles at me for saying this, I believe Grant County should vote wet.

Now that the noose has been tied, I would like to offer a few observations on the water cooler hot topic of the moment, the upcoming wet/dry vote.

To begin, I am amazed at the number of people who do not want this issue to see the light of the ballot box. What happened to democracy? What happened to majority rule?

If anything, I would think dry proponents would want to organize, rally, and stomp the wet people into the dirt.

I would think supporters of a dry county would want to stand up and point out why living in a wet county is wrong, using the power of their vote to drive the point home.

Instead, it seems like the wets are trying to sweep the issue under the rug. If wet/dry is kept off the ballot, it will come up again twice as fast. A strong vote dry would kill the issue for another 10 years, right?

Yes, and if Grant County remains dry for another 10 years, major businesses will continue to pass over the area when they want to expand. Big grocery chains will not bring us their lower prices if they are not allowed to sell alcohol in their stores. Fine dining restaurants will not consider opening their doors in our cities if they can't offer a glass of wine with dinner.

Unfortunately, when a passionate issue like wet/dry surfaces, logic and common sense can be tossed aside in favor of faith and emotion.

For example, a letter in a recent issue of Grant County News said: "It is a proven fact, from the Temperance League of Kentucky, that opening the door to Alcohol sales in every community has led to a degradation of society."

Does one measure degradation in feet, pounds, or kilograms?

Who decides when degradation has occurred? Maybe it happens when teenage girls become pregnant, or when people in the community are stricken by poverty. Maybe it hap-

[23] 10 October 1996. *Grant County News.*

pens when department stores move onto farm land, or when kids drop out of high school. Who makes the call?

Should we let the Temperance League decide for us? After all, the League thinks alcohol is bad for the community.

No kidding. And the United Beer Drinkers Union, if such a thing exists, would promote opening a tavern on every block in town.

Perhaps the signs of degradation differ for everyone, and like the imaginary Beer Drinkers Union, the Temperance League has an agenda. No matter the situation, the League will preach the evils of alcohol.

Maybe the Temperance League and other supporters of a dry Grant County do not want alcohol here because it kills people.

After all, you can't argue with fact. Drunk drivers kill the people we love because of their pathetic need to have a drink and get behind the wheel. Nobody is suggesting we legalize drunk driving.

However, our county has been dry for a long time, and we have always had drunk drivers. Turn to the police reports in this newspaper for further details.

Voting wet will not bring drunk drivers to the county. They are already here, and you can hole up inside of your house and pull the drapes closed, or you can go on with your life. The sun will still shine, the birds will still fly into your patio door, and alcohol will continue to kill people, wet county or dry.

Wet county or dry, cigarettes will kill people too. In fact, tobacco products kill many more people each year than alcohol, yet I do not see anybody circulating a petition to put an end to the Grant County's number one cash crop.

When all is said and done, I think Grant County will remain dry. The drinkers among us have been driving to other counties to fulfill their needs for quite a while, like little kids who sneak a Marlboro out of their father's pack. To stand up in Grant County and say 'I believe we should be wet' is to put your neck on the chopping block. It's just not worth causing any trouble.

So us wets probably will continue to make small sacrifices to keep the peace with our neighbors. Truly, it's a small price to pay.

(And to those of you who like to blow the froth off a thick, brown Guinness after you've mowed the lawn on a 90 degree August afternoon... I'll see you at the pong keg.)[24]

County Judge Rejects Wet/Dry Petitions

Grant County Judge Executive Shirley Howard has rejected a petition requesting a special election on alcohol sales.

Howard said he rejected the petition because it asked for the election to be held on Dec. 7, a Saturday.

According to a state law, elections, including special ones not in conjunction with a general election must be held on a Tuesday.

Howard said he consulted with the county attorney before deciding to reject the petitions.

Boyd Kiser, a retired state police officer, who began the petition drive, could not be reached for comment on whether he intended to file the petitions with a new date.

Despite the judge's rejection of the petitions, local church leaders plan to meet on Wednesday to discuss the issue.

Information from that meeting can be found in next week's Grant County News.[25]

Walters Sees Wet/Dry Debate As A Moral Issue

In reference to the article Personally. Speaking, written by your staff writer, David Thomas:

First, Mr. Thomas is not a resident of Grant County. He has no vote here, so, the issue of wet or dry is none of his business or affair.

Secondly, Mr. Thomas' article was placed beside another article which contained in large black print, Editorial Comment. Whether intentional or not, this indicated to the readers that Grant County News had taken the stand to vote our county wet. Unless I missed something, there was

[24] 10 October 1996. *Grant County News.* David Thomas,Staff Writer.

[25] 17 October 1996. *Grant County News.*

no place in the article that stated, this was only the opinion of Mr. Thomas, and our Grant County News was remaining neutral, as it should. Maybe we can use the words of your editorial comments on keeping freedom of information strong. You wrote it was the People's Law, and the media, more than others kept watch over that law, fighting to keep it strong on behalf of everyone. By allowing a staff writer, from another county, to print such an article did not represent me.

I'm glad Mr. Thomas could have his two beers and it had no effect on him, at least for now. But I reject the idea of paying taxes to support alcoholism, because of the many folks who were unable to stop with two beers.

America is a land of choice. I have many friends in the county who choose to take a drink. But those same people will vote opposition to liquor being sold across the street.

But as for me, after a hard time mowing my lawn, I sit back and drink a Sprite. This also has no effect on me, especially if it is diet.

And if the baby needs milk, I can run to the carry out without any danger of being DUI. Neither is my neighbor endangered when I meet him on the road.

Many of our voters are much younger than me. But I remember when Grant County was wet. I also remember why it was voted dry. We simply could not afford the cost.

Now, as to logic and common sense. Someone much higher than a staff writer, or myself, decides when degradation occurs.

Common sense tells me the sale of alcohol will cost our people dearly. Remember how the lottery was to solve our school problems?

Common sense and knowledge tells me that alcohol kills more of our people than anything else. It begins when the mind is altered, whether at home or away.

Common sense tells me there will always be drinking drivers in the county. But, this will increase when they meet at the pub.

Common sense tells me: (1) We will need more police protection; (2) Our premiums will increase for insurance; (3) The value of many properties will decrease.

Common sense says we do not have space in our jail now, or the money to build another one.

Common sense says we have enough domestic violence and child abuse.

Yes!! The sale of alcohol will cost the people.

Yes!! The sale of alcohol will add more pressure to our court officials and our courts are overcrowded now.

Common sense tells me that our kids don't need a daily reminder to wonder what kind of high they can get from drinking. Most will try it soon enough, but let's not tempt them to have one sooner.

A word to the citizens of Grant County. Make sure you vote. To stay away from the polls is a vote for the county to be wet.

By the way, I am a Christian and church leader, and the wet/dry issue is definitely a moral issue.[26]

Lyons Gives Her Opinion On Wet Versus Dry Issue

Dear Editor,

In reference to the Personally Speaking column by Dave Thomas in the Grant County News on Oct. 10, "Common Sense Needed When Voting Wet or Dry."

Yesterday after a long day of of teaching, house cleaning, cooking and yard work, I took a frosted mug from my freezer and poured a bubbly glass of pop. When it was gone, I fried the family some crispy country chicken, freshly mashed potatoes and cornbread. We all washed this down with a cold sparkling soda.

What happened? Absolutely nothing! No one stumbled to the nearest tavern, there was no abuse, no one crashed into a busload of children - killing them, not one of us robbed anyone, but we would have been much more likely to if we had alcohol in our body.

Every church leader in Grant County certainly won't be throwing Bibles, simply because they respect the Word of God much more than that, sir.

What happened to democracy and majority rule? Nothing, that's why Grant County has remained dry. That's the choice of Grant County citizens. For the most part, folks from other counties are the ones trying to push it in this county.

If anything I would think the wet proponents would like to form a rally

[26] 17 October 1996. *Grant County News.* Charlie Walters, Guest Editorial.

and stomp us dry of Grant County into dirt, using the power of a vote to keep the point home.

A dry vote would kill the issue of wet/dry for 10 more years? Yes, and that's what I pray for.

Don't be fooled, alcohol will not bring money to Grant, it will bring the need for more police, more jail space, more court hearings. The revenue from the sale of alcohol goes to the federal and state government. not to the county. The only revenue from Grant County would be a space license fee. Now, will big chain stores bring us cheaper food prices? Write down a long list of of products you use and the weight of products, go to Florence or Lexington and compare prices, as we have, see for yourselves.

I am glad and proud Grant Countians can place common sense aside for faith and emotion. These two virtues are much more honorable.

These are folks who drink in our or county and no one condemns them, and yes, cigarettes do kill also but I've never heard of a bus full of kids being killed because someone smoked a cigarette.

And to those of you who like a frosted glass of soda after a long day at work...I'll see you at the polls to vote "no" against wet.[27]

Mary Marlene Lyons
Dry Ridge

Is your News subscription paid?

Ministers Group, Citizens Form Keep It Dry, Safe Committee

Local ministers and county residents met last week to form a group to combat a drive that would put a wet/dry alcohol issue on a special election ballot.

Rev. Willie Ailstock, pastor of Dry Ridge Baptist Church, was selected as the chairman of Grant County's Keep It Dry And Safe (KIDS) committee.

Jim Simpson was chosen as the vice chairman, along with Charlie Walters as secretary and Terry Peer as treasurer. They will be working to get volunteers to help with the effort to keep the county dry.

Boyd Kiser of Dry Ridge submitted a petition seeking a special election on the wet/dry issue. The county judge-executive denied his petition based on the date.

Kiser is expected to re-file the petition after the Nov. 5 election. The earliest a special election could be held would be January.[28]

Schoenman Says Alcohol Does Not Cause Problems

Dear Editor,

Yesterday, after a long day of welding, operating machinery, and conferring with prospective business clients, I took a frosted mug from my freezer and poured myself a nice, cold beer to go along with the pizza I made with my children. During dinner, at which my children washed I lay down their pizza with a lovely glass of ice cold milk (milk being much better for growing children than sugary soda pop), I savored the taste of my ice cold beer. Also during dinner, my children and I had a stimulating conversation on their school day and on the upcoming presidential election.

What happened after dinner? Absolutely nothing! I didn't stumble to the nearest tavern looking for another beer. I didn't beat my children in a drunken frenzy. I did not get behind the wheel of my car looking for a busload of nuns to crash into. I did not rob the nearest business establishment. Even though I had a moderate amount of alcohol in my system, I had no inclination to commit any of these atrocities.

I understand that many of the people in this community don't want bars, taverns and carryouts. Then simply restrict the licensing to beer and wine sales at the grocery stores, no hard liquor sales. The voters of Grant County have the power to decide how, where, and what kind of is alcohol is to be sold here. Many of us have moved here from "other counties" as well as many native Grant Countians would appreciate the freedom to purchase beer/wine locally instead of driving to Florence, again.

Further I resent the implication that since I occasionally drink a beer

[27] 24 October 1996. *Grant County News.*
[28] 31 October 1996. *Grant County News.*
[29] 7 November 1996. *Grant County News.*

or two that I am more likely to lie, cheat, steal and kill. To the majority of Americans, drinking moderate amounts of alcohol is not a condemnable sin.[29]

Sincerely,
James Schoenman
Williamstown

Sipple Offers Reasons To Keep Grant County Dry

Dear Editor,

I agree with the "Personally Speaking" column in the News by David Thomas, "Common sense needed with voting wet or dry." (The column appeared in the Oct. 10 issue of the Grant County News.) The column made five points I would like to comment on.

Point number one - "Now that the noose has been tied." I assume he is referring to his neck. I would not want to use a noose, tar and feather maybe, but no noose.

Point number two - "Major business will continue to pass over the area when they want to expand." A major corporation's decision on where to locate is based on availability of work force, low wages, tax incentives by state and local governments, proximity of an airport and accessibility to an interstate system. Not whether a county or town is wet or dry.

Point number three - "Fine dining restaurants will not consider opening their doors in our cities if they can't offer a glass of wine with dinner." I have dined at a few fine restaurants over the years. Unfortunately even with reservations you will be directed to the bar until a table becomes available. Instead of enjoying a fine meal and conversation in quiet, many times I have had to listen to a loud-mouth with a snoot full of liquor.

Point number four - "The big grocery chains will not bring us their lower prices if they are not allowed to sell alcohol in their stores." I suggest the writer do a shopping comparison between the big grocery chains and our local stores. He might be surprised to find our local groceries are very competitive in price without selling alcohol.

Point number five - "Tobacco." I want to bring the writer to task for bringing the subject of tobacco into the wet and dry issue. My blood pressure went up 10 points reading that part of the column. I may change my mind about the noose. I do not believe every statistic about the harm of tobacco. What is a tobacco-related death? Is it a fatality when a person fell out of a barn housing tobacco? No, a tobacco-related death is affixed to every disease know to man; if the person was a smoker. What if the person also was a beer drinker, had a stressful job, did not eat properly, did not exercise? Would that be a tobacco smoking, beer drinking, stressed out, out of shape, did not eat properly related death? By the statistics, it would be only tobacco-related.

Why is Grant County one of the leading counties in Kentucky in population growth? Could it be because it is a dry county? Why do we have a low fatality rate due to drunk drivers? Could it be because we are a dry county?

I was born in Grant County but lived most of my young adult life out of the county. The reason I returned was the relaxed style of living, the friendly people of Grant County, and the roots of my family. I have lived in wet counties but would prefer to live in a dry county. I like to drink an occasional beer, but I am foresighted enough to buy a twelve pack when I am in a wet county for consumption at home. No noose -just tar and feather.[30]

Gaylon Sipple
Dry Ridge

Sixteen Year Old Fields Weighs In On Wet/Dry Issue

Dear Editor,

I am writing to you as a concerned young adult about the "Wet/Dry" issue. I'm 16-years old, and I fail to see 'an issue,' for there really shouldn't be one. Too many teenagers, as well as adults, have already died in our country alone, due to drunk driving.

Call me young, or immature or say that I don't have any idea what it's all about, but sadly enough, I

[30] 7 November 1996. *Grant County News.*

alone have lost over four family members due to alcohol. So I do know first-hand what the effects of alcohol really are. I soon hope to get my license after driver's education, but what good does it do, if you know how to drive...and perhaps you may be the best driver you could possibly be? You still have to watch out for the 'other' person on the road. And what's going to happen when bars are placed right here in our own county? Maybe even next door to our schools, churches, homes, etc. Drunk driving won't be the half of it. Innocent lives are that much more at risk, than they are now.

People, adults, can say that nothing happens to you by drinking a couple of beers, but let me say this, alcohol is a drug, and it effects every person differently. And if teenage parties aren't bad enough in places where their parents are, or should be aware of, how much more at risk are the 'newly skilled' drivers who are drunk or under the influence after these parties. The fact is, that alcohol does affect the mind and the body. A 'couple' of beers may not have a huge affect on one certain person, but for us younger generations, we could have one or two and it kill us. Crazy? No. It has happened before. Some people react differently than others to drugs...like alcohol. We must also consider other factors to drinking as well. Such as doing things that we normally wouldn't do unless otherwise under the influence, because your judgment is clouded. Thus winding up pregnant, AIDS, or other sexually transmitted diseases, not to mention breaking the law.

I don't want to be "just another victim," because of someone who wasn't responsible enough to take authority over this matter. I am sorry to say this, but if this issue is passed, the leaders of our community have allowed the next generation and every generation living here to be victims of an addiction. And we will all pay the price. You can say whatever you want, and blame it on religious morals or churches not wanting this in their county, but it's a sad day when adults can't be adult enough to blame themselves, because what they're wanting for their children is wrong. What a legacy to leave your child. At least someone cares enough (like the churches), to stand up and fight for what is right.

Also as a future taxpayer, I believe it will be hard enough for our generation to get by let alone have to pay higher taxes due to things like: increased crime, increased law enforcement for the crimes, additional medical assistants for the crimes, different courthouse hours for the added crime, added cleanup maintenance, etc.

I also find it funny that some of the people that are involved or voicing their opinions on this issue are not even from this country. Why should they even have a say so?

Please just consider the past deaths alone. We already read about so many each and every week in the paper. Statistics show that every hour there are two people who die due to alcohol in our country alone: Although we can't foresee the future, we can look at the figures from other counties and compare their crime rate from being dry to the crime rate after becoming wet and you will see that there is a large increased number of crimes and death due to alcohol related incidences. With that being said, also consider this, if our county's going wet means there will be only two more deaths due to alcohol, isn't that two too many? And who might it be? Someone close to you or me?

I have lived in this community all my life and of all the people that I know, whom I love, respect and look up to they are the ones who have made this community what it is today and I am proud to be a part of it. Let's not continue to cut generations of life short, due to a bottle or can or even "an issue."

Stand up and be united, or one day you may see your child, grandchild, mother, father, sister, brother, friend, etc. in the obituary because of this so-called 'harmless' "wet/dry" issue. Let me end by saying this, they may force the vote, but they cannot force it wet. So you may be forced to vote but you are not forced to vote wet.[31]

Thank you,
Jennifer Fields
Dry Ridge

Is your News subscription paid?

Wolfe Gives Reasons To Prove Wet Is Wrong In Grant

---

[31] 7 November 1996. *Grant County News.*

Dear Editor,

In a recent edition of your paper, you encouraged folks to write in and express their views on the wet/dry issue. I lived in the city for a while and since alcohol is sold on just about every street corner in Covington and Cincinnati, I have seen the gradual degradation of property and lives resulting from the sale of alcohol.

I thank God for Grant County and for the people who are working to keep it "dry." I urge those people who want to let liquor sold in our county to consider these facts:

Ninety to ninety-five percent of inmates in jail are there as a result of alcohol or drug-related offenses.

The "Wets" are telling us that the sale of alcohol will bring in other businesses and help the county to grow. I heard at a meeting the other evening that Grant County was the third fastest growing county in the state. If we follow the rationale of the Wets, this is impossible, because we are a dry county and you can only grow if you allow the sale of alcohol. We can't build schools fast enough now to handle the growth. We don't need the type growth these people are referring to. It will result in more taxes for judges, jails, police and counselors for those with drinking problems and their families. We need to spend our tax money on the upkeep of roads, installation of water lines, better schools - things which benefit everyone.

I call upon everyone who believes as I do - that Grant County should remain a dry county - to stand up and make your voice heard. Don't let those who only care about financial gain cause our county to inherit the problems resulting from the sale of alcohol.[32]

Yours truly,
H. David Wolfe
Williamstown

Lusby Responds To Recent Arguments On Wet/Dry

Dear Editor,

Some things in the paper demand a response.

A father savoring the taste of ice cold beer at dinner with his children is not a picture of idyllic family life. It is a lesson for the children that alcohol, a mind-altering, behavior-affecting drug is an enjoyable, acceptable beverage.

The children have milk, because beer drinking is for adults. Venturesome youngsters are eager to try this grown-up thing. We read that some are alcoholics by age 12, some starting as young as age 8.

Soon this father may find out that his children and their friends are "savoring the taste of beer" more than just a cold one with dinner. If one of them becomes an alcoholic or if, while under the influence, kills himself or someone else with a car, dad may spend the rest of his days answering some soul-wrenching questions.

Who needs beer and wine at the neighborhood grocery? Another message to children and youth. And what about the temptation to a recovering alcoholic? "It is better not to...drink wine or to do anything that will cause your brother to fall." Romans 14:21.

We hear the term "problem drinker." It seems to me that if one can't enjoy eating a meal, watching TV, playing a game, visiting with friends without alcohol, he's got a problem.

Further, a "bouquet of roses" to 16-year old Jennifer Fields for her well-reasoned treatment of the wet/dry issue.[33]

Thanks for listening,
Sadie Evelyn Lusby
Mason

Drinkers Should Move To Wet Area, Suggests Covey

Dear Editor,

First of all I would like to say I appreciate these people speaking up for our dry county. Thanks goes to Jennifer Fields. She's a young lady who said it all. I can't add much only to say we personally, as a family, know what drinking does to a person's mind, chemical imbalance, believe me you don't want this in your family.

My grandparents, parents, also us, are all farmers. There is no harder

[32] 7 November 1996. *Grant County News.*

[33] 14 November 1996. *Grant County News.*

work. When we come in tired we sure don't need a frosted glass of beer to relax like some people. Look in the paper each week. Half of these people are DUI and no insurance in a dry county. Can you imagine it being wet?

The ones who want this county wet don't like it dry. I suggest they move to a county that is wet.[34]

Wanda Covey
Dry Ridge

Cummins Hopes County Stays Dry

Dear Editor,

Well, everyone else in Grant County has voiced their opinion on wet and dry. So now I would like to voice my opinion.

I'm 56-years old and at one time or another I've probably been in every beer joint from here to Cincinnati, as I've lived in all the wet surrounding counties. I started drinking when I was 15-years old and drank until I was 46. In those 31-years, I learned that the closer the beer joint. the more often I drank. I moved out here in 1984 and I slacked off on my drinking, because it was too far and too risky to go out drinking and then try to get back home without getting arrested for DUI. I finally quit drinking in 1986. I really enjoy driving through Dry Ridge, Williamstown and all of our cities in Grant County without seeing beer signs and drunks standing on the corners or in parking lots.

If we let Grant County or any part of it become wet, we'll have to hire more police, get more or bigger jails and have more outsiders coming to our county to check out our beer joints.

Bringing beer and booze to our county would be like putting candy in front of small children and saying, "No, no." It can turn light drinkers into heavy drinkers. It will make teenagers who drink and don't have transportation more able to get what they want to drink, as there is always someone of age that will buy it for them.

There are enough alcohol problems in Grant County now without bringing it in by the truckload.

Well. I didn't say much, but what I did say is from experience. I know there are more people out there who feel the same as I do. Our county does not have to be wet to survive. People can go to a restaurant and eat without any loud noise from drinkers. My wife and I eat out often and yow can't imagine the difference it is between eating in the wet counties and our dry county. It's more relaxing to eat without noise.

Well, I'm starting to repeat myself, so I'll sign off, saying "Let's keep Grant County dry" - people be proud - keep our county clean and dry.[35]

Thanks,
Alvin L. Cummins Sr.
Williamstown

County Should Remain Dry

Dear Editor,

Freedom. That is what I hear every time I read a letter advocating the sale of alcohol in our county. People should have the right and freedom to drink whatever they choose with their dinner. The words "Americans" and "Freedom" were in the very title of the original petition to make clear it's purpose.

I agree that freedom is an admirable goal but I don't believe it is on target with wet/dry issue. As I understand it, Grant County allows the freedom for you to consume any kind of alcoholic beverage you want. You simply have to drive north to buy it. No one in our county is upset because they can't drink beer. People are upset because it is not available on the nearest corner. Not one resident is complaining that they can't drink alcohol in restaurants. They are saying they can't drink in nearby restaurants. The right and the freedom to consume is available, it's just not five minutes away. In my mind that is not a question of freedom but a question of convenience.

Now I would admit that for someone who drinks, a dry county would certainly be inconvenient. The benefits of living in this dry county, however, far outweigh any troubles you may endure. It is because we are a dry county we have safer roads. All drinking and driving occurs between two points, the alcohol source and

[34] 21 November 1996. *Grant County News.*
[35] 28 November 1996. *Grant County News.*

the person's destination. If the alcohol source is Boone or Kenton county and the destination of the driver is Grant County, how will most DUI offenders get here? The answer is I-75 and U.S. 25. These two roads work as a funnel for DUI offenders in our county because it is dry. Stop and think, where do you see sobriety check points most often? The Crittenden, Dry Ridge and Williamstown exits are great hunting for DUI's because they are smack in-between the alcohol source and the driver's destination. Did you know that we have a better batting average for picking up drunk drivers than our neighbors to the north.

The Enquirer reported that in 1995, Grant County averaged 16.8 DUI arrests per thousand while Boone County averaged only 14.6. We don't have the population or civic resources that Boone or Kenton counties have but because of our county's geography and because we are dry, we can pick off DUI's before they get into our neighborhoods.

Now, let's spread the source of alcohol throughout our county. Let one of these irresponsible drinkers get good and drunk at a local restaurant or bar. Which back street, alley or county road are we going to watch? The hunting will not be nearly as easy, more DUI's will slip through, more people will be put in danger. To top it off, this man or woman will have started their deadly trip just a few blocks or a few miles from our homes. They aren't weaving through Boone or Kenton before even approaching our neighborhoods. We gave them a head start by bringing the source of the problem closer to home. People are going to drink and drive. In fact, as Grant County grows in population, the number of people who drink and drive will increase. The only question is how many will be caught before they pull on to your street or mine?

This county is dry but people are still free to drink. No First Amendment right has been violated. It is simply inconvenient and that inconvenience is pulling more DUI offenders off the roads before they weave too close to our children and homes.[36]

Sincerely,
David Tucker
Dry Ridge

Caldwell Against Wet County

Dear Editor,

I am responding to a letter that was in the paper a few weeks ago. The letter was from a man trying to share his opinion about the wet/dry issue that people who want alcohol in Grant County are trying to get passed.

His opinion is that the sale of alcohol in Grant County would be great for the economical and population growth in the community.

The letter contained some information that really bothered me. He told the community that when he gets home from a long day of work he sits down and eats dinner and enjoys a nice cold glass of beer, while his kids drank a glass of milk. Later in the letter he complains about how he wouldn't go out after dinner and get in his car, rob a bank, or hit a bus full of nuns.

Then he later says that the things he does, is not reflected upon his children. When I finished reading this letter I could not imagine what he was thinking about when he wrote it. Maybe he already had one too many drinks when he was writing it. I truly feel that the father's drinking has affected the rest of his family's attitudes toward drinking.

If parents are giving their children alcohol today, what will the parents and families do when adults can go down to the nearest gas station or grocery store, and buy as much alcohol as they please.

I know alcohol would be good for Grant County's economy and growth, but I feel it is not worth the consequences of higher crime, abuse, murders, DUI's and other more severe drug problems.

I hope that when the wet/dry I issue vote occurs the people will make the right decision and vote dry so our community will stay a safe and secure society.[37]

Sincerely,
Chad Caldwell

---

[36] 5 December 1996. *Grant County News.*
[37] 12 December 1996. *Grant County News.*

McMillan Speaks Out On Wet Vote For Community

Dear Editor,

I'm writing in response to a letter published in your Dec. 19 edition.

A young Grant Countian was speaking of the evil of alcohol at the expense of a previous writer and his family. The young man made the assumption that a father could not drink a beer with his dinner without negative effects on his children.

Is this true? Are we not capable of using our best judgment? We are a wonderful community with many intelligent adults with common sense to use alcohol responsibly.

It is your choice Grant County. Either stand idly by as misinformed residents continue to persuade each other to believe we can't handle the responsibility of purchasing liquor in our town or show all the pessimists that as adults, we can make our own decision, intelligently and responsibly.[38]

Joe McMillan
Williamstown

Corinth Man Arrested For Illegal Liquor Sales

A Corinth man was selling cases of beer from his Lawrenceville Road home, according to Sheriff's Chief Deputy Chuck Dills.

Donald L. Martin, was arrested on Jan. 22, 1998 at 11:30 p.m.

He was charged with carrying a concealed deadly weapon and illegal sale of alcohol in a dry territory.

Martin pleaded guilty on March 10 in Grant District Court.

He was sentenced to one year in jail for both charges and was fined $100 plus court costs. Martin will have to only serve 30 days of the jail sentence.

In addition, he agreed to forfeit a .32 caliber handgun. $2,500 in cash and 12 cases of beer.

The sheriff's office will receive $2,250 and the Williamstown Police Department will receive $250 of the forfeited funds because they assisted with the case.

Dills said the sheriffs office received information, Martin was selling alcohol from his trailer. The police were then able to keep him under surveillance and make a controlled buy from Martin.

Dills said after the beer was purchased, police obtained a search warrant and seized the cash and beer.

This is the only the second time Dills said he could remember the sheriff's department investigating an illegal liquor sales case.

Under the state's forfeiture laws, police departments can seize money, homes, vehicles, etc.

Money from seizures such as this must be used to purchase equipment for the police department.

The Grant County Sheriff's office has used seized drug money, along with an annual contribution from the Grant County Fiscal Court to purchase a 1998 Ford Explorer.[39]

[38] 2 January 1997. *Grant County News.*

[39] 19 March 1998. *Grant County News.* Jamie Baker-Nantz, Editor.

2000s

Bingham Against Liquor Sales

Dear Editor,

I understand a drive for registered voters is underway to bring the issue before the voters of Grant County to sell liquor. A very few will benefit.

Personally, I hate to see the temptation brought before our young people. I grew up in Grant County when slot machines and saloons prevailed. Certainly we think enough of our young people to help them adjust to a good life.

Common sense tells us it will cost taxpayers more to have liquor available to profit just a few, plus the moral influence it brings to our county.[1]

Donald Bingham
Dry Ridge

Williamstown Student Speaks Out On Alcohol

Dear Editor,

My name is Jessica and I am 10-years-old and live in Grant County.

Please do not let the alcohol issue come to a vote in our county. I do not want alcohol to be sold in Grant County.

For example, what if a bus driver bought alcohol? What if another drunk driver ran into a school bus? Innocent children could be killed.

We do not need alcohol problems in Grant County.[2]

Jessica Napier
Fourth grade student at
Williamstown Elementary

Youth Can Live Dreams By Staying Alcohol Free

To the editor:

If we did better in preventing kids from drinking, our community would be a safer place. But all to often our prevention efforts are limited to telling kids to say "no" to alcohol and other drugs.

While "no-use" messages are important, they are only part of the solution to a problem that stubbornly refuses to go away. According to the latest government survey, about 10.5 million Americans from ages 12 to 20 had at least one drink last month; of these, 5.1 million were "binge" drinkers, meaning that they had consumed five or more drinks in a row on a single occasion.

Parents sometimes deny the seriousness of the underage drinking problem by pretending it does not exist or that it's a "rite of passage" all teenagers must go through before reaching adulthood. Unfortunately, in the aggregate, alcohol use by youth costs America more than $58 billion a year, including traffic accidents, violent crime, burns, drowning, suicide attempts, fetal alcohol syndrome, alcohol poisonings and treatment. Few parents contemplate the negative consequences of drinking until their child suffers from one such as these.

Teenagers, on the other hand, see drinking all around them - in their homes, in restaurants and at sporting events. It's a new experience that for the most part seems to be positive and almost essential to having a good time if they believe the countless beer commercials they are exposed to every time they watch television. Studies show that teenagers also tend to believe that more of their peers drink than actually do.

What they do not hear enough about are the rewards of not drinking.

[1] 9 March 2000. *Grant County News.*
[2] 30 March 2000. *Grant County News.*

New York Yankees shortstop Derek Jeter is doing his best to change that. As honorary chair of Alcohol Awareness Month in April, the rising young baseball star is helping to send a powerful message to the nation's young people.

"You can live your dreams as I am, by staying away from alcohol and other drugs," says Jeter.

It is hard to argue with a professional athlete who may one day inherit the legendary status of a Babe Ruth or a Joe DiMaggio. Jeter is not the only athlete to publicly acknowledge how he hasn't allowed the use of alcohol or other drugs to interfere with his goals.

"When my friends and I go to a restaurant or bar, the person buying the drinks always comes back with a full glass of water for me. They don't bother asking if I want a beer; the answer has always been 'no'," says T.J. Lavin, a bicycle stunt rider in the 1999 X-Games.

There are plenty of young men and women right here in Northern Kentucky with similar attitudes who are excelling in their studies, at sports, and in their efforts. By helping and encouraging our young people to say "yes" to their lives, and giving them greater recognition in our homes, schools and our community, we're giving them the best possible reason to say no to alcohol and other drugs.[3]

Shelly Micham, M.S. Ed.
NorthKey Regional
Prevention Center
Florence

Walters' Class Against Alcohol Sales In County

To the editor:

Our class has learned that there is the possibility that the alcohol issue may come to vote in Grant County.

If alcoholic beverages were sold in our community, there could be an increase in drinking and driving accidents. Innocent families with small children could be killed by drunk drivers.

If adults model irresponsible drinking, children may want to drink alcohol too. For example, if a parent drinks too much, he or she might physically abuse their children. This only teaches the children to grow up with the same bad behavior.

Alcohol damages the human body. For example, drinking too much alcohol can damage the liver. A person under the influence of alcohol cannot think clearly. Do we want this for the citizens of Grant County?

Some of the citizens may choose to disagree with our viewpoint. They might think that drinking is fun and tastes good. The fun won't last forever. Some may say people will bring alcohol in from other counties anyway. We believe that we should not make excuses for people who may abuse alcohol.

One young lady of our class wanted to remind Grant County readers that many young women might choose to drink while carrying an unborn child. Is it fair to the child to be born with birth defects because their mother chose to drink alcohol purchased in the community or elsewhere?

Think before we allow alcohol to be sold in our community. We must think before we drink.[4]

Marcia Walters' Fourth Grade
Students
Williamstown Elementary

McAdams Upset Over Wallace's Interest In Club

To the editor,

I fully recognize Bob Wallace's legal right to invest his money in a "strip club" operation in Gallatin County. I also recognize my right, and perhaps obligation, to register a voice of indignation.

For over 50 years, as a pan of my life's work, I have endeavored to champion the sacredness of marriage and human sexuality and to focus on family values. Also, I have on occasion been called upon to help put broken families back together and heal marital wounds. In recent years, with increasing frequency, I have found pornography and the pursuit of sexually-oriented adult entertainment to be a contributing factor in destroyed lives and homes. For a local businessman and acquaintance

[3] 27 April 2000. *Grant County News*.
[4] 4 May 2000. *Grant County News*.

to enter into and defend such as business is akin to a professional slap in the face.

I would think that among those with strong moral values, who have patronized Grant County Drugs over a period of many years, that there would be a sense of betrayal at seeing one man's profits, to which they have contributed, be used to promote values directly opposed to the moral principles of a strong family life. Also, it is characteristic for young people to look to those who are successful and see them as role models. Men of Mr. Wallace's stature have a trust. Jesus Christ put it like this, "From everyone who has been given much, of him they will ask all the more." (Luke 12:48)

In my personal view, Mr. Wallace has violated that trust.

In an article appearing in the April 25 issue of the Kentucky Enquirer, it was reported that some have suggested boycotting Grant County Drugs. In my mind this raises both a question and an observation.

The question is this: Why penalize Mr. Wallace's partner, and their staff, for Mr. Wallace's lack of moral judgment?

The observation is one that can be made so often. The violation of what is morally right always produces a ripple effect; bringing hurt and disappointment to other lives nearby.

I am not a long-time resident of Grant County, having lived here for the past 11 years. During that time I have taken a goodly number of prescriptions to Grant County Drugs. The owners, Mr. Spears and Mr. Wallace, and their staff, have always treated me with courtesy and respect. This has not been an easy letter to write. But a sense of revulsion and moral indignation has demanded it. The convictions expressed are my own. It is for others to decide if I may have spoken for them as well.[5]

Respectfully,
Henry McAdams
Dry Ridge

Resident Concerned Over Decline In Family Values

To the editor,

My heart became heavy as I read in another paper the news of a "strip bar" possibly opening soon in a neighboring county (or perhaps in Grant County in the near future).

We appear to be troubled concerning the deterioration of family life and values. Many of our children are growing up in an environment lacking in love, security and guidance. They are being influenced, daily, by scenes of violence and immorality on television. Many of our children are in desperate need of a positive male role model or image.

Will men watching a "stripper" in a bar cause a family to be stronger? Will this cause a man to return home and be a loving husband? Will it encourage a father to be more loving and interested in his children? Will this cause a man to be that role model? I think not! A business of this nature is only a breeding ground for other problems.

It is very sad to think that businessmen have to bring this sort of immoral attraction in beside a sporting event.

We cannot, as Christians, or concerned citizens sit complacently by and let another "negative" influence be added to the lives of our families.

I encourage our churches and organizations to band together, take a stand on moral issues and begin addressing relevant needs of our community. We can no longer stay within our "four walls" and expect it to make a difference in the lives of our next generation.[6]

Sincerely,
Irma Parks
Dry Ridge

Wet/Dry Petition Filed With Clerk

Judge To Verify Signatures

If you would like to see alcohol available for sale in Grant County. you may get the chance to vote on the issue.

A petition asking for a special election for voters to choose to keep Grant County a "dry" county or vote in favor of allowing alcohol to be sold

[5] 11 May 2000. *Grant County News.*
[6] 11 May 2000. *Grant County News.*

here, was given to County Clerk Judy Fortner on May 5.

The stack of petitions contained over 900 names including addresses, birth dates or Social Security numbers and the date the petition was signed.

Fortner, in turn, notified Grant County Judge Executive Darrell Link. Link, by law, must now verify that each person who signed the petition is a registered voter and was eligible to vote in the last election.

Kentucky law allows a wet/dry election to be placed on the ballot if the petition contains at least 25 percent of the number of votes cast in the last election.

Once Link has verified the names as registered voters he then will order a special election.

The election must then be held no earlier than 60 days nor more than 90 after the petitions were filed at the courthouse or within 30 days preceding or following a regular election.

Kentucky law allows that a wet/dry vote can't be held more than once in three years.

The county will pay the cost of the special election which will probably be held in August.

Local ministers were not surprised that a petition had been filed.

"We knew it was probably going to happen because of other legislation that the General Assembly considered." said Willie Ailstock. pastor of Dry Ridge Baptist Church and president of the Grant County Ministerial Association.

Membership in the ministerial association is open to any local minister. A monthly meeting is held at different churches.

"We expected it to happen sooner or later. so now we just have to get organized." Ailstock said.

'We expected it to happen sooner or later, so now we just have to get organized.'

- Willie Ailstock, president of the Grant County Ministerial Association

■

7

Ailstock said ministers had been encouraging their members to register to vote for the last several months in case the issue did make it to the ballot.

An officers' meeting for the association was planned for Wednesday, May 10, followed by an open meeting on May 31 at the Williamstown Christian Church.[8]

Court Adopts Entertainment Regulations

Nude Dancing, Alcohol Banned

The Grant County Fiscal Court has adopted rules for adult entertainment in Grant County.

In an unanimous decision, fiscal court members approved the second reading of a 26-page ordinance that regulates the establishment of a strip club, adult store or adult theater.

"This is basically to regulate any type of business that is adult-oriented," said County Judge Executive Darrell Link. "We want to protect the wholesomeness of this county."

Link said the court's intention was not to encourage an adult entertainment business, but to regulate one if an application is made.

"The court thought if a business like this did come in, then we would have some controls and regulations already in place." Link said.

The ordinance, which graphically defines terms specifically bans nude dancing, any form of sexual activity and straddle dances.

The ordinance will require anyone who wants to open an adult establishment to make an application along with a $750 processing fee. Anyone making an application must also post a $5,000 surety bond to the county.

[7] Circa May 2000. *Grant County News.*

[8] 11 May 2000. *Grant County News.* Jamie Baker-Nantz,Editor.

The ordinance also prohibits liquor sales at an adult establishment and prohibits patrons from personally tipping the entertainers. Any tips must be placed in a container, not on a performer.

The ordinance also requires that the management of any adult business maintain an employee registration containing the employee's legal name, any and all aliases, current address and phone number, date of birth, gender, Social Security number, date of employment, specific job duties, wage rate, both current and historical and tip income.

Anyone applying for a license to operate an establishment must provide the same information as well as whether they have within three years, been convicted of any criminal act.

The county judge-executive will serve as the adult use commissioner. The judge will appoint an adult use commission.

Establishments would be allowed to operate between noon and midnight Monday through Saturday, but would not he open on Sunday or any legal state or federal holiday.

The new ordinance applies to all of Grant County and each city except the city limits of Corinth. Because Corinth's boundaries fall between two counties, the county's ordinance will not apply.

The adoption of the adult entertainment ordinance was not prompted by the opening of a restaurant/strip club in Gallatin County.

Dick Austin, magistrate of the 1st district, discussed the need for an adult entertainment ordinance in January.

"I knew the issue had been an ongoing fight in Lexington and Northern Kentucky, so I thought it would be better to he prepared for it when it came," said Austin.

"Sometimes you think stuff that happens in big cities won't happen here, but I felt like if we were going to have it here, the best thing the court could do is regulate it. We're not endorsing adult entertainment." he added.

'We're not endorsing adult entertainment.'

- Dick Austin, magistrate of the 1st district

■

9

Members of the Grant County Ministerial Association were given an opportunity to examine the language in the ordinance. Several attended the court meeting when the ordinance was given a first reading and spoke in favor of the language, Link said.[10]

Wet/Dry Issue Headed To Voters

Voters will get the chance to vote on whether they want alcohol sales in Grant County.

A special election on the issue has been set for Tuesday, July 25.

A petition, asking for the special election, was given to County Clerk Judy Fortner on May 5.

The petition contained over 1,000 signatures. Grant County Judge Executive Darrell Link was required by law to verify that the petition contained at least 827 names (which was 25 percent of the votes cast in the last election.)

Link said the petitions contained some duplication of names, as well as some names of deceased singers and actors, but there were enough valid signatures to order a special election.

The fiscal court will pay for the cost of the special election.

Anyone wishing to register to vote has until Monday, June 24 to do so. According to County Clerk Judy Fortner, voter registration closes one month prior to an election, per Kentucky law.

All registered voters will be deciding whether they want to allow liquor sales in Grant County.

Kentucky law allows for a wet/dry county-wide election to be held only once in three years.

After the petition was filed, the Grant County Ministerial Association, composed of ministers of area churches, met to discuss the wet/dry issue.

David Tucker, pastor of Sherman Baptist Church and a member of the

[9] Circa June 2000. *Grant County News.*

[10] 8 June 2000. *Grant County News.* Jamie Baker-Nantz,Editor.

ministerial association, said it's not about telling members how to vote.

"I am going to encourage them on a personal level to knock on doors and encourage people to get out and vote," he said. "You've got to vote your conscience."

"As an individual I have some safety concerns," Tucker said. "There is a great opportunity to pick up those who are driving under the influence before they get to our door."

A group of concerned citizens has formed Keep It Dry and Safe (K.I.D.S.) The group is planning a community meeting at 2 p.m. on June 11 at the Cornerstone Church of God, 22 Warsaw Road in Dry Ridge. For more information call XXX-XXXX or e-mail the group at XXXX@XXXX.XXX.[11]

---

[11] 8 June 2000. *Grant County News.* Jamie Baker-Nantz,Editor.

CLIP AND SEND

Yes, I want to take advantage of the 4th of July offer.
Enclosed is $15 for 10 months.
Send to: Grant County News, P.O. Box 247, Williamstown, Ky. 41097
Name___
Address___
Phone___
Offer expires July 14, 2000 - not valid with other specials or discounts.
☐ New ☐ Renew

12

[12]Circa June 2000. *Grant County News.*

Local Minister Says Wet/Dry Issue Is One Of Safety

To the editor:

With the county's special election on July 25, we will decide one simple issue for our community safety. Now, many will claim it's about freedom, saying that we don't allow alcohol or drinking in our county. Others may complain that we will never grow economically without alcohol sales to bring in business. Don't be fooled, these arguments are groundless.

Let's look at argument number one. Are people really not free to drink in our county? No. Alcohol and drinking have always been permitted, even in this "dry" county. Any person with a refrigerator may choose to stock it, top to bottom, with beer if they so desire. Their real issue is the "inconvenience" of traveling 30 seconds across the county line to the package store to purchase it. Any group wishing to go out and eat in a restaurant where they sell alcohol with the meal can do so. Again, their only issue is the "inconvenience" of traveling 10 to 20 minutes into the next county. People in this county can and do drink alcohol, the only problem is that it isn't convenient enough.

Let's look at argument number two. Will our county wither away economically simply because there are no alcohol sales? No, of course not, just open your eyes to the change in our community. In the last three years, we've grown by leaps and bounds. In Crittenden, nine new businesses have opened their doors and the city is now running out of land for commercial use. In Dry Ridge, 20 new businesses have opened up and Mayor Bill Cull says that in 99 percent of his negotiations with future businesses, alcohol is not an issue. Alcohol is definitely not the Miracle-Gro of a county's economy.

Now let's look at the real issue at stake, our community's safety. I have long believed that because we are dry and because there are only two major entries into our community, we have safer roads and homes. Anyone who wants to tie one on must leave the county for the bars up north. Their problem is that once drunk, they must return by one of two heavily-patrolled roads, Interstate 75 or U.S. 25. They can take their chances on the back roads but if they are good and drunk, they will meet a tree or wall long before they see our county line. Now, 25 is straighter but any drunk can tell you that on 25 they will be passing by city police, county police and state police headquarters.

As one former state trooper said, "All you have got to do is sit up on U.S. 25, south of Kenton County, and it's like shooting fish in a bucket." (1)

I spoke with our present county sheriff, Randy Middleton, and he agreed that there is a kind of funnel effect and that the majority of their DUI arrests come right off U.S. 25. All of this topped off with our county's DUI conviction rate of 95 percent, and the result is clear. (2) A dry county means safer streets for your family and mine.

So this issue at the ballot box is not about the freedom to drink or trying to help our county's economy grow. It is all about helping law enforcement officers pick up and lock away danger at the county line instead of your front yard. Please vote for safety by voting "No" to the sale of alcohol in Grant County.[13]

Sincerely,
David Tucker
Dry Ridge

(1) Boyd Kiser as quoted by the Cincinnati Enquirer, Sept. 29, 1996.

(2) Research Report KTC-99-56 by the Kentucky Transportation Center College of Engineering in cooperation with the Kentucky State Police.

If Grant County Is Safe, Why Do DUI Cases Clog Courts?

To the editor:

Mr. David Tucker has concluded that the wet/dry vote is a matter of safety and I am inclined to agree with him, only for the opposite reason. In our county, you must drive across the county line to purchase alcohol, or to have a drink with your meal. Once you have done so, you must then travel back across the county line into our "front yards" as he so eloquently put it. I have yet to see that anywhere is it stated that our county

[13] 15 June 2000. *Grant County News.*

will "wither away economically" as grounds for the sale of alcohol.

The real issue at stake is safety - ours. Why should we continue to pay 25 percent higher insurance due to DUIs in our county and force those who wish to have a few drinks to drive "10 or 20 minutes into the next county?" The revenue that could possibly be gained by the sale of alcohol could actually benefit you. To quote Mr. Tucker's letter. "One former state trooper said, 'all you have to do is go up on U.S. 25 south of Kenton County and it is like shooting fish in a bucket.' " So, what you're really saying is that you don't want to make it hard on the officers who have to catch the DUI drivers. Not to say that this will solve it but if people have a chance to get it close to home, the chances that it will be drank at home is substantially higher than if they have to drive to another county to buy it. The result: not fewer caught DUI drivers, but fewer altogether.

In the Bible it states that Jesus turned water into wine. If it is such a sin to drink, then why not Kool-Aid or Tang? The only sin is gluttony and you can't force a drinker not to drink any more than you can force an overeater not to eat. They have to want it. Some of us enjoy a mug of beer or a glass of wine with dinner, so why should we suffer because some can't control themselves?

Also, I would like to ask Mr. Tucker if our county is so safe, why do we have so many cases of DUI under the district court docket clogging our system?

So, in conclusion, I have to disagree with Mr. Tucker who seems to think that our forefathers were mistaken when they concluded that the sale of alcohol was a liberty that should be granted to all of our citizens within a legal age, not just those outside of Grant County.[14]

Sincerely,
Maria L. Gregory
Dry Ridge

Kinmon Encourages Voters To Keep County Dry

To the editor:

I have lived in Grant County my entire life. The fact of our county becoming wet scares me to death.

I am a Christian but this isn't just about religion. If Grant County becomes wet, I'm sure we will have many deaths due to drunk driving. One of the biggest arguments for a wet county is having steakhouses. The steakhouses aren't that far away and I, for one, would rather drive a few extra minutes than to have to fear for the life of my loved ones due to those who make poor decisions and drink and drive. I know we have people who drive while drinking already in Grant County, but the police are able to monitor this problem. They do a wonderful job. If Grant County becomes wet, this is only the first of many poor decisions that will be made.

Yes, I am a Christian but that isn't my point. My point is I someday want to have children and raise them in this area.

I hope and pray they are given the privilege of growing up in a safe environment like I did. Some people may call me old-fashioned but I'm anything but that. At the age of 21, I'm just planning for the future when I have a family.

Please think about the safety of not myself but the safety of those you love. Think about the future of children today before you vote.[15]

Carolyn M. Kinmon
Dry Ridge

Personally Speaking

Mixing Alcohol With Business

Wet or dry? That is the question. Whether tis nobler in the county to suffer the slings and arrows of higher crime or to take votes against the seas of troubles, and by opposing them, bring more revenue and restaurants.

And what money may lie with such a decision? Ay, there's the rub.

Maybe William Shakespeare doesn't lend well to the wet/dry issue facing the county, but it seemed to fit the situation.

Grant County, want it or not, now finds itself embroiled in an issue that can literally divide people within it.

[14] 22 June 2000. *Grant County News.*
[15] 22 June 2000. *Grant County News.*

Man, woman, black, white, senior citizen or young adult, everyone seems to have an opinion on which choice is most beneficial to the county and its economy.

On the one hand, proponents of Grant County remaining dry suggest allowing the sale of alcohol will bring more crime, more drunk driving accidents, and prove detrimental in the long run.

The other side, those who want Grant County wet, throw the gauntlet of more money flowing into local business, more entertainment and restaurants being lured into the county's borders, and being able to compete with areas such as Northern Kentucky and Lexington for revenue.

Now let's separate fact from fiction.

Fact: Becoming a wet county will allow people to buy beer at Wal-Mart, Alice's and Bruce's Grocery.

That's true, so long as those businesses choose to sell alcohol. If having convenience of buying alcohol is what you want, vote for this bill because that's about all it will do.

Fiction: Alcohol sales will entice new entertainment and restaurants to build in Grant County.

Grant County doesn't have entertainment because Grant Countians don't support it. Talking to people around the county, you hear them speak of how Grant County needs a movie theater, bowling alley, roller rink, skating rink, or something. Yet the truth is Grant Countians didn't support a batting cage, so why would they support something else. Pro Maker's owners sold the batting cage, not because they didn't want to run it, but simply because no one patroned the establishment enough to make it profitable. And what's the first rule of a business? To be profitable.

As far as luring new, alcohol selling, restaurants to the area, it correlates directly with no entertainment. Eateries such as Ruby Tuesdays, Applebees, and T. G. I. Fridays locate near shopping malls, college campuses, or entertainment venues.

Quickly, think of the three Applebees locations in Northern Kentucky. Where are they? Turfway Road (Near the horse racing track, a movie theater, and shopping areas), Turkeyfoot Road (Near Thomas More College and Crestview Hills Mall), and Covington Landing (Across the river from the baseball and football stadiums and located in the renovated downtown Covington riverfront). Grant County has nothing like that in which to attract new business, alcohol sales withstanding.

Let's also look at the plight of Cracker Barrel. Cracker Barrel sells no alcoholic beverages, yet developers have lamented for years about not being able to attract the restaurant. Why? Nothing in the immediate area will help funnel customers into the restaurant.

Grant County's inability to match revenue made "Up North" isn't because of beer, wine, and liquor. It's because Grant Countians don't use Grant County businesses, which result in them closing shop and moving away. Grant County residents have gotten accustomed to traveling 30 minutes north or south for entertainment and shopping and alcohol will do little to change that learned behavior.

As a comparison, look at Boyle County. Boyle County, located south of Frankfort, was listed by Time Magazine as one of the top 10 small towns in America. They have two steak restaurants, a McDonalds, Dairy Queen, Fazoli's, Long John Silvers, K-mart, Wal-Mart, a movie theater, and countless other ventures. The year's vice presidential debate will take place in Boyle's largest city, Danville, and their Brass Band Festival attracts people from across the globe.

All that and Boyle County is a dry county.

Why can Boyle County be so successful? Boyle's citizens utilize the businesses, entertainment, and restaurants they have. The movie theater has people flowing in and out of its doors. The restaurants have plenty of customers ordering food. Can we say the same thing about Grant County, where two local grocery stores closed down within a month of each other and local businesses struggle on a weekly basis?

The simple fact of the matter is without support, local business dies and that doesn't look tempting to any outside entrepreneur looking to set up a franchise in Grant County.

Alcohol sales can't and won't solve that problem.

And finally, three more facts. Crittenden is the tenth fastest growing city in Kentucky. Dry Ridge has seen an explosion of development in just the last five years. And Grant County

[16] 22 June 2000. *Grant County News.* Wayne Yeager, Sports Writer.

is the second fastest growing county in the state.

You know the old saying. 'If it ain't broke, don't fix it.'[16]

(Personally Speaking is the opinion of the writer and does not necessarily reflect the editorial opinion of the newspaper.)

Grant County Doesn't Need Saloons

Editor's Note: Velda Turner requested this to be published in the Grant County News. It first appeared 15 years ago when the county was voting on whether to allow alcohol sales.

Dear editor,

Although I'm only 10, I feel I know what could happen to my county if we make the wrong decisions. I'm not old enough to vote no, and I will never change my mind about it. So please put in a vote for me.

Drunk driving kills millions of people each year. We have a little county but it has many corners that would have saloons on them that are loud and stink very much. I am sure that is what you do not want at every corner of Grant County.

Our county is very beautiful, so don't tear it up with stinking saloons. Leave it beautiful for our sake.[17]

Velda Turner
10 years old
Dry Ridge

Alcohol (Part One)

Alcohol creates an atmosphere for family failure Genesis 9:21 says, "And he drank of the wine, and was drunken, and he was uncovered within his tent." Alcohol is a drug that takes away the user's ability to make wise decisions. Noah failed after passing the great test of building the ark by faith. His weakness created family problems for generations to come. He failed to see the danger of using a product that disarms you.

Alcohol increases moral failure among its users. Habakkuk 2:15 says, "Woe unto him that giveth his neighbour drink that puttest thy bottle to him and makest him drunken also that thou mayest look on their nakedness." Proverbs 23:33 says, "Thine eyes shall behold strange women and thine heart shall utter perverse things." The result of being involved with alcohol is often disgrace, shame and in our day, even a slow agonizing death. Those who do not heed the warnings suffer great personal damage.

Alcohol mocks the users and opens them up to violence. Proverbs 20:1 says, "Wine is a mocker, strong drink is a brawler, and whoever is led astray by it is not wise." One advertisement used to say, "Know when to say, No." The only problem is the product advertised gradually removes from the user the ability to decide between safe and unsafe, good and evil.

Alcohol perverts judgment in the land. Proverbs 31:4-5 says, "It is not for kings, O Lemuel, it is not for kings to drink wine, nor for princes strong drink. Lest they drink, and forget the law, and pervert the judgment of any of the afflicted." All who are in authority should avoid mind altering drugs at all costs.

The Bible is filled with examples and warnings of failing to be under the control of God, the Holy Spirit. Let us beware![18]

Brother Lynn White is the pastor of Mt. Pleasant Church in Williamstown.

Dry Vote Won't Stop People From Buying Alcohol

To the editor,

I would like to comment on the question of wet or dry facing the Grant County voters.

It seems most everyone has a strong opinion, whatever their opinion is. Therefore, I may as well as air my opinion also.

First off, I can't believe anyone seriously believes that a wet vote would result in our highway turning into a soggy bumper car area where your chances of instant death greatly increases. If this is true, then my heart

[17] 29 June 2000. *Grant County News.*

[18] 6 July 2000. *Grant County News.* Lynn White, Weekly Devotional

goes out to those worried people and the stress they undergo each time they must bravely venture into Boone, Kenton, Harrison or Fayette counties, where they don't have to watch for their neighbors coming back from making a beer run. But once there, [they must watch for] all the other people who surely must be drunkards, for after all, they live in wet counties.

Also, it has been said that we in Grant County won't support entertainment as proven by the fact that a batting cage was unsuccessful. This also I find incredible. I know when I was a young man looking for female companionship, the batting cage was the first place I'd look, and after I married, if my wife had a choice of me taking her out for a dinner and a movie or to the local batting cage, well, there was no question at all, it was the batting cage every time.

Finally, I would like to comment on the Christian side of this issue. My holy Bible, which is the old King James version which Christians relied on for over 300 years, simply says, "Thou shalt not be a drunkard." "Have a little wine as it is good for the digestive system" as well as "Jesus turned the water into wine." As I live in New Testament times, I believe my salvation is through Jesus Christ, not on whether or not I consume a can of beer or glass of wine occasionally.

To sum up, I guess my opinion is that voting this county either wet or dry is 1) not going to change it much; 2) a batting cage is hardly the ultimate test of our willingness to support entertainment; and 3) that our churches would do well to preach only the word and quit adding or subtracting to it or from it.

Ultimately, with Cincinnati-Northern Kentucky spreading south and Lexington-Georgetown spreading north, if Grant County votes wet it may help some businesses who may be at the point of making a profit or not, decide to stay here or locate here, but voting dry will not prevent one person that wants a drink from getting one.[19]

Denny A. Roberts
Corinth

Business Can Be Successful Without Submitting To Pressure

To the editor:

To many of you who are new residents of Grant County within the last three and a half years, you did not have the privilege of knowing my late husband, Kelly Bruce, then owner of Bruce's at Mason, Ky.

Allow me to let you have an insight on some of his thoughts. When the Kentucky Lottery was getting a foothold, it wasn't discussed as an issue whether, Bruce's One Stop Family Store would participate in the program. Not for one moment did he think it was a good program.

First, many would buy tickets when they should have been buying food for their children, likewise, if alcoholic beverages are allowed, perhaps the wife could be neglected. Second, has the lottery helped education as much as publicized? If so, why are students selling magazines and other items for those things not provided through the lottery?

Now the real issue of this letter in relating to the column written by Wayne Yeager in the June 22 issue of the Grant County News.

I hurriedly read the article and seeing the name, "Bruce's," I reread the article more carefully. It is true whatever the outcome of the wet/dry election, the same opinion would be carried over to my sons, Lee and Scott, the present owners of Bruce's, from their dad and that decision whether to sell alcohol if the law allowed, the results or answer would be the same as for the lottery NO.

Other decisions that Lee and Scott make now, ask themselves the question, "Would dad have it done it this way?"

A business can be successful without submitting to outside pressures such as alcoholic beverages. The ingredients to doing this is to show compassion, concern and respect for your customers. The familiar saying concerning Bruce's is, "If you can't find what you want elsewhere, go to Bruce's. If they don't have it, they'll have it on the next order." Why not go there first? Save your gas.

I liked the last paragraph Mr. Yeager wrote, "If it ain't broke, don't fix

[19] 6 July 2000. *Grant County News.*
[20] 6 July 2000. *Grant County News.*

it," as well as the text of the entire column.

Thank you from a concerned mother, grand-mother and voter.[20]

Jewel Bruce
Mason

Alcohol (Part Two)

One of the driving forces behind alcohol is a desire to escape problems brought about as a result of violating the principles in God's word. Proverbs 31:6-7 says, "Give strong drink unto him that is ready to perish, and wine unto those that be of heavy hearts. Let him drink, and forget his poverty, and remember his misery no more." Dealing with problems without God is a painful experience.

Alcohol is not a solver of problems, it only delays finding real solutions. The following verses list six problems associated with alcohol and then states the source and results of the problems. Proverbs 23:29-32 says, "Who hath woe? who hath sorrow? who hath contentions? who hath babbling? who hath wounds without cause? who hath redness of eyes? They that tarry long at the wine; they that go to seek mixed wine. Look not thou upon the wine when it is red, when it giveth his colour in the cup, when it moveth itself aright. At the last it biteth like a serpent, and stingeth like an adder."

The shock of accidents, crime, violence, loss of health, family destruction and loss of jobs are just a few of the biting and stinging results of alcohol.

Alcohol is often associated with "the good life," meaning no work and all pleasures fulfilled. Proverbs 21:17 says, "He that loveth pleasure shall be a poor man: he that loveth wine and oil shall not be rich." The failure to have a strong moral standard is so often seen most dramatically in the "next" generation. What one generation allows in moderation, the next generation excuses in excess. By its very nature, all addictions must increase the amounts for our bodies and minds to get the same high of previous experiences.

Let us face life's difficulties without the clouding effects of alcohol or other drugs that dull our spiritual senses and seek God, our creator and true source of answers.[21]

Brother Lynn White is the pastor of Mt. Pleasant Church in Williamstown.

Alcohol Contributes To Domestic, Child Abuse Cases

To the editor:

One of my primary concerns regarding the possibility of Grant County joining the minority of Kentucky counties which are already "wet" is my concern for Grant County families. Three out of five reported incidents of domestic abuse and child abuse are alcohol-related. The facts ring clear from a host of sources alcohol affects families.

Being in a position where I am called to counsel and help disrupted and troubled families, it is not uncommon to find alcohol as one source of problems in the home. The bottom line happens when frustration mounts, communication lessens, tempers flare, and so often the bottle is sought for the answer. The answer to a troubled family is not found at the bottom of the bottle. Many times a root problem for families is strained financial burdens either from inadequate income or poor management of household income, and here again, spending necessary utility, rent payment, clothing, and food money on alcohol only adds to the problem. Also, it is proven that worker absenteeism and work-related injuries increase with even casual or occasional drinking, which immediately affect families.

Now, I know quite well that every person who buys a six-pack or drinks a glass of wine is not going home to beat up their wife/husband or abuse their children or skip work the next day. However, making alcohol more readily available and more commonplace in our community, I'm convinced, will raise a subtle but powerful question to the families of our community where can we find answers to our problems when they arise in a bottle to which we surrender control of our actions and words, or in sitting down, talking sensibly and finding solutions based on high

[21] 13 July 2000. *Grant County News.* Lynn White, Weekly Devotional

moral standards and responsible behavior and decisions?

Sure alcohol is already present in many families and homes, but bringing it closer to home and making it more readily available can only make a serious problem worse. Let's keep Grant County dry, for the family's sake.[22]

Terry L. Peer
Dry Ridge

For Christians, Voting Is Solemn Obligation

To the editor:

Grant Countians will go to the polls July 25 to exercise their responsibility as citizens of Grant County in a wet-dry issue ballot. Sadly, however, the opportunity to vote is often taken for granted and is altogether neglected and ignored by too many citizens including Christians.

For the Christian, voting is a solemn obligation, a sacred duty. Called to be salt and light in their world (Matthew 5:13-14), Christians can have an impact in Grant County through the voting machines this election day.

Every registered voter in this county will have the opportunity to keep this wonderful, God-blessed land free from alcoholic beverages by simply casting their vote against being wet. That is why Christians must be involved to cast their votes together, men and women of moral and spiritual conviction who will stand up for Godly values in our county.

Those who don't do anything, who don't participate, don't vote, will never have an impact for good. Every person in this county, whether Christian or not, has an obligation to do the right thing to be a part of our local government. God expects it of us. If we don't stand up together and vote no, our Lord and Savior will not be honored by our actions.

Righteousness exalts a nation, but sin is a disgrace to any people. (Proverbs 14:34)[23]

Jerry T. Martin
Serving the Lord at
Corinth Baptist Church

Grant County Hasn't Missed Out By Being Dry

To the editor:

I have been proud to have lived in Grant County and raised my family these past 30-plus years. The county has been dry all this time and we missed nothing. In fact, I rather enjoy walking in Williamstown, Dry Ridge, Crittenden, etc., without passing saloons or bars. In the grocery I did not have to look at the beer, or in the drug stores, liquor.

I lived in Covington and Erlanger growing up so I know what influence these places have on young people and older people. I know the results fights, drunks, shootings, unattended children, broken homes, etc. If anyone says this will not happen here, they are fooling themselves and others.

Let's not be a party to alcohol for the revenue, the problems will far outweigh the money. Let's keep Grant County dry for us and our children and grandchildren.

"Woe unto him that giveth his neighbour drink, that puttest thy bottle to him, and makest him drunken also, that thou mayest look on their nakedness." Habakkuk 2:15

I want Grant County to be the quiet, peaceful farming country I moved to, where people care about people. I believe this happened due to the fact there is no easy accessible beer or alcohol. I do not want to see saloons, bars, beer in groceries, alcohol in drug stores, no liquor stores at interstate exits ,and no carry-outs. I do not eat in places that serve beer or alcohol.

Don't get worn down with this wet/dry issue. Let's get out on July 25 and vote dry.[24]

Thank you,
Sondra Bailey
Verona

---

[22] 13 July 2000. *Grant County News.*
[23] 13 July 2000. *Grant County News.*
[24] 13 July 2000. *Grant County News.*

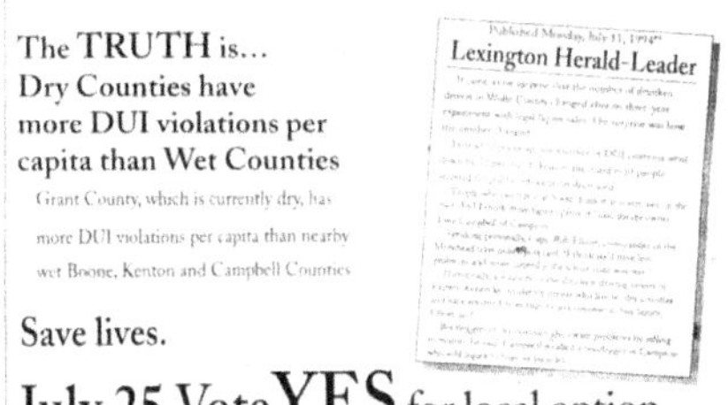

[25]

Wet/Dry Issue Divides County; Voters To Decide July 25

The clock is winding down for the day, July 25, when voters will decide whether to allow alcohol sales in Grant County.

If voters approve the measure then alcohol could be sold by the drink in local restaurants and in package liquor stores.

According to Dan Gahafer with the Alcohol Beverage Control in Frankfort, no liquor licenses are available until a wet/dry election is held. If voters then approve alcohol sales, the number of licenses available is based on the population of the county and the classification of the largest city in the county.

In Grant County, there would be one liquor license for every 2,500 people or approximately eight licenses.

Gahafer said there are several different types of licenses available (per drink, package and retail). Anyone wishing to make an application for a liquor license must get approval from the ABC and then pay for the license.

"None of these licenses are available until the vote is wet," said Gahafer.

Dara Florek of Dry Ridge is the treasurer of the Citizens for Freedom of Choice, which has placed ads in the Grant County News and Grant County Express encouraging voters to vote in favor of allowing alcohol sales.

Florek was responsible for organizing the petition drive to get the issue on the ballot. She collected over 1,000 signatures by going door to door, sending out letters and placing petitions in area gas stations.

Florek said she's the only member of Citizens for Freedom of Choice and the reason she got involved with the issue to give Grant County resident's a choice.

"I knew back in 1996 there was a petition drive, but the issue didn't make it on the ballot," she said. "So, I just thought it was time again to have people vote whether they want it here."

Florek said she believes the public doesn't understand that the population of the county will determine how many liquor licenses are available.

"There won't be bars or liquor stores on every corner," she said.

Florek said she also supports alcohol sales locally for convenience sake.

"Whenever someone comes over for dinner and you want to serve a drink, it's inconvenient to have to drive across county lines and buy alcohol," she said.

Florek said she doesn't believe it is a safety issue.

"I grew up here and I don't see more problems if the county was wet. It might cut down on problems because statistics show there are more DUIs (driving under the influence) in dry counties than wet ones," she added.

But the biggest reason Florek supports alcohol sales is because of the revenue she believes is being lost.

"I don't see a need to give Kenton County our tax money," she said.

Local ministers and some officials, however, don't agree.

"There is no money that will come into this local government on this wet/dry issue," said County Judge Executive Darrell Link.

The only way the county would benefit from alcohol sales, according to Link, is if more businesses located here and the county received property tax revenue from them. Link said the county's revenue comes from property taxes (including real estate and personal property) and the county's host agreement with the landfill.

"The county does not get any portion of our money based on sales tax, so it's not a large economic boom to Grant or any other county," Link said.

Link said he also sees costs for patrol of roads and incarceration for more DUI offenses increasing by alcohol being readily available.

Opponents to allowing alcohol sales in the county, including area ministers and church members, formed an organization, K.I.D.S. (Keep It Dry and Safe) in Grant County.

---

[25]Circa July 2000. *Grant County News.*

This group has also been placing ads in the Grant County News and Grant County Express, as well as undertaking a door-to-door campaign to encourage voters to vote against alcohol sales.

The last time the issue came before Grant County voters was in 1985. Voters defeated the measure by a 2-1 margin. If it is defeated, a countywide wet/dry vote can only be held once every three years.

Officials are predicting a heavy turnout for the special election on Tuesday, July 25. The polls will be open from 6 a.m. to 6 p.m. For information on polling places, call County Clerk Judy Fortner at XXX-XXXX.[26]

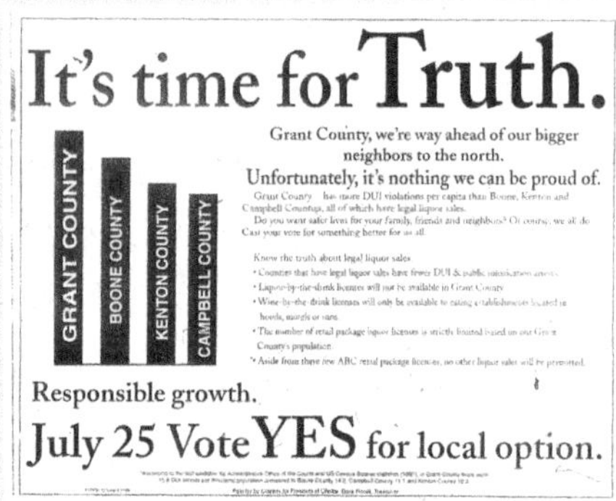

27

Alcohol (Part Three)

Reasons why we, as Christians, should never partake of alcohol.

- Even if we could control alcohol in our life, we are responsible for our weaker brother who cannot. Romans 14:21 says, "It is good neither to eat flesh, nor to drink wine, nor any thing whereby thy brother stumbleth, or is offended, or is made weak." The example we set before the world will be judged by God as to whether we walked in true love or self-gratification without considering other's spiritual growth.

- If we truly want to "get high," God recommends the Holy Spirit to fill us with excitement, joy, peace and source of wisdom and direction. Ephesians 5:18 "And he not drunk with wine, wherein is excess [a source of riot], but be filled with the Spirit."

- It was the prayer of the Lord Jesus Christ that his followers would be in the world, but not of the world [John 17:15]. Participating in a product that lowers our spiritual standards and conforms us to the world violates His will for us. Daniel purposed in his heart not to "defile" himself with the wine which the king drank [Daniel 1:8].

There are two types of wine mentioned in the Bible: unfermented wine was called "new wine." It was freshly squeezed grapes (grape juice). When some on the day of Pentecost wanted to mock the apostles speaking other languages which were present at that celebration of the giving of the law, they accused the apostles of being drunk on "new wine." [Acts 2:13] Fermented wine was an intoxicating beverage ("strong drink"). Several methods were used in Jesus' day to keep grape juice from fermenting: boiling down the grape juice into syrup, bottling the grape juice and storing it in a pond of cool water for 30 days or soaking raisins in water until juice was reconstituted. Grape juice that ferments on its own without control becomes spoiled grape juice.

When Jesus turned the water into wine at the wedding feast in Cana of Galilee, they had already drunk up the wine they had. Some of these feasts lasted several days. Yet, the host of the banquet immediately recognized the drink as superior in quality, demonstrating an alert perception, not drunkenness. Jesus made between 160 to 180 gallons of wine that day. Which type of wine do you believe the son of God put into the hands of man that day? Did he encourage the use of a destructive drink all scripture warns us about or the "new wine" of fresh pressed grape juice? Let us allow the Holy Spirit to be our "high."[28]

Brother Lynn White is the pastor at Mt. Pleasant Church in Williamstown.

An All Purpose Remover

To the editor,

I'm writing to say, vote "No" on alcohol. Keep us dry. Let's keep Grant County dry.

Alcohol, the all-purpose remover.

[26] 13 July 2000. *Grant County News.* Jamie Baker-Nantz,Editor.

[27] Circa July 2000. *Grant County News.*

[28] 20 July 2000. *Grant County News.* Lynn White, Weekly Devotional

Alcohol, used in sufficient quantity, will remove clothes from men, women and children.

Alcohol will remove furniture from a home.

Alcohol will remove food from the table.

Alcohol will remove lining from the stomach.

Alcohol removes vision from the eyes.

Alcohol removes judgment from the mind.

Alcohol removes reputations, jobs, friends, happiness, sanity, freedom and families.

Alcohol removes the ability to live with one another.

Alcohol, as a remover, has no equal. It can remove even life itself.[29]

Sincerely,
Jim Scudder Cordova

Bates Encourages Voters To Keep County Dry

To the editor:

As I awoke this morning my mind drifted back to childhood memories of Corinth, where I was raised. It was a pleasant place to grow up with one exception. That was the years from 1933, when the 18th Amendment was repealed until the citizens of Grant County had enough putting up with the liquor traffic and it was voted out.

I don't know what went on in the other communities but it was a bad time for Corinth. Liquor flowed freely, especially beer, and some people became addicted. There were drunk people weaving up and down the streets which made it unsafe for children. There were a lot of fights and several town officials were shot including the town marshal and one man was killed. These were all alcohol-related.

Since liquor was voted out in Grant County, things, for the most part, have calmed down.

We now have nice little peaceful communities where are children as well as adults can have a good life.

I hope that all Christians and others who seek the best for their families will vote "No" on July 25.[30]

Vivian Bates
Crittenden

County Needs Alcohol Sales Like It Needs Nuclear Explosion

To the editor,

Grant County needs the sale of alcoholic drinks like we need a nuclear explosion. We often hear, "Alcohol and drugs;" it should be "alcohol and other drugs."

Alcohol is a narcotic. (Get out your encyclopedia.) It depresses the central nervous system; at first the inhibitory functions of the brain are depressed, next the intellectual functions, then the sensory and reflex activities, the motor functions. If large amounts are ingested, vital nerve-centers of respiration and circulation can be depressed, resulting in death.

Alcohol depresses the cerebral centers, which control judgment, sense of responsibility, moral integrity, inhibitions. (Sound like anybody you know?) In today's fast and heavy traffic, drivers need all their skills intact. We don't need drinking drivers, drunken parties, abusive spouses and parents, and other alcohol-related crimes.

Further, if we vote "Wet," we send our young people the message that drinking alcohol is acceptable.

Some extol the economic benefits to the county. What dollar-value would you put on the life of a loved one, taken by an intoxicated driver or a violent "drunk." What about a precious young son or daughter becoming an addict because it's readily available and seen as acceptable?

There is not one good thing to be said for alcohol. Vote!

"Wine is a mocker and beer a brawler: whoever is led astray by them is not wise." (Proverbs 20: 1 NIV)

"Who has woe? ... sorrow? ... bruises?... When will I wake up so I can find another drink?" (excerpts from Proverbs 23:29-35 NIV)

God said it. that settles it![31]

Sadie Evelyn Lusby

---

[29] 20 July 2000. *Grant County News.*
[30] 20 July 2000. *Grant County News.*
[31] 20 July 2000. *Grant County News.*

Mason

Don't Ignore What Is Already Attracting People To Area

To the editor:

In the ongoing discussion over legalizing alcohol sales in Grant County, several arguments have been offered as sufficient reasons for making the sale of alcohol legal in our county. I would like to address several of these reasons and offer some observations.

It is proposed that we should make alcohol sales legal in Grant County because all of the counties are doing this. This fails to be a sufficient cause for legalization for two reasons. First, not all of the other counties are doing this. In an article published in The Kentucky Post on May 12, 2000 and written by Patrick Wood, the following figures are offered: there are eight Northern Kentucky counties that are wet, one is partially wet and three are dry. Those that are wet include Boone, Bracken, Campbell, Carroll, Gallatin, Harrison, Kenton and Mason counties. Those that are dry include Grant, Owen and Robertson counties. One county, Pendleton, is partially wet.

In looking at the state as a whole, 75 of Kentucky's 120 counties are dry (George Hunter, The Detroit News, Feb. 18, 2000). Realistically, not all of the other counties are offering legalized alcohol sales. Second, it should also be pointed out that simply because someone is doing something, regardless of how many are involved in the act, does not make it right. To offer that a substantial number of counties are offering alcohol for sale therefore it is right to sell alcohol is simply faulty reasoning. The same argument can be used for illegal drugs, adultery, child abuse or any other issue. Some things are always wrong regardless of how many are engaged in the act.

The argument has also been offered that by legalizing alcohol sales it would aid in the prosperity and growth of the county. Again, a careful look at the facts seems to tell a different story. In an article that appeared in The Cincinnati Enquirer and written by Mark Crowley, we find that Grant County is the second-fastest growing county in the Greater Cincinnati area. Its population increased 26 percent, from 15,737 in 1990 to 19,828 in 1997. Also, there are many restaurants that do business every day without selling alcohol. We are blessed with some good eating establishments now. The best way to attract other businesses is not by lowering our standards and offering alcohol for sale, but by patronizing the businesses that are here.

Success attracts more attention than anything else. Actually, we should ask the question why is our county growing now? I believe it is because it is a good, safe place to live and raise a family. Our schools are excellent, the crime rate is low and unemployment is equally low. These are all attributes that many communities envy. By seeking to legalize alcohol sales, we are ignoring what is already working to attract people to our community.

Finally, it has also been proposed that if we legalize the sale of alcohol in our county, it will actually result in safer highways because people will not have to drive as far for a drink. This argument ignores the fact that if the availability of alcohol increases, so too, will the chances that accidents will occur. According to Mothers Against Drunk Driving, 15,935 people are killed in alcohol-related traffic crashes an average of one every 33 minutes. These deaths constituted approximately 38.4 percent of the total of 41,471 traffic fatalities (NHTSA, 1999). However, in Kentucky, the percentage of accidents that are alcohol-related falls to 33.3 percent. The difference is the fact that 75 of 120 counties in Kentucky are dry and alcohol is more difficult to obtain. Proposing that the length of the trip to buy alcohol has a greater influence over the accident rate than the availability of alcohol is poor reasoning.

I simply would like to ask people to think about the upcoming referendum. Do we want to place a greater risk on our population by making alcohol more available? It is true that some people will always drink, but we have an obligation and responsibility to do what is right and best for our population as a whole, including those that do not drink. This includes not only adults who can choose to drink or not, but also children who have to live with the consequences of such a choice. Possibly, the bottom line of this whole issue has nothing to with the rights of the drinker, but with the desire to make some money.

We, as a community, should never allow financial success to become so important that we would be willing to sacrifice the quality of life that we enjoy here in Grant County. I ask you to please consider these matters and to vote responsibly on July 25.[32]

Thank you,
Rev. David Wiggins
Vine Run Baptist Church
Dry Ridge

Instead Of Speaking Out, Make A Real Difference

To the editor:

If there is anything that "chaps my cheeks," it is someone who tries to use God's word for their own personal gain. It is a fact that the Bible does speak out against drunkards and strong drink. But these products are fermented to create alcohol. And we all know what alcohol does if it is consumed. Jesus did turn the water into wine, but this is plain grape juice, not fermented. But the real kicker is the abuse of 1 Timothy 5:23. This is not meant to give us permission to drink. The word "wine" is the same as Jesus used: nothing more than plain grape juice. The interpretation of this passage of scripture is to use wine as a medicine, not a beverage. If ignorance is bliss, then some people are living in ecstasy. If you intend to interpret the Bible, then at least get an analytical concordance and a good set of commentaries. I stand against alcohol, and will vote as such. No good has ever come of it.

Secondly, God does not have a Top Ten List. Using terms like this makes His word sound unimportant. God set the standard for all to follow. Jesus followed that standard, setting the example. Jesus did not sin because he kept his eyes on the will of the Father. He sought after the kingdom of God. We are told to do the same. In order for that to be, we must let Jesus live through us, being submissive to the Fathers' will. Jesus was armed with the word of God, being the living word. That is all he needed, since His purpose on earth was different than ours. He had no reason to carry a weapon. Owning a gun is no different than owning a knife. Both have their proper uses.

Jesus rode on a boat and a donkey. But mostly he walked everywhere. So, as Christians, should we give up our motor vehicles, bicycles, etc., to do as Jesus did? Should pastors earn money for something they claim God has called them to do? Or should the church take care of them in the same fashion as the early churches? And what about music directors, piano players, organist, et cetera, that use their talents to glorify God in the church. Should they be paid also, even though that talent came from God?

Many people profess to be Christians, which means to be Christ-like. The problem is, people want to be like Christ in their own way. God gave us all sovereignty, the power to make our own choices. Some choose to kill, abort, maim, rape, destroy, lie, cheat, speed, play games of chance, smoke, drink, and so on. There are just too many to mention. We are smart enough to know when something we are doing or are about to do is wrong. We suffer the consequences of our actions.

It is not up to any one person or any group to tell others what to do when personal choices are involved. If a Christian wants to own a gun and use it responsibly, then who are we to say otherwise? The church has tried for too long to set standards in communities. God has already set the standard. The church simple needs to follow it, and in doing so, will set the example for others to follow. There is nothing wrong with speaking out against something that is immoral. But instead of just speaking out, why not do something that would make a real difference. Jesus did.[33]

Carl Floyd
Dry Ridge

Making People Drive To Get Alcohol Won't Stop Them

To the editor,

The wet/dry issue to be voted upon in Grant County has been a

[32]20 July 2000. *Grant County News.*
[33]20 July 2000. *Grant County News.*

hotly debated topic in recent weeks. The prospect of allowing alcohol sales within the county has received a lot of negative publicity from people who overestimate or misconstrue the effects of alcohol sales on Grant County and its citizens.

It seems to me that a lot of the people who have adamantly opposed allowing liquor sales within Grant County are under the assumption that just because the county is currently dry, residents do not have access to alcohol. This is absolutely not true. There are two liquor stores just over the Kenton County line. Many residents of Crittenden can obtain alcohol in closer proximity to their home than I could from my home in Boone County.

Furthermore, having to drive a few miles will not stop those who really want to drink from doing so. If a person feels that they need alcoholic beverages, they will take the necessary steps to obtain them. Those who abuse alcohol are not deterred by the fact that alcohol is not sold in the country. Allowing alcohol sales in the county will, however, make it easier for those who drink socially and responsibly to bring alcohol into their homes, where it can be consumed in a safe environment.

Another concern of opponents of alcohol sales in Grant County is an increased incidence of drinking and driving. Strangely enough, however, Grant County already has a higher DUI violation rate than several surrounding counties which are currently wet. Perhaps if the county does allow liquor sales, it will encourage drinkers to buy locally and consume alcohol in the privacy of their own homes, rather than going to bars in surrounding counties to drink and then driving home while intoxicated.

Others express concerns about bars and saloons popping up on every street corner. This simply will not happen. There would only be a limited number of liquor licenses available, approximately eight according to recent information, so simple mathematics tells-us that this would not amount to a bar on every street corner.

Many people who have responded in support of remaining dry have either directly stated or insinuated that allowing alcohol to be sold in the county will lead to the demise of the home and family. I have lived in Boone County for most of my life and the fact that alcohol is sold within the county does not make Boone County residents any more dysfunctional than those in any other county.[34]

Maria R. Russell
Verona

News Editorial

Not Voting = No Right To Gripe

Therels a choice to be made on Tuesday, July 25.

Grant County voters will decide whether or not to allow alcohol sales in the county.

It's been a hotly contested debate the last few weeks. Grant County citizens, for and against, have found themselves quoted in area and national newspapers. Some even found a few minutes of fame when they were interviewed by some television statements.

But the time for talk is nearly over and the time for action is just five days away.

Whether you agree or disagree with alcohol sales in Grant County isn't at issue. Everyone is free to make their own choice.

What is at issue is your responsibility to take the time to go to the polls and express your opinion.

Sitting around the morning coffee table with your buddies, or blowing off at the mouth with your Euchre friends or even being interviewed for a story or for TV doesn't matter a lick if you don't vote.

Voter turnout in the last couple of elections in Grant County has been pathetic and there's no excuse for it.

Everyone has a choice, just like they have an opinion. When voters make the conscious choice to stay away from the polls on election day, then they just lost their right to complain whatever the outcome.

The polls are open 6 a.m. to 6 p.m. If you don't know where to vote call Judy Fortner, the county clerk, at XXX-XXXX and ask. If you're not going to be in the county on July 25, you have until July 24 to vote by absentee ballot.

It's pretty simple. If you don't vote, then you don't have any right

[34] 20 July 2000. *Grant County News.*

whatsoever to gripe about the decision you let others make.

Don't ever be fooled. Every vote should and does count.

Editorials published in the Grant County News are the collective opinion of the News editorial team.[35]

Life is our Greatest Natural Resource.

Please keep Grant County Dry.

VOTE NO

July 25th.

Sponsored by Grant County Farm Bureau Federation Board of Directors.

36

Taylor Encourages Keeping Community Quiet And Small

To the editor:

Throughout the last few weeks, we have all read the statistics published on wet and dry counties. We have all read about the added income it could bring into the county and the new businesses that may choose to locate in our community if alcohol sales were permitted. Maybe we should all just take a minute and look at the social issues that accompany the issue.

There are things in today's society we all accept, like the tobacco issue. Everyone has become accustomed to the fact that most establishments have become smoke-free environments. Being a smoker myself, I now go to the mall and I do not smoke until I leave. I may sit through a whole meal if smoking is not available.

The same will hold true with alcohol being readily available. At 10 p.m. at night when someone wants alcohol you would be a lot more inclined to drive to town as opposed to crossing the line. Society has proven over and over we are easy prey to convenience, whether it be fast food, at-home shopping, paying bills electronically, whatever the case may be in the hectic fast-paced lives we have become accustomed to living, convenience is what we are looking for. If anyone thinks the convenience of obtaining alcohol would be any less abused, we are kidding ourselves.

We have a small, quiet community why can't we keep it that way? Our children are influenced by what they grow up around, seeing alcohol sales on a daily basis they grow up thinking that is just a part of life, it is not. I want my children to have the same opportunities I had growing up in this county. When I went through town I saw people I knew and local business people not neon signs and the weekly special on beer. It is our commitment to the children of this community for us to cast our vote and keep this county dry.[37]

Shelia Marksberry Taylor
Williamstown

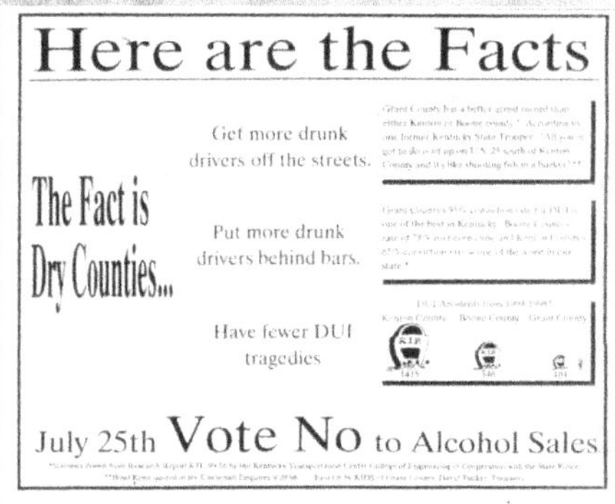

38

Wet/Dry Issue Sparks Debate

DRY RIDGE The KIDS (Keep It Dry and Safe) in Grant County are taking their message door to door.

Last week, the group who wants the county to remain dry covered Dry Ridge, Mt. Zion and Four Corners by knocking on doors and asking residents to vote next Tuesday, July 25 on the issue.

If no one is home, they are leaving flyers hanging on the door knob. This week the group, composed of local church members , plan to move to Williamstown and surrounding areas.

"Our main focus has been knocking on doors," said Willie Ailstock, pastor at Dry Ridge Baptist Church and president of the Grant County Ministerial Association, which helped organize KIDS.

Ailstock and members of the Dry Ridge Baptist Church found themselves in television last week when reporters from Channel 9 News showed up Sunday morning to tape interviews with some of the members.

---

[35]20 July 2000. *Grant County News.*
[36]Circa July 2000. *Grant County News.*
[37]20 July 2000. *Grant County News.*
[38]Circa July 2000. *Grant County News.*

Ailstock was also interviewed by a reporter from the New York Times about the upcoming wet/dry election.

"I have been surprised by the coverage, but I think it's been positive. We are hoping for more voter turnout because we think it will be better for us," Ailstock said.

Ailstock, along with several other members of Dry Ridge Baptist, left July 19 for a mission trip to Ecuador but before he left he cast his vote by absentee ballot.

According to County Clerk Judy Fortner, there have been about 75 absentee ballots cast as of Tuesday July 18.

"That's heavy," she said. "I don't recall recently having that many in any other election," Fortner said.

Voting by absentee ballot will be allowed until July 24 for anyone not going to be in the county on election day.

Grant County has 12,552 registered voters and Fortner is expecting a large turnout on July 25. The polls will be open from 6 a.m. to 6 p.m. For information on where to vote, call Fortner at XXX-XXXX.

If Grant County voters approve alcohol sales in the county, there will be a limited number of licenses available.

According to Dan Gahater, deputy commissioner of the state department of Alcohol Beverage Control, there will be approximately eight licenses available for restaurants in Grant County to sell alcohol. That number is based on one license for every 2,500 residents. The restaurants must have 100 seats and derive at least 70 percent of their sales from food.

Those licenses are calculated independently from the number of retail liquor licenses that are allowed. The state allows one retail liquor license for every 2,300 residents or approximately eight in Grant County.

The state has no quota on beer licenses. Once a county is voted wet, establishments wishing to sell beer have to make an application and pay for the license.

No liquor licenses exist for Grant County at this time, but once the voters approve alcohol sales, then anyone wishing to sell alcohol may apply for them.

Currently there are 75, of 120 counties in Kentucky, which do not allow alcohol sales. Thirty counties allow alcohol sales and 15 are dry counties with cities that allow alcohol sales.

Once a county holds a wet/dry vote, another one can not be taken for at least three years. However, a new law approved by the 2000 General Assembly, which took effect July 14, 2000 has changed that.

Senate Bill 247 will allow any dry city or county to vote on whether it wants just restaurants to be able to serve alcohol. If the wet/dry option is defeated in Grant County, then it would be 2003 before a county-wide election could be held again, but under Senate Bill 247, any city in the county could hold a wet/dry vote at any time.

According to a memo released by the Legislative Research Commission, precincts within a wet county may have a vote to consider banning alcohol sales, but a precinct in a dry city or county may not have an election to vote to be wet.

The last county to vote to approve alcohol sales, according to Gahafer, was Wolfe County and that vote took place in 1991.

With all the interest recently, Fortner is expecting a heavy turnout.

"Seems like a lot of people are talking about it." she said. "It has generated more talk than other recent elections."

Until the last vote is counted, Ailstock and those who support keeping Grant County dry, are remaining optimistic.

"We're hoping for a good voter turnout and from the people we've talked to, it seems like most everyone wants to keep the county dry," he said.[39]

See next Thursday's Grant County News for results from Tuesday's wet/dry vote.

What are the people saying?

The issue of whether Grant County should remain dry or should allow alcohol sales seems to have the citizens divided.

The Grant County News randomly called residents from the telephone book to ask their opinion on the issue. Some of those took the time to answer, some politely declined to answer and others just hung up the phone.

Here are some of the comments:

■ "I would prefer it to be dry. The county would be better off and safer," said Richard Evans.

■ "It should be wet because I think it would benefit the restaurant trade in Grant County. I don't think it will encourage too many drive-thru liquor stores," said Mary Lile.

■ "I would vote dry because it is not safe. I've raised seven kids and I know very well the dangers of alcohol. I don't drink and I don't care for anyone who does. If it passed, it would make it more convenient for young kids to get it," said Beldie Miracle.

■ "My personal opinion is it should be wet. People have to drive 50 miles to get their liquor. If it were closer, I think the people that drive out so far to get it are either drunk or they are drinking while they drive back. If it were closer, I think people would wait those last few moments to get home," said Annette Gadd.

40

---

[39] 20 July 2000. *Grant County News.* Jamie Baker-Nantz,Editor.

[40] Circa July 2000. *Grant County News.*

Wet Vote Won't Bring Rampant Drunkenness To County

To the editor,

I would like to comment again on the ism of wet or dry for Grant County.

It dismays me to see so many comments dealing primarily with rampant drunkenness in this county if we vote wet. I would like to appeal to these folks to stick with the issue at hand and not confuse our many citizens who like to relax with a can of beer or glass of wine after a hard day or week, at work and dealing with life in general, with those who overindulge drinking.

Those who live to drink already do so, as a few miles between them and the alcohol they love is no problem at all. If you look at this with your mind and not your fear, you know this is true.

So then the question is really should we force our citizens who work hard and lead lawful lives to drive past our stores and go elsewhere because they would like to have a 12-pack. They may as well do all their shopping elsewhere, where they can buy their groceries and a beer at one stop.

I challenge anyone to quote me a Bible verse that condemns the minor use of alcohol.

So far all quotes deal with drunkenness and the truth is drinking a beer or a glass of wine doesn't make a person a drunk anymore than eating a bologna sandwich makes a person a glutton.

To Mrs. Kelly Bruce, I would like to say that it is very refreshing to know of someone who puts principle ahead of money; we could all benefit by following this example. However, no one questions your right to choose whether to carry a legal product or nor, the many people in Grant County who use alcohol occasionally should be allowed to choose where to buy it. By where, I mean what county, not what store.

Driving up U.S. 25, 1 can't help notice that several stores have closed their doors. I can't help but wonder how many sales they lost simply because they couldn't carry everything people wanted so they, the customer passed on by to another place where they could buy what they wanted.

In closing, let me just say that if you believe voting wet will cause your neighbors to become drunkards, then by all means vote dry. But if you're like me and believe the drunks are here anyway, then stop forcing decent, law-abiding citizens to shop elsewhere. It's just that simple.[41]

Denny A. Roberts

Corinth

THE GRANT COUNTY BOARD OF ELECTION WILL INSPECT VOTING MACHINES FOR THE WET/DRY ELECTION ON JULY 14, 2000 AT 9:00 A.M. AT THE GRANT COUNTY COURTHOUSE.

42

Woodyard Says Experience More Truthful Than Figures

To the editor,

Yes, it is time for truth, but let's get the real truth. Experience is much more truthful than figures.

I'm almost 85 years-old and have more experience than most when it comes to the wet or dry question. I have lived through both and played music with my own band for a long time, mostly in northern Kentucky. Much of the time it was every night in the week and I know that very few drunks are arrested in a wet county even with an officer there. They said if you are allowed to drink it, why bother them if they drink a little too much.

But it's different if the county is dry. A wet county has more bootleggers so the officer says the county is wet, so what. Yes, I saw bootleggers sell it on Main Street, not so when it was dry so you cannot go

[41] 20 July 2000. *Grant County News.*

[42] Circa July 2000. *Grant County News.*

by the numbers you read in the papers. I have seen wives stand outside a saloon waiting for their husbands to come out. Many people that have moved from northern counties remark how much better it is in Grant County.

The only one making money will be the one who sells it.

The old excuse, Jesus made wine, is a poor one. Jesus did this under a special occasion to show his power and he made a special wine.

The most important thing is how does God look on this if you vote wet and help some young one get killed. What are you going to tell God?[43]

Thank you,
Wilbur "Bo" Woodyard
Williamstown

Is your News subscription paid?

Attention Voters

July 25, 2000 is a very important day for all citizens of Grant County. You and I can help keep Grant County a great place to live by voting NO to alcohol sales in our county. Did you know that a county does not receive any taxes from the sale of alcoholic beverages? This means no new taxes for our schools, county or city government. Did you know that Grant County, Scott County (Georgetown) and Boyle County (Danville) are among the fastest growing places in the state? None of these have alcohol sales. Compare these to Walton or Falmouth where alcohol is sold. Alcohol sales do not benefit the community.

We know that many of you who enjoy wine or other alcoholic beverages are responsible users. We also believe there are some, including our young people, who are more likely to abuse its use the more readily available it is.

We know of several families who have moved to Grant County in recent years because they believe that it is a good place to raise a family. We agree. We can not think of any way that the sale of alcoholic beverages in our county would make it a better place to live. The financial benefit for a few businesses would not offset the potential negatives for many of our citizens. We are sure that it would not reduce the work of our law enforcement agencies and our court system.

BE A RESPONSIBLE CITIZEN AND VOTE ON AUGUST 25. BE A WISE CITIZEN. VOTE NO.

Dr. Steve Sterneberg, Dr. Clay Parks, Bill Cull

44

Voters Decide To Keep County Dry

WILLIAMSTOWN - Forty-one percent of Grant County's registered voters have spoken and the county will remain a dry county.

By just over a 2-1 margin, a petition to allow alcohol sales in Grant County was defeated by 1,962 votes on Tuesday, July 25.

There were 1,591 votes cast in favor of allowing alcohol sales as opposed to 3,553 votes against. The issue was defeated in all of Grant County's 17 voting precincts.

As the results were read aloud following the vote count from each precinct, there were cries of joy from those opposing alcohol sales.

"I've lived here 27 years and it's been dry and I think we should keep it that way," said Edna Adams of Crittenden.

Adams shouted "Yes!" as returns were called out and it was obvious the county would stay dry.

Adams said she ate in Dry Ridge on Sunday and people were standing in line to be seated.

"We drank coffee and tea and had a great time," she said. "We don't need alcohol to do that."

Adams said she believed the voters would choose to keep the county dry, but waited tensely for results.

"It was a little scary with all of the new people in the county, but I'm very happy it turned out this way," she said.

The crowd broke out into cheers and clapped heartily as the last of the returns were announced.

"I believed it would be voted down 2-1 and I was right," said Judge Executive Darrell Link, who expressed his desire for the county to remain dry.

"I believe the new people moved out here for a reason." he added, "With the vote being slightly greater than 2-1, hopefully this is sending a message that we won't have to deal with this issue again in three years."

Once a wet/dry vote is held in a county, Kentucky laws requires a three year wait before a petition drive to get the issue on the ballot can be held.

Danny Link, Darrell's brother, booed as the results were announced.

"Eventually it will go wet," Danny said.

Danny Link said he respected the vote, but was sorry the county would not allow alcohol sales because it would limit the number and type of restaurants that would locate here.

"I wish it had passed," Danny said. "I would have liked to go to Dry Ridge or Williamstown to eat at Red Lobster or Applebee's. I don't eat at fast food places and it would have been nice not to have to drive to Florence to eat somewhere nice."

Rep. Royce Adams, D-Dry Ridge, wasn't surprised by the outcome.

"The Associated Press in New York called me yesterday and I told them it would stay dry by about a 2-1 margin," Adams said.

---

[43] 20 July 2000. *Grant County News.*
[44] Circa July 2000. *Grant County News.*

Adams said that he believes many of the statistics that appeared in advertisements encouraging people to vote in favor of alcohol sales were misleading, but the churches in the county were organized in attempting to get voters to go to the polls.

Local churches in Grant County formed a group called KIDS (Keep It Dry and Safe) in Grant County. Volunteers knocked on doors and passed out flyers encouraging church goers to vote against alcohol sales.

"This sends a message that the people aren't ready for alcohol to be served in Grant County," Adams said.

Adams said that while many of the signatures that appeared on the petition asking for a wet/dry election were from the Crittenden area, he believes that segment of the county's population isn't interested.

"I feel Crittenden is largely a transient population and (they) probably don't care what happens. A lot of people live in apartments and work up north. If they want alcohol they just stop and pick it up on the way home," Adams added.[45]

Editor's Note: Rebecca Russo, editorial assistant, assisted with this article.

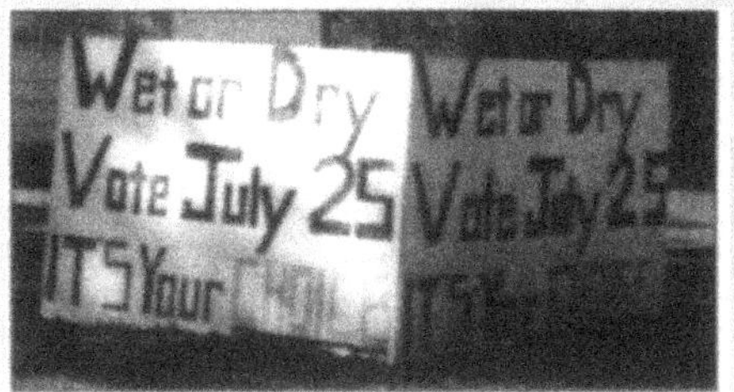

[46]

Liquor Store Robbed

In less than two minutes on April 2, a knife-wielding bandit made off with an undetermined amount of cash from County Line Liquors located north of Crittenden on the Grant/Kenton county line

"The employee in the store saw him and even people outside did, but nobody wrote down a license plate number or anything," said Ralph Deitz, owner of the store.

He added that the store has been robbed once before since opening in July 1996.

The robber was a white male in his late teens or early 20s, approximately 5 feet, 2 inches tall with a skinny build. It is possible he had a blonde mustache.

He left the scene in a white, 2-door car with a cracked windshield and headed south on U.S. 25.

Another person was waiting inside the car, but police aren't sure whether it was a male or female.

Deitz is offering a $1,000 reward for information leading to the arrest and conviction of the robber.

Call Detective Chris Middle at XXX-XXXX with any information.[47]

Children Should Be Taught Alcohol Is Not Essential To Good Time

---

To the editor:

Recent newspaper articles and television news stories on "malternative" beverage marketing speak to an issue that is very important to me, and to Kentucky. Children see and hear messages about alcohol every day. Billboards and promotions for alcoholic beverages often display attractive young people or cartoon characters, encouraging kids to think that alcohol use is accepted,expected, and essential to having a good time. It's clear that these messages are reaching our children. The Center for Science in the Public Interest's recent poll reported that underage drinkers were more likely to try these sweetened "alcopops," and that 41 percent of 14- to 18-year olds said they had actually tried an alcohol pop drink.

Studies show that more than 2.1 million minors are considered to be heavy drinkers, and that more than 100,000 12-13 year olds binge drink every month. The danger to our youth is clear. Preliminary studies now indicate that heavy, regular drinking can damage the developing brains of teens as well, and impair brain cells involved in learning and memory. And this problem doesn't just affect the kids who are drinking. A re-

[45] 27 July 2000. *Grant County News.* Jamie Baker-Nantz,Editor.

[46] Circa July 2000. *Grant County News.*

[47] 11 April 2001. *Grant County News.* Rebecca Russo, Editorial Assistant.

cent study at the University of Washington found that alcohol abuse by seventh-grade students also had a negative impact upon learning and performance of non-drinking students in the class. Since children are drinking more and at earlier ages, the implications of this research for our children's health and future success must be taken seriously.

As a member of the Leadership to Keep Children Alcohol Free, I have joined with 28 other governor's spouses to address this issue and prevent children from using alcohol. Alcohol is our children's number-one drug of choice. It is time we faced the issues openly and honestly. Alcohol is not a rite of passage, and its use by children is every bit as dangerous as illegal drugs. As First Lady, I am committed to raising public awareness to this issue and I invite parents, businesses, the media, opinion-leaders and policy makers to take action to prevent this silent epidemic.[48]

Judy Patton
First Lady of Kentucky
Leadership to Keep Children
Alcohol Free

Surprised To Find Beer Cans

To the editor,

Hi! I'm Kara Caldwell from Williamstown Schools. I participated in a trash pick-up for the Athletic Boosters earlier this year.

I think people should not litter because it makes our roadsides look bad. I was surprised to find a lot of beer cans. People who are drinking and driving - please stop!

So stick with me and if you see any trash on the side of the road, please pick it up. Better yet, don't litter at all.[49]

Sincerely,
Kara Caldwell
Mrs. Popham's fifth grade

Corinth To Vote On Alcohol Sales

The residents of Corinth may get the opportunity to decide if they want to have liquor sales inside the city limits.

The Kentucky Court of Appeals handed down a decision last week that reversed a ruling by Grant County Circuit Judge Stephen Bates that denied a local option election in Corinth. A three-judge panel has returned the case to Grant County Circuit Court.

The case was appealed by Anna Francis "Frankie" Dalton who owns Freeway Restaurant in Corinth who had submitted a petition for a local option election to Judge-Executive Darrell Link last year.

Dalton's petition contained 59 valid signatures, which was enough to qualify for the ballot. However, Link refused to set an election and was upheld by the circuit court.

Bates ruled in June 2002 that a law allowing cities in dry counties to hold special elections did not apply to towns as small as Corinth. A law passed by the General Assembly in 2000, allows cities to decide whether to allow liquor sales in restaurants that seat at least 100 people and derive 70 percent of their receipts from food sales.

Cities in Kentucky are classified from 1 to 6, with 1 being the largest. Cities of 999 or fewer residents are classified as a sixth class city. Corinth has a population of 200 residents.

Link said the law was unclear and he was advised by the county attorney that to allow the election to go forward would be illegal.

Link said he had not received any official notification of the Court of Appeals' ruling as of Oct. 13.

"At least the law is clarified now, so we know what a higher court will uphold." he said.

"The General Assembly obviously believed that these cities and counties also have economic needs that can be met by the limited sale of alcohol in otherwise dry territories," Chief Judge Tom Emberton wrote in his decision.

The case was returned to the Grant County Circuit Court for further proceedings, which means Bates will order Link to schedule a vote. It is too late for the issue to be included on the ballot for the upcoming Nov. 4 election, which means a special elec-

[48] 31 May 2001. *Grant County News.*
[49] 3 July 2003. *Grant County News.*

tion will probably be held in January 2004.

"There just isn't enough time to get it on the ballot which means there will have to be a special election," said Robert Gettys, a Covington attorney who represented Dalton.

"I was confident throughout this ordeal and everything is still in place with the developers. This would be a terrific boon to that little town because there will be jobs and new people moving in and those people will need services," Gettys said.

Billy Hill, mayor of Corinth, is glad that local residents will be able to make the decision.

"This vote isn't about having bars on every corner, but it's about allowing alcohol sales by the drink in restaurants and golf courses and that will very much benefit the city," Hill said.

The City of Corinth annexed 1,800 acres two years ago after property owners approached them about the possibility of a golf course/resort style development. That annexation more than tripled the city's size.

"We annexed that property with the intention of bringing jobs and economic development here," Hill said.

Hill said he personally had not seen plans for the development, but had seen brochures of other developments by Tee to Green Inc., a division of Landmark Golf. Hill said he had also stayed at one of Landmark's developments in Myrtle Beach.

"It was simply beautiful," he said. "I hate to hang an entire development on one issue, but the developers have to know they'll be able to sell alcohol before they go forward."

Walt Ramey, a real estate agent with Jim Huff Realty spent the last two years wrangling to keep the developers interested in the project.

"It's totally ridiculous that we had to go to all this trouble," Ramey said. "We told the administration in Grant County what the law said, but they fought us every step of the way."

Tee to Green Inc. is still "very much interested" in developing a project in Corinth that would include two to three golf courses, a restaurant with a least 100 seats, a large destination hotel with a lounge and meeting rooms as well as a housing development, Ramey said.

"We're not talking red neck bars, but fine dining establishments, but we can't do anything until we get these stumbling blocks out of our way," he said.

We're not talking red neck bars, but fine dining establishments, but we can't do anything until we get these stumbling blocks out of our way.

—WALT RAMEY
REAL ESTATE DEVELOPER

50

Bob Wallace was counting on the election taking place. That's why he purchased nearly 900 acres in Corinth.

"We're talking a project that is over $100 million and there's already a couple of restaurants who have bought land and are just waiting to see what the decision would be," Wallace said. "It would be a shame if the county decided to appeal the court's ruling, it might be the last straw."

The county has 30 days to appeal the Court of Appeals' ruling.

For Hill and the Corinth City Commission, its like walking a tight rope.

'We're just trying to make ends meet," he said. "But just being allowed to vote on the issue is a victory. Voting is one of the last great privileges that we have and it was a shame that we were being denied that opportunity."

For the county, the appellate court's decision, could have larger ramifications.

"The Court of Appeals has just ruled this is applicable to any city or precinct so that means that any city or precinct can petition for a wet/dry vote, so when you reduce it to a smaller geographic area and say that it's only for restaurants that seat 100, it's more palatable to many. I think it's the first of many to come," Link said.[51]

'Moist' Election Set For Jan. 20

---

[50]Circa October 2003. *Grant County News.*

[51] 16 October 2003. *Grant County News.* Jamie Baker-Nantz,Editor.

Residents in Corinth will get the opportunity to vote on alcohol sales in a special election on Jan. 20, 2004.

Circuit Judge Stephen Bates ordered Grant County Judge-Executive Darrell Link last week to set a date for the local option election. That same day, Dec. 17, Link issued an executive order on alcohol sales inside the city limits of Corinth.

Voters in precincts #9 and #19 will be deciding whether alcohol can be sold, by the drink, in restaurants that seat at least 100 people and derive at least 70 percent of their receipts from food sales.

"We basically had a short window because of the time that had elapsed. We had to pick up where the clock stopped," Link said.

Allowing alcohol sales in restaurants is an issue that began in January 2002, when Anna Frances "Frankie" Dalton filed a petition containing 59 valid signatures to Link, asking for a special election on the issue.

Link refused, saying Corinth didn't meet the requirements as set forth by Kentucky law that allowed a local election on alcohol sales.

A law passed by the General Assembly in 2000, allows cities to decide whether to allow liquor sales in restaurants that seat at least 100 people and derive 70 percent of their receipts from food sales.

Bates upheld Link's decision when he ruled in June 2002, that a law allowing cities in dry counties to hold special elections did not apply to towns as small as Corinth.

Corinth, with a population of 200 residents, is classified as a sixth class city. Cities in Kentucky are classified from 1 to 6, with 1 being the largest. Cities with a population less than 999 or fewer residents are classified as a sixth class city.

However, the Kentucky Court of Appeals issued a ruling in October 2003, that Bates should order Link to set a date for the special election.

Dalton, who operates Freeway Restaurant in Corinth, and other surrounding land owners, have said alcohol sales are necessary to land a golf course resort development for the southern end of the county.

Dalton, who has lived in Corinth most of her life, said she's not interested in alcohol sales, but it would be for developers who've expressed an interest in Corinth.

"This has been a long time coming and I think people deserve the right to vote on it," Dalton said. "My intentions aren't to have alcohol sales at my restaurant."

This has been a long time coming. This is going to be good for the economy and it's going to create jobs. Without jobs this area is dead.

—FRANKIE DALTON
OWNER OF FREEWAY REST.

[52]

The city of Corinth annexed 1,800 acres two years ago after property owners approached them about the possibility of a golf course/resort style development. That annexation more than tripled the city's size.

Walt Ramey, a real estate agent with Jim Huff Realty, has spent the last two years wrangling to keep the developers interested in the project.

Tee to Green Inc. is still "very much interested" in developing a project in Corinth that would include two to three golf courses, a restaurant with a least 100 seats, a large destination hotel with a lounge and meeting rooms as well as a housing development, Ramey said.

"This is going to be good for the economy and it's going to create jobs. Without jobs this area is dead." Dalton said.

However, there are some residents of Corinth who were not pleased about the possiblity that alcohol may be sold in their community.

"I was saddened to hear the court over-rode Judge Bates' decision," said Rev. Bob Stun, pastor of Corinth Baptist Church.

"I want to see this community grow, but not at the expense of alcohol," he added. "It opens the door for too many other things to take place in our community. We're one of the few cities along Interstate-75 that isn't troubled by problems associated with alcohol. I believe in my heart when an economy has to have alcohol, it's in trouble. Why can't we have golf courses without it?"

Mic Bowen, pastor of Corinth Christian Church doesn't want to see the close-knit community split over the vote.

[52]Circa December 2003. *Grant County News.*

"My own personal belief is that I don't think alcohol sales are necessary to improve a community, but I do think we should have the right to vote on the issue," Bowen said.

Both ministers said they understand that in order for the community to prosper, more businesses are needed.

"I think we need to encourage more development, but what concerns me is that a large entity from out of town would be dictating to us what our community must do in order to grow," Bowen said.

"This has opened a can of worms," said Sain. "I hope a compromise can be reached, but not at the expense of alcohol sales."

Link, who grew up in the Corinth area, said he was never opposed to the voters in Corinth having a say on whether alcohol sales should be allowed, but rather he believed he was following the law.

"Who in their right mind would be against Corinth having something good?" Link said. "I just hope and pray for the people's sake in Corinth, there is a development. I believe the legislation has opened up a Pandora's box and we will see petitions for alcohol sales on every exit in Grant County."[53]

Personally Speaking

Alcohol Sales: You Choose, You Lose

In a little less than two weeks, the citizens of Corinth will get the option of voting for or against alcohol sales in their city.

This won't allow bars and taverns to set up shop in Corinth. Instead, it'll allow restaurants with at least 100 seats to sell alcohol by the drink if 70 percent of their sales come from food.

And while Corinth does deserve the right to vote on such a proposal, they don't need to vote yes.

The arguments for alcohol sales are well-documented. It will bring growth, in particular a golfing resort by Tee to Green Inc. that will include two or three golf courses. a hotel and a restaurant. The hope by proponents of a "yes" vote is that additional restaurants (those that sell alcohol with dinner) will take up residence in Corinth, the only city on the I-75 corridor between Walton and Georgetown that would be "wet."

But the question remains, who will benefit from a "wet" vote?

Will it be the citizens of Corinth who don't own some of the coveted land wanted by developers? Not likely. They can't sell their land for lots of money. They won't see the "benefits" of the golf course or the possible restaurants.

Counterpoint

Will it be the citizens of Corinth looking for a job? Not unless they want minimum wage jobs at the new golf resort. The jobs Tee To Green Inc. will bring will be bus boys, servers, groundskeepers, custodians and the like. There is nothing wrong with those jobs, but corporations do not pay top dollar for those positions, especially in an area where there aren't a lot of other competitors for good employees.

Will it be the citizens of Corinth looking for more civil services from their city government? Depends on what services they want. There's no doubt this development will bring more tax revenue to Corinth. However, this development will also bring with it the need for other services, like more police. With a new housing development, a new golf resort and a restaurant, Corinth will need to provide safety for their citizens and their new businesses. Not to mention, there will be the increased potential for drunk driving and domestic abuse, which again, will need more police.

So, who does this proposal benefit again? Well, obviously those with land to sell. They'll be the ones making the money in this deal.

And let's not forget the Landmark Golf Company. Landmark Golf Company, out of California, is the parent corporation of Tee to Green Inc. They will be the ultimate winner. They will have convinced a small town in Kentucky that going "wet" was in their best interest. They will build their golf course and they will take in the money Corinthians and others will pay to eat at their restaurant, play on their course and stay at their hotel.

If Landmark is the ultimate winner, then all of Grant County will be the ultimate loser in a "yes" vote for alcohol sales.

You see, though this is a vote limited just to Corinth, a "yes" vote will impact the entire county.

[53] 25 December 2003. *Grant County News.* Jamie Baker-Nantz,Editor.

It will start with Corinth. Then the focus will shift to Williamstown. After all, they have new expressway [] cultivate and a need to develop at a pace similar to Dry Ridge and Crittenden. From there, a movement will begin to get Crittenden to approve alcohol sales. And once three of the four major cities of Grant County are wet, a county-wide initiative will have no trouble passing.

Is that just a worst-case scenario? Maybe, but it is a very real possibility. After all, sometimes going after the sum of your parts is greater than taking on the whole, and the whole of Grant County voted down the last wet/dry initiative by a large margin.

Some are going to say this election is all about choices. They'll paint a wonderful picture of all the development that will come to Corinth to make that choice hard to pass up. When they do, ask the same questions above.

If you do, you'll likely come to the same conclusions, which will leave you no choice at all.[54]

Wayne Yeager is the sports writer at the Grant County News. He can be reached at XXXX@XXXX.XXX

(Personally Speaking is the opinion of the writer and does not necessarily reflect the editorial opinion of the newspaper.)

City Residents To Get Say In Jan. 20 Vote

There might be 1,304 registered voters in the #9 and #19 precincts in Corinth, but less than 10 percent of those will be eligible to vote in the Jan. 20 special election which will determine whether alcohol can be sold in restaurants that seat 100 people and derive 70 percent of their receipts from food sales.

Corinth Mayor Billy Hill is concerned that because interest is high in the alcohol issue, voter turnout will be larger than normal, but some voters may come to the polls only to be turned away.

Only residents who live in the city limits will be able to vote in the election.

"If you pay city taxes or live in an apartment inside the city limits, then you can vote," Hill said.

He said residents from Corinth had been calling the city building inquiring about whether they could vote or not.

"So many of the people who have a Corinth address think they can vote, but that's not the way it is," he added.

Hill estimated that less than 100 of the 1,300 registered voters in the #9 and #19 precincts were eligible to vote.

"1 wish that it was a nice big square area, so it would be easy to determine who could vote and who can't but it's not that way," Hill said. "Precinct workers will have to be diligent to determine who actually lives in the city limits."

Hill said precinct workers would have a map at the polling place to aid them.

City roads and streets in Corinth include Hwy. 330 (through 325 Owenton Road), Main Street (210 through 420), U.S. 25 (10865 through 11180 Dixie Hwy.), Old Corinth-Owenton Road (235 through 430), Woods Lane (225 through 240), Knox Lane (215 through 245), Corinth Road (215 through 255), Depot Street or Depot Road (210 through 240), Church Street (220 through 255), Hamilton Lane (210 through 280), Stringtown Road (235 through 270), Thomas Lane (215 through 300), Rook Circle (210 through 250), Owenton Road (on west side of U.S. 25 up to 1865 Owenton Road) and Morgan Creek Road (all residences on right side of road 245, 295 and 505).

Both of Corinth's precincts are housed in the Corinth City Building on Thomas Lane. The polls will be open from 6 a.m. to 6 p.m. City offices will be closed that day.

In order to be eligible to vote in the election, voters had to register by Dec. 23, 2003.

"We've had one lady who called up and wanted to know how to get registered, but the deadline has passed, so if you haven't already registered to vote, you won't be able to on Jan. 20," said County Clerk Judy Fortner.

Allowing alcohol sales in restaurants is an issue that began in January 2002, when Anna Frances "Frankie" Dalton, who operates Free-

[54] 8 January 2004. *Grant County News.* Wayne Yeager, Sports Writer

way Restaurant in Corinth, asked for a special election on the issue.

Grant County Judge-Executive Darrell Link refused saying Corinth didn't meet the requirements as set forth by Kentucky law that allowed a local election on alcohol sales.

A law passed by the General Assembly in 2000, allows cities to decide whether to allow liquor sales in restaurants that seat at least 100 people and derive 70 percent of their receipts from food sales.

Circuit Judge Stephen Bates upheld Link's decision when he ruled in June 2002 that a law allowing cities in dry counties to hold special elections did not apply to towns as small as Corinth.

Corinth. with a population of 200 residents, is classified as a sixth class city. Cities in Kentucky are classified from 1 to 6. with 1 being the largest. Cities with a population less than 999 or fewer residents are classified as a sixth class city.

However, the Kentucky Court of Appeals, issued a ruling in October 2003, that Bates should order Link to set a date for the special election, which Link set for Jan. 20.[55]

Is your News subscription paid?

Personally Speaking

Moist Vote Wets Developers' Lips

Voter turnout should be near 100 percent on Tuesday, Jan. 20 when the residents of Corinth vote on alcohol sales during a special election.

On the ballot will be whether or not alcohol can be sold, by the drink, in restaurants that serve at least 100 people and derive at least 70 percent of their receipts from food sales.

Obviously a contentious possibility, there are those on both sides of the issue - who oppose and support the sale of alcohol in Corinth who feel that if the city votes to go "moist," then other cities, and the county, are sure to follow.

This may or may not be the case, as only time will tell, but as for now the "liquid matter" will be resolved among Corinth's voting-age population.

A petition with 59 valid signatures got the issue on the ballot, but the end result remains to be seen.

If the sale of alcohol was the only factor involved in most people's decisions, then I suspect the moral majority would vote against the issue and the city would remain dry.

But this is not just about alcohol. It's about money. It's about development. It's about jobs. It's about the future.

And before every future, there is a definite past.

Over two years ago, the city of Corinth annexed 1,800 acres and more than tripled the city's size on the behest of nearby property owners who informed the city commission on the possibility of a golf course/resort development for that area.

Tee to Green Inc. is still interested in the Corinth project, which would include two to three golf courses, a minimum 100-seat restaurant and destination hotel, as well as housing developments. But first they want to make sure that alcohol will be on their menu.

The question is: are the voters of Corinth interested in a future that involves alcohol?

In an ideal world they would not need alcohol sale incentives to attract economic boom. But this is the real world; and it's far from ideal.

The reality is, most Corinth residents have noticed the sweeping increases in both residential and commercial development elsewhere in the county from Williamstown to Crittenden.

They have read and heard the comments from public officials and real estate agents who agree that Corinth's varied landscape does not lend itself to most development that has occurred on flat ridges to the north.

And they have entertained the thought, I suspect, that if they don't answer the phone on this one, another large-scale development might never call again.

Like it or not, the economic future of the city and by some extent, possibly the county could depend on a few votes.

So while I don't live in Corinth and I don't have a vote, I'll respect whatever decision they make. At least there is a choice.

Somewhat obscured amid the ongoing debate of alcohol or no alcohol is the fact that the people will decide this issue as they should.

[55] 8 January 2004. *Grant County News.* Jamie Baker-Nantz,Editor.

Collectively, Corinth may chose to go "moist," but the individual choice to drink or not to drink will always remain.

It's advantageous, from an economical perspective, for menus to be as diverse as possible in their beverage selection.

The same goes for cities seeking development - the more diverse, the better.

Sure, a "yes" vote on alcohol sales doesn't necessarily mean a "yes" vote for a golf course in Corinth. Acres of tobacco farmland, long since profitable, may or may not become fairways and putting greens.

But if it does happen, and golf courses succeed in opening up the southern part of the county to more development and a stronger, local economy...

I'll drink to that.[56]

Jason Feldmann is a staff writer ar the Grant County News. He can he reached at jfeldmann@grantky.com

---

(Personally Speaking is the opinion of the writer and does not necessarily reflect the editorial opinion of the newspaper.)

Question Remains Whether Alcohol Sales Will Spur Development

The issue that went from Corinth all the way to Court of Appeals will now be settled by the voters when city residents will vote on whether to allow alcohol sales by the drink in restaurants that seat 100 and derive 70 percent of their receipts from food sales.

Registered voters who live within the city limits of Corinth will have from 6 a.m. to 6 p.m. on Jan. 20 to vote for or against alcohol sales in Grant County's smallest city.

If voters approve alcohol sales, they will join a number of other small cities in Kentucky who have decided to attempt to bring economic prosperity to their communities who have difficulty competing for businesses and industry with their larger sister cities.

Currently, Kentucky has 30 counties that are considered wet where alcohol is sold in restaurants and in package liquor stores. Sixteen counties are considered moist or allow alcohol to be sold in cities that are located in dry counties, 12 counties have limited alcohol sales which means alcohol is sold only by the drink in restaurants that seat 100 and derive 70 percent of receipts from food sales. There are seven golf courses and 10 wineries in the state that allow alcohol sales.

Sixty-one of Kentucky's 120 counties are dry where alcohol sales are prohibited.

Anna Frances "Frankie" Dalton, who operates Freeway Restaurant in Corinth, filed a petition in January 2002, petitioning Judge Darrell Link to order a special election on the issue. Link declined, saying the law did not allow cities as small as Corinth to have a special election on alcohol. The case finally ended up with the Kentucky Court of Appeals who issued a ruling in October 2003 that Link should order a special election.

Dalton and other property owners in the area contend that without alcohol sales, a golf course/resort-style development won't happen.

Walt Ramey, a real estate agent with Jim Huff Realty, said he has spent the last two years keeping developers such as Landmark Golf Company interested in building two 18-hole golf courses, a hotel and restaurant on 1,800 acres that the city annexed in 2002.

For Kuttawa, a city of 600 residents in Lyon County, allowing alcohol sales was intended to bring development to the city.

"Since the wet vote we have three restaurants and one marina that have opened," said Steve Long, the city clerk/treasurer of Kuttawa. After voters approved alcohol sales, Long was given the added responsibility to being the city's Alcohol Beverage Commission administrator. He is responsible for checking licenses and monitoring restaurants for violations or he investigates if he receives a complaint.

"I think alcohol sales have helped our community," he said. "We are a tourist destination because of the lake, but we think it has generated more business because we have people who are traveling to our city to eat because they can buy a drink."

"People have also been employed because of it," he added. "I'd say we haven't had any more of a DUI (driv-

[56] 8 January 2004. *Grant County News.* Jason Feldman,Staff Writer.

ing under the influence) problem than before."

However, others aren't so sure that alcohol sales are a good thing for a community.

"I think it would help it a lot. We need something up here. Everything goes to the other end of the county. This end of the county needs something." said Josie Blake. a 85-year-old Corinth resident.

She doesn't care much about golf, but likes the idea of something coming to Corinth.

Blake plans on voting, and is hopeful that others will do the same.

"I don't know how many will show up [to vote], but I hope it's a lot." she said.

Although he doesn't drink alcohol, personally, City Commissioner Ted Fisk believes that a "moist" vote could be good for economic development in the southern end of the county.

"I think it will help if the development goes through," said Fisk. "We have the room to grow. We just need some people with [development] interest."

Restaurants would be a welcome addition, he said.

Meanwhile, although he respects the views of those who wish the city to remain dry, Fisk said he doesn't agree with alcohol-infested doomsday scenarios.

"Drive around the city and you can see beer bottles and beer cans in ditches," he said, pointing out that no matter what the vote, the presence of alcohol in the city will remain.

Like the many bottles and cans that currently litter the roadways, the allure of new jobs is one factor that Fisk can't ignore.

"If it happens, then there will definitely be a few jobs in the area. Jobs will help. I'm not sure about minimum wage or not - I certainly won't belong to the country club - but also some restaurants and housing developments could give people more offerings," said Fisk.

More housing equals more people equals more taxes. Fisk added.

"As far as growing, a city should build from there with the tax revenue," he said.

The city commission needs to address a host of issues, said Fisk, among them law enforcement, street repair and improved infrastructure.

Heather Delaney is a Corinth resident who is opposed to alcohol sales.

"I don't think that it will be a good thing because if they serve it, people will be drinking too much and getting on the road. We will need more police to watch for drunk driving," said Delaney.

In her opinion, alcohol sales and the proposed golf course development by are not the best fit for Corinth.

"I don't think that it fits in this area. Unless people drive up here from other places. I don't think that it will bring a lot of business up here." said Delaney.

Also, if businesses do come to the area because the city votes to go partially wet, Delaney doesn't hold too much hope that quality jobs will follow.

"I wouldn't think that it would bring high-paying jobs. Maybe $6 an hour," said Delaney.

After moving to Corinth last year from Dry Ridge, Delaney hopes that the community, and her six acres, remains a peaceful area.

"Amen to that." said her husband, Richard. "I didn't move up here to be in the hustle and bustle. I like the quiet."

"It needs to stay dry up here because it's always been dry up here, and that's the way I like it. Why change a good thing?" said Richard.

"Besides," added Heather, "I think that it will go onto Williamstown, Dry Ridge and Crittenden. Then it will all be wet. It will be a start and it will keep on going once they get the yes."

Then she's worried about the slippery slope that the city's initial "moist" vote could do for the entire county. She foresees alcohol being sold not only by the drink, but eventually by the case.

"I don't see the difference. If it's wet, it's wet. If people can go and have some drinks then go home, I don't see the difference with buying it and then taking it home."

Howard Beauman. executive director of the Kentucky League on Alcohol and Gambling Problems, formerly known as the Kentucky Temperance League, agrees with Delaney.

"People say there will be no bars, but that's not true because an Applebee's is nothing more than a bar surrounded by a restaurant, so really there will be bars just with food sales," he said.

Beauman traveled to a meeting in Grant County of residents who requested information they could circulate in the community on alcohol statistics.

"I'll challenge anyone to prove that there's a positive economic impact from the sale of alcohol," he added.[57]

Is your News subscription paid?

Corinth 'moist'/dry vote:
■ Jan. 20
■ Only registered voters who live in the city limits can vote
■ Polls open 6 a.m. to 6 p.m.
■ Polling place - Corinth City Building

58

In Our Opinion

Vote On Alcohol Shouldn't Divide Community

Voters in Corinth wanted to have a say in whether their city should be allowed to have alcohol sales and they will get the chance to make that decision on Jan. 20.

Only registered voters who live in the city limits will be allowed to vote in the special election which will determine whether restaurants that seat at least-100 people and derive 70 percent of their receipts from food sales can serve alcohol by the drink.

It's only natural that Corinth residents want their city to grow and prosper and share in the wealth like other parts of the county, but voters should weigh their yes or no vote carefully because if Corinth residents do indeed vote in favor of allowing alcohol sales, it will have a dramatic impact on the rest of the county.

The other cities and residents in the rest of the county are anxiously waiting on the results from Jan. 20 because it will send a message that the time is ripe for other cities to follow suit which will mean that opponents of alcohol sales had better get busy.

Whatever the outcome of the election, let's hope both factions can live peaceably with the result because one of the things that makes Corinth a unique place is it's ability to ban together.

The issue of whether alcohol is sold or not should not he allowed to destroy that.[59]

Editorials published in the Grant County News are the collective opinion of the News staff.

The Grant County News - Where Grant County Comes Together

Alcohol Sales Are Not A Solution For Corinth

To the editor, God bless Wayne Yeager for his viewpoint on alcohol sales in Corinth, published in the Jan. 8 Grant County News.

He made good comments and his views were right on the money about alcohol sales. It all comes down to money. I hope the good people of Corinth read his viewpoint and thought about his comments before they voted. I feel the people of Corinth have been misinformed and promised more than they'll ever get.

I agree, Corinth has the right to vote but when it impacts a whole county, other people should get to vote on it too. Oh! That's right, we did vote - twice - not to allow alcohol sales in Grant County. Isn't it ironic that a town of 100-200 people get to decide on something that will affect over 1,000 people or more.

People of Corinth do not want to work for minimum wages. If you don't believe me, ask any business in Corinth. They can't get people who want to work for minimum wage.

Certain people will profit from land sales and from more tax money, however, the majority will not. Most of Corinth voters will never profit anything from this vote. They may even live to regret a yes vote.

The big fish will remain big and eat up all the little fish. Give them an inch and they'll take a mile. As to a golf course, I bet that of 100 voters in Corinth, not more than 10 have ever played golf.

[57] 15 January 2004. *Grant County News.* Jamie Baker-Nantz & Jason Feldmann
[58] Circa January 2004. *Grant County News.*
[59] 15 January 2004. *Grant County News.*

The same people who want alcohol sales in Grant County could not get the whole county to go wet so they went after a small community in need of money to do it for them. The promise of wealth and fortune; at what cost?

I only hope the citizens of Corinth thought real hard what this actually (not what you've been told) means to us all. Drinks will be sold but not only with meals. Restaurants have bars to wait and drink without food. Think hard and long about some drunk driving up your street and maybe hitting someone near and dear to you. It happens all the time. Alcohol is not the answer - no matter what the question.

I cannot conceive of a person who attends church (even pastors or deacons) who would vote yes for alcohol. We do have choices and we do pay for our choices. When you stand before God one day, you will have to justify your choices. So, I hope you thought about your vote and voted wisely for yourself, not because someone said so. I pray you can live with your choice and what you reap from it.

And, Jason Feldmann, I will not drink to that.[60]

Carolyn Switzer
Corinth

Corinth Goes 'Moist'

Voters Approve Alcohol Sales By A Vote Of 84 To 21

CORINTH - In decisive fashion, the voters of Corinth have approved alcohol sales by the drink in restaurants that seat at least 100 people and derive at least 70 percent of their receipts from food sales.

In Grant County, the total vote count was 82 "yes" votes compared to 21 "no" votes. In the #9 precinct the vote was 60-16. In the #19 precinct it was 19-5.

All three absentee votes were "yes," including one paper and two machine.

However, the total vote count in the wet/dry ballot issue was 84-21, because the Corinth city limits stretch into Scott County, thus enabling two "wet" votes from Sadieville.

According to state figures sent to the Grant County clerk's office, there were 171 eligible voters for this special election.

Voter turnout came to approximately 61 percent as a total of 105 ballots were cast in the Jan. 20 election.

Among them was first-time voter Amanda Rose, 23, who decided to make her vote count because the issue was so important to the future of the city

"I think over here needs a change," said Rose after casting her vote during her lunch hour from work. "I think [a yes vote] will have a good impact. We need something over here. This place is dead."

Roland Motley agrees that a "yes" vote was not only in the best interest of the city, it was needed to revive a dying city.

While he chose not to theorize on what kind of effect the "moist" vote might have on the rest of Grant County, Motley instead focused primarily on the impact it will have on the southern end of the county.

"I'll put it to you this way," said Motley. "If it doesn't go wet, Corinth might as well jump in the river. It'll be dead."

The successful wet vote will help the city in a variety of ways, including economic development and increased tax revenue, Motley added.

"It's good for the whole city taxes wise," said Motley, a Corinth resident since 1946. "And it'll help put a lot of people to work."

Linda Dalton was unsure how the vote would ultimately turn out when she cast her vote in the early afternoon, but she was sure that change was needed.

"We need new businesses out here," said Dalton, a Corinth resident for the last eight years.

The possibility of growth and new jobs to the area was also a selling point made by Shane Stakelin after he cast his vote shortly before 1 pm.

"I don't believe the town is going to grow any at all without the alcohol sales. They sell it to the north and the south of us. There's no reason for [business] to come here without it," said Stakelin.

Melinda Hudson, 24, reserved judgment after casting her vote, instead admitting that she was unsure what future affects the vote may or may not bring.

"There will be people against it anyway you go, but I think it will be great for the county. For growth and

---

[60] 22 January 2004. *Grant County News.*

jobs, it will be great for the city," said Hudson.

Most importantly, Hudson said she hopes the city's vote to go "moist" will lead eventually to more recreational options for the city's youth.

As a mother of three children, ages 2, 5, and 6 respectively, Hudson is looking to the future and believes that increased tax revenues will bolster the city's budget and bring about something good for the city's youth.

Although there are 1,304 registered voters in the #9 and #19 precincts in Corinth, only residents who live in the city limits were permitted to vote on the issue.

According to poll workers, there were no complaints or problems from residents thinking they could vote, but who actually could not.

"We've had no problems at all," said election officer Lila McDaniel.[61]

Corinth's Moist Vote Opens Pandora's Box

To the editor,

It's scary to think that 81 voters of Corinth on Jan. 20 decided the future of Grant County.

I have heard both sides of the story and think that it is very selfish of Corinth voters to think only of themselves and not what the impact would be for the rest of us. This vote will open the box and I don't think anyone knows what the impact will be 5, 10, or 15 years down the road. Many people live here in Grant County because they feel it's a safe place to raise a family. After Jan. 20 this will be questionable.

Now that this vote passed will Williamstown be next? When the first drunk driving accident happens from alcohol sold in Grant County and there are injuries, who do we hold accountable? If alcohol sales are the only thing Corinth has to offer developers, then it's time to explore other avenues. There are many golf courses in the state that do not sell alcohol. They've been in business for a long time and seem to be doing well and the same goes for restaurants, hotels, motels, resorts and the list goes on and on.

It's not that I wouldn't like to see Corinth grow but grow in a way that not only would benefit Corinth greatly but in a way that will shine for all of Grant County. Alcohol is not the answer. It's the beginning of a problem. Many thanks to the 21 voters who voted no.[62]

Jeff Baker
Mount Zion

Reader 'Ashamed' Of Corinth Wet Vote

To the editor,

I was always proud to live in Grant County because it is a beautiful place. The people in Grant County were always so friendly, loving, honest and would help a friend or stranger at the drop of a hat. I raised my children here, went to school here.

When Corinth voted to go "wet," I was ashamed of my county and cried myself to sleep. I just could not understand how we got to this crossroads. People were not honest with their votes. People did not write to the paper in objection. One Corinth resident called me a "no-good rotten coward." He said anyone who writes in the paper is a coward. So now, I know why no one else has written.

God bless you Jeff Baker for writing to the editor. I don't feel so lonely. Also that same resident felt I needed his family's approval to write a letter to the editor.

Corinth may have voted to go wet but they did not vote to take my constitutional rights from me. As I remember, freedom of speech is still a right for all, however, the way the people in power keep changing the Constitution it could become another lost right. Look at the Ten Commandments, prayer in schools, freedom of religion - things of the past. Why? Because we as people stood back and let government officials vote for us. We did not use our freedom of speech.

People, voice your opinion. One person can make a difference.[63]

Thank you,
Carolyn Switzer
Corinth

---

[61] 22 January 2004. *Grant County News.* Jason Feldmann, Staff Writer.
[62] 12 February 2004. *Grant County News.*
[63] 11 March 2004. *Grant County News.*

Zero Tolerance For Drinking And Driving

If you ask people in this county whether or not alcohol should be served locally, you don't know what answer you'll get because people's morals, religious beliefs and mores control what they think is good for the community. However, if you ask people in this county whether or not people should be allowed to drive under the influence of alcohol, almost all will resoundingly respond with a no.

There is a great distinction between drinking and driving under the influence, and in the wake of the recent "alcohol by the drink" referendum, it bears reminding all of us that the two are and should be thought about differently in the legal sense. Having a drink at a restaurant is now okay. But after having too many, and then drive, is not OK.

I write this article as a reminder to all Grant Countians that they should not now nor ever forget that distinction. Just because we, as a community, are beginning to tolerate public alcohol sales is no reason to think that we should let down our guard and start tolerating illegal drinking and driving. The DUI laws have not changed in this county and they won't unless you let it happen.

What do I mean by this? According to a University of Kentucky, Kentucky Transportation Center study on DUI conviction rates, from 1996 to 2000 Grant County distinguished itself by having the highest conviction rate per number of arrests of any other county in the state (89.1 percent of those people charged with DUI were convicted of it. Some counties were below 60 percent, which, at that rate, in this county would mean that 357 people charged with DUI would not have been convicted during that period.) This high conviction rate was and still is certainly attributable to aggressive police enforcement and prosecution, but these numbers would not be attainable if the community at large did not support it.

The point is that Grant County set the standard for what tolerance levels are to be met when it comes to drinking and driving. When a charge of DUI is brought, the officer who brought it and the prosecutor both know that the defendant has to consider what a jury of Grant Countians will do with the case if it is tried. In the past and presently, those juries have been tough, clearly indicating this community's disfavor of people who drive under the influence. With this knowledge, criminals and criminal defense lawyers have been and are often reluctant to take DUI's to trial for fear of what a jury might do. Consequently, this often results in a plea without a trial to the charge. In a close case the jury will hear it, but when the facts support a good case, there is a greater reluctance by a defendant to "chance it" with the jury.

That's the bar set by Grant Countians, and that's the message people who drink and drive have when they get charged in Grant County. There is no plea to a lesser charge, there is only a plea to the charge, or the case goes to trial. Defendants respect our juries and the tough stance they have taken up to now. This system should not change because now, instead of drinking in another county, we allow drinking in this county. In many of those counties that have low conviction rates, prosecutors rightfully (at least to some extent) point to the lack of ability to obtain jury convictions as the reason. Criminals have no fear of taking a case to a jury because they know they have a decent chance of getting off, even in the face of good evidence. When this happens the system starts to fail. Without that fundamental support of the community, prosecutors cannot rely on the fear that the defendant might get a stiffer sentence if he goes to a jury trial. The ability to obtain a plea to the DUI is jeopardized, and, to complete the domino effect, police will be reluctant to charge "close" but good fact cases.

On this advent of local alcohol sales, I can assure you there will be no change in the attitudes and procedures by which police charge a person and there will be no change in the way my office prosecutes a case. The only thing that could change is the way Grant County juries treat these cases. Will you lower your standards now? I hope not.

So, it is my plea to you to not let your guard down as a community when it comes to tolerating driving under the influence. Do yourself, your families and the community a service, and do not allow yourselves

[64] 18 March 2004. *Grant County News*. Ed Lorenz, County Attorney.

to become complacent with respect to DUI's just because we are now a "moist" county.[64]

Is your News subscription paid?

Moist Vote On Tap

Williamstown Voters May Get To Decide

WILLIAMSTOWN - A local husband and wife are attempting to get the ball rolling on a vote that would make alcohol sales legal at restaurants in the city of Williamstown.

Tom and Tammy Robertson recently mailed hundreds of petitions to registered voters in the four Williamstown precincts, asking them to sign their names in favor of holding a special election to decide whether the city should be "moist." The election will allow voters to decide whether they are in favor of the sale of alcoholic beverages by the drink in Williamstown at restaurants and dining facilities with a seating capacity of at least 100 persons and which derive at least 70 percent of their gross receipts from the sale of food.

According to Grant County Clerk Judy Fortner, 203 signatures are required in order for the position to be presented in her office. At first, the Robertsons thought they only needed 109 signatures, but Tom Robertson said they had mistakenly calculated the number based on voters in the last primary election instead of the general election. When they found out, they already had 170 signatures.

"We had to go back and send out more petitions." Tom Robertson said.

In order for a petition to be effective, at least 25 percent of the residents who voted in the last general election must sign the petition, he explained.

Robertson said he and his wife got a list of voters in precincts 1, 2, 3 and 20 and mailed petitions to randomly-selected homes. Enclosed with the petition was a self-addressed stamped-envelope and letter explaining their plight.

The letter opens by claiming that the sale of adult beverages will allow local restaurants to compete on a more level playing field with restaurants in northern Kentucky, Cincinnati, Georgetown and Lexington.

"This issue is not about your personal stance on the use of alcohol. Rather, this issue pertains to the economic development of our area," the letter reads. "We have all dined in restaurants that serve drinks with meals and make our own choice as to whether we are going to enjoy an adult beverage with our meal. You will still have that choice!"

Robertson said he and his wife have no vested financial interest in a moist vote, but they were interested in seeing Williamstown grow stronger economically. He said taxes from alcohol sales will help the city.

"I have no financial gain or interest in it," he said. "The only reason I am doing it is because I'd like to see some restaurants in Williamstown. I'm tired of going all the way to Florence. Plus, it'd be good for our city and it would help our tax base."

---

[65]Circa June 2004. *Grant County News.*

The only reason I'm doing it it because I'd like to see some restaurants in Williamstown. I'm tired of going all the way to Florence.

—TOM ROBERTSON
WILLIAMSTOWN

65

He added that he has young children and he thinks the additional tax money would benefit the schools. Robertson said he expects to present the petitions to Fortner in the next few days. Fortner said after she receives the petitions, they will go to Grant County Judge-Executive Darrell Link, whose office will be responsible for verifying that the signatures are valid. Once they are confirmed, it is up to Link to set a date for the election.

But it won't be all smooth sailing, as two Williamstown pastors say they expect their churches will encourage residents to vote against the sale of alcohol by the drink.

"Historically, it (a vote on alcohol sales) has usually made the churches of Grant County get organized and work together to defeat something like that," said Mike McGinnis, pastor of Williamstown Christian Church, adding that he has been vocal about his opinion in the past and would do so again. "But I can't speak for my church and what we're going to do until I speak with the leaders and elders of the church."

However, McGinnis said he thinks it is likely that Williamstown churches will band together to encourage residents to vote against the moist measure.

Steve Rice, pastor of Williamstown Baptist Church, said he would not vote in favor of restaurants being allowed to sell alcohol, and he hopes his church would take a stand against it as well.

"I don't want to speak for the church without talking to them," he said. "I know there's lots of other factors - business factors and such - and I know they're wanting to bring in restaurants. But with alcohol brings lots of other issues and problems. I certainly would not vote for it."

In January, the city of Corinth voted in favor of legalizing alcohol sales by the drink in restaurants. As of June 14, no one has applied for a liquor license in the city.[66]

Personally Speaking

Williamstown Doesn't Need Alcohol Sales

This is one of those instances where I hate to admit that I was right.

I really, really, really wanted to be wrong. I hoped and prayed my words wouldn't prove to be prophetic.

But down deep, even as I said them, I knew they would.

Grant County may soon be facing another "moist" vote.

As seen in a story in this week's News, residents of Williamstown have seen a petition for a vote to allow alcohol sales by the drink. As of now, the petition has not garnered enough signatures, but it doesn't mean it won't.

And it doesn't mean that others won't follow.

Once Corinth voted to go moist, it was only a matter of time before an eager resident or residents decided to challenge for a vote in their community. And let's face it, with Corinth moist, it makes selling the idea of alcohol sales that much easier.

Which is why it's so important to take a stand now. Why wait until the issue is on the ballot? Why wait until it's a simple "yes" vote away from being passed? As a community, as a county, we need to say no to a moist vote. We do that by letting our voices be heard, by not signing any petitions and by making others aware of our feelings that Grant County remain a dry community.

I said it a few months ago when Corinth faced this issue and I'll say it again now. Alcohol is not the economic savior for a community. Applebees and TGI Fridays and Longhorn Steakhouse are not going to open up locations in Williamstown or Grant County just because we're suddenly able to sell liquor by the drink.

Other businesses, like shopping malls and movie theaters, attract

[66] 17 June 2004. *Grant County News.* Lori Love.

those kinds of restaurants to the area. Right now, Grant County is deficient of those types of businesses, and alcohol by the drink isn't going to entice an entrepreneur to open a movie theater in the county.

I know it's only been a few months, but look at Corinth. How much growth have they seen after their moist vote? What new restaurant has opened up? What development has been sparked by the vote?

Before you answer the alcohol question, consider this piece of information gleamed from a restaurant owner in the county. Offering alcohol by the drink increases the insurance premiums on restaurants that choose to sell it, in addition to the new liquor license fees. When those extra costs are added, it tends to offset the benefits, and profits, of selling alcohol.

In fact, the owner went as far to say that if alcohol sales were approved, they would not add alcohol to the menu. It would be too cost prohibitive.

What that adds up to is Williamstown does not need alcohol sales to add growth. On the contrary, Williamstown can see new development without adding beer from the tap. Barnes Road, with some structural improvement to the road, will be an excellent opportunity to see new businesses locate to the area. Also, with the relocation of the Grant County Board of Education office, that leaves open the possibility of future development along US 36.

That being said, Williamstown's residents would do well to nix the idea of alcohol sales. It's not going to improve their city and it definitely won't improve the county. It'll just increase the chances of drunk drivers, underage drinking and alcoholism and by association, domestic violence, broken families and broken marriages.

Like or not, Williamstown, it seems you're the next front on the battle to keep our county dry and safe. You won't be the only such city to face this problem, but you can be the one that takes a stand against alcohol sales. I foresee Crittenden, Dry Ridge, and eventually, all of Grant County battling this within the next few years. A resounding "no thanks" from Williamstown would be a big step toward winning the battle countywide.

For now, the ball is in your court. Only you can choose to throw away the petition. Only you can fight the battle for now.

The choice is yours. What are you going to do?[67]

Wayne Yeager is the sports writer for the Grant County News. You can e-mail him at XXX@XXXX.XXX.

(*Personally Speaking is the opinion of the writer and does not necessarily reflect the editorial opinion of the newspaper.*)

VisionQuest Gets Praise

Alcohol Brings Tax Revenue

To the editor,

As a future county resident (we are moving to the city of Mason in August) I have read your newspaper online with some interest since the first of the year. The edition of June 17, 2004, had two prominent articles, which I found to be of particular interest.

One was on the VisionQuest2004. Apparently, this committee has done much praiseworthy work and should continue to do so. Moreover, these ideas should be a blueprint to the future. From what I have learned in talking to the residents of the county, something like this has been needed in the county for over 30 years. Many of these ideas should have been implemented years ago to allow Grant County to compete with surrounding counties. And yes, like it or not, there is a real competition going on.

Second was Wayne Yeager's column surrounding the apparent controversy on alcohol sales in Williamstown. I wish to take exception to several points in his article.

1. He says that although Corinth has been moist for several months, that no new businesses have opened. While this is true, it should also be noted that most of the better restaurants do market surveys in the areas that they intend to open in. Most of these surveys take an average of 18-24 months to complete and will not even be started until after the voters have approved the issue. Only af-

[67] 17 June 2004. *Grant County News.* Wayne Yeager, Sports Writer

ter these surveys are completed will they begin to seek building locations, property acquisition, etc.

2. He also says in his column information concerning increased operating costs to current restaurants that would probably not be offset by profits of alcohol sales. This information can only be based on current sales figures of any restaurant and no accurate projections on exactly what their increase in revenue (and profits) can even be determined now. It may have been more accurate to conduct a survey of county residents to determine how much money was spent in restaurants outside of the county.

3. Furthermore, he says that approval of such an issue would only result in a decrease of safety for the county residents as well as a moral decline. I have yet to see a restaurant owner twist someone's arm to buy a drink. It always has been, and will remain, a personal choice. If a person wants to consume alcohol, it is not that difficult to merely drive to an adjoining county, make their purchase and return home. And while they are there make some other purchases as well that could have been made in their home county, using the idea "Well, we had to come here anyway so while we are here, we can go ahead and do the grocery shopping and get gas."

I have lived all over the United States, in rural, suburban and urban areas. And in dry counties. This has been quite a learning experience as you can imagine. This is what I have learned about this particular issue:

1. I have personally seen people who live in dry counties drive outside the county and return with literally a pickup truck load of alcohol products for private parties at their homes. End result: a) They still had their alcohol. b:) county where alcohol was purchased gained tax revenue while home county received nothing, and c:) the possibility of someone leaving the party and driving under the influence was equal to or greater than the chances of that occurring when leaving a restaurant.

2. I have personally seen a city lose the placement of a major sports complex within their boundaries due to a ban on alcohol sales. Estimated loss to the city was 33 million dollars a year in new revenue from taxes, tourism dollars, etc.

3. I have seen two separate counties lose the locations of corporate office because the executives of these companies did not have the availability of finer restaurants and sports activities because of alcohol bans. Loss to these counties was over 10 million in annual revenue not to mention the additional jobs that would have been created in those counties.

While I do agree with Mr. Yeager that alcohol sales is not nor cannot be the economic savior of any entity, whether it be city, county or state, I do have to question if any of those entities can afford to turn down that amount of potential revenue. We are all well aware that the cost of operating any government is escalating just in normal purchases such as fuel, vehicle maintenance, etc. Is this cost going to escalate our taxes proportionately? Or will the people affected not only allow but demand for the powers that be to do what is necessary to bring tenants to the area to help shoulder this increased fiscal burden. Just food for thought.

And just for those who are interested, myself and my entire family are non-drinkers.[68]

Sincerely,
Tina L. Hurysz
Webster, N.Y.

Voters Get Say On Moist Issue

Williamstown Precincts To Vote On Alcohol Sales Nov. 2

Williamstown voters will get the chance to decide whether they want alcohol sales by the drink at the Nov. 2 election.

Tom and Tammy Robertson, a husband and wife who live on Lake Williamstown, presented a petition containing 219 signatures on Sept. 3 to County Clerk Judy Fortner.

Fortner said that 203 signatures were required to make the petition valid.

Only voters who live in the Williamstown city limits in each of the four Williamstown precincts will be able to vote on the issue.

The Robertsons began mailing out hundreds of petitions this summer. At first, they believed they only

[68] 1 July 2004. *Grant County News.*

needed 109 signatures based on voters in the last primary election. In reality, they needed 203 signatures because it was based on the number of voters in the last general election.

For a petition to be effective, at least 25 percent of the residents who voted in the last general election must sign the petition.

Once Fortner received the petitions, she sent them to Grant County Judge-Executive Darrell Link. Link certified the petition and verified 205 of the 217 as valid signatures.

Link ordered the local option election to be held on Nov. 2, which is the general election.

The election will allow voters to decide whether they are in favor of the sale of alcoholic beverages by the drink in Williamstown in restaurants and dining facilities that seat 100 persons and derive at least 70 percent of their gross receipts from food sales.

In a story published in the June 17 issue of the Grant County News, Robertson said, "The only reason I'm doing it is because I'd like to see some restaurants in Williamstown. I'm tired of going all the way to Florence."

Before beginning their petition drive, the Robertsons got a list of voters in precincts 1, 2, 3 and 20 and mailed petitions to randomly-selected homes. Enclosed with the petition was a self-addressed stamped-envelope and letter explaining what they wanted voters to do.

"The issue is not about your personal stance on the use of alcohol. Rather, this issue pertains to the economic development of our area," the letter stated. "We have all dined in restaurants that serve drinks with meals and make our own choice as to whether we are going to enjoy an adult beverage with our meal. You will still have that choice."

Williamstown Mayor Glenn Caldwell doesn't deny that there will be an economic impact if alcohol sales are allowed, but said it won't be from taxes.

"The only economic impact to the city would be an additional tax base and the utility sales for any restaurants that move in," Caldwell said. "The city would not actually make any money off the sale of alcohol."

Taxes charged on alcohol sales are state taxes.

However, Caldwell does believe that if the city allows alcohol sales and businesses locate here, then more businesses will follow. Caldwell, along with several other city employees, signed the petition.

"Anytime we can create more businesses within the city it's a plus because one business will feed another business," he added.

Some ministers were taken by surprise over the petition.

G.R. Stone of Hands of Jesus Ministry said he would work with other churches to form a coalition against alcohol sales.

"I didn't know a petition had been filed," he said. "I had talked with other ministers about what we would do if one were filed and just the other day we had prayer that Williamstown wouldn't go wet," Stone said.[69]

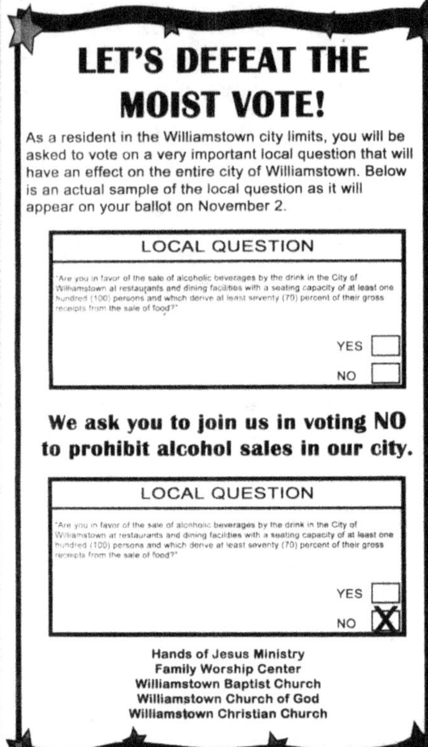

[70]

Voters Get Chance To Be Counted Nov. 2

Decisions Abound on Alcohol, National, State and Local Candidates

G.R. Stone used to drink a case of beer every night and a quart of whiskey on most days.

He describes himself as a loner and didn't like people back then.

"I was an alcoholic and I hated people," he said.

That was over 20 years ago, before Stone, now the pastor of Hands

[69] 16 September 2004. *Grant County News.* Jamie Baker-Nantz,Editor.

[70] Circa September 2004. *Grant County News.*

of Jesus Ministry in Williamstown accepted Jesus Christ.

"I've been preaching for 20 years and as far as I'm concerned, we don't need alcohol," he said.

Stone is one of four ministers in Williamstown who has taken a stand on the upcoming moist vote on Nov. 2 by taking out a full page ad in the Grant County News (see page 12 of this issue) and in the Oct. 25 issue of the Express encouraging their members to vote no.

Residents who live inside Williamstown's city limits in precincts 1, 2, 3 and 20 will get the chance to decide whether they want alcohol sales by the drink in Williamstown in restaurants and dining facilities that seat 100 persons and derive at least 70 percent of their gross receipts from food sales.

"I've been talking to people and letting them know what's going on," Stone said. "I'm not telling them what to do but trying to inform them because if it does pass then it's because people want it and that's part of the democratic process."

Stone said he's heard from many of his church members who are planning to go to the polls this time.

He gave an example of a 69-year-old member that has never voted before.

"We've tried to tell our people to be informed and read everything before they vote on it because they may think they are voting one way but it's really the other way," Stone said.

He used the same sex marriage amendment, which will also be on the ballot, as an example. See story on the same sex marriage amendment below.

"If people don't agree with same sex marriage and cast a no vote, then they have said they actually approve of redefining the law, so we're encouraging everyone to make sure they understand the wording on these issues before they vote," Stone said.

Gwendola Riley, one of 205 registered voters who signed the petition requesting the alcohol sales issue to be placed on the ballot, believes voting to allow alcohol sales will mean more restaurant options for the community.

"I'm not a drinker, but I'm for nice restaurants," Riley said. "I like to sit down and eat a nice steak and we can't do that in Williamstown now. Georgetown did it and they have restaurants like Applebee's and O'Charley's and they've got jobs for people."[71]

Williamstown Approves Alcohol Sales

Williamstown has gone moist.

Citizens of the city of Williamstown voted, 856 to 579, in favor of allowing the limited sale of alcohol in the city limits.

Alcohol sales will now be permitted in restaurants and dining facilities that seat at least 100 people and derive at least 70 percent of their revenue from food sales.

The moist vote will not allow bars or liquor stores to open in the city of Williamstown, and all restaurants wanting to obtain a liquor license will have to be approved and regulated by the Kentucky Alcohol Beverage Control.

Although the votes are in and the decision has been made, citizens of Williamstown are still torn on the issue.

G.R. Stone, the pastor of Hands of Jesus Ministry in Williamstown, was one of four ministers in Williamstown to speak out against the moist vote before Tuesday's election. Stone is not especially surprised by the moist vote, he just feels it is time to change his strategy.

"This is part of the democratic process, and the only thing we can do is live with it and change our ways" said Stone. "Our idea is to get people into church because if they are serving God they won't want to drink.

"The people spoke, and that's the way they want it."

One of the citizens who spoke in favor of the moist vote was Melissa Meece, of Williamstown, when she signed a petition earlier this year to get the moist issue put on the ballot.

Meece is a mother and factory worker, and is excited to see better job opportunities in Williamstown.

"I work in a factory, and it's long hours," said Meece. "There are no jobs in Williamstown now and this will bring great opportunities to working moms."

Ed Clemons, owner of Edwardo's Pizza and Subs, is pleased about the moist vote in Williamstown. Ed-

[71] 28 October 2004. *Grant County News.* Jamie Baker-Nantz,Editor.

wardo's is one of only five restaurants in Williamstown, and seats 102 people.

Clemons plans to contact the ABC and apply for his liquor license as soon as possible.

"It's good to see that the people of Williamstown are ready for a change," Clemons said. "We hope that this vote will bring new businesses to the city so that we may progress to the future and go back to a time when Williamstown led the community in growth and prosperity.

Only those from precincts 1, 2, 3 and 20 that lived in the city limits of Williamstown were allowed to vote on the moist issue.

"We have no plan in place if the vote does go in favor of alcohol sales," Glen Caldwell said before the election occurred. "When you get right down to it, the city won't gain any tax dollars from alcohol sales."

Caldwell said, however, the city would gain from new businesses coming to the city, as well as property taxes and profits on the sale of utilities to any new businesses.

Caldwell said he was aware of a couple of developers who were waiting to see if the voters approved alcohol sales.

"Whether you like it (alcohol) or not, it usually lends itself to other businesses or economic development," Caldwell said.

He also said the city will be able to accommodate business and residential growth for the next few years.

The city council, though, will need to keep their eye on expansions for the sewer plant and, eventually, the water plant.

"Our long-range goal is to expand our waste water treatment plant and we have identified a potential site for a new one," Caldwell said. "Right now we've got room for growth, but a lot depends on how fast it comes."[72]

City Adopts Rules On Alcohol Sales

No Sales Allowed On Sunday

Citizens of the city of Williamstown voted to allow the limited sale of alcohol in Williamstown on Nov. 2, but there is still work to be done before restaurants can begin utilizing the outcome.

Now that the city has gone moist, meaning alcohol sales are allowed at restaurants seating over 100 people and deriving 70 percent of their profit from food sales, the city council must pass ordinances outlining and regulating the sale of alcohol.

In a special meeting on Tuesday, Nov. 16, the Williamstown city council approved the first reading of two ordinances pertaining to the sale of alcoholic beverages and responsible server training.

City ordinances must have a second reading before they become law.

According to Jeff Shipp, Williamstown city atttorney, the Sale of Alcoholic Beverages ordinance was modeled after similar ordinances used across the state. This ordinance details what is required for restaurants to receive liquor licenses. For example, restaurants must seat 100 people permanently. Patio seating and bar stools will not be considered in the occupancy count.

The Sale of Alcoholic Beverages ordinance also establishes an $800 application and licensing fee that must be paid to the city of Williamstown before a liquor license can be obtained. This fee was set at the same price as Georgetown's fee, and it must be paid annually for renewal. This does not include money paid to the Alcoholic Beverages Control (ABC) Commission.

This ordinance establishes a mandate that restaurants hire an auditor to review their books annually to ensure they are deriving at least 70 percent of their profit from sales other than alcohol. These audits will be reviewed by the city.

The city of Williamstown will set business operating hours from 6 a.m. to midnight for restaurants serving alcohol during the week and extend operating hours until 1 a.m. on weekends, they will establish that alcohol is only served Monday through Saturday, and they will require that the kitchen staff be on the clock as long as alcohol is being served through this ordinance.

A second ordinance, also based on ordinances across the state, will require that training programs be attended by restaurant employees serving alcohol. (Note: There is a state law prohibiting restaurant employees from serving alcohol if they are under the age of 18.)

[72] 4 November 2004. *Grant County News.* Jamie Baker-Nantz & Sarah Adams.

Employees will be trained to look for fake identification and underage drinkers at restaurants where they work. They will also be trained to know when and how to refuse alcohol sales to customers.

If situations arise where restaurant customers become threatening or begin to cause a problem, the Williamstown Police Department will be able to assist restaurant employees and protect business patrons.

Williamstown Chief of Police Bobby Webb does not see the sale of alcohol being a problem in the city, and he does not see alcohol sales as a need for more police personnel.

"I don't see a big increase in police personnel in the first year, but every year we get more subdivisions," Webb said. "As the city grows, all of the city departments will grow to meet their needs.

"We have a high rate of convictions for DUIs in Grant County. We just don't put up with it, and I think people know that."

Webb's prediction that alcohol sales will not cause crime in Williamstown has become a reality in Georgetown, Ky.

Capt. Scott Stames, patrol section of the Georgetown police department, said that Georgetown did not see an increase in crimes or driving offenses after the city went moist.

"We did a study on that after Georgetown went moist a couple of years ago, and there was no significant change at all," Stames said. "The percentage of DUI arrests went down from the year before the moist vote to the first full year we were moist."

"We were expecting an increase, but there was not an increase in DUIs, and we have not had an increase in crime."

We were expecting an increase, but there was not an increase in DUIs and we have not had an increase in crime.

—CAPT. SCOTT STARNES
GEORGETOWN POLICE

[73]

The city of Georgetown has seen economic growth since voting to allow the limited sale of alcohol. According to Sue Lewis, the city clerk in Georgetown, restaurants such as Applebee's came to the area because of the alcohol vote.

Wade Gutman, director of the Grant County Chamber of Commerce, has not been approached by possible restaurant developers, but his office has had requests for Grant County demographic information from land owners, including traffic counts, population projections, current population estimates, tax information and the projected number of households.

Property and business owners like Ed Rawls and Tom Link are undecided on utilizing the limited sale of alcohol.

Rawls owns property on Main Street in Williamstown and thinks the moist vote will help bring business to the downtown area, but he is not sure if it will be a business he opens.

Link owns Josie's Country Kitchen and thinks adding the sale of alcohol to his restaurant, which seats well over 100 people, would increase business, but he is still not sure if he will add alcohol to his menu.

"I think I would lose some local business, but I think I would gain local business too," Link said. "Alcohol sales would help business with travelers coming off the interstate to stay at nearby motels."[74]

Dry Ridge Voters Tackle Moist Issue

Dry Ridge voters will get the chance to decide whether they want alcohol sales by the drink at a special election in January.

J.B. Barnes presented a petition to County Clerk Judy Fortner on Sept. 29. Fortner forwarded it on to Grant County Judge-Executive Dana Link.

Link rejected the petition because it did not have enough valid signatures.

[73] Circa November 2004. *Grant County News.*

[74] 18 November 2004. *Grant County News.* Sarah Adams,Staff Writer.

The petition was presented again on Oct. 28 and contained 144 signatures.

Link certified 113 of those which met the requirement that a petition requesting a special election must contain signatures of 25 percent of the residents who voted in the last general election.

Only voters who live in the Dry Ridge city limits in precincts 4, 5 and 13 will be able to vote on the issue.

Precinct 4 contains 749 registered voters, while precinct 5 has 790 followed by precinct 13 with 1,028. However, all those voters do not live in the city limits.

According to Fortner, precinct workers will be verifying addresses of those who come out to vote.

"Voters are coded in our system so that precinct workers will know whether they live in the city limits or not. but they can also consult an address list, as well as a city map Fortner said.

Link ordered the local option election to be held on Tuesday, Jan. 11.

The election will allow voters to decide whether they are in favor of the sale of alcoholic beverages by the drink in Dry Ridge in restaurants and dining facilities that seat 100 persons and derive at least 70 percent of their gross receipts from food sales.

Dry Ridge Mayor Bill Cull said since word of a moist vote has gotten out, the city has been flooded with calls from restaurants requesting demographics of the area.

"People have a choice whether to drink or not, so it's up to the citizens to vote yes or no on the issue." Cull said.

The desire to have more dining out options, was reason enough for some to sign the petition getting a moist vote before the voters.

"That's why I signed it." said Jerry Ellis "I would like to see some nice restaurants come to the area."

Ellis said he's lived in the city for nearly 13 years and is tired of making the trek to northern Kentucky when he wants to eat out.

Sharon Rider secs it as an opportunity for existing businesses to expand.

"If restaurants come, then there could be more development," she said. Sharon and her husband Charlie, have been developers in the community for 15 years. They developed the property where Food Lion is located, as well as the Arbors Apartments and Hogan's Mill Subdivision.

"I think it can be good for the whole community because of the job opportunities," she said.[75]

Moist Vote Set For Jan. 11

Dry Ridge voters will get the chance to decide whether they want alcohol sales by the drink at a special election next week.

On Jan. 11, voters who live in the Dry Ridge city limits in precincts 4, 5 and 13 will he able to vote on the issue at the JMB Center on Taft Highway.

Precinct 4 contains 749 registered voters, while precinct 5 has 790 followed by precinct 13 with 1,028. However, all those voters do not live in the city limits.

The polls will open at 6 a,m. and remain open until 6 p.m. Poll workers will be verifying addresses using an address list and city map, said County Clerk Judy Fortner.

The election will allow voters to decide whether they are in favor of the sale of alcoholic beverages by the drink in Dry Ridge in restaurant, and dining facilities that seat 100 persons and derive at least 70 percent of their gross receipts from food sales.

Jerry Barnes, of Dry Ridge, circulated the petition to get the issue on a special election ballot.

For Barnes, a retired locomotive engineer for CSX Railroad, it's about having dining options.

"There's no doubt it will be a plus to the economy," he said.

Barnes said it took him about four weeks to circulate the petition, by mailing it and taking it door to door, to get enough signatures on it to present it to Grant County Judge Executive Darrell Link.

Link rejected the petition in September because it didn't contain a valid number of signatures, but when he presented it again on Oct. 28, it had more than necessary to call a special election.

Barnes, in an effort to get voters out for the special election, placed an ad in this issue of the Grant County News, encouraging the public to turn out.

[75] 9 December 2004. *Grant County News.* Jamie Baker-Nantz,Editor.

The ad states "It's the future of our town, so make sure your opinion is counted. VOTE."

Barnes, a lifelong resident of Grant County, said he's seen a lot of progress in Dry Ridge in the last few years and he sees alcohol sales by the drink another way to continue that progress.

"Dry Ridge has really developed and people need some nice restaurants to go along with that," Barnes said. "Dry Ridge is a booming community and we don't need to stay in the dark ages."

For Mayor Bill Cull, alcohol sales may boost his city's economy, but it's his religious convictions that will guide him when he votes.

"I've heard a lot of citizens say that they'd like to see Dry Ridge stay dry because people will still come and that the community will grow without alcohol," he said.

Cull said on the other hand, though, there are nice restaurants that do serve alcohol.

"Citizens can choose to drink or not to drink and to vote yes or no." he said.

While Cull is mayor of Dry Ridge, he's also a deacon at Dry Ridge Baptist Church.

"As a representative for the citizens of Dry Ridge, I'm going to have to take a stance that I'd rather not see alcohol come into the city at this point because I'm afraid the crime rate will go up and then we'll need more police," he said.

For Clay Parks, also a deacon at Dry Ridge Baptist Church, the decision is an easy one.

"I've been here 40 years and if someone would show me any good it's done for a community, but I haven't seen any," he said.

Parks said that approving alcohol sales would be sending the wrong message to young people.

"All the big restaurants might go to Walton, but they've been moist for years and I haven't seen any rushing to locate there." he added.

Park, said information concerning alcohol use had been included in Dry Ridge Baptist Church's bulletin.

"We simply tried to make our church members aware of what we feel is our responsibility of the citizens to the community," he said.

While Dry Ridge Baptist Church, as well as other churches in Dry Ridge, didn't organize a campaign against the issue, church leaders are in hopes their members will exercise their right to vote.

"We haven't taken a stand, as a church, on this issue and we typically don't," said Jetty Summers, pastor at Dry Ridge Christian Church. "We are leaving it to each person to make their own choice. Everyone should vote and vote their conscience."

Earlier this year, voters in the city limits of Corinth and Williamstown approved liquor sales. To date, a liquor license has not been issued to any restaurants in those cities.[76]

Wet vs. Dry

Corinth, Williamstown Approves Alcohol Sales

Corinth and Williamstown became the first cities in Grant County to allow alcohol sales.

The two cities voted to allow alcohol by the drink in restaurants that seat at least 100 people and derive 70 percent of their sales from food.

Corinth was the first city in Grant County to allow alcohol sales.

On Jan. 20, in a special election, Corinth voters approved alcohol sales by a vote of 84-21. Sixty-one percent of registered voters turned out to the polls.

"I think over here needs a chance," said Amanda Rose, 23, after casting her ballot. "I think (a yes vote) will have a good impact. We need something over here. This place is dead."

Proponents of the "moist" vote had hoped a yes would lure Landmark Golf Company to build a resort in Corinth. Landmark Gold Company had proposed two 18-hole golf courses, a restaurant and new housing development for its golf resort, but would not consider Corinth unless alcohol sales were allowed.

So far, no golf resort has been built and no Corinth business has applied for an alcohol license.

Williamstown was the next city to approve a "moist" vote.

On Nov. 2, while Americans cast their ballot in the presidential elections, Williamstown residents also approved alcohol sales by a vote of 856 to 579.

"This is part of the democratic process, and the only thing we can do is live with it and change our ways," said G.R. Stone, the pastor of Hands of Jesus Ministry in Williamstown,

[76]6 January 2005. *Grant County News.* Jamie Baker-Nantz,Editor.

one of four ministers in Williamstown to speak out against the moist vote.

"It's good to see that the people of Williamstown are ready for a change," said Ed Clemons, owner of Edwardo's Pizza and Subs in Williamstown. "We hope that this vote will bring new businesses to the city so that we may progress to the future and go back to a time when Williamstown led the community in growth and prosperity."

Edwardo's has plans for alcohol sales.

Dry Ridge will be the next city to consider the "moist" question. Dry Ridge citizens will go to the polls on Jan. 11 to vote for or against alcohol sales in the city.[77]

Voters Reject Alcohol Sales

Dry Ridge To Stay Dry

If you were hoping that you'd soon be having a drink with dinner in Dry Ridge, you'll have to wait.

Voters in the city limits of Dry Ridge rejected alcohol sales on Jan. 11 inside restaurants that seat 100 people and derive at least 70 percent of their sales from food.

The measure was defeated by 14 votes.

Only voters who lived inside the city limits of Dry Ridge in precincts 4, 5 and 13 were eligible to vote. Only 304 total votes were cast in the special election.

Voters in those three precincts cast 159 votes against the measure and 145 votes in favor of alcohol sales.

Jerry Barnes, of Dry Ridge, filed the petition requesting that Grant County Judge-Executive Darrell Link set a special election. Link rejected the first petition saying it didn't have enough valid signatures on it, but Barnes presented another petition containing 113 signatures and Link ordered the special election to be held on Tuesday.

"I'm a little shocked," said Barnes, after the votes had been counted. "I expected it to go moist, but it's just postponing the inevitable."

Barnes placed a couple of ads in the Grant County News during the last couple of weeks reminding people to go out and vote. He said he also made some phone calls reminding people to vote, but found it difficult to get people interested.

For Dr. Clay Parks the fact that alcohol sales won't be allowed in Dry Ridge was reason to celebrate.

"I was pleased and not at all surprised," Parks, a Dry Ridge resident and member of Dry Ridge Baptist Church, said. "I'm glad we still have people who have principles and stand up for them."

Parks said he didn't anticipate a large voter turnout, but was glad of those who did venture out on a wet, gloomy day and cast their vote.

"Low turnout could be indifference, which has become generally true in elections, but we'll take what we can get," Parks said.

Betty Webster, a resident of Dry Ridge was thrilled to learn her city won't be allowing alcohol sales.

"I am so surprised," she said. "All the others went wet, Corinth and Williamstown. I can't believe it. I'm elated."

Corinth and Williamstown voters both approved alcohol sales last year. To date, no applications from a restaurant have been filed, but some have expressed an interest in doing so.

According to Kentucky law, it will be three years before a vote on alcohol sales can be put on the ballot in Dry Ridge.

But Barnes will wait.

"I was disappointed, but I'm not going to give up," he said. "The next time I bring it up I'm going for the whole thing - the full blown wet issue so that grocery stores can sell it if they want to."[78]

---

[77] 6 January 2005. *Grant County News.*

[78] 13 January 2005. *Grant County News.* Jamie Baker-Nantz,Editor.

WHAT'S ON TAP?

COUNTY HAS FIRST ALCOHOL SALES IN 62 YEARS

Frances Reynolds made history in Grant County on March 25 by spending $2.75 on a bottle of Miller Light at Edwardo's Pizza and Subs in Williamstown. Reynolds' purchase seemed small, but alcohol has not been sold in Grant County in over 62 years.

Grant County citizens voted to become a dry county on Dec. 12, 1942, but citizens of the city of Williamstown voted to change their alcohol status on Nov. 2, 2004. by making it the second moist city in Grant County. (Corinth was the first city to pass a moist vote on Jan. 20. 2005. See related story.)

Ed Clemons, owner of Edwardo's Pizza and Subs in Williamstown, knew he wanted to serve alcohol at his restaurant the night the moist vote passed.

"It's good to see that the people of Williamstown are ready for a change," Clemons said after hearing the elections results on Nov. 2, 2004.

Citizens of Grant County continue to debate the issue of alcohol sales (Dry Ridge citizens voted against making alcohol sales legal in their city on Jan. 11, 2005) but Clemons said he was never concerned about a negative backlash for serving alcohol.

"We haven't had any negative feedback," Clemons said. "It seems like the community has embraced the idea."

Clemons went through a long process to receive his liquor license on March 24, but said it has all been worth it.

"This has been an exciting process;" Clemons said. "We're even hoping to expand and add a sports bar in May because we have our full service liquor license."

Reynolds did not know Edwardo's was serving alcohol when she entered the restaurant with her husband, Mike Reynolds, on Friday afternoon to pick up a pizza for lunch.

"Pizza and beer just go hand-in-hand." Mike said.

Frances said she is not concerned about a negative stigma being associated with people who drink at Edwardo's.

"I don't care what people say, but I think there will be people that look down on other people who drink," Frances said. "People don't have to drink if they don't want to."

Edwardo's, in Williamstown, became the first restaurant in Grant County to sell alcohol since 1942. The voters of Williamstown approved alcohol sales in November.

Mike is a prime example of someone who doesn't drink when he goes out with his wife.

"I don't drink when we go out. Peer pressure is everywhere and it's an individual's choice." Mike said. "I'm her (Frances') designated driver everywhere we go."

After Frances finished her drink, she had Clemons sign the bottle as a memento.

"I'm going to sell this on E-bay," Frances joked.

Clemons said he planned to hang one of Frances' dollars on the wall as a memento of his first alcohol sale too.

Clemons expects business to pick-up in the next few weeks as the word spreads.

"I think next week will be busier because it will take people a while to hear about it," Clemons said.

Clemons celebrated the end of his first day of business with alcohol sales by watching the University of Kentucky basketball game and selling alcohol at Edwardo's.

Friends, family and customers gathered in front of the new big-screen television in Edwardo's back room and cheered the Wildcats to victory in their game against Utah.

Good Friday was truly good for Clemons. After months of work Clemons made history by selling alcohol, watched his team win a spot in the Elite Eight of the NCAA tournament and celebrated both with his friends.

What did it take to get a license?

- The Nov. 2, 2004 election results were certified in mid-December.

- Ed Clemons had to wait 60 days after the election was certified to begin the application process.

- Clemons had to increase the seating capacity at Edwardo's from 84 to 104 to meet the Williamstown city ordinance saying that 100 or more seats are required in a restaurant for alcohol sales to be allowed. Clemons increased his seating capacity by adding a bar area in the front of Edwardo's.

- The new seating capacity and alcohol equipment had to be approved by the state fire marshal.

- Clemons had to be approved through the city of Williamstown, which included paperwork.

"The city has been very helpful through this process," Clemons said.

- Edwardo's employees able to serve alcohol (employees 20-years-old and older) attended server training offered by the Alcohol Beverage Control, ABC. Clemons said they hired 10 new employees over 20-years-old to serve alcohol. Clemons also said it is a myth that servers have to be 20 and a day to serve.

"No minors are allowed to handle beer, even empty bottles and glasses," Clemons said. "They have to be 20-years-old to serve. There is no day. It's just 20. I don't know where that wives' tale got started.

- The ABC did an on site inspection of Edwardo's and approved the site on their first visit.

- Edwardo's received its liquor license on March 24, 2005.[79]

Where Do We Go From Here?

Alcohol is now being sold in the city of Williamstown, but the question still remains whether or not alcohol sales will bring growth to Grant County.

The Williamstown city council unanimously approved the first reading of two ordinances for developments on Barnes Road and Baton Rouge Road during a special council meeting on March 15.

Williamstown Mayor Glenn Caldwell said the developers of the Barnes Road project are hoping to bring shopping centers, stand-alone stores and restaurants to Williamstown.

Williamstown city administrator Doug Beckham will be working with developers to oversee these two projects for the city. Beckham will also be responsible for making sure businesses that serve alcohol derive 70 percent of their revenues from food sales.

Beckham declined to comment on this issue.

While development on Barnes Road is still in the planning stages, a Dry Ridge restaurant will be opening a second location in Williamstown in order to serve alcohol.

Manuel Albares, owner of Cazador's restaurant in Dry Ridge, will be opening a second location within two months.

Albares said the new restaurant, El Jalisco, is in the final stages of the liquor licensing process.

"We are just waiting for our state inspection," Albares said. "We will have our liquor, beer and wine license so we can serve all types of drinks."

El Jalisco will be located on Skyway Drive, in Williamstown, next to the Best Value Inn and Suites.[80]

Alcohol Sales OK'd But Corinth Still Dry

Voters in Corinth approved alcohol sales by the drink in January 2004, but no liquor has been served yet in Grant County's southern community.

"We are at the first of many stages," said Mayor Billy Hill.

The first step for the city commission was to adopt ordinances that would govern alcohol sales. The council did this in June 2004.

The ordinance establishes the position of an alcoholic beverage control administrator, license requirements and fees, as well as hours when alcohol can be sold.

"This will give us some teeth," said Hill. "We don't want bars, saloons or strip joints. The city wants to have some control."

Hill, as mayor, will serve as the city's alcoholic beverage control administrator. As such, he can inspect businesses that sell alcohol and also inspect the books and records of any businesses that sell alcohol.

Liquor licenses will be good for one year and will cost $800.

According to Corinth's ordinance, alcohol by the drink can only be sold between 6 a.m. and midnight with no sales on Sunday or any time the polls are open for an election.

The city's ordinance also governs the type of signs that are permitted to advertise alcohol. The ordinance allows one sign, not over 2-square-feet that must be displayed from the inside of the business.

No flashing lights are permitted. The liquor license holder is

[79] 31 March 2005. *Grant County News.* Sarah Adams,Staff Writer.

[80] 31 March 2005. *Grant County News.* Sarah Adams,Staff Writer.

also barred from distributing flyers or cards to advertise alcohol sales.

Voters approved alcohol sales in Corinth by an 84 to 21 vote, but alcohol can only be sold by the drink in restaurants that seat at least 100 people and derive 70 percent of their receipts from food sales.

Frankie Dalton, owner of Freeway Restaurant, was the only business owner that met the criteria. She is also the one who filed the petition asking the issue to be put decided by voters who live in the city limits of Corinth.

Dalton originally said she did not plan on applying for a liquor license and has since closed her restaurant.

While Noble's Truck Stop does seat at least 100 people and derives 70 percent of its receipts from food sales, it does not sit inside city limits.

In 2003, 10 property owners encompassing over 1,660 acres asked for their land to be annexed into the city limits.

To date, no one has made an application with the Kentucky Alcohol Beverage Control in Frankfort for a liquor license.

According to city officials and developers of a golf course eyeing Corinth, voters had to approve alcohol sales if they wanted to see growth come to that end of the county.

Hill is hoping the project will eventually happen and bring jobs to his town.

He has met periodically with the developers of the proposed golf course.

"I think we're talking two to five years, at least, " Hill said. "If you're going to do something like this, it can't be done overnight. We did tell them to get off square one because the city had done what they needed to and now it was up to them."

Walt Ramey, the real estate developer from Fort Mitchell, who was working with the developers said the project isn't dead.

"We've basically been in meetings since the vote went down and we have a rough draft of the first 18 holes of the golf course and we're still doing the feasibility study," Ramey said.

He projected that it'll be another year before dirt is moved on the site.

"We couldn't spend any more money until we found out if the wet/dry vote would go in our favor," he added.

"This is the beginning of a long process, so those who thought they'd get a drink quickly in Corinth were sadly mistaken," said Hill. "It's possible that the people on this city council won't even be in office when it happens."[81]

Deputy Jailer Charged With DUI Following Accident In County Vehicle

---

The operations officer, at the Grant County Detention Center was arrested and charged with driving under the influence after police say he wrecked a county vehicle.

Dennis R. Narramore, 44, of Williamstown, was arrested after police were called to KY 36 at 11:09 pm. on May 9.

According to police, Charlie Hutchison, who lives at the corner of Ashbrook Road and KY 36 went outside to feed his dogs and found Narramore hiding in the bushes.

Hutchison's wife dialed 911 and Deputy Rick Kells and Deputy Kevin Burke responded.

According to the police citation, Burke said. "(Narramore) was very unstable on his feet with slurred speech; blood shot eyes and unable to do a field sobriety test."

Deputies took Narramore to the Grant County Detention Center. When he was given a breath test at the jail, he tested a .252 at the jail, which is twice the legal limit of .08 for alcohol intoxication.

Narramore, who is chief of operations at the detention center, has a staff vehicle which he drives to and from work. It received minor damage in the accident.

"He was not on duty at the time," said Jailer Steve Kellam. "I don't know what he was doing in the vehicle because I haven't had a chance to interview him at this time."

After he was brought to the detention center, Narramore was not placed in a cell.

"He was housed in an area, not a jail cell because there were safety concerns of putting him in with prisoners, but in a place where he could be watched by a jail employee," Kellam said.

[81] 31 March 2005. *Grant County News.* Jamie Baker-Nantz,Editor.

Narramore was later released on a $500 bond. His next court appearance is scheduled for May 23.

The jail, according to Kellam, has three staff vehicles that are driven by himself, Chief Deputy Greg Wells and Narramore. The rest of the jail's vehicles remain on site when deputies are not on duty.

As chief of operations, Kellam said Narramore was responsible for transporting prisoners and evidence, as well as taking calls from the center when he was not on duty.

"He's been a good employee," said Kellam. "He served his country in Desert Storm, and he's done a good job, but this time he used bad judgment."

Narramore was placed on administrative leave while an investigation is conducted into the incident.

According to Grant County Sheriff's Chief Deputy Chuck Dills, the situation was difficult.

"Our deputies followed procedure, but it was an awkward position to be in because he was someone we worked with, but we had to follow the law and what we were sworn to do," Dills said.[82]

Williamstown Man Seeks Alcohol Answer About Lake

To the editor,

A few friends and I have a question. Since Williamstown was voted moist and Williamstown Lake is in the city limits, are we allowed to take our coolers full of beer to the lake when we go on a picnic, go boating or fishing, or just sitting and admiring the lake?

I've asked everyone and no one seems to know what the answer is. So maybe someone out there can give us the answer.[83]

Thank you,
Alvin L. Cummons Sr.
Williamstown

DUI, Assault Charges Filed Against Trooper After Wreck

A 12-year police veteran is now facing charges of assault, drunken driving and wanton endangerment following a wreck on Warsaw Road, five miles outside Dry Ridge, on July 4.

Larry E. "Buddy" Carey, 38, of Dry Ridge. was traveling eastbound in a 1996 Acura when investigators say it crossed the center line and struck a 1986 Nissan pickup head on.

Edwin C. Gregory, 28, of Williamstown, the driver of the pickup, remains in critical condition at University Hospital in Cincinnati.

His wife, Maria Gregory, 27, underwent surgery on July 10 at University Hospital and is in serious condition.

The couple's two children, Lisa Ann Gregory, 10, and Jonathon Gregory, 3, were taken to Cincinnati Children's Hospital Medical Center where they were treated but have since been released.

Carey followed in his father and uncle's footsteps and became a trooper with the Kentucky State Police. He was the officer who stopped Oprah Winfrey and her entourage on Interstate 75 as she was filming from a vehicle on a cross-country trek for her talk show. Winfrey later flew Carey to Chicago to appear on the show.

Carey has been moved from University Hospital in Cincinnati to Gateway Rehabilitation Hospital in Florence. He has several broken bones and it may be several months before he can be released.

Carey was off duty at the time of the accident. He has been suspended with pay, pending the criminal and administrative investigations.

According to Sgt. Travis Tennill, a KSP media relations specialist, Carey's toxicology results have been sent to Commonwealth Attorney James Crawford.

Crawford has filed a criminal complaint against Carey.

Tennill said Carey could be arrested following his release from the rehabilitation facility.

"He's not been charged or arrested as of yet," Terrill said.

Tennill refused to discuss the results of the toxicology reports and said he didn't know if speed was a factor or not.

[82] 12 May 2005. *Grant County News.* Jamie Baker-Nantz,Editor.
[83] 25 August 2005. *Grant County News.*

"If and when charges are brought will be up to the Commonwealth Attorney's office, Tennill said.

The Kentucky State Police handled the investigation into the accident which is the protocol the agency follows when a trooper is involved in an accident, Tennill said.

"It's common practice that we investigate all accidents involving state police," he said.[84]

Trooper Arrested

A Kentucky State Police trooper who was indicted July 11 on charges of driving under the influence and other offenses is behind bars after warrants were executed against him on July 25 in Grant County.

Larry E. "Buddy" Carey, 38, was off-duty and driving his personal 1996 Acura on July 4 when he crossed the centerline on Warsaw Road, five miles west of Dry Ridge, and struck an oncoming 1986 Nissan pickup driven by Edwin Gregory.

Gregory, 28, and his wife, Maria, 27, were both seriously injured in the wreck, along with their children, 10-year-old Lisa Ann and 3-year-old Jonathan. They are still recovering from their injuries.

All five were wearing seat belts at the time of the crash.

Carey, a 12-year veteran of the KSP, has been suspended from duty without pay, pending both criminal and administrative investigations, according to a press release issued by KSP Lt. Phil Crumpton in Frankfort.

Other charges in the indictment include two counts of first-degree assault, two counts of first-degree wanton endangerment and having no insurance.

Carey is best known as the trooper who pulled over Oprah Winfrey's entourage during a cross-country trek last year.

He is lodged in the Grant County Detention Center in Williamstown.[85]

Ex-Trooper Pleads Guilty In Wreck

Larry E. "Buddy" Carey raised his right hand, like he'd done many times before, and swore to tell the truth.

But this time, Carey, a former Kentucky State Police trooper, wasn't giving testimony against a drunk driver, he was entering a plea to driving under the influence and causing a wreck on July 4 which injured a Dry Ridge couple.

Carey, 38, was indicted July 11 by a Grant County grand jury on two counts of first-degree assault, two counts of wanton endangerment, one count of operating his vehicle under the influence and one count of not having insurance.

His trial was scheduled to begin December, but instead, Carey, who is no longer employed by the state police, entered a guilty plea to amended charges of assault, driving under the influence and wanton endangerment. He will receive a 10-year prison sentence.

Carey also agree to pay $700 monthly to Edwin and Maria Gregory, the couple whose truck he hit, up to $250,000 to cover their medical expenses, which total more than $300,000.

His guilty plea and the restitution he agreed to pay will not shield him from the Gregorys filing a civil lawsuit if they choose to. A charge of not maintaining required insurance was dropped in exchange for his guilty plea.

Carey entered the courtroom on Oct. 3, walking slowly behind his attorney, Steve Howe. Carey was injured in the accident and recently underwent surgery. He is still wearing a protective boot.

Carey stood with his hands clasped behind his back as Judge Stephen Bates asked him questions about the proceeding, to which he gave only yes or no answers.

"Are you pleading guilty because you are guilty?" Bates asked him.

"Yes," Carey said.

Formal sentencing is scheduled for Dec. 19. He is supposed to report to the Grant County Detention Center that day to being serving his sentence.

Carey was a 12-year veteran of the state police. He is the trooper who pulled over Oprah Winfrey as she was making a cross-country car trip for her television show. Winfrey later flew Carey to Chicago for a tap-

[84] 12 July 2007. *Grant County News.* Jamie Baker-Nantz,Editor.

[85] 2 August 2007. *Grant County News.* Rebecca Russo, Editorial Assistant.

[86] 8 November 2007. *Grant County News.* Jamie Baker-Nantz,Editor.

ing of a show where he appeared as a guest.[86]

Alcohol Violation Forces Coach To Step Down

For four seasons, Buck Walter has served as lead coach of the Williamstown High School baseball team. However, when the season comes to an end, so will Walter's tenure following his resignation. At press time, Walter's overall record is 50-65-1 and inherited the program in 2005, replacing Marlin Gregg.

The resignation comes as a result of a violation of a Williamstown Independent School Board policy while on a school-related trip.

"This is not an easy decision to make and was finalized after long thought and consideration," Walter wrote in his letter of resignation.

According to papers obtained though an open records request, Walter violated Board Policy 03.23251, which pertains to the use of alcohol while in the workplace.

The policy states, "district employees shall not manufacture, distribute, dispense, be under the influence of, purchase, possess, use or attempt to purchase or obtain, sell or transfer any of the following in the workplace or in the performance of duties: alcoholic beverages, controlled substances, prohibited drugs and substances, and drug paraphernalia; and substances that look like' a controlled substance."

Walter admitted he violated the policy by having a beer in a restaurant following a baseball game on April 19.

Following an investigation by principal Bob Elliott, Williamstown superintendent Charles Ed Wilson conducted a conference with Walter, who indicated that he "did drink a beer while sitting with other parents in another area of the restaurant while the players and coaches ate lunch."

In his report, Wilson wrote that Walter admitted he made a mistake in judgment and "did not realize this was an issue."

Walter was suspended for the April 21 game against Pendleton County and the April 22 game against Walton-Verona, in addition to a practice on April 23. The Demons lost 3-0 to Pendleton County and 8-0 to Walton-Verona.

Wilson reinstated Walter under the conditions that he resign after the last game of the season.

"I value the students I've worked with and the faculty that assisted me during my tenure. I feel it is time to move onto new opportunities," Walter wrote.[87]

Carey Denied Probation

A motion for shock probation for Larry E. "Buddy" Carey Jr. was denied on June 17 in Grant County circuit court.

"As grounds, it is stated that to grant the defendant shock probation would unduly deprecate the seriousness of his crimes," ruling Circuit Judge Stephen Bates wrote.

Commonwealth Attorney James Crawford also opposed the motion.

Carey, a former Kentucky State Police trooper, is serving 10 years for pleading guilty to assault, driving under the influence and wanton endangerment after his 1996 Acura was involved in an accident on July 4, 2007, which injured Eddie and Maria Gregory and their two children.

Carey, who was 38 years old when the accident occurred, was off-duty at the time. He began serving his sentence on Dec. 19, 2007.

Several letters were written in support of shock probation for Carey including those from Gallatin County Judge-Executive Kenny French, Vic Lavender, Joe and Donna Whelan, Coy Cox, Marie Arnold and Lt. Gary Peace.[88]

Wet Or Dry?

Dry Ridge Voters Get To Decide

With plenty of signatures, a petition was filed to allow the sale of alcoholic beverages by the drink in Dry Ridge.

J.B. Barnes filed the petition on Aug. 14 with Leatha Conrad, county

[87] 15 May 2008. *Grant County News.* Paul Gable,Staff Writer.

[88] 26 June 2008. *Grant County News.* Rebecca Russo, Editorial Assistant.

clerk. If voters decide to pass the petition, alcohol will be available by the drink at restaurants and dining facilities with a seating capacity of at least 100 people and which derive at least 70 percent of their gross receipts from the sale of food. Previous petitions have been filed, with the last one being rejected by voters in 2005.

The issue will be on the Nov. 4 ballot and only residents living in the city limits of Dry Ridge can vote on the issue.

"We need some better restaurants and that won't happen until Dry Ridge goes moist," Barnes said. "I would say 95 percent of the people we approached signed the petition. There was no real negative feedback. The main and only reason for this petition is for the restaurants. This would be exactly like Williamstown. I hope it passes."

Dry Ridge City Council member Encil Webster was one of the people who signed the petition.

"I feel that we need some controlled growth," Webster said. "It's a way of further developing and helping Dry Ridge's future, particularly with restaurants. We all know that if want to get other restaurants in the area, Dry Ridge will have to become moist. The local restaurants are nice, but to bring in additional national chains, the city will have to go moist. It's up to the voters.

"I think it's good for the growth of the city as far as food service and tax revenue," Webster said. "The potential of abusing is always there, but I've not seen it happen thus far. If someone wants to get a drink, all they have to do is go seven miles north. This is about having a glass of wine or a beer with your dinner. I can see it as a positive, certainly not a negative. Williamstown and Corinth have already done this and if Dry Ridge doesn't follow, I'm afraid of new business not coming."

Former Grant County Sheriff Randy Middleton also put his name on the petition.

"I hope to get better restaurants," he said. "I'm not for package stores or bars, but I'm not against a restaurant selling drinks to get steakhouses or better restaurants here. I'm assuming it might bring growth to Dry Ridge."

As former sheriff, Middleton has seen the dangers of drinking and driving and believes that the number of DUI's will not increase.

"I'm against drunk driving," he said. "I don't think it will increase though. I talked to the sheriff of Scott County before I left office and he told me they had not had any complaints of anyone leaving the restaurants under the influence. There are a lot of people who drive to Florence for a sit-down family restaurant. People will save gas on driving and I think it will increase the city's revenue. It doesn't matter if the petition passes or not, but that's the way I feel."

Dry Ridge Mayor Clay Crupper has decided to let the citizens of Dry Ridge resolve whether they want their city to become moist.

"I'm not getting involved in it," Crupper said. "I'm going to let the voters decide. It's going to be up to the people whether they want it or not. It's new and I haven't heard much from the community about it."

Rev. Jerry Summers serves the people of Dry Ridge Christian Church, but will only encourage people to vote, not how to vote.

"I believe that everyone should educate themselves on the issue and when the time comes to vote, be ready and vote their conscience," Summers said. "When I found out the petition was filed, I thought yet again. We keep coming back to this issue. It is certainly not something that is settled. I think we're going to struggle as a community with the alcohol issue for many years to come, no matter the outcome.

"I think the positive thing is that the community has the power to decide," he said. "I promise that I will preach that everyone should get up and vote and let their feelings be known. I will not tell the people I serve how to vote. I will only strongly encourage them to vote. I think everyone should participate in the joy of our democracy. The right to vote is a precious thing."[89]

---

[89] 28 August 2008. *Grant County News.* Ryan Naus,Staff Writer.

[90] Circa August 2008. *Grant County News.*

The question of whether alcohol sales, by the drink, will be allowed in Dry Ridge will be on the Nov. 4 ballot.

90

Dry Ridge Moist Issue Questioned

The Dry Ridge moist vote hit a possible snag Friday, Oct. 17, after court papers were filed asking a judge to decide if the local option election can continue on the ballot in its current language.

Grant County Attorney Jack Gatlin filed a petition for declaratory judgement on behalf of Grant County Clerk Leatha Conrad in circuit court after a question arose about the difference in wording in the certified petition filed by J.B. Barnes and the state law that allows for a local option election on alcohol sales.

"I felt we wanted to make sure that whatever vote was cast on Nov. 4 was counted," Gatlin said. "We wanted to minimize the potential for litigation."

"I felt we wanted to make sure that whatever vote was cast on Nov. 4 was counted. We wanted to minimize the potential for litigation."

-JACK GATLIN
County Attorney

91

The petition filed on Aug. 14 which contained 97 signatures of Dry Ridge voters, asked for a special election to decide whether or not the voters are in favor of "the sale of alcoholic beverages by the drink in Dry Ridge at restaurants and dining facilities with a seating capacity of at least 100 persons and which derive at least 70 percent of their gross receipts from the sale of food."

The petition's language was similar to the wording of a state law (KRS 242.185) that was last amended in 2000.

However, after Conrad certified the petition, but prior to putting the question on the ballot, the county clerk's office became aware of a newer state law (KRS 242.1244) that changes the minimum seating capacity for restaurants and dining facilities from 100 to 50.

The more recent law, which became effective in June 2007, also requires that a meal be purchased with an alcohol beverage, prohibits the operation of an open bar within the restaurant or dining facility and includes a limitation that no alcohol beverage can be served more than 30 minutes after a meal is completed.

When placed on the ballot, which some absentee voters have already cast, the question uses the 50-person seating capacity instead of the 100-person seating capacity in the original petition.

"Although case law only requires that the petition language and the ballot language be substantially similar, the question has now arisen as to whether the language used on the ballot meets this standard," the court document filed by Gatlin states.

The motion is scheduled to be heard at 9 a.m. Wednesday, Oct 21 at the Grant County Courthouse by Judge Stephen L Bates.

The motion asks the judge to declare whether the local option election can continue with the current language on the ballot, and if not, whether the county clerk should amend the language on the ballot to more closely reflect the language of the older state law that uses a 100-person seating capacity.

If the language is changed on the current ballot, the judge also is asked to decide how to account for any bal-

[91] Circa October 2008. *Grant County News.*

lots that have already been cast under the current language.

Gatlin, who described alcohol laws as "confusing and convoluted" said Conrad and her office would have been scrutinized regardless of how the question was put on the ballot.

"If she would have put the 100-seat question on the ballot, then folks would have said. 'The most recent law is 50 seats, why didn't she put that on it??' he said. "If she put 50 seats on, people would say, Why didn't she match it up with the petition?' If she would have said 'This language doesn't match up with current law. I'm not putting it on the ballot,' people would say, 'The petition was very similar to that new law, so why didn't you put it on the ballot.'

"All I'm trying to do is clarify the situation," Gatlin said "There's plenty of time to change the ballot and to allow those folks who have already cast ballots, which is very minimal, to recast their vote. This is really a non-issue. If I would have thought that by filing this there would have been a risk of coming off the ballot, I wouldn't have filed it."[92]

Citizens Urge Voters To Just Say No

We urge all eligible voters to vote for the candidates of their choice on Nov. 4. Your vote does count. Hopefully the winners will work faithfully for our best interest.

We also urge Dry Ridge voters to vote no to alcohol sales in our city. Consider the following when you vote on this issue:

The sale of alcohol does not assure that we would have great growth of business or new restaurants. Walton and Falmouth have been wet for longer than we remember and Williamstown for four years. Where is their great growth and fine restaurants?

If the yes vote passes, you can be sure that an attempt will soon be made to vote all of Grant County wet, so that bars and carry out stores would exist anywhere in the county.

Consider this before you vote. The next "First and Last Chance" or "Racers" could be near you. Also, drug stores and groceries would be licensed to sell by the bottle or case. Consider the motives of those who have been pushing for this for years. Perhaps there is more of a personal interest than the good of our citizens. Are they concerned about the additional society problems, such as public drunkenness and DUI?

The more available alcohol is, the more prevalent these problems. A wet city or county will not lower your taxes, but would likely raise them to cover increased law enforcement costs.

Vote to keep Dry Ridge and Grant County a great place to live and raise a family.

Vote no to alcohol sales in Dry Ridge.[93]

Clay Parks
Bill Cull
Charlie Conrad
Dry Ridge

Moist Vote Goes To Dry Ridge Voters

Dry Ridge residents will be choosing more than their pick for the next U.S. president or local office on election day.

Voters will once again decide if they want their city to go moist.

J.B. Barnes filed a signed petition on Aug. 14 to get the vote on the ballot that, if passed, would make alcohol available by the drink at restaurants and dining facilities with a seating capacity of at least 100 people and which derive at least 70 percent of their gross receipts from the sale of food.

"We need some better restaurants and that won't happen until Dry Ridge goes moist," Barnes previously said. "I would say 95 percent of the people we approached signed the petition. There was no real negative feedback. The main and only reason for this petition is for the restaurants. This would be exactly like Williamstown. I hope it passes."

Previous petitions have been filed, with the last one being rejected by voters in 2005.

In the January 2005 vote, only 304 voters were cast 159 against and 145 in favor of alcohol sales.

According to Kentucky law, three years had to pass before a vote on al-

[92] 23 October 2008. *Grant County News.* Bryan Marshall,Staff Writer.
[93] 30 October 2008. *Grant County News.*

cohol sales could be put back on the ballot in Dry Ridge.

Dry Ridge Mayor Clay Crupper said he is staying neutral on the issue.

"I believe in letting the people say," he said. "If they do, they do. If they don't, they don't."

"I hear talk both ways," Crupper said about whether he thinks the city will go moist. "I've heard some people who are for it and some who are against it"

Regardless of his stance, Crupper admitted it could possibly be beneficial if the voters choose to allow alcohol sales.

"I've had a couple calls about it, chain-type restaurants wanting to know about it," he said "They just wanted to know if it was going to be on the ballot"

In order to get on the ballot, the petition was required to have signatures from at lest 25 percent of Dry Ridge voters in the last general election, said Grant County Clerk Leatha Conrad.

"There was plenty of signatures," she said about the 97 residents who signed the petition.

Once the petition was certified, Grant County Judge-Executive Darrell Link ordered that the local option election be conducted Nov. 4.

Only residents living in the city limits of Dry Ridge can vote on the issue.

Five precincts 4, 5, 13, 21 and 23 will have the local option vote on its ballot.

There has been some opposition to the idea that alcohol could be served in local restaurants.

"I think that some people who are probably in favor of it are either misinformed or misled," said Rev. Joe Kitchens of the Dry Ridge Baptist Church. "One of the things I hear a lot is that with the sale of alcohol the economy will grow and without the sale of alcohol an economy can't grow. If you come south from Florence all the way north to Georgetown, that 40-mile stretch, and look at Walton, Williamstown, Corinth, and Dry Ridge has really been outgrowing all of them. There is more hotels and restaurants in Dry Ridge than at Walton and that's wet, or Williamstown, which has liquor, or Corinth. The argument that an economy can't grow without liquor is false. The argument that an economy will grow with liquor is also false."

Kitchens said the ultimate goal of the people pushing for this vote is to have a wet Grant County.

"If we have a wet Grant County, then we're going to have bars," he said. "We're going to have liquor stores. I don't think people want that next to their home or next to their churches or having their kids pass it two or three times a day on the way to school."

Kitchens, along with David Tucker, Bobby Barnes, Greg Nimmo and Conrad Hefner, also submitted a letter to the editor to the Grant County News opposing to alcohol sales.

"If liquor is the cure all for financial woes and stalled growth, then where are the home owners asking for a bar beside their home?" the letter states. "Where are the land speculators promising to improve roads, community services and create family friendly bars? Where are the studies to show that alcohol will improve the workforce of Dry Ridge? Where are the school officials promising with liquor sales that new schools will be built? The sad truth is, while some individuals may benefit from the alcohol sales, families will suffer because of it."

Corinth and Williamstown voters approved alcohol sales by the drink in 2004.

While he did not know what to expect at first, Williamstown Police Chief Bobby Webb said the availability of alcohol has not increased crime in the city.

"It's not caused our DUI rate to go up at all," he said "We've not had any calls as far as fights or any type of disturbance at either restaurant in town. I believe it's all in how you manage your business. I think Ed (Clemons of Edwardo's Pizza) and the guy who runs El Jalisco do a good job."

Clemons, owner of Edwardo's Pizza, said he expected his business to be impacted financially more than it has since Williamstown went moist.

"There has not been a substantial impact," he said. "But, we haven't really marketed beer that much. We like to have more of a family atmosphere. We're not really after the bar crowd."

As for the likelihood that there will be enough votes cast for Dry Ridge to join Williamstown as moist cities, Crupper said he thinks the local option has a chance to pass.

[94] 30 October 2008. *Grant County News.* Bryan Marshall,Staff Writer.

"It was close last time," he said. "There's been a lot of new people who've moved in."[94]

Alcohol Sales Get Thumbs Up

Dry Ridge will be dry no more after a convincing majority of voters chose to make the city moist.

With a total of 742 votes, 488 were in favor of making alcohol available in the city by the drink at restaurants and dining facilities with a seating capacity of at least 100 people and which derive at least 70 percent of their gross receipts from the sale of food.

Only 254 residents voted no in the local option that was spurred by a signed petition filed Aug. 14 by J.B. Barnes.

"Of course, I'm happy that the people voiced their opinion," Barnes said. "It's what the people wanted and it's what they got. It will be good for the community. It will be good if we can get some decent restaurants here. You're not going to have that without cocktails. It will create jobs and it will be good for the business community and taxes. I think it's a real good decision. Had it gone the other way, I would not have had any complaints."

"It's what the people wanted and it's what they got. It will create jobs and it will be good for the business community and taxes."

- J.B. Barnes
of Dry Ridge

[95]

Previous petitions have been filed, with the last one being rejected by voters in 2005.

In the January 2005 vote, only 304 votes were cast 159 against and 145 in favor of alcohol sales.

According to Kentucky law, three years had to pass before a vote on alcohol sales could be put back on the ballot in Dry Ridge.

Corinth and Williamstown voters approved alcohol sales by the drink in 2004.

Dry Ridge Mayor Clay Crupper, who has remained neutral on the issue, said he will have to wait to see what potential impact the vote will have on the city.

"The people have spoken and we're going to do what the people say," he said. "We'll just have to wait to the future and see what happens. We might get a steakhouse or some good restaurants out of it to help the city draw business in. We'll see what comes out of it."

Although the local option passed easily, there were some vocal opponents to alcohol sales being allowed in Dry Ridge.

Rev. Joe Kitchens of the Dry Ridge Baptist Church previously said that the ultimate goal of the people pushing the vote is to have a wet Grant County.

"If we have a wet Grant County, then we're going to have bars," he said. "We're going to have liquor stores. I don't think people want that next to their home or next to their churches or having their kids pass it two or three times a day on the way to school."

Kitchens, along with David Tucker, Bobby Barnes, Greg Nimmo and Conrad Hefner, also submitted a letter to the editor of the Grant County News opposing to alcohol sales.

"If liquor is the cure all for financial woes and stalled growth, then where are the home owners asking for a bar beside their home?" the letter states. "Where are the land speculators promising to improve roads, community services and create family friendly bars? Where are the studies to show that alcohol will improve the workforce of Dry Ridge? Where are the school officials promising with liquor sales that new schools will be built? The sad truth is, while some individuals may benefit from the alcohol sales, families will suffer because of it."

[95] Circa October 2008. *Grant County News.*

Barnes, who said he thought the vote would be a landslide victory, said his reasons for the petition were wrongly portrayed by some who were against alcohol sales.

"I know they said they'll be bars on every corner, but that's not the issue at all," he said. "It's just to get some restaurants here. As far as getting the whole county or city wet with bars and beer joints and packaged liquor stores, that's not the issue at all.

"They tried to scare the people into that to try to change their minds on how to vote, but it didn't work," he said. "They were very negative and untrue about the whole matter. Of course, that's their prerogative. If they want to be that way, that's fine. I have no hard feelings toward them. They have a right to voice their opinions."[96]

Dry Ridge Adopts Rules Governing Alcohol

The Dry Ridge City Council took the next step Monday, Dec. 15, in making the city moist.

The council heard a first reading of an ordinance allowing alcohol sales by the drink at restaurants and dining facilities with a seating capacity of at least 100 people and which derive at least 70 percent of their gross receipts from the sale of food.

The ordinance comes after voters passed a local option to allow alcohol sales in the November election.

J.B. Barnes filed a signed petition on Aug. 14 to get the vote on the ballot after previous petitions had been filed, with the last one being rejected by voters in 2005.

In the January 2005 vote, only 304 voters were cast 159 against and 145 in favor of alcohol sales.

According to Kentucky law, three years had to pass before a vote on alcohol sales could be put back on the ballot in Dry Ridge.

Mayor Clay Crupper said an ordinance needs to be passed within 60 days after the election.

A second reading of the ordinance will be voted on by the council during a special-called meeting at 5:30 p.m. Monday, Dec. 22.

Crupper decided to use the same ordinance that Williamstown City Council passed when voters there chose to make the city moist.

Williamstown modeled their ordinance from one used by Georgetown.

"I don't want us an hour or two later or earlier," Crupper said about the hours of operation for facilities selling alcohol in the two cities. "They already have their ordinance in place so I plan on going by theirs. (Williamstown Mayor Glenn Caldwell) said they haven't had any problem with theirs. I was pleased. He didn't see anything that we would need to change."

In the proposed ordinance, restaurants and dining facilities must seat a minimum of 100 people in permanent seating, excluding bar-type stools, patio seating or temporary chairs.

The sale of alcoholic beverages also shall be an accessory to food sales, offered only during times in which the licensee's kitchen and food service staff is on duty.

Businesses wanting to sell alcohol must file an application and pay an $800 fee.

Applicants who receive a license will have to provide periodic information demonstrating compliance with the required 70 percent of business income from food sales.

A license must be renewed annually, along with an $800 renewal fee.

No licensed restaurant or dining facility can open for business earlier than 6 a.m. or later than midnight Monday through Thursday in the ordinance.

On Friday and Saturday, the business can not be open before 6 a.m. and no later than 1 a.m.

There are no Sunday sales of alcoholic beverages permitted in the ordinance.

Violations of the ordinance are punishable by a fine up to $500 for each offense. Complaints alleging violations may be filed in Grant District Court.

Appropriate actions by the mayor or designated appointee can include a warning and probationary period in which the violations is corrected, a license suspension or license revocation.

Suspensions may be satisfied with a $50 fine per day.

A responsible beverage server ordinance dealing with the required

[96] 6 November 2008. *Grant County News.* Bryan Marshall,Staff Writer.

training of servers of alcoholic beverages, also had its first reading.

When the council votes on the issue, they can decide to alter any language in the proposed ordinance.

Since the moist vote passed, Crupper said there has been some calls to the city inquiring about the requirements to sell alcohol by potential new businesses.

"I don't know anything that has sold for sure," he said. "They called to find out more or less what they needed to do. They really didn't even tell us who they was. I guess they didn't want the word to get out."

Pizza Hut, which has recently done some remodeling to open up space, wants a license, but they need to build on to have the required number of seats, Crupper said.

"I think it's going to bring some businesses. I really do," he said. 'This exit is a busy exit. It's easy access to get on and off. There's a lot of traffic. I think it might be a year or two before we see anything big, but I think we'll get one or two good chain outfits coming here."[97]

Dry Ridge Is Moist

Dry Ridge officially is moist.

The city council adopted an ordinance on Monday, Dec. 22, allowing alcohol sales by the drink at restaurants and dining facilities with a seating capacity of at least 100 people and which derive at least 70 percent of their gross receipts from the sale of food.

The ordinance came after voters passed a local option to allow alcohol sales in the November election.

Mayor Clay Crupper said an ordinance needed to be passed within 60 days after the election.

The sale of alcoholic beverages also shall be an accessory to food sales, offered only during times in which the licensee's kitchen and food service staff is on duty.

Businesses wanting to sell alcohol must file an application and pay an $800 fee.[98]

Country Grill To Reopen, Serve Alcohol

The Country Grill will soon reopen its doors after major renovations and the addition of alcohol sales.

The restaurant closed Oct. 20, 2008, and shortly after was deeded back to its original owner, John DiGirolamo.

He opened The Country Grill with his wife, Barbara, Nov. 22, 1988, before selling it in 1999.

DiGirolamo originally planned to sell the restaurant after recently retaining ownership.

"We had some bites, but a lot of people wanted to lease it," he said. "I didn't really want to lease it."

Then, his step-son, Mike Hare of Williamstown, and his friend, Joey Nugent of Fort Wright, formed a partnership and asked if they could lease the restaurant with an option to purchase it in the future.

DiGirolamo agreed and a lease was signed.

Hare and Nugent will receive a helping hand from the original owners to get The Country Grill back on its feet.

"Barbara and I are committed to help them open it and renovate it and stay with them for the duration of whatever it takes for that to be reestablished again like once it was," DiGirolamo said.

The renovations will be major, including "stripping everything out except the tables and chairs," he said.

"The wall paper's gone," DiGirolamo said. "Our (old) carpet will be gone. It's just a complete renovation. We even got the automatic flusher toilets and urinals going in."

"It's going to be modern, tastefully done, with some of the old touches back in," he said about the decor. "There won't be any big surprises. We hope it to be very pleasant to the eye of the public and comfortable. It will be a good environment to enjoy a good meal. That's basically what we always did before and that's what we're doing again."

There also will be new equipment in the kitchen.

While the menu is no completed yet, DiGirolamo said he promises a lot of the old favorites, along with some new items.

One new addition will be the limited sale of alcohol by the drink.

The restaurant recently applied for an alcohol license, making it the

[97] 18 December 2008. *Grant County News.* Bryan Marshall,Staff Writer.

[98] 25 December 2008. *Grant County News.*

first in Dry Ridge since a moist vote passed in November.

DiGirolamo said he believes the sale of alcohol will positively impact the business and the community.

"In the years when I opened the restaurant, there always was a request from the traveling public to have a glass of wine with their meal," he said. "So, those people are going to be happy now. It certainly may help us manage our bottom line and our sales a little bit. I don't know that we're going to kill the world with that, but it's going to be a good addition to the fare we offer."

Dry Ridge Mayor Clay Crupper said other businesses have inquired about locating to the city after the moist vote passed, but none have come to fruition.

He said alcohol sales at The Country Grill likely will help the local economy.

"I think it may attract other businesses if they see a successful restaurant," Crupper said.

The original goal was to reopen The Country Grill on June 15, but DiGirolamo said things may be behind schedule.

Tentatively, the restaurant will likely open between mid- and late-June, he said.

"We're hoping to get it open as soon as possible," DiGirolamo said. "The public has been very encouraging. It's really been unbelievable just how many people have missed us. I'm so glad to hear that. Hopefully, half of them will show up to eat there."[99]

Country Grill in Dry Ridge has applied for a liquor license. The restaurant is expected to re-open by the end of the month.

If approved, it will be the first restaurant in the city to begin serving alcohol by the drink since a moist vote passed in November 2008.

[100]

[99] 4 June 2009. *Grant County News.* Bryan Marshall,Staff Writer.

[100] Circa June 2009. *Grant County News.*

2010s

Alcohol Proponents Start Wet Petition

A group of Dry Ridge residents would like to see alcohol sales all over Grant County so they've begun a petition drive to put the issue on the ballot.

Darren Spahr, along with his wife, Kellee, is leading the petition drive.

"We are putting this in the hands of the voters of Grant County," said Spahr, a Dry Ridge resident. "The people should decide the issue and we believe they will support it."

Grant County businessman Bob Wallace is also involved in the effort and said alcohol sales will boost the local economy.

"With county-wide alcohol sales, we would see an influx of new restaurants, hotels and other businesses, and our existing retail stores would enjoy more business through the sale of alcohol," Wallace said.

Wallace is owner of Grant County Drugs.

"That means more jobs and opportunities for our residents, and more tax dollars for local governments and schools, which could offer additional services with additional revenue," Wallace said.

Under Kentucky law, voters must approve the sale of alcohol in a county-wide election, also known as a "wet election."

For a wet election to be held, state law requires that petitions must be signed by the number of registered voters equal to 25 percent of all the votes cast in the last county election.

That means the signatures of 1,700 registered voters must be collected to put the issue on the ballot.

In addition to their name, voters must also list their date of birth and the day they signed the petition.

Currently, there are three locations where voters can sign the petition. They include:

- Dave's Barber Shop, 33 Broadway, Dry Ridge
- Pro Image Cleaners, 118 S. Main, Dry Ridge
- Tobacco Mart, 26 Taft Highway, Dry Ridge

The effort for Grant County to become wet is being called "End Grant County Prohibition." Registered voters can learn more about the movement, as well as download a petition by going to

www.EndGrantCounty
Prohibition.com

"Interstate 75 already brings hundreds of thousands of people through our county every year, but most pass through our county. Why not take advantage of this built-in customer base," Wallace said.

"Williamstown Lake already brings people to our community and the new Ark Encounter is going to bring even more people. Let's keep these dollars that many people will spend on lodging, relaxing and dining in Grant County."

When a sufficient number of signatures are collected, the petitions will be turned into the county clerk. After the clerk certifies the petitions by validating the signatures, the county judge-executive can order the wet election to be held.

Certain requirements exist about when the election can be held:

- The election has to be at least 60 days after the petitions are filed with the county clerk.
- The election cannot be held more than 90 days after the petitions are filed.
- The wet election cannot be held on the same day at the November election or within 30 days of the election.

Wallace, who has spearheaded similar efforts in the past, said he is hopeful that when the issue is put before the voters, it will pass.

"We've waited long enough," Wallace said. "The time has come to improve our economy, give our residents more convenience, provide them with leisure activities found in

[1]22 July 2015. *Grant County News.* Jamie S. Baker.

other communities and once and for all, End Grant County Prohibition."

The wet election is likely to be held in September or early October.[1]

'Wet' Petition Is Now In Clerk's Hands

Those interested in seeing Grant County have alcohol sales have amassed more than 2,000 signatures. The petition containing 2,409 signatures was delivered to the Grant County Clerk's office on Monday, Oct. 8.

The minimum number of signatures needed for the petition was 1,613, but Darren Spahr, a Dry Ridge resident, who leads the wet drive wanted the petition to include more than the law required in case some of the names are not valid.

Under Kentucky law, voters must approve the sale of alcohol in a county-wide election, also known as a "wet election."

For a wet election to be held, state law requires that petitions must be signed by the number of registered voters equal to 25 percent of all the votes cast in the last county election.

"We have ended the petition phase of the campaign, now is the time for us to focus our efforts on fundraising to ensure we are successful in getting voters to approve this issue," Spahr said.

Spahr said the group "End Grant County Prohibition" received a favorable response for their efforts. The wet issue will not be on the November ballot. Kentucky law requires that a wet election cannot be decided on the same day as the November election or within 30 days of that election.

Signatures were collected at various businesses, as well as during the Grant County Fair.

The next step will be for Tabatha Clemons, county clerk, to verify the signatures and pass the issue to Grant County Judge-Executive Steve Wood who will then order the wet election to be held.

The election has to be at least 60 days after the petitions are filed with the county clerk and cannot be held more than 90 days after the petitions are filed.

"My wife, Kellee, and I moved to Dry Ridge a little over three years ago to raise our family in a small town setting surrounded by nature but we found that Grant County could really use some of the conveniences and amenities that our neighbors driving to Florence and Georgetown to enjoy," Spahr said.

He believes if the campaign is successful, it will bolster existing businesses and attract new businesses to the county.

"With the economy being reasonably steady and the Ark on the horizon, now is the time to put as many economic development tools in our toolbox as possible," he said.[2]

Wet Vote Set For Dec. 22

The decision whether or not Grant County goes "wet" will be in the hands of the voters on Dec. 22.

Judge-Executive Stephen Wood has issued an order setting a vote on the county-wide sale of alcohol after a citizen petition was certified allowing the special election.

"There are certain constraints in the statute as to when you are to set wet dry votes and having just completed a general election, this is the first date that works at a time when the schools are not in session and can be used as polling places," Wood said.

The group End Grant County Prohibition gathered 256 pages of signatures for the petition and turned it into Grant County Clerk Tabatha Clemons' office.

A review team spent more than 70 hours researching signatures, dates of birth and comparing them with voter files to insure that at least 1,613 of the petitioners were registered voters.

Wood said some of the names were difficult to read, and in many cases the signatures were from people outside the county.

"We would like to thank all the registered voters that signed petitions and all of the retailers, businesses and others who assisted in soliciting and gathering signatures to End Grant County Prohibition," said Darren Spahr of End Grant County Prohibition. "The level of support is a clear indication that Grant County residents and businesses recognize that the time has come for Grant County to attract new development and jobs, keep tax dollars in the county and stop forcing residents to drive to

[2] 7 October 2015. *Grant County News.* Jamie S. Baker.

other communities that offer restaurants, entertainment districts, live music venues and a legal product - alcohol - that is already responsibly enjoyed by thousands of our local residents."

Wood said the issue now will be decided by voters, although he lamented the cost of a special election.

"While I am a strong believer in the power of the people and their right to vote, I am disheartened that because of the way election laws are written, the full cost of the special election, based on recent history will cost us $30,000 to $35,000," Wood said. "The full amount of this will be borne by the residents of Grant County. There is no state reimbursement on special elections, so this will be a costly exercise in democracy."

Spahr said campaign updates and information can be found on the group's website at

www.EndGrantCounty
Prohibition.com

and on Facebook.[3]

Wet Proponents Say 'Yes' Vote Will Bring Growth

Darren Spahr believes the community could reap economic benefits if the voters approve a measure allowing alcohol sales in Grant County on Dec. 22.

Spahr, a Dry Ridge resident who led a petition drive to get the issue to a vote, said Grant County could enjoy an increase in jobs, which in turn could mean an increased tax base.

"If you look at other towns who've gone wet, such as Elizabethtown, Somerset and Danville, there's an increase because of the license fees, anywhere from $470,000 to $600,000," Spahr said. "In a short time, you're looking at license and registration fees that the cities will receive as revenue."

Spahr and a group called "End Grant County Prohibition" gathered over 2,000 signatures to get the issue before the voters.

That special election has been set for Tuesday, Dec. 22 and will be held at regular polling places throughout the county.

"We know we're running up against the holiday and that it will have an impact on the vote," Spahr said. "That's why we want to get the word out that if someone isn't going to be in town that day, they can vote by absentee ballot."

Spahr said if voters favor alcohol sales in Grant County, the decision could mean more restaurant choices, which means more employment opportunities for Grant County residents.

"We've put out the welcome mat," he said. "So you're looking at increasing employment and property values, which then will hopefully provide amenities to grow the housing market."

Spahr said the "wet" proponents have hung out signs and plan to make phone calls in an effort to get the issue passed.

"So far, we've had a positive response," he said. "Hopefully, people are ready for it."

For more information about End Grant County Prohibition, go to the group's Facebook page or

www.EndGrantCounty
Prohibition.com[4]

Citizens Organize Against Wet Vote

A group called Citizens Against a Wet Grant County has organized to fight the possibility of county-wide alcohol sales.

A wet vote will be held Dec. 22 that, if approved, will allow for the county-wide sale of alcoholic beverages at bars and restaurants as well as at liquor, grocery and convenience stores.

The special election comes after the group, End Grant County Prohibition, submitted a petition to the county.

Fifty-five people attended the first meeting of Citizens Against a Wet Grant County on Nov. 17.

Tim Seevers, minister at Sherman Church of Christ, was named chairman of the committee.

"As a minister I have dealt with many families where alcohol has destroyed relationships," Seevers said.

[3] 11 November 2015. *Grant County News.* Bryan Marshall.

[4] 2 December 2015. *Grant County News.* Jamie S. Baker.

From underage drinking and child abuse to health risks, Seevers believes alcohol abuse can cause harm to the county.

Among the statistics he cites, 77 percent of all child abuse cases are alcohol-related while 12 percent of all alcohol consumed in Kentucky is consumed by underage drinkers.

Locally, Seevers said a survey showed that 25.6 percent of all 10th graders and 30.2 percent of all 12th grade students reported being drunk at least once within the previous 30 days.

Seevers also said alcohol can be a gateway drug for marijuana and other illicit substances and cause negative effect to families, lost labor and bring a need for additional law enforcement.

Grant County Sheriff Chuck Dills, however, said he does not believe a wet Grant County will greatly impact the crime rate.

"When the county went moist, we never noticed any increase in thefts or DUIs," he said. "If people are able to get a 12 pack of beer (in Grant County,) they are going to run up the street and get it and take it on home. Common sense says that most likely if they drive up north to get it, they will possibly drink some before they get home. We're still going to have DUIs, whether or wet or not wet."

While proponents believe a wet Grant County will provide a much-needed economic boost with additional restaurants opening, Seevers is not sold on the idea.

"With the exception of Crittenden, every exit is moist," he said. "If restaurants want to come to the area, they can already do so. They choose not to because there are not enough residents here to make it profitable."

As the Ark Encounter prepares to open in July 2016, the local economy will already see a boost without the need for more alcohol, said Seevers.

"With the Ark opening up next summer, there will already be a boost to our economy," he said. "The patrons to the Ark park, which is estimated to be near 1.5 to 2ă million the first year, are not going to be the people who will frequent the bar scene nor run into a liquor store. But they will be spending money in Grant County, which will be the economic boost that is far greater than the sale of alcohol."

Seevers said the issue is more about having liquor stores and bars than bringing in new restaurants.

"According to the criteria established by law with our current 24,500 residents in the county, there could be as many as 10 (quota packaging) licenses issued at the rate ofă one per every 2,400 residents," he said. "These are licenses for the sale of distilled spirits and wine by the package for consumption off the premises. These are licenses that are usually associated with liquor stores."

Quota Drink licenses at the rate of one per every 2,500 residents also could be issued for the sale of distilled spirits and wine by the drink for consumption on the premises, said Seevers.

These licenses are usually associated with bars, he said.

"This does not include all the different licenses for sale of packaged beer at grocery stores, convenient marts and gas stations," Seevers said. "There are six licenses in all that could be issued for Grant County. Also, once the county goes wet there could be licenses issued for Temporary Drinks. These are permits to allow drink sales at civic or charitable events such as fairs, festivals or carnivals with specific guidelines."

The next step for Citizens Against a Wet Grant County is to raise money for an advertising campaign.

Along with ads, the group plans on having yard signs, making phone calls and sending a mailer to all 11,500 households in the county.

Since the initial meeting, the group has already raised $4,700, said Seevers.

Those who would like to donate can call XXX-XXXX or mail a check to: Citizens Against a Wet Grant County at XXXXX Dry Ridge, KY 41035.

"There will also be an organized prayer effort on the part of Grant County churches that will take place on a weekly basis at various churches around the county," Seevers said.

Absentee voting for those eligible began Nov. 30 at the Grant County Clerk's Office.

The deadline for applying for a mail-in absentee ballot is Dec. 15.

The completed application for an absentee ballot must be received by the county clerk by mail or in person by the deadline.

The absentee ballot must be received in the county clerk's office by

[5]2 December 2015. *Grant County News.* Bryan Marshall.

6 p.m. on Election Day for the ballot to be counted.

For voting questions, contact Grant County Clerk Tabatha Clemons at XXX-XXXX.[5]

Myths Vs. Realities In The Wet/Dry Debate

Political campaigns – whether for an elective office or a policy issue, such as the "wet" ballot issue Grant Countians will vote for on Dec. 22 often come with their share of rhetoric.

It's often hard to separate the myths from the realities. However, in this column, I want to share with you some facts about alcohol sales and their impact on local communities to address some of the rhetoric you may be hearing.

Myth: Approving alcohol sales will increase DUIs and alcohol-related crashes in Grant County. Reality: Statistics and studies show that alcohol-related crashes and DUIs stay flat or actually go down after alcohol sales are approved in dry counties.

Records from the Kentucky State Police show that dry counties tend to have higher rates of DUI-related car crashes than wet ones – presumably because when you live in a dry county, you have to drive farther to get your booze.

In Pulaski County, Kentucky, where the City of Somerset went wet in 2012 and the City of Burnside went moist in 2004, then fully wet in 2014, alcohol-related crashes actually decreased from a high of 80 in 2002 to just over 30 in 2014, according to statistics from the Kentucky State Police.

In Danville, Ky., another Kentucky community that went wet, Police Chief and ABC Administrator Thomas Bustle said "alcohol-related arrests have remained pretty close to the same" and "overall, alcohol-related arrests have stayed flat" since the county voted to go wet.

The Southwest Journal of Criminal Justice conducted a study of a Texas county with similar alcohol policies as Grant County: beer and wine or liquor could not be sold or purchased in stores within the boundaries of the County, but it was freely sold by the drink in 20 restaurants and clubs and alcohol in all forms could be easily obtained by a relatively short drive (10-15 minutes).

While this county was legally and technically dry, it was functionally and practically wet. Therefore, this study and many other studies – find no statistically significant increase in DUI arrests or alcohol-related accidents after countywide alcohol sales are permitted.

Myth: Approving alcohol sales will increase drug use and drug-related deaths in Grant County.

Reality: Studies show that drug use and drug-related deaths actually decrease after alcohol sales are approved in dry counties.

A 2005 paper in the Journal of Law and Economics found that when Texas counties changed from dry to wet, the incidences of drug-related mortality decreased by 14 percent as people substituted alcohol for other drugs.

In addition, "dry counties" that prohibit alcohol sales seem to have a bigger meth problem than other counties.

That's the thought-provoking conclusion a study by researchers at the University of Louisville that was recently reported in The Washington Post.

The Louisville researchers noticed that dry counties had higher rates of meth lab busts, as well as higher rates of meth crimes overall.

And the effect is significant: "If all counties (in Kentucky) were to become wet, the total number of meth lab seizures in Kentucky would decline by about 25 percent," the study found.

In other words, people who buy alcohol in places where it's illegal become accustomed to dealing with the black market.

Interestingly, under policies enacted by the Kentucky Alcoholic Beverage Control Commission, some of the state funds generated by alcohol sales are returned to local law enforcement agencies in the communities where alcohol is sold.

When Elizabethtown, Ky. became wet, the city was able to hire additional police officers because of state funds it received from the sale of alcohol. The same would likely happen in Grant County.

Myth: Approving alcohol sales will not create jobs or improve Grant County's economy.

Reality: All Kentucky communities that have gone "wet" have seen new jobs created and tremendous economic benefit in their communities.

Kentucky communities such as Danville, Elizabethtown, Corbin, and Somerset have all benefited by going "wet" in recent years. As a result, a number of new businesses and a significant number of jobs were created in these communities because voters approved the sale of alcohol.

In the City of Danville, the city has received an additional $600,000 in revenue because of the vote to go from "moist" to "wet" and tourism dollars have risen more than nine percent in Boyle County.

Jody Lassister, president and CEO of the Danville-Boyle County Economic Development Partnership, which includes the Boyle County Industrial Foundation, the tourism bureau, the Chamber of Commerce, said the "wet" vote has been a "boon" for Boyle County, helping both the county and the City of Danville grow.

Since July 2010, alcohol sales in Danville have totaled $22 million.

He said that only $3 million has come from restaurants – "ironically" the same amount that they were bringing in before the "wet" vote. "The lion's share" of the other $19 million has come from package retail sales of beer and liquor, he said.

After the City of Somerset voted to allow alcohol sales, the overall economic impact to the city because of this vote was $12 million, including more than $470,000 that was paid to the city in regulatory fees.

ǎ"Sales are quite high," said Nick Bradley, Somerset's Alcoholic Beverage Control (ABC) administrator.

"More than what we make in the fees, the overall impact you're looking at is probably around $12 million. It's made a big difference."

In Corbin, ABC administrator Bruce Rains said:

"We broke $14,000 (in license fees) the first day. This is instant money that will be pumped back into the community."

The truth of the matter is that Grant County has a higher unemployment rate than its bordering counties – Boone and Kenton – while having an extremely low number of employees in the service industry, i.e. workers in hotels, restaurants, bars, etc.

The service industry only accounts for 5.6 percent of all jobs in Grant County. However, it accounts for 48.1 percent of all jobs in the labor markets in our neighboring counties. This is an employee category we need to grow and allowing alcohol sales in the city will do just that.

The Reality Check

The reality is that a "yes" vote on Dec. 22 will create new businesses and more jobs, attract more tourists and young professionals who want to live in Grant County, provide more tax revenue to our local governments.

And as other communities have discovered after they go "wet," it will not adversely affecting the quality of life in our community.

Please vote "yes" on Dec. 22 for the future of Grant County.[6]

Wet Or Dry? Vote Is Dec. 22

The voters of Grant County will go to the polls on Tuesday, Dec. 22 and decide whether all of the county will be wet' or whether it will remain moist' with liquor by the drink allowed in the city limits of Corinth, Dry Ridge and Williamstown.

Those supporting the end of prohibition say that the impact will be a boost to the economy and increased revenue for the county's budget.

Those who oppose alcohol sales say it's about keeping the problems at bay that easy availability of alcohol could bring.

The issue lands before voters after the group "End Grant County Prohibition" garnered enough signatures on a petition to put the issue on the ballot.

Darren Spahr, a Dry Ridge resident, said it's an economic issue and the county cannot afford to miss out on revenue because people will drive to other communities that offer more variety of restaurants.

"With the Ark coming we're set to grow the tourism sector," Spahr said. "If this passes, a lot of our people who go to Boone and Kenton counties to work and patronize establishments there may be able to work and seek entertainment closer to home."

Spahr and others such as Bob Wallace, owner of Grant County Drugs, organized the petition drive and put up signs around Grant County encouraging voters to approve alcohol sales.

Opponents to more alcohol sales in Grant County say the community doesn't need the social problems such

[6] 9 December 2015. *Grant County News*. Bill Adkins.

as more police calls and patrols and impact to families that making alcohol easier to get will bring.

Tim Seevers, minister at Sherman Church of Christ, said that he's ministered to many families where alcohol has destroyed relationships.

He pointed out that people coming to view the Ark, more than likely won't be the ones frequenting bars or buying alcohol.

"They will be spending money in Grant County, which will be the economic boost that is far greater than the sale of alcohol," Seevers said.

Seevers and others formed "Citizens Against A Wet Grant County" group and has worked through the churches to encourage voters to go to the polls on Dec. 22 and say no to additional alcohol sales.

On Tuesday, Dec. 15, across Grant County, at Mason Baptist Church, the senior center at the Williamstown City Building, Beans Café and Bakery in Dry Ridge, Sherman Church of Christ and Macedonia Baptist Church in Jonesville held prayer vigils.

The group is also asking for prayers for 24 hours prior to the wet election starting at 6 p.m. on Dec. 21 and continuing to 6 p.m. on Dec. 22. To sign up to be part of the prayer vigil and for more details, go to

http://doodle.come/poll/
dukk3enmhcudz6sg

The group will gather at 6 p.m. on Dec. 22 at Beans Café.

"Regardless of the outcome, we believe it is very important to move forward prayerfully and unified in our effort to reach our community for Christ," the Citizens Against A Wet Grant County said in a flyer.

The election itself will be like any other, said County Clerk Tabatha Clemons.

Polls will open at 6 a.m. on Dec. 22 and close at 6 p.m.

Voting places are the same as they were for the Nov. 3 election for statewide offices including governor.

For a list of polling sites, see page 20 of this issue.

Anyone with questions about voting or where they can vote, should call the county clerk's office at XXX-XXXX.

If alcohol sales are approved, Grant County would become wet 60 days after the board of elections certify the election.

According to information on the Alcohol Beverage Control website, local governments have the option to get involved in issuing licenses and providing enforcement.

A county-wide vote on alcohol sales was last held on July 25, 2000. There were 3,553 votes against the county being wet and 1,591 for allowing alcohol sales.

In Grant County, three of the four cities are moist' and allow alcohol sales by the drink in restaurants that seat at least 100 persons and derive 70 percent of its gross receipts from the sale of food.

Corinth was the first city to become moist in January 2004, followed by Williamstown in November 2004 and then Dry Ridge in January 2005.

The special election on alcohol is expected to cost $30,000 to $35,000.[7]

County Goes 'Wet'

By a 525-vote margin, voters were in favor of county-wide alcohol sales during the Dec. 22 local option election.

There were 2,424 votes in favor and 1,899 in opposition. Dry Ridge, Williamstown and Corinth are already "moist," meaning alcohol sales by the drink are allowed in qualifying restaurants.

However, being "wet" allows for broader alcohol and liquor sales, including packaged beer, by qualified licensed businesses.

A 60-day waiting period must elapse before individuals and businesses can start applying for licenses to sell alcohol and liquor.

"Today's vote was a historic event in Grant County and we confident that it will prove to be a springboard for future economic development in our county," said Darren Spahr, chairman of End Grant County Prohibition, the group who petitioned for the special election. "We believe this vote will bring new businesses, new residents and new energy to our community."

Tim Seevers, chairman of Citizens Against A Wet Grant County, said he was disappointed in the outcome but not surprised at the result.

"The opposition did a great job of selling their point to the local government officials," he said. "This was

[7] 16 December 2015. *Grant County News.* Jamie S. Baker.

not a moral or ethical decision, but a financial one. The ones who will get the benefit of this decision are the ones who will be selling it."

Seevers said local churches have already come together to start a counseling center in Dry Ridge in preparation for more alcohol sales in the county.

"We will offer support to help families deal with addictions," he said. "We need to be able to support people and families who need help."

Turnout for the local option election was about 24 percent, compared to 22.92 percent in the November governor's race.

"Turnout was higher so (poll workers) were a little busier," said Grant County Clerk Tabatha Clemons. "In my mind, that can help prepare them for the presidential primary in May. Still, overall, it's sad that only 24 percent of our voting population turned out. I want to see elections where everyone votes. You want to see higher turnout so everyone's voice is heard."

Several elected officials were pleased with the potential economic impact the vote could have on Grant County and its cities.

"I'm tickled to death," said Dry Ridge Mayor Jim Wells. "I'm happy that the voters decided that there was more to the issue than just alcohol. I'm ecstatic for the turnout. The turnout was amazing for a special election. That says a lot right there. People were engaged and wanted their voice to be heard."

The immediate impact of the vote is going to be the surge of new business, said Wells, who believes restaurants, conferences and other businesses that were not previously available before could look at locating in the county.

"We don't know exactly what that number will be," he said. "We may only have five licenses that we're able to issue or we could have 15. I don't know. Regardless, we're going to see a surge of new businesses for the city. That has a domino effect in the community." Williamstown Mayor Rick Skinner said the vote was about economic development, not alcohol consumption.

"For the future for us, with the Ark Encounter and tourism, it was something we needed," he said. Both mayors said they have already been fielding questions from interested parties.

During the 60-day waiting period, mayors and county officials will meet with state Alcohol Beverage Commission (ABC) officials to prepare for the county officially becoming "wet."

"That 60 days is really for the county and cities to get ordinances in place allowing for the applications (for alcohol licenses,)" Skinner said. "ABC in Frankfort is coming down to speak to the mayors and the judge about the process and what is going on."

Wells said he has been looking at ordinances from other cities and counties to get possible revenue stream ideas that could benefit Dry Ridge.

"I like what Georgetown did by instituting the 6-percent tax, so to speak, on the sale," he said. "That's a direct revenue to the city and it only effects the people who are going to consume the product. It's not a tax to the public. It's a tax on consumption. That's going to create the revenue to enforce the rest of the ordinance so it's not an unfunded requirement."

Grant County Judge-Executive Steve Wood, who has had 14 calls about licenses already, said he was surprised that the "wet" vote was successful.

"I didn't think it would pass," he said. "I had no opinion on it. I'm not a drinker, but it looks like hopefully it will be good for the county financially. I hope and pray that it will be good for the county. I just want what's good for the county."[8]

Alcohol Voted In Now What?

Grant County will soon be officially wet and alcohol and liquor sales will be available for purchase.

The result of the Dec. 22 local option election has left many with questions. Here are some of the answers residents may be wondering about. When does the wet vote results become effective?

Residents obviously were not able to go out immediately the following day after the Dec. 22 local option election and buy beer and liquor.

In fact, the election approving alcohol sales becomes effective 60 days after the vote is certified, which in this case was the night of the election.

[8] 30 December 2015. *Grant County News.* Bryan Marshall.

That would mean the vote would become effective around Feb. 20.

However, there are still other regulations that push the date back further when businesses can get a license to sell beer and/or liquor.

What kind licenses will be available?

There are six main retail license types related to alcohol sales, according to the ABC Commission.

Of those, there are two quota licenses: Quota Retail Package (QP) license and Quota Retail Drink licenses (QD).

QP licenses permit the sale of distilled spirits and wine by the package for consumption off of the premises.

These licenses are usually associated with a package liquor store.

Businesses must obtain another license in order to sell beer by the package.

QP licenses may not be issued to grocery or convenience store, however like several Krogers, a grocery store owner may qualify for a QP licenses immediately adjacent to the store if there is a separate entrance not accessible inside the grocery store.

The number of QP licenses available is based on the population of the county.

There is one license available per every 2,300 residents.

Depending on the population number used, Grant County could have anywhere from nine to 11 licenses available that would allow for liquor stores.

Quota Retail Drink (QD) licenses permit the sale of distilled spirits and wine by the drink for consumption on the premises such as a bar or small restaurant.

Since Grant County does not have a city with 8,000 residents, no QD licenses will be available, meaning there will be no standalone bars.

A city with 3,000 or more residents is permitted to have a second local option election to permit QD licenses in the city limits.

There are also several types of Non-Quota Retail Drink licenses.

NQ-2 Retail Drink licenses may be issued to a restaurant with seating for 50 people or a hotel with 50 sleeping units and dining facilities for 50 people.

Hotels and restaurants with a NQ-license must maintain food sales that are at least 50 percent of their gross receipts from the sale of alcohol and food combined.

The NQ Retail Malt Beverage license, usually associated with grocery and convenience stores, authorizes the sale of beer only by the package for consumption off the premises.

Convenience stores selling gas cannot obtain a NQ package license unless they maintain an inventory of $5,000 worth of food, groceries and related products.

Temporary drink licenses permit alcoholic beverage drink sales at civic or charitable events such as fairs and festivals.

Strict requirements exist for temporary licenses.

Who will oversee licenses?

Grant County Judge-Executive Steve Wood or another appointed person may be the local county ABC administrator.

The county ABC administrator has jurisdiction over the portion of the county that lies outside the limits of a city with its own city ABC administrator and licenses.

The county ABC administer issues local county licenses created by ordinance and has the same authority for county licenses as state ABC administrators have for state licenses.

The Grant County Fiscal Court and each city in the county must create licenses by ordinance in order to collect licensing fees and regulate alcoholic beverage sales.

In addition to licensing fees, "qualified" cities and counties containing a qualified city, may also levy an additional regulatory licensing fee based on a percentage of a licensees' gross sales, but it is not considered an alcohol tax.

The additional fee must be "reasonably estimated to fully reimburse the cost of additional policing, regulatory and administrative expenses."

The funds cannot be used to build parks, sidewalks or anything else.

Wet cities with 3,000 or more resident must have a local city ABC administrator.

Those cities with less than 3,000 residents have the option to have a local city administrator or not.

The city ABC administrator has the same authority and duties as a county ABC administrator.

If a city does not create local ABC licenses, a business only needs a state license in order to sell alcoholic beverages.

If a county or city does create licenses, applicants must first submit their applications and get approval locally before filing for a state license.

County and city officials will be meeting this week with ABC officials to discuss regulations, ordinances and laws.

What is included in the application process for a license?

Applications for local licenses must first be approved before a state license can be applied for.

Cities and counties may use their own forms or use the state application form on the ABC website at http://abc.ky.gov.

Along with the application, there are several other requirements.

Applicants must first advertise in the newspaper their intention to apply for a license.

The ad must be published not before 60 days after the election.

A license application must be filed within 90 days of the ad being published.

Anyone can file a protest against a license application and a license may not be issued until 30 days after a protest period.

Applicants for a state license also may obtain a criminal background check and a department investigator will visit the proposed premises to complete a field inspection report.

Because of the inspection report, it takes about 45 to 60 days to process an application.

How can a license be denied?

The mandatory ways licenses can be denied include not complying fully with ABC laws and regulations, not complying with all city and county regulations or making false statements on the application.

A person also is disqualified from holding a license by law if they have been convicted of a felony with the past five years, convicted of a KRS Chapter 218A controlled substance crimes within two years, convicted of an alcoholic beverage-related misdemeanor within two years, under 21 years old or is not a United States citizen or resident of Kentucky.

A department administrator also has discretion to deny a license for any reasonable reason including: public sentiment in the area; number of licensed outlets in the area; potential for future growth; type of area involved and financial potential of the area.

What laws/regulations regulate alcohol sales?

By state law, license holders cannot sell alcohol to intoxicated persons, permit gambling on premises, give away free alcohol or sell for less than cost, permit crimes on property and employ a felon or person with two alcohol-related misdemeanors in past two years if they serve or sell alcohol.

Hours of sale under state law are 6 a.m. to midnight Monday through Saturday with no Sunday sales. However, cities with 3,000 residents and a county with such a city, may enact ordinances extending the hours and permitting Sunday sales.[9]

Bottoms Up

First Alcohol Sales On Tap

It was termed a "historic event in Grant County" by Darren Spahr, chairman of the group that petitioned for the Dec. 22, 2015 special election, turning the county from moist to wet. Now, four months since the vote, some people may be asking, where are the changes?

The wheels of bureaucracy turn slowly and there has been a state-required 60-day waiting period after the election. This time allowed for certification of the vote and for government officials to set up guidelines for licensing and fees, and to name Alcohol Beverage Control (ABC) administrators.

Because of the election outcome, the Grant County Fiscal Court was required to participate and regulate alcoholic beverage sales. Although not required to participate, Corinth, Crittenden, Dry Ridge and Williamstown chose to collect fees and regulate sales. They also had to enact their own ordinances and each respective mayor is acting as the ABC administrator.

The administrator for the city of Dry Ridge is Mayor Jim Wells.

"We obviously opted to want to have controlbecause it is really about how we want to shape where these locations are and what kind of added rules we want to put on it," Wells said.

There are many waiting periods from the time an entity applies for a license and the product is placed on a store shelf. Applicants first had to advertise in the newspaper their intention to apply for a license, and file the application within 90 days of the ad being published. During that time,

[9] 13 January 2016. *Grant County News.* Bryan Marshall.

protests against an application could have been filed and a license may not be issued until 30 days after the protest period. There is also a criminal background check and a field inspection report.

"Dry Ridge and Williamstown's ordinance is based closely on that of Georgetown," Wells said. Mayor (Rick) Skinner and I worked really hard on making sure that our ordinances were as identical as possible."

According to Wells, officials in Williamstown wanted to have a cafe presence downtown, where they could have shops with tables outside. Therefore, Dry Ridge included that in their ordinance, as well, even if that wasn't something that the city was pursuing.

However, there are differences between the two cities.

"One of those deals with Sunday sales," Wells said. "Williamstown allowed their Sunday sales to go to 1 a.m. and ours stops at midnight. Williamstown wanted to have it a little bit later, because they want to have some different things downtown."

The other major difference may be seen in pricing. According to state law, a city must have a population of 3,000 citizens before charging a regulatory fee. As of the 2013 Census, the population of Williamstown was 3,952; therefore, a regulatory fee of 5 percent will be added to the cost of products. In that same census, Dry Ridge had a population 2,212, below the requirement number to tack on a regulatory fee. By statute, the regulatory fee can only be used in the administration of the ABC program.

In Williamstown, Rulers and Ezy Stop are in the protest portion of the licensing process.

At the time of this report, the following businesses within the City of Dry Ridge have valid licenses: The Speedway gas stations on Taft Highway and Broadway are permitted to sell malt beverages (beer) only. LaRosas, El Rio Grande and Happy Dragon Chinese Restaurant all have permits for alcohol sales.

There are four licenses pending approval, by the state, for the city of Crittenden, according to Mayor James Livingood.

Two of those are for Eagle Creek Country Club: one for retail drink sales and a special Sunday drink sales permit. The others are for the Shell Station and Ezy Stop, both for malt beverages.

Bobby Newman, Grant County ABC administrator and magistrate for the third district, handles anything outside a particular city's jurisdiction.

No entities have completed the licensing process to date, but three are pending approval at the state level. One business is in the Crittenden area and there are two others in the Corinth area, according to Newman.

"A lot of these business that are already established have their own corporate lawyers assisting them and filling out their applications," Newman said. "But these Mom and Pop' places that don't have corporate lawyersit takes a little time to meet the criteria of the state. It's a lengthy process."[10]

---

[10] 27 April 2016. *Grant County News.* Linda Lawrence.

Digestif

[1]

[1]Courtesy the Lester S. Levy Collection of Sheet Music, Sheridan Libraries, Johns Hopkins University.

2

[2]Courtesy the Lester S. Levy Collection of Sheet Music, Sheridan Libraries, Johns Hopkins University.

[3]

[3]Courtesy the Lester S. Levy Collection of Sheet Music, Sheridan Libraries, Johns Hopkins University.

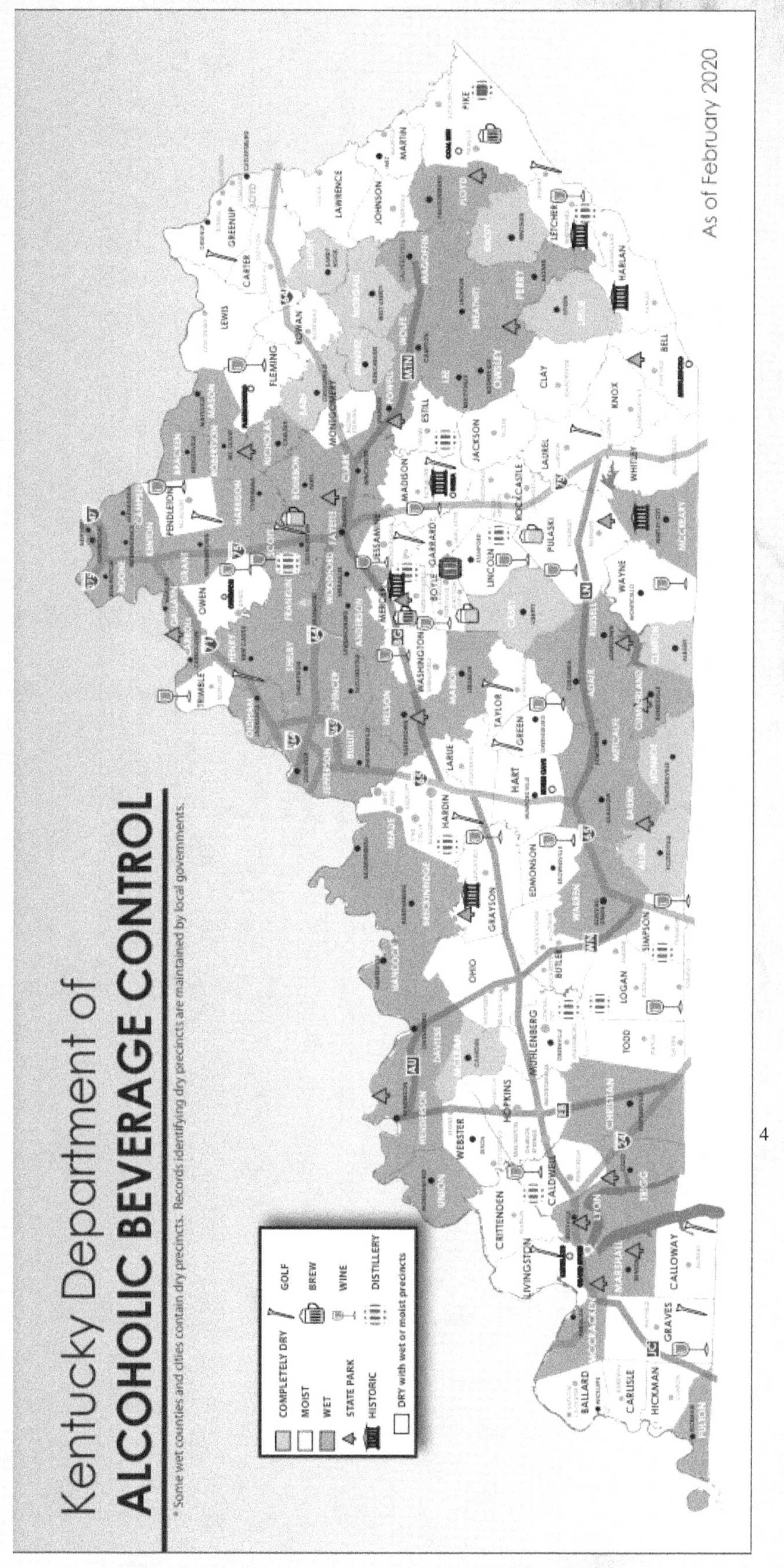

[4]

[4]Courtesy, Department of Alcoholic Beverage Control, abc.ky.gov. Check ABC website for more updated maps.

www.ingramcontent.com/pod-product-compliance
Lightning Source LLC
Chambersburg PA
CBHW081209230426
43666CB00015B/2685

* 9 7 8 0 9 8 1 6 4 6 6 8 8 *